GREAT
WORLD WAR II
STORIES

GREAT
WORLD WAR II
STORIES

A 50th ANNIVERSARY COLLECTION

CHARTWELL
BOOKS, INC.

This volume first published in Great Britain in 1989 by

The Octopus Group Limited
Michelin House
81 Fulham Road
London SW3 6RB

for
CHARTWELL BOOKS, INC.
A Division of BOOK SALES, INC.
110 Enterprise Avenue
Secaucus, New Jersey 07094

Jacket illustration by David Harding

ISBN 1 55521 478 9

Printed and bound in Great Britain by
William Clowes Limited, Beccles and London

CONTENTS

A Perfect Morning

Irwin Shaw

The Platoon Lieutenant had been killed in the morning and Christian was in command when the order came to fall back. The Americans had not been pushing much and the battalion had been beautifully situated on a hill overlooking a battered village of two dozen houses in which three Italian families grimly continued to live.

'I have begun to understand how the Army operates,' Christian heard a voice complain in the dark, as the platoon clanked along, scuffling in the dust. 'A Colonel comes down and makes an examination. Then he goes back to Headquarters and reports. "General," he says, "I am happy to report that the men have warm, dry quarters, in safe positions which can only be destroyed by direct hits. They have finally begun to get their foot regularly, and the mail is delivered three times a week. The Americans understand that their position is impregnable and do not attempt any activity at all." "Ah, good," says the General. "We shall retreat."'

Christian recognized the voice. Private Dehn, he noted down silently for future reference.

He marched dully, the Schmeisser on its sling already becoming a nagging burden on his shoulder. He was always tired these days, and the malaria headaches and chills kept coming back, too mildly to warrant hospitalization, but wearying and unsettling. Going back, his boots seemed to sound as he limped in the dust, going back, going back. . . .

At least, he thought heavily, we don't have to worry about the planes in the dark. That pleasure would be reserved for later, when the sun came up. Probably back near Foggia, in a warm room, a young American lieutenant was sitting down to a breakfast of grapefruit juice, oatmeal, ham and eggs, and real coffee with cream, preparing to climb into his plane a little later and come skimming over the hills, his guns spitting at the black, scattered blur of men, crouched insecurely in shallow holes along the road, that would be Christian and the platoon.

As he plodded on, Christian hated the Americans. He hated them more for the ham and eggs and the real coffee than for the bullets and the planes. Cigarettes, too, he thought. Along with everything else, they have all the cigarettes they want. How could you beat a country that had all those cigarettes?

His tongue ached for the healing smoke of a cigarette. But he had only two cigarettes in his packet, and he had rationed himself to one a day.

Christian thought of the faces of the American pilots he had seen, men who had been shot down behind the German lines and had waited to be taken, insolently smoking cigarettes, with arrogant smiles on their empty, untouched faces. Next time, he thought, next time I see one of them, I'm going to shoot him, no matter what the orders are.

Then he stumbled in a rut. He cried out as the pain knotted in his knee and hip.

'Are you all right, Sergeant?' asked the man behind him.

'Don't worry about me,' Christian said. 'Stay on the side of the road.'

He limped on, not thinking about anything any more, except the road in front of him.

The runner from the battalion was waiting at the bridge, as Christian had been told he would.

The platoon had been walking for two hours, and it was broad daylight by now. They had heard planes, on the other side of the small range of hills the platoon had been skirting, but they had not been attacked.

The runner was a corporal, who had hidden himself nervously in the ditch alongside the road. The ditch had six inches of water in it, but the Corporal had preferred safety to comfort, and he rose from the ditch muddy and wet. There was a squad of Pioneers on the other side of the bridge, waiting to mine it after Christian's platoon had gone through. It was not much of a bridge, and the ravine which it crossed was dry and smooth. Blowing the bridge wouldn't delay anyone more than a minute or two, but the Pioneers doggedly blew everything blowable, as though they were carrying out some ancient religious ritual.

'You're late,' said the Corporal nervously. 'I was afraid something had happened to you.'

'Nothing has happened to us,' said Christian shortly.

'Very well,' said the Corporal. 'It's only another three kilometres. The Captain is going to meet us, and he will show you where you are to dig in.' He looked around nervously. The Corporal always looked like a man who expects to be shot by a sniper, caught in an open field by a strafing plane, exposed on a hill to a direct hit by an artillery shell. Looking at him, Christian was certain that the Corporal was going to be killed very shortly.

Christian gestured to the men and they started over the bridge behind the Corporal. Good, Christian thought dully, another three kilometres and then the Captain can start making decisions. The squad of Pioneers regarded them thoughtfully from their ditch, without love or malice.

Christian crossed the bridge and stopped. The men behind him halted automatically. Almost mechanically, without any conscious will on his part, his eye began to calculate certain distances, probable approaches, fields of fire.

'The Captain is waiting for us,' said the Corporal, peering shiftily past the platoon, down the road on which later in the day the Americans would appear. 'What are you stopping for?'

'Keep quiet,' Christian said. He walked back across the bridge. He stood in the middle of the road, looking back. For a hundred metres the road went straight, then curved back round a hill, out of sight. Christian turned again and stared through the morning haze at the road and the hills before them. The road wound in mounting curves through the stony, sparsely shrubbed hills in that direction. Far off, eight hundred, a thousand metres away, on an almost cliff-like drop, there was an outcropping of boulders. Among those boulders, his mind registered automatically, it would be possible to set up a machine-gun and it would also be possible to sweep the bridge and its approach from there.

The Corporal was at his elbow. 'I do not wish to annoy you, Sergeant,' the Corporal said, his voice quivering, 'but the Captain was specific. "No delays, at all," he said. "I will not take any excuses."'

'Keep quiet,' said Christian.

The Corporal started to say something. Then he thought better of it. He swallowed and rubbed his mouth with his hand. He stood at the first stone of the bridge and stared unhappily towards the south.

Christian walked slowly down the side of the ravine to the dry stream bed below. About ten metres back from the bridge, he noticed, his mind still working automatically, the slope leading down from the road was quite gentle, with no deep holes or boulders. Under the bridge the stream bed was sandy and soft, with scattered worn stones and straggling undergrowth.

It could be done, Christian thought, it would be simple. He climbed slowly up to the road again. The platoon had cautiously got off the bridge by now and were standing at the edge of the road on the other side, ready to jump into the Pioneers' ditches at the sound of an aeroplane.

Like rabbits, Christian thought resentfully, we don't live like human beings at all.

The Corporal was jiggling nervously up and down at the entrance to the bridge. 'All right, now, Sergeant?' he asked. 'Can we start now?'

Christian ignored him. Once more he stared down the straight hundred metres towards the turn in the road. He half closed his eyes and he could almost imagine how the first American, flat on his belly, would peer around the bend to make sure nothing was waiting for him. Then the head would disappear. Then another head, probably a lieutenant's (the American Army seemed to have an unlimited number of lieutenants they were willing to throw away), would appear. Then, slowly, sticking to the side of the hill, peering nervously down at their feet for mines, the squad, or platoon, even the company would come around the bend, and approach the bridge.

Christian turned and looked again at the clump of boulders high up on the cliff-like side of the hill a thousand metres on the other side of the bridge. He was almost certain that from there, apart from being able to command the approach to the bridge and the bridge itself, he could observe the road to the south where it wound through the smaller hills they had just come through. He would be able to see the Americans for a considerable distance before they moved behind the hill from which they would have to emerge on the curve of the road that led up to the bridge.

He nodded his head slowly, as the plan, full-grown and thoroughly worked out, as though it had been fashioned by someone else and presented to him, arranged itself in his mind. He walked swiftly across the bridge. He went over to the Sergeant who was in command of the Pioneers.

The Pioneer Sergeant was looking at him inquisitively. 'Do you intend to spend the winter on this bridge, Sergeant?' the Pioneer said.

'Have you put the charges under the bridge yet?' Christian asked.

'Everything's ready,' said the Pioneer. 'One minute after you're past we light the fuse. I don't know what you think you're doing, but I don't mind telling you you're making me nervous, parading up and down this way. The Americans may be along at any minute and then . . .'

'Have you a long fuse?' Christian asked. 'One that would take, say, fifteen minutes to burn?'

'I have,' said the Pioneer, 'but that isn't what we're going to use. We have a one-minute fuse on the charges. Just long enough so that the man who sets them can get out of the way.'

'Take it off,' said Christian, 'and put the long fuse on.'

'Listen,' said the Pioneer, 'your job is to take these scarecrows back over my bridge. My job is to blow it up. I won't tell you what to do with your platoon, you don't tell me what to do with my bridge.'

Christian stared silently at the Sergeant. He was a short man who miraculously had remained fat. He looked like the sort of fat man who also had a bad stomach, and his air was testy and superior. 'I will also require ten of those mines,' Christian said, with a gesture towards the mines piled haphazard near the edge of the road.

'I am putting those mines in the road on the other side of the bridge,' said the Pioneer.

'The Americans will come up with their detectors and pick them up one by one,' said Christian.

'That's not my business,' said the Pioneer sullenly. 'I was told to put them in here and I am going to put them in here.'

'I will stay here with my platoon,' said Christian, 'and make sure you don't put them in the road.'

'Listen, Sergeant,' said the Pioneer, his voice shivering in excitement, 'this is no time for an argument. The Americans . . .'

'Pick those mines up,' Christian said to the squad of Pioneers, 'and follow me.'

'See here,' said the Pioneer in a high, pained voice, 'I give orders
to this squad, not you.'

'Then tell them to pick up those mines and come with me,' said
Christian coldly, trying to sound as much like Lieutenant Hardenburg as possible. 'I'm waiting,' he said sharply.

The Pioneer was panting in anger and fear now, and he had caught
the Corporal's habit of peering every few seconds towards the bend,
to see if the Americans had appeared yet. 'All right, all right,' he
said. 'It doesn't mean anything to me. How many mines did you say
you want?'

'Ten,' said Christian.

'The trouble with this Army,' grumbled the Pioneer, 'is that there
are too many people in it who think they know how to win the war
all by themselves.' But he snapped at his men to pick up the mines,
and Christian led them down into the ravine and showed them where
he wanted them placed. He made the men cover the holes carefully
with brush and carry away in their helmets the sand they had dug
up.

Even while he supervised the men down below, he noticed, with a
grim smile, that the Pioneer Sergeant himself was attaching the long
fuses to the small, innocent-looking charges of dynamite under the
span of the bridge.

'All right,' said the Pioneer gloomily, when Christian came up on
the road again, the mines having been placed to his satisfaction, 'the
fuse is on. I do not know what you are trying to do, but I put it on to
please you. Now, should I light it now?'

'Now,' said Christian, 'please get out of here.'

'It is my duty,' said the Pioneer pompously, 'to blow up this bridge
and I shall see personally that it is blown up.'

'I do not want the fuse lighted,' Christian said, quite pleasantly
now, 'until the Americans are almost here. If you wish personally to
stay under the bridge until that time, I personally welcome you.'

'This is not a time for jokes,' said the Pioneer with dignity.

'Get out, get out,' Christian shouted at the top of his voice, fiercely,
menacingly, remembering with what good effect Hardenburg had
used that trick. 'I don't want to see you here one minute from now.
Get back or you're going to get hurt!' He stood close to the Pioneer,
towering ferociously above him, his hands twitching, as though he

could barely restrain himself from knocking the Pioneer senseless where he stood.

The Pioneer backed away, his pudgy face paling under his helmet. 'Strain,' he said hoarsely. 'No doubt you have been under an enormous strain in the line. No doubt you are not quite yourself.'

'Fast!' said Christain.

The Pioneer turned hurriedly and strode back to where his squad was again assembled on the other side of the bridge. He spoke briefly, in a low voice, and the squad clambered up from the ditch. Without a backward glance they started down the road. Christian watched them for a moment, but did not smile, as he felt like doing, because that might ruin the healthful effect of the episode on his own men.

'Sergeant.' It was the Corporal, the runner from battalion, again, his voice drier and higher than ever. 'The Captain is waiting. . . .'

Christian wheeled on the Corporal. He grabbed the man's collar and held him close to him. The man's eyes were yellow and glazed with fright.

'One more word from you,' Christian shook his roughly, and the man's helmet clicked painfully down over his eyes, on to the bridge of his nose. 'One more word and I will shoot you.' He pushed him away.

'Dehn!' Christian called. A single figure slowly broke away from the platoon on the other side of the bridge and came towards Christian. 'Come with me,' said Christian when Dehn had reached him. Christian half-slid, half-walked down the side of the ravine, carefully avoiding the small minefield he and the Pioneers had laid. He pointed to the long fuse that ran from the dynamite charge down the northern side of the arch.

'You will wait here,' he said to the silent soldier standing beside him, 'and when I give the signal, you will light that fuse.'

Christian heard the deep intake of breath as Dehn looked at the fuse. 'Where will you be, Sergeant?' he asked.

Christian pointed up the mountain to the outcropping of boulders about eight hundred metres away. 'Up there. Those boulders below the point where the road turns. Can you see it?'

There was a long pause. 'I can see it,' Dehn whispered finally.

The boulders glittered, their colour washed out by distance, and sunlight, against the dry green of the cliff. 'I will wave my coat,' said Christian. 'You will have to watch carefully. You will then set the fuse and make sure it is going. You will have plenty of time. Then get out on the road and run until the next turn. Then wait until you hear the explosion here. Then follow along the road until you reach us.'

Dehn nodded dully. 'I am to be all alone down here?' he asked.

'No,' said Christian, 'we will supply you with two ballet dancers and a guitar player.'

Dehn did not smile.

'Is it clear now?' Christian asked.

'Yes, Sergeant,' said Dehn.

'Good,' Christian said. 'If you set off the fuse before you see my coat, don't bother coming back.'

Dehn did not answer. He was a large, slow-moving young man who had been a stevedore before the war, and Christian suspected that he had once belonged to the Communist party.

Christian took a last look at his arrangements under the bridge, and at Dehn standing stolidly, leaning against the curved, damp stone of the arch. Then he climbed up to the road again. Next time, Christian thought grimly, that soldier will be less free with criticism.

It took fifteen minutes, walking swiftly, to reach the clump of boulders overlooking the road. Christian was panting hoarsely by the time he got there. The men behind him marched doggedly, as though resigned to the fact that they were doomed to march, bent under their weight of iron, for the rest of their lives. There was no trouble about straggling, because it was plain to even the stupidest man in the platoon that if the Americans got to the bridge before the platoon turned away out of sight behind the boulders, the platoon would present a fair target, even at a great distance, to the pursuers.

Christian stopped, listening to his own harsh breathing, and peered down into the valley. The bridge was small, peaceful, insignificant in the winding dust of the road. There was no movement to be seen anywhere, and the long miles of broken valley seemed deserted, forgotten, lost to human use.

Christian smiled as he saw that his guess had been right about the vantage point of the boulders. Through a cut in the hills it was possible to see a section of the road some distance from the bridge. The Americans would have to cross that before they disappeared momentarily from sight behind a spur of rock, around which they would then have to turn and appear again on the way to the bridge.

Even if they were going slowly and cautiously, it would not take them more than ten or twelve minutes to cover the distance, from the spot at which they would first come into sight, to the bridge itself.

'Heims,' Christian said, 'Richter. You stay with me. The rest of you go back with the Corporal.' He turned to the Corporal. The Corporal now looked like a man who expects to be killed, but feels that there is a ten per cent chance he may postpone the moment of execution till tomorrow. 'Tell the Captain,' Christian said, 'we will get back as soon as we can.'

'Yes, Sergeant,' the Corporal said, nervous and happy. He started walking, almost trotting, to the blessed safety of the turn in the road. Christian watched the platoon file by him, following the Corporal. The road was high on the side of the hill now. When they walked the men were outlined heroically and sadly against the shreds of cloud and wintry blue sky, and when they made their turns, one by one, in towards the hill, they seemed to step off into windy blue space. Heims and Richter were a machine-gun team. They were standing heavily, leaning against the roadside boulders, Heims holding the barrel and a box of ammunition, and Richter sweating under the base and more ammunition. They were dependable men, but, looking at them standing there, sweating in the cold, their faces cautious but non-committal, Christian felt suddenly that he would have preferred, at this moment, to have with him now the men of his old platoon, dead these long months in the African desert. He hadn't thought about his old platoon for a long time, but somehow, looking at the two machine-gunners, left behind on another hill this way, brought to mind the night more than a year before when the thirty-six men had thoughtfully and obediently dug the lonely holes which would a little later be their graves.

Somehow, looking at Heims and Richter, he felt that these men could not be depended upon to do their jobs as well. They belonged, by some slight, subtle deterioration in quality, to another army, an army whose youth had left it, an army that seemed, with all its experience, to have become more civilian, less willing to die. If he left the two men now, Christian thought, they would not stay at their posts for long. Christian shook his head. Ah, he thought, I am getting silly. They're probably fine. God knows what they think of me.

The two men leaned, thickly relaxed against the stones, their eyes

warily on Christian, as though they were measuring him and trying
to discover whether he was going to ask them to die this morning.

'Set it up here,' Christian said, pointing to a level spot between
two of the boulders which made a rough V at their joining. Slowly
but expertly the men set up the machine-gun.

When the gun was set up, Christian crouched down behind it and
traversed it. He shifted it a little to the right and peered down the
barrel. He adjusted the sight for the distance, allowing for the fact
that they would be shooting downhill. Far below, caught on the fine
iron line of the sight, the bridge lay in sunlight that changed
momentarily to shadow as rags of cloud ghosted across the sky.

'Give them plenty of chance to bunch up near the bridge,' Christian
said. 'They won't cross it fast, because they'll think it's mined. When
I give you the signal to fire, aim at the men in the rear, not at the
ones near the bridge. Do you understand?'

'The ones in the rear,' Heims repeated. 'Not the ones near the
bridge.' He moved the machine-gun slowly up and down on its
rocker. He sucked reflectively at his teeth. 'You want them to run
forward, not back in the direction they are coming from. . . .'

Christian nodded.

'They won't run across the bridge, because they are in the open
there,' said Heims thoughtfully. 'They will run for the ravine, under
the bridge, because they are out of the field of fire there.'

Christian smiled. Perhaps he had been wrong about Heims, he
thought, he certainly knew what he was doing here.

'Then they will run into the mines down there,' said Heims flatly.
'I see.'

He and Richter nodded at each other. There was neither approval
nor disapproval in their gesture.

Christian took off his coat, so that he would be able to wave in it
signal to Dehn, under the bridge, as soon as he saw the enemy. Then
he sat on a stone behind Heims, who was sprawled out behind the
gun. Richter knelt on one knee, waiting with a second belt of
cartridges. Christian lifted the binoculars he had taken from the dead
lieutenant the evening before. He fixed them on the break between
the hills. He focused them carefully, noticing that they were good
glasses.

There were two poplar trees, dark green and funereal, at the break
in the road. They swayed glossily with the wind.

It was cold on the exposed side of the hill, and Christian was sorry he had told Dehn he would wave his coat at him. He could have done with his coat now. A handkerchief would probably have been good enough. He could feel his skin contracting in the cold and he hunched inside his stiff clothes uncomfortably.

'Can we smoke, Sergeant?' Richter asked.

'No,' said Christian, without lowering the glasses.

Neither of the men said anything. Cigarettes, thought Christian, remembering, I'll bet he has a whole packet, two packets. If he gets killed or badly wounded in this, Christian thought, I must remember to look through his pockets.

They waited. The wind, sweeping up from the valley, circled weightily within Christain's ears and up his nostrils and inside his sinuses. His head began to ache, especially around the eyes. He was very sleepy. He felt that he had been sleepy for three years.

Heims stirred as he lay outstretched, belly down, on the rockbed in front of Christian. Christian put down the glasses for a moment. The seat of Heims's trousers, blackened by mud, crudely patched, wide and shapeless, stared up at him. It is a sight, Christian thought foolishly, repressing a tendency to giggle, a sight completely lacking in beauty. The human form devine.

His forehead burned. The malaria. Not enough the English, not enough the French, the Poles, the Russians, the Americans, but the mosquitoes, too. Perhaps, he thought feverishly and cunningly, perhaps when this is over, I will have a real attack, one that cannot be denied, and they will have to send me back. He raised the glasses once more to his eyes, waiting for the chills to come, inviting the toxin in his blood to gain control.

Then he saw the small mud-coloured figures slowly plodding in front of the poplars. 'Quiet,' he said warningly, as though the Americans could hear Heims and the other man if they happened to speak.

The mud-coloured figures, looking like a platoon in any army, the fatigue of their movement visible even at this distance, passed in two lines, on each side of the road, across the binocular's field of vision. Thirty-seven, thirty-eight, forty-two, forty-three, Christian counted. Then they were gone. The poplars waved as they had waved before, the road in front of them looked exactly the same as it had before. Christian put down the glasses. He felt wide awake now, unexcited.

He stood up and waved his coat in large, deliberate circles. He could imagine the Americans moving in their cautious, slow way along the edge of the ridge, their eyes always nervously down on the ground, looking for mines.

A moment later he saw Dehn scramble swiftly out from beneath the bridge and run heavily up to the road. Dehn ran along the road, slowing down perceptibly as he tired, his boots kicking up minute puffs of dust. Then he reached a turn and he was out of sight.

Now the fuse was set. It only remained for the enemy to behave in a normal, soldierly manner.

Christian put on his coat, grateful for the warmth. He plunged his hands in his pockets, feeling cosy and calm.

The two men at the machine-gun lay absolutely still.

Far off there was the drone of plane engines. High, to the south-west, Christian saw a formation of bombers moving slowly, small specks in the sky, moving north on a bombing mission. A pair of sparrows swept, chirping, across the face of the cliff, darting in a flicker of swift brown feathers across the sights of the gun.

Heims belched twice. 'Excuse me,' he said politely.

They waited. Too long, Christian thought anxiously, they're taking too long. What are they doing back there? The bridge will go up before they get to the bend. Then the whole thing will be useless.

Heims belched again. 'My stomach,' he said aggrievedly to Richter. Richter nodded, staring down at the magazine on the gun, as though he had heard about Heims's stomach for years.

Hardenburg, Christian thought, would have done this better. He wouldn't have gambled like this. He would have made more certain, one way or another. If the dynamite didn't go off, and the bridge wasn't blown, and they heard about it back at Division, and they questioned that miserable Sergeant in the Pioneers and he told them about Christian . . . Please, Christian prayed under his breath, come on, come on, come on. . . .

Christian kept the glasses trained on the approach to the bridge. The glasses shook, and he knew that the chills were coming, although he did not feel them at that moment. There was a rushing, tiny noise, near him, and, involuntarily, he put the glasses down. A squirrel scurried up to the top of a rock ten feet away, then sat up and stared with beady, forest eyes at the three men. Another time, another place, Christian remembered, the bird strutting on the road through the woods outside Paris, before the French road-block, the overturned farm cart and the mattresses. The animal kingdom, curious for a moment about the war, then returning to its more important business.

Christian blinked and put the glasses to his eyes again. The enemy were out on the road now, walking slowly, crouched over, their rifles ready, every tense line shouting that their flesh inside their vulnerable clothing understood that they were targets.

The Americans were unbearably slow. They were taking infinitely small steps, stopping every five paces. The dashing, reckless young men of the New World. Christian had seen captured newsreels of them in training, leaping boldly through rolling surf from landing barges, flooding on to a beach like so many sprinters. They were not sprinting now. 'Faster, faster,' he found himself whispering, 'faster . . .' What lies the American people must believe about their soldiers!

Heims belched. It was a rasping, ugly, old man's noise. Each man reacted to a war in his own way, and Heims's reaction was from the stomach. What lies the people at home believed about Heims and his comrades. *What were you doing when you won the Iron Cross? Mother, I was belching.* Only Heims and he and Richter knew what the truth was, only they and the forty-three men tenderly approaching the old stone of the bridge that had been put up by slow Italian labourers in the sunlight of 1840. They knew the truth, the machine-gunners and himself, and the forty-three men shuffling through the dust across the gunsights eight hundred metres away, and they were more connected by that truth than to anyone else who wasn't there that morning. They knew of each other that their stomachs were contracting in sour spasms, and that all bridges are approached with timidity and a sense of doom. . . .

Christian licked his lips. The last man was out from behind the bend now, and the officer in command, the inevitable childish Lieutenant, was waving to a man with the mine detector, who was moving regretfully up towards the head of the column. Slowly, foolishly, they were bunching, feeling a little safer closer together now, feeling that if they hadn't been shot yet they were going to get through this all right.

The man with the mine detector began to sweep the road twenty metres in front of the bridge. He worked slowly and very carefully, and as he worked, Christian could see the Lieutenant, standing in the middle of the road, put his binoculars to his eyes and begin to sweep the country all around him. Zeiss binoculars, no doubt, Christian's mind registered automatically, made in Germany. He could see the binoculars come up and almost fix on their boulders, as though some nervous, latent military sense in the young Lieutenant recognized instinctively that if there were any danger ahead of him, this would be the focus of it. Christian crouched a little lower, although he was certain that they were securely hidden. The binoculars passed over them, then wavered back.

'Fire,' Christian whispered. 'Behind them. Behind them.'

The machine-gun opened up. It made an insane, shocking noise as it broke the mountain stillness, and Christian couldn't help blinking again and again. Down on the road two of the men had fallen. The others were still standing there stupidly, looking down in surprise at the men on the ground. Three more men fell on the road. Then the others began to run down the slope towards the ravine and the protection of the bridge. They are sprinting now, Christian thought, where is the camera-man? Some were carrying and dragging the men who had been hit. They stumbled and rolled down the slope, their rifles thrown away, their arms and legs waving grotesquely. It was remote and disconnected, and Christian watched almost disinterestedly, as though he were watching the struggle of a beetle dragged down into a hole by ants.

Then the first mine went off. A helmet hurtled end over end, twenty metres straight up in the air, glinting dully in the sunlight, its straps whipping in its flight.

Heims stopped firing. Then the explosions came one on top of another, echoing and re-echoing along the walls of the hills. A large dirty cloud of dust and smoke bloomed from the bridge.

The noise of the explosions died slowly, as though the sound was moving heavily through the draws and along the ridges to collect in other places. The silence, when it came, seemed unnatural, dangerous. The two sparrows wheeled erratically, disturbed and scolding, across the gun. Down below, from beneath the arch of the bridge, a single figure came walking out, very slowly and gravely, like a doctor from a deathbed. The figure walked five or six metres, then just as slowly sat down on a rock. Christian looked at the man through his glasses. The man's shirt had been blown off him, and his skin was pale and milky. He still had his rifle. While Christian watched, the man lifted his rifle, still with that lunatic deliberation and gravity. Why, thought Christian with surprise, he's aiming at us!

The sound of the rifle was empty and flat and the whistle of the bullets was surprisingly close over their heads. Christian grinned. 'Finish him,' he said.

Heims pressed the trigger of the machine-gun. Through his glasses, Christian could see the darting spurts of dust, flickering along a savage, swift line in an arc around the man. He did not move. Slowly, with the unhurried care of a carpenter at his workbench, he was putting a new clip in his rifle. Heims swung the machine-gun, and the arc of dust splashes moved closer to the man, who still refused to notice them. He got the clip in his rifle and lifted it once more to his naked shoulder. There was something insane, disturbing, about the shirtless, white-skinned man, an ivory blob against the green and brown of the ravine, sitting comfortably on the stone with all his comrades dead around him, firing in the leisurely and deliberate way at the machine-gun he could not quite make out with his naked eye, paying no attention to the continuous, snapping bursts of bullets that would, in a moment or two, finally kill him.

'Hit him,' Christian murmured irritably. 'Come on, hit him.'

Heims stopped firing for a moment. He squinted carefully and jiggled the gun. It made a sharp, piercing squeak. The sound of the rifle came from the valley below, meaningless and undangerous, although again and again there was the whine of a bullet over Christian's head, or the plunk as it hit the hard-packed dirt below him.

Then Heims got the range and fired one short burst. The man put down his gun drunkenly. He stood up slowly and took two or three sober steps in the direction of the bridge. Then he lay down as though he were tired.

At that moment, the bridge went up. Chunks of stone spattered against the trees along the road, slicing white gashes in them and knocking branches off. It took a long time for the dust to settle, and when it did, Christian saw the lumpy, broken mud-coloured uniforms sticking out here and there, at odd angles from the debris. The half-naked American had disappeared under a small avalanche of earth and stones.

Christian sighed and put down his glasses. Amateurs, he thought, what are they doing in a war?

Heims sat up and twisted round. 'Can we smoke now?' he asked.

'Yes,' said Christian, 'you can smoke.'

He watched Heims take out a packet of cigarettes. Heims offered one to Richter, who took it silently. The machine-gunner did not offer a cigarette to Christian. The miserly bastard, thought Christian bitterly, and reached in and took out one of his two remaining cigarettes.

He held the cigarette in his mouth, tasting it, feeling its roundness for a long time before he lit it. Then, with a sigh, feeling, well, I've earned it, he lit the cigarette. He took a deep puff and held the smoke in his lungs as long as he could. It made him feel a little dizzy, but relaxed. I must write about this to Hardenburg, Christian thought, taking another pull at the cigarette, he'll be pleased, he wouldn't have been able to do better himself. He leaned back comfortably, taking a deep breath, smiling at the bright blue sky and the pretty little clouds racing overhead in the mountain wind, knowing that he would have at least ten minutes to rest before Dehn got there. What a pretty morning, he thought.

Then he felt the long, quivering shiver sliding down his body. Ah, he thought deliciously, the malaria, and this is going to be a real attack, they're bound to send me back. A perfect morning. He shivered again, then took another pull at his cigarette. Then he leaned back happily against the boulder at his back, waiting for Dehn to arrive, hoping Dehn would take his time climbing the slope.

Lunghua Camp

J. G. Ballard

Voices fretted along the murmuring wire, carried like stressed notes on the strings of a harp. Fifty feet from the perimeter fence, Jim lay in the deep grass beside the pheasant trap. He listened to the guards arguing with each other as they conducted their hourly patrol of the camp. Now that the American air attacks had become a daily event, the Japanese soldiers no longer slung their rifles over their shoulders. They clasped the long-barrelled weapons in both hands, and were so nervous that if they saw Jim outside the camp perimeter they would shoot at him without thinking.

Jim watched them through the netting of the pheasant trap. Only the previous day they had shot a Chinese coolie trying to steal into the camp. He recognized one of the guards as Private Kimura, a large-boned farmer's son who had grown almost as much as Jim in his years at the camp. The private's strong back had burst through his faded tunic, and only his ammunition webbing held the tattered garment together.

Before the war finally turned against the Japanese, Private Kimura often invited Jim to the bungalow he shared with three other guards and allowed him to wear his kendo armour. Jim could remember the elaborate ceremony as the Japanese soldiers dressed him in the metal and leather armour, and the ripe smell of Private Kimura's body that filled the helmet and shoulder guards. He remembered the burst of violence as Private Kimura attacked him with the two-handed sword, the whirlwind of blows that struck his helmet before he could fight back. His head had rung for days. Giving him his orders, Basie had been forced to shout until he woke the men's dormitory in E Block, and Dr Ransome had called Jim into the camp hospital and examined his ears.

Remembering those powerful arms, and the quickness of Private Kimura's eyes, Jim lay flat in the long grass behind the trap. For once he was glad that the trap had failed to net a bird. The two Japanese had stopped by the wire fence and were scanning the group of abandoned buildings that lay outside the north-west perimeter of Lunghua Camp. Beside them, just within the camp, was the derelict hulk of the assembly hall, the curved balcony of its upper circle open to the sky. The camp occupied the site of a teacher training college that had been bombed and overrun during the fighting around Lunghua Aerodrome in 1937. The damaged buildings nearest to the airfield had been excluded from the camp, and it was here, in the long grass quadrangles between the gutted residence halls, that Jim set his pheasant traps. After roll-call that morning he had slipped through the fence where it emerged from a bank of nettles surrounding a forgotten blockhouse on the airfield perimeter. Leaving his shoes on the blockhouse steps, he waded along a shallow canal, and then crawled through the deep grass between the ruined buildings.

The first of the traps was only a few feet from the perimeter fence, a distance that had seemed enormous to Jim when he first crept through the barbed wire. He had looked back at the secure world of the camp, at the barrack huts and water tower, at the guardhouse and dormitory blocks, almost afraid that he had been banished from them forever. Dr Ransome often called Jim a 'free spirit', as he roved across the camp, hunting down some new idea in his head. But here, in the deep grass between the ruined buildings, he felt weighted by an unfamiliar gravity.

For once making the most of this inertia, Jim lay behind the trap. An aircraft was taking off from Lunghua Airfield, clearly silhouetted against the yellow façade of the apartment houses in the French Concession, but he ignored the plane. The soldier beside Private Kimura shouted to the children playing in the balcony of the assembly hall. Kimura was walking back to the wire. He scanned the surface of the canal and the clumps of wild sugar cane. The poor rations of the past year – the Japanese guards were almost as badly fed as their British and American prisoners – had drawn the last of the adolescent fat from Kimura's arms. After a recent attack of tuberculosis his strong face was puffy and coolie-like. Dr Ransome had repeatedly warned Jim never to wear Private Kimura's kendo armour. A fight between them would be less one-sided now, even though Jim was only fourteen. But for the rifle, he would have liked to challenge Kimura . . .

As if aware of the threat within the grass, Private Kimura called to his companion. He leaned his rifle against the pine fencing-post, stepped through the wire and stood in the deep nettles. Flies rose from the shallow canal and settled on his lips, but Kimura ignored them and stared at the strip of water that separated him from Jim and the pheasant traps.

Could he see Jim's footprints in the soft mud? Jim crawled away from the trap but the clear outline of his body lay in the crushed grass. Kimura was rolling his tattered sleeves, ready to wrestle with his quarry. Jim watched him stride through the nettles. He was certain that he could outrun Kimura, but not the bullet in the second soldier's rifle. How could he explain to Kimura that the pheasant traps had been Basie's idea? It was Basie who had insisted on the elaborate camouflage of leaves and twigs, and who made him climb through the wire twice a day, even though they had never seen a bird, let alone caught one. It was important to keep in with Basie, who had small but reliable sources of food. He could tell Kimura that Basie knew about the secret camp radio, but then the extra food would cease.

What most worried Jim was the thought that, if Kimura struck him, he would fight back. Few boys of his own age dared to touch Jim, and in the last year, since the rations had failed, few men. However, if he fought back against Kimura he would be dead.

He calmed himself, calculating the best moment to stand up and surrender. He would bow to Kimura, show no emotion and hope that the hundreds of hours he had spent hanging around the guardhouse – albeit at Basie's instigation – would count in his favour. He had once given English lessons to Kimura, but although they were clearly losing the war, the Japanese had not been interested in learning English.

Jim waited for Kimura to climb the bank towards him. The soldier stood in the centre of the canal, a bright black object gleaming in his hand. The creeks, ponds and disused wells within Lunghua Camp held an armoury of rusting weapons and unstable ammunition abandoned during the 1937 hostilities. Jim peered through the grass at the pointed cylinder, assuming that the tidal water in the canal had uncovered an old artillery shell or mortar bomb.

Kimura shouted to the second soldier waiting by the barbed wire. He brushed the flies from his face and spoke to the object, as if murmuring to a baby. He raised it behind his head, in the position taken by the Japanese soliders throwing a grenade. Jim waited for the explosion, and then realized that Private Kimura was holding a large fresh-water turtle. The creature's head emerged from its carapace, and Kimura began to laugh excitedly. His tubercular face resembled a small boy's, reminding Jim that Private Kimura had once been a child, as he himself had been before the war.

After crossing the parade ground, the Japanese soldiers disappeared among the lines of ragged washing between the barrack huts. Jim emerged from the damp cavern of the blockhouse. Wearing the leather golfing shoes given to him by Dr Ransome, he climbed through the wire. In his hand he carried Kimura's turtle. The ancient creature contained at least a pound of meat, and Basie, almost certainly, would know a special recipe for turtle. Jim could imagine Basie tempting it out of its shell with a live caterpillar, then skewering its head with his jack-knife . . .

In front of Jim was Lunghua Camp, his home and universe for the past three years, and the suffocating prison of nearly two thousand Allied nationals. The shabby barrack huts, the cement dormitory blocks, the worn parade ground and the guardhouse with its leaning watch-tower lay together under the June sun, a rendezvous for every fly and mosquito in the Yangtze basin. But once he stepped through the wire fence Jim felt the air steady around him. He ran along the cinder path, his tattered shirt flying from his bony shoulders like the tags of washing between the huts.

In his ceaseless journeys around the camp Jim had learned to recognize every stone and weed. A sun-bleached sign, crudely painted with the words 'Regent Street', was nailed to a bamboo pole beside the pathway. Jim ignored it, as he did the similar signs enscribed 'Piccadilly', Knightsbridge' and 'Petticoat Lane' which marked the main pathways within the camp. These relics of an imaginary London – which many of the Shanghai-born British prisoners had never seen – intrigued Jim but in some way annoyed him. With their constant talk about pre-war London, the older British families in the camp claimed a special exclusiveness. He remembered a line from one of the poems that Dr Ransome had made him memorize – 'a foreign field that is for ever England . . .' But this was Lunghua, not England. Naming the sewage-stained paths between the rotting huts after a

vaguely remembered London allowed too many of the British prisoners to shut out the reality of the camp, another excuse to sit back
when they should have been helping Dr Randome to clear the septic
tanks. To their credit, in Jim's eyes, neither the Americans nor the
Dutch and Belgians in the camp wasted their time on nostalgia. The
years in Lunghua had not given Jim a high opinion of the British.

And yet the London street signs fascinated him, part of the magic
of names that he had discovered in the camp. What, conceivably,
were Lord's, the Serpentine, and the Trocadero? There were so few
books or magazines that an unfamiliar brand-name had all the
mystery of a message from the stars. According to Basie, who was
always right, the American fighters with the ventral radiators that
strafed Lunghua Airfield were called 'Mustangs', the name of a wild
pony. Jim relished the name; to know that the planes were Mustangs
was more important to him than the confirmation that Basie had his
ear to the camp's secret radio. He hungered for names.

Jim stumbled on the worn path, unable to control the golf shoes.
Too often these days he became light-headed. Dr Ransome had
warned him not to run, but the American air attacks and the
imminent prospect of the war's end made him too impatient to walk.
Trying to protect the turtle, he grazed his left knee. He limped across
the cinder track and sat on the steps of the derelict drinking-water
station. Here brackish water taken from the ponds in the camp had
once been boiled by the prisoners. There was still a small supply of
coal in the camp store-rooms, but the work gang of six Britons who
stoked the fires had lost interest. Although Dr Ransome remonstrated
with them, they preferred to suffer from chronic dysentery rather
than make the effort of boiling the water.

While Jim nursed his knee the members of the gang sat outside the
nearby barrack hut, watching the sky as if they expected the war to
end within the next ten minutes. Jim recognized Mr Mulvaney, an
accountant with the Shanghai Power Company who had often swum
in the pool at Amherst Avenue. Beside him was the Reverend Pearce,
a Methodist missionary whose Japanese-speaking wife openly collab-
orated with the guards, reporting to them each day on the prisoners'
activities.

No one criticized Mrs Pearce for this, and in fact most of the
prisoners in Lunghua were only too keen to collaborate. Jim vaguely
disapproved, but agreed that it was probably sensible to do anything

to survive. After three years in the camp the notion of patriotism meant nothing. The bravest prisoners – and collaboration was a risky matter – were those who bought their way into the favour of the Japanese and thereby helped their fellows with small supplies of food and bandages. Besides, there were few illicit activities to betray. No one in Lunghua would dream of trying to escape, and everyone rightly ratted on any fool about to step through the wire, for fear of the reprisals to come.

The water-workers scraped their clogs on the steps and stared into the sun, moving only to pick the ticks from between their ribs. Although emaciated, the process of starvation had somehow stopped a skin's depth from the skeleton below. Jim envied Mr Mulvaney and the Reverend Pearce – he himself was still growing. The arithmetic that Dr Ransome had taught him made it all too clear that the food supplied to the camp was shrinking at a faster rate than that at which the prisoners were dying.

In the centre of the parade ground a group of twelve-year-old boys were playing marbles on the baked earth. Seeing the turtle, they ran towards Jim. Each of them controlled a dragonfly tied to a length of cotton. The blue flames flicked to and fro above their heads.

'Jim! Can we touch it?'

'What is it?'

'Did Private Kimura give it to you?'

Jim smiled benignly. 'It's a bomb.' He held out the turtle and generously allowed everyone to inspect it. Despite the gap in years, several of the boys had been close friends in the days after his arrival in Lunghua, when he had needed every ally he could find. But he had outgrown them and made other friends – Dr Ransome, Basie and the American seamen in E Block, with their ancient pre-war copies of the *Reader's Digest* and *Popular Mechanics* that he devoured. Now and then, as if recapturing his lost childhood, Jim re-entered the world of boyish games and would play tops and marbles and hopscotch.

'Is it dead? It's moving!'

'It's bleeding!'

A smear of blood from Jim's knee gave the turtle's head a piratical flourish.

'Jim, you killed it!'

The largest of the boys, Richard Pearce, reached out to touch the reptile, but Jim tucked it under his arm. He disliked and slightly feared Richard Pearce, who was almost as big as himself. He envied Richard the extra Japanese rations which his mother fed to him. As well as the food, the Pearces had a small library of confiscated books which they guarded jealously.

'It's a blood bond,' Jim explained grandly. By rights turtles belonged to the sea, to the open river visible a mile to the west of the camp, that broad tributary of the Yangtze down which he had once dreamed of sailing with his parents to the safety of a world without war.

'Watch out . . .' He waved Richard aside. 'I've trained it to attack!'

The boys backed away from him. There were times when Jim's humour made them uneasy. Although he tried to stop himself, Jim resented their clothes – hand-me-downs stitched together by their mothers, but far superior to his own rags. More than this, he resented that they had mothers and fathers at all. During the past year Jim had gradually realized that he could no longer remember what his parents looked like. Their veiled figures still entered his dreams, but he had forgotten their faces.

THE CUBICLE

'Young Jim . . .!'

An almost naked man wearing clogs and ragged shorts shouted to him from the steps of G Block. In his hands he held the shafts of a wooden cart with iron wheels. Although the cart carried no load, its handles had almost wrenched the man's arms from their sockets. He spoke to the English women sitting on the concrete steps in their faded cotton frocks. As he gestured to them his shoulder blades seemed to be working themselves loose from his back, about to fly across the barbed wire.

'I'm here, Mr Maxted!' Jim pushed Richard Pearce aside and ran along the cinder path to the dormitory block. Seeing the empty food cart, it occurred to him that he might have missed the daily meal. The fear of being without food for even a single day was so intense that he was ready to attack Mr Maxted.

'Come on, Jim. Without you it won't taste the same.' Mr Maxted glanced at Jim's golf shoes, these nailed brogues that had a life of their own and propelled his scarecrow figure on his ceaseless rounds of the camp. To the women he remarked: 'Our Jim's spending all his time at the 19th hole.'

'I promised, Mr Maxted. I'm always ready . . .' Jim had to stop as he reached the entrance to G Block. He worked his lungs until the dizziness left his head, and ran forward again. Turtle in hand, he raced up the steps into the foyer and swerved between two old men stranded like ghosts in the middle of a conversation they had forgotten.

On either side of the corridor was a series of small rooms, each furnished with four wooden bunks. After the first winter in the camp, when many of the children in the uninsulated barracks had died, families with children were moved into the residence halls of the former training college. Although unheated, the rooms with their cement walls remained above freezing point.

Jim shared his room with a young English couple, Mr and Mrs Vincent, and their six-year-old son. He had lived within inches of the Vincents for two and a half years, but their existences could not have been more separate. On the day of Jim's arrival Mrs Vincent had hung an old bedspread around his nominal quarter of the room. She and her husband – a broker on the Shanghai Stock Exchange – never ceased to resent Jim's presence, and over the years they had strengthened his cubicle, stringing together a worn shawl, a petticoat and the lid of a cardboard box, so that it resembled one of the miniature shanties that seemed to erect themselves spontaneously around the beggars of Shanghai.

Not content with walling Jim into his small world, the Vincents had repeatedly tried to encroach upon it, moving the nails and string from which the bedspread hung. Jim had defended himself, first by bending the nails until, to the Vincents's horror, the entire structure collapsed one night as they were undressing, and then by calibrating the wall with a ruler and pencil. The Vincents promptly retaliated by superimposing their own system of marks.

All this Jim took in his stride. For some reason he still liked Mrs Vincent, a handsome if frayed blonde, although her nerves were always stretched and she had never made the slightest attempt to care for him. He knew that if he starved to death in his bunk she would find some polite reason for doing nothing to help him. During the first year in Lunghua the few single children were neglected, unless they were prepared to let themselves be used as servants. Jim alone had refused, and had never fetched and carried for Mr Vincent.

Mrs Vincent was sitting on her straw mattress when he burst into the room, her pale hands folded onher lap like a forgotten pair of gloves. She stared at the whitewashed wall above her son's bunk, as if watching an invisible film projected on to a screen. Jim worried that Mrs Vincent spent too much of her time watching these films. As he peered at her through the cracks in his cubicle he tried to guess what she saw – a home-made cine film, perhaps, of herself in England before she was married, sitting on one of those sunlit lawns that seemed to cover the entire country. Jim assumed that it was those lawns that had provided the emergency airfields for the Battle of Britain. As he was aware from his observations in Shanghai, the Germans were not too keen on sunlit lawns. Was this why they had lost the Battle of Britain? Many of his ideas were hopelessly confused in a way that even Dr Ransome was too tired to disentangle.

'You're late, Jim,' Mrs Vincent told him disapprovingly, her eyes on his golf shoes. Like everyone else, she was unable to cope with their intimidating presence. Already Jim felt that the shoes gave him a special authority. 'The whole of G Block has been waiting for you.'

'I've been with Basie, hearing the latest war news. Mrs Vincent, what's the 19th hole?'

'You shouldn't work for Basie. The things those Americans ask you to do . . . I've told you that we come first.'

'G Block comes first, Mrs Vincent.' Jim meant it. He ducked under the flap into his cubicle. Catching his breath, he lay on the bunk with the turtle inside his shirt. The reptile preferred its own company, and Jim turned his attention to his new shoes. With their polished toecaps and bright studs, they were an intact piece of the pre-war world that he could stare at for hours, like Mrs Vincent and her films. Laughing to himself, Jim lay back as the hot sunlight shone through the wall of the cubicle, outlining the curious stains on the old bedspread. Looking at them, he visualized the scenes of air-battles and armadas, the sinking of the *Petrel*, and even the garden at Amherst Avenue.

'Jim, kitchen time . . .!' he heard someone call from the steps below the window. But Jim rested on his bunk. It was a long haul to the kitchens, and there was no point in being early. The Japanese had celebrated VE Day in their own way, by cutting the already meagre

rations in half. The first arrivals often received less than the later
ones, when the cooks realized how many of the prisoners had died or
were too ill to collect their rations.

Besides, there was no obligation on Jim to help with the food cart
– nor, for that matter, on Mr Maxted. But as Jim had noticed, those
who were prepared to help their fellow prisoners tended to do so, and
this did nothing to stop those too lazy to work from endlessly
complaining. The British were especially good at complaining, something the Dutch and Americans never did. Soon Jim reflected with a
certain grim pleasure, they would be too sick even to complain.

He gazed at his shoes, consciously imitating the childlike smile on
Private Kimura's lips. The wooden bunk filled the cubicle, but Jim
was at his happiest in this miniature universe. On the walls he had
pinned several pages from an old *Life* magazine that Basie had given
to him. There were photographs of Battle of Britain pilots sitting in
armchairs beside their Spitfires, of a crashed Heinkel bomber, of St
Paul's floating like a battleship on a sea of fire. Next to them was a
full-page colour advertisement for a Packard motorcar, as beautiful
in Jim's eyes as the Mustang fighters which strafed Lunghua Airfield.
Did the Americans bring out a new-model Mustang every year or
every month? Perhaps there would be an air raid that afternoon,
when he could check the latest design modifications to the Mustangs
and Superfortresses. Jim looked forward to the air raids.

Besides the Packard was a small section that Jim had cut from a
larger photograph of a crowd outside the gates of Buckingham Palace
in 1940. The blurred images of a man and a woman standing arm-in-
arm reminded Jim of his parents. This unknown English couple,
perhaps dead in an air raid, had almost become his mother and
father. Jim knew that they were complete strangers, but he kept the
pretence alive, so that in turn he could keep alive the lost memory of
his parents. The world before the war, his childhood in Amherst
Avenue, his class at the Cathedral School, belonged to that invisible
film which Mrs Vincent watched from her bunk.

Jim allowed the turtle to crawl across his straw mat. If he carried
it around with him Private Kimura or one of the guards might guess
that he had left the camp. Now that the war was ending the Japanese
guards were convinced that the British and American prisoners were
constantly trying to escape – the last notion, in fact, to cross their
minds. In 1943 a few Britishers had escaped, hoping to be sheltered

by neutral friends in Shanghai, but had soon been discovered by the
army of informers. Several groups of Americans had set out in the
summer of 1944 for Chungking, the Nationalist Chinese capital nine
hundred miles to the west. All had been betrayed by Chinese villagers
terrified of reprisals, handed over to the Japanese and executed. From
then on escape attempts ceased altogether. By June 1945, the
landscape around Lunghua was so hostile, roamed by bandits,
starving villagers and deserters from the puppet armies, that the
camp and its Japanese guards offered the only security.

With his finger Jim stroked the turtle's ancient head. It seemed a
pity to cook it – Jim envied the reptile its massive shell, a private
fortress against the world. From below his bunk he pulled out a
wooden box, which Dr Ransome had helped him to nail together.
Inside were his possessions – a Japanese cap badge given to him by
Private Kimura; three steel-bossed fighting tops; a chess set and a
copy of Kennedy's *Latin Primer* on indefinite loan from Dr Ransome;
his Cathedral School blazer, a carefully folded memory of his younger
self; and the pair of clogs he had worn for the past three years.

Jim placed the turtle in the box and covered it with the blazer. As
he raised the flap of his cubicle Mrs Vincent watched his every move.
She treated him like her Number Two Coolie, and he was well aware
that he tolerated this for reasons he barely understood. Like all the
men and older boys in G Block, Jim was attracted to Mrs Vincent,
but her real appeal for Jim lay elsewhere. Her long hours staring at
the whitewash, and her detachment even from her own son – she fed
the dysentery-ridden boy and changed his clothes without looking at
him for minutes at a time – suggested to Jim that she remained
forever above the camp, beyond the world of guards and hunger and
American air attacks to which he himself was passionately committed.
He wanted to touch her, less out of adolescent lust than simple
curiosity.

'You can use my bunk, Mrs Vincent, if you want to sleep.'

As Jim reached to her shoulder she pushed his hand away. Her
distracted eyes could come to a remarkably sharp focus.

'Mr Maxted is still waiting, Jim. Perhaps it's time you went back
to the huts . . .'

'Not the huts, Mrs Vincent,' he pretended to groan. Not the huts,
he repeated fiercely to himself as he left the room. The huts were
cold, and if the war lasted beyond the winter of 1945 many more

people would die in those freezing barracks. However, for Mrs
Vincent perhaps he would go back to the huts . . .

THE UNIVERSITY OF LIFE

All over the camp there sounded the scraping of iron wheels. In the
windows of the barrack huts, on the steps of the dormitory blocks,
the prisoners were sitting up, roused for a few minutes by the memory
of food.

Jim left the foyer of G Block, and found Mr Maxted still holding
the wooden handles of the food cart. Having made the effort twenty
minutes earlier to lift the handles, he had exhausted his powers of
decision. The former architect and entrepreneur, who had represented so much that Jim most admired about Shanghai, had been
sadly drained by his years in Lunghua. After arriving at the camp
Jim had been glad to find him there, but by now he realized how
much Mr Maxted had changed. His eyes forever watched the
cigarette butts thrown down by the Japanese guards, but only Jim
was quick enough to retrieve them. Jim chafed at this, but he
supported Mr Maxted out of nostalgia for his childhood dream of
growing up one day to be like him.

The Studebaker and the afternoon girls in the gambling casinos
had prepared Mr Maxted poorly for the world of the camp. As Jim
took the wooden handles he wondered how long the architect would
have stood on the sewage-stained path. Perhaps all day, watched
until he dropped by the same group of British prisoners who sat on
the steps without once offering to help. Half-naked in their ragged
clothes, they stared at the parade ground, uninterested even in a
Japanese fighter that flew overhead. Several of the married couples
held their mess-plates, already forming a queue, a reflex response to
Jim's arrival.

'At last . . .'

'. . . that boy . . .'

'. . . running wild.'

These mutters drew an amiable smile from Mr Maxted. 'Jim you're
going to be blackballed by the country club. Never mind.'

'I don't mind.' When Mr Maxted stumbled Jim held his arm. 'Are you all right, Mr Maxted?'

Jim waved to the men sitting on the step, but no one moved. Mr Maxted steadied himself. 'Let's go, Jim. Some work and some watch, and that's all there is to it.'

For the past year there had been a third member of the team, Mr Carey, the owner of the Buick agency in Nanking Road. But six weeks earlier he had died of malaria, and by then the Japanese had cut the food ration to a point where only two of them were needed to push the cart.

Propelled by his new shoes, Jim sped along the cinder path. The iron wheels struck sparks from the flinty stones. Mr Maxted held his shoulder, panting to keep up.

'Slow down, Jim. You'll get there before the war ends.'

'When will the war end, Mr Maxted?'

'Jim . . . is it going to end? Another year, 1946. You tell me, you listen to Basie's radio.'

'I haven't heard the radio, Mr Maxted,' Jim answered truthfully. Basie was far too canny to admit a Britisher into the secret circle of listeners. 'I know the Japanese surrendered at Okinawa. I hope the war ends soon.'

'Not too soon, Jim. Our problem might begin then. Are you still giving English lessons to Private Kimura?'

'He isn't interested in learning English,' Jim had to admit. 'I think the war's really ended for Private Kimura.'

'Will the war really end for you, Jim? You'll see your mother and father again.'

'Well . . .' Jim preferred not to talk about his parents, even with Mr Maxted. The two of them had formed a long-standing partnership, though Mr Maxted did little to help Jim and rarely referred to his son Patrick or to their visits to the Shanghai clubs and bars. Mr Maxted was no longer the dapper figure who fell into swimming-pools. What worried Jim was that his mother and father might also have changed. Soon after arriving in Lunghua he heard that his parents were interned in a camp near Soochow, but the Japanese refused to consider the notion of a transfer.

They crossed the parade ground and approached the camp kitchens behind the guardhouse. Some twenty food carts and their teams were drawn up beside the serving hatch, jostling together like a crowd of rickshaws and their coolies. As Jim had estimated, he and Mr Maxted would take their place halfway down the queue. Late-comers clattered along the cinder paths, watched by hundreds of emaciated prisoners. One day during the previous week there had been no food, as a reprisal for a Superfortress raid that had devastated Tokyo, and the prisoners had continued to stare at the kitchens until late afternoon. The silence had unsettled Jim, reminding him of the beggars outside the house in Amherst Avenue. Without thinking, he had removed his shoes and hidden them among the graves in the hospital cemetery.

Jim and Mr Maxted took their places in the queue. Outside the guardhouse a work party of British and Belgian prisoners were strengthening the fence. Two of the prisoners unwound a coil of barbed wire, which the others cut and nailed to the fencing posts. Several of the Japanese soldiers were working shoulder to shoulder with their prisoners, ragged uniforms barely distinguishable from the faded khaki of the inmates.

The object of this activity was a group of thirty Chinese camped outside the gates. Destitute peasants and villagers, soldiers from the puppet armikes and abandoned children, they sat in the open road, staring at the barbed-wire gates being strengthened against them. The first of these impoverished people had appeared three months earlier. At night some of the more desperate would climb through the wire, only to be caught by the internees' patrols. Those who survived in the guardhouse till dawn were taken down to the river by the Japanese and clubbed to death on the bank.

As they moved forward to the serving hatch Jim watched the Chinese. Although it was summer the peasants still wore their quilted winter clothes. Needless to say, none of the Chinese was ever admitted to Lunghua Camp, let alone fed. Yet still they came, attracted to this one place in the desolate land where there was food. Worryingly for Jim, they stayed until they died. Mr Maxted was right when he said that with the conclusion of the war the prisoners' real problems would not end, but begin.

Jim worried about Dr Ransome and Mrs Vincent, and the rest of his fellow-prisoners. How would they survive, without the Japanese to look after them? He worried especially for Mr Maxted, whose tired repertory of jokes about the country club meant nothing in the real world. But at least Mr Maxted was trying to keep the camp going, and it was the integrity of the camp on which they depended.

During 1943, when the war was still moving in Japan's favour, the prisoners had worked together. The entertainments committee, of which Mr Maxted had been chairman, organized a nightly programme of lectures and concert parties. This was the happiest year of Jim's life. Tired of his cramped cubicle and Mrs Vincent's nail-tapping aloofness, he spent every evening listening to lectures on an endless variety of topics: the construction of the pyramids, the history of the world land-speed record, the life of a district commissioner in Uganda (the lecturer, a retired Indian Army officer, claimed to have named after himself a lake the size of Wales, which amazed Jim), the infantry weapons of the Great War, the management of the Shanghai Tramways Company, and a score of others.

Sitting in the front row of the assembly hall, Jim devoured these lectures, many of which he attended two or three times. He helped to copy the parts for the Lunghua Players' productions of *Macbeth* and *Twelfth Night*, he moved scenery for *The Pirates of Penzance* and *Trial by Jury*. For most of 1944 there was a camp school run by the missionaries, which Jim found tedious by comparison with the evening lectures. But he deferred to Basie and Dr Ransome. Both agreed that he should never miss a class, if only, Jim suspected, to give themselves a break from his restless energy.

But by the winter of 1944 all this had ended. After the American fighter attacks on Lunghua Airfield, and the first bombing raids on the Shanghai dockyards, the Japanese enforced an evening curfew. The supply of electric current to the camp was switched off for good, and the prisoners retreated to their bunks. The already modest food ration was cut to a single meal each day. American submarines blockaded the Yangtze estuary, and the huge Japanese armies in China began to fall back to the coast, barely able to feed themselves.

The prospect of their defeat, and the imminent assault on the Japanese home islands, made Jim more and more nervous. He ate every scrap of food he could find, aware of the rising numbers of deaths from beri beri and malaria. Jim admired the Mustangs and Superfortresses, but sometimes he wished that the Americans would return to Hawaii and content themselves with raising their battleships at Pearl Harbor. Then Lunghua Camp would once again be the happy place that he had known in 1943.

*   *   *

When Jim and Mr Maxted returned with the rations to G Block the prisoners were waiting silently with their plates and mess-tins. They stood on the steps, the bare-chested men with knobbed shoulders and birdcage ribs, their faded wives in shabby frocks, watching without expression as if about to be presented with a corpse. At the head of the queue were Mrs Pearce and her son, followed by the missionary couples who spent all day hunting for food.

Hundreds of flies hovered in the steam that rose from the metal pails of cracked wheat and sweet potatoes. As he heaved on the wooden handles Jim winced with pain, not from the strain of pulling the cart, but from the heat of the stolen sweet potato inside his shirt. As long as he remained doubled up no one would see the potato, and he put on a pantomime of grimaces and groans.

'Oh, no . . . oh, my God . . .'

'Worthy of the Lunghua Players, Jim.' Mr Maxted had watched him remove the potato from the pail as they left the kitchens, but he never objected. Crouching forward, Jim abandoned the cart to the missionaries. He ran up the steps, past the Vincents, who stood plates in hand – it never occurred to them, nor to Jim, that they should bring his plate with them. He dived through the curtain into his cubicle and dropped the steaming potato under his mat, hoping that the damp straw would smother the vapour. He seized his plate, and darted back to the foyer to take his place at the head of the queue. Mr Maxted had already served the Reverend and Mrs Pearce, but Jim shouldered aside their son. He held out his plate and received a ladle of boiled wheat and a second sweet potato which he had pointed out to Mr Maxted within moments of leaving the kitchens.

Returning to his bunk, Jim relaxed for the first time. He drew the curtain and lay back, the warm plate like a piece of the sun against his chest. He felt drowsy, but at the same time light-headed with hunger. He rallied himself with the thought that there might be an American air raid that afternoon – who did he want to win? The question was important.

Jim cupped his hands over the sweet potato. He was almost too hungry to enjoy the grey pith, but he gazed at the photograph of the man and woman outside Buckingham Palace, hoping that his parents, wherever they were, also had an extra potato.

When the Vincents returned with their rations Jim sat up and folded back the curtain so that he could examine their plates. He liked to watch Mrs Vincent eating her meals. Keeping a close eye on her, Jim studied the cracked wheat. The starchy grains were white and swollen, indistinguishable from the weevils that infested these warehouse sweepings. In the early years of the camp everyone pushed the weevils to one side, or flicked them through the nearest window, but now Jim carefully husbanded them. Often there was more than a hundred insects in three rows around the rim of Jim's plate, though recently even their number was in decline. 'Eat the weevils,' Dr Ransome had told him, and he did so, although everyone else washed them away. But there was protein in them, a fact that Mr Maxted seemed to find depressing when Jim informed him of it.

After counting the eighty-seven weevils – their numbers, Jim calculated, wsere falling less steeply than the ration – he stirred them into the cracked wheat, an animal feed grown in northern China, and swallowed the six spoonfuls. Giving himself a breather, he waited for Mrs Vincent to begin her sweet potato.

'Must you, Jim?' Mr Vincent asked. No taller than Jim, the stockbroker and former amateur jockey sat on his bunk beside his ailing son. With his black hair and lined yellow face like a squeezed lemon, he reminded Jim of Basie, but Mr Vincent had never come to terms with Lunghua. 'You'll miss this camp when the war's over. I wonder how you'll take to school in England.'

'It might be a bit strange,' Jim admitted, finishing the last of the weevils. He felt sensitive about his ragged clothes and his determined efforts to stay alive. He wiped his plate clean with his finger, and remembered a favourite phrase of Basie's. 'All the same, Mr Vincent, the best teacher is the university of life.'

Mrs Vincent lowered her spoon. 'Jim, could we finish our meal? We've heard your views on the university of life.'

'Right. But we should eat the weevils, Mrs Vincent.'

'I know, Jim. Dr Ransome told you so.'

'He said we need the protein.'

'Dr Ransome is right. We should all eat the weevils.'

Hoping to brighten the conversation, Jim asked: 'Mrs Vincent, do you believe in vitamins?'

Mrs Vincent stared at her plate. She spoke with true despair. 'Strange child . . .'

The rebuff to bother Jim. Everything about this distant woman with her thinning blond hair intrigued him, although in many ways he distrusted her. Six months earlier, when Dr Ransome thought that Jim had contracted pneumonia, she had done nothing to look after him, and Dr Ransome was forced to come in every day and wash Jim himself. Yet the previous evening she had helped him with his Latin homework, matter-of-factly pointing out the distinction between gerunds and gerundives.

Jim waited until she began her sweet potato. After confirming that his own potato was the largest of the four in the room, and deciding not to save any for the turtle under his bunk, he broke the skin and swiftly devoured the warm pulp. When the last morsel had gone he lay back and lowered the curtain. Alone now – the Vincents, although only a few feet away from him, might as well have been on another planet – Jim pondered the jobs ahead of him that day. First, there was the second potato to be smuggled from the room. There were his Latin homework for Dr Ransome, errands to be run for Basie and Private Kimura, and then the afternoon air raid – all in all, a full programme until the evening curfew, when he would probably roam the G Block corridors with his chess set, ready to take on all comers.

The Kennedy *Primer* in hand, Jim stepped from his cubicle. The second potato bulged in his trouser pocket, but for several months the presence of Mrs Vincent had sometimes given him an unexpected erection, and he relied on the confusion to make his escape.

His spoon halfway to his mouth, Mr Vincent stared at the bulge with an expression of deep gloom. His wife gazed in her level fashion at Jim, who side-stepped quickly from the room. Glad as always to be free of the Vincents, he skipped down the corridor to the external door below the fire-escape, and vaulted over the children squatting on one step. As the warm air ruffled the ragged strips of his shirt he ran off into the familiar and reassuring world of the camp.

The Journey

Nevil Shute

Kuala means the mouth of a river, and Kuala Panong is a small town at the entrance to the Panong River. There is a District Commissioner stationed there. By the time the truck reached his office it was loaded with about forty men, women, and children picked up for forcible evacuation from the surrounding estates. Most of these were English-women of relatively humble birth, the wives of foremen engineers at the tin mines or gangers on the railway. Few of them had been able to appreciate the swiftness and the danger of the Japanese advance. Plantation managers and those in the Secretariat and other Government positions had had better sources of information and more money to spend, and these had got their families away to Singapore in good time. Those who were left to be picked up by truck at the last moment were the least competent.

The truck halted at the DC's office and the subaltern went inside; the DC came out presently, a very worried man, and looked at the crowded women and children, and the few men amongst them. 'Christ,' he said quietly as he realized the extent of the new responsibility. 'Well, drive them to the accounts office over there; they must sit in the veranda for an hour or two and I'll try and get something fixed up for them. Tell them not to wander about too much.' He turned back into the office. 'I can send them down in fishing-boats, I think,' he said. 'There are some of those left. That's the best I can do. I haven't got a launch.'

The party were unloaded on to the veranda of the accounts office, and here they were able to stretch and sort themselves out a little. There were chatties of cold water in the office and the veranda was shady and cool. Jean and Bill Holland left Eileen sitting on the veranda with her back against the wall with the children about her, and walked into the village to buy what they could to replace the luggage they had lost. They were able to get a feeding-bottle for the

baby, a little quinine, some salts for dysentery, and two tins of
biscuits and three of tinned meat; they tried for mosquito nets, but
they were all sold out. Jean got herself a few needles and thread, and
seeing a large canvas haversack she bought that, too. She carried that
haversack for the next three years.

They went back to the veranda about teatime and displayed their
purchases, and had a little meal of biscuits and lemon squash.

Towards sunset the lighthouse-keepers at the river mouth telephoned to the DC that the *Osprey* was coming into the river. The
Osprey was the customs launch that ran up and down the coast
looking for smugglers from Sumatra across the Malacca Strait; she
was a large Diesel-engined vessel about a hundred and thirty feet
long, normally stationed at Penang; a powerful, seagoing ship. The
DC's face lit up; here was the solution to his problems. Whatever was
the mission of the *Osprey* she must take his evacuees on board, and
run them down the coast out of harm's way. Presently he left his
office, and walked down to the quay to meet the vessel as she berthed,
to interview the captain.

She came round the bend in the river, and he saw that she was
loaded with troops, small stocky men in grey-green uniforms with
rifles and fixed bayonets taller than themselves. With a sick heart he
watched her as she came alongside, realizing that this was the end of
all his endeavour.

The Japanese came rushing ashore and arrested him immediately,
and walked him back up the jetty to his office with guns at his back,
ready to shoot him at the slightest show of resistance. But there were
no troops there to resist; even the officer with the truck had driven off
in an attempt to join his unit. The soldiers spread out and occupied
the place without a shot; they came to the evacuees sitting numbly in
the veranda of the accounts office. Immediately, with rifles and
bayonets levelled, they were ordered to give up all fountain-pens and
wristwatches and rings. Advised by their men folk, the women did so
silently, and suffered no other molestation. Jean lost her watch and
had her bag searched for a fountain-pen, but she had packed it in her
luggage.

An officer came presently, when night had fallen, and inspected
the crowd on the veranda in the light of a hurricane lamp; he walked
down the veranda thrusting his lamp forward at each group, a couple
of soldiers hard on his heels with rifles at the ready and bayonets

fixed. Most of the children started crying. The inspection finished, he made a little speech in broken English. 'Now you are prisoners,' he said. 'You stay here tonight. Tomorrow you go to prisoner camp perhaps. You do good things, obedience to orders, you will receive good from Japanese soldiers. You do bad things, you will be shot directly. So, do good things always. When officer come, you stand up and bow, always. That is good thing. Now you sleep.'

One of the men asked, 'May we have beds and mosquito nets?'

'Japanese soldiers have no beds, no mosquito nets. Perhaps tomorrow you have beds and nets.'

Another said, 'Can we have some supper?' This had to be explained. 'Food.'

'Tomorrow you have food.' The officer walked away, leaving two sentries on guard at each of the veranda.

Kuala Panong lies in a marshy district of mangrove swamps at the entrance to a muddy river; the mosquitoes are intense. All night the children moaned and wailed fretfully, preventing what sleep might have been possible for the adults. The night passed slowly, wearily on the hard floor of the veranda; between the crushing misery of captivity and defeat and the torment of the mosquitoes few of the prisoners slept at all. Jean dozed a little in the early hours and woke stiff and aching and with swollen face and arms as a fresh outburst from the children heralded the more intense attack from the mosquitoes that comes in the hour before the dawn. When the first light came the prisoners were in a very unhappy state.

There was a latrine behind the account office, inadequate for the numbers that had to use it. They made the best of that, and there was nothing then to do but to sit and wait for what would happen. Holland and Eileen made sandwiches for the children of tinned meat and sweet biscuits, and after this small breakfast they felt better. Many of the others had some small supplies of food, and those that had none were fed by those who had. Nothing was provided for the prisoners that morning by the Japanese.

In the middle of the morning an interrogation began. The prisoners were taken by families to the DC's office, where a Japanese captain, whom Jean was to know later as Captain Yoniata, sat with a lieutenant at his side, who made notes in a child's penny exercise book. Jean went in with the Hollands; when the captain enquired who she was she explained that she was a friend of the family travelling with them, and told him what her job was in Kuala Lumpur. It did not take long. At the end the captain said, 'Men go to prisoner camp today, womans and childs stay here. Men leave in afternoon, so you will now say farewell till this afternoon. Thank you.'

They had feared this, and had discussed it in the veranda, but they had not expected it would come so soon. Holland asked, 'May we know where the women and children will be sent to? Where will their camp be?'

The officer said, 'The Imperial Japanese Army do not make war on womans and on childs. Perhaps not go to camp at all, if they do good things, perhaps live in homes. Japanese soldiers always kind to womans and to childs.'

They went back to the veranda and discussed the position with the other families. There was nothing to be done about it, for it is usual in war for men to be interned in separate camps from women and children, but none the less it was hard to bear. Jean felt her presence was unwanted with the Holland family, and went and sat alone on the edge of the veranda, feeling hungry and wondering, with gloom tempered by the buoyancy of youth, what lay ahead of her. One thing was certain; if they were to spend another night upon the veranda she must get hold of some mosquito repellent. There was a chemist's shop just up the village that they had visited the afternoon before; it was probable that in such a district he had some repellent.

As an experiment she attracted the attention of the sentry and pointed to her mosquito bites; then she pointed to the village and got down from the veranda on to the ground. Immediately he brought his bayonet to the ready and advanced towards her; she got back on to the veranda in a hurry. That evidently wouldn't do. He scowled at her suspiciously, and went back to his position.

There was another way. The latrine was behind the building up against a wall; there was no sentry there because the wall prevented any exit from the accounts office except by going round the building to the front. She moved after a time and went out of the back door. Sheltered from the view of the sentries by the building, she looked around. There were some children playing in the middle distance.

She called softly in Malay, 'Girl. You, you girl. Come here.'

The child came towards her; she was about twelve years old. Jean asked, 'What is your name?'

She giggled shyly, 'Halijah.'

Jean said, 'Do you know the shop that sells medicine? Where a Chinese sells medicine?'

She nodded. 'Chan Kok Fuan.'

Jean said, 'Go to Chan Kok Fuan, and if you give my message to him so that he comes to me, I will give you ten cents. Say that the Mem has Nyamok bites' – she showed her bites – 'and he should bring ointments to the veranda, and he will sell many to the Mems. Do this, and if he comes with ointments I will give you ten cents.'

The child nodded and went off. Jean went back to the veranda and waited; presently the Chinaman appeared carrying a try loaded with little tubes and pots. He approached the sentry and spoke to him, indicating his wish to sell his wares; after some hesitation the sentry agreed. Jean got six tubes of repellent and the rest was swiftly taken by the other women. Halijah got ten cents.

Presently a Japanese orderly brought two buckets of a thin fish soup and another half full of boiled rice, dirty and unappetizing. There were no bowls or utensils to eat with. There was nothing to be done but to eat as best they could; at that time they had not fallen into the prisoner's mode of life in which all food is strictly shared out and divided scrupulously, so that some got much more than others, who got little or none. There were still food supplies, however, so they fell back on the biscuits and the private stocks to supplement the ration.

That afternoon the men were separated from their families, and marched off under guard. Bill Holland turned from his fat, motherly wife, his eyes moist. 'Goodbye, Jean,' he said heavily. 'Good luck.' And then he said, 'Stick with them, if you can, won't you?'

She nodded. 'I'll do that. We'll all be in the same camp together.'

The men were formed up together, seven of them, and marched off under guard.

The party then consisted of eleven married women, and two girls, Jean and an anaemic girl called Ellen Forbes who had been living with one of the families; she had come out to be married, but it hadn't worked out. Besides these there were nineteen children varying in age from a girl of fourteen to babies in arms; thirty-two persons in all. Most of the women could speak no language but their own; a few of them, including Eileen Holland, could speak enough Malay to control their servants, but no more.

They stayed in the accounts office for forty-one days.

The second night was similar to the first, except that the doors of the offices were opened for then and they were allowed to use the rooms. A second meal of fish soup was given to them in the evening, but nothing else whatever was provided for their use – no beds, no blankets, and no nets. Some of the women had their luggage with them and had blankets, but there were far too few to go round. A stern-faced woman, Mrs Horsefall, asked to see the officer; when Captain Yoniata came she protested at the condition and asked for beds and nets.

'No nets, no beds,' he said. 'Very sorry for you. Japanese womans sleep on mat on floor. All Japanese sleep on mat. You put away proud thoughts, very bad thing. You sleep on mat like Japanese womans.'

'But we're English,' she said indignantly. 'We don't sleep on the floor like animals.!'

His eyes hardened; he motioned to the sentries, who gripped her by each arm. Then he hit her four stinging blows upon the face with the flat of his hand. 'Very bad thoughts,' he said, and turned upon his heel, and left them. No more was said about beds.

He came to inspect them the next morning and Mrs Horsefall, undaunted, asked for a water supply; she pointed out that washing was necessary for the babies and desirable for everyone. A barrel was brought into the smallest office that afternoon and was kept filled by coolies; they turned this room into a bathroom and washhouse. In those early days most of the women had money, and following the example of Chan Kok Fuan the shopkeepers of the village came to sell to the prisoners, so they accumulated the bare essentials for existence.

Gradually they grew accustomed to their hardships. The children quickly learned to sleep upon the floor without complaint; the younger women took a good deal longer, and the women over thirty seldom slept for more than half an hour without waking in pain – but they did sleep. It was explained to them by Captain Yoniata that until the campaign was over the victorious Japanese had no time to construct prison camps for women. When all Malaya had been conquered they would be moved into a commodious and beautiful camp which would be built for them in the Cameron Highlands, a noted health resort up in the hills. There they would find beds and mosquito nets and all the amenities to which they were accustomed, but to earn these delights they must stay where they were and do good things. Doing good things meant getting up and bowing whenever he approached. After a few faces had been slapped and shins had been kicked by Captain Yoniata's army boots, they learned to do this good thing.

The food issued to them was the bare minimum that would support life, and was an unvarying issue of fish soup and rice, given to them twice a day. Complaint was useless and even dangerous; in the view of Captain Yoniata these were proud thoughts that had to be checked for the moral good of the complaint. Meals, however, could be supplied by a small Chinese restaurant in the village, and while money was available most of the families ordered one cooked meal a day from this restaurant.

They received no medical attention and no drugs whatsoever. At the end of a week dysentery attacked them, and the nights were made hideous by screaming children stumbling with their mothers to the latrine. Malaria was always in the background, held in check by the quinine that they could still buy from Chan Kok Fuan at an ever increasing price. To check the dysentery Captain Yoniata reduced the soup and increased the rice ration, adding to the rice some of the dried, putrescent fish that had formerly made the soup. Later, he added to the diet a bucket of tea in the afternoon, as a concession to English manners.

Through all this time, Jean shared with Mrs Holland the care of the three Holland children. She suffered a great deal from weakness and a feeling of lassitude induced, no doubt, by the change in diet, but she slept soundly most nights until wakened, which was frequently. Eileen Holland suffered much more. She was older, and could not sleep so readily upon the floor, and she had lost much of the resilience of her youth. She lost weight rapidly.

On the thirty-fifth day, Esmé Harrison died.

Esmé was a child of eight. She had had dysentery for some time and was growing very thin and weak; she slept little and cried a great deal. Presently she got fever, and for two days ran a temperature of a hundred and four as the malaria rose in her. Mrs Horsefall told Captain Yoniata that the child must see a doctor and go to hospital. He said he was very sorry, but there was no hospital. He would try and get a doctor, but the doctors were all fighting with the victorious army of the Emperor. That evening Esmé entered on a series of convulsions, and shortly before dawn she died.

She was buried that morning in the Moslem cemetery behind the village; her mother and one other woman were allowed to attend the burial. They read a little of the service out of a prayer book before the uncomprehending soliders and Malays, and then it was over. Life went on as before in the accounts office, but the children now had nightmares of death to follow them to sleep.

At the end of six weeks Captain Yoniata faced them after the morning inspection. The women stood worn and draggled in the shade of the veranda facing him, holding the children by the hand. Many of the adults, and most of the children, by that time were thin and ill.

He said, 'Ladies, the Imperial Japanese Army has entered Singapore, and all Malaya is free. Now prisoner camps are being built for men and also for womans and childs. Prisoner camps are at Singapore and you go there. I am very sad your life here has been uncomfortable, but now will be better. Tomorrow you start to Kuala Lumpur, not more than you can go each day. From Kuala Kumpur you go by train to Singapore, I think. In Singapore you will be very happy. Thank you.'

From Panong to Kuala Lumpur is forty-seven miles; it took a minute for his meaning to sink in. Then Mrs Horsefall said, 'How are we to travel to Kuala Lumpur? Will there be a truck?'

He said, 'Very sorry, no truck. You walk, easy journeys, not more than you can go each day. Japanese soldier help you.'

She said, 'We can't walk, with these children. We *must* have a truck.'

These were bad thoughts, and his eyes hardened. 'You walk,' he repeated.

'But what are we to do with all the luggage?'

He said, 'You carry what you can. Presently the luggage is sent after you.' He turned, and went away.

For the remainder of the day they sat in stunned desperation; those who had luggage sorted hopelessly through their things, trying to make packs that would hold the essentials and yet which would not be too heavy. Mrs Horsefall, who had been a schoolmistress in her time and had assumed the position of leader, moved among them, helping and advising. She had one child herself, a boy of ten called

John; her own position was better than most, for it was possible for a woman to carry the necessities for one boy of that age. The position of the mothers with several younger children was bad indeed.

Jean and Mrs Holland had less of a problem, for having lost their luggage they had less to start with and the problem of selection did not arise. They had few clothes to change into, and what they had could easily go into Jean's haversack. They had acquired two blankets and three food bowls between them, and three spoons, and a knife and fork; they decided to make a bundle of these small possessions in the blankets, and they had a piece of cord to tie the bundle with and to make a sling, so that one could carry the haversack and one the bundle. Their biggest problem was their shoes, which had once been fashionable and were quite unsuitable for marching in.

Towards evening, when the children had left them and they were alone with the baby in a corner, Mrs Holland said quietly, 'My dear, I shan't give up, but I don't think I can walk very far. I've been so poorly lately.'

Jean said, 'It'll be all right,' although deep in her mind she knew that it was not going to be all right at all. 'You're much fitter than some of the others,' and this possibly was true. 'We'll have to take it very slowly, because of the children. We'll take several days over it.'

'I know, my dear. But where are we going to stay at night? What *are* they going to do about that?'

Nobody had an answer to that one.

Rice came to them soon after dawn, and at about eight o'clock Captain Yoniata appeared with four soldiers, who were to be their guard upon the journey. 'Today you walk to Ayer Penchis,' he said. 'Fine day, easy journey. Good dinner when you get to Ayer Penchis. You will be very happy.'

Jean asked Mrs Horsefall, 'How far is Ayer Penchis?'

'Twelve or fifteen miles, I should think. Some of us will never get that far.'

Jean said, 'We'd better do what the soldiers do, have a rest every hour. Hadn't we?'

'If they'll let us.'

It took an hour to get the last child out of the latrine and get the women ready for the march. The guards squatted on their heels; it was a small matter to them when the march started. Finally Captain Yoniata appeared again, his eyes hard and angry. 'You walk now,' he said. 'Womans remaining here are beaten, beaten very bad. You do good thing and be happy. Walk now.'

There was nothing for it but to start. They formed into a little group and walked down the tarmac road in the hot sun, seeking the shade of trees wherever they occurred. Jean walked with Mrs Holland carrying the bundle of blankets slung across her shoulders as the hottest and the heaviest load, and leading the four-year-old Jane by the hand. Seven-year-old Freddie walked beside his mother, who carried the baby, Robin, and the haversack. Ahead of them strolled the Japanese sergeant; behind came the three privates.

The women went very slowly, with frequent halts as a mother and child retired into the bushes by the roadside. There was no question of walking continuously for an hour and then resting; the dysentery saw to that. For those who were not afflicted at the moment the journey became one of endless, wearisome waits by the roadside in the hot sun, for the sergeant refused to allow the party to move on while any remained behind. Within the limits of their duty the Japanese soldiers were humane and helpful; before many hours had passed each was carrying a child.

Slowly the day wore on. The sergeant made it very clear at an early stage that there would be no food and no shelter for the party till they got to Ayer Penchis, and it seemed to be a matter of indifference to him how long they took to get there. They seldom covered more than a mile and a half in the hour, on that first day. As the day went on they all began to suffer from their feet, the older women especially. Their shoes were quite unsuitable for walking long distances, and the heat of the tarmac swelled their feet, so that before long many of them were limping with foot pains. Some of the children went barefoot and got along very well. Jean watched them for a time, then stooped and took her own shoes off, savouring the unaccustomed road surface gingerly with her bare feet. She walked on carrying her shoes, picking her way with her eyes upon the ground, and her feet ceased to pain her though from time to time the tarmac grits hurt her soft soles. She got along better barefoot, but Eileen Holland refused to try it.

They stumbled into Ayer Penchis at about six o'clock that evening, shortly before dark. This place was a Malay village which housed the labour for a number of rubber plantations in the vicinity. The latex-processing plant of one stood near at hand and by it was a sort of

palm thatch barn, used normally for smoking sheets of the raw rubber
hung on horizontal laths. It was empty now and the women were
herded into this. They sank down wearily in a stupor of fatigue;
presently the soldiers brought a bucket of tea and a bucket of rice
and dried fish. Most of them drank cup after cup of the tea, but few
had any appetite for the food.

With the last of the light Jean strolled outside and looked around.
The guards were busy cooking over a small fire; she approached the
sergeant and asked if she might go into the village. He understood
that, and nodded; away from Captain Yoniata discipline was lax.

In the village she found one or two small shops, selling clothes,
sweets, cigarettes, and fruit. She saw mangoes for sale, and bought a
dozen chaffering over the price with the Malay woman to conserve
her slender cash. She ate one at once and felt better for it; at Kuala
Panong they had eaten little fruit. She went back to the barn and
found that the soldiers had provided one small lamp with an open
wick fed by coconut oil.

She distributed her mangoes to Eileen and the Holland children
and to others, and found they were a great success. Armed with
money from the women she went down to the village again and got
four dozen more, and presently all the women and children were in
mango up to their ears. The soldiers came in with another bucket of
tea and got a mango each for their pains, and so refreshed the women
were able to eat most of the rice. They slept, exhausted, weak, and
ill.

The barn was full of rats, which ran over them and round them all
night through. In the morning it was found that several of the
children had been bitten.

They woke aching in new places with the stiffness and fatigue of
the day before; it did not seem possible that they could march again.
The sergeant drove them on; this time the stage was to a place called
Asahan. It was a shorter stage than the day before, about ten miles,
and it had need to be, because they took as long getting to it. This
time the delay was chiefly due to Mrs Collard. She was a heavy
woman of about forty-five with two children, Harry and Ben, aged
about ten and seven. She had suffered from both malaria and
dysentery at Panong, and she was now very weak; she had to stop
and rest every ten minutes, and when she stopped they all stopped
since the sergeant would not allow them to separate. She was relieved

of all load and the younger women took turns to walk by her and
help her along.

By the afternoon she had visibly changed colour; her somewhat
ruddy face had now gone a mottled blue, and she was complaining of
pains in her chest. When they finally reached Asahan she was
practically incapable of walking alone. Their accommodation was
another rubber-curing barn. They half carried Mrs Collard into it
and sat her up against the wall, for she said that lying down hurt her,
and she could not breathe. Somebody went to fetch some water, and
bathed her face, and she said, 'Thank you, dearie. Give some of that
to Harry and Ben, there's a dear.' The woman took the children
outside to wash them, and when she came back Mrs Collard had
fallen over on her side, and was unconscious. Half an hour later she
died.

That evening Jean got more fruit for them, mangoes and bananas,
and some sweets for the children. The Malay woman who supplied
the sweets refused to take money for them. 'No, mem,' she said. 'It is
bad that Nippon soldiers treat you so. This is our gift.' Jean went
back to the barn and told the others what had happened, and it
helped.

In the flickering light of the cooking fire outside the barn Mrs
Horsefall and Jean held a conference with the sergeant, who spoke
only a very few words of English. They illustrated their meaning with
pantomime. 'Not walk tomorrow,' they said. 'No. Not walk. Rest –
sleep – tomorrow. Walk tomorrow, more women die. Rest tomorrow.
Walk one day, rest one day.'

They could not make out if he understood or not. 'Tomorrow,' he
said, 'woman in earth.'

It would be necessary to bury Mrs Collard in the morning. This
would prevent an early start, and would make a ten-mile stage almost
impossible. They seized upon this as an excuse. 'Tomorrow bury
woman in earth,' they said. 'Stay here tomorrow.'

They had to leave it so, uncertain whether he understood or not;
he squatted down on his heels before the fire with the three privates.
Later he came to Jean, his face alight with intelligence. 'Walk one
day, sleep one day,' he said. 'Womans not die.' He nodded vigorously
and she called Mrs Horsefall, and they all nodded vigorously
together, beaming with good nature. They were all so pleased with

each other and with the diplomatic victory that they gave him a banana as a token of esteem.

All that day Jean had walked barefoot; she had stubbed her toes two or three times and had broken her toenails; but she felt fresher that evening than she had felt for a long time. The effect of the march upon the women began to show itself that night in very different forms, according to their age. The women under thirty, and the children, were in most cases actually in better condition than when they left Panong; they were cheered by the easier discipline, and stimulated by the exercise and by the improvement in the diet brought by fruit and sweets. The older women were in much worse case. For them exhaustion outweighed these benefits; they lay or sat listlessly in the darkness, plagued by their children and too tired to eat. In many cases they were too tired even to sleep.

In the morning they buried Mrs Collard. There was no burial ground at hand but the Malay headman showed them where they could dig the grave, in a corner of the compound, near a rubbish heap. The sergeant got two coolies and they dug a shallow grave; they lowered Mrs Collard into it covered by a blanket, and Mrs Horsefall read a little out of the Prayer Book. Then they took away the blanket because they could not spare that, and the earth was filled in. Jean found a carpenter who nailed a little wooden cross together for them, and refused payment; he was a Moslem or perhaps merely an animist, but he knew what the Tuans did for a Christian burial. They wrote JULIA COLLARD on it and the date of death with an indelible pencil, hoping it would survive the rain, and then they had a long discussion over the text to put underneath it. This interested every woman in the party, and kept them happy and mentally stimulated for half an hour. Mrs Holland, rather surprisingly, suggested Romans, xiv, 4; 'Who art thou that judgest another man's servant? to his own master he standeth or falleth', meaning the sergeant who had made them march that day. But the other women did not care for that, and finally they compromised. 'Peace, perfect peace, with loved ones far away'. That pleased everybody.

They sat around and washed their clothes after the burial was over. Soap was getting scarce amongst them, but so was money. Mrs Horsefall held a sort of meeting after rice and examined the money situation; half the women had no money left at all, and the rest had only about fifteen dollars between them. She suggested pooling this, but the mothers who had money left preferred to keep it for their own children; as there was so little in any case it did not seem worth while to worry them by making an issue of it. They all agreed, however, to share rations equally, and after that their feeding times were much better organized.

Captain Yoniata turned up about midday, driving into Kuala Lumpur in the District Commissioner's car. He stopped and got out, angry to find that they were not upon the road. He abused the sergeant for some minutes in Japanese; the man stood stiffly to attention, not saying a word in explanation or defence. Then he turned to the women. 'Why you not walk?' he demanded angrily. 'Very bad thing. You not walk, no food.'

Mrs Horsefall faced him. 'Mrs Collard died last night. We buried her this morning over there. If you make us walk every day like this, we shall all die. These women aren't fit to march at all. You know that.'

'What woman die of?' he inquired. 'What illness?'

'She had dysentery and malaria, as most of us have had. She died of exhaustion after yesterday's march. You'd better come inside and look at Mrs Frith and Judy Thomson. They couldn't possibly have marched today.'

He walked into the barn, and stood looking at two or three women sitting listless in the semi-darkness. Then he said something to the sergeant and walked back to his car. At the door he turned to Mrs Horsefall. 'Very sad woman die,' he said. 'Perhaps I get a truck in Kuala Lumpur. I will ask.' He got into the car and drove away.

His words went round the women quickly; he had gone to get a truck for them, and they would finish the journey to Kuala Lumpur by truck; there would be no more marching. Things weren't so bad, after all. They would be sent by rail from Kuala Lumpur to Singapore, and there they would be put into a proper camp with other Englishwomen, where they could settle down and organize their lives properly, and get into a routine that would enable them to look after the children. A prison camp would have a doctor, too, and there was always some kind of a hospital for those who were really ill. They became much more cheeful, and the most listless ones revived, and came out and washed and made themselves a little more presentable. Their appearance was a great concern to them that afternoon. Kuala

Lumpur was their shopping town where people knew them; they must get tidy before the truck came for them.

Captain Yoniata appeared again about an hour before sunset; again he spoke to the sergeant, who saluted. Then he turned to the women. 'You not go to Kuala Lumpur,' he said. 'You go to Port Swettenham. English destroy bridges, so railway to Singapore no good. You go to Port Swettenham now, and then ship to Singapore.'

There was a stunned silence. Then Mrs Horsefall asked, 'Is there goin g to be a truck to take us to port Swettenham?'

He said, 'Very sorry no truck. You walk slow, easy stages. Two days, three days, you walk to Port Swettenham. Then ship take you to Singapore.'

From Asahan to Port Swettenham is about thirty miles. She said, 'Captain Yoniata, please be reasonable. Many of us are quite unfit to walk any further. Can't you get some transport for the children, anyway?'

He said, 'Englishwomans have proud thoughts, always. Too good to walk like Japanese womans. Tomorrow you walk to Bakri.' he got into his car and went away; that was the last they ever saw of him.

Bakri is eleven miles in the general direction of Port Swettenham. The change in programme was the deepest disappointment to them, the more so as it showed irresolution in their destiny. Mrs Holland said despairingly, 'I don't see why he shouldn't have known at Panong that the bridges were down, and not sent us to Kuala Lumpur at all. It makes one wonder if there's going to be a ship when we get to Port Swettenham. . . .'

There was nothing for it, and next morning they started on the road again. They found that two of the privates had been taken away, and one remained to guard them, with the sergeant. This was of no consequence to their security because they had no desire to attempt to escape, but it reduced by half the help the guards had given them in carrying the younger children, so that it threw an extra burden on the mothers.

That day for the first time Jean carried the baby, Robin: Mrs Holland was walking so badly that she had to be relieved. She still carried the haversack and looked after Freddie, but Jean carried the bundle of blankets and small articles, and the baby, and led Jane by the hand. She went barefoot as before; after some experiments she found that the easiest way to carry the baby was to perch him on her hip, as the Malay women did.

The baby, curiously, fave them the least anxiety of any of the children. They fed it on rice and gravy from the fish soup or stew, and it did well. Once in the six weeks it had seemed to be developing dysentery and they had given it a tiny dose or two of Glauber's salt, and it recovered. Mosquitoes never seemed to worry it, and it had not had fever. The other children were less fortunate. Both had had dysentery from time to time, and though they seemed now to be free of it they had gone very thin.

They slept that night in the bungalow that had belonged to the manager of the Bakri tin mine, an Englishman. In the seven or eight weeks since he had abandoned it it had been occupied by troops of both sides and looted by the Malays; now little remained of it but the bare walls. Marvellously, however, the bath was still in order though filthily dirty, and there was a store of cut wood for the furnace that heated water. The sergeant, true to his promise, allowed them a day of rest here, and they made the most of the hot water for washing their clothes and themselves. With the small improvement in conditions their spirits revived.

'I should think there'd be hot water on the ship,' said Mrs Holland. 'There usually is, isn't there?'

They marched again next day to a place called Dilit; this was mostly a day spent marching down cart tracks in the rubber plantations. The tracks were mostly in the shade of the trees and this made it pleasant for them, and even the older women found the day bearable. They had some difficulty in finding the way. The sergeant spoke little Malay and had difficulty in understanding the Malay women latex-tappers that he asked for directions from time to time. Jean found that she could understand the answers that the women gave, and could converse with them, but having got the directions they required she had some difficulty in making the sergeant understand. They reached an agreement by the end of the day that she should talk to the women, who talked to her less shyly in any case, and she developed a sign language which the sergeant understood. From that time onwards Jean was largely responsible for finding the shortest way for the party to go.

In the middle of the afternoon Ben Collard, the younger son of Mrs Collard who had died, trod on something while walking barefoot in the grass that bit him with poison fangs and got away. He said afterwards that it looked like a big beetle; possibly it was a scorpion. Mrs Horsefall took charge and laid him on the ground and sucked the wound to draw the poison from it, but the foot swelled quickly and the inflammation travelled up the leg to the knee. It was obviously painful and he cried a great deal. There was nothing to be done but carry him, and this was no easy matter for the women in their feeble condition because he was a boy of seven and weighed five stone. Mrs Horsefall carried him for an hour and after that the sergeant took him and carried him the rest of the way. By the time they got to Dilit the ankle was enormous and the knee was stiff.

At Dilit there was no accommodation for them and no food. The place was a typical Malay village, the houses built of wood and palm thatch raised about four feet from the ground on posts, leaving a space beneath where dogs slept and fowls nested. They stood or sat wearily while the sergeant negotiated with the Malay headman: very soon he called for Jean, and she joined the tri-lingual discussion. The village had rice and could prepare a meal for them, but the headman wanted payment, and was only with difficulty induced to agree to provide rice for so many on the word of the sergeant that they would be paid some day. As regards accommodation he said flatly that there was none, and the party must sleep under the houses with the dogs and poultry; later he agreed to move the people from one house, so that the thirty prisoners had a roof to sleep under on a floor about fifteen feet square.

Jean secured a corner for their party, and Eileen Holland settled into it with the children and the baby. A few feet from them Mrs Horsefall was working on Ben Collard. Somebody had some permanganate crystals and someone else an old razor blade; with this they cut the wound open a little, in spite of the child's screams, and put in crystals and bound it up; then they applied hot fomentations. There was nothing Jean could do, and she wandered outside.

There was a sort of village kitchen, and here the Japanese private was superintending the activities of women of the village who were preparing rice. At a house nearby the headman was sitting at the head of the steps leading up to his house, squatting on his heels and smoking a long pipe: he was a grey-haired old man wearing a sarong and what once had been a khaki drill jacket. Jean crossed to him and said rather shyly in Malay, 'I am sorry we have been forced to come here, and have made trouble for you.'

He stood up and bowed to the Mem. 'It is no trouble,' he said. 'We are sorry to see Mems in such a state. Have you come far?'

She said, 'From Bakri today.'

He made her come up into the house: there was no chair and she sat with him on the floor at the doorless entrance. He asked their history, and she told him what had happened, and he grunted. Presently the wife came from within the house bearing two cups of coffee without sugar or milk; Jean thanked her in Malay, and she smiled shyly, and withdrew into the house again.

Presently the headman said, 'The Short One' – he meant the Japanese sergeant – 'says you must stay here tomorrow.'

Jean said, 'We are too weak to march each day. The Japanese allow us to rest a day between each day of marching. If we may stay here tomorrow it will help us a great deal. The sergeant says he can get money for the food.'

'The Short Ones never pay for food,' the headman said. 'Nevertheless you shall stay.'

She said, 'I can do nothing but thank you.'

He raised his grey old head. 'It is written in the Fourth Surah, "Men's souls are naturally inclined to covetousness; but if ye be kind towards women and fear to wrong them, God is well acquainted with what ye do".'

She sat with the old man till rice was ready; then she left him and went to her meal. The other women looked at her curiously. 'I saw you sitting with the headman, chatting away,' said one. 'Just as if you were old chums.'

Jean smiled. 'He gave me a cup of coffee.'

'Just fancy that! There's something in knowing how to talk to them in their own language, isn't there? What did he talk about?'

Jean thought for a minute. 'This and that – about our journey. He talked about God a little.'

The women stared at her. 'You mean, his own God? Not the real God?'

'He didn't differentiate,' Jean said. 'Just God.'

They rested all next day and then marched to Klang, three or four miles outside Port Swettenham. Little Ben Collard was neither better nor worse: the leg was very much swollen. The chief trouble with him now was physical weakness: he had eaten nothing since the injury for nothing would stay down, and none of the children by that time had any reserves of strength. The headman directed the villagers to make a litter for him in the form of a stretcher of two long bamboo poles with spreaders and a woven palm mat between and they put him upon this and took turns at carrying it.

They got to Klang that afternoon, and here there was an empty schoolhouse: the sergeant put them into this and went off to a Japanese encampment near at hand, to report and to arrange rations for them.

Presently an officer arrived to inspect them, marching at the head of a guard of six soldiers. This officer, whom they came to know as Major Nemu, spoke good English. He said, 'Who are you people? What do you want here?'

They stared at him. Mrs Horsefall said, 'We are prisoners, from Panong. We are on our way to the prisoner-of-war camp in Singapore. Captain Yoniata in Panong sent us here under guard, to be put on a ship to Singapore.'

'There are no ships here,' he said. 'You should have stayed in Panong.'

It was no good arguing, nor had they the energy. 'We were sent here,' she repeated dully.

'They had no right to send you here,' he said angrily. 'There is no prison camp here.'

There was a long, awkward silence: the women stared at him in blank despair. Mrs Horsefall summoned up her flagging energy again. 'May we see a doctor?' she asked. 'Some of us are very ill — one child especially. One woman died upon the way.'

'What did she die of?' he asked quickly. 'Plague?'

'Nothing infectious. She died of exhaustion.'

'I will send a doctor to examine you all. You will stay here for tonight, but you cannot stay for long. I have not got sufficient rations for my own command, let alone feeding prisoners.' He turned and walked back to the camp.

A new guard was placed upon the schoolhouse: they never saw the friendly sergeant or the private again. Presumably they were sent back to Panong. A Japanese doctor, very young, came to them within an hour; he had them all up one by one and examined them for infectious disease. Then he was about to take his departure, but they made him stay and look at little Ben Collard's leg. He ordered them to continue with the hot fomentations. When they asked if he could not be taken into hospital he shrugged his shoulders and said, 'I inquire.'

They stayed in that schoolhouse under guard, day after day. On the third day they sent for the doctor again, for Ben Collard was obviously worse. Reluctantly the doctor ordered his removal to the hospital in a truck. On the sixth day they heard that he had died.

Jean Paget crouched down on the floor beside the fire in my sitting-room; outside a change of wind had brought the London rain beating against the window.

'People who spent the war in prison camps have written a lot of books about what a bad time they had,' she said, staring into the embers. 'They don't know what it was like, not being in a camp.'

They stayed in Klang eleven days, not knowing what was to become of them. The food was bad and insufficient, and there were no shops in the vicinity: if there had been shops they could not have done much with them, because their money was now practically gone. On the twelfth day Major Nemu paraded them at half an hour's notice, allocated one corporal to look after them, and told them to walk to Port Dickson. He said that there might be a ship there to take them down to Singapore; if there was not they would be walking in the general direction of the prison camps.

That was about the middle of March 1942. From Klang to Port Dickson is about fifty miles, but by this time they were travelling more slowly than ever. It took them till the end of the month; they had to wait several days in one village because Mrs Horsefall went down with malaria and ran a temperature of a hundred and five for some time. She recovered and was walking, or rather tottering, within a week, but she never recovered her vigour and from that time onwards the leadership fell more and more upon Jean's shoulders.

By the time they reached Port Dickson their clothes were in a deplorable condition. Very few of the women had a change of any sort, because burdens had been reduced to an absolute minimum.

Jean and Mrs Holland had nothing but the thin cotton frocks that they had worn since they were taken; these were now torn and ragged from washing. Jean had gone barefoot since the early stages of the march and intended to go on without shoes: she now took another step towards the costume of the Malay woman. She sold a little brooch for thirteen dollars to an Indian jeweller in Salak, and with two of the precious dollars she bought a cheap sarong.

A sarong is a skirt made of a tube of cloth about three feet in diameter; you get into it and wrap it round your waist like a towel, the surplus material falling into pleats that permit free movement. When you sleep you undo the roll around your waist and it then lies over you as a loose covering that you cannot roll out of. It is the lightest and coolest of all garments for the tropics, and the most practical, being simple to make and to wash. For a top, she cut down her cotton frock into a sort of tunic which got rid of the most tattered part, the skirt, and from that time she was cooler and more at ease than any of them. At first the other women strongly disapproved of this descent to native dress: later most of them followed her example as their clothes became worn out.

There was no haven for them at Port Dickson, and no ship. They were allowed to stay there, living under desultory guard in a copra barn, for about ten days; the Japanese commander then decided that they were a nuisance, and put them on the road to Seremban. He reasoned, apparently, that they were not his prisoners and so not his responsibility; it was the duty of those who had captured them to put them into camp. His obvious course was to get rid of them and get them out of his area before, by their continued presence, they forced him to divert food and troops and medical supplies from the Imperial Japanese Army to sustain them.

At Siliau, between Port Dickson and Seremban, tragedy touched the Holland family, because Jane died. They had stayed for their day of rest in a rubber-smoking shed: she had developed fever during the day's march and one of the two Japanese guards they had at that time had carried her for much of the day. Their thermometer had been broken in an accident a few days before and they had now no means of telling the temperature of malaria patients, but she was very hot. They had a little quinine left and tried to give it to her, but they could not get her to take much of it till she grew too weak to resist, and then it was too late. They persuaded the Japanese sergeant to allow them to stay at Siliau rather than to risk moving the child, and Jean and Eileen Holland stayed up with her, sleepless, fighting for her life in that dim, smelly place where the rats scurried round at night and hens walked in and out by day. On the evening of the second day she died.

Mrs Holland stood it far better than Jean had expected that she would. 'It's God's will, my dear,' she said quietly, 'and He'll give her Daddy strength to bear it when he hears, just as He's giving us all strength to bear our trials now.' She stood dry-eyed beside the little grave, and helped to make the little wooden cross. Dry-eyed she picked the text for the cross: 'Suffer little children to come unto Me'. She said quietly, 'I think her Daddy would like that one.'

Jean woke that night in the darkness, and heard her weeping.

Through all this the baby, Robin, throve. It was entirely fortuitous that he ate and drank nothing but food that had been recently boiled; living on rice and soup, that happened automatically, but may have explained his relative freedom from stomach disorders. Jean carried him every day, and her own health was definitely better than when they had left Panong. She had had five days of fever at Klang, but dysentery had not troubled her for some time, and she was eating well. With the continual exposure to the sun she was getting very brown, and the baby that she carried on her hip got browner.

Seremban lies on the railway, and they had hoped that when they got there there would be a train down to Singapore. They got to Seremban about the middle of April, but there was no train for them; the railway was running in a limited fashion but probably not through to Singapore. Before very long they were put upon the road to Tampin, but not till they had lost another member of the party.

Ellen Forbes was the unmarried girl who had come out to get married and hadn't, a circumstance that Jean could well understand by the time she had lived in close contact with her for a couple of months. Ellen was a vacuous, undisciplined girl, good humoured, and much too free with Japanese troops for the liking of the other women. At Seremban they were accommodated in a schoolhouse on the outskirts of the town, which was full of soldiers. In the morning Ellen simply wasn't there, and they never saw her again.

Jean and Mrs Horsefall asked to see the officer and stated their case, that a member of their party had disappeared, probably abducted by the soldiers. The officer promised to make inquiries, and nothing happened. Two days later they received orders to march down the road to Tampin, and were moved off under guard.

They stayed at Tampin for some days, and got so little food there that they practically starved; at their urgent entreaty the local commandant sent them down under guard to Malacca, where they hoped to get a ship. But there was no ship at Malacca and the officer in charge there sent them back to Tampin. They plodded back there in despair; at Alor Gajah Judy Thomson died. To stay at Tampin meant more deaths, inevitably, so they suggested it was better for them to continue down to Singapore on foot, and a corporal was detailed to take them on the road to Gemas.

In the middle of May, at Ayer Kuning, on the way to Gemas, Mrs Horsefall died. She had never really recovered from her attack of malaria or whatever fever it was that had attacked her two months previously; she had had recurrent attacks of low fever which had made Jean wonder sometimes if it was malaria that she had had at all. Whatever it was it had made her very weak; at Ayer Kuning she developed dysentery again, and died in two days, probably of heart failure or exhaustion. The faded little woman Mrs Frith, who was over fifty and always seemed to be upon the point of death and never quite made it, took over the care of Johnnie Horsefall and it did her a world of good; from that day Mrs Frith improved and gave up moaning in the night.

They got to Gemas three days later; here as usual in towns they were put into the schoolhouse. The Japanese town major, a Captain Nisui, came to inspect them that evening; he had known nothing about them till they appeared in his town. This was quite usual and Jean was ready for it; she explained that they were prisoners being marched to camp in Singapore.

He said, 'Prisoner not go Singapore. Strict order. Where you come from?'

She told him. 'We've been travelling for over two months,' she said, with the calmness borne of many disappointments. 'We must get into a camp, or we shall die. Seven of us have died upon the road already – there were thirty-two when we were taken prisoner. Now there are twenty-five. We can't go on like this. We *must* get into camp at Singapore. You must see that.'

He said, 'No more prisoner to Singapore. Very sorry for you, but strict order. Too many prisoner in Singapore.'

She said, 'But, Captain Nisui, that can't mean women. That means men prisoners, surely.'

'No more prisoner to Singapore,' he said. 'Strict order.'

'Well, can we stay here and make ourselves a camp, and have a doctor here?'

His eyes narrowed. 'No prisoner stay here.'

'But what are we to do? Where can we go?'

'Very sad for you,' he said. 'I tell you where you go tomorrow.'

She went back to the women after he had gone. 'You heard all that,' she said calmly. 'He says we aren't to go to Singapore after all.'

The news meant very little to the women; they had fallen into the habit of living from day to day, and Singapore was very far away. 'Looks as if they don't want us anywhere,' Mrs Price said heavily. 'Bobbie, if I see you teasing Amy again I'll wallop you just like your father. Straight, I will.'

Mrs Frith said, 'If they'd just let us alone we could find a little place like one of them villages and live till it's all over.'

Jean stared at her. 'They couldn't feed us,' she said slowly. 'We depend upon the Nips for food.' But it was the germ of an idea, and she put it in the back of her mind.

'Precious little food we get,' said Mrs Frith. 'I'll never forget that terrible place Tampin in all my born days.'

Captain Nisui came the next day. 'You go now to Kuantan,' he said. 'Woman camp in Kuantan, very good. You will be very glad.'

Jean did not know where Kuantan was. She asked, 'Where is Kuantan? Is it far away?'

'Kuantan on coast,' he said. 'You go there now.'

Behind her someone said, 'It's hundreds of miles away. It's on the east coast.'

'Okay,' said Captain Nisui. 'On east coast.'

'Can we go there by railway?' Jean inquired.

'Sorry, no railway. You walk, ten, fifteen miles each day. You get there soon. You will be very happy.'

She said quietly, 'Seven of us are dead already with this marching, Captain. If you make us march to this place Kuantan more of us will die. Can we have a truck to take us there?'

'Sorry, no truck,' he said. 'You get there very soon.'

He wanted them to start immediately, but it was then eleven in the morning and they rebelled. With patient negotiation Jean got him to agree that they should start at dawn next day; this was the most that she could do. She did, however, get him to provide a good supper for them that night, a sort of meat stew with the rice, and a banana each.

From Gemas to Kuantan is about a hundred and seventy miles; there is no direct road. They left Gemas in the last week of May; on the basis of their previous rate of progress Jean reckoned that it would take them six weeks to do the journey. It was by far the longest they had had to tackle; always before there had been hope of transport of some sort at the end of fifty miles or so. Now six weeks of travelling lay ahead of them, with only a vague hope of rest at the end. None of them really believed that there were prison camps for them at Kuantan.

'You made a mistake, dearie,' said Mrs Frith, 'saying what you did about us staying and making a camp here. I could see he didn't like that.'

'He just wants to get rid of us,' Jean said wearily. 'They don't want to bother with us – just get us out of the way.'

They left next morning with a sergeant and a private as a guard. Gemas is a railway junction and the East Coast railway runs north from there; the railway was not being used at all at that time, and there was a rumour that the track was being taken up and sent to some unknown strategic destination in the north. The women were not concerned with that; what concerned them was that they had to walk along the railway line, which meant nearly walking in the sun most of each day, and there was no possibility of getting a ride in a train.

They went on for a week, marching about ten miles every other day; then fever broke out among the children. They never really knew what it was; it started with little Amy Price, who came out in a rash and ran a high temperature, with a running nose. It may have been measles. It was impossible in the conditions of their life to keep the children segregated, and in the weeks that followed it spread from child to child. Amy Price recovered, but by the time she was fit to walk again seven of the other children were down with it. There was nothing they could do except to keep the tired, sweating little faces bathed and cool, and change the soaked clothes for what fresh ones they could muster. They were at a place called Bahau when the sickness was at its height, living at the station in the ticket office and the waiting-room, and on the platform. They had bad luck because there had been a doctor in Bahau three days before they arrived, a Japanese army doctor. But he had gone on in his truck in the direction of Kuala Klawang, and though they got the headman to send runners after him they never made contact with him. So they had no help.

At Bahau four children died, Harry Collard, Susan Fletcher, Doris Simmonds, who was only three, and Freddie Holland. Jean was most concerned with Freddie, as was natural, but there was so little she could do. She guessed from the first day of fever that he was going to die; by that time she had amassed a store of sad experience. There was something in the attitude of people, even tiny children, to their illness that told when death was coming to them, a listlessness, as if they were too tired to make the effort to live. By that time they had all grown hardened to the fact of death. Grief and mourning had ceased to trouble them; death was a reality to be avoided and fought, but when it came – well, it was just one of those things. After a person had died there were certain things that had to be done, the straightening of the limbs, the grave, the cross, the entry in a diary saying who had died and just exactly where the grave was. That was the end of it; they had no energy for afterthoughts.

Jean's care now was for Mrs Holland. After Freddie was buried she tried to get Eileen to care for the baby; for the last few weeks the baby had been left to Jean to feed and tend and carry, and she had grown very much attached to it. With both the older children dead Jean gave the baby, Robin, back to its mother, not so much because she wanted to get rid of it as because she felt that an interest must be found for Eileen Holland, and the baby would supply it. But the experiment was not a great success; Eileen by that time was so weak that she could not carry the baby on the march, and she could not summon the energy to play with it. Moreover, the baby obviously preferred the younger woman to its mother, having been carried by her for so long.

'Seems as if he doesn't really belong to me,' Mrs Holland said once. 'You take him, dear. He likes being with you.' From that time on they shared the baby; it got its rice and soup from Eileen, but it got its fun from Jean.

They left four tiny graves behind the signal box at Bahau and went on down the line carrying two litters of bamboo poles; the weakest children took turns in these. As was common on this journey, they found the Japanese guards to be humane and reasonable men, uncouth in their habits and mentally far removed from western ideas, but tolerant to the weaknesses of women and deeply devoted to children. For hours the sergeant would plod along carrying one child piggyback and at the same time carrying one end of the stretcher, his rifle laid beside the resting child. There was the usual language difficulty. The women by that time were acquiring a few words of Japanese, but the only one who could talk Malay fluently was Jean, and it was she who made inquiries at the villages and sometimes acted as interpreter for the Japanese.

Mrs Frith surprised Jean very much. She was a faded, anaemic little woman of over fifty. In the early stages of the journey she had been very weak and something of a nuisance to them with her continued prognostications of evil; they had trouble enough in the daily round without looking forward and anticipating more. Since she had adopted Johnnie Horsefall Mrs Frith had taken on a new lease of life; her health had improved and she now marched as strongly as any of them. She had lived in Malaya for about fifteen years; she could speak only a few words of the language but she had a considerable knowledge of the country and its diseases. She was quite happy that they were going to Kuantan. 'Nice over there, it is,' she said. 'Much healthier than in the west, and nicer people. We'll be all right once we get over there. You see.'

As time went on, Jean turned to Mrs Frith more and more for comfort and advice in their predicaments.

At Ayer Kring Mrs Holland came to the end of her strength. She had fallen twice on the march and they had taken turns in helping her along. It was impossible to put her on the litter; even in her emaciated state she weighed eight stone, and they were none of them strong enough by that time to carry such a load very far. Moreover, to put her on a litter meant turning a child off it, and she refused even to consider such a thing. She stumbled into the village on her own feet, but by the time she got there she was changing colour as Mrs Collard had before her, and that was a bad sign.

Ayer Kring is a small village at a railway station; there were no station buildings here, and by negotiation the headman turned the people out of one house for them, as had been done several times before. They laid Mrs Holland in a shady corner and made a pillow for her head and bathed her face; they had no brandy or any other stimulant to give her. She could not rest lying down and insisted on sitting up, so they put her in a corner where she could be supported by the walls. She took a little soup that evening but refused all food. She knew herself it was the end.

'I'm so sorry, my dear,' she whispered in the night. 'Sorry to make so much trouble for you. Sorry for Bill. If you see Bill again, tell him not to fret. And tell him not to mind about marrying again, if he can find somebody nice. It's not as if he was an old man.'

An hour or two later she said, 'I do think it's lovely the way baby's taken to you. It *is* lucky, isn't it?'

In the morning she was still alive, but unconscious. They did what they could, which wasn't very much, but her breathing got weaker and weaker, and at about midday she died. They buried her in the Moslem village cemetery that evening.

At Ayer Kring they entered the most unhealthy district they had passed through yet. The central mountains of Malaya were now on their left, to the west of them as they marched north, and they were coming to the head waters of the Pahang river, which runs down to the east coast. Here the river spreads out into numerous tributaries, the Menkuang, the Pertang, the Belengu, and many others, and these tributaries running through flat country make a marshy place of swamps and mangroves that stretched for forty miles along their route, a country full of snakes and crocodiles, and infested with mosquitoes. By day it was steamy and hot and breathless; at night a cold wet mist came up and chilled them unmercifully.

By the time they had been two days in this country several of them were suffering from fever, a fever that did not seem quite like the malaria that they were used to, in that the temperature did not rise so high; it may have been dengue. They had little by that time to treat it with, not so much because they were short of money as because there were no drugs at all in the jungly villages that they were passing through. Jean consulted with the sergeant, who advised them to press on, and get out of this bad country as soon as possible. Jean was running a fever herself at the time and everything was moving about her in a blur; she had a cracking headache and it was difficult to focus her eyes. She consulted with Mrs Frith, who was remarkably well.

'What he says is right, dearie,' Mrs Frith declared. 'We won't get any better staying in this swampy place. I think we ought to walk each day, if you ask me.'

Jean forced herself to concentrate. 'What about Mrs Simmonds?'

'Maybe the soldiers would carry her, if she gets any worse. I don't know, I'm sure. It's cruel hard, but if we've got to go we'd better go and get it over. That's what I say. We shan't do any good hanging around here in this nasty place.'

They marched each day after that, stumbling along in fever, weak, and ill. The baby, Robin Holland, that Jean carried, got the fever; this was the first ailment he had had. She showed him to the headman in the village of Mentri, and his wife produced a hot infusion of some bark in a dirty coconut shell; Jean tasted it and it was very bitter, so she judged it to be a form of quinine. She gave a little to the baby and took some herself; it seemed to do them both good during the night. Before the day's march began several of the women took it, and it helped.

It took them eleven days to get through the swamps to the higher ground past Temerloh. They left Mrs Simmonds and Mrs Fletcher behind them, and little Gillian Thomson. When they emerged into the higher, healthier country and dared to stay a day to rest, Jean was very weak but the fever had left her. The baby was still alive, though obviously ill; it cried almost incessantly during its waking hours.

It was Mrs Frith who now buoyed them up, as she had depressed them in the earlier days. 'It should be getting better all the time from now on,' she told them. 'As we get nearer to the coast it should get better. It's lovely on the east coast, nice beaches to bathe on, and always a sea breeze. It's healthy, too.'

They came presently to a very jungly village on a hilltop; they never learned its name. It stood above the river Jengka. By this time they had left the railway and were heading more or less eastwards on a jungle track that would at some time join a main road that led down to Kuantan. This village was cool and airy, and the people kind and hospitable; they gave the women a house to sleep in and provided food and fresh fruit, and the same bark infusion that was good for fever. They stayed there for six days revelling in the fresh, cool breeze and the clear, healthy nights, and when they finally marched on they were in better shape. They left a little gold brooch that had belonged to Mrs Fletcher with the headman as payment for the good and kindness that they had received, thinking that the dead woman would not have objected to that.

Four days later, in the evening, they came to Maran. A tarmac road runs through Maran crossing the Malay peninsula from Kuantan to Kerling. The road runs through the village, which has perhaps fifty houses, a school, and a few native shops. They came out upon the road half a mile or so to the north of the village; after five weeks upon the railway track and jungle paths it overjoyed them to see evidence of civilization in this road. They walked down to the village with a fresher step. And there, in front of them, they saw two trucks and two white men working on them while Japanese guards stood by.

They marched quickly towards the trucks, which were both heavily loaded with railway lines and sleepers; they stood pointing in the direction of Kuantan. One of them was jacked up on sleepers taken from the load, and both of the white men were underneath it working on the back axle. They wore shorts and army boots without socks; their bodies were brown with sunburn and very dirty with the muck from the back axle. But they were healthy and muscular men, lean, but in good physical condition. And they were white, the first white men that the women had seen for five months.

They crowded round the trucks; their guard began to talk in staccato Japanese with the truck guards. One of the men lying on his back under the axle, shifting spanner in hand, glanced at the bare feet and the sarongs within his range of vision and said slowly, 'Tell the mucking Nip to get those mucking women shifted back so we can get some light.'

Some of the women laughed, and Mrs Frith said, 'Don't you go using that language to me, young man.'

The men rolled out from under the truck and sat staring at the women and the children, at the brown skins, the sarongs, the bare feet. 'Who said that?' asked the man with the spanner. 'Which of you speaks English?' He spoke deliberately in a slow drawl, with something of a pause between each word.

Jean said laughing, 'We're all English.'

He stared at her, noting the black hair plaited in a pigtail, the brown arms and feet, the sarong, the brown baby on her hip. There was a line of white skin showing on her chest at the V of her tattered blouse. 'Straits-born?' he hazarded.

'No, real English – all of us,' she said. 'We're prisoners.'

He got to his feet; he was a fair-haired powerfully built man about twenty-seven or twenty-eight years old. 'Dinky-die?' he said.

She did not understand that. 'Are you prisoners?' she asked.

He smiled slowly. 'Are we prisoners?' he repeated. 'Oh my word.'

There was something about this man that she had never met before. 'Are you English?' she asked.

'No fear,' he said in his deliberate way. 'We're Aussies.'

She said, 'Are you in camp here?'

He shook his head. 'We come from Kuantan,' he said. 'But we're driving trucks all day, fetching this stuff down to the coast.'

She said, 'We're going to Kuantan, to the women's camp there.'

He stared at her. 'That's crook for a start,' he said slowly. 'There isn't any women's camp at Kuantan. There isn't any regular prisoner camp at all, just a little temporary camp for us because we're truck drivers. Who told you that there was a women's camp at Kuantan?'

'The Japanese told us. They're supposed to be sending us there.' She sighed. 'It's just another lie.'

'The bloody Nips say anything.' He smiled slowly. 'I thought you were a lot of boongs,' he said. 'You say you're English, dinky-die? All the way from England?'

She nodded. 'That's right. Some of us have been out here for ten or fifteen years, but we're all English.'

'And the kiddies – they all English too?'

'All of them,' she said.

He smiled slowly. 'I never thought the first time that I spoke to an English lady she'd be looking like you.'

'You aren't exactly an oil painting yourself,' Jean said.

The other man was talking to a group of the women; Mrs Frith and Mrs Price were with Jean. The Australian turned to them. 'Where do you come from?' he inquired.

Mrs Frith said, 'We got took in Panong, over on the west coast, waiting for a boat to get away.'

'But where did you come from now?'

Jean said. 'We're being marched to Kuantan.'

'Not all the way from Panong?'

She laughed shortly. 'We've been everywhere – Port Swettenham, Port Dickson – everywhere. Nobody wants us. I reckon that we've walked nearly five hundred miles.'

'Oh my word,' he said. 'That sounds a crook deal to me. How do you go on for tucker, if you aren't in a camp?'

She did not understand him. 'Tucker?'

'What do you get to eat?'

'We stay each night in a village,' she said. 'We'll have to find somewhere to stay here. Probably in a place like this it'll be the school. We eat what we can get in the village.'

'For Christ's sake,' he said. 'Wait while I tell my cobber.' he swung round to the other. 'You heard about the crook deal that they got?' he said. 'Been walking all the time since they got taken. Never been inside a prison camp at all.'

'They've been telling me,' the other said. 'The way these bloody Nips go on. Makes you chunda.'

The first man turned back to Jean. 'What happens if any of you get sick?'

She said cynically. 'When you get sick, you get well or you die. We haven't seen a doctor for the last three months and we've got practically no medicines left, so we mostly die. There were thirty-two of us when we were taken. Now we're seventeen.'

The Australian said softly. 'Oh my word.'

Jean said, 'Will you be staying here tonight?'

He said, 'Will you?'

'We shall stay here,' she said. 'We shall be here tomorrow too, unless they'll let us ride down on your trucks. We can't march the children every day. We walk one day and rest the next.'

He said, 'If you're staying, Mrs Boong, we're staying too. We can fix this bloody axle so it will never roll again, if needs be.' He paused in slow thought. 'You got no medicines?' he said. 'What do you want?'

She said quickly, 'Have you got any Glauber's salt?'

He shook his head. 'Is that what you want?'

'We haven't got any salts at all,' she said. 'We want quinine, and something for all these skin diseases that the children have got. Can we get those here?'

He said slowly, 'I'll have a try. Have you got any money?'

Mrs Frith snorted. 'After being six months with the Japs? They took everything we had. Even our wedding rings.'

Jean said, 'We've got a few little bits of jewellery left, if we could sell some of those.'

He said, 'I'll have a go first, and see what I can do. You get fixed up with somewhere to sleep, and I'll see you later.'

'All right.'

She went back to their sergeant and bowed to him because that pleased him and made things easier for them. She said, 'Gunso, where yasme tonight? Children must yasme. We see headman about yasme and mishi?'

He came with her and they found the headman, and negotiated for the loan of the school building for the prisoners, and for the supply of rice for mishi. They did not now experience the blank refusals that they formerly had met when the party was thirty strong; the lesser numbers had made accommodation and food much easier for them. They settled into the school building and began the routine of chores and washing that occupied the bulk of their spare time. The news that there was no women prisoners' camp in Kuantan was what they had all secretly expected, but it was a disappointment, none the less. The novelty of the two Australians made up for this, because by that time they were living strictly from day to day.

At the trucks the Aussies got back to their work. With heads close together under the axle, the fair-haired man that Jean had talked to said to his cobber, 'I never heard such a crook deal. What can we do to fix this bastard so as we stay here tonight? I said I'd try and get some medicines for them.'

They had already rectified the binding brake that had heated up the near side hub and caused the stoppage. The other said, 'Take the whole bloody hub off for a dekko, 'n pull out the shaft from the diff. That makes a good show of dirty bits. Means sleeping in the trucks.'

'I said I'd try and get some medicines.' They worked on for a little.

'How you going to do that?'

'Petrol, I suppose. That's easiest.'

It was already growing dark when they extracted four feet of heavy metal shafting, splined at both ends, from the back axle; dripping with black oil they showed it to the Japanese corporal in charge of them as evidence of their industry. 'Yasme here tonight,' they said. The guard was suspicious, but agreed; indeed, he could do nothing else. He went off to arrange for rice for them, leaving them in charge of the private who was with him.

On the excuse of a benjo, the fair-haired man left the trucks and in the half light retired behind a house. He slipped quickly down behind a row of houses, and came out into the street a couple of hundred yards down, towards the end of the village. Here there was a Chinaman who ran a decrepit bus; the Australian had noted this place on various journeys through Maran; they plied regularly up and down this road.

In his deliberate manner he said quietly, 'Johnnie, you buy petrol? How much you give?' It is extraordinary how little barrier an unknown language makes between a willing buyer and a willing seller. At one point in the negotiation they resorted to the written word, and the Australian wrote GLAUBER'S SALT and QUININE and SKIN DISEASE OINTMENT in block letters on a scrap of wrapping paper.

He slunk back behind the houses carrying three two-gallon cans and a length of rubber hose, which he hid behind the latrine. He came back to the trucks presently, ostentatiously buttoning his shorts.

In the darkness, early in the night, he came to the schoolhouse; it may have been about ten o'clock. One of the Japanese soldiers was supposed to be on guard all night, but in the five weeks that they had been with this pair of guards the women had not shown the slightest inclination to escape, and their guards had long given up watching them at night. The Australian had made sure where they were, however, and when he had seen them squatting with the truck guards he came silently to the school.

At the open door he paused, and said quietly, 'Which of you ladies was I talking to this afternoon? The one with the baby.'

Jean was asleep; they woke her and she pulled up her sarong and slipped her top on, and came to the door. He had several little packages for her. 'That's quinine,' he said. 'I can get more of that if you want it. I couldn't get Glauber's, but this is what the Chinese take for dysentery. It's all written in Chinese, but what he says it means if three of these leaves powdered up in warm water every four hours. That'll be for a grown-up person. If it's any good, keep the label and maybe you could get some more in a Chinese drug shop. I got this Zam-Buk for the skin, and there's more of that if you want it.'

She took them gratefully from him. 'That's marvellous,' she said softly. 'How much did it all cost?'

'That's all right,' he said in his deliberate manner. 'The Nips paid, but they don't know it.'

She thanked him again. 'What are you doing here?' she asked. 'Where are you going with the trucks?'

'Kuantan,' he said. 'We should be back there tonight, but Ben Leggatt – he's my cobber – he got the truck in bits so we had to give it away. Get down there tomorrow, or we might stretch it another day if it suits, though it'ld be risky, I think.' He told her that there were six of them driving six trucks for the Japanese; they drove regularly from Kuantan up-country to a place upon the railway called Jerantut, a distance of about a hundred and thirty miles. They would drive up one day and load the truck with sleepers and railway lines taken up from the track, and drive back to Kuantan the next day, where the railway material was unloaded on to the quayside to be taken away by ship to some unknown destination. 'Building another railway somewhere, I suppose,' he said. A hundred and thirty miles is a long way to drive a heavily loaded truck in a day in tropical conditions, and they sometimes failed to reach Kuantan before dark; when that happened they spent the night in a village. Their absence would not be remarked particularly at Kuantan.

He had been taken somewhere in Johore, and had been driving trucks from Kuantan for about two months. 'Better than being in a camp,' he said.

She sat down on the top step of the three that led up to the school, and he squatted down before her on the ground. His manner of sitting intrigued her, because he sat down on one heel somewhat in the manner of a native, but with his left leg extended. 'Are you a truck driver in Australia?' she asked.

No bloody fear,' he said. 'I'm a ringer.'

She asked, 'What's a ringer?'

'A stockman,' he said. 'I was born in Queensland out behind Cloncurry, and my people, they're all Queenslanders. My dad, he came from London, from a place called Hammersmith. He used to drive a cab and so he knew about horses, and he came out to Queensland to work for Cobb and Co., and met Ma. But I've not been back to the Curry for some time. I was working in the Territory over to the west, on a station called Wollara. That's about a hundred and ten miles south-west of the Springs.'

She smiled. 'Where's the Springs, then?'

'Alice,' he said. 'Alice Springs. Right in the middle of Australia, half way between Darwin and Adelaide.'

She said, 'I thought the middle of Australia was all desert?'

He was concerned at her ignorance. 'Oh my word,' he said deliberately. 'Alice is a bonza place. Plenty of water in Alice; people living there, they leave the sprinkler on all night, watering the lawn. That's right, they leave the sprinkler on all night. Course, the Territory's dry in most parts, but there's usually good feed along the creeks. Come to that, there's water all over if you look for it. You take a creek that only runs in the wet, now, say a couple of months in the year, or else not that. You get a sandy billabong, and you'll get water there by digging not a foot below the surface, like as not – even in the middle of the dry.' his slow, even tones were strangely comforting. 'You go to a place like that and you'll find little diggings all over the sand, where the kangaroos and euros have dug for water. They know where to go. There's water all over in the outback, but you've got to know where to find it.'

'What do you do at this place Wollara?' she asked. 'Do you look after sheep?'

He shook his head. 'You don't find sheep around the Alice region,' he said. 'It'd be too hot for them. Wollara is a cattle station.'

'How many cattle have you got?'

'About eighteen thousand when I come away,' he said. 'It goes up and down, according to the wet, you know.'

'Eighteen thousand? How big is it?'

'Wollara? About two thousand seven hundred.'

'Two thousand seven hundred acres,' she said. 'That's a big place.'

He stared at her. 'Not acres,' he said. 'Square miles. Wollara's two thousand seven hundred square miles.'

She was startled. 'But is that all one place – one farm, I mean?'

'It's one station,' he replied. 'One property.'

'But however many of you does it take to run it?'

His mind ran lovingly around the well-remembered scene. 'There's Mr Duveen, Tommy Duveen – he's the manager, and then me – I'm the head stockman, or I was. Tommy said he'd keep a place for me when I got back. I'd like to get back to Wollara again, one day . . .' He mused a little. 'We had three other ringers – whites,' he said. 'Then there was Happy, and Moonlight, and Nugget, and Snowy, and Tarmac . . .' He thought for a minute. 'Nine boongs we had,' he said. 'That's all.'

'Nine what?'

'Black boys – black stockmen. Abos.'

'But that's only thirteen men,' she said.

'That's right. Fourteen if you count Mr Duveen.'

'But can fourteen men look after all those cattle?' she asked.

'Oh yes,' he said thoughtfully. 'Wollara is an easy station, in a way, because it hasn't got any fences. It's fences make the work. We've got the Palmer River and the Levi Range to the north, and the sand country over to the west; the cattle don't go there. Then there's the Kernot Range to the south and Mount Ormerod and the Twins to the east. Fourteen men is all right for a station like that; it would be easier if we had more whites, but you can't get them. These bloody boongs, they're always going walkabout.'

'What's that?' she asked.

'Walkabout? Why, an Abo ringer, he'll come up one day and he'll say, "Boss, I go walkabout now." You can't keep him. He'll leave the station and go wandering off just in a pair of pants and an old hat with a gun if he's got one, or a spear and a throwing stick, maybe, and he'll be away two or three months.'

'But where does he go to?' she asked.

'Just travels. They go a long way on a walkabout – oh my word,' he said. 'Four or five hundred miles, maybe. Then when he's had enough, he'll come back to the station and join up for work again. But the trouble with the boongs is, you never know if they'll be there next week.'

There was a short silence; they sat quietly in the tropic night together on the steps of the atap schoolhouse, exiles far from their homes. Over their heads the flying foxes swept in the moonlight with a dry rustling of leathery wings. 'Eighteen thousand cattle . . .' she said thoughtfully.

'More or less,' he said. 'Get a good wet, and it'll maybe rise to twenty-one or twenty-two thousand. Then you get a dry year, and it'll go right down to twelve or thirteen thousand. I reckon we lose about three thousand every year by drought.'

'But can't you get them to water?'

He smiled slowly. 'Not with fourteen men. There's enough cattle die of thirst each year in the Territory and Northern Queensland to feed the whole of England. Course, the horses make it worse on Wollara.'

'Horses?'

'Oh my word,' he said. 'We've got about three thousand brumbies, but you can't do nothing with them – they're vermin. Wollara used to be a horse station years ago, selling horses to the Indian Army, but you can't sell horses now. We use a few, of course – maybe a hundred, with packhorses and that. You can't get rid of them except by shooting, and you'll never get a ringer to shoot horses. They eat the feed the cattle ought to get, and spoil it, too. Cattle don't like feeding where a horse has been.'

She asked, 'How big is Wollara – how long, and how wide?'

He said, 'Oh, I'd say about ninety miles from east to west, and maybe forty-five to fifty, north to south, at the widest part. But it's a good station to manage, because the homestead is near the middle, so it's not so far in any one way. Over to the Kernot Range is the furthest; that's about sixty miles.'

'Sixty miles from the homestead? That's where you live?'

'That's right.'

'Are there any other homesteads on it?'

He stared at her. 'There's only the one homestead on each station. Some have an outstation, a shack of some kind where the boys can leave blankets and maybe a little tucker, but not many.'

'How long does it take you to get to the furthest point, then – to the Kernot Range?'

'Over to the Range? Oh well, to go there and come back might take about a week. That's with horses; in a utility you might do it in a day and a half. But horses are best, although they're a bit slow. You never take a packhorse faster'n a walk, not if you can help it. It isn't like you see it on the movies, people galloping their horses everywhere – oh my word. You'd soon wear out a horse if you used him that way in the Territory.'

They sat together for over an hour, talking quietly at the entrance to the schoolhouse. At the end the ringer got up from his strange posture on the ground, and said, 'I mustn't stay any longer, case those Nips come back and start creating. My cobber, too – he'll be wondering what happened to me. I left him to boil up.'

Jean got to her feet. 'It's been terribly kind of you to get us these things. You don't know what they mean to us. Tell me, what's your name?'

'Joe Harman,' he said. 'Sergeant Harman – Ringer Harman, some

of them call me.' He hesitated. 'Sorry I called you Mrs Boong today,'
he said awkwardly. 'It was a silly kind of joke.'

She said, 'My name's Jean Paget.'

'That sounds like a Scotch name.'

'It is,' she said. 'I'm not Scotch myself, but my mother came from
Perth.'

'My mother's family was Scotch,' he said. 'They came from
Inverness.'

She put out her hand. 'Goodnight, Sergeant,' she said. 'It's been
lovely talking to another white person.'

He took her hand; there was great comfort for her in his masculine
handshake. 'Look, Mrs Paget,' he said. 'I'll try if I can get the Nips
to let your party ride down on the truck with us. If the little bastards
won't wear it, then we'll have to give it away. In that case I'll see
you on the road again before you get to Kuantan, and I'll make darn
sure there's something crook with the truck. What else do you
want?'

'Soap,' she said. 'Could you possibly get us soap?'

'Should be able to,' he said.

'We've got no soap at all,' she observed. 'I've got a little gold
locket that one of the women had who died, a thing with a bit of
hair in it. I was going to see if I could sell that here, and get some
soap.'

'Keep it,' he said. 'I'll see you get soap.'

'We want that more than anything, now that you've got these
medicines for us,' she said.

'You'll have it.' He hesitated, and then said, 'Sorry I talked so
much, boring you with the outback and all that. There's times when
you get down a bit – can't make yourself believe you'll ever see it
again.'

'I wasn't bored,' she said softly. 'Goodnight, Sergeant.'

'Goodnight.'

In the morning Jean showed the women what she had got. 'I heard
you talking to him ever so long,' Mrs Price said. 'Nice young man,
I'd say.'

'He's a very homesick young man,' Jean said. 'He loves talking
about the cattle station he comes from.'

'Homesick!' Mrs Price said. 'Aren't we all?'

The Australians had a smart argument with their guard that

morning, who refused point-blank to let the women ride down on the trucks. There was some reason in this from their point of view, because the weight of seventeen women and children added to two grossly overloaded trucks might well be the last straw that would bring final breakdown, in which case the guards themselves would have been lucky to escape with a flogging at the hands of their officer. Harman and Leggatt had to put the back axle together again; they were finished and ready for the road about the middle of the morning.

Joe Harman said, 'Keep that little bastard busy for a minute while I loose off the union.' He indicated the Jap guard. Presently they started, Harman in the lead, dribbling a little petrol from a loosened pipe joint, unnoticed by the guard. It was just as well to have an alibi when they ran out of fuel, having parted with six gallons to the Chinaman.

From Maran to Kuantan is fifty-five miles. The women rested that day at Maran, and next day began the march down the tarmac road. They reached a village called Buan that night. Jean had looked for Joe Harman's truck all day, expecting to see it returning; she was not to know that it had been stranded overnight at Pohoi, short of petrol, and was a day late in the return journey. They stayed next day at Buan in an atap shed; the women took turns with Jean watching for the truck. Their health already was somewhat improved. After the railway track and the jungle paths the tarmac road was easy walking, and the medicines were already having an effect. The country, too, was growing higher and healthier, and the more imaginative of them were already saying they could smell the sea. And finally their contact with the two Australians had had a marked effect on their morale.

They did not see Joe Harman's truck as it passed through. Instead, a Malay girl came to them in the evening with a brown paper parcel of six cakes of Lifebuoy soap; it was addressed to Mrs Paget. Written on the parcel was a note which read,

DEAR LADY,
  I send some soap which is all that we can find just at present but I will get more later on. I am sorry not to see you but the Nip won't let us stop so I have given this to the Chinaman at Maran and he says he will get it to you. Look out for us on the way back and I will try and stop then.
                                                              JOE HARMAN

The women were delighted. 'Lifebuoy,' said Mrs Warner, sniffing it ecstatically. 'You can just smell the carbolic in it! My dear, wherever do you think they got it?'

'I'd have two guesses,' Jean replied. 'Either they stole it, or they stole something to buy it with.' In fact, the latter was correct. At Pohoi their Japanese guard had taken off his boots to wash his feet at the village well; he washed his feet for about thirty seconds and turned round, but the boots had vanished; it could not have been either of the Australians because they both appeared immediately from the other direction. The mystery was never cleared up. Ben Leggatt, however, was most helpful and stole a pair from a sleeping Japanese that evening and gave them to their guard, who was so relieved that he gave Ben a dollar.

The next day the women marched to Berkapor. They were coming out into much better country now, a pleasant, relatively healthy part where the road wound round hillsides and was mostly shaded by the overhanging trees. That day for the first time they got coconuts. Mrs Price had an old worn-out pair of slippers that had belonged to Mrs Horsefall; she had carried them for weeks and had never really used them; they traded these at Berkapor as soon as they got in for milk coconuts, one for each member of the party, thinking that the vitamins contained in the fluid would be good for them. At Berkapor they were accommodated in a large atap copra shed beside the road, and just before dusk the two familiar trucks drew up in the village, driven by Ben Leggatt and Joe Harman. As before, they were headed for the coast and loaded high with railway lines and sleepers.

Jean and several of the others walked across the road to meet them, with the Japanese sergeant; the Japanese guards fell into conversation together. Joe Harman turned to Jean. 'We couldn't get loaded at Jerantut in time to make it down to Kuantan tonight,' he said. 'Ben's got a pig.'

'A pig?' They crowded round Ben's truck. The corpse was lying upon the top of the load, a black, long-nosed Oriental pig, somewhat mauled and already covered in flies. Somewhere near the Tekam River Ben, whose truck was in the lead, had found this pig upon the road and had chased it with the truck for a quarter of a mile. The Japanese guard beside him had fired six shots at it from his rifle and had missed it every time till with the seventh he had wounded it and so enabled Ben to run over it with one of the front wheels. They had stopped and Harman coming close behind them had stopped too, and the two Aussies and the Japanese guard had heaved the pig on to the load and got moving again before the infuriated Chinese storekeeper had caught up with them to claim his property. Harman said quietly to Jean, 'We'll have to let the bloody Nips eat all they can and carry away a bit. Leave it to me; I'll see there's some for you.'

That night the women got about thirty-five pounds of boiled pig meat, conveyed to them surreptitiously in several instalments. They made a fire of coconut shells behind the copra store and made a stew with their rice ration, and ate all of this that seemed prudent to them; at that there was enough meat left for the three meals that they would have before they took the road again. They sat about in the shed or at the roadside after they had finished, replete with the first really nourishing meal that they had had for months, and presently the Australians came across to talk to them.

Joe Harman came to Jean. 'Sorry I couldn't send over more of that pig,' he said in his slow Queensland drawl. 'I had to let the bloody Nips have most of it.'

She said, 'It's been splendid, Joe. We've been eating and eating, and there's still lots left for tomorrow. I don't know when we last had such a meal.'

'I'd say that's what you need,' he observed. 'There's not a lot of flesh on any of you, if I may say so.'

He squatted down upon the ground beside the women, sitting on one heel in his peculiar way.

'I know we're pretty thin,' Jean said. 'But we're a darned sight better than we were. That Chinese stuff you got us as the substitute for Glauber's salt – that's doing the trick all right. It's stopping it.'

'Fine,' he said. 'Maybe we could get some more of that in Kuantan.'

'The pig was a god-send,' she said. 'That, and the fruit – we got some green coconuts today. We've been very lucky so far that we've had no beriberi, or that sort of thing.'

'It's because we've had fresh rice,' said Mrs Frith unexpectedly. 'Being in the country parts we've had fresh rice all through. It's old rice that gives you beriberi.'

The Australian sat thoughtful, chewing a piece of stick. 'Funny sort of a life for you ladies,' he said. 'Living in a place like this, and eating like the boongs. These Nips'll have something coming to them, when it's all added up.'

He turned to Jean. 'What were you all doing in Malaya?' he asked.

'Most of us were married,' she said. 'Our husbands had jobs here.'

Mrs Frith said, 'My hubby's District Engineer on the railway. We had ever such a nice bungalow at Kajang.'

Harman said, 'All the husbands got interned separately, I suppose?'

'That's right,' said Mrs Price. 'My Arthur's in Singapore. I heard about him when we was in Port Dickson. I think they're all in Singapore.'

'All comfortable in a camp while you go walking round the country,' he said.

'That's right,' said Mrs Frith. 'Still, it's nice to know that they're all right, when all's said and done.'

'It seems to me,' said Harman, 'the way they're kicking you around, they just don't know what they can do with you. It might not be too difficult for you to just stay in one place, as it might be this, and live till the war's over.'

Mrs Frith said, 'That's what I've been thinking.'

Jean said, 'I know. I've thought of this ever since Mrs Frith suggested it. The trouble is, the Japs feed us – or they make the village feed us. The village never gets paid. We'd have to earn our keep somehow, and I don't see how we could do it.'

Harman said, 'It was just an idea.'

He said presently, 'I believe I know where I could get a chicken or two. If I can I'll drop them off for you when we come up-country, day after tomorrow.'

Jean said, 'We haven't paid you for the soap yet.'

'Forget about it,' he said slowly. 'I didn't pay cash for it myself. I swapped it for a pair of Nip rubber boots.' With slow, dry humour he told them about the boots. 'You got the soap, the Nip got another pair of boots, and Ben got a dollar,' he said. 'Everybody's happy and satisfied.'

Jean said, 'Is that how you're going to get the chicken?'

'I'll get a chicken for you, one way or another,' he said. 'You ladies need feeding up.'

She said, 'Don't take any risks.'

'You attend to your own business, Mrs Boong,' he said, 'and take what you get. That's what you have to do when you're a prisoner, just take what you can get.'

She smiled, and said, 'All right.' The fact that he had called her Mrs Boong pleased her; it was a little tenuous bond between herself and this strange man that he should pull her leg about her sunburn, her native dress, and the baby that she carried on her hip like a Malay woman. The word boong put Australia into her mind, and the aboriginal stockmen, and she asked a question that had occurred to her, partly from curiosity and partly because she knew it pleased him to talk about his own country. 'Tell me,' she said, 'is it very hot in Australia, the part you come from? Hotter than this?'

'It's hot,' he said. 'Oh my word, it can be hot when it tries. At Wollara it can go to a hundred and eighteen – that's a hot day, that is. But it's not like this heat here. It's a kind of a dry heat, so you don't sweat like you do here.' He thought for a minute. 'I got thrown once,' he said, 'breaking in a brumby to the saddle. I broke my thigh, and after it was set in the hospital they used to point a sort of lamp at it, a sunray lamp they called it, to tone up the muscles or something. Do you have those things in England?'

She nodded. 'It's like that, is it?'

'That's right,' he said. 'It's a kind of warm, dry heat, the sort that does you good and makes you thirsty for cold beer.'

'What does the country look like?' she inquired. It pleased the man to talk about his own place and she wanted to please him; he had been so very kind to them.

'It's red,' he said. 'Red around Alice and where I come from, red earth and then, the mountains are all red. The Macdonnells and the Levis and the Kernots, great red ranges of bare hills against the blue sky. Evenings they go purple and all sorts of colours. After the wet there's green all over them. In the dry, parts of them go silvery white with the spinifex.' He paused. 'I suppose everybody likes his own place,' he said quietly. 'The country round about the Springs is my place. People come up on the 'Ghan from Adelaide and places in the south, and they say Alice is a lousy town. I only went to Adelaide once, and I thought that was lousy. The country round about the Springs is beautiful to me.'

He mused. 'Artists come up from the south and try and paint it in pictures,' he said. 'I only met one that ever got it right, and he was an Abo, an Abo called Albert out at Hermannsburg. Somebody gave him a brush and some paints one time, and he started in and got it better than any of them, oh my word, he did. But he's an Abo, and he's painting his own place. I suppose that makes a difference.'

He turned to Jean. 'What's your place?' he asked. 'Where do you come from?'

She said, 'Southampton.'

'Where the liners go to?'

'That's it,' she said.

'What's it like there?' he asked.

She shifted the baby on her hip, and moved her feet in the sarong. 'It's quiet, and cool, and happy,' she said thoughtfully. 'It's not particularly beautiful, although there's lovely country round about – the New Forest, and the Isle of Wight. It's my place, like the Springs is yours, and I shall go back there if I live through this time, becaue I love it so.' She paused for a moment. 'There was an ice rink there,' she said. 'I used to dance upon the ice, when I was a girl at school. One day I'll get back there and dance again.'

'I've never seen an ice rink,' said the man from Alice. 'I've seen pictures of them, and on the movies.'

She said, 'It was such fun . . .'

Presently he got up to go; she walked across the road with him towards the trucks, the baby on her hip, as always. 'I shan't be able to see you tomorrow,' he said. 'We start at dawn. But I'll be coming back up the road the day after.'

'We shall be walking to Pohoi that day, I think,' she said.

'I'll see if I can get you those chickens,' he said.

She turned and faced him, standing beside her in the moonlit road, in all the noises of the tropic night. 'Look, Joe,' she said. 'We don't want meat if it's going to mean trouble. It was grand of you to get that soap for us, but you did take a fearful risk, pinching that chap's boots.'

'That's nothing,' he said slowly. 'You can run rings round these Nips when you learn how.'

'You've done a lot for us,' she said. 'This pig, and the medicines, and the soap. It's made a world of difference to us in these last few days. I know you've taken risks to do these things. Do, please, be careful.'

'Don't worry about me,' he said. 'I'll try and get the chickens, but if I find things getting hot I'll give it away. I won't go sticking out my neck.'

'You'll promise that?' she asked.

'Don't worry about me,' he said. 'You've got enough troubles on your own plate, my word. But we'll come out all right, so long as we just keep alive, that's all we got to do. Just keep alive another two years, till the war's over.'

'You think that it will be as long as that?' she asked.

'Ben knows a lot more than I do about things like that,' he said. 'He thinks about two years.' He grinned down at her. 'You'd better have those chickens.'

'I'll leave that with you,' she said. 'I'd never forgive myself if you got caught in anything, and bought it.'

'I won't,' he said. He put out his hands as if to take her own, and then dropped it again. 'Goodnight, Mrs Boong,' he said.

She laughed. 'I'll crack you with a coconut if you say Mrs Boong again. Goodnight, Joe.'

'Goodnight.'

They did not see him next morning, though they heard the trucks go off. They rested that day at Berkapor, as was their custom, and the next day they marched on to Pohoi. The two trucks driven by Harman and Leggatt passed them on the road about midday going up empty to Jerantut; each driver waved to the women as they passed, and they waved back. The Japanese guards seated beside the drivers scowled a little. No chickens dropped from the trucks and the trucks did not stop; in one way Jean was rather relieved. She knew something of the temper of these men by now, and she knew very well that they would stop at nothing, would be deterred by no risk, to get what they considered to be helpful for the women. No chickens meant no trouble, and she marched on for the rest of the day with an easy mind.

That evening, in the house that they had been put into at Pohoi, a little Malay boy came to Jean with a green canvas sack; he said that he had been sent by a Chinaman in Gambang. In the sack were five black cockerels, alive, with their feet tied. Poultry is usually transported in the East alive.

Their arrival put Jean in a difficulty, and she consulted with Mrs Frith. It was impossible for them to kill, pluck and cook five cockerels without drawing the attention of their guards to what was going on, and the first thing that the guards would ask was, where had the cockerels come from? If Jean had known the answer to that one herself it would have been easier to frame a lie. It would be possible, they thought, to say that they had bought them with money given to them by the Australians, but that was difficult if the sergeant wanted to know where they had bought them in Pohoi. It was unfortunate that Pohoi was a somewhat unfriendly village; it had been genuinely difficult for the village to evacuate a house for the women, and it was not to be expected that they would get much co-operation from the villagers in any deceit. Finally they decided to say that they had bought them with money given to them by the Australians, and that they had arranged at Berkapor for the poultry to be sent to them at Pohoi from a village called Limau, two or three miles off the road. It was a thin tale and one that would not stand up to a great deal of investigation, but they saw no reason why any investigation should take place.

They decided regretfully that they would have to part with one of the five cockerels to their guards; the gift of a chicken would make the sergeant sweet and involve him in the affair, rendering any serious investigation unlikely. Accordingly Jean took the sack and went to find the sergeant.

She bowed to him, to put him in a good temper. 'Gun so,' she said, 'good mishi tonight. We buy chickens.' She opened the sack and showed him the fowls lying in the bottom. Then she reached down and pulled out one. 'For you.' She smiled at him with all the innocence that she could muster.

It was a great surprise to him. He had not known that they had so much money; they had never been able to buy anything but coconuts or bananas before, since he had been with them. 'You buy?' he asked.

She nodded. 'From Limau. Very good mishi for us all tonight.'

'Where get money?' he inquired. Suspicion had not dawned, for they had never deceived him before; he was just curious.

For one fleeting moment Jean toyed with the idea of saying they had sold some jewellery, with a quick, intuitive feeling that it would be better not to mention the Australians. But she put the idea away; she must stick to the story that they had prepared and considered from all angles. 'Man prisoner give us money for chicken,' she said. 'They say we too thin. Now we have good mishi tonight, Japanese and prisoner also.'

He put up two fingers. 'Two.'

She went up in a sheet of flame. 'One, not two, gunso,' she said. 'This is a present for you, because you have been kind and carried children, and allowed us to walk slowly. Five only, five.' She showed him the sack, and he counted them carefully. It was only then that she took note of the fact that the birds were rather unusually large for the East, and jet black all over. 'One for you, four for us.'

He let the sack fall, and nodded; then he smiled at her, tucked the cockerel under his arm, and walked off with it towards the kitchen where his meal was in preparation.

That day there was a considerable row in progress at Kuantan. The local commanding officer was a Captain Sugamo, who was executed by the Allied War Crimes Tribunal in the year 1946 after the trial for atrocities committed at Camp 302 on the Burma-Siam railway in the years 1943 and 1944: his duty in Kuantan at that time was to see to the evacuation of the railway material from the eastern railway in Malaya and to its shipment to Siam. He lived in the house formerly occupied by the District Commissioner of Kuantan, and the District Commissioner had kept a fine little flock of about twenty black Leghorn fowls, specially imported from England in 1939. When Captain Sugamo woke up that morning, five of his twenty black Leghorns were missing, with a green sack that had once held the mail for the District Commissioner, and was now used to store grain for the fowls.

Captain Sugamo was a very angry man. He called the Military Police and set them to work; their suspicion fell at once upon the Australian truck drivers, who had a record for petty larceny in that district. Moreover, they had considerable opportunities, because the nature of their work allowed them a great deal of freedom; trucks had to be serviced and refuelled, often in the hours of darkness when it was difficult to ascertain exactly where each man might be. Their camp was searched that day for any sign of telltale feathers, or the sack, but nothing was discovered but a cache of tinned foods and cigarettes stolen from the quartermaster's store.

Captain Sugamo was not satisfied and he became more angry than ever. A question of face was now involved, because this theft from the commanding officer was a clear insult to his position, and so to the Imperial Japanese Army. He ordered a search of the entire town of Kuantan: on the following day every house was entered by troops

working under the directions of the military Police to look for signs of
the black feathers or the green sack. It yielded no result.

Brooding over the insults levelled at his uniform, the captain
ordered the barracks of the company of soldiers under his command
to be searched. There was no result from that.

There remained one further avenue. Three of the trucks, driven by
Australians, were up-country on the road to or from Jerantut. Next
day Sugamo dispatched a light truck up the road manned by four
men of his military police, to search these trucks and to interrogate
the drivers and the guards, and anybody else who might have
knowledge of the matter. Between Pohoi and Blat they came upon a
crowd of women and children walking down the road loaded with
bundles; ahead of them marched a Japanese sergeant with his rifle
slung over one shoulder and a green sack over the other. The truck
stopped with a squeal of brakes.

For the next two hours Jean stuck to her story, that the Australian
had given her money and she had bought the fowls from Limau.
They put her through a sort of third degree there on the road, with
an insistent reiteration of questions: when they felt that her attention
was wandering they slapped her face, kicked her skins, or stamped
on her bare feet with army boots. She stuck to it with desperate
resolution, knowing that it was a rotten story, knowing that they
disbelieved her, not knowing what else she could say. At the end of
that time a convoy of three trucks came down the road; the driver of
the second one, Joe Harman, was recognized by the sergeant immediately, and brought before Jean at the point of the bayonet. The
sergeant of the Military Police said, 'Is this man?'

Jean said desperately, 'I've been telling them about the four dollars
you gave me to buy the chickens with, Joe, but they won't believe
me.'

The military policeman said, 'You steal chicken from the shoko.
Here is bag.'

The ringer looked at the girl's bleeding face and at her bleeding
feet. 'Leave her alone, you bloody mucking bastards,' he said angrily
in his slow Queensland drawl. 'I stole those mucking chickens, and I
gave them to her. So what?'

Darkness was closing down in my London sitting-room, the early
darkness of a stormy afternoon. The rain still beat upon the window.

The girl sat staring into the fire, immersed in her sad memories. 'They crucified him,' she said quietly. 'They took us all down to Kuantan, and they nailed his hands to a tree, and beat him to death. They kept us there, and made us look on while they did it.'

'My dear,' I said. 'I am so very sorry.'

She raised her head. 'You don't have to be sorry,' she replied. 'It was one of those things that seem to happen in a war. It's a long time ago, now – nearly six years. And Captain Sugamo was hung – not for that, but for what he did upon the railway. It's all over and done with now, and nearly forgotten.'

There was, of course, no women's camp in Kuantan, and Captain Sugamo was not the man to be bothered with a lot of women and children. The execution took place at midday at a tree that stood beside the recreation ground overlooking the tennis courts: as soon as the maimed, bleeding body hanging by its hands had ceased to twitch Captain Sugamo stood them in parade before him.

'You very bad people,' he said. 'No place here for you. I send you to Kota Bahru. You walk now.'

They stumbled off without a word, in desperate hurry to get clear of that place of horror. The same sergeant that had escorted them from Gemas was sent with them, for he also was disgraced as having shared the chickens. It was as a punishment that he was ordered to continue with them, because all prisoners are disgraceful and dis-honourable creatures in the eyes of the Japanese, and to guard them and escort them is an insulting and a menial job fit only for the lowest type of man. An honourable Japanese would kill himself rather than be taken prisoner. Perhaps to emphasize this point the private soldier was taken away, so that from Kuantan onwards the sergeant was their only guard.

So they took up their journey again, living from day to day. They left Kuantan about the middle of July. It is about two hundred miles from Kuantan to Kota Bahru: allowing for halts of several days for illness Jean anticipated it would take them two months at least to get there.

They got to Besarah on the first day: this is a fishing village on the sea, with white coral sand and palm trees at the head of the beach. It is a very lovely place but they slept little, for most of the children were awake and crying in the night with memories of the horror they had seen. They could not bear to stay so close to Kuantan and travelled on next day another short stage to Balok, another fishing village on another beach with more palm trees. Here they rested for a day.

Gradually they came to realize that they had entered a new land. The north-east coast of Malaya is a very lovely country, and comparatively healthy. It is beautiful, with rocky headlands and long, sweeping, sandy beaches fringed with palm trees, and usually there is a fresh wind from the sea. Moreover there is an abundance of fresh fish in all the villages. For the first time since they left Panong the women had sufficient protein with their rice, and their health began to show an improvement at once. Most of them bathed in the warm sea at least once every day, and certain of the skin diseases that they suffered from began to heal with this salt water treatment, though not all. For the first time in months the children had sufficient energy to play.

They all improved, in fact, except the sergeant. The sergeant was suspicious of them now; he seldom carried a child or helped them in any way. He seemed to feel the reproofs that he had been given very much, and he had now no companion of his own race to talk to. He moped a great deal, sitting sullenly aloof from them in the evenings; once or twice Jean caught herself consciously trying to cheer him up, a queer reversal of the role of prisoner and guard. Upon this route they met very few Japanese. Occasionally they would find a detachment stationed in a river village or at an airstrip; when they came to such a unit the sergeant would smarten himself up and go and report to the officer in charge, who would usually come and inspect them. But there is very little industry between Kuantan and Kota Bahru and no town larger than a fishing village, nor was there any prospect of an enemy attack upon the eastern side of the Malay Peninsula. On several occasions a week passed without the women seeing any Japanese at all except the sergeant.

As they travelled slowly up the coast the condition of the women

and the children altered greatly for the better. They were now a very
different party from the helpless people who had started off from
Panong nearly six months before. Death had ruthlessly eliminated
the weakest members and reduced them to about half the original
numbers, which made all problems of billeting and feeding in the
villages far easier. They were infinitely more experienced by that
time, too. They had learned to use the native remedies for malaria
and dysentery, to clothe themselves and wash and sleep in the native
manner; in consequence they now had far more leisure than when
they had been fighting to maintain a western style of life in primitive
conditions. The march of ten miles every other day was now no
longer a great burden; in the intervening day they had more time for
the children. Presently Mrs Warner, who at one time had been an
elementary schoolmistress, started a class for the children, and school
became a regular institution on their day of rest.

Jean began to teach her baby, Robin Holland, how to walk. He
was quite fit and healthy again, and getting quite a weight for her to
carry, for he was now sixteen months old. She never burdened him
with any clothes in that warm climate, and he crawled about naked
in the shade of palm or casuarina trees, or in the sun upon the sand,
like any Malay boy. He got nearly as brown as one, too.

In the weeks that followed they moved slowly northwards up the
coast, through all the many fishing villages. Ular and Chendar and
Kalong and Penunjok and Kemasik and many others. They had a
little sickness and spent a few days here and there while various
members of the party sweated out a fever, but they had no more
deaths. The final horror at Kuantan was a matter that they never
spoke about at all, each fearing to recall it to the memory of the
others, but each was secretly of the opinion that it had changed their
luck.

With Mrs Frith this impression struck much deeper. She was a
devout little woman who said her prayers morning and evening with
the greatest regularity. It was Mrs Frith who always knew when
Sunday was: on that day she would read the Prayer Book and the
Bible for an hour aloud to anyone who came to listen to her. If it was
their rest day she would hold this service at eleven o'clock as near as
she could guess it, because that was the correct time for Matins.

Mrs Frith sought for the hand of God in everything that happened
to them. Brooding over their experiences with this in mind, she was

struck by certain similarities. She had read repeatedly about one Crucifixion; now there had been another. The Australian, in her mind, had had the power of healing, because the medicines he brought had cured her dysentery and Johnnie Horsefall's ringworm. It was beyond all doubt that they had been blessed in every way since his death for them. God had sent down His Son to earth in Palestine. What if He had done it again in Malaya?

Men and women who are in great and prolonged distress and forced into an entirely novel way of life, divorced entirely from their previous association, frequently develop curious mental traits. Mrs Frith did not thrust her views upon them, yet inevitably the matter that she was beginning to believe herself became known to the other women. It was received with incredulity at first, but as a matter that required the most deep and serious thought. Most of the women had been churchgoers when they got the chance, mostly of Low Church sects; deep in their hearts they had been longing for the help of God. As their physical health improved throughout these weeks, their capacity for religious thought increased, and, as the weeks went on, accurate memory of the Australian began to fade, and was replaced by an awed and roseate memory of the man he had not been. If this incredible event that Mrs Frith believed could possibly be true, it meant indeed that they were in the hand of God; nothing could touch them then; they would win through and live through all their troubles and one day they would regain their homes, their husbands, and their western way of life. They marched on with renewed strength.

Jean did nothing to dispel these fancies, which were evidently helpful to the women, but she was not herself impressed. She was the youngest of all of them, and the only one unmarried; she had formed a very different idea of Joe Harman. She knew him for a very human, very normal man; she had grown prettier, she knew, when he had come to talk to her, and more attractive. It had been a subconscious measure of defence that had led her to allow him to continue to refer to her as Mrs Boong; if the baby on her hip had misled him into classing her with all the other married women, that was just as well. In those villages, in the hot tropic nights when they wore little clothing, in that place of extraordinary standards or no standards at all, she knew that anything might have happened between them if he had known that she was an unmarried girl, and it might well have happened very quickly. Her grief for him was more real and far deeper than that of the other women, and it was not in the least because she thought that he had been divine. She was entirely certain in her own mind that he wasn't.

Toward the end of August they were in a village called Kuala Telang about half way between Kuantan and Kota Bahru. The Telang is a short, muddy river that wanders through a flat country of rice fields to the sea; the village stands on the south bank of the river just inside the sand bar at the mouth. It is a pretty place of palm and casuarina trees and long white beaches on which the rollers of the South China Sea break in surf. The village lives upon the fishing and on the rice fields. About fifteen fishing-boats operate from the river, big open sailing-boats with strange, high, flat figureheads at bow and stern. There is a sort of village square with wood and palm-leaf native shops grouped round about it; behind this stands a godown for the rice beside the river bank. This godown was empty at the time, and it was here that the party was accommodated.

The Japanese sergeant fell ill with fever here, probably malaria. He had not been himself since Kuantan; he had been sullen and depressed, and he seemed to feel the lack of companionship very much. As the women had grown stronger so he had grown weaker, and this was strange to them at first, because he had never been ill before. At first they had been pleased and relieved that this queer, ugly, uncouth little man was in eclipse, but as he grew more unhappy they suffered a strange reversal of feeling. He had been with them for a long time and he had done what was possible within the limits of his duty to alleviate their lot; he had carried their children willingly and he had wept when children died. When it was obvious that he had fever they took turns at carrying his rifle and his tunic and his boots and his pack for him, so that they arrived in the village as a queer procession, Mrs Warner leading the little yellow man clad only in his trousers, stumbling about in a daze. He walked more comfortably barefoot. Behind them came the other women carrying all his equipment as well as their own burdens.

Jean found the headman, a man of about fifty called Mat Amin bin Taib, and explained the situation to him. 'We are prisoners,' she said, 'marching from Kuantan to Kota Bharu, and this Japanese is our guard. He is ill with fever, and we must find a shady house for him to lie in. He has authority to sign chits in the name of the Imperial Army for our food and accommodation, and he will do this for you when he recovers, he will give you a paper. We must have a place to sleep ourselves, and food.'

Mat Amin said, 'I have no place where white Mems would like to sleep.'

Jean said, 'We are not white mems any longer; we are prisoners and we are accustomed to living as your women live. All we need is a shelter and a floor to sleep on, and the use of cooking pots, and rice, and a little fish or meat and vegetables.'

'You can have what we have ourselves,' he said, 'but it is strange to see mems living so.'

He took the sergeant into his own house and produced a mattress stuffed with coconut fibre and a pillow of the same material; he had a mosquito net which was evidently his own and he offered this, but the women refused it because they knew the sergeant needed all the cooling breezes he could get. They made him take his trousers off and get into a sarong and lie down on the bed. They had no quinine left, but the headman produced a draught of his own concoction and they gave the sergeant some of this, and left him in the care of the headman's wife, and went to find their own quarters and food.

The fever was high all that night; in the morning when they came to see how he was getting on they did not like the look of him at all. He was still in a high fever and he was very much weaker than he had been; it seemed to them that he was giving up, and that was a bad sign. They took turns all that day to sit with him and bathe his face, and wash him; from time to time they talked to him to try and stimulate his interest, but without a great deal of success. In the evening Jean was sitting with him; he lay inert upon his back, sweating profusely; he did not answer anything she said.

Looking for something to attract his interest, she pulled his tunic to her and felt in the pocket for his paybook. She found a photograph in it, a photograph of a Japanese woman and four children standing by the entrance to a house. She said, 'Your children gunso?' and gave it to him. He took it without speaking and looked at it; then he gave it back to her and motioned to her to put it away again.

When she had laid the jacket down she looked at him and saw that tears were oozing from his eyes and falling down to mingle with the sweat beads on his cheeks. Very gently she wiped them away.

He grew weaker and weaker, and two days later he died in the night. There seemed no particular reason why he should have died,

but the disgrace of Kuantan was heavy on him and he seemed to
have lost interest and the will to live. They buried him that day in
the Moslem cemetery outside the village, and most of them wept a
little for him as an old and valued friend.

The death of the sergeant left them in a most unusual position, for
they were now prisoners without a guard. They discussed it at some
length that evening after the funeral. 'I don't see why we shouldn't
stay here, where we are,' said Mrs Frith. 'It's a nice place, this is, as
nice as any that we've come to. That's what He said, we ought to
find a place where we'd be out of the way, and just live there.'

Jean said, 'I know. There's two things we'd have to settle though.
First, the Japs are bound to find out sometime that we're living here,
and then the headman will get into trouble for having allowed us to
stay here without telling them. They'd probably kill him. You know
what they are.'

'Maybe they wouldn't find us, after all,' said Mrs Price.

'I don't believe Mat Amin is the man to take that risk,' Jean said.
'There isn't any reason why he should. If we stay he'll go straight to
the Japanese and tell them that we're here.' She paused. 'The other
thing is that we can't expect this village to go on feeding seventeen of
us for ever just because we're white mems. They'll go and tell the
Japs about us just to get rid of us.'

Mrs Frith said, 'If we were growing rice like that, maybe perhaps.
Half the paddy fields we walked by coming in haven't been planted
this year.'

Jean stared at her. 'That's quite right – they haven't. I wonder
why that is?'

'All the men must have gone to the war,' said Mrs Warner.
'Working as coolies taking up that railway line, or something of that.'

Jean said slowly, 'What would you think of this? Suppose I go and
tell Mat Amin that we'll work in the rice fields if he'll let us stay
here? What would you think of that?'

Mrs Price laughed. 'Me, with my figure? Walking about in mud
and water up to the knee planting them little seedlings in the mud,
like you see the Malay girls doing?'

Jean said apologetically, 'It was just a thought.'

'And a very good one, too,' said Mrs Warner. 'I wouldn't mind
working in the paddy fields if we could stay here and live comfortable
and settled.'

Mrs Frith said, 'If we were growing rice like that, maybe they'd let us stay here – the Japs I mean. After all, in that way we'd be doing something useful, instead of walking all over the country like a lot of whipped dogs with no home.'

Next morning Jean went to the headman. She put her hands together in the praying gesture of greeting, and smiled at him and said in Malay, 'Mat Amin, why do we see the paddy fields not sown this year. We saw so many of them as we came to this place, not sown at all.'

He said, 'Most of the men, except the fishermen, are working for the army.' He meant the Japanese Army.

'On the railway?'

'No. They are at Gong Kedak. They are making a long piece of land flat, and making roads, and covering the land they have made flat with tar and stones, so that aeroplanes can come down there.'

'Are they coming back soon to plant paddy?'

'It is in the hand of God, but I do not think they will come back for many months. I have heard that after they have done this thing at Gong Kedak, there is another such place to be made at Machang, and another at Tan Yongmat. Once a man falls into the power of the Japanese it is not easy for him to escape and come back to his home.'

'Who, then, will plant the paddy, and reap it?'

'The women will do what they can. Rice will be short next year, not here, because we shall not sell the paddy that we need to eat ourselves. We shall not have enough to sell to the Japanese. I do not know what they are going to eat, but it will not be rice.'

Jean said, 'Mat Amin, I have serious matters to discuss with you. If there were a man amongst us I would send him to talk for us, but there is no man. You will not be offended if I ask you to talk business with a woman, on behalf of women?' She now knew something of the right approach to a Mohammedan.

He bowed to her, and led her to his house. There was a small rickety veranda; they went up to this and sat down upon the floor facing each other. He was a level-eyed old man with close-cropped hair and a small, clipped moustache, naked to the waist and wearing a sarong; his face was firm, but not unkind. He called sharply to his wife within the house to bring out coffee.

Jean waited till the coffee appeared, making small talk for politeness; she knew the form after six months in the villages. It came in two thick glasses, without milk and sweet with sugar. She bowed to him, and lifted her glass and sipped, and set it down again. 'We are in a difficulty,' she said frankly. 'Our guard is dead, and what now will become of us is in our own hands – and in yours. You know our story. We were taken prisoner at Panong, and since then we have walked many hundreds of miles to this place. No Japanese commander will receive us and put us in a camp and feed us and attend to us in illness, because each commander thinks that these things are the duty of the other; so they march us under guard from town to town. This has been going on now for more than six months, and in that time half of our party have died upon the road.'

He inclined his head.

'Now that our gunso is dead,' she said, 'what shall we do? If we go on until we find a Japanese officer and report to him, he will not want us; nobody in all this country wants us. They will not kill us quickly, as they might if we were men. They will get us out of the way by marching us on to some other place, perhaps into a country of swamps such as we have come through. So we shall grow ill again, and one by one we shall all die. That is what lies ahead of us, if we report now to the Japanese.'

He replied, 'It is written that the angels said, "Every soul shall taste of death, and we will prove you with evil and with good for a trial of you, and unto us shall ye return."'

She thought quickly; the words of the headman at Dilit came into her mind. She said, 'It is also written, "If ye be kind towards women and fear to wrong them, God is well acquainted with what ye do."'

He eyed her steadily. 'Where is that written?'

She said, 'In the Fourth Surah.'

'Are you of the Faith?' he asked incredulously.

She shook her head. 'I do not want to deceive you. I am a Christian; we are all Christians. The headman of a village on our road was kind to us, and when I thanked him he said that to me. I do not know the Koran.'

'You are a very clever woman,' he said. 'Tell me what you want.'

'I want our party to stay here, in this village,' she said, 'and go to work in the paddy fields, as your women do.' He stared at her, astonished. 'This will be dangerous for you,' she said. 'We know that very well. If Japanese officers find us in this place before you have reported to them that we are here, they will be very angry. And so, I want you to do this. I want you to let us go to work at once with one or two of your women to show us what to do. We will work all day for our food alone and a place to sleep. When we have worked so for two weeks, I will go myself and find an officer and report to him, and tell him what we are doing. And you shall come with me, as headman of this village, and you shall tell the officer that more rice will be grown for the Japanese if we are allowed to continue working in the rice fields. These are the things I want.'

'I have never heard of white mems working in the paddy fields,' he said.

She asked, 'Have you ever heard of white mems marching and dying as we have marched and died?'

He was silent.

'We are in your hands,' she said. 'If you say, go upon your way and walk on to some other place, then we must go, and going we must die. That will then be a matter between you and God. If you allow us to stay and cultivate your fields and live with you in peace and safety, you will get great honour when the English Tuans return to this country after their victory. Because they will win this war in the end; these Short Ones are in power now, but they cannot win against the Americans and all the free peoples of the world. One day the English Tuans will come back.'

He said, 'I shall be glad to see that day.'

They sat in silence for a time, sipping the glasses of coffee. Presently the headman said, 'This is a matter not to be decided lightly, for it concerns the whole village. I will think about it and I will talk it over with my brothers.'

Jean went away, and that evening after the hour of evening prayer she saw a gathering of men squatting with the headman in front of his house; they were all old men, because there were very few young ones in Kuala Telang at that time, and young ones probably would not have been admitted to the conference in any case. Later that evening Mat Amin came to the godown and asked for Mem Paget; Jean came out to him, carrying the baby. She stood talking to him in the light of a small oil lamp.

'We have discussed this matter that we talked about,' he said. 'It is a strange thing, that white mems should work in our rice fields, and some of my brothers are afraid that the white Tuans will not understand when they come back, and that they will be angry, saying we have made you work for us against your will.'

Jean said, 'We will give you a letter now, that you can show them if they should say that.'

He shook his head. 'It is not necessary. It is sufficient if you tell the Tuans when they come back that this thing was done because you wished it so.'

She said, 'That we will do.'

They went to work next day. There were six married women in the party at that time, and Jean, and ten children including Jean's baby. The headman took them out to the fields with two Malay girls, Fatimah binti Darus and Raihana binti Hassan. He gave them seven small fields covered in weeds to start upon, an area that was easily within their power to manage. There was a roofed platform nearby in the fields for resting in the shade; they left the youngest children here and went to work.

The seven women were all fairly robust; the journey had eliminated the ones who would have been unable to stand agricultural work. Those who were left were women of determination and grit, with high morale and a good sense of humour. As soon as they became accustomed to the novelty of working ankle-deep in mud and water they did not find the work exacting, and presently as they became accustomed to it they were seized with an ambition to show the village that white mems could do as much work as Malay women, or more.

Paddy is grown in little fields surrounded by a low wall of earth, so that water from a stream can be led into the field at will to turn it into a shallow pool. When the water is let out again the earth bottom is soft mud, and weeds can be pulled out by hand and the ground hoed and prepared for the seedlings. The seedlings are raised by scattering the rice in a similar nursery field, and they are then transplanted in rows into the muddy field. The field is then flooded again for a few days while the seedlings stand with their heads above the water in the hot sun, and the water is let out again for a few days to let the sun get to the roots. With alternating flood and dry in that hot climate the plants grow very quickly to about the height of wheat, with feathery ears of rice on top of the stalks. The rice is harvested by cutting off the ears with a little knife, leaving the straw standing, and is taken in sacks to the village to be winnowed. Water buffaloes are then turned in to eat the straw and fertilize the ground and tramp it all about, and the ground is ready for sowing again to repeat the cycle. Two crops a year are normally got from the rice fields, and there is no rotation of crop.

Working in these fields is not unpleasant when you get accustomed to it. There are worse things to do in a very hot country than to put on a large conical sun-hat of plaited palm leaves and take off most of your clothes, and play about with mud and water, damming and diverting little trickling streams. By the end of the fortnight the women had settled down to it and quite liked the work, and all the children loved it from the first. No Japanese came near the village in that time.

On the sixteenth day Jean started out with the headman, Mat Amin, to go and look for the Japanese; they carried the sergeant's rifle and equipment, and his uniform, and his paybook. There was a place called Kuala Rakit twenty-seven miles away where a Japanese detachment was stationed, and they went there.

They took two days to walk this distance, staying overnight at a place called Bukit Perah. They stayed with the headman there, Jean sleeping in the back quarters with the women. They went on next day and came to Kuala Rakit in the evening; it was a very large village, or small town. Here Mat Amin took her to see an official of the Malay administration at his house, Tungku Bentara Raja. Tungku Bentara was a little thin Malay who spoke excellent English; he was genuinely concerned at the story that he heard from mat Amin and from Jean.

'I am very, very sorry,' he said at last. 'I cannot do much to help you directly, because the Japanese control everything we do. It is terrible that you should have to work in the rice fields.'

'That's not terrible at all,' Jean said. 'As a matter of fact, we rather like it. We want to stay there, with Mat Amin here. If the Japanese have got a camp for women in this district I suppose they'll put us into that, but if they haven't, we don't want to go on marching all over Malaya. Half of us have died already doing that.'

'You must stay with us tonight,' he said. 'Tomorrow I will have a talk with the Japanese Civil Administrator. There is no camp here for women, anyway.'

That night Jean slept in a bed for the first time in nearly seven months. She did not care for it much; having grown used to sleeping on the floor she found it cooler to sleep so than to sleep on a mattress. She did not actually get out of bed and sleep upon the floor, but she came very near to it. The bath and shower after the bath taken by holding a gourd full of water over her head, however, were a joy, and she spent a long time washing.

In the morning she went with Tungku Bentara and Mat Amin to the Japanese Civil Administrator, and told her tale again. The Civil Administrator had been to the State University of California and spoke first-class American English; he was sympathetic, but declared that prisoners were nothing to do with him, being the concern of the Army. He came with them, however, to see the military commanding officer, a Colonel Matisaka, and Jean told her tale once more.

It was quite clear that Colonel Matisaka considered women prisoners to be a nuisance, and he had no intention whatsoever of diverting any portion of his force to guarding them. Left to himself he would probably have sent them marching on, but with Tungku Bentara and the Civil Administrator in his office and acquainted with the facts he could hardly do that. In the end he washed his hands of the whole thing and told the Civil Administrator to make what arrangements he thought best. The Civil Administrator told Bentara that the women could stay where they were for the time being, and Jean started back for Kuala Telang with Mat Amin.

They lived there for three years.

The Birth of an Idea

Ewen Montague

In the graveyard of the Spanish town of Huelva there lies a British subject. As he died, alone, in the foggy damp of England in the late autumn of 1942, he little thought that he would lie forever under the sunny skies of Spain after a funeral with full military honours, nor that he would, after death, render a service to the Allies that saved many hundred of British and American lives. In life he had done little for his country; but in death he did more than most could achieve by a lifetime of service.

It all really started through a wild idea of George's. He and I were members of a small inter-Service and inter-departmental committee which used to meet weekly to deal with questions of the security of intended operations. We exchanged and discussed information that had been obtained from all kinds of sources – from our own Services and other sources at home as well as from neutral countries, together with intelligence reports from enemy countries. With all this and the latest information as to Allied 'intentions' – not only immediate and probable, but also 'long-term possible' – we had to try to detect any leakages that might have occurred and any 'intelligent anticipation' that the enemy might already have made, and also to guard against such leakages and anticipations in the future.

It was not an easy task, but the committee was a good one: it comprised not only Regular officers of considerable knowledge and experience, but also temporary officers and civilians with most varied backgrounds; we were a mixed lot, and between us we could view any item of information as it would strike observers from any walk of life; we had a thoroughly variegated fund of knowledge and there were few spheres of activity with which we had no contacts.

George produced his idea during a discussion over a report with which we had been supplied from occupied Europe; as happened from time to time, we were puzzled whether it was genuine or had been planted by the Germans for transmission to the Allies.

George had one of those subtle and ingenious minds which is forever throwing up fantastic ideas – mostly so ingenious as either to be impossible of implementation or so intricate as to render their efficacy problematical, but every now and again quite brilliant in their simplicity. As we puzzled whether this particular report was genuine, or whether the Germans had captured the agent concerned and were sending reports through him or for him, George remembered a recent warning that had been issued reminding officers that it was forbidden for secret documents to be carried in aircraft lest they should be shot down in enemy territory.

Starting from that, George suddenly suggested that as a check on such reports we should try to get the Germans to plant something on us that we knew was planted, so that we could see what their line was and how they put it over: if we could drop a resistance workers' wireless set into France (he suggested) and it started working it would be difficult to tell whether the Germans or a friendly Frenchman was working it, but if it dropped accompanied by a dead body attached to a badly opened parachute, the task of checking might be easier. A Frenchman would probably tell us what had occurred, whereas the Germans would be more likely to conceal what had happened and work the set as if the agent was still alive. It would not be certain, but it did not involve much effort and might be worth trying. 'Does anyone know whether we can get a body?' asked George.

This was not one of his better inspirations, and we rapidly demolished it; agents did not carry their codes on their routine and system for sending messages with them for anyone to find, so how would the Germans transmit messages?

Also, if a parachute failed, whatever was hanging from it would be bound to hit the ground with a considerable bump; if it was a body, this would almost certainly result in a broken limb as well as grazes and scratches, and injuries inflicted after death can always be detected. There was therefore no hope of dropping a dead body attached to a partially opened parachute without the finder being able to tell that the body had been dead for some time before it hit the ground. Besides, even if we could get a dead body (and no one knew whether we could), our field of choice would indeed be limited if it had to be that of someone who had died through falling from a height! No; this was one of George's failures, and we quickly turned back to our report: was it genuine or not? But some months later George's wild idea produced results.

By the summer of 1942 our little committee was in the midst of its first big job. 'Operation Torch', the invasion of North Africa, was being mounted, and the experience that we had gained in trying to guard the security of small-scale operations, involving relatively few units, was receiving its first full test.

In spite of all that could be done in the way of security, it was obviously impossible to prevent the enemy knowing that something was brewing. In the first place, it was apparent to everyone that the Allies would not just sit back indefinitely: there must be an invasion somewhere. Secondly, there could be no restriction on foreign diplomats: they moved around the country and they met and spoke to people, not only people in the know, but also some of the thousands who were bound to see the congregation of ships or of troops before they left this country; and whatever view had to be taken officially, none of us had any illusions as to the neutrality of a number of the diplomats. Besides, even a pro-British diplomat had a job to do: he had to report to his government what was going on over here, and once the report got to his country there could be no doubt that there would be at least one official or minister over there who was either paid, or at any rate ideologically ready, to pass the information to the Germans. Thirdly, there were neutral business-men and sailors travelling between this country and the Continent.

Therefore we could not hope to prevent the Germans knowing that there *was* an operation afoot. What we could hope to do was to prevent the vital information of 'When?' and 'Where?' leaking.

Until the invasion of North Africa had taken place the Allies had no foothold on the continent of Europe, and the war in North Africa consisted of a campaign in which we were pushing from east to west with our armies based on the Canal Zone. As a result of this situation there was no reason why the Allies should not make an attack at almost any point. As far as the Germans knew, we might land in Norway, in the Low Countries or in France, or try to push up through Spain; we might seize the Canaries or the Azores to help in the war against U-boats; or we might land in Libya to attack Rommel's army in its rear. Except in Egypt, we were wholly uncommitted, and anywhere in German-held Europe or neutral countries was open to assault.

In these circumstances all that it was necessary for our committee to try to ensure, when we attacked Dieppe or the Lofoten Islands or planned any other assault, was that the actual target and date did not get over to the enemy. That involved nothing more than leaking a false target to the troops concerned, perhaps backing such leaks up with papers about an issue of sun helmets – if they were in fact going to the Lofoten Islands – or something of that kind, and then working really hard to reduce, as much as possible, the bits of information which would inevitably get out of this country. In other words, our principle was to try to make security as complete as possible, and then to try to prevent any leakage that *did* get by our precautions being such as would give away the true target.

When 'Operation Torch' was being launched against North Africa we could still operate on this basis and, as we studied our Intelligence reports and learned of the movements that the Germans made, we realised that this system had worked as the potential targets were so many that the Germans could not get a definite idea even of where we would strike.

But our problem would be entirely different after 'Operation Torch' had been completed. At that stage of the war the Allies would have command of the whole of the North African coast and would be poised ready to strike at what the Prime Minister called 'the soft under-belly of Europe'. Our committee was kept in touch with the strategic thinking of our Chiefs of Staff and also with that of the Americans. We knew that there were some differences of opinion, but there was a definite probability that we would strike there, and our committee had to be prepared to play our part when the Allies attacked.

With the whole North African coast in Allied hands it was pretty obvious that we would not turn round and transport all those troops back to England for an invasion of France across the Channel, and at least some of them were bound to be used across the Mediterranean. They could form part of an army for the conquest of Italy or they could be used for landing in the South of France or in Greece. Any one of these campaigns was a possibility, and our committee had to be prepared to deal with whatever might eventually be decided upon. We might perhaps have been able to cope with this task on the system which had worked so well up till then had that been the whole story, but there was one feature of the strategic situation which created a new problem.

Sicily lay in the middle of the Mediterranean like a football at the toe of Italy, and until it had been captured the passing of a convoy through the Mediterranean was a major operation attended by enormous losses, and this situation would remain even when the airfields in North Africa were finally in our hands. It was made clear to our committee that the reduction of Sicily would almost certainly have to be undertaken before any of the other operations could take place. As we always had to make our preparations long before an operation was launched, we were considering this next job, the security of the invasion of Sicily, even before 'Torch' was finally mounted.

And here we foresaw trouble. If Sicily was a clear probability to us, once North Africa was in Allied hands, it would be just as clear a probability to the Germans. Indeed, as the Prime Minister eventually said, when approving this operation of ours, it did not matter taking some risk of revealing Sicily as the target, as 'anybody but a damn' fool would *know* it is Sicily.' How would we be able, when the time came, to prevent the Germans from reinforcing the defences of Sicily to a dangerous extent as the result of the same strategic reasoning which had caused the Allies to attack it?

As we were puzzling over this problem, the penny suddenly dropped, and George's fantastic idea of some time before justified itself. 'Why,' I said, 'shouldn't we get a body, disguise it as a staff officer, and give him really high-level papers which will show clearly that we are going to attack somewhere else. We won't have to drop him on land, as the aircraft might have come down in the sea on the way round to the Med. He would float ashore with the papers either in France or in Spain; it won't matter which. Probably Spain would be best, as the Germans wouldn't have as much chance to examine the body there as if they got it into their own hands, while it's certain that they will get the documents, or at least copies.' So the idea was born. Excitedly, we discussed its potentialities. We would have to check on a number of points: What sort of condition would a body be in after an aircraft crash in the sea? What were the usual causes of death in such cases? What would a *post mortem* reveal? Could we get a suitable body – indeed, could we get *any* body? Such were the first questions to which we would have to get answers. If those were satisfactory the plan was worth studying with care, for we none of us doubted that, given the chance, the Spaniards would play the part for which we had cast them, and then what a chance we would have given ourselves!

PRELIMINARY ENQUIRIES

We had talked glibly of 'getting a body', but we had realised that there would be difficulties; we had yet to learn how difficult it would actually be. None of us, indeed, entirely liked the idea, for even in the stress of war one's natural respect for the sanctity of the human body remains a powerful instinct. But for us that instinct was overborne by a realisation of the lives that could be saved by the temporary use of a body that we were confident would eventually receive a proper and decent burial. The difficulty with which we were immediately faced was that imposed by security. How could we go to relatives in their hour of sorrow and ask to be allowed to take without explanation the remains of the son or husband or brother whom they mourned? And if we had to explain, what could we say? In fiction one could, perhaps, expect that we would meet a man who happened to be the sole relative of someone who had just died a death suitable for our plan – a man of that rare type who would just agree to our taking the body and would ask no questions as to why we wanted it. In fiction, perhaps, but not in real life!

Before we started our search, we had first to make sure what kind of body we needed. If the Germans were to accept the body as that of the victim of an aircraft crash at sea, we would have to present them with someone whose body did not afford signs of a cause of death inconsistent with that.

It seemed to me that the best approach to this question would be from the point of view of the man who would do the *post mortem*. What would a pathologist expect to find and what would he expect not to find in the body of a man who had drifted ashore after an aircraft had been lost at sea? For, after all, the aircraft need not have actually crashed.

My thoughts at once turned to Sir Bernard Spilsbury. No one had more experience of pathology than he had, and I felt that no better security risk existed: one could be certain that he at any rate would not gossip or even pass what I said to him on 'in confidence to someone whom he could trust'. In this respect, there had never been any difference between Sir Bernard and an oyster. And he had one even rarer quality: I felt sure that he would not ask any questions other than those needed for the solution of the problem put to him; *he* would just take the fact that we wanted the Germans and Spaniards to accept a floating body as that of a victim of an aircraft disaster, and would neither ask me why nor seek to find an answer elsewhere.

So I rang up Sir Bernard and we arranged a meeting at his club, the Junior Carlton. There, over a glass of sherry, I put our problem to him. After a moment or two of thought, he gave me one of those concise, yet complete, expositions that had convinced so many juries – and even so many judges. His advice gave me hope. If the body was floating in a 'Mae West' when it was recovered, we could use one of a man who had either drowned or died from any but a few of the 'natural causes'; victims of an aircraft disaster at sea sometimes died from an injury received in the crash and some died from drowning, but many died from exposure or even from shock; our field of search was less narrow than I had feared it might be.

My opinion of Sir Bernard was fully justified; that extraordinary man listened to my questions and gave me his answers without ever for a moment giving vent to the curiosity which he must have felt. He asked me some questions which bore on the pathological problem that I was putting to him, but never once did he ask why I wanted to know or what I was proposing to do.

But even then the quest was not easy. We could not make any open inquiries – at all costs we had to avoid anything which might start talk. We could not risk anyone remembering that someone had been trying to obtain a dead body, and such a search was just the sort of thing that is likely to start gossip: 'Have you heard? It's frightfully odd. So-and-So was asking such-and-such the other day where he could get a dead body.' And so, very quietly, our search went on. There we were, in 1942, surrounded all too often by bodies, but none that we could take. We felt like the ancient Mariner – bodies, bodies, everywhere, nor any one to take! We felt like Pirandello – 'Six officers in search of a corpse.'

At one time we feared that we might have to do a body-snatch –

'do a Burke and Hare' as one of us put it; but we did not like the idea, if we could possibly avoid it. We managed to make some very guarded enquiries from a few Service medical officers whom we could trust; but when we heard of a possibility, either the relatives were unlikely to agree or we could not trust those whose permission we would need not to mention to other close relatives what had happened – or there were some other snags, such as a complication in the cause of death.

At last, when we had begun to feel that it would have either to be a 'Burke and Hare' after all or we would have to extend our inquiries so widely as to risk suspicion of our motives turning into gossip, we heard of someone who had just died from pneumonia after exposure: pathologically speaking, it looked as if he might answer our requirements. We made feverish inquiries into his past and about his relatives; we were soon satisfied that these would not talk or pass on such information as we could give them. But there was still the crucial question: could we get permission to use the body without saying what we proposed to do with it and why? All we could possibly tell anyone was that we could guarantee that the purpose would be a really worthwhile one, as anything that was done would be with approval on the highest level, and that the remains would eventually receive proper burial, though under a false name.

Permission, for which our indebtedness is great, was obtained on condition that I should never let it be known whose corpse it was. It must therefore suffice for me to say that the body was that of a young man in his early thirties. He had not been very physically fit for some time before his death, but we could accept that for, as I said to a senior officer who queried the point, 'He does not have to look like an officer – only like a staff officer.'

As a precaution, I had another chat with Sir Bernard Spilsbury. He was quite satisfied: the pneumonia was a help, for there would tend to be some liquid in the lungs, as might well be the case if the man had died while floating in a rough sea. If a *post mortem* examination was made by someone who had formed the preconceived idea that the death was probably due to drowning there was little likelihood that the difference between this liquid, in lungs that had started to decompose, and sea water would be noticed. Sir Bernard closed our talk with the characteristically confident statement: 'You have nothing to fear from a Spanish *post mortem*; to detect that this young man had not died after an aircraft had been lost at sea would need a pathologist of my experience – and there aren't any in Spain.'

So we arranged for the body to be kept in suitable cold storage until we were ready for it.

'OPERATION MINCEMEAT'

I now had to get general approval for the principle of the operation. The first step, as always before any operation, was to get a code name; except in the case of a few major operations for which the Prime Minister himself invented the names, these were always taken from lists issued by us to the Service departments and the various Commands. I therefore went to see what names had been allocated for Admiralty use, and there I found that the word 'Mincemeat' had just been restored after employment in a successful operation some time before. My sense of humour having by this time become somewhat macabre, the word seemed to be one of good omen – and 'Operation Mincemeat' it became.

I had next to decide where we were to send the body, and I chose Huelva as the best destination, if delivery there was possible. For we knew that there was a very active German agent at Huelva who had excellent contacts with certain Spaniards, both officials and others. If the body reached Huelva, the odds were very heavy that this agent would be given any papers or other objects of importance that might be with it; even if circumstances prevented that happening, there was no doubt whatsoever that he would either get copies or be given detailed information, and we could then be sure that he would alert his superiors in Madrid who would intercept the documents at a higher level. Our only risk was that the body and papers would be handed straight over to the British Vice-Consul so quickly that no one could intercept anything. But the co-operation between the Spaniards and the Germans was so complete that such a proper procedure was most improbable: if there were a Spaniard who proposed to do that, I had little doubt but that there would be several others who would step in and prevent it.

Huelva had a further advantage in that it was not too near to Gibraltar; we did not want the Spaniards to send the body for burial there. The arrival at Gibraltar of the body of an officer who did not really exist might give rise to talk which would be almost certain to be picked up by the many German agents who obtained information through the Spaniards who entered and left that area each day.

So I went to the Hydrographer of the Navy at the Admiralty and made some inquiries about weather and tidal conditions at various points off the coast of Spain at various times of the year. Our luck was holding. Although the tidal stream would not be too helpful and would set along the coast, the south-westerly wind, which would be the prevailing wind in April, would be 'onshore'. Indeed, the Hydrographer thought that 'an object' would probably drift in towards the shore, and a body in a 'Mae West' would be comparatively more affected by the wind than would the sort of object which I had led him to envisage.

So Huelva was decided on. There was practically no doubt that the body would float inshore: then, if the normal procedure was followed, the body would be handed over to the British Vice-Consul for burial. And, as I have said, we were confident that the efficiency of the local German agent would ensure that any papers, or at least copies of them, would eventually reach the Germans. Our confidence in him was not misplaced.

While we were going into the exact location for 'Mincemeat's' arrival, a means of transportation had to be devised. He could not be dropped for fear of injury, which left three methods of placing him in the sea: submarine, flying boat or a temporary diversion of one of the ships which escorted the convoys up the coast of Spain. Of these a submarine could clearly get much the closest inshore without risk of detection. I therefore asked permission from the Vice-Chief of Naval Staff (Home) to discuss possibilities with Admiral Barry, the Flag Officer commanding our submarines: it was, of course, on the basis that our planning was purely tentative, so that a complete scheme could be worked out for submission to the Chiefs of Staff.

Admiral Barry readily saw the possibilities of the idea, and I had a preliminary talk with his Chief Staff Officer. He decided that 'Mincemeat' could be carried in a submarine on passage to Malta, as these quite frequently took important but not too bulky articles to that island. We discussed whether the body should be transported in the casing (that is under what would normally be called the deck) or inside the actual pressure hull of the submarine. In spite of the size of the container, which would have to be some 6 feet 6 inches long and about 2 feet in diameter, he considered that it could be accommodated inside the pressure hull and brought up through the conning tower for launching at sea. This greatly eased our problem, as it meant that we would only have to get an airtight canister and not a pressure-proof container, which would have had to be much heavier and more complicated. The question remained whether the body could be kept in a plain canister for the necessary time, after removal from cold storage, without decomposition being too great — or would we have to try to get some form of enormous thermos flask?

So I consulted Sir Bernard Spilsbury once more. He took the view that temperature would be of comparatively minor importance if the body was really cold when it was put into the container. The important thing was to exclude as much oxygen as possible, as it was that which hastened decomposition. He advised that the best method for us to use would be to stand our container on one end and fill it with dry ice; as that melted into carbon dioxide, it would prevent air from entering. We should then lower the body carefully into the canister and pack it round once more with dry ice. If that was done carefully, there should be little oxygen left in the container, and the rate of decomposition would be so slowed down that, if the body was picked up shortly after launching its condition would be consistent with a few days' immersion floating in from an aircraft crash some distance offshore.

So we arranged for a container to be made of two skins of 22–gauge sheet steel welded together, with asbestos wool between the skins; at the top there was a similar lid which was bedded on to an airtight rubber gasket by sixteen nuts; a box-spanner was chained to the lid, to which it was clipped when not in use; a lifting handle was provided at each end, for it would weigh over 400 lb with the body inside.

To complete the account of this part of our preparations, I should record that later on I saw Admiral Barry again and told him that the plan was going ahead and that, if we got final approval, we would want the operation carried out at about the end of April. This would also have the advantage from the submarine's point of view of there being little or no moon, so as to render detection close inshore less likely. He decided that H. M. Submarine *Seraph* might be used, as she could delay her departure from Malta by a fortnight, spending the time 'working up' in home waters. The chance of using *Seraph* was fortunate, as she was commanded by Lieutenant Jewell, and he and his ship's company had already had experience of special operations in connection with the North Africa landings; they had picked up General Giraud on his escape from captivity and it was they who had put General Mark Clark ashore on the coast of North Africa when he made secret contact with the French, and then taken him off again.

I had prepared tentative 'operation orders' for the Captain of the submarine, and these Admiral Barry approved; but, at his suggestion, Lieutenant Jewell came to the Flag Officer, Submarines Headquarters, where he and I could talk over the whole matter.

I gave him the 'operation orders', which were as follows:

OPERATION MINCEMEAT

1. *Object*

To cause a briefcase containing documents to drift ashore as near as possible to HUELVA in Spain in such circumstances that it will be thought to have been washed ashore from an aircraft which crashed at sea when the case was being taken by an officer from the UK to Allied Forces HQ in North Africa.

2. *Method*

A dead body dressed in the battle-dress uniform of a Major, Royal Marines, and wearing a 'Mae West', will be taken out in a submarine, together with the briefcase and a rubber dinghy.

The body will be packed fully clothed and ready (and wrapped in a blanket to prevent friction) in a tubular air-tight container (which will be labelled as 'Optical Instruments').

The container is just under 6 feet 6 inches long and just under 2 feet in diameter and has no excrescences of any kind on the sides. The end which opens has a flush-fitting lid which is held tightly in position by a number of nuts and has fitted on its exterior in clips a box-spanner with a permanent tommy-bar which is chained to the lid.

Both ends are fitted with handles which fold down flat. It will be possible to lift the container by using both handles or even by using the handle in the lid alone, but it would be better not to take the whole weight on the handle at the other end, as the steel of which the container is made is of light gauge to keep the

weight as low as possible. The approximate total weight when
the container is full will be 400 lb.

When the container is closed the body will be packed round
with a certain amount of dry ice. The container should therefore
be opened on deck, as the dry ice will give off carbon dioxide.

3. *Position*

The body should be put into the water as close inshore as
prudently possible and as near to HUELVA as possible preferably to the north-west of the river mouth.

According to the Hydrographic Department, the tides in that
area run mainly up and down the coast, and every effort should
therefore be made to choose a period with an onshore wind.
South-westerly winds are in fact the prevailing winds in that
area at this time of year.

The latest information about tidal streams in that area, as
obtained from the Superintendent of Tides, is attached.

4. *Delivery of the Package*

The package will be brought up to the port of departure by road
on whatever day is desired, preferably as close to the sailing day
as possible. The briefcase will be handed over at the same time
to the Captain of the submarine. The rubber dinghy will also be
a separate parcel.

5. *Disposal of the Body*

When the body is removed from the container all that will be
necessary will be to fasten the chain attached to the briefcase
through the belt of the trench-coat, which will be the outer
garment on the body. The chain is of the type worn under the
coat, round the chest and out through the sleeve. At the end is a
'dog-lead' type of clip for attaching to the handle of the briefcase
and a similar clip for forming a loop round the chest. It is this
loop that should be made through the belt of the trench-coat as
if the officer has slipped the chain off for comfort in the aircraft,
but has nevertheless kept it attacheed to him so that the bag
should not either be forgotten or slide away from him in the
aircraft.

The body should then be deposited in the water, as should

also be the rubber dinghy. As this should drift at a different speed from the body, the exact position at which it is released is unimportant, but it should be near the body, but not too near if that is possible.

6. *Those in the Know at Gibraltar*
Steps have been taken to inform F.O.I.C.[1] Gibraltar and his S.O.(I).[2] No one else there will be in the picture.

7. *Signals*
If the operation is successfully carried out, a signal should be made 'MINCEMEAT completed'. If that is made from Gibraltar the S.O.(I) should be asked to send it addressed to D.N.I.[3] (PERSONAL). If it can be made earlier it should be made in accordance with orders from F.O.S.[4]

8. *Cancellation*
If the operation has to be cancelled a signal will be made 'Cancel MINCEMEAT'. In that case the body and container should be sunk in deep water; as the container may have positive buoyancy, it may either have to be weighted or water may have to be allowed to enter. In the latter case care must be taken that the body does not escape. The briefcase should be handed to the S.O.(I) at Gibraltar, with instructions to burn the contents unopened, if there is no possibility of taking the course earlier. The rubber dinghy should be handed to the S.O.(I) for disposal.

9. *Abandonment*
If the operation has to be abandoned, a signal should be made 'MINCEMEAT abandoned' as soon as possible (see Para. 7 above).

10. *Cover*
This is a matter for consideration. Until the operation actually takes place, it is thought that the labelling of the container

---

[1] Flag Officer in Charge.   [3] Director of Naval Intelligence.
[2] Staff Officer, Intelligence.   [4] Flag Officer, Submarines (Admiral Barry).

'Optical Instruments' will provide sufficient cover. It is suggested that the cover after the operation has been completed should be that it is hoped to trap a very active German agent in this neighbourhood, and it is hoped that sufficient evidence can be obtained by this means to get the Spaniards to eject him. The importance of dealing with this man should be impressed on the crew, together with the fact that any leakage that may *ever* take place about this will compromise our power to get the Spaniards to act in such cases; also that they will never learn whether we were successful in this objective, as the whole matter will have to be conducted in secrecy with the Spaniards or we won't be able to get them to act.

It is in fact most important that the Germans and Spaniards should accept these papers in accordance with Para. 1. If they should suspect that the papers are a 'plant', it might have far-reaching consequences of great magnitude.

(*Signed*) E. E. S. MONTAGU,

Lt.-Cdr., R.N.V.R.

31.3.43.

We then discussed the operation and filled in points of detail.

While all these things were being arranged, we had been busy over the more interesting matters. What document could we provide which could be so impressive that it would make the Germans alter their planning and disposition of forces? How could we provide the document with a sufficiently convincing background to make them accept it as genuine; for Pooh-Bah was right when he spoke of '. . . corroborative detail, intended to give artistic verisimilitude to an otherwise bald and unconvincing narrative.'

The Big Day

James Jones

Milt Warden did not really get up early the morning of the big day. He just had not been to bed.

He had gone around to the Blue Chancre, after Karen had gone home at 9:30, on a vague hunch that Prewitt might be there. Karen had asked him about him again and they had discussed him a long time. Prewitt hadnt been there, but he ran into Old Pete and the Chief; Pete was helping the Chief to celebrate his last night in town before going back into his garrison headquarters at Choy's. They had already made their bomb run on the whorehouse and dropped their load on Mrs Kipfer's New Congress. After Charlie Chan closed up the Blue Chancre, the four of them had sat out in the back room and played stud poker for a penny a chip while drinking Charlie's bar whiskey.

It was always a dull game; Charlie could not play poker for peanuts; but he always let them have the whiskey at regular wholesale prices and if they complained loud enough he would even go in on it and pay a full share, although he drank very little. So they were always willing to suffer his poker playing. They would always overplay a hand to him now and then to keep him from finding out how lousy he was.

When they had drunk as much as they could hold without passing out, it was so late the Schofield cabs had stopped running. They had hired a city cab to take them back because there was nowhere else to go at 6:30 on Sunday morning.

Besides, Stark always had hotcakes-and-eggs and fresh milk on Sundays. There is nothing as good for a hangover as a big meal of hotcakes-and-eggs and fresh milk just before going to bed.

They were too late to eat early chow in the kitchen, and the chow line was already moving slowly past the two griddles. Happily drunkenly undismayed, the three of them bucked the line amid the ripple of curses from the privates, and carried their plates in to eat at the First-Three-Graders' table at the head of the room.

It was almost like a family party. All the platoon sergeants were there, and Stark was there in his sweated undershirt after getting the cooks started, and Malleaux the supply sergeant. Even Baldy Dhom was there, having been run out by his wife for getting drunk last night at the NCO Club. All of this in itself did not happen often, and today being Sunday nobody was less than half tight and since there had been a big shindig dance at the Officers' Club last night none of the officers had shown up, so that they did not have to be polite.

The conversation was mostly about Mrs Kipfer's. That was where Pete and the Chief had wound up last night, and most of the others had gone there. Mrs Kipfer had just got in a shipment of four new beaves, to help take care of the influx of draftees that was raising Company strengths all over Schofield. One was a shy dark-haired little thing who was apparently appearing professionally for the first time, and who showed promise of someday stepping into Lorene's shoes when Lorene went back home. Her name was Jeanette and she was variously recommended back and forth across the table.

At least one officer was always required to eat the men's food in the messhall, either Lt Ross, or Chicken Culpepper, or else one of the three new ROTC boys the Company had been issued during the last week; the five of them passed the detail around them; but whichever one got it, it was still always the same and put a damper over the noncoms' table. But today it was just like a big family party. Minus the mother-in-law.

Stark was the only one, outside of Warden and Baldy, who had not been around to Mrs Kipfer's last night. But he was drunk, too. Stark had picked himself off a shackjob down at the Wailupe Naval Radio Station while they had had the CP out at Hanauma Bay. Some of them had seen her, and she was a hot-looking, wild. I'll-go-as-far-as-you-will wahine, but Stark would not talk about her. So he did not enter the conversation much at the table; but he listened. He had not spoken to Warden since the night at Hickam Field except in the line of duty, and at the table he ignored Warden and Warden ignored him.

It was a typical Sunday morning breakfast for the first weekend after payday. At least a third of the Company was not home. Another third was still in bed asleep. But the last third more than made up for the absences in the loudness of their drunken laughter and horseplay and the clashing of cutlery and halfpint milk bottles.

Warden was just going back for seconds on both hotcakes and eggs, with that voracious appetite he always had when he was drunk, when this blast shuddered by under the floor and rattled the cups on the tables and then rolled on off across the quad like a high wave at sea in a storm.

He stopped in the doorway of the KP room and looked back at the messhall. He remembered the picture the rest of his life. It had become very quiet and everybody had stopped eating and looked up at each other.

'Must bed doin some dynamitin down to Wheeler Field,' somebody said tentatively.

'I heard they was clearin some ground for a new fighter strip,' somebody else agreed.

That seemed to satisfy everybody. They went back to their eating. Warden heard a laugh ring out above the hungry gnashings of cutlery on china, as he turned back into the KP room. The tail of the chow line was still moving past the two griddles, and he made a mental note to go behind the cooks' serving table when he bucked the line this time, so as not to make it so obvious.

That was when the second blast came. He could hear it a long way off coming toward them under the ground; then it was there before he could move, rattling the cups and plates in the KP sinks and the rinsing racks; then it was gone and he could hear it going away northeast toward the 21st Infantry's football field. Both the KPs were looking at him.

He reached out to put his plate on the nearest flat surface, holding it carefully in both hands so it would not get broken while he congratulated himself on his presence of mind, and then turned back to the messhall, the KPs still watching him.

As there was nothing under the plate, it fell on the floor and crashed in the silence, but nobody heard it because the third groundswell of blast had already reached the PX and was just about to them. It passed under, rattling everything, just as he got back to the NCOs' table.

'This is it,' somebody said quite simply.

Warden found that his eyes and Stark's eyes were looking into each other. There was nothing on Stark's face, except the slack relaxed peaceful look of drunkenness, and Warden felt there must not be anything on his either. He pulled his mouth up and showed his teeth in a grin, and Stark's face pulled up his mouth in an identical grin. Their eyes were still looking into each other.

Warden grabbed his coffee cup in one hand and his halfpint of milk in the other and ran out through the messhall screendoor onto the porch. The far door, into the dayroom, was already so crowded he could not have pushed through. He ran down the porch and turned into the corridor that ran through to the street and beat them all outside but for one or two. When he stopped and looked back he saw Pete Karelsen and Chief Choate and Stark were all right behind him. Chief Choate had his plate of hotcakes-and-eggs in his left hand and his fork in the other. He took a big bite. Warden turned back and swallowed some coffee.

Down the street over the trees a big column of black smoke was mushrooming up into the sky. The men behind were crowding out the door and pushing those in front out into the street. Almost everybody had brought his bottle of milk to keep from getting it stolen, and a few had brought their coffee too. From the middle of the street Warden could not see any more than he had seen from the edge, just the same big column of black smoke mushrooming up into the sky from down around Wheeler Field. He took a drink of his coffee and pulled the cap off his milk bottle.

'Gimme some of that coffee,' Stark said in a dead voice behind him, and held up his own cup. 'Mine was empty.'

He turned around to hand him the cup and when he turned back a big tall thin red-headed boy who had not been there before was running down the street toward them, his red hair flapping in his self-induced breeze, and his knees coming up to his chin with every step. He looked like he was about to fall over backwards.

'Whats up, Red?' Warden hollered at him. 'Whats happening? Wait a minute! Whats going on?'

The red-headed boy went on running down the street concentratedly, his eyes glaring whitely at them.

'The Japs is bombing Wheeler Field!' he hollered over his shoulder. 'The Japs is bombing Wheeler Field! I seen the red circles on the wings!'

He went on running down the middle of the street, and quite suddenly right behind him came a big roaring, getting bigger and bigger; behind the roaring came an airplane, leaping out suddenly over the trees.

Warden, along with the rest of them, watched it coming with his milk bottle still at his lips and the twin red flashes winking out from the nose. It came over and down and up and away and was gone, and the stones in the asphalt pavement at his feet popped up in a long curving line that led up the curb and puffs of dust came up from the grass and a line of cement popped out of the wall to the roof, then back down the wall to the grass and off out across the street again in a big S-shaped curve.

With a belated reflex, the crowd of men swept back in a wave toward the door, after the plane was already gone, and then swept right back out again pushing the ones in front into the street again.

Above the street between the trees Warden could see other planes down near the smoke column. They flashed silver like mirrors. Some of them began suddenly to grow larger. His shin hurt from where a stone out of the pavement had popped him.

'All right, you stupid f – !' he bellowed. 'Get back inside! You want to get your ass shot off?'

Down the street the red-haired boy lay sprawled out floppy-haired, wild-eyed, and silent, in the middle of the pavement. The etched line on the asphalt ran up to him and continued on on the other side of him and then stopped.

'See that?' Warden bawled. 'This aint jawbone, this is for record. Thems real bullets that guy was isin.'

The crowd moved reluctantly back toward the dayroom door. But one man ran to the wall and started probing with his pocketknife in one of the holes and came out with a bullet. It was a .50 caliber. Then another man ran out in the street and picked up something which turned out to be three open-end metal links. The middle one still had a .50 caliber casing in it. The general movement toward the dayroom stopped.

'Say! Thats pretty clever,' somebody said. 'Our planes is still usin web machinegun belts that they got to carry back home!' The two men started showing their finds to the men around them. A couple of other men ran out into the street hurriedly.

'This'll make me a good souvenir,' the man with the bullet said contentedly. 'A bullet from a Jap plane on the day the war started.'

'Give me back my goddam coffee!' Warden hollered at Stark. 'And help me shoo these dumb bastards back inside!'

'What you want me to do?' Chief Choate asked. He was still holding his plate and fork and chewing excitedly on a big bite.

'Help me get em inside,' Warden hollered.

Another plane, on which they could clearly see the red discs, came skidding over the trees firing and saved him the trouble. The two men hunting for metal links in the street sprinted breathlessly. The crowd moved back in a wave to the door, and stayed there. The plane flashed past, the helmeted head with the square goggles over the slant eyes and the long scarf rippling out behind it and the grin on the face as he waved, all clearly visible for the space of a wink, like a traveltalk slide flashed on and then off of a screen.

Warden, Stark, Pete and the Chief descended on them as the crowd started to wave outward again, blocking them off and forcing the whole bunch back inside the dayroom.

The crowd milled indignantly in the small dayroom, everybody talking excitedly. Stark posted himself huskily in the doorway with Pete and the Chief flanking him. Warden gulped off the rest of his coffee and set the cup on the magazine rack and pushed his way down to the other end and climbed up on the pingpong table.

'All right, all right, you men. Quiet down. Quiet down. Its only a war. Aint you ever been in a war before?'

The word war had the proper effect. They began to yell at each other to shut up and listen.

'I want every man to go upstairs to his bunk and stay there,' Warden said. 'Each man report to his squad leader. Squad leaders keep your men together at their bunks until you get orders what to do.'

The earth shudders rolling up from Wheeler Field were already a commonplace now. Above it, they heard another plane go roaring machinegun-rattling over.

'The CQ will unlock the rifle racks and every man get his rifle and hang onto it. *But stay inside at your bunks*. This aint no maneuvers. You go runnin around outside you'll get your ass shot off. And you cant do no good anyway. You want to be heroes, you'll get plenty chances later; from now on. You'll probly have Japs right in your laps, by time we get down to beach positions.

'Stay off the proches. *Stay inside*. I'm making each squad leader responsible to keep his men *inside*. If you have to use a rifle butt to do it, thats okay too.'

There was a mutter of indignant protest.

'You heard me!' Warden hollered. 'You men want souvenirs, buy them off the widows of the men who went out after them. If I catch anybody runnin around outside, I'll personally beat his head in, and then see he gets a goddam general court martial.'

There was another indignant mutter of protest.

'What if the f – bomb us?' somebody hollered.

'If you hear a bomb coming, you're free to take off for the brush,' Warden said. 'But not unless you do. I dont think they will. If they was going to bomb us, they would of started with it already. They probly concentratin all their bombs on the Air Corps and Pearl Harbor.'

There was another indignant chorus.

'Yeah,' somebody hollered, 'but what if they aint?'

'Then you're shit out of luck,' Warden said. 'If they *do* start to bomb, get everybody outside – on the side *away* from the quad – not *into* the quad – and disperse; *away* from the big buildings.'

'That wont do us no good if they've already laid one on the roof,' somebody yelled.

'All right,' Warden hollered, 'can the chatter. Lets move. We're wasting time. Squad leaders get these men upstairs. BAR men, platoon leaders and first-three-graders report to me here.'

With the corporals and buck sergeants haranguing them, the troops gradually began to sift out through the corridor to the porch stairs. Outside another plane went over. Then another, and another. Then what sounded like three planes together. The platoon leaders and guides and BAR men pushed their way down to the pingpong table that Warden jumped down off of.

'What you want me to do, First?' Stark said; his face still had the same expression of blank, flat refusal – like a stomach flatly refusing food – that he had had in the messhall; 'what about the kitchen force? I'm pretty drunk, but I can still shoot a BAR.'

'I want you to get your ass in the kitchen with every man you got and start packing up,' Warden said, looking at him. He rubbed his hand hard over his own face. 'We'll be movin out for the beach as soon as this tapers off a little, and I want that kitchen all packed and ready to roll. Full field. Stoves and all. While you're doin that, make a big pot of coffee on the big stove. Use the biggest #18 pot you got.'

'Right,' Stark said, and took off for the door into the messhall.

'Wait!' Warden hollered. 'On second thought, make two pots. The two biggest you got. We're going to need it.'

'Right,' Stark said, and went on. His voice was not blank, his voice was crisp. It was just his face, that was blank.

'The rest of you guys,' Warden said.

Seeing their faces, he broke off and rubbed his own face again. It didnt do any good. As soon as he stopped rubbing it settled right back into it, like a campaign hat that had been blocked a certain way.

'I want the BAR men to report to the supplyroom right now and get their weapons and all the loaded clips they can find and go up on the roof. When you see a Jap plane, shoot at it. Dont worry about wasting ammo. Remember to take a big lead. Thats all. Get moving.'

'The rest of you guys,' Warden said, as the BAR men moved away at a run. 'The rest of you guys. The first thing. The main thing. Every platoon leader is responsible to me personally to see that all of his men stay inside, except the BAR men up on the roof. A rifleman's about as much good against a low flying pursuit ship as a boy scout with a sling-shot. And we're going to need every man we can muster when we get down to beach positions. I dont want none of them wasted here, by runnin outside to shoot rifles at airplanes. Or by goin souvenir huntin. The men stay inside. Got it?'

There was a chorus of hurried vacant nods. Most of the heads were on one side, listening to the planes going over and over in ones twos and threes.

It looked peculiar to see them all nodding on one side like that. Warden found himself wanting to laugh excitedly.

'The BARs will be up on the roof,' he said. 'They can do all the shooting that we can suppy ammo for. Anybody else will just be getting in the way.'

'What about my MGs Milt?' Pete Karelsen asked him.

The easy coolness in old Pete's voice shocked Warden to a full stop. Drunk or not, Pete seemed to be the only one who sounded relaxed, and Warden remembered his two years in France.

'Whatever you think, Pete,' he said.

'I'll take one. They couldnt load belts fast enough to handle more than one. I'll take Mikeovitch and Grenelli up with me to handle it.'

'Can you get the muzzle up high enough on those ground tripods?'

'We'll put the tripod over a chimney,' Pete said. 'And then hold her down by the legs.'

'Whatever you think, Pete,' Warden said, thinking momentarily how wonderful it was to be able to say that.

'Come on, you two,' Pete said, almost boredly, to his two section leaders. 'We'll take Grenelli's because we worked on it last.'

'Remember,' Warden said to the rest of them as Pete left with his two machinegunners. 'The men stay inside. I dont care how you handle it. Thats up to you. I'm going to be up on the roof with a BAR. If you want to get in on the fun, go yourself. Thats where I'm going to be. But make damn sure your men are going to stay *inside*, off the porches, before you go up.'

'Like hell!' Liddell Henderson said. 'You aint goin to catch this Texan up on no roof. Ah'll stay down with ma men.'

'Okay,' Warden said, jabbing a finger at him. 'Then you are hereby placed in charge of the loading detail. Get ten or twelve men, as many as you can get in the supplyroom, and put them to loading BAR clips and MG belts. We're going to need all the ammo we can get. Anybody else dont want to go up?'

'I'll stay down with Liddell,' Champ Wilson said.

'Then you're second-in-command of the loading detail,' Warden said. 'All right, lets go. If anybody's got a bottle laying around, bring it up with you. I'm bringing mine.'

When they got out to the porch, they found a knot of men arguing violently with S/Sgt Malleaux in front of the supplyroom.

'I dont give a damn,' Malleaux said. 'Thats my orders. I cant issue any live ammo without a signed order from an officer.'

'But there aint no goddamned officers, you jerk!' somebody protested angrily.

'Then there aint no live ammo,' Malleaux said.

'The officers may not get here till noon!'

'I'm sorry, fellows,' Malleaux said. 'Thats my orders. Lt Ross give them to me himself. No signed order, no ammo.'

'What the f – hell is all this?' Warden said.

'He wont let us have any ammo, Top,' a man said.

'He's got it locked up and the keys in his pocket,' another one said.

'Gimme them keys,' Warden said.

'Thats my orders, Sergeant,' Malleaux said, shaking his head. 'I got to have a signed order from an officer before I can issue any live ammo to an enlisted man.'

Pete Karelsen came out of the kitchen and across the porch wiping his mouth off with the back of his hand. From the screendoor Stark disappeared inside putting a pint bottle back into his hip pocket under his apron.

'What the hells the matter?' Pete asked his two machinegunners happily.

'He wont give us no ammo, Pete,' Grenelli said indignantly.

'Well for – Jesus Christ!' Pete said disgustedly.

'Thats my orders, Sergeant,' Malleaux said irrefragably.

From the southeast corner of the quad a plane came over firing, the tracers leading irrevocably in under the porch and up the wall as he flashed over, and the knot of men dived for the stairway.

'F – your orders!' Warden bawled. 'Gimme them goddam keys!'

Malleaux put his hand in his pocket protectively. 'I cant do that, Sergeant. I got my orders from Lt Ross himself.'

'Okay,' Warden said happily, 'Chief, bust the door down.' To Malleaux he said, 'Get the hell out of the way.'

Choate, and Mikeovitch and Grenelli the two machinegunners, got back for a run at the door, the Chief's big bulk towering over the two lightly built machinegunners.

Malleaux stepped in front of the door. 'You cant get by with this, Sergeant,' he told Warden.

'Go ahead,' Warden grinned happily at the Chief. 'Bust it down. He'll get out of the way.' Across the quad, there were already two men up on top of the Headquarters Building.

Chief Choate and the two machinegunners launched themselves at the supply room door like three blocking backs bearing down on an end. Malleaux stepped out of the way. The door rattled ponderously.

'This is your responsibility, Sergeant' Malleaux said to Warden. 'I did my best.'

'Okay,' Warden said. 'I'll see you get a medal.'

'Remember I warned you, Sergeant,' Malleaux said.

'Get the f – out of my way,' Warden said.

It took three tries to break the wood screws loose enough to let the Yale night lock come open. Warden was the first one in. The two machinegunners were right behind him, Mikeovitch burrowing into a stack of empty belt boxes looking for full ones while Grenelli got his gun lovingly out of the MG rack. There were men up on both the 3rd and 1st Battalion roofs by now, to meet the planes as they came winging back, on first one then the other of the cross legs of their long figure 8.

Warden grabbed a BAR from the rack and passed it out with a full bag of clips. Somebody grabbed it and took off for the roof, and somebody else stepped up to receive one. Warden passed out three of them from the rack, each with a full bag of clips, before he realized what he was doing.

'To hell with this noise,' he said to Grenelli who was unstrapping his tripod on his way out the door. 'I could stand here and hand these out all day and never get up on the roof.'

He grabbed a BAR and clip bag for himself and pushed out the door, making a mental note to eat Malleaux's ass out. There were a dozen bags of full clips in there, left over from the BAR practice firing in August. They should have been unloaded and greased months ago.

Outside, he stopped beside Henderson. Pete, Grenelli and Mikeovitch were already rounding the stair landing out of sight with the MG and eight belt boxes.

'Get your ass in there and start passing them out,' Warden told Henderson, 'and start loading clips. And belts. Have Wilson go up and get a detail of men. Soons you get a batch loaded send a couple men up with them. Put three men on belts, the rest on BAR clips.'

'Yes, Sir,' Henderson said nervously.

Warden took off for the stairs. On the way up he stopped off at his room to get the full bottle that he kept in his footlocker for emergencies.

In the squadroom men were sitting on their bunks with their helmets on holding their empty rifles in black despair. They looked up hopefully and called to him as he passed.

'What gives, Sarge?' 'Whats the deal, First?' 'Are we going up on the roofs now?' 'Where the hells the ammunition, Top?' 'These guns aint worth nothing without no ammunition.' 'Hell of a note to sit on your bunk with an empty rifle and no ammunition while they blow your guts out.' 'Are we soljers? or boy-scouts?'

Other men, the ones who had slept through breakfast and were now getting up tousle-headed and wide-eyed, stopped dressing and looked up hopefully to see what he'd say.

'Get into field uniforms,' Warden said, realizing he had to say something. 'Start rolling full field packs,' he told them ruthlessly in an iron voice. 'We're moving out in fifteen minutes. Full field equipment.'

Several men threw their rifles on their beds disgustedly.

'Then what the hell're you doin with a BAR?' somebody hollered.

'Field uniforms,' Warden said pitilessly, and went on across the squadroom. 'Full field equipment. Squad leaders, get them moving.'

Disgustedly, the squad leaders began to harangue them to work.

In the far doorway onto the outside porch Warden stopped. In the corner under an empty bunk that had three extra mattresses piled on it, S/Sgt Turp Thornhill from Mississippi lay on the cement floor in his underwear with his helmet on hugging his empty rifle.

'You'll catch a cold, Turp,' Warden said.

'Dont go out there, First Sergeant!' Turp pleaded. 'You'll be killed! They shootin it up! You'll be dead! You'll not be alive any more! Dont go out there!'

'You better put your pants on,' Warden said.

In his room on the porch splinters of broken glass lay all over Warden's floor, and a line of bullet holes was stitched across the top of his foot-locker and up the side of Pete's locker and across its top. Under Pete's locker was a puddle and the smell of whiskey fumes was strong in the air. Cursing savagely, Warden unlocked his footlocker and flung back the lid. A book in the tray had a slanting hole drilled right through its center. His plastic razor box was smashed and the steel safety razor bent almost double. Savagely he jerked the tray out and threw it on the floor. In the bottom of the locker two .30 caliber bullets were nestled in the padding of rolled socks and stacked underwear, one on either side of the brown quart bottle.

The bottle was safe.

Warden dropped the two bullets into his pocket and got the unbroken bottle out tenderly and looked in his wall locker to make sure his record-player and records were safe. Then he hit the floor in the broken glass, holding the bottle carefully and under him, as another plane went over going east over the quad.

As he beat it back out through the squadroom the men were beginning bitterly to roll full field packs. All except Turp Thornhill, who was still under the bunk and four mattresses in his helmet and underwear; and Private Ike Galovitch, who was lying on top his bunk with his rifle along his side and his head under his pillow.

On the empty second floor, from which men were hurriedly carrying their full field equipment downstairs to roll into packs, at the south end of the porch by the latrine Readall Treadwell was going up the ladder in the latrine-supplies closet to the roof hatch carrying a BAR and grinning from ear to ear.

'First time in my goodam life,' he yelled down; 'I'm really goin to git to shoot a BAR, by god. I wount never of believe it.'

He disappeared through the hatch and Warden followed him on up, and out into the open. Across G Company's section of roof most of G Company's first-three-graders were waiting to meet the enemy from behind one of the four chimneys, or else down on their knees in one of the corners, the BAR forearms propped on the crotch-high wall, or a chimney top, their muzzles looking eagerly into the sky, and their bottles of whisky sitting beside them close up against the wall. Reedy Treadwell, who did not have a bottle, was just dropping down happily beside Chief Choate, who did. Two of the first-three-graders had hopped across the wall onto F Company's roof and were standing behind two of their chimneys. A knot of first-three-graders from F Co. were just coming up through their own hatch. They crossed the roof and began to argue violently with the two first-three-graders from G Co., demanding their chimneys. All down the 2nd Battalion roof, and on the 1st and 3rd Battalion roofs, first-three-graders were coming up through the hatches eagerly with BARs, rifles, pistols, and here and there a single MG. There were a few buck sergeants visible among them, but the only privates visible anywhere were Readall Treadwell and the two other BAR men from G Co.

'Throw your empty clips down into the Compny Yard,' Warden hollered as he moved down the roof. 'Pass it along. Throw your empty clips down in the Compny Yard. The loading detail will pick em up. Thrown your empty – '

A V of three planes came winging over from the southeast firing full blast, and the waiting shooters cheered happily like a mob of hobos about to sit down to their first meal in years. All the artillery on all the roofs cut loose in a deafening roar and the earth stopped. The argument on F Co.'s roof also stopped, while both sides all dived behind the same chimney. Warden turned without thinking, standing in his tracks, and fired from the shoulder without a rest, the bottle clutched tightly between his knees.

The big BAR punched his shoulder in a series of lightning left jabs.

On his right Pete Karelsen was happily firing the little air-cooled .30 caliber from behind the chimney while Mikeovitch and Grenelli hung grimly onto the bucking legs of the tripod laid over the chimney, bouncing like two balls on two strings.

The planes sliced on over, unscathed, winging on down to come back up the other leg of the big figure 8. Everybody cheered again anyway, as the firing stopped.

'Holymarymotherofgod,' Chief Choate boomed in his star basso that always took the break-line of the Regimental song uncontested. 'I aint had so much fun since granmaw got her tit caught in the wringer.'

'Shit!' old Pete said disgustedly in a low voice behind Warden. 'He was on too much of an angle. Led him too far.'

Warden lowered his BAR, his belly and throat tightening with a desire to let loose a high hoarse senseless yell of pure glee. This is *my* outfit. These are *my* boys. He got his bottle from between his knees and took a drink that was not a drink but an expression of feeling. The whiskey burned his throat savagely joyously.

'Hey, Milt!' Pete called him. 'You can come over here with us if you want. We got enough room for you and the bottle.'

'Be right with you!' Warden roared. Gradually his ears had become aware of a bugle blowing somewhere insistently, the same call over and over. He stepped to the inside edge of the roof and looked down over the wall.

In the corner of the quad at the megaphone, among all the men running back and forth, the guard bugler was blowing The Charge.

'What the f – are *you* doing,' Warden bellowed.

The bugler stopped and looked up and shrugged sheepishly. 'You got me,' he yelled back. 'Colonel's orders.' He went on blowing.

'Here they come, Pete!' Grenelli hollered. 'Here comes one!' His voice went off up into falsetto excitedly.

It was a single, coming in from the northeast on the down leg of the 8. The voice of every gun on the roofs rose to challenge his passage, blending together in one deafening roar like the call of a lynch mob. Down below, the running men melted away and the bugler stopped blowing and ran back under the E Company porch.

Warden screwed the cap back on his bottle and ran crouching over to Pete's chimney and swung around to fire, again with no rest. His burst curved off in tracer smoke lines well behind the swift-sliding ship that was up, over, and then gone. Got to take more lead.

'Wouldnt you know it?' Pete said tragically. 'Shot clear behind that one.'

'Here, Mike,' he said. 'Move back a little and make room for the 1st/Sgt so he can fire off the corner for a rest. You can set the bottle down right here, Milt. Here,' he said, 'I'll take it for you.'

'Have a drink first,' Warden said happily.

'Okay.' Pete wiped his soot-rimmed mouth with the back of his sleeve. There were soot flecks on his teeth when he grinned. 'Did you see what they done to our room?'

'I seen what they done to your locker,' Warden said.

From down below came the voice of the bugle blowing The Charge again.

'Listen to that stupid bastard,' Warden said. 'Colonel Delbert's ordedrs.'

'I dint think the Colonel's be up this early,' Pete said.

'Old Jake must of served his first hitch in the Cavalry,' Warden said.

'Say, listen,' Grenelli said, 'listen, Pete. When you going to let me take it a while?'

'Pretty soon,' Pete said, 'pretty soon.'

'Throw your empty clips down in the Compny Yard, you guys!' Warden yelled around the roof. 'Throw your empty clips down in the Compny Yard. Pass it along, you guys.'

Down along the roof men yelled at each other to throw the empties down into the yard and went right on piling them up beside them.

'God damn it!' Warden roared, and moved out from behind the chimney. He walked down along behind them like a quarterback bolstering up his linemen. 'Throw them clips down, goddam you Frank. Throw your clips down, Teddy.'

'Come on, Pete,' Grenelli said behind him. 'Let me take it a while now, will you?'

'I got first on it,' Mikeovitch said.

'Like hell!' Grenelli said. 'Its my gun aint it?'

'Shut up,' Pete said. 'Both of you. You'll both get your chance. Pretty soon.'

Warden was behind the Chief and Reedy Treadwell on the inside edge when the next ones came in, a double flying in in echelon from the northeast like the single, and he dropped down beside them. Down below the bugler stopped blowing and ran back in under the E Company porch again.

Straight across from Warden on the roof of the Headquarters Building there were only two men up. One of them he recognized as M/Sgt Big John Deterling, the enlisted football coach. Big John had a .30 caliber water-cooled with no tripod, holding it cradled in his left arm and firing it with his right. When he fired a burst, the recoil staggered him all over the roof.

The winking noseguns of the incoming planes cut two foot-wide swathes raising dust across the quad and up the wall and over the D Co. Roof like a wagon road through a pasture. Warden couldnt fire at them from laughing at Big John Deterling on the Headquarters roof. This time Big John came very near to falling down and spraying the roof. The other man up over there had wisely put the chimney between him and Big John, instead of between him and the planes.

'Look at that son of a bitch,' Warden said, when he could stop laughing.

Down below the loading detail dived out to pick up the clips in the lull, and the bugler ran back to the megaphone.

'I been watching him,' Chief grinned. 'The son of a bitch is drunk as a coot. He was down to Mrs Kipfer's last night when me and Pete was there.'

'I hope his wife dont find out,' Warden said.

'He ought to have a medal,' Chief said still laughing.

'He probly will,' Warden grinned.

As it turned out, later, he did. M/Sgt John L. Deterling; the Silver Star; for unexampled heroism in action.

Another V of three flashed sliding in from the southeast and Warden turned and ran back to Pete's chimney as everybody opened up with a joyous roar. Firing with the BAR forearm resting on his hand on the chimney corner, he watched his tracers get lost in the cloud of tracers around the lead plane spraying the nose, spraying the cockpit, and on back into the tail assembly. The plane shivered like a man trying to get out from under a cold shower and the pilot jumped in his seat twice like a man tied to a hot stove. They saw him throw up his arms helplessly in a useless try to ward it off, to stop it pouring in on him. There was a prolonged cheer. A hundred yards beyond the quad, with all of them watching it now in anticipatory silence, the little Zero began to fall off on one wing and slid down a long hill of air onto one of the goalposts of the 19th Infantry football field. It crashed into flames. A vast happy college-yell cheer went up from the quad and helmets were thrown into the air and backs were slapped as if our side had just made a touchdown against Notre Dame.

Then, as another V of three came in from the northeast, there was a wild scramble for helmets.

'You got him, Pete!' Grenelli yelled, bobbing around on the bucking tripod leg, 'you got him!'

'Got him hell,' Pete said without stopping firing. 'Nobody'll ever know who got that guy.'

'Hey, Milt!'

In the lull, Chief Choate was yelling at him from the roof edge.

'Hey, Milt! Somebody's yellin for you down below.'

'Coming up!' Warden bawled. Behind him as he ran, Grenelli was pleading:

'Come on, Pete. Let me take it for a while now. You got one already.'

'In a minute,' Pete said. 'In a minute. I just want to try one more.'

Looking down over the wall, Warden saw Lt Ross standing in the yard looking up angrily, large bags under his eyes, a field cap on his uncombed head, his pants still unbuttoned, and his shoes untied and his belt unbuckled. He started buttoning his pants without looking down.

'What the hell are you doing up there, Sergeant?' he yelled. 'Why arent you down here taking care of the Company? We're going to move out for the beach in less than an hour. Its probably alive with Japs already.'

'Its all taken care of,' Warden yelled down. 'The men are rolling full field packs right now in the squadroom.'

'But we've got to get the kitchen and supply ready to move, too, goddam it,' Lt Ross yelled up.

'The kitchen is bein pack,' Warden yelled down. 'I gave Stark the orders and he's doing it now. Should be all ready in fifteen minutes.'

'But the supply – ' Lt Ross started to yell up.

'They're loading clips and belts for us,' Warden yelled down. 'All they got to do is carry the water-cooled MGs for the beach out to the trucks and throw in Leva's old field repair kit and they ready to go.

'And,' he yelled, 'they makin coffee and sandwiches in the kitchen. Everything's all taken care of. Whynt you get a BAR and come on up?'

'There arent any left,' Lt Ross yelled up angrily.

'Then get the hell under cover.' Warden yelled down as he looked up. 'Here they come.'

Lt Ross dived under the porch for the supplyroom as another single came blasting in from the southeast and the roaring umbrella of fire rose from the roofs to engulf it. It seemed impossible that he could fly right through it and come out untouched. But he did.

Right behind him, but flying due north along Waianae Avenue and the Hq Building, came another plane; and the umbrella swung that way without even letting go of its triggers.

The plane's gastank exploded immediately into flames that engulfed the whole cockpit and the plane veered off down on the right wing, still going at top speed. As the belly and left under-wing came up into view, the blue circle with the white star in it showed plainly in the bright sunlight. Then it was gone, off down through some trees that sheered off the wings, and the fuselage, still going at top speed, exploded into some unlucky married officer's house quarters with everyone watching it.

'That was one of ours!' Reedy Treadwell said in a small still voice. 'That was an American plane!'

'Tough,' Warden said, without stopping firing at the new double coming in from the northeast. 'The son of a bitch dint have no business there.'

After the Jap double had flashed past, unscathed, Warden turned back and made another circuit up and down the roof, his eyes screwed up into that strained look of having been slapped in the face that he sometimes got, and that made a man not want to look at him.

'Be careful, you guys,' he said. Up the roof. Down the roof. 'That last one was one of ours. Try and be careful. Try and get a look at them before you shoot. Them stupid bastards from Wheeler liable to fly right over here. So try and be careful after this.' Up the roof. Down the roof. The same strained squint was in his voice as was in his eyes.

'Sergeant Warden!' Lt Ross roared up from down below. 'God damn it! Sergeant *Warden!*'

He ran back to the roof edge. 'What now?'

'I want you down here, god damn it!' Lt Ross yelled up. He had his belt buckled and his shoes tied now and was smoothing back his hair with his fingers under his cap. 'I want you to help me get this orderly room ready to move out! You have no business up there! Come down!'

'Goddamn it, I'm busy!' Warden yelled. 'Get Rosenberry. Theres a goddamn war on, Lieutenant.'

'I've just come from Col. Delbert,' Lt Ross yelled up. 'And he has given orders we're to move out as soon as this aerial attack is over.'

'G Company's ready to move now,' Warden yelled down. 'And I'm busy. Tell that goddam Henderson to send up some clips and belts.'

Lt Ross ran back under the porch and then ran back out again. This time he had a helmet on.

'I told him,' he yelled up.

'And tell Stark to send us up some coffee.'

'*God damn it!*' Lt Ross raged up at him. 'What is this? a Company picnic? Come down here, Sergeant! I want you! Thats an order! Come down here immediately! You hear me? thats an order! All Company Commanders have orders from Col. Delbert personally to get ready to move out within the hour!'

'Whats that?' Warden yelled. 'I cant hear you.'

'I said, we're moving out within the hour.'

'What?' Warden yelled. 'What? Look out,' he yelled; 'here they come again!'

Lt Ross dove for the supplyroom and the two ammo carriers ducked their heads back down through the hatch.

Warden ran crouching back to Pete's chimney and rested his BAR on the corner and fired a burst at the V of three that flashed past.

'Get that goddam ammo up here!' he roared at them in the hatchway.

'Milt!' Chief Choate yelled. 'Milt Warden! They want you downstairs.'

'You cant find me,' Warden yelled. 'I've gone someplace else.'

Chief nodded and relayed it down over the edge. 'I cant find him, Lootenant. He's gone off someplace else.' He listened dutifully down over the edge and then turned back to Warden. 'Lt Ross says tell you we're moving out within the hour,' he yelled.

'You cant find me,' Warden yelled.

'Here they come!' Grenelli yelled from the tripod.

They did not move out within the hour. It was almost another hour before the attack was all over. And they did not move out until early afternoon three and a half hours after the attack was over. G Company was ready, but it was the only company in the Regiment that was.

Warden stayed up on the roof, by one subterfuge or another, until the attack was over. Lt Ross, it turned out, stayed down in the supplyroom and helped load ammunition. The Regimental fire umbrella claimed one more positive, and two possibles that might have been hit by the 27th and already going down when they passed over the quad. Stark himself, personally, with two of the KPs, brought them up coffee once, and then still later brought up coffee and sandwiches. In gratitude for which, Pete Karelsen let him take the MG for a while.

After it was all over, and the dead silence which no sound seemed able to penetrate reigned, they all smoked a last cigarette up on the roof and then, dirty-faced, red-eyed, tired happy and let-down, they trooped down reluctantly into the new pandemonium that was just beginning below and went to roll their full field packs. Nobody had even been scratched. But they could not seem to get outside of the earringing dead silence. Even the pandemonium of moving out could not penetrate it.

Warden, instead of rolling his pack, went straight to the orderly room. In the three and a half hours before they finally left he was in the orderly room all the time, getting it packed up. Lt Ross, whose Company was the only one that was ready ahead of time, had already forgotten to be angry and came in and helped him. So did Rosenberry. Warden had plenty of time and to spare, to pack the orderly room. But he did not have any time left to roll his full field pack or change into a field uniform. Or, if he did, he forgot it.

The result of this was that he had to sleep in the popcorn vendor's wagon at Hanauma Bay without blankets for five days before he could get back up to Schofield to get his stuff, and he would have welcomed even a woolen OD field-uniform shirt. He did not see how the hell he could have possibly have forgotten that.

One by one, each company's consignment of trucks lined up before its barracks in a double file and settled down to wait. One by one, the platoons of troops filed out into their company yards and sat down on their packs holding their rifles and looked at the waiting trucks. The Regiment moved as a unit.

No two companies were going to the same place. And when they got there each company would be a separate unit on its own. But one company, that was ready, did not leave out by itself for its beach position ahead of the other companies, that were not ready. The Regiment moved as a unit.

Everywhere trucks. Everywhere troops sitting on their packs. The quad filled up with trucks until even the Colonel's jeep could not worm through between them. The yards filled up with troops until even the Colonel's adjutants and messengers could not work through them. There was much swearing and sweaty disgust. The Regiment moved as a unit.

And in the G Co. orderly room, Warden chortled to himself smugly, as he worked.

Once, when Lt Ross had gone to the supply room, Maylon Stark stuck his head in at the door. 'The kitchen truck's loaded and ready to roll.'

'Right,' Warden said, without looking up.

'I want you to know I think you done a hell of a swell job,' Stark said reluctantly sttrangledly. 'It'll be two hours, anyway, before any other kitchen in this outfit is ready; and some of them probly have to stay behind to get loaded and come down later.'

'You done a good job yourself,' Warden said, still not looking up.

'It wasnt me,' Stark said. 'It was you. And I just want you to know I think you done a hell of a job.'

'Okay,' Warden said, 'thanks,' and went on working without looking up.

He rode down in the jeep at the head of the Company's convoy with Lt Ross, Weary Russell driving. There was terrific traffic. The roads were alive with trucks and taxis as far as the eye could see, bumper to bumper. The trucks were taking them down, to beach positions; the taxis were taking them up, to Schofield, where their outfits would already be gone. Recons and jeeps slithered in and out among the long lines of trucks, but the big two-and-a-halfs could only lumber on, a few feet at a time, stopping when the truck in front of them stopped in back of the truck in front of him, waiting to move on until the truck in front of them moved on a little in back of the truck in front of him.

The trucks had been stripped of their tarps and one man with his BAR or machinegun mounted over the cab rode standing on the truckbed wall. Helmeted heads were poked above the naked ribs watching the sky like visitors inspecting the dinosaur's skeleton in the Smithsonian Institute.

In the jeep, riding up and down haranguing on the road shoulder alongside the Company's column, Warden saw them all, a lot of times. Their faces were changed and they did not look the same any more. It was somewhat the same look as Stark had had in the messhall, only the drunkenness was evaporating out of it leaving only the hard set of the dry plaster. Out here on the highway, lost among hundreds of other outfits, the idea was not only clearer but bigger, much bigger, than back at your home barracks in your own quad. Chief Choate, riding with a BAR up, looked down at him from above his truck cab and Warden looked back.

They had all left everything behind, civilian clothes, garrison shoes and uniforms, campaign hat collections, insignia collections, photograph albums, private papers. To hell with all that. This was war. We wont need that. They brought nothing but the skeletal field living equipment, and the only man who packed in anything comfortable to bring with him was Pete Karelsen. Pete had been in France.

Gradually, foot by foot, the trucks moved on down toward Honolulu and whatever waited on the beaches. Up till now it had been a day off, it had been fun.

Pearl Harbor, when they passed it, was a shambles. Wheeler Field had been bad, but Pearl Harbor numbed the brain. Pearl Harbor made a queasiness in the testicles. Wheeler Field was set back quite a ways from the road, but parts of Pearl Harbor were right on the highway. Up till then it had been a big lark, a picnic; they had fired from the roofs and been fired at from the planes and the cooks had served them coffee and sandwiches and the supply detail had brought them up ammo and they had got two or three planes and only one man in the whole Regiment had been hit (with a .50 caliber in the fleshy part of his calf, didnt even hit a bone, he walked up to the dispensary by himself), and he was getting himself a big Purple Heart. Almost everybody had had a bottle and they all had been half-drunk anyway when it started and it had all been a sort of super-range-season with live targets to shoot at. The most exciting kind: Men. But now the bottles were fast wearing off and there was no immediate prospect of getting any more and there were no live targets to shoot at. Now they were thinking. Why, it might be months – even years – before they could get hold of a bottle again! This was a big war.

As the trucks passed through the new Married NCO Quarters that had been added onto Pearl Harbor recently, women and children and an occasional old man standing in the yards cheered them. The troops rode on through in silence, staring at them dully.

Going through the back streets of town, all along the route, men, women and children stood on porches fences cartops and roofs and cheered them roundly. They waved Winnie Churchill's V-for-Victory sign at them, and held their thumbs up in the air. Young girls threw them kisses. Mothers of young girls, with tears in their eyes, urged their daughters to throw them more kisses.

The troops, looking wistfully at all this ripe young stuff running around loose that they could not get into, and remembering the old days when civilian girls were not allowed – and did not desire – to speak to soldiers on the street in broad daylight let alone at night in a bar, gave them back the old one-finger salute of the clenched fist fabbing the stiff middle finger into the air. They returned Winnie Churchill's V-for-Victory sign with an even older one of their own, in which the fist is clenched and the middle finger and thumb are extended and pinched repeatedly together.

The ecstatic civilians, who did not know that this last was the Old Army sign for the female, or that the first meant 'F – you!' cheered them even more roundly and the troops, for the first time since they'd left Schofield, grinned a little bit at each other, slyly, and redoubled with their saluting.

From Waikiki on east, the trucks in the Company's convoy began to peel off to deliver the various three- and four-man details each with its noncom to their various beach positions. By the time they reached the rise up over the Kioko Head saddle where the road turned off down to the CP at Haunauma Bay, there were only four trucks left. The two for Position 28 at Makapuu Head, one for the CP personnel and Position 27, and the kitchen truck. The first two, the CP truck and the kitchen truck, pulled off onto the side road and stopped and the last two bound for Makapuu went on, then, past them. They had all had their big day with the civilians, which most of them had waited from two to five years for, and now they were preparing to pay for it.

Among the troops in the trucks there was a certain high fervor of defense and patriotism that exploded into a weak feeble cheer in the heavy perpetual wind, as they passed Lt Ross and The Warden who had climbed out of the jeep on the road-shoulder to watch them go past. A few fists were shaken in the air up between the bare truck ribs and Friday Clark, current-rifleman and ex-apprentice-Company-bugler, shook a wildly promising two-finger V-for-Victory sign at Lt Ross from over the tailgate of the last truck as they pulled on away.

This general patriotic enthusiasm lasted about three days.

Lt Ross, standing beside his jeep to watch his men go off to possible maiming and death, certainly off to a war that would last a long time, looked at Friday sadly and without acknowledgement from across a great gulf of years pity and superior knowledge, his eyes set in a powerful emotion, a look of great age and fearful responsibility on his face.

1st/Sgt Warden, standing beside his Company Commander and watching his face, wanted to boot his Company Commander hard in the ass.

It was perhaps the stringing of the barbed wire, more than anything else, that ate into the patriotism of the troops in the next few days. The men who had acquired the new unknown disease of aching veins in their arm joints from the building of these positions now found it coming back on them doubly powerfully from putting up barbed wire to protect these positions. So that even when they were not pulling guard at night, they couldnt sleep anyway. The stringing of the barbed wire, after the first day, was an even more powerful astringent to the patriotism than their getting crummy with no prospect of a shower, or their getting itchy with beard and no prospect of a shave, or their having to sleep on the rocks with nothing but a single shelterhalf and two blankets over them when it rained.

Actually, this war that had started out so well Sunday morning and given them such high hopes of the future, was turning out to be nothing more than an extended maneuvres. With the single difference that this showed no prospect of ending.

It was five days before things were organized enough to allow the sending of a detail back to Schofield for the rest of their stuff, that they had not thought they'd need, and the Company's quota of pyramidal tents. But even these didnt do the men at Makapuu any good since out there there werent any trees to set them up under.

Warden, armed with the request list of each man which altogether covered an entire pad of legal-size scratch paper, led the detail of three trucks. Pete Karelsen, who was the only man in the Company who had been anywhere near comfortable in the five days, was his second-in-command. They pulled into the quad with their three trucks to find another outfit already moved into the barracks and the footlockers and wall lockers of G Company thoroughly rifled. Their lists were useless. Pete Karelsen, again, had been practically the only man in the Company who had bothered to lock either his footlocker or wall locker that Sunday morning. But even Pete's extra set of false teeth, which had been out on the table, were gone.

And, of course, none of the new tenants they talked to knew a damn thing about it.

Warden's records and player were gone, also his $120 Brooks Bros. Suit, saddle-stitched Forstmann jacket, and the white dinner jacket and tux pants he had bought but never worn yet, together with all of his uniforms. Also, the brand new $260 electric guitar, still less than half paid for, that Andy and Friday had bought while Prew was in the Stockade, was gone too, speaker jackplug and all.

If it had not been for 1st/Sgt Dedrick of A Company, who was about his size and had remembered to lock his wall locker, he would not have even been able to scare up two whole field uniforms. Just about the only thing that had been left untouched were the folded pyramidal tents in the supply room.

By the end of the seventh day, when they had got the tents back downtown and disturbuted out to the positions and set up ready to occupy, every man on the Company roster – including the two men serving time in the Stockade who had been released with the rest of the prisoners – had shown up and reported for duty. With the single exception of Prewitt.

Abducting the General

W. Stanley Moss

DOING

27 April

Well, we've done it.

It's a lovely morning; and the General, Manoli, and I are sitting beside a mountain stream about one mile from the village of Anoyia. The General, looking a trifle pained because of a bump on the leg which he got last night, is sitting on a rock at the water's edge, his trousers rolled up to his knees, washing his feet. Contrary to his behaviour of yesterday evening, he is quite subdued and no longer very talkative. His chief worry appears to be that at some stage of last night's journey he lost his Knight's Cross of the Iron Cross – a decoration which he would normally wear round his neck. I told him that it would be easy enough to have a replica made as soon as we reached Cairo. But no, he replied, that would not be the same thing – he would have to be content to wear the medal in his heart. To this he added that he considered I was being pretty optimistic in thinking that we should ever reach Cairo, and then, with a shrug of the shoulders, he clambered down to the rock on which he is now sitting.

Among ourselves we call him 'Theophilus', so that he shall not know when we are talking about him, but at present he is taking very little interest in the world around him. He is brooding, and I think also he is feeling tired after his long march. It seems that he is doing a lot of speculatiing as he sits there, shoulders hunched, drying his feet, and from time to time rubbing the sore place on his leg. I see that he has a lesser variety of the Iron Cross pinned low upon his breast. Perhaps this will in some way compensate for the loss of his prized medal.

I find it impossible to go to sleep because of the benzedrine which

I took last night, so I shall try to put on paper all that I can remember of the events of the past twelve hours.

It was eight o'clock when we reached the T-junction. We had met a few pedestrians on the way, none of whom seemed perturbed at seeing our German uniforms, and we had exchanged greetings with them with appropriate Teutonic gruffness. When we reached the road we went straight to our respective posts and took cover. It was now just a question of lying low until we saw the warning torch-flash from Mitso, the buzzer-man. We were distressed to notice that the incline in the road was much steeper than we had been led to believe, for this meant that if the chauffeur used the foot-brake instead of the hand-brake when we stopped him there would be a chance of the car's running over the edge of the embankment as soon as he had been disposed of. However, it was too late at this stage to make any changes in our plan, so we just waited and hoped for the best.

There were five false alarms during the first hour of our watch. Two *Volkswagen*, two lorries, and one motor-cycle combination trundled past at various times, and in each of them, seated primly upright like tailors' dummies, the steel-helmeted figures of German soldiers were silhouetted against the night sky. It was a strange feeling to be crouching so close to them – almost within arm's reach of them – while they drove past with no idea that nine pairs of eyes were so fixedly watching them. It felt rather like going on patrol in action, when you find yourself very close to the enemy trenches, and can hear the sentries talking or quietly whistling, and can see them lighting cigarettes in their cupped hands.

It was already one hour past the General's routine time for making his return journey when we began to wonder if he could possibly have gone home in one of the vehicles which had already passed by. It was cold, and the canvas of our German garb did not serve to keep out the wind.

I remember Paddy's asking me the time. I looked at my watch and saw that the hands were pointing close to half-past nine. And at that moment Mitso's torch blinked.

'Here we go.'

We scrambled out of the ditch on to the road. Paddy switched on his red lamp and I held up a traffic signal, and together we stood in the centre of the junction.

In a moment – far sooner than we had expected – the powerful headlamps of the General's car swept round the bend and we found ourselves floodlit. The chauffeur, on approaching the corner, slowed down.

Paddy shouted, 'Halt!'

The car stopped. We walked forward rather slowly, and as we passed the beams of the headlamps we drew our ready-cocked pistols from behind our backs and let fall the life-preservers from our wrists.

As we came level with the doors of the car Paddy asked, '*Ist dies das General's Wagen?*'

There came a muffled '*Ja, ja*' from inside.

Then everything happened very quickly. There was a rush from all sides. We tore open our respective doors, and our torches illuminated the interior of the car – the bewildered face of the General, the chauffeur's terrified eyes, the rear seats empty. With his right hand the chauffeur was reaching for his automatic, so I hit him across the head with my kosh. He fell forward, and George, who had come up behind me, heaved him out of the driving-seat and dumped him on the road. I jumped in behind the steering-wheel, and at the same moment saw Paddy and Manoli dragging the General out of the opposite door. The old man was struggling with fury, lashing out with his arms and legs. He obviously thought he was going to be killed, and started shouting every curse under the sun at the top of his voice.

The engine of the car was still ticking over, the hand-brake was on, everything was perfect. To one side, in a pool of torchlight in the centre of the road, Paddy and Manoli were trying to quieten the General, who was still cursing and struggling. On the other side George and Andoni were trying to pull the chauffeur to his feet, but the man's head was pouring with blood, and I think he must have been unconscious, because every time they lifted him up he simply collapsed to the ground again.

This was the critical moment, for if any other traffic had come along the road we should have been caught sadly unawares. But now Paddy, Manoli, Nikko, and Stratis were carrying the General towards the car and bundling him into the back seat. After him clambered George, Manoli, and Stratis – one of the three holding a knife to the General's throat to stop him shouting, the other two with the Marlin guns poking out of either window. It must have been quite a squash.

Paddy jumped into the front seat beside me.

The General kept imploring, 'Where is my hat? Where is my hat?'

The hat, of course, was on Paddy's head.

We were now ready to move. Suddenly everyone started kissing and congratulating everybody else; and Micky, having first embraced Paddy and me, starting screaming at the General with all the pent-up hatred he held for the Germans. We had to push him away and tell him to shut up. Andoni, Grigori, Nikko, and Wallace Beery were standing at the roadside, propping up the chauffeur between them, and now they waved us good-bye and turned away and started off on their long trek to the rendezvous on Mount Ida.

We started.

The car was a beauty, a brand-new Opel, and were delighted to see that the petrol-gauge showed the tanks to be full.

We had been travelling for less than a minute when we saw a succession of lights coming along the road towards us; and a moment later we found ourselves driving past a motor convoy, and thanked our stars that it had not come this way a couple of minutes sooner. Most of the lorries were troop transports, all filled with soldiery, and this sight had the immediate effect of quietening George, Manoli, and Stratis, who had hitherto been shouting at one another and taking no notice of our attempts to keep them quiet.

When the convoy had passed Paddy told the General that the two of us were British officers and that we would treat him as an honourable prisoner of war. He seemed mightily relieved to hear this and immediately started to ask a series of questions, often not even waiting for a reply. But for some reason his chief concern still appeared to be the whereabouts of his hat – first it was the hat, then his medal. Paddy told him that he would soon be given it back, and to this the General said, *'Danke, danke.'*

It was not long before we saw a red lamp flashing in the road before us, and we realized that we were approaching the first of the traffic-control posts through which we should have to pass. We were, of course, prepared for this eventuality, and our plan had contained alternative actions which we had hoped would suit any situation, because we knew that our route led us through the centre of Heraklion, and that in the course of our journey we should probably have to pass through about twenty control posts.

Until now everything had happened so quickly that we had felt no emotion other than elation at the primary success of our venture; but as we drew nearer and nearer to the swinging red lamp we experienced our first tense moment.

A German sentry was standing in the middle of the road. As we approached him, slowing down the while, he moved to one side, presumably thinking that we were going to stop. However, as soon as we drew level with him – still going very slowly, so as to give him an opportunity of seeing the General's pennants on the wings of the car – I began to accelerate again, and on we went. For several seconds after we had passed the sentry we were all apprehension, fully expecting to hear a rifle-shot in our wake; but a moment later we had rounded a bend in the road and knew that the danger was temporarily past. Our chief concern now was whether or not the guard at the post behind us would telephone ahead to the next one, and it was with our fingers crossed that we approached the red lamp of the second control post a few minutes later. But we need not have had any fears, for the sentry behaved in exactly the same manner as the first had done, and we drove on feeling rather pleased with ourselves.

In point of fact, during the course of our evening's drive we passed twenty-two control posts. In most cases the above-mentioned formula sufficed to get us through, but on five occasions we came to road-blocks – raisable one-bar barriers – which brought us to a standstill. Each time, however, the General's pennants did the trick like magic, and the sentries would either give a smart salute or present arms as the gate was lifted and we passed through. Only once did we find ourselves in what might have developed into a nasty situation – but of that I shall write in a moment.

Paddy, sitting on my right and smoking a cigarette, looked quite imposing in the General's hat. The General asked him how long he would have to remain in his present undignified position, and in reply Paddy told him that if he were willing to give his parole that he would neither shout nor try to escape we should treat him, not as a prisoner, but, until we left the island, as one of ourselves. The General gave his parole immediately. We were rather surprised at this, because it seemed to us that anyone in his position might still entertain reasonable hopes of escape – a shout for help at any of the control posts might have saved him.

According to our plan, I should soon be having to spend twenty-four hours alone with Manoli and the General, so I thought it best to find out if we had any languages in common (for hitherto we had been speaking a sort of anglicized German). Paddy asked him if he spoke any English.

'*Nein,*' said the General.

'Russian?' I asked. 'Or Greek?'

'*Nein.*'

In unison: '*Parlez-vous français?*'

'*Un petit peu.*'

To which we could not resist the Cowardesque reply, 'I never think that's quite enough.'

But it was in French that we spoke, and continue to do so. The quality is scarcely commendable.

Presently we found ourselves approaching the Villa Ariadne. The sentries, having recognized the car from a distace, were already opening the heavily barbed gates in anticipation of our driving inside. I hooted the horn and did not slow down. We drove swiftly past them, and it was with considerable delight that we watched them treating us to hurried salutes.

We were now approaching Heraklion, and coming towards us we saw a large number of lorries. We remembered that Micky had told us that there was to be a garrison cinema-show in the town that evening, so we presumed that these lorries were transporting the audience back to various billets. We did not pass a single vehicle which was travelling in the same direction as ourselves.

Soon we had to slow down to about 25 kph, because the road was chock-full of German soldiers. The were quick to respond to the hooting of our horn, however, and when they saw whose car it was they dispersed to the sides of the road and acknowledged us in passing. It was truly unfortunate that we should have arrived in the town at this moment; but once again luck was with us, and, apart from a near-miss on a cyclist, who swerved out of our way only just in time, we drove down the main street without let or hindrance. By the time we reached the market square in the centre of the town we had already left the cinema crowd behind us, and we found the large, open space, which by daylight is usually so crowded, now almost completely deserted. At this point we had to take a sharp turning to the left, for our route led us westward through the old West Gate to the Retimo road.

The West Gate is a relic of the old days when Heraklion was completely surrounded by a massive wall, and even to-day it remains a formidable structure. The gate itself, at the best of times not very wide, has been further narrowed by concrete anti-tank blocks; and a German guard is on duty there for twenty-four hours a day.

I remember saying 'Woops' as I saw the sentry signalling us to stop. I had proposed to slow down, as on the previous occasions, and then to accelerate upon drawing level with the sentry; but this time this was impossible, for the man did not move an inch, and in the light of the headlamps we saw several more Germans standing behind him. I was obliged to take the car forward at a snail's pace. We had previously decided that in the event of our being asked any questions our reply would be simply, 'General's Wagen,' coupled with our hopes for the best. If any further conversation were called for Paddy was to do the talking.

George, Manoli, and Stratis held their weapons at the ready and kept as low as they could in the back seat. The General was on the floor beneath them. Paddy and I cocked our pistols and held them on our laps.

The sentry approached Paddy's side of the car.

Before he had come too near Paddy called out that this was the General's car – which, after all, was true enough – and without awaiting the sentry's next word I accelerated and we drove on, calling out 'Gute Nacht!' as we went. Everyone saluted.

We drove fast along the next stretch of road.

The General, coming to the surface, said he felt sorry for all the sentries at the control posts, because they would surely get into terrible trouble on the morrow.

The road was clear of traffic, and it was not long before we had put several kilometres between ourselves and Heraklion. Soon we had passed the last of the control posts, and the road began to rise from the plain and wind gradually uphill. Up and up we went. We had seen the massive mountain forms in front of us as a target, but now we were among them; and high above, like a white baby curled upon a translucent canopy, we saw the crescent of the moon. Suddenly we felt quite distant from everything that had just happened – a terrific elation – and we told one another that three-quarters of the job was now over, and started discussing what sort of celebration we would have when we got back to Cairo. We sang The Party's over; and then I lit a cigarette, which I thought was the best I had ever smoked in my life.

At a quarter-past eleven we arrived at the point on the road where Manoli, Stratis, the General, and I were to leave the car. We had been driving for an hour and three-quarters, and during the latter part of the journey the road had spiralled up and up, so that we were now at a considerable altitude, and we felt that until dawn at least we were out of harm's way.

As Paddy and I got out of the car the General called to us, begging us not to leave him alone with the Cretans – so dramatically, in fact, that I'm sure he imagined he would have his throat slit the moment our backs were turned. Paddy assured him that he was not going to be left alone, that I was going to accompany him; and on hearing this the General gave a great sigh of relief. We told him to come out of the car, and he hastily obeyed. Paddy gave him a smart salute, saying that he would meet him, together with the rest of us, on the morrow at Anoyia; and then he clambered into the driving-seat with George next to him.

Paddy had not driven a car for over five years, and it was with fits of suppressed laughter that we watched him trying to put the hand-brake into gear and pressing the horn instead of the starter. After several starts and stalls, off he went, and we watched the car going on up the road, swerving from side to side and grinding along in bottom gear, until the tail-lamp disappeared round a bend. With only two kilometres to go, I hope he made the journey all right.

We set off with the General in a southerly direction. There was no path or track, and we were obliged to scramble up and down cliffs, across streams, and through heavy undergrowth. This was very hard going for the General, and although he was quite co-operative and did not try to hinder us in any way, it was inevitable that we travelled very slowly. Stratis, contrary to his assurances, had little idea of the route which we were trying to follow, and consequently our progress was more or less guided by our reading of the stars. The General said that his leg had been badly hurt when he had been dragged out of his car, and indeed he walked with a pronounced limp. I considered it unnecessary to continue walking behind him and with my revolver at his back, so I searched him for concealed arms – he had none – and then walked with him, helping him over obstacles and, with Manoli's assistance, carrying him across streams. We were foolish enough not to drink from these streams, for it was not long before we came to a dry expanse of country, and it was three o'clock in the morning before we reached a spring.

The spring was almost dry, and in order to get any water out of it we had to tie some string round the lid of an emergency-ration tin, which we let down some twenty feet and dragged in the mud until it was full. It took us a long time to quench our thirsts, for we were only able to bring up about a quarter of an inch of water each time. The General said that he was very hungry, for he had eaten nothing since luncheon, so I gave him a few raisins which were mixed up with the dust in my pockets, and for these he was more than thankful.

We moved on again. The General became talkative and started discussing General Brauer's* reactions to hearing of this 'Hussar Act', as he called it. He supposed that Paddy and I must be very happy and pleased with ourselves, but added that the job was not over yet. And then he asked me if we were Regular soldiers. When I replied that we were not he seemed greatly upset, for he had just realized, it appeared, that his career had ceased to exist. He was the thirteenth child, he said, of a family of fifteen; and his father, a poor man, was a pastor, so it was really he himself who was the family's breadwinner. A major-general's pay, he explained, was pretty good in the German Army, and, what was more, he had been expecting his promotion to the rank of lieutenant-general to come through at any moment. (He was, in fact, already wearing the insignia of a lieutenant-general, but I think this was due rather to his local appointment than to eager anticipation.)

During the German evacuation of Greece I discovered in Salonika a certain Major von Schenk, who had been an ADC to General Lohr, but had deserted and given himself up. He said that the story of Kreipe's disappearance had at the time been a big joke in Vienna, but the most ironic thing about it had been that his promotion to lieutenant-general had come through on the very day after his abduction.

At about five o'clock in the morning we found ourselves within a short distance of Anoyia, but since we were not going to enter the

* General Brauer was Commander of the Fortress of Crete, as opposed to Kreipe, who was the Divisional Commander. Both Brauer and Kreipe's predecessor, General Muller, were sentenced to death at a War-crimes trial in Athens in December 1945.

village itself, but wait for Paddy and George in a near-by river-bed, we decided to stay where we were until first light and then to set off to find a suitably secluded hiding-place.

The General was feeling very cold, so Stratis gave him his Greek policeman's overcoat. Then we sat down and talked.

The General told me it was a strange thing, but he had always felt that if anything were to happen to him in Crete it would be at the very spot where the ambush actually took place – so certain of this had he been, in fact, that he had already given instructions for a guard-post to be mounted on that selfsame T-junction. (It is possible that when he saw us there last night he thought that we were the sentries guarding the new post.) Even stranger, he added, was the fact that on the way home he had had a premonition that something was going to happen, and had remarked on it to his chauffeur. Then he went on to ask me about the chauffeur's fate, and I told him – with little conviction, I fear – that the man would be joining us on Mount Ida in a day or two.

As the darkness began to leave the sky, and the first colour of day, like violet ink rising through the veins of a tulip, fanned out to the east, I was able to have a good look at the General for the first time. He is a thick-set man, and his face possesses most of the regular Teutonic features – thin lips, bull neck, blue eyes, and a fixed expression. His skin is fair, almost delicate; and his hair, cut guardsman-fashion, is slightly grey at the temples. I should say that he is between forty-five and fifty years of age.

As soon as it was light enough to discover our exact whereabouts we moved on again. Stratis said that he knew of a pleasant and sheltered spot not far distant, whereupon he led us to the boulder-strewn stream where we now remain.

I immediately wrote two short letters, which I gave to Stratis, telling him to go to Anoyia and find two trust-worthy messengers who would deliver my notes to Sandy, in the Lasithi Mountains, and Tom Dumbabin,* who should be on Mount Ida. The note to Sandy was to tell him that our escapade had been successful, that the General was quite a pleasant catch and not the raving Nazi he might well have been, and to ask him to look after Vassily and Ivan as best

---

* The British agent with the wireless set whom we were hoping to contact on the mountain.

he could until I returned from Egypt. The note to Tom Dumbabin was to ask him to inform Cairo via his set that we had succeeded with the abduction so far, and to ask headquarters, as previously arranged, to have announcements made over the wireless and pamphlets dropped on the island.*

I told Stratis to keep a look-out for Paddy and George and to bring them here if he was to meet them; and I also told him that he should have some food and wine sent to us as soon as possible, because we were all pretty hungry.

The General, tired after the night's march, took off his coat and lay down. It was then that he discovered the loss of his Iron Cross, and this upset him a great deal. Without his medal and his hat he felt decidedly naked. He told me that he had won the award while in command of the push against Leningrad on the Russian Front. Later, he said, he had fought for a long time in the Kuban, and it was with nostalgia in his voice that he recalled his main diet there – caviare. After two years on the Russian Front he had been sent to Crete for a 'rest cure', and it was now only five weeks since his arrival here. He's going to have a nice long rest, I imagine, but not in Crete. The lesser variety of Iron Cross which he wears was won, he told me, at Verdun during the last war; so it certainly seems that he has done a lot of fighting in his time.

It is now three o'clock in the afternoon. At midday a basket of food and wine was brought to us from the village by a jovial little man who tells me that he is an old friend of Paddy's. He fulfilled Stratis's request for provisions, and it was with real pleasure that we sat

---

* Our original plan had included an arrangement with headquarters that, as soon as we had caught the General, pamphlets should be dropped all over Crete stating in both Greek and German that the operation had been carried out by a British raiding party. By this method we had further hoped to prevent reprisals being taken on the islanders.

The second arrangement concerned the BBC and other broadcasting stations. When the news of the kidnapping was being broadcast it had been agreed that the announcer should say that General Kreipe was *already on his way to Cairo*, which would not be untrue. In this way we hoped to give the Germans the impression that we had already left the island, thus giving ourselves a fair chance of making our way to the south coast without being chased or hemmed in.

As things turned out, however, the pamphlets were never dropped at all, owing to bad flying conditions; and all the radio broadcasts, including those from the BBC, stated that the General *was being taken off the island*. This, needless to say, made matters very much worse for us, and was responsible for the Germans' launching of a full-scale man-hunt.

ourselves on some rocks in the sunlight and ate and drank our fill.
The General tucked into the meal like a schoolboy.

Sleepy now with sun and wine, I feel ready to doze until dusk.

GOING

29 April
Soon after I had made my last entry in this diary and fallen asleep in
the sunlight I was awakened by somebody shaking me. I heard
agitated voices, and when I opened my eyes I saw Manoli crouching
over me, his face all excitement.

'Germans coming!' he said. 'Plenty Germans in village!'

I was glad to see that the General had also been roused and was
already putting on his boots. He was being quite quick about it.

Paddy's friend from Anoyia said that he knew of a good cave close
at hand, so we hurriedly threw our kit on to our backs and made off
along the bank of the stream. The General, though never ceasing to
complain about the pain in his leg, walked well and kept up a good
pace. We had not gone far before our guide led us across the stream
and up a narrow gorge. Five minutes later we reached a steep cliff-
face, and up it we scrambled, heaving the General from foothold to
foothold, until we found ourselves at the entrance of a tiny cave.
Somehow we managed to clamber inside, all four of us squeezing into
a space which would not comfortably have housed two men. We filled
up the entrance of the cave with bracken, leaving ourselves peep-
holes through which we should be able to see up and down the gorge.

The General had been rather amused by our haste to conceal
ourselves, and his face wore an I-told-you-so expression. But now,
with his knees tucked under his chin, he somehow contrived to go to
sleep, and it was not long before the whistle of his heavy breathing
filled the corners of the cave.

For two hours we watched and waited, but no one – not even a
shepherd – passed up or down the gorge.

It was at half-past five that we heard an aeroplane flying very low
above us. I poked out my head to have a look at it and saw a Fieseler-
Storch – the German equivalent of our own 'Shufti' 'plane – hovering
at an altitude of no more than a hundred feet immediately over our

heads. It was travelling so slowly that I was easily able to see the occupant of the back seat surveying the countryside through a pair of binoculars. (Later, when I met Paddy, he told me that numbers of these 'planes had patrolled the entire area for over three hours.)

Suddenly the air was full of bits of paper, which came fluttering down in a thick cloud, and some of them landed within a few yards of our hideout. We felt certain that the messages on these pamphlets must be referring to us, but, much as we wanted to read them, we did not dare to leave the cave for fear of being seen.

Presently, however, when the sky was growing dark and there appeared to be no one in the immediate vicinity, we crawled out of our hiding-place, stretched our limbs to get rid of cramp, then scrambled down the cliff-face. We collected a number of pamphlets. They were written in Greek, and by the look of the blurred type and scrappy paper it seemed that they had been turned out with the greatest of haste. As best he could, Manoli translated the matter to me, and this was the gist of it:

TO ALL CRETANS

Last night the German General Kreipe was abducted by bandits. He is now being concealed in the Cretan mountains, and his whereabouts cannot be unknown to the populace. If the General is not returned within three days all rebel villages in the HERAKLION DISTRICT will be razed to the ground and the severest measures of reprisal will be brought to bear on the civilian population.

It seemed obvious that the Germans could not yet have discovered the abandoned car with the letter on the front seat. At all events, we had and still have high hopes that the BBC broadcast and the British-dropped pamphlets will repair this situation; but it certainly looks as though the Germans mean business.

As soon as it was dark enough we set off uphill towards Anoyia. Within half an hour we were within a short distance of the village, so we hid in a ditch while Manoli went to fetch Paddy and George.

He found them within five minutes of leaving us and straightway brought them to the place where we were waiting. With them they had a muleteer and a mule for the General. We were certainly pleased to see Paddy and George safe and sound after their shaky drive; but it appeared that everything had gone well after they had left us. Paddy had ditched the car near the coast at a spot, once used as a submarine beach, which was well known to the Germans, and this was a good corroborative detail in giving the impression that we had already left the island. After leaving the 'clues' (a commando beret and a great-coat) in the back of the car, he and George had marched to Anoyia and arrived there at midday. They had been eating luncheon with the village priest when the Germans had arrived; but there had not been a house-to-house search. The Germans, who had come in considerable numbers, had left the village at six o'clock.

Paddy, who like myself was still wearing German uniform, said that while walking through the streets of Anoyia he had received some pretty dirty looks from the notoriously lawless villagers!

Now that the Germans had gone we felt that we should be safe until daybreak, for Anoyia has a fine reputation in Crete as being a village of fighting-men; and, owing to its sympathy for all that is British, it is often jokingly referred to by Cretans as 'the British Colony'. It is the largest village in the island, and its history is a tale of wars against anyone who ever came to challenge its freedom.

As a reprisal for certain operations carried out in this area during July and August 1944 the Germans burned down and dynamited every house in Anoyia. For good measure they also dive-bombed it, with the result that there is now only rubble where the nine-hundred-year-old village used to stand. The Germans in Crete used to conduct their reprisals on the basis of ten Cretans for every German killed, and this often resulted in the extermination of the population of an entire village or even district, and as many as two thousand civilians were once slaughtered in the matter of a few days. The people of Anoyia were both clever and fortunate enough to escape to the mountains as soon as they discovered that trouble was coming to them, and only a handful of them were caught by the Germans; but in most cases such as this the enemy would descend swiftly and suddenly, round up all the inhabitants, lining them up against a wall and machine-gunning them to death, regardless of age, sex, or condition. Often the brutality went much further than this, and it was no uncommon thing for villagers to be thrown into their own blazing homes to perish in the flames.

Manoli's brother was once the hero of such an incident. The entire population of a small village had been drawn up in line against the wall of the church, and a German machine-gunner was already squatting behind his weapon, awaiting the order to fire. It was at this moment that Manoli's brother, who unobserved had clambered up a near-by rock, shot the German with deadly accuracy through the head. The remainder of the German force, doubtless imagining that a full-scale ambush was about to take place, immediately took to their heels and fled; whereupon the happy villagers returned to their houses, collected their belongings, and wasted no time in making their way to the sanctuary of the mountains.

German brutality in Crete nearly always took the form of simple and methodical mass murder. There was none of that artistic subtlety about it which permits one to have a sneaking admiration for the Borgias, the Duke of Milan, the Malatestas of this world. It was blatant and crude, and even its perverted or sexual varieties found the outlet in a fitting manner, for it was the mules and donkeys of the island which suffered in consequence.

One can perhaps find the most typical story of the Hun mentality in the simplest of stories: A little boy was crossing a road when a German staff car, travelling at great speed, swept round a bend. The driver, an officer, was unable to pull up in time and swerved into a ditch. On getting out of the car he saw that a mudguard had been scratched; so he called the little boy to him. Shyly smiling, the boy approached. The officer said nothing, but merely grasped the child's arm and broke it in half across his knee.

The General, Manoli, George, Stratis, Paddy, and I sat down among some rocks and ate a meal of hard-boiled eggs, cheese, and bread. This done, we helped the General on to the mule. He was very happy to know that he would not have to walk.

We set off due south, our route taking us up a steady gradient along a goat-track which frequently lost itself among rocks and shingle. The night's march should not have been a long one, but because the mule had to follow the zigzagging track we were unable to take any short cuts, and when at two o'clock we found ourselves approaching a sheep-fold we were still several hours' march from our destination. The shepherd, a dear old man with white whiskers and almost no teeth, was delighted to see us, and immediately asked us into his hut so that we could rest and warm ourselves in front of the fire.

The interior of the hut was lined with stone shelves, upon which were stacked row upon row of cheeses. Beneath the shelves were some stone seats, so we sat down and clustered round the bracken fire which was blazing in the centre of the floor. The shepherd gave us cheese to eat, and with it some rock bread, which was first left to soak in a stone jug. The General was very tired and fell asleep as he sat at the fireside, so we decided not to wake him, but to let him sleep until four o'clock. Whereupon, having asked the shepherd to give us a shake in a couple of hours, we all settled down to have a short rest.

As good as his word, the old man roused us punctually, though how he was able to estimate the time I cannot imagine. We gave him a fond farewell and were soon on our way again.

> *The entire Psiloriti area through which we were now travelling was a forbidden zone, but many shepherds preferred to risk staying there. Often, on this and other operations when we were being chased by Germans, it was under a shepherd's care that we were able to find concealment. No cave, track, or hiding-place was unknown to them; and of this the Germans were fully aware. Many shepherds were caught and put to death. The man, for instance, of whom I have just written, is now dead. He was shot in the back after having been greeted by a German patrol, and his flock was driven off to the mess-rooms of the garrison.*

It was approaching dawn when we found ourselves within a short distance of the rendezvous. The sky grew pink above the Lasiti Mountains, while against it, seen in silhouette upon his mule, the General looked for all the world like Napoleon in the retreat from Moscow. And we, as jaded-looking a rabble as ever fought an enemy, must have perfectly suited this picture.

Now, as we approached the local *andarte* headquarters, we saw sentries on each successive crest; and these men would whistle and shout to warn the rest of the band of our arrival, and then come running down the slopes to greet us. Very soon we were surrounded by *andartes*, all of them kissing us, embracing us, asking us a million questions. They led us along a gully, conducting us as though we were some royal *cortège*, and brought us to their lair – a well-concealed cave half-way up a rock-face. At its entrance we were greeted by the *andarte* leader, a handsome man with snow-white hair, whose name, well known the length and breadth of the island, is Mihale Xilouris. And behind him we saw, to our great surprise and delight, no less than three British colleagues. One was a lieutenant, another a corporal, and the third a wireless operator. The lieutenant, John Houseman, I had seen only a few weeks previously, but already his

appearance had undergone a considerable change. The youthful
cavalry officer had been transformed into a long-haired, turbaned
peasant with a moustache, albeit still of only pubescent density,
which is full of promise. His companion, the corporal, I have found
to be an immensely likeable person. He has gone completely native
both in speech and manner, and were one ignorant of his identity it
would be impossible to tell him apart from his Cretan fellows. He
wears an imposing beard, a matted *capota*, turban, top-boots, and a
pair of breeches which, he says, he has not taken off since his arrival
on the island a year ago. His name is John Lewis, and his appearance
as I have described it is in complete contrast to that of the wireless
operator. The latter, a man of dry humour and philosophical saws, is
always the transplanted British farmer. He prefers to teach the
Cretans to speak English than to learn their language for himself; but
at the same time he has picked up all their mannerisms – knuckle-
cracking, thumb biting, lapel tugging, and so forth. His stay on the
island has been a long one, and he hopes to go on leave to Egypt
pretty soon; but in the meantime he sums up his attitude as 'Give me
a bottle of *raki*, and heigho for rain, snow, and the Germans!'

We sat down to have a conference to make arrangements for our
departure; but no sooner had the first words been spoken than our
troubles started.

The messenger who had been detailed to take my letter to Tom
Dumbabin arrived suddenly at the entrance of our cave. He said that
he had searched the entire area for Tom, but had found no trace of
him, nor had anyone in the district a notion of his whereabouts. This
was sad news indeed; but we consoled ourselves with the knowledge
that Tom's wireless set and operator were here with us. We straightway composed a message for transmission to Cairo, asking headquarters to send a motor-launch to pick us up in four days' time.
This the wireless operator enciphered, then went to his set with the
intention of contacting Cairo. An hour later he returned. Try as he
would, he said, he was unable to make the set work. It had been
behaving peculiarly during the past few days, he explained, but now
it seemed to have packed up altogether. He had taken it to pieces to
try to discover what was wrong, and had found that a most important
part of it had been broken beyond repair. There was nothing for it,
he added, but to await the sending of a replacement from Cairo.

Thus, with Tom Dumbabin missing and the wireless set out of

action, there was only one course left for us to take: to send
messengers to the other British-operated stations on the island – one
to Sandy, in the east, the second to another agent, Dick Barnes by
name, in the west – asking them to transmit our message to
headquarters. In both cases, we realized the journey would take the
fleetest of runners at least two days to reach his destination, a further
day to await Cairo's reply, and another two days in which to return
to us. There was nothing else to be done, so we resigned ourselves to
remaining here while awaiting developments. Sad prospect!

During the afternoon a scout reported that he had spotted Andoni,
Wallace Beery, Nikko, and Grigori in the distance. We asked him if
they were bringing a German soldier with them, but he shook his
head and grinned.

Looking amazingly fresh after their long trek, the four of them
arrived a few minutes later. They told us that the hue and cry in the
plain had grown more and more intense with the days. There were
full-scale drives, they said, launched in every direction, and they
themselves had only just escaped capture. Then we asked them about
the chauffeur. It was Andoni who answered, his eyes diverted as he
spoke. The wretched man had expired on the way, he explained, as a
result of the blow he had received on the head. They had buried him
discreetly beneath a large pile of rocks and shingle, and there would
be little chance of the body's being discovered until it started to smell.
Altogether, he concluded, it had been a good thing that the man had
died, because he had walking so slowly that, had he lived, he would
probably have been responsible for the capture of the whole party. At
this, Wallace Beery, Nikko, and Grigori nodded grave agreement.

Andoni's story, we supposed, was a roundabout way of telling us
that his knife now had another notch on its handle; but we let the
matter rest. We decided not to tell the General of his chauffeur's fate,
for it seems that he was rather attached to the man. Amen.

From time to time until dusk we were visited by *andartes* of a
neighbouring band who had come to have a look at the General. The
General did not appear to object to these visits, and in fact he
remained throughout in quite a good humour; but I am sure that the
knowledge that he was an exhibition like this must have pained his
pride to no small extent. After a little coaxing he allowed John
Houseman to take some photographs of him, but only on the
condition, he stipulated, that they were not for publication in the

Press. We did not argue the point. When confronted by a camera he adopts a stylized photo-expression – the grim, dejected look of conquered heroes brought in captivity to Rome.

Once the sun had gone down the air became very cold. We had some supper, watched the *andartes* playing a game of buzz-buzz,* then retired to our cave. We dreamed of being able to light a fire by which to warm ourselves; but the *andartes* told us that the light would be visible for miles, so we took heed of their warning and remained shivering in the darkness. For a long time we sat and talked. Paddy discovered that the General is a fair Greek scholar, and, much to the amusement of our Cretan colleagues, the two of them entertained each other by exchanging verses from Sophocles.

The cave, we were shortly to discover, was alive with fleas, and these pests showed a marked preference for the General and me. Coupled with this unpleasantness was the fact that we had only one blanket between the three of us, so Paddy and I, our chivalry not extending to the sacrifice of this threadbare necessity, placed ourselves on either side of the General, stretched the blanket lengthways across our bodies, and tried to go to sleep. But sleep was impossible. John Lewis, noticing our misery, very gallantly sacrificed most of his bedding; but even so the situation was little improved. We gave the General a large swig of *raki*, and this had the eventual effect of sending him to sleep; but the soporific qualities of the same medicine, though internally warming, were lost upon the two of us. We cursed Pavlo, who was supposed to have brought our bedding and warm clothing up from the river-bed at Skalani;† but curses were of little avail. Every now and again the General would turn over and drowsily scratch a flea-bite, and from time to time he would pause in his snoring to butt one of us amidships with his knees. It must have been at about midnight that we finally talked ourselves into a doze; but

* This game consists of little more than seeing who can hit his neighbour's face the hardest.

† We never saw either Pavlo or our kit again, and we heard much later that he had made off with it to the mountains. But this action, by Cretan standards, was fair enough. I should perhaps explain that *klepsi-klepsi* – translatable into English as 'swiping' or 'pinching', but hardly 'stealing' – is something of a Cretan sport. On the mainland it is an institution rather than a pastime, and therefore provides little amusement for the foreigner, but in both places sympathy is usually on the side of the 'pincher' rather than on the loser. If you allow someone to steal from you, it is you who are the mug, he the clever fellow. It's quite simple really.

three hours later we awoke, chilled to the marrow, and so we remained, sitting up and chain-smoking until dawn. Two hours later the General woke up. He said that he had spent a rotten night because we had periodically kicked him in our sleep! We didn't find anything very amusing about that remark.

Before we had breakfast several *andarte* runners arrived. They all told the same story, bringing reports that large numbers of Germans are concentrating around the foothills of this mountain and that there is every reason to believe that a full-scale drive over the area is imminent. We have decided that the best course for us is to make the long climb over Ida's crest and the descent down its southern slopes before the German action has time to develop. Still no news of Tom Dumbabin,* nor, despite constant efforts at improvisation by the wireless operator, a glimmer of life in the radio set. Our lines of communication appear to have completely broken down.

It is now almost noon. Shortly we shall have some food, and then, allowing ourselves six hours in daylight marching, we shall start climbing the northern slope of the mountain.

30 April

A terribly long walk – twelve hours at a snail's pace over the summit of Ida.

We had set off from Mihale Xilouris's headquarters in good time, the *andartes* giving us a heartening send-off, and the three Englishmen, standing at the cave's entrance, waving to us and wishing us well (and the wireless operator, upon seeing the General in the saddle, whistling *Going to Heaven on a Mule!*).

At the foot of the summit-slope we found some fresh guides and scouts awaiting us, and these, we learned, were men from the neighbouring *andarte* band. We had left Xilouris's area, it appeared, and were now approaching a territory which is the lair of the largest guerrilla band in Crete. Its headquarters are practically on Ida's summit, a spot as impregnable as the Krak des Chevaliers, and from it, mist permitting, one commands a view of the length and breadth of the island.

---

* It was some time later that we heard that Tom had been in hiding owing to a severe attack of malaria; and so it was that during our journey we never saw him, nor even heard from him. He was evacuated to Cairo in June, but returned to the island a few months later.

Here we were met by the leader of this new band. He is a fine figure of a man – tall, bearded, appropriately bedecked in warlike apparel, and possessed of a face full of strength, humour, and quiet assurance. His name is Petrakoiorgis – in other words, 'Peter George', or just 'P.G.' to us – and Paddy tells me that he was a wealthy and influential merchant before he took to the mountains and set himself up as a chief of guerrillas. Until armed and subsidized by the British he had maintained the band at his own expense, and this had given him a flying start over other would-be leaders.

At this point we sent Andoni and several *andartes* ahead of us, telling them to arrange a system of fire-signals on the southern slopes of the mountain, so that when we, the main party, reached the top we should be able to see if the coast were clear. We expected that the climb would take us at least twice the normal time, because the gradient was much too steep for the General's mule, and we were obliged to make the old man climb all the way up on foot – this, in ten-minute shifts, interspersed with pauses for resting or the smoking of a cigarette. Paddy and I thought the General managed it pretty well, for he plodded up step by step without complaint, whereas he could easily have pleaded incapability and thus have made things very difficult for us. But the Cretans thought otherwise, and they consistently insisted that he was going slowly on purpose. Even George and Manoli nagged us to do something to make him go faster; but we ignored their complaints, considering that a misplaced word now could well result in his refusal to climb another step.

When we reached the snowline the climbing became more difficult – slippery where the surface had iced over and treacherous where holes or gaps were loosely filled with snow. Then it began to drizzle, and as we reached the shaved scalp of the mountain an icy wind swept into our faces and cut through our clothes.

It was almost dusk when finally we found ourselves overlooking the southern coast of Crete – or, to be more accurate, in the direction of the southern coast, for the mountain mist had reduced visibility to less than two hundred yards. However, we decided to take no chances of being sighted, and it was agreed that we should wait until darkness fell before starting to make the descent. We took shelter in a disused shepherd's hut which had been so battered by the wind and the weather that its roof and two of its walls had crumbled to the ground. In this riddled retreat we sat and waited, listening the while to the continued grumblings of our henchmen. They were all out of temper and made little effort to conceal their ill-feelings towards the General; and, although he did not understand a word they said, I think he must have sensed the atmosphere of antagonism, for he kept very quiet and sat by himself in a corner, not speaking.

We had brought no food with us, and the cold served to accentuate the emptiness in our stomachs. Paddy and I went out of the hut and searched among rocks for those mountain dandelions which have such a pleasant, bitter taste. To the casual observer, I suppose, we might have been hunting for gentians in an Alpine snow; but no gentian could at that moment have been so satisfying as the grey-leafed weeds which we greedily stuffed into our mouths.

As the last light of day was swept off the mountain-top a scout came to us and said that he had spotted the first of Andoni's fire-signals on the southern slope.

We began the descent.

Everyone was cold and hungry, and the night had suddenly enveloped us with so complete a blackness that you could not go more than a few steps downward without slipping, stumbling, or falling. It took us two hours to reach the bottom of the snow-belt, and then we found ourselves groping between the wind-curved branches of stunted trees. Twigs would snap back into our face, and brambles would tear at your clothes and hands. The oaths and curses on all sides were a fitting mirror to the ugly mood of our companions, and there were times when Paddy and I felt seriously for the safety of the wretched General in our midst.

We were descending so slowly that it soon became apparent that we could not hope to reach our intended destination before daylight, so after a brief conference with our *andarte* guides we decided to make for a near-by sheepfold. The shepherd there, we were assured, was a good friend of P.G.'s band, and his discretion could be trusted with confidence.

At three o'clock in the morning we reached the sheepfold. The shepherd was delighted to see us, telling George and Manoli that he was greatly honoured that we had selected his hut to which to bring the General. He gave us water, cheese, and a little bread to eat, and these we swallowed ravenously. The General was very tired and, as before, he fell asleep while sittiing in front of the fire. We allowed him to sleep undisturbed for an hour or two; but then the shepherd said it was time we were moving to a cave where we could hide during the day, so we roused the General and moved on once more.

The cave was not far distant, and we reached it with over an hour to spare before dawn. Its entrance was small and perpendicular, and its interior was as musty as a catacomb, with dripping walls and a floor soaked by subterranean humidity. But it was deep enough for the lighting of a fire, so we built up a large pile of logs and started a smoky blaze. Everyone crowded round the flames, and some managed to go to sleep, but for most of us the cold dampness allowed us to do no more than doze off for a few moments at a time. We piled wet logs on to the fire, which filled the cave with a blanket of smoke, but we persevered, and somehow managed to keep alive what little warmth there was.

Dawn broke, but scarcely a glimmer of light found its way down to us, and presently, when the sun began to shine upon the outer world, it was tantalizing to find that the temperature in the cave did not rise by one degree. In a vain attempt to warm ourselves we lit a second fire in another part of the cave, and we have kept these two blazes going all day long; but sleep is out of the question, for it is only possible to heat one side of your body while the other freezes.

This cave, we have been told, was a renowned hiding-place during the Cretan's war with the Turks, and our *andarte* guides said that if we cared to look for ourselves we should discover how, in its depths, there was room enough to house literally hundreds of men.*

Paddy and I resolved to do some exploring, so we equipped ourselves with torches, descended to the bottom of the cave, and crawled downward through a concealed entrance which was no bigger than a coal-hole. We groped along a low passageway, then suddenly found ourselves standing at the entrance to a large chamber. The floor was sprinkled with rushes, and in odd corners we saw numbers of animals' skulls. From this chamber there spread three further tunnels, and it was along one of these that we crawled – what price Ariadne's thread of scarlet? – until we found ourselves in an even larger chamber, which was so thickly speared with stalactites and stalagmites that we had the impression of standing at the end of some vast and colonnaded hall.

* This, too, might well have been the Dictean cave, the birthplace of Zeus, and many Cretans will tell you that there is no question but that it is so. Of all the caves on Mount Ida it is certainly the one which is most eligible for such a distinction.

To have explored any farther would perhaps have been to run the risk of losing ourselves, so we contented ourselves with peering into the hollow roots of passageways that gaped at us on all sides. To speculate upon the size of this labyrinthine cave would serve to bring accusations of exaggeration upon one's head, and I can only say that as we returned to the outer air we felt that we had just seen something wonderful and rare. I should like one day to return here and explore the place from end to end, for there is no knowing what one might discover in its depths. (And to think that one used to complain of not being able to find one's bedroom at the Royal Danieli!)

After our midday bread and cheese – (waterless, despite the dampness of the cave, for the local spring has run dry) – a messenger arrived with a note from Andoni. This told us, first, that despite their threats the Germans had as yet taken no reprisals in the Heraklion district (which led us to believe that our letter in the car must have been discovered), and secondly, that during the morning considerable numbers of lorried infantry had arrived in all the foothill villages preparatory to the drawing of a cordon around the base of the mountain. To-morrow, the message continued, the Germans would in all probability start an organized drive up the mountain, so it would be best for us if we were immediately to leave this hideout and try to break through the cordon before it was too late.

It certainly seems that the Germans have a good idea of our whereabouts, though how they've got their information I can't imagine. We have decided to act on Andoni's advice and make a dash for it to-night.

I hope the General stands up to the continuance of our march. He has had little sleep to-day, and the descent from Ida left him extremely tired. A few minutes ago I asked him what he thought of having to march again to-night. He shrugged his shoulders and replied that physically he could manage it, but that spirutally he was filled with a *post coitum triste* feeling. He smiled as he spoke – a hopeless sort of smile – in a way that made one feel a kind of sympathy for the mental anguish from which he is so obviously suffering.

The sun has left the sky, and soon we shall be on our way.

1 May
Last night we set off soon after dark and travelled as quickly and as

quietly as possible. Fortunately a good, strong mule had been brought for the General, so our progress was not hindered by his slow walking. We marched for three hours without a stop, making for a rendezvous where Andoni, we believed, was waiting to meet us before leading us along a special route towards the coast.

When we reached the rendezvous we found no trace of either Andoni or anyone else; so after waiting a few moments we sent George and Manoli, both of whom know this district very well, to search for any place in the vicinity which might answer the same description as the spot at which we had arrived – for there was certainly a chance that we had missed our mark or mistaken our direction in the dark. However, after half an hour of searching, George and Manoli returned. They said they had gone to every likely spot in the area and that they had found no sign whatever of Andoni.

We waited until midnight. It was very cold, and we tried to keep ourselves warm by running around in circles or pommelling one another. Then we began to grow anxious. It appeared either that there had been some drastic misunderstanding or else that Andoni had been captured while we, all unwittingly, were being surrounded.

It was now that Paddy suddenly thought of re-reading the note which Andoni had sent us during the afternoon; and so, with a torch hooded under his coat, he slowly read out the message. I cannot describe our feelings when he had finished – for it transpired that Manoli (who had originally read us the message in the cave) had misinterpreted the substance of the most important sentence. What Andoni had really said was. 'Do *not* try to come through to-night.'

Then it began to pour with rain. We had no alternative but to take shelter in a covered-in ditch which was close at hand . . . and it is in that same ditch that we are still hiding.

It rained incessantly all this morning, and our boots are inches deep in water. We have eaten nothing since yesterday evening, but needless to say we have had all that we want in the way of God's good drink. Yesterday there was food but no water, and to-day it's the other way round. That's how it goes. Wallace Beery's moustaches are drooping and dripping; Grigori's plate-like beret has wilted like a candle in the tropics; Nikko's little calpac number looks as sorry as a kitchen rag; and even George and Manoli, though struggling to smile if one grins at them, are a picture of storm-ridden orphanhood. The General, looking supremely dejected (and understandably so), is crouched in the ditch with a dripping blanket tented over his head. The fact that the ditch is overgrown with saplings and creepers does not serve to exclude the rain, but merely means that where ordinarily there would be ten small drops there is now one big one.

At ten o'clock in the morning Andoni arrived, looking very surprised to see us. He explained that last night the Germans had drawn a cordon of a thousand men around the foot of Ida, and it had been for this reason (since he had learned of the proposed German move earlier in the day) that he had considered it best to advise us against trying to get through. Thus it appears that we, in complete ignorance, have overcome our greatest danger. How close we passed to the German posts last night I scarcely dare to think, but it must have been a very near thing.

All day we have been wondering if the Germans have yet put their threats into practice. So far, thank goodness, we have heard no reports of reprisals; but, on the other hand, it appears that our ruse of leaving the car close to the submarine beach has not deceived the Germans into believing that we have left the island. Their increased activity in this area is only too obvious a proof that they have a shrewd idea of our movements and intentions.

To-day we have received no messages from anybody, so there is nothing for us to do but wait. I wish we could find a more attractive hideout. This ditch is hell. The only good piece of news we have heard is that Andoni's home village is not far distant from here, and to-night he intends to go to his house to bring us some food.

Paddy and I are feeling the anticlimax of this business acutely. It seems that we now have everything to lose and nothing whatsoever to gain, and the only sort of excitement left to us is of the unpleasant kind. Ah me!

2 May
Still in the same ditch, still no messages.

It rained all night long and most of this morning. Everything, including the pages of this diary, is soaking wet, and our morale in general is at a pretty low ebb. It is a blessing that Andoni has successfully been able to organize the food situation, for both before dawn and after sunset various members of his family bring us baskets of meat, eggs, cheese, and bread.

We heard at midday from Andoni that Cairo Radio broadcast the news of the kidnapping on 30 April and 1 May, but the announcer had said that 'Kreipe is *being* taken off the island.' Small wonder that the Germans weren't taken in by our letter!

The General has again been complaining of the pain in his leg, and this may well be due to the dampness of his clothes, but on the whole he has been behaving most reasonably and causes us little trouble. I think he realizes now that in the event or our being caught he himself would stand little chance of escaping with his life. For him dreams and reality appear to be jumbled up in his mind, one beginning before the other ends, so that at one moment he will be talkative and cheerful, and at the next, as he suddenly remembers his sorry plight, morose and brooding. This morning he was speculating on what he would say to von Arnim and other captive generals when he meets them in England; but he seemed to come to no decision.

Still no news of Tom Dumbabin. I wonder what's happened to him?

16.00

A German aeroplane has been flying over the district this afternoon dropping more pamphlets. We have managed to find a few of them. Their tone is distinctly milder than in the previous ukase, and the blame now rests, they say, upon Communists and that section of the population 'sold to the British'. These elements, they continue, will be ruthlessly pursued and exterminated. The implied corollary of all this is the exoneration of the Cretans as a whole and the placing of the blame on a selected few; so it seems that our letter did, in fact, serve its own especial purpose. The tone of the pamphlet as a whole reflects a remarkable come-down on the part of the Germans, and the General says that, since they are bound to look foolish whichever course they take in the matter of reprisals, the whole business is, in his own words, 'an awful slap in the face for General Brauer'.

The General appears to be a little hurt because, as far as he has seen, the Germans have not made any serious attempts to recapture him. He would certainly think differently if he were to know what a close shave we had two nights ago, but we have told him nothing about it, and are doing our best to make him believe that we are miles away from any German positions. In actual fact, the nearest enemy post is a quarter of a mile away, but so far we have seen no signs of patrolling or other activity in this direction.

If the messages which we are expecting arrive, and if luck stays with us, we can cherish a faint hope of leaving Crete in a couple of days. Will it really be the 4th again?

3 May

Last night we moved to a new hiding-place – a thicket of brambles and saplings – which is not far from the old ditch, but altogether a pleasanter spot. It is situated on the eastern slope and close to the top of a hillock, and owing to the steepness of the gradient the earth is much drier under foot. There is no shelter, however, and if there is more rain we shall once again be soaked to the skin. Mercifully the weather has cheered up to-day and, although the sky is heavy with clouds, not a drop of rain has fallen.

All day long we have waited in vain for messages.

Early this morning our scouts arrived with the most distressing news that two hundred Germans are now stationed on the very beach which we had intended to use for our departure. This means that we have no hope of leaving Crete until we have (*a*) found a new and suitable beach, (*b*) made contact with a wireless set, (*c*) sent a fresh message to Cairo informing headquarters of the change, and (*d*) waited several days for a motor-launch to arrive. Even now there may not be time to warn Brian Coleman that the beach to which he is coming is manned by Germans, for it is possible that he may be having a try to-night.

We have arrived at the following plan:

Paddy will go now to contact a set personally, and he will remain with it so as to be able to maintain direct communication with headquarters. I, in the meantime, together with the General and a few henchmen, will journey slowly westward in a line more or less parallel to the coast. Paddy and I will keep in touch by runner, and shall meet again as soon as he has arranged a date for our departure from the island.

The nearest wireless set – that belonging to Dick Barnes in the west – is at least a day's journey from here, so Paddy proposes to leave us after dark to-night and to complete the distance to-morrow. He is going to take George with him, while the rest of the party will remain with me.

At midday Micky and Elias arrived from Heraklion. They had made most of the journey by bus, but owing to our constant change of position they had found difficulty in locating us, and had been obliged to walk a considerable distance. Rather to our amusement, the were both extremely regretful that they had come in their slick town shoes instead of wearing heavy boots like the rest of us, and as soon as they arrived they sat down, removed their footwear, and with sorry faces nursed their blistered toes. They were both full of stories about German reactions and activities around Heraklion, and, best of all, were able to confirm the fact that no reprisals have yet been taken against the populace. They also told us that the General's ADC and the sentries at the Villa Ariadne have been arrested by the Gestapo.

We passed on this latter bit of news to the General. He said that he did not mind a scrap about his ADC's arrest, because the man was an idiot and would shortly have got the sack in any case; but he felt sorry for the sentries, for he considered that they were not to be blamed. We thought that this might be a good moment to ask him about the circumstances which had led to his leaving his headquarters on the night of the ambush with neither companions nor escort. In reply he said that he and certain other officers, including the ADC, had decided to have a game of cards before returning to their billets. He had telephoned to the Villa Ariadne and ordered his dinner to be served at 21.30 (instead of at eight), and so, although at 21.15 the card came was still in progress, he had announced his intention of going home. None of his companions, however, had felt inclined to leave the game, so he had told his ADC to follow along in one of the other cars when the party broke up. A few minutes later, alone with his chauffeur, he had met with our little reception. He again mentioned the strange premonition he had had that something unpleasant was going to happen to him at the road junction; and then, shaking his head, he relapsed once more into that dream-world which occupies so much of his time.

It is growing dark now, and I can see Andoni coming towards us up the slope with a basket of food under his arm. So we shall soon have a meal, and then Paddy and George will set off on their journey.

4 May
It rained all night long, and, as was inevitable, we are once again soaked to the skin. Around me I see a picture of human misery, and

I know that if my companions feel half as uncomfortable as I do they must be feeling terrible.

During the night the General and I had to share a blanket. First he would wake up and drag it over to his side, then I in turn would repeat the action for my own benefit. Thus, with the rain playing its unwelcome music on the leaves above and large drops of water splashing on to our faces, we slept extremely little. This morning, now that the sun has risen and the day is clear, we have had quite a good laugh about our duel. The General does not grudge me my claims on the blanket; but for my part I know that I am on the losing side, for he has the ability of being able to sleep at any hour of the day – a thing I cannot do – and therefore the loss of a few hours' rest at night-time means only slight discomfort to him. I know his secret, but have in vain tried to apply it to my own ends. He always takes an enormous swig of *raki*, of which he has become very fond, just before turning in, and this sleeping-draught has him slumbering soundly within a matter of minutes. I am all envy.

I have noticed that he is growing quite fond of Manoli, and have seen the two of them back-chatting on several occasions – though how they converse I cannot imagine, for they have scarcely a word of any language in common. This attachment is a welcome event, because hitherto the General has always grown anxious whenever Paddy and I have left him alone with the Cretans. I think he is slowly coming to realize that the island folk are not the barbarians he imagined them to be.

14.00
And now, as I suppose one might have expected, no sooner has Paddy gone than messages have started to pour in from every direction. There is a letter from Sandy, another from Dick Barnes in the west, and a third from the headquarters on Ida.

The message from Dick Barnes tells us that a motor-launch did actually come for us on the night of 2 May, but on receiving no signal from the shore it had left without sending a landing-party to the beach.. For the next four nights, the message continues, a boat will come to the same spot to try to make contact with us. How infuriating it is to know that all this is happening at a beach which is no more than a few hours' walk from here and that we can do absolutely nothing about it. The two hundred Germans are still stationed there, and it is quite possible that they will not move for weeks. The only thing for us to do is to leave this hideout to-night and start on our journey westward. It is obvious that we cannot hope to leave the island inside a week, but the farther west we travel the less chance there is of our being caught. When finally we do leave it seems that we may have to go by submarine.

Sandy sends a charming little note attached to his factual letter:

Dear Billy,

All my rosiest and sincerest and completest congratulations on presenting everyone with quite the best war story yet! You must certainly come back – thanks for your note – and I will getin touch with Zahari and see that your Russians are well cared for until your return. I shall look forward immensely, needless to say, to hear full details later. I'm so glad the old man is a charmer – so much nicer than if he was grumpy. Bless you – and once more I raise an aged, tattered, almost historic but very respectful hat – and all the best of luck for the rest of the journey.

SANDY

P.S. Please send any spare sleeping tablets, with instructions if possible, back to me with this messenger. And could you post the enclosed letter to Mrs R. when you get back to Cairo?

I have completely run out of reading matter, so spend my day like any Cretan, contemplating.

All being well, we should leave here soon after dark this evening.

5 May

Just before dusk last night Andoni arrived with the news that our route westward had been blocked by Germans, who had moved in large numbers to form a cordon covering the very area through which we are hoping to pass. It looks as though another enemy drive is about to develop, but Andoni's news was not details enough to give us a complete picture of what is likely to happen, so I straightway sent him off again to try to discover the enemy's dispositions and to select some mountain track which might lead us through the cordon. It was obvious enough that we should not attempt the journey last night, so we have remained in this thicket for an extra day; but it is essential that we should leave to-night, for to delay any longer would probably result in our being completely surrounded.

At all events, the weather to-day is fine, and with any luck it will continue to be so, for the sky is bright and clear. It is not yet warm, and the nights are very cold, but so long as there is no rain one's powers of resistance are much stronger. If only we had the spare clothing and blankets which we left at Pavlo's house it would make all the difference to our comfort, but Manoli assures me that we shall never see our kit again. He says he knows Pavlo well enough to believe that that rogue is now a very well-dressed guerrilla, handsomely equipped with British arms and apparel.

I have had a bit of a row with the General.

All morning he has been complaining – about the food, the pain in his leg and a new-found pain in his stomach, the lack of sleep, the absence of anything to read, and on and on – and I began to be a little fed up with this constant moan. From the very beginning both Paddy and I have been aware of his discomfort, and by way of compensation we have fed him as best we could, have treated him with respect (synthetic but apparent), and done everything possible to make things easier for him. It seemed that these attentions had escaped his notice, and I rather naturally resented his grumbling, but I said nothing and did my best to humour him. At midday, however, we heard a number of explosions coming from the direction of the Mesara plain, and soon afterwards a scout came andtold us that three villages – Lochria, Kamares, and Magarikari – had been blown up as reprisals for a gun-running affair which had taken place last month, and also for some indiscretions on the part of P.G.'s gang during the Easter celebrations. I passed on this information to the General; whereupon he grinned – an expression on his face which I have not seen before – and said that it was so easy and so practical for the Germans to kill Cretans or destroy villages as reprisals for anything the British did. I was not at all polite in my reply, and told him that if he didn't change his tune I should be obliged to treat him as the prisoner he was. So now I am in the ridiculous position of sitting beside him and not speaking to him. It's the sort of tragi-comic situation which could only arise in circumstances such as these. Manoli has developed a suspicion that the old man may try to escape while we are sleeping; so I now detail members of our band to watch him day and night and to follow him whenever he makes his frequent but necessary departures into the depths of the thicket. We sleep with our weapons under our heads.

Still no news of British pamphlets' having been dropped. But in any case it would now be too late.

To-day the sun is strong enough for us to put out our clothes to dry, and during the morning we began to feel warm for the first time since leaving Pavlo's house. I hear birds singing, cicadas in close harmony, and Wallace Beery humming Turkish love-songs in an undertone. We await Andoni's return.

The Landing on Kuralei

James A. Michener

We would have captured Kuralei according to plan if it had not been for Lt Col Kenjuro Hyaichi. An honor graduate from California Tech, he was a likely choice for the job the Japs gave him.

As soon as our bombers started to soften up Konora, where we built the airstrip, the Jap commander on Kuralei gave Hyaichi his instructions: 'Imagine that you are an American admiral. You are going to invade this island. What would you do?'

Hyaichi climbed into a plane and had the pilot take him up 12,000 feet. Below him Kuralei was like a big cashew nut. The inside bend faced north, and in its arms were two fine sandy bays. They were the likely places to land. You could see that even from the air.

But there was a small promontory protruding due south from the outside bend. From the air Hyaichi studied that promontory with great care. 'Maybe they know we have the two bays fortified. Maybe they will try that promontory.'

The colonel had his pilot drop to three thousand feet and then to five hundred. He flew far out to sea in the direction from which our search planes came. He roared in six times to see if he could see what an American pilot, scared and in a hurry, would think he saw.

Then he studied the island from a small boat. Had it photographed from all altitudes and angles. He studied the photographs for many days. He had two Jap spies shipped in one night from Truk. They crept ashore at various points. 'What did you see?' he asked them. 'Did you think the bay was defended? What about that promontory?'

He had two trained observers flown over from Palau. They had never seen Kuralei before. When their plane started to descend, they were blindfolded. 'The bays?' Hyaichi asked. 'And that promontory?

Did you think there was sand in the two small beaches there? Did you see the cliffs?'

Jap intelligence officers brought the colonel sixty-page and seventy-page reports of interrogations of American prisoners. They showed him detailed studies of every American landing from Guadalcanal to Konora. They had a complete book on Admiral Kester, an analysis of each action the admiral had ever commanded. At the end of his study Lt Col Hyaichi ruled out the possibility of our landing at the promontory. 'It couldn't be done,' he said. 'That coral shelf sticking out two hundred yards would stop anything they have.'

But before the colonel submitted his recommendations that all available Jap power be concentrated at the northern bays, a workman in Detroit had a beer. After his beer this workman talked with a shoe salesman from St Louis, who told a brother-in-law, who passed the word on to a man heading for Texas, where the news was relayed to Mexico and thence to Tokyo and Kuralei that 'General Motors is building a boat that can climb over the damnedest stuff you ever saw.'

Lt Col Hyaichi tore up his notes. He told his superiors: 'The Americans will land on either side of the promontory.' 'How can they?' he was asked. 'They have new weapons,' he replied. 'Amphibious tanks with treads for crossing coral.' Almost a year before, Admiral Nimitz had decided that when we hit Kuralei we would not land at the two bays. 'We will hit the promontory. We will surprise them.'

Fortunately for us, Lt Col Hyaichi's superiors were able to ignore his conclusions. It would be folly, they said, to move defenses from the natural northern landing spots. All they would agree to was that Hyaichi might take whatever material he could find and set up secondary defenses at the promontory. How well he did his job you will see.

At 0527 our first amphibs hit the coral shelf which protruded underwater from the shore. It was high tide, and they half rode, half crawled toward land. They had reached a point twenty feet from the beach, when all hell ripped loose. Lt Col Hyaichi's fixed guns blasted our amphibs right out of the water. Our men died in the air before they fell back into the shallow water on the coral shelf. At low tide their bodies would be found, gently wallowing in still pools of water.

A few men reached shore. They walked the last twenty feet through a haze of bullets.

At 0536 our second wave reached the imaginary line twenty feet from shore. The Jap five-inch guns ripped loose. Of nine craft going in, five were sunk. Of the three hundred men in those five amphibs, more than one hundred were killed outright. Another hundred died wading to shore. But some reached shore. They formed a company, the first on Kuralei.

It was now dawn. The LSC-108 had nosed in toward the coral reef to report the landings. We sent word to the flagship. Admiral Kester started to sweat at his wrists. 'Call off all landing attempts for eighteen minutes,' he said.

At 0544 our ships laid down a gigantic barrage. How had they missed those five-inch guns before? How had anything lived through our previous bombardment? Many Japs didn't. But those hiding in Lt Col Hyaichi's special pillboxes did. And they lived through this bombardment, too.

On the small beach to the west of the promontory 118 men huddled together as the shells ripped overhead. Our code for this beach was Green, for the one to the east, Red. The lone walkie-talkie on Green Beach got the orders: 'Wait till the bombardment ends. Proceed to the first line of coconut trees.' Before the signalman could answer, one of our short shells landed among the men. The survivors re-formed, but they had no walkie-talkie.

At 0602 the third wave of amphibs set out for the beach. The vast bombardment rode over their heads until they were onto the coral shelf. Then a shattering silence followed. It was full morning. The sun was rising. Our amphibs waddled over the coral. At the fatal twenty-foot line some Japs opened up on the amphibs. Three were destroyed. But eight got through and deposited their men ashore. Jap machine gunners and snipers tied into tall trees took a heavy toll. But our men formed and set out for the first line of coconut trees.

They were halfway to the jagged stumps when the Japs opened fire from carefully dug trenches behind the trees. Our men tried to outfight the bullets but could not. They retreated to the beach. The coconut grove was lined with fixed positions, a trench behind each row of trees.

As our men withdrew they watched a hapless amphib broach to on the coral. It hung suspended, turning slowly. A Jap shell hit it full in the middle. It rose in the air. Bodies danced violently against the rising sun and fell back dead upon the coral. 'Them poor guys,' the Marines on the beach said.

At 0631 American planes appeared. F6F's. They strafed the first trench until no man but a Jap could live. They bombed. They ripped Green Beach for twelve minutes. Then the next wave of amphibs went in. The first two craft broached to and were blown to shreds of steaming metal. 'How can those Japs live?' the man at my side said. In the next wave four more amphibs were sunk.

So at 0710 the big ships opened up again. They fired for twenty-eight minutes this time, concentrating their shells about sixty yards inland from the first row of coconut stumps. When they stopped, our men tried again. This time they reached the trees, but were again repulsed. Almost four hundred men were ashore now. They formed in tight circles along the edge of the beach.

At 0748 we heard the news from Red Beach, on the other side of the promontory. 'Repulsed four times. First men now safely ashore!' Four times! we said to ourselves. Why, that's worse than here! It couldn't be! Yet it was, and when the tide started going out on Red Beach, the Japs pushed our men back onto the coral.

This was fantastic! When you looked at Alligator back in Noumea you knew it was going to be tough. But not like this! There were nine rows of coconut trees. Then a cacao grove. The edge of that grove was Line Albany. We had to reach the cacaos by night. We knew that an immense blockhouse of sod and stone and concrete and coconut trees would have to be reduced there before night. We were expected to start storming the blockhouse by 1045. That was the schedule.

At 1400 our men were still hudddled on the beach. Kester would not withdraw them. I don't think they would have come back had he ordered them to do so. They hung on, tried to cut westward but were stopped by the cliffs, tried to cut eastward but were stopped by fixed guns on the promontory.

At 1422 Admiral Kester put into operation his alternative plan. While slim beachheads were maintained at Red and Green all available shock troops were ordered to hit the rugged western side of the promontory. We did not know if landing craft could get ashore. All we knew was that if they could land, and if they could establish a beach, and if they could cut a path for men and tanks down through the promontory, we might flank each of the present beachheads and have a chance of reaching the cacaos by dark.

At 1425 we got our orders. 'LCS-108. All hands to Objective 66.' The men winked at one another. They climbed into the landing barges. The man whose wife had a baby girl. The young boy who slept through his leave in Frisco. They went into the barges. The sun was starting to sink westward as they set out for the shore.

Lt Col Hyaichi's men waited. Then two fixed guns whose sole purpose was to wait for such a landing fired. Shells ripped through the barges. One with men from 108 turned in the air and crushed its men to death. They flung their arms outward and tried to fly free, but the barge caught them all. A few swam out from under. They could not touch bottom, so they swam for the shore, as they had been trained to do. Snipers shot at them. Of the few, a few reached shore. One man shook himself like a dog and started into the jungle. Another made it and cried out to a friend. 'Red Beach! Green Beach! Sonova Beach!' You can see that in the official reports. 'At 1430 elements from LCS-108 and the transport *Julius Kennedy* started operations at Sonova Beach.'

The hidden guns on the promontory continued firing. Kester sent eight F6F's after them. They dived the emplacements and silenced one of the guns. I remember one F6F that seemed to hang for minutes over a Jap gun, pouring lead. It was uncanny. Then the plane exploded! It burst into a violent puff of red and black. Its pieces were strewn over a wide area, but they hurt no one. They were too small.

At 1448 a rear-admiral reported to Kester, 'Men securely ashore at Objective 66.' The admiral diverted all available barges there. Sonova Beach was invaded. Barges and men turned in the air and died alike with hot steel in their guts, but the promontory was invaded. Not all our planes nor all our ships could silence those damned Jap gunners, but Sonova Beach, that strip of bleeding coral, it was invaded.

At 1502 Admiral Kester sent four tanks ashore at Sonova with orders to penetrate the promontory and to support whichever beach seemed most promising. Two hundred men went along with axes and shovels. I watched the lumbering tanks crawl ashore and hit their first banyan trees. There was a crunching sound. I could hear it above the battle. The tanks disappeared among the trees.

At 1514 came the Japs' only airborne attack that day. About thirty bombers accompanied by forty fighters swept in from Truk. They tried for our heavy ships. The fleet threw up a wilderness of flak. Every ship in the task force opened up with its five-inchers, Bofors, Oerlikons, three-inchers and .50 calibers. The air was heavy with lead. Some Jap planes spun into the sea. I watched a bomber spouting flames along her port wing. She dived to put them out. But a second shell hit her amidships. The plane exploded and fell into the ocean in four pieces. The engine, badly afire, hit the water at an angle and ricocheted five times before it sank in hissing rage.

One of our transports was destroyed by a Jap bomb. It burst into lurid flame as it went down. Near by, a Jap plane plunged into the sea. Then, far aloft an F6F came screaming down in a mortal dive. 'Jump!' a thousand voices urged. But the pilot never did. The plane crashed into the sea right behind the Jap bomber and burned.

A Jap fighter, driven low, dived at the 108 and began to strafe. I heard dull spats of lead, the firing of our own guns, and a cry. The Jap flashed past, unscathed. Men on the 108 cursed. The young skipper looked ashen with rage and hurried aft to see who had been hit.

The Japs were being driven off. As a last gesture a fighter dived into the bridge of one of our destroyers. There were four explosions. The superstructure was blown away with three dozen men and four officers. Two other fighters tried the same trick. One zoomed over the deck of a cruiser and bounced three times into a boiling sea. The other came down in a screaming vertical spin and crashed deep into the water not far from where I stood. There were underwater explosions and a violent geyser spurting high in the air.

Our planes harried the remaining Japs to death, far out at sea. Our pilots, their fuel exhausted, went into the sea themselves. Some died horribly of thirst, days later. Others were picked up almost immediately and had chicken for dinner.

While the Jap suicide planes were crashing into the midst of the fleet, a Jap shore battery opened up and hit an ammunition ship. It disintegrated in a terrible, gasping sound. Almost before the last fragments of that ship had fallen into the water, our big guns found the shore battery and destroyed it.

Meanwhile power had been building up on Green Beach. At 1544, with the sun dropping lower toward the ocean, they tried the first row of coconut trees again. They were driven back. This time, however, not quite to the coral. They held onto some good positions fifteen or twenty yards inland.

At 1557 Admiral Kester pulled them back onto the coral. For the last time that day. He sent the planes in to rout out that first trench. This time with noses almost in the coconut stumps, our fliers roared up and down the trenches. They kept their powerful .50's aimed at the narrow slits like a woman guiding a sewing machine along a predetermined line. But the .50's stitched death.

At 1607 the planes withdrew. At a signal, every man on that beach, every one, rose and dashed for the first trench. The Japs knew they were coming, and met them with an enfilading fire. But the Green Beach boys piled on. Some fell wounded. Others died standing up and took a ghostly step toward the trench. Some dropped from fright and lay like dead men. But most went on, grunting as they met the Japs with bayonets. There was a muddled fight in the trench. Then things were quiet. Some Americans started crawling back to pick up their wounded. That meant our side had won.

Japs from the second trench tried to lead a charge against the exhausted Americans. But some foolhardy gunners from a cruiser laid down a pinpoint barrage of heavy shells. Just beyond the first trench. It was dangerous, but it worked. The Japs were blown into small pieces. Our men had time to reorganize. They were no longer on coral. They were inland. On Kuralei's earth.

At 1618 Admiral Kester made his decision. Green Beach was our main chance. To hell with Red. Hang on, Red! But everything we had was thrown at Green. It was our main chance. 'Any word from the tanks?' 'Beating down the peninsula, sir.' It was no use banging the table. If the tanks could get through, they would.

At 1629 about a hundred amphibs sped for Green Beach. They were accompanied by a tremendous barrage that raked the western end of the beach toward the cliffs. Thirty planes strafed the Jap part of the promontory. A man beside me started yelling frantically. A Jap gun, hidden somewhere in that wreckage, was raking our amphibs. 'Get that gun!' he shouted. 'It's right over there! ' He jumped up and down and had to urinate against the bulkhead. 'Get that gun!' Two amphibs were destroyed by the gun. But more than ninety made the beach. Now, no matter how many Japs counterattacked, we had a chance to hold the first trench.

'A tank!' our lookout shouted. I looked, but saw none. Then, yes!

There was a tank! But it was a Jap tank. Three of them! The Jap general had finally conceded Lt. Col. Hyaichi's point. He was rushing all moveable gear to the promontory. And our own tanks were still bogged down in the jungle.

'LCS-108! Beach yourself and use rockets!' The order came from the flagship. With crisp command the young skipper got up as much speed as possible. He drove his small craft as near the battle lines as the sea would take it. We braced ourselves and soon felt a grinding shock as we hit coral. We were beached, and our bow was pointed at the Jap tanks.

Our first round of rockets went off with a low swish and headed for the tanks. 'Too high!' the skipper groaned. The barrage shot into the cacao trees. The Jap tanks bore down on our men in the first ditch. Our next round of rockets gave a long hisss. The first tank exploded loudly and blocked the way of the second Jap.

At this moment a Jap five-incher hit the 108. We heeled over to port. The men at the rocket-launching ramps raised their sights and let go with another volley. The second tank exploded. Japs climbed out of the manhole. Two of them dived into the cacaos. Two others were hit by rifle fire and hung head downward across the burning tank.

The third Jap tank stopped firing at our men in the first trench and started lobbing shells at LCS-108. Two hit us, and we lay far over on the coral. The same foolhardy gunners on the cruiser again ignored our men in the first trench. Accurately they plastered the third tank. We breathed deeply. The Japs probably had more tanks coming, but the first three were taken care of.

Our skipper surveyed his ship. It was lost. It would either be hauled off the reef and sunk or left there to rot. He felt strange. His first command! What kind of war was this? You bring a ship all the way from Norfolk to stop two tanks. On land. You purposely run your ship on a coral reef. It's crazy. He damned himself when he thought of that Jap plane flashing by. It had killed two of his men. Not one of our bullets hit that plane. It all happened so fast. 'So fast!' he muttered. 'This is a hell of a war!'

At 1655 the Marines in trench one, fortified by new strength from the amphibs, unpredictably dashed from the far western end of their trench and overwhelmed the Japs in the opposite part of trench two. Then ensued a terrible, hidden battle as the Marines stolidly swept down the Jap trench. We could see arms swinging above the trench, and bayonets. Finally, the men in the eastern end of trench one could stand the suspense no longer. Against the bitterest kind of enemy fire, they rushed past the second row of coconut stumps and joined their comrades. Not one Jap survived that brutal, silent, hidden struggle. Trench two was ours.

At 1659 more than a thousand Jap reinforcements arrived in the area. Not yet certain that we had committed all our strength to Green Beach, about half the Japs were sent to Red. Lt. Col. Hyaichi, tight-lipped and sweating, properly evaluated our plan. He begged his commanding officer to leave only a token force at Red Beach and to throw every ounce of man and steel against Green. This was done. But as the reserves moved through the coconut grove, the skipper of the LCS-108 poured five rounds of rockets right into their middle. Results passed belief. Our men in trench two stared in frank astonishment at what the rockets accomplished. Then, shouting, they swamped the third Jap trench before it could be reinforced.

At 1722, when the sun was beginning to eat into the treetops of Kuralei, our tanks broke loose along the shore of the promontory. Sixty sweating footslogging axmen dragged themselves after the tanks. But ahead lay an unsurmountable barrier of rock. The commanding officer of the tanks appraised the situation correctly. He led his ménage back into the jungle. The Japs also foresaw what would happen next. They moved tank destroyers up. Ship fire destroyed them. We heard firing in the jungle.

At 1740 our position looked very uncertain. We were still six rows from Line Albany. And the Japs had their blockhouse right at the edge of the cacaos. Our chances of attaining a reasonably safe position seemed slight when a fine shout went up. One of our tanks had broken through! Alone, it dashed right for the heart of the Jap position. Two enemy tanks, hidden up to now, swept out from coconut emplacements and engaged our tank. Bracketed by shells from each side, our tank exploded. Not one man escaped.

But we soon forgot the first tank. For slowly crawling out of the jungle came the other three. Their treads were damaged. But they struggled on. When the gloating Jap tanks saw them coming, they hesitated. Then, perceiving the damage we had suffered, the Japs charged. Our tanks stood fast and fired fast. The Japs were ripped up and down. One quit the fight. Its occupants fled. The other came on to its doom. Converging fire from our three tanks caught it. Still it came. Then, with a fiery gasp, it burned up. Its crew did not even try to escape.

At 1742 eleven more of our tanks landed on Sonova Beach. You would have thought their day was just beginning. But the sun was on their tails as they grunted into the jungle like wild pigs hunting food.

An endless stream of barges hit Green Beach. How changed things were! On one wave not a single shot from shore molested them. Eight hundred Yanks on Kuralei without a casualty. How different that was! We got Admiral Kester's message: 'Forty-eight minutes of daylight. A supreme effort.'

At 1749 the Japs launched their big counter-attack. They swept from their blockhouse in wild assault. Our rockets sped among them, but did not stop them. It was the men in trench three that stopped them.

How they did so, I don't know. Japs swarmed upon them, screaming madly. With grenades and bayonets the banzai boys did devilish work. Eighty of our men died in that grim assault. Twelve had their heads completely severed.

But in the midst of the melee, two of our three tanks broke away from the burning Jap tanks and rumbled down between trench three and trench four. Up and down that tight area-way they growled. A Jap suicide squad stopped one by setting it afire. Their torches were their own gasoline-soaked bodies. Our tankmen, caught in an inferno, tried to escape. From trench three, fifty men leaped voluntarily to help them. Our men surrounded the flaming tank. The crewmen leaped to safety. In confusion, they ran not to our lines but into trench four. Our men, seeing them cut down, went mad. They raged into trench four and killed every Jap. In a wild spontaneous sweep they swamped trench five as well!

Aboard the LCS-108 we could not believe what we had seen. For in their rear were at least a hundred and twenty Japs still fighting. At this moment reinforcements from the amphibs arrived. The Japs were caught between heavy fire. Not a man escaped. The banzai charge from the blockhouse had ended in complete rout.

At 1803 Admiral Kester sent his message: 'You can do it. Twenty-seven minutes to Line Albany!' We were then four rows from the blockhouse. But we were sure that beyond trench seven no trenches had been dug. But we also knew that trenches six and seven were

tougher than anything we had yet tackled. So for the last time
Admiral Kester sent his beloved planes in to soften up the trenches.
In the glowering dusk they roared up and down between the charred
trees, hiccuping vitriol. The grim, terrible planes withdrew. There
was a moment of waiting. We waited for our next assault. We waited
for new tanks to stumble out of the promontory. We waited in itching
dismay for that tropic night. We were so far from the blockhouse!
The sun was almost sunk into the sea.

What we waited for did not come. Something else did. From our
left flank, toward the cliffs, a large concentration of Jap reinforcements broke from heavy cover and attacked the space between
trenches one and two. It was seen in a flash that we had inadequate
troops at that point. LCS-108 and several other ships made an
instantaneous decision. We threw all our fire power at the point of
invasion. Rockets, five-inchers, eight-inchers and intermediate fire hit
the Japs. The were stopped cold. Our lines held.

But I can still see one flight of rockets we launched that day at
dusk. When the men in trench two saw the surprise attack coming on
their flank, they turned sideways to face the new threat. Three
Americans nearest the Japs never hesitated. Without waiting for a
command to duty they leaped out of their trench to meet the enemy
head on. Our rockets crashed into the advancing Japs. The three
voluntary fighters were killed. By their own friends.

There was no possible escape from this tragedy. To be saved, all
those men needed was less courage. It was nobody's fault but their
own. Like war, rockets once launched cannot be stopped.

It was 1807. The sun was gone. The giant clouds hanging over
Kuralei turned gold and crimson. Night birds started coming into the
cacao grove. New Japs reported to the blockhouse for a last stand.
Our own reinforcements shuddered as they stepped on dead Japs.
Night hurried on.

At 1809, with guns spluttering, eight of our tanks from Sonova
Beach burst out of the jungle. Four of them headed for the blockhouse.
Four tore right down the alleyway between trenches five and six.
These took a Jap reinforcement party head on. The fight was foul
and unequal. Three Japs set fire to themselves and tried to immolate
the tank crews. They were actually shot to pieces. The tanks rumbled
on.

At the blockhouse it was a different story. Tank traps had been well built in that area. Our heavies could not get close to the walls. They stood off and hammered the resilient structure with shells.

'Move in the flame-throwers. Everything you have. Get the block-house.' The orders were crisp. They reached the Marines in trench five just as the evening star became visible. Eight husky young men with nearly a hundred pounds of gear apiece climbed out of the trench. Making an exceptional target, they blazed their way across six and seven with hundreds of protectors. They drew a slanting hailstorm of enemy fire. But if one man was killed, somebody else grabbed the cumbersome machinery. In the gathering darkness they made a weird procession.

A sergeant threw up his hands and jumped. 'No trenches after row seven!' A tank whirled on its right tread and rumbled over. Now, with tanks on their right and riflemen on their left, the flame-throwers advanced. From every position shells hit the blockhouse. It stood. But its defenders were driven momentarily away from the portholes. This was the moment!

With hoarse cries our flame-throwers rushed forward. Some died and fell into their own conflagration. But three flame-throwers reached the portholes. There they held their spuming fire. They burned away the oxygen of the blockhouse. They seared eyes, lips, and more than lungs. When they stepped back from the portholes, the blockhouse was ours.

Now it was night! From all sides Japs tried to infiltrate our lines. When they were successful, our men died. We would find them in the morning with their throats cut. When you found them so, all thought of sorrow for the Japs burned alive in the blockhouse was erased. They were the enemy, the cruel, remorseless, bitter enemy. And they would remain so, every man of them, until their own red sun sank like the tired sun of Kuralei.

Field headquarters were set up that night on Green Beach. I went ashore in the dark. It was strange to think that so many men had died there. In the wan moonlight the earth was white like the hair of an old woman who has seen much life. But in spots it was red, too. Even in the moonlight.

Unit leaders reported. 'Colonel, that schedule for building the airstrip is busted wide open. Transport carrying LARU-8 hit. Heavy casualties.' I grabbed the man's arm.

'Was that the transport that took a direct hit?' I asked.

'Yes,' he said, still dazed. 'Right in the belly.'

'What happened?' I rattled off the names of my friends in that unit. Benoway, in the leg. The cook, dead. The old skipper, dead. 'What happened to Harbison?' I asked.

The man looked up at me in the yellow light. 'Are you kidding, sir?'

'No! I know the guy.'

'*You* know him? Hmmm. I guess you don't! You haven't heard?' His eyes were excited.

'No.'

'Harbison pulled out four days before we came north. All the time we were on Efate he couldn't talk about anything but war. 'Hold me back, fellows. I want to get at them!' But when our orders came through he got white in the face. Arranged it by airmail through his wife's father. Right now he's back in New Mexico. Rest and rehabilitation leave.'

'That little Jewish photographic officer you had?' I asked, sick at the stomach.

'He's dead,' the man shouted. He jumped up. 'The old man's dead. The cook's dead. But Harbison is back in New Mexico.' He shouted and started to cry.

'Knock it off!' a Marine colonel cried.

'The man's a shock case,' I said. The colonel came over.

'Yeah. He's the guy from the transport. Fished him out of the drink. Give him some morphine. But for Christ's sake shut him up. Now where the hell *is* that extra .50 caliber ammo?'

The reports dragged in. We were exactly where Alligator said we should be. Everything according to plan. That is, all but one detail. Casualties were far above estimate. It was that bastard Hyaichi. We hadn't figured on him. We hadn't expected a Cal Tech honors graduate to be waiting for us on the very beach we wanted.

'We'll have to appoint a new beachmaster,' a young officer reported to the colonel.

'Ours get it?' the colonel asked.

'Yessir. He went inland with the troops.'

'Goddam it!' the colonel shouted. 'I told Fry a hundred times . . .'

'It wasn't his fault, sir. Came when the Japs made that surprise attack on the flank.'

There was sound of furious firing to the west. The colonel looked up.

'Well,' he said. 'We lost a damned good beachmaster. You take over tomorrow. And get that ammo in and up.'

I grabbed the new beachmaster by the arm. 'What did you say?' I whispered.

'Fry got his.'

'Tony Fry?'

'Yes. You know him?'

'Yes,' I said weakly. 'How?'

'If you know him, you can guess.' The young officer wiped his face. 'His job on the beach was done. No more craft coming in. We were attacking the blockhouse. Fry followed us in. Our captain said, 'Better stay back there, lieutenant. This is Marines' work.' Fry laughed and turned back. That was when the Japs hit from the cliffs. Our own rockets wiped out some of our men. Fry grabbed a carbine. But the Japs got him right away. Two slugs in the belly. He kept plugging along. Finally fell over. Didn't even fire the carbine once.'

I felt sick. 'Thanks,' I said.

The colonel came over to look at the man from LARU-8. He grabbed my arm. 'What's the matter, son? You better take a shot of that sleeping stuff yourself,' he said.

'I'm all right,' I said. 'I was thinking about a couple of guys.'

'We all are,' the colonel said. He had the sad, tired look that old men wear when they have sent young men to die.

Looking at him, I suddenly realized that I didn't give a damn about Bill Harbison. I was mad for Tony Fry. That free, kind, independent man. In my bitterness I dimly perceived what battle means. In civilian life I was ashamed until I went into uniform. In the States I was uncomfortable while others were overseas. At Noumea I thought, 'The guys on Guadal! They're the heroes!' But when I reached Guadal I found that all the heroes were somewhere farther up the line. And while I sat in safety aboard the LCS-108 I knew where the heroes were. They were on Kuralei. Yet, on the beach itself only a few men ever really fought the Japs. I suddenly realized that from the farms, and towns, and cities all over America an unbroken line ran straight to the few who storm the blockhouses. No matter where along that line you stood, if you were not the man at the end of it, the ultimate man with his sweating hands upon the blockhouse, you didn't know what war was. You had only an intimation, as of a bugle blown far in the distance. You might have flashing insights, but you did not know. By the grace of God you would never know.

Alone, a stranger from these men who had hit the beaches, I went out to dig a place to sleep. Two men in a foxhole were talking. Eager for some kind of companionship, I listened in the darkness.

'Don't give me that stuff,' one was saying. 'Europe is twice as tough as this!'

'You talk like nuts,' a younger voice retaliated. 'These yellows is the toughest fighters in the world.'

'I tell you not to give me that crap!' the older man repeated. 'My brother was in Africa. He hit Sicily. He says the Krauts is the best all round men in uniform!'

'Lend me your lighter.' There was a pause as the younger man used the flameless lighter.

'Keep your damned head down,' his friend warned.

'If the Japs is such poor stuff, why worry?'

'Like I said,' the other reasoned. 'Where did you see any artillery barrage today? Now if this was the Germans, that bay would of been filled with shells.'

'I think I saw a lot of barges get hell,' the young man argued.

'You ain't seen nothing! You mark my words. Wait till we try to hit France! I doubt we get a ship ashore. Them Krauts is plenty tough. They got mechanized, that's what they got!'

'You read too many papers!' the second Marine argued. 'You think when they write up this war they won't say the Japs was the toughest soldier we ever met?'

'Look! I tell you a thousand times. We ain't met the Jap yet. Mark my words. When we finally tangle with him in some place like the Philippines . . .'

'What were we doin' today? Who was them little yellow fellows? Snow White and the Seven Dwarfs? Well, where the hell was Snow White?'

'Now wait! Now wait just a minute! Answer me one question. Just one question! Will you answer me one question?'

'Shoot!'

'No *ifs* and *ands* and *buts*?'

'Shoot!'

'All right! Now answer me one question. Was it as tough as you thought it would be?'

There was a long moment of silence. These were the men who had landed in the first wave. The young man carefully considered the facts. 'No,' he said.

'See what I mean?' his heckler reasoned.

'But it wasn't no pushover, neither,' the young man defended himself.

'No, I didn't say it was. But it's a fact that the Nips wasn't as tough as they said. We got ashore. We got to the blockhouse. Little while ago I hear we made just about where we was expected to make.'

'But on the other hand,' the young Marine said, 'it wasn't no picnic. Maybe it *was* as tough as I thought last night!'

'Don't give me that stuff! Last night we told each other what we thought. And it wasn't half that bad. Was it? Just a good tough tussle. I don't think these Japs is such hot stuff. Honest to God I don't!'

'You think the way the Germans surrendered in Africa makes them tougher?'

'Listen, listen. I tell you a hundred times. They was pushed to the wall. But wait till we hit France. I doubt we get a boat ashore. That's one party I sure want to miss.'

There was a moment of silence. Then the young man spoke again. 'Burke?' he asked. 'About last night. Do you really think he'll run for a fourth term?'

'Listen! I tell you a hundred times! The American public won't stand for it. Mark my words. They won't stand for it. I thought we settled that last night.'

'But I heard Colonel Hendricks saying . . .'

'Please, Eddie! You ain't quotin' that fathead as an authority, are you?'

'He didn't do so bad gettin' us on this beach, did he?'

'Yeah, but look how he done it. A slaughter!'

'You just said it was easier than you expected.'

'I was thinkin' of over there,' Burke said. 'Them other guys at Red Beach. Poor bastards. We did all right. But this knuckle-brain Hendricks. You know, Eddie, honest to God, if I had a full bladder I wouldn't let that guy lead me to a bathroom!'

'Yeah, maybe you're right. He's so dumb he's a colonel. That's all. A full colonel.'

'Please, Eddie! We been through all that before. I got a brother wet the bed till he was eleven. He's a captain in the Army. So what? He's so dumb I wouldn't let him make change in my store. Now he's a captain! So I'm supposed to be impressed with a guy that's a colonel! He's a butcher, that's what he is. Like I tell you a hundred times, the guy don't understand tactics.'

This time there was a long silence. Then Eddie spoke, enthusiastically. 'Oh, boy! When I get back to Bakersfield!' Burke made no comment. Then Eddie asked, 'Tell me one thing, Burke.'

'Shoot.'

'Do you think they softened this beach up enough before we landed?'

Burke considered a long time. Then he gave his opinion: 'It's like I tell you back in Noumea. They got to learn.'

'But you don't think they softened it up enough, do you, Burke?'

'Well, we could of used a few more big ones in there where the Japs had their guns. We could of used a few more in there.'

Silence again. Then: 'Burke, I was scared when we hit the beach.'

'Just a rough tussle!' the older man assured him. 'You thank your lucky stars you ain't goin' up against the Krauts. That's big league stuff!'

Silence and then another question: 'But if the Japs is such pushovers, why you want me to stand guard tonight while you sleep?'

Burke's patience and tolerance could stand no more. 'Goddammit,' he muttered. 'It's war! If we was fighting the Eyetalians, we'd still stand guard! Plain common sense! Call me at midnight. I'll let you get some sleep.'

Shall I Live for a Ghost?

Richard Hillary

I was falling. Falling slowly through a dark pit. I was dead. My body, headless, circled in front of me. I saw it with my mind, my mind that was the redness in front of the eye, the dull scream in the ear, the grinning of the mouth, the skin crawling on the skull. It was death and resurrection. Terror, moving with me, touched my cheek with hers and I felt the flesh wince. Faster, faster . . . I was hot now, hot, again one with my body, on fire and screaming soundlessly. Dear God, no! No! Not that, not again. The sickly smell of death was in my nostrils and a confused roar of sound. Then was all quiet. I was back.

Someone was holding my arms.

'Quiet now. There's a good boy. You're going to be all right. You've been very ill and you mustn't talk.'

I tried to reach up my hand but could not.

'Is that you, nurse? What have they done to me?'

'Well, they've put something on your face and hands to stop them hurting and you won't be able to see for a little while. But you mustn't talk: you're not strong enough yet.'

Gradually I realized what had happened. My face and hands had been scrubbed and then sprayed with tannic acid. The acid had formed into a hard black cement. My eyes alone had received different treatment; they were coated with a thick layer of gential violet. My arms were propped up in front of me, the fingers extended like witches' claws, and my body was hung loosely on straps just clear of the bed.

I can recollect no moments of acute agony in the four days which I spent in that hospital; only a great sea of pain in which I floated almost with comfort. Every three hours I was injected with morphia, so while imagining myself quite coherent, I was for the most part in a semi-stupor. The memory of it has remained a confused blur.

Two days without eating, and then periodic doses of liquid food taken through a tube. An appalling thirst, and hundreds of bottles of ginger beer. Being blind, and not really feeling strong enough to care. Imagining myself back in my plane, unable to get out, and waking to find myself shouting and bathed in sweat. My parents coming down to see me and their wonderful self-control.

They arrived in the late afternoon of my second day in bed, having with admirable restraint done nothing the first day. On the morning of the crash my mother had been on her way to the Red Cross, when she felt a premonition that she must go home. She told the taxi-driver to turn about and arrived at the flat to hear the telephone ringing. It was our Squadron Adjutant, trying to reach my father. Embarrassed by finding himself talking to my mother, he started in on a glamorized history of my exploits in the air and was bewildered by my mother cutting him short to ask where I was. He managed somehow after about five minutes of incoherent stuttering to get over his news.

They arrived in the afternoon and were met by Matron. Outside my ward a twittery nurse explained that they must not expect to find me looking quite normal, and they were ushered in. The room was in darkness; I just a dim shape in one corner. Then the blinds were shot up, all the lights switched on, and there I was. As my mother remarked later, the performance lacked only the rolling of drums and a spotlight. For the sake of decorum my face had been covered with white gauze, with a slit in the middle through which protruded my lips.

We spoke little, my only coherent remark being that I had no wish to go on living if I were to look like Alice. Alice was a large country girl who had once been our maid. As a child she had been burned and disfigured by a Primus stove. I was not aware that she had made any impression on me, but now I was unable to get her out of my mind. It was not so much her looks as her smell I had continually in my nostrils and which I couldn't dissociate from the disfigurement.

They sat quietly and listened to me rambling for an hour. Then it was time for my dressings and they took their leave.

The smell of ether. Matron once doing my dressing with three orderlies holding my arms; a nurse weeping quietly at the head of the bed, and no remembered sign of a doctor. A visit from the lifeboat crew that had picked me up, and a terrible longing to make sense when talking to them. Their inarticulate sympathy and assurance of quick recovery. Their discovery that an ancestor of mine had founded the lifeboats, and my pompous and unsolicited promise of a subscription. The expectation of an American ambulance to drive me up to the Masonic Hospital (for Margate was used only as a clearing station). Believing that I was already in it and on my way, and waking to the disappointment that I had not been moved. A dream that I was fighting to open my eyes and could not: waking in a sweat to realize it was a dream and then finding it to be true. A sensation of time slowing down, of words and actions, all in slow motion. Sweat, pain, smells, cheering messages from the Squadron, and an overriding apathy.

Finally I was moved. The ambulance appeared with a cargo of two somewhat nervous ATS women who were to drive me to London, and, with my nurse in attendance, and wrapped in an old grandmother's shawl, I was carried aboard and we were off. For the first few miles I felt quite well, dictated letters to my nurse, drank bottle after bottle of ginger beer, and gossiped with the drivers. They described the countryside for me, told me they were new to the job, expressed satisfaction at having me for a consignment, asked me if I felt fine. Yes, I said, I felt fine; asked my nurse if the drivers were pretty, heard her answer yes, heard them simpering, and we were all very matey. But after about half an hour my arms began to throb from the rhythmical jolting of the road. I stopped dictating, drank no more ginger beer, and didn't care whether they were pretty or not. Then they lost their way. Wasn't it awful and shouldn't they stop and ask? No, they certainly shouldn't: they could call out the names of the streets and I would tell them where to go. By the time we arrived at Ravenscourt Park I was pretty much all-in. I was carried into the hospital and once again felt the warm September sun burning my face. I was put in a private ward and had the impression of a hundred excited ants buzzing around me. My nurse said good-bye and started to sob. For no earthly reason I found myself in tears. It had been a lousy hospital, I had never seen the nurse anyway, and I was now in very good hands; but I suppose I was in a fairly exhausted state. So there we all were, snivelling about the place and getting nowhere. Then the charge nurse came up and took my arm and asked me what my name was.

'Dick,' I said.

'Ah,' she said brightly. 'We must call you Richard the Lion Heart.'

I made an attempt at a polite laugh but all that came out was a dismal groan and I fainted away. The house surgeon took the opportunity to give me an anaesthetic and removed all the tannic acid from my left hand.

At this time tannic acid was the recognized treatment for burns. The theory was that in forming a hard cement it protected the skin from the air, and encouraged it to heal up underneath. As the tannic started to crack, it was to be chipped off gradually with a scalpel, but after a few months of experience, it was discovered that nearly all pilots with third-degree burns so treated developed secondary infection and septicaemia. This caused its use to be discontinued and gave us the dubious satisfaction of knowing that we were suffering in the cause of science. Both my hands were suppurating, and the fingers were already contracting under the tannic and curling down into the palms. The risk of shock was considered too great for them to do both hands. I must have been under the anaesthetic for about fifteen minutes and in that time I saw Peter Pease killed.

He was after another machine, a tall figure leaning slightly forward with a smile at the corner of his mouth. Suddenly from nowhere a Messerschmitt was on his tail about 150 yards away. For two seconds nothing happened. I had a terrible feeling of futility. Then at the top of my voice I shouted, 'Peter, for God's sake look out behind!'

I saw the Messerschmitt open up and a burst of fire hit Peter's machine. His expression did not change, and for a moment his machine hung motionless. Then it turned slowly on its back and dived to the ground. I came-to, screaming his name, with two nurses and the doctor holding me down on the bed.

'All right now. Take it easy, you're not dead yet. That must have been a very bad dream.'

I said nothing. There wasn't anything to say. Two days later I had a letter from Colin. My nurse read it to me. It was very short, hoping that I was getting better and telling me that Peter was dead.

Slowly I came back to life. My morphia injections were less frequent and my mind began to clear. Though I began to feel and think again coherently I still could not see. Two VADs fainted while helping with my dressings, the first during the day and the other at night. The second time I could not sleep and was calling out for someone to stop the beetles running down my face, when I heard my nurse say fiercely, 'Get outside quick: don't make a fool of yourself here!' and the sound of footsteps moving towards the door. I remember cursing the unfortunate girl and telling her to put her head between her knees. I was told later that for my first three weeks I did little but curse and blaspheme, but I remember nothing of it. The nurses were wonderfully patient and never complained. Then one day I found that I could see. My nurse was bending over me doing my dressings, and she seemed to me very beautiful. She was. I watched her for a long time, grateful that my first glimpse of the world should be of anything so perfect. Finally I said:

'Sue, you never told me that your eyes were so blue.'

For a moment she stared at me. Then, 'Oh, Dick, how wonderful,' she said. 'I told you it wouldn't be long'; and she dashed out to bring in all the nurses on the block.

I felt absurdly elated and studied their faces eagerly, gradually connecting them with the voices that I knew.

'This is Anne,' said Sue. 'She is your special VAD and helps me with all your dressings. She was the only one of us you'd allow near you for about a week. You said you liked her voice.' Before me stood an attractive fair-haired girl of about twenty-three. She smiled and her teeth were as enchanting as her voice. I began to feel that hospital had its compensations. The nurses called me Dick and I knew them all by their Christian names. Quite how irregular this was I did not discover until I moved to another hospital where I was considerably less ill and not so outrageously spoiled. At first my dressings had to be changed every two hours in the daytime. As this took over an hour to do, it meant that Sue and Anne had practically no time off. But they seemed not to care. It was largely due to them that both my hands were not amputated.

Sue, who had been nursing since seventeen, had been allocated as my special nurse because of her previous experience of burns, and because, as Matron said, 'She's our best girl and very human.' Anne had been married to a naval officer killed in the *Courageous*, and had taken up nursing after his death.

At this time there was a very definite prejudice among the regular nurses against VADs. They were regarded as painted society girls, attracted to nursing by the prospect of sitting on the officers' beds and holding their hands. The VADs were rapidly disabused of this idea, and, if they were lucky, were finally graduated from washing bed-pans to polishing bed-tables. I never heard that any of them grumbled, and they gradually won a reluctant recognition. This prejudice was considerably less noticeable in the Masonic than in most hospitals: Sue, certainly, looked on Anne as a companionable and very useful lieutenant to whom she could safely entrust my dressings and general upkeep in her absence. I think I was a little in love with both of them.

The Masonic is perhaps the best hospital in England, though at the time I was unaware how lucky I was. When war broke out the Masons handed over a part of it to the services; but owing to its vulnerable position very few action casualties were kept there long. Pilots were pretty quickly moved out to the main Air Force Hospital, which I was not in the least eager to visit. Thanks to the kind-hearted duplicity of my house surgeon, I never had to; for every time they ran up and asked for me he would say that I was too ill to be moved. The Masonic's great charm lay in that it in no way resembled a hospital; if anything it was like the inside of a ship. The nursing staff were very carefully chosen, and during the regular blitzing of the district, which took place every night, they were magnificent.

The Germans were presumably attempting to hit Hammersmith Bridge, but their efforts were somewhat erratic and we were treated night after night to an orchestra of the scream and crump of falling bombs. They always seemed to choose a moment when my eyes were being irrigated, when my poor nurse was poised above me with a glass undine in her hand. At night we were moved into the corridor, away from the outside wall, but such was the snoring of my fellow sufferers that I persuaded Bertha to allow me back in my own room after Matron had made her rounds.

Bertha was my night nurse. I never discovered her real name, but to me she was Bertha from the instant that I saw her. She was large and gaunt with an Eton crop and a heart of gold. She was engaged to a merchant seaman who was on his way to Australia. She made it quite clear that she had no intention of letting me get round her as I did the day staff, and ended by spoiling me even more. At night when I couldn't sleep we would hold long and heated arguments on the subject of sex. She expressed horror at my ideas of love and on her preference for a cup of tea. I gave her a present of four pounds of it when I was discharged. One night the Germans were particularly persistent, and I had the unpleasant sensation of hearing a stick of bombs gradually approaching the hospital, the first some way off, the

next closer, and the third shaking the building. Bertha threw herself
across my bed; but the fourth bomb never fell. She got up quickly,
looking embarrassed, and arranged her cap.

'Nice fool I'd look if you got hit in your own room when you're
supposed to be out in the corridor,' she said, and stumped out of the
room.

An RASC officer who had been admitted to the hospital with the
painful but unromantic complaint of piles protested at the amount of
favouritism shown to me merely because I was in the RAF. A
patriotic captain who was in the same ward turned on him and said:
'At least he was shot down defending his country and didn't come in
here with a pimple on his bottom. The Government will buy him a
new Spitfire, but I'm damned if it will buy you a new arse.'

One day my doctor came in and said that I could get up. Soon
after I was able to totter about the passages and could be given a
proper bath. I was still unable to use my hands and everything had
to be done for me. One evening during a blitz, my nurse, having led
me along to the lavatory, placed a prodigiously long cigarette-holder
in my mouth and lighted the cigarette in the end of it. Then she went
off to get some coffee. I was puffing away contentedly when the
lighted cigarette fell into my pyjama trousers and started smouldering. There was little danger that I would go up in flames, but I
thought it advisable to draw attention to the fact that all was not
well. I therefore shouted 'Oi!' Nobody heard me. 'Help!' I shouted
somewhat louder. Still nothing happened, so I delivered myself of my
imitation of Tarzan's elephant call of which I was quite proud. It
happened that in the ward opposite there was an old gentleman who
had been operated on for a hernia. The combination of the scream of
the falling bombs and my animal cries could mean only one thing.
Someone had been seriously injured, and he made haste to dive over
the side of the bed. In doing so he caused himself considerable
discomfort: convinced of the ruin of his operation and the imminence
of his death, he added his cries to mine. His fears finally calmed, he
could see nothing humorous in the matter and insisted on being
moved to another ward. From then on I was literally never left alone
for a minute.

For the first few weeks, only my parents were allowed to visit me
and they came every day. My mother would sit and read to me by
the hour. Quite how much she suffered I could only guess, for she

gave no sign. One remark of hers I shall never forget. She said: 'You should be glad this has to happen to you. Too many people told you how attractive you were and you believed them. You were well on the way to becoming something of a cad. Now you'll find out who your real friends are.' I did.

When I was allowed to see people, one of my first visitors was Michael Cary (who had been at Trinity with me and had a First in Greats). He was then private secretary to the Chief of Air Staff. He was allowed to stay only a short time before being shoo'd away by my nurses, but I think it may have been time enough to shake him. A short while afterwards he joined the Navy as an AB. I hope it was not as a result of seeing me, for he had too good a brain to waste polishing brass. Colin came down whenever he had leave from Hornchurch and brought me news of the Squadron.

Ken MacDonald, Don's brother who had been with 'A' Flight at Dyce, had been killed. He had been seen about to bale out of his blazing machine at 1,000 feet; but as he was over a thickly populated area he had climbed in again and crashed the machine in the Thames.

Pip Cardell had been killed. Returning from a chase over the Channel with Dexter, one of the new members of the Squadron, he appeared to be in trouble just before reaching the English coast. He jumped; but his parachute failed to open and he came down in the sea. Dexter flew low and saw him move. He was still alive, so Dexter flew right along the shore and out to sea, waggling his wings to draw attention and calling up the base on the RT. No boat put out from the shore, and Dexter made a crash landing on the beach, drawing up ten yards from a nest of buried mines. But when they got up to Pip he was dead.

Howes had been killed, even as he had said. His Squadron had been moved from Hornchurch to a quieter area, a few days after I was shot down. But he had been transferred to our Squadron, still deeply worried because as yet he had failed to bring anything down. The inevitable happened; and from his second flight with us he failed to return.

Rusty was missing, but a clairvoyant had written to Uncle George swearing that he was neither dead nor captured. Rusty, he said (whom he had never seen), had crashed in France, badly burned, and was being looked after by a French peasant.

As a counter to this depressing news Colin told me that Brian, Raspberry, and Sheep all had the DFC, and Brian was shortly to get a bar to his. The Squadron's confirmed score was nearing the hundred mark. We had also had the pleasure of dealing with the Italians. They had come over before breakfast, and together with 41 Squadron we were looking for them. Suddenly Uncle George called out:

'Wops ahead.'

'Where are they?' asked 41 Squadron.

'Shan't tell you,' came back the answer. 'We're only outnumbered three to one.'

Colin told me that it was the most unsporting thing he had ever had to do, rather like shooting sitting birds, as he so typically put it. We got down eight of them without loss to ourselves and much to the annoyance of 41 Squadron.

Then one day I had an unexpected visitor. Matron opened the door and said 'Someone to see you,' and Denise walked in. I knew at once who she was. It was unnecessary for her to speak. Her slight figure was in mourning and she wore no make-up. She was the most beautiful person I have ever seen.

Much has been written on Beauty. Poets have excelled themselves in similes for a woman's eye, mouth, hair; novelists have devoted pages to a geometrically accurate description of their heroines' features. I can write no such description of Denise. I did not see her like that. For me she had an inner beauty, a serenity which no listing of features can convey. She had a perfection of carriage and a grace of movement that were strikingly reminiscent of Peter Pease, and when she spoke it might have been Peter speaking.

'I hope you'll excuse me coming to see you like this,' she said; 'but I was going to be married to Peter. He often spoke of you and wanted so much to see you. So I hope you won't mind me coming instead.'

There was so much I wanted to say, so many things for us to talk over, but the room seemed of a sudden unbearably full of hurrying jolly nurses who would not go away. The bustle and excitement did little to put her at her ease, and her shyness was painful to me. Time came for her to leave, and I had said nothing I wanted to say. As soon as she was gone I dictated a note, begging her to come again and to give me a little warning. She did. From then until I was able to get out, her visits did more to help my recovery than all the expert nursing and medical attention. For she was the very spirit of courage. It was useless for me to say to her any of the usual words of comfort for the loss of a fiancé, and I did not try. She and Peter were two halves of the same person. They even wrote alike. I could only pray that time would cure that awful numbness and bring her back to the fullness of life. Not that she was broken. She seemed somehow to have gathered his strength, to feel him always near her, and was determined to go on to the end in the cause for which he had given his life, hoping that she too might be allowed to die, but feeling guilty at the selfishness of the thought.

She believed passionately in freedom, in freedom from fear and oppression and tyranny, not only for herself but for the whole world.

'For the whole world.' Did I believe that? I still wasn't sure. There was a time – only the other day – when it hadn't mattered to me if it was true or not that a man could want freedom for others than himself. She made me feel that this might be no mere catch-phrase of politicians, since it was something to which the two finest people I had ever known had willingly dedicated themselves. I was impressed. I saw there a spirit far purer than mine. But was it for me? I didn't know. I just didn't know.

I lay in that hospital and watched summer turn to winter. Through my window I watched the leaves of my solitary tree gradually turn brown, and then, shaken by an ever-freshening wind, fall one by one. I watched the sun change from a great ball of fire to a watery glimmer, watched the rain beating on the glass and the small broken clouds drifting a few hundred feet above, and in that time I had ample opportunity for thinking.

I thought of the men I had known, of the men who were living and the men who were dead; and I came to this conclusion. It was to the Carburys and the Berrys of this war that Britain must look, to the tough practical men who had come up the hard way, who were not fighting this war for any philosophical principles or economic ideals; who, unlike the average Oxford undergraduate, were not flying for aesthetic reasons, but because of an instinctive knowledge that this was the job for which they were most suited. These were the men who had blasted and would continue to blast the Luftwaffe out of the sky while their more intellectual comrades would alas, in the main be killed. They might answer, if asked why they fought, 'To smash

Hitler!' But instinctively, inarticulately, they too were fighting for the things that Peter had died to preserve.

Was there perhaps a new race of Englishmen arising out of this war, a race of men bred by the war, a harmonious synthesis of the governing class and the great rest of England; that synthesis of disparate backgrounds and upbringings to be seen at its most obvious best in RAF squadrons? While they were now possessed of no other thought than to win the war, yet having won it, would they this time refuse to step aside and remain indifferent to the peace-time fate of the country, once again leave government to the old governing class? I thought it possible. Indeed, the process might be said to have already begun. They now had as their representative Churchill, a man of initiative, determination, and no Party. But they would not always have him; and what then? Would they see to it that there arose from their fusion representatives, not of the old gang, deciding at Lady Cufuffle's that Henry should have the Foreign Office and George the Ministry of Food, nor figureheads for an angry but ineffectual Labour Party, but true representatives of the new England that should emerge from this struggle? And if they did, what then? Could they unite on a policy of humanity and sense to arrive at the settlement of problems which six thousand years of civilization had failed to solve? And even though they should fail, was there an obligation for the more thinking of them to try to contribute, at whatever personal cost 'their little drop,' however small, to the betterment of mankind? Was there that obligation, was that the goal towards which all those should strive who were left, strengthened and confirmed by those who had died? Or was it still possible for men to lead the egocentric life, to work out their own salvation without concern for the rest; could they simply look to themselves – or, more important, could I? I still thought so.

The day came when I was allowed out of the hospital for a few hours. Sue got me dressed, and with a pair of dark glasses, cotton-wool under my eyes, and my right arm in a sling, I looked fairly presentable. I walked out through the swing-doors and took a deep breath.

London in the morning was still the best place in the world. The smell of wet streets, of sawdust in the butchers' shops, of tar melted on the blocks, was exhilarating. Peter had been right: I loved the capital. The wind on the heath might call for a time, but the facile glitter of the city was the stronger. Self-esteem, I suppose, is one cause; for in the city, work of man, one is somebody, feet on the pavement, suit on the body, anybody's equal and nobody's fool; but in the country, work of God, one is nothing, less than the earth, the birds, and the trees; one is discordant – a blot.

I walked slowly through Ravenscourt Park and looked into many faces. Life was good, but if I hoped to find some reflection of my feeling, I was disappointed. One or two looked at me with pity, and for a moment I was angry; but when I gazed again at their faces, closed in as on some dread secret, their owners hurrying along, unseeing, unfeeling, eager to get to their jobs, unaware of the life within them, I was sorry for them. I felt a desire to stop and shake them and say: 'You fools, it's you who should be pitied and not I; for this day I am alive while you are dead.'

And yet there were some who pleased me, some in whom all youth had not died. I passed one girl, and gazing into her face became aware of her as a woman: her lips were soft, her breasts firm, her legs long and graceful. It was many a month since any woman had stirred me, and I was pleased. I smiled at her and she smiled at me. I did not speak to her for fear of breaking the spell, but walked back to lunch on air. After this I was allowed out every day, and usually managed to stay out until nine o'clock, when I drove back through the blitz and the black-out.

'London can take it' was already becoming a truism; but I had been put out of action before the real fury of the night attacks had been let loose, and I had seen nothing of the damage. In the hospital, from the newspapers, and from people who came to see me, I gained a somewhat hazy idea of what was going on. On the one hand I saw London as a city hysterically gay, a city doomed, with nerves so strained that a life of synthetic gaiety alone prevented them from snapping. My other picture was of a London bloody but unbowed, of a people grimly determined to see this thing through, with manpower mobilized; a city unable, through a combined lack of inclination, facility, and time, to fritter away the war in the night-haunts of the capital. I set out to see for myself.

London night-life did exist. Though the sirens might scream and the bombs fall, restaurants and cocktail bars remained open and full every night of the week. I say restaurants and cocktail bars, for the bottle parties and strip-tease cabarets which had a mushroom growth at the beginning of the war had long been closed. Nor was prostitution abroad. Ladies of leisure whose business hours were from eleven till three were perhaps the only citizens to find themselves completely baffled by the black-out. London was not promiscuous: the diners-out in a West End restaurant were no longer the clientele of café society, for café society no longer existed in London. The majority of the so-called smart set felt at last with the outbreak of war a real vocation, felt finally a chance to realize themselves and to orientate themselves to a life of reality. They might be seen in a smart restaurant; but they were there in another guise – as soldiers, sailors, and airmen on forty-eight hours' leave; as members of one of the women's services seeking a few hours' relaxation before again applying themselves wholeheartedly to their jobs; or as civil servants and Government workers who, after a hard day's work, preferred to relax and enjoy the bombing in congenial company rather than return to a solitary dinner in their own flats.

While the bombs were dropping on London (and they were dropping every night in my time in the hospital), and while half London was enjoying itself, the other half was not asleep. It was striving to make London as normal a city by night as it had become by day. Anti-aircraft crews, studded around fields, parks, and streets, were momentarily silhouetted against the sky by the sudden flash of their guns. The Auxiliary Fire Service, spread out in a network of squads through the capital, was standing by, ready at a moment's notice to deal with the inevitable fires; air-raid wardens, tireless in their care of shelters and work of rescue, patrolled their areas watchfully. One heavy night I poked my nose out of the Dorchester, which was rocking gently, to find a cab calmly coasting down Park Lane. I hailed it and was driven back to the hospital. The driver turned to me: 'Thank God, sir,' he said, 'Jerry's wasting 'is time trying to break our morale, when 'e might be doing real damage on some small town.'

With the break of day London shook herself and went back to work. Women with husbands in Government jobs were no longer to be seen at noon draped along the bars of the West End as their first appointment of the day. They were up and at work with determined efficiency in administrative posts of the Red Cross, the women's voluntary services, and the prisoners of war organizations. The Home Guards and air-raid wardens of the previous night would return

home, take a bath, and go off to their respective offices. The soldier
was back with his regiment, the airman with his squadron; the
charming frivolous creatures with whom they had dined were themselves in uniform, effective in their jobs of driving, typing, or nursing.

That, I discovered, was a little of what London was doing. But
what was London feeling? Perhaps a not irrelevant example was an
experience of Sheep Gilroy's when flying with the Squadron. He was
sitting in his bath when a 'flap' was announced. Pulling on a few
clothes and not bothering to put on his tunic, he dashed out to his
plane and took off. A few minutes later he was hit by an incendiary
bullet and the machine caught fire. He baled out, quite badly burned,
and landed by a parachute in one of the poorer districts of London.
With no identifying tunic, he was at once set upon by two hundred
silent and coldy angry women, armed with knives and rolling-pins.
For him no doubt it was a harrowing experience, until he finally
established his nationality by producing all the most lurid words in
his vocabulary; but as an omen for the day when the cream of Hitler's
Aryan youth should attempt to land in Britain it was most interesting.

All this went on at a time when night after night the East End was
taking a terrible beating, and it was rumoured that the people were
ominously quiet. Could their morale be cracking? The answer was
provided in a story that was going the rounds. A young man went
down to see a chaplain whom he knew in the East End. He noticed
not only that the damage was considerable but that the people were
saying practically nothing at all. 'How are they taking it?' He asked
nervously. The chaplain shook his head. 'I'm afraid,' he said, 'that
my people have fallen from grace: they are beginning to feel a little
bitter towards the Germans.'

The understatement in that remark was impressive because it was
typical. The war was practically never discussed except as a joke.
The casual observer might easily have drawn one of two conclusions:
either that London was spent of all feeling, or that it was a city
waiting like a blind man, unseeing, uncaring, for the end. Either
conclusions would have been wide of the mark. Londoners are slow
to anger. They had shown for long enough that they could take it;
now they were waiting on the time when it would be their turn to
dish it out, when their cold rage would need more than a Panzer
division to stamp it out.

Now and then I lunched at home with my mother, who was

working all day in the Prisoners of War Organization, or my father would leave his desk long enough to give me lunch at his club. On one of these occasions we ran into Bill Aitken, and I had coffee with him afterwards. He was still in Army Co-operation and reminded me of our conversation at Old Sarum. 'Do you remember,' he asked, 'telling me that I should have to eat my words about Nigel Bicknell and Frank Waldron? Well, you were certainly right about Nigel.'

'I haven't heard anything,' I said, 'but you sound as though he had renounced his career as Air Force psychologist.'

Bill laughed. 'He's done more than that. He was flying his Blenheim to make some attack on France when one engine cut. He carried on, bombed his objective, and was on his way back when the other engine cut out, too, and his machine came down in the sea. For six hours, until dawn when a boat saw him, he held his observer up. He's got the DFC.'

'I must write to him,' I said. 'But I was right about Frank too. Do you remember your quotation that war was "a period of great boredom, interspersed with moments of great excitement"; and how you said that the real test came in the periods of boredom, since anyone can rise to a crisis?'

'Yes, I remember.'

'Well, I think I'm right in saying that Frank has come through on that score. He's in the Scots Guards with very little to do; but he's considerably more subdued than you'll remember him. When he first got out of the Air Force he thought he could waltz straight into the Guards, but they wouldn't take him until he had been thorugh an OCTU. That was his first surprise. The second was when there was no vacancy in the OCTU for three months. Our Frank, undismayed, hied himself off to France and kicked up his heels in Megève with the *Chasseurs Alpins*, and then in Cannes with the local lovelies. But he came back and went through his course. He was a year behind all his friends – or rather all those that were left, and it sobered him up. I think you'd be surprised if you saw him now.'

Bill got up to leave. 'I should like to see him again,' he said with a smile, 'but of the ex-bad boys, I think you are the best example of a change for the better.'

'Perhaps it's as well that you can't stay,' I said. 'I'm afraid it wouldn't take you long to see that you're mistaken. If anything, I believe even more strongly in the ideas which I held before. Sometime we'll discuss it.'

I spent most evenings with Denise at the house in Eaton Place. It was the usual London house, tall, narrow, and comfortable. Denise was living there alone with a housekeeper, for her father was about to marry again and had moved to the country. At tea-time I would come and find her curled up on the sofa behind the tray, gazing into the fire; and from then until eight o'clock, when I had to drive back to the Masonic, we would sit and talk – mostly of Peter, for it eased her to speak of him, but also of the war, of life, and death, and many lesser things.

Two years before the war she had joined the ATS. Sensiblity and shyness might well have made her unsuited for this service, but when her familiy said as much, they merely fortified her in her determination. After she was commissioned, she fainted on her first parade, but she was not deterred, and she succeeded. She had left the ATS to marry Peter. I was not surprised to learn that she had published a novel, nor that she refused to tell me under what pseudonym, in spite of all my accusations of inverted snobbery. She wished to see nobody but Colin and me, Peter's friends; and though often she would have preferred to be alone, she welcomed me every day, nevertheless. So warm and sincere was her nature, that I might almost have thought myself her only interest. Try as I would, I could not make her think of herself; it was as if she considered that as a person she was dead. Minutes would go by while she sat lost in reverie, her chin cupped in her hand. There seemed nothing I could do to rouse her to consciousness of herself, thaw out that terrible numbness, breathe life into that beautiful ghost. Concern with self was gone out of her. I tried pity, I tried understanding, and finally I tried brutality.

It was one evening before dinner, and Denise was leaning against the mantelpiece, one black heel resting on the fender.

'When are you coming out of mourning?' I asked.

She had been standing with her chin lowered; and now, without lifting it, she raised her eyes and looked at me a moment.

'I don't know,' she said slowly. 'Maybe I never shall.'

I think she sensed that the seemingly innocent question had been put deliberately, though she couldn't yet see why. It had surprised her; it had hurt her, as I had meant it to. Up to now I had been at pains to tread delicately. Now the time had come, I felt, for a direct attack upon her sensibility under the guise of outward stupidity.

'Oh, come, Denise,' I said. 'That's not like you. You know life better than that. You know there's no creepiing away to hide in a dream world. When something really tragic happens – the cutting-off of a man at a moment when he has most reason to live, when he has planned great things for himself – the result for those who love him isn't a whimpering pathos; it's growth, not decline. It makes you a richer person, not a poorer one; better fitted to tackle life, not less fitted for it. I loved Peter, too. But I'm not going to pretend I feel sorry for you; and you ought to be grateful to the gods for having enriched you. Instead, you mope.'

I knew well enough that she wouldn't go under, that this present numb resignation was transitory. But I had been worried too long by her numbness, her rejection of life, and I wanted to end it. She said nothing, and I dared not look at her. I could see her fingers move as I went doggedly on.

'You can't run away from life,' I said. 'You're a living vital person. Your heart tells you that Peter will be with you always, but your senses know that absence blots people out. Your senses are the boundaries of your feeling world, and their power stops with death. To go back and back to places where you were happy with Peter, to touch his clothes, dress in black for him, say his name, is pure self-deception. You drug your senses in a world of dreams, but reality cannot be shut out for long.'

Still she said nothing, and I had a quick look at her. This was far worse than badgering Peter in the train. Her face was tense, slightly flushed, and her eyes were wide open and staring with what I hoped was anger, not pain. I wished to rouse her, and prayed only that I would not reduce her to tears.

'Death is love's crucifixion,' I said brutally. 'Now you go out with Colin and me because we were his friends, we are a link. But we are not only his friends, we are men. When I leave you and say good night, it's not Peter's hand that takes yours, it's mine. It's Colin's touch you feel when he helps you on with your coat. Colin will go away. I shall go back to hospital. What are you going to do then? Live alone? You'll try, but you won't be able. You will go out again – and with people who didn't know Peter, people your senses will force you to accept as flesh and blood, and not fellow players in a tragedy.'

She went over to a sofa opposite me and sat looking out of the window. I could see her breast rise and fall with her breathing. Her face was still tense. The set of her head on her shoulders was so graceful, the lines of her figure were so delicate as she sat outlined against the light, that I became aware with a shock of never before having thought of her as a woman, a creature of flesh and blood. I who had made the senses the crux of my argument had never thought of her except as disembodied spirit. Minutes passed; she said no word; and her silence began almost to frighten me. If she should go on saying nothing, and I had to do all the talking, I didn't know quite what I should end by saying. I was about to attack her again when she spoke, but in a voice so gentle that at first I had trouble hearing her.

'You're wrong, Richard,' she said. 'You are so afraid of anything mystical, anything you can't analyse, that you always begin rationalizing instinctively, in self-defence, fearing your own blind spots. You like to think of yourself as a man who sees things too clearly, too realistically, to be able to have any respect for the emotions. Perhaps you don't feel sorry for me; but I do feel sorry for you.

'I *know* that everything is not over for Peter and me. I know it with all the faith that you are so contemptuous of. We *shall* be together again. We are together now. I feel him constantly close to me; and that is my answer to your cheap talk about the senses. Peter lives within me. He neither comes nor goes, he is ever-present. Even while he was alive there was never quite the tenderness and closeness between us that now is there.'

She looked straight at me and there was a kind of triumph in her face. Her voice was now so strong that I felt there was no defeating her any more, no drawing her out of that morass of mysticism from which I so instinctively recoiled.

'I suppose you're trying to hurt me to give me strength, Richard,' she said; 'but you're only hurting yourself. I have the strength. And let me explain where it comes from, so that we need never revert to the subject again. I believe that in this life we live as in a room with the blinds down and the lights on. Once or twice, perhaps, it is granted us to switch off the lights and raise the blinds. Then for a moment the darkness outside becomes brightness, and we have a glimpse of what lies beyond this life. I believe not only in life after death, but in life before death. This life is to me an intermission lived in spiritual darkness. In this life we are in a state not of being, but of becoming.

'Peter and I are eternally bound up together; our destinies are the same. And you, with your unawakened heart, are in some curious way bound up with us. Oh, yes, you are! In spite of all your intellectual subterfuges and attempts to hide behind the cry of self-realization! You lay in hospital and saw Peter die as clearly as if you had been with him. You told me so yourself. Ever since Peter's death you have been different. It has worked on you; and it's only because it has that I tell you these things. Colin says he would never have believed that anyone could change as you have.'

'That,' said I, 'was pure hallucination. I don't pretend to account for it exactly, but it was that hundredth example of instinct, or intuition, that people are always boasting of while they never mention the ninety-nine other premonitions that were pure fantasy.'

'Please, Richard,' she said, 'let's not talk about Peter and me any more. Your self-realization theory is too glib to stand a real test. To pass coldly through the death and destruction of war, to stand aloof and watch your sensibility absorb experience like a photographic plate, so that you may store it away to use for your own self-development – that's what you had hoped to do, I believe?'

'Of course it is,' I admitted. She was really roused now, and I was pleased.

'Well, you can't! You know you can't, despite that Machiavellian pose of yours. You tell me women are not as I am. I tell you, men are not as you are. Or rather, were. You remember those photographs taken of you before the crash that I saw the other day? Well, I believe that then, before the crash, you could and possibly did feel as you say you still do. I could never have liked you when you looked like that, looked like the man of the theory you still vaunt. Have you read Donne's *Devotions*?'

'Looked through them,' I said.

'In one of them he says this: "Any man's death diminishes me, because I am involved in Mankind." You, too, are involved, Richard; and so deeply that you won't always be able to cover up and protect yourself from the feelings prompted in you by that involvement. You talk about my self-deception: do you really believe you can go through life to the end, always taking and never giving? And do you really imagine that you haven't given to me, haven't helped me? Well, you

have. And what have you got out of it? Nothing! You have given to
me in a way that would have been impossible for you before Peter's
death. You are still giving. You are conferring value on life by feeling
Peter's death as deeply as you do. And you are bound to feel the
death, be recreated by the death, of the others in the Squadron – if
not in the same degree, certainly in the same way. Certainly you are
going to "realize" yourself; but it won't be by leading the egocentric
life. The effect that you will have on everybody you meet will come
not only from your own personality, but from what has been added
to you by all the others who are now dead – what you have so
ungratefully absorbed from them.'

She spoke with great feeling and much of what she said struck
home. It was true that Peter was much in my thoughts, that I felt
him somewhere near me, that he was in fact the touchstone of my
sensiblity at the moment. It was true that the mystical experience of
his death was something which was outside my understanding, which
had still to be assimilated, and yet, and yet . . . I could not help but
feel that with the passage of time this sense of closeness, of affinity,
must fade, that its very intensity was in part false, occasioned by
being ill, and by meeting Denise so shortly afterwards; a Denise who
was no mere shadow of Peter, but Peter's reincarnation; thus serving
to keep the memory and the experience always before my eyes. While
here were two people of an intense lyrical sensiblity, two people so
close in thought, feeling, and ideals, that although one was dead and
the other living they were to me as one, yet I could not feel that their
experience was mine, that it could do more than touch me in passing,
for that I had been of any help to Denise was in a large part due to
the fact that we were so dissimilar. While her thoughts came trailing
clouds of glory, mine were of the earth earthy, and at such a time
could help to strike a balance between the mystical flights of her
mind and the material fact of high-explosive bombs landing in the
next street. But though we might travel the same road for a time,
lone voyagers eager for company, yet the time must come when our
ways should part. Right or wrong, her way was not mine and I
should be mistaken in attempting to make it so. We must live how
we can.

Billy Pilgrim

Kurt Vonnegut

Listen:

Billy Pilgrim has come unstuck in time.

Billy has gone to sleep a senile widower and awakened on his wedding day. He has walked through a door in 1955 and come out another one in 1941. He has gone back through that door to find himself in 1963. He has seen his birth and death many times, he says, and pays random visits to all the events in between.

He says.

Billy is spastic in time, has no control over where he is going next, and the trips aren't necessarily fun. He is in a constant state of stage fright, he says, because he never knows what part of his life he is going to have to act in next.

Billy was born in 1922 in Ilium, New York, the only child of a barber there. He was a funny-looking child who became a funny-looking youth – tall and weak, and shaped like a bottle of Coca-Cola. He graduated from Ilium High School in the upper third of his class, and attended night sessions at the Ilium School of Optometry for one semester before being drafted for military service in the Second World War. His father died in a hunting accident during the war. So it goes.

Billy saw service with the infantry in Europe, and was taken prisoner by the Germans. After his honorable discharge from the Army in 1945, Billy again enrolled in the Ilium School of Optometry. During his senior year there, he became engaged to the daughter of the founder and owner of the school, and then suffered a mild nervous collapse.

He was treated in a veteran's hospital near Lake Placid, and was given shock treatments and released. He married his fiancée, finished his education, and was set up in business in Ilium by his father-in-law. Ilium is a particularly good city for optometrists because the General Forge and Foundry Company is there. Every employee is required to own a pair of safety glasses, and to wear them in areas where manufacturing is going on. GF&F has sixty-eight thousand employees in Ilium. That calls for a lot of lenses and a lot of frames.

Frames are where the money is.

Billy became rich. He had two children, Barbara and Robert. In time, his daughter Barbara married another optometrist, and Billy set him up in business. Billy's son Robert had a lot of trouble in high school, but then he joined the famous Green Berets. He straightened out, became a fine young man, and he fought in Vietnam.

Early in 1968, a group of optometrists, with Billy among them, chartered an airplane to fly them from Ilium to an international convention of optometrists in Montreal. The plane crashed on top of Sugarbush Mountain, in Vermont. Everybody was killed by Billy. So it goes.

While Billy was recuperating in a hospital in Vermont, his wife died accidentally of carbon-monoxide poisoning. So it goes.

When Billy finally got home to Ilium after the airplane crash, he was quiet for a while. He had a terrible scar across the top of his skull. He didn't resume practice. He had a housekeeper. His daughter came over almost every day.

And then, without any warning, Billy went to New York City, and got on an all-night radio program devoted to talk. He told about having come unstuck in time. He said, too, that he had been kidnapped by a flying saucer in 1967. The saucer was from the planet Tralfamadore, he said. He was taken to Tralfamadore, where he was displayed naked in a zoo, he said. He was mated there with a former Earthling movie star named Monatana Wildhack.

Some night owls in Ilium heard Billy on the radio, and one of them called Billy's daughter Barbara. Barbara was upset. She and her husband went down to New York and brought Billy home. Billy insisted mildly that everything he had said on the radio was true. He said he had been kidnapped by the Tralfamadorians on the night of his daughter's wedding. He hadn't been missed, he said, because the

Tralfamadorians had taken him through a time warp, so that he could be on Tralfamadore for years, and still be away from Earth for only a microsecond.

Another month went by without incident, and then Billy wrote a letter to the Ilium *News Leader*, which the paper published. It described the creatures from Tralfamadore.

The letter said that they were two feet high, and green, and shaped like plumber's friends. Their suction cups were on the ground, and their shafts, which were extremely flexible, usually pointed to the sky. At the top of each shaft was a little hand with a green eye in its palm. The creatures were friendly, and they could see in four dimensions. They pitied Earthlings for being able to see only three. They had many wonderful things to teach Earthlings, especially about time. Billy promised to tell what some of those wonderful things were in his next letter.

Billy was working on his second letter when the first letter was published. The second letter started out like this:

'The most important thing I learned on Tralfamadore was that when a person dies he only *appears* to die. He is still very much alive in the past, so it is very silly for people to cry at his funeral. All moments, past, present, and future, always have existed, always will exist. The Tralfamadorians can look at all the different moments just the way we can look at a stretch of the Rocky Mountains, for instance. They can see how permanent all the moments are, and they can look at any moment that interests them. It is just an illusion we have here on Earth that one moment follows another one, like beads on a string, and that once a moment is gone it is gone forever.

'When a Tralfamadorian sees a corpse, all he thinks is that the dead person is in bad condition in that particular moment, but that the same person is just fine in plenty of other moments. Now, when I myself hear that somebody is dead, I simply shrug and say what the Tralfamadorians say about dead people, which is "So it goes."'

And so on.

Billy was working on this letter in the basement rumpus room of his empty house. It was his housekeeper's day off. There was an old typewriter in the rumpus room. It was a beast. It weighed as much as a storage battery. Billy couldn't carry it very far very easily, which was why he was writing in the rumpus room instead of somewhere else.

The oil burner had quit. A mouse had eaten through the insulation of a wire leading to the thermostat. The temperature in the house was down to fifty degrees, but Billy hadn't noticed. He wasn't warmly dressed, either. He was barefoot, and still in his pajamas and a bathrobe, though it was late afternoon. His bare feet were blue and ivory.

The cockles of Billy's heart, at any rate, were glowing coals. What made them so hot was Billy's belief that he was going to comfort so many people with the truth about time. His door chimes upstairs had been ringing and ringing. It was his daughter Barbara up there, wanting in. Now she let herself in with a key, crossed the floor over his head, calling, 'Father? Daddy, where are you?' And so on.

Billy didn't answer her, so she was nearly hysterical, expecting to find his corpse. And then she looked into the very last place there *was* to look – which was the rumpus room.

'Why didn't you answer me when I called?' Barbara wanted to know, standing there in the door of the rumpus room. She had the afternoon paper with her, the one in which Billy described his friends from Tralfamadore.

'I didn't *hear* you,' said Billy.

The orchestration of the moment was this: Barbara was only twenty-one years old, but she thought her father was senile, even though he was only forty-six – senile because of damage to his brain in the airplane crash. She also thought that she was head of the family, since she had had to manage her mother's funeral, since she had to get a housekeeper for Billy, and all that. Also, Barbara and her husband were having to look after Billy's business interests, which were considerable, since Billy didn't seem to give a damn for business any more. All this responsibility at such an early age made her a bitchy flibbertigibbet. And Billy meanwhile, was trying to hang onto his dignity, to persuade Barbara and everybody else that he was far from senile, that, on the contrary, he was devoting himself to a calling much higher than mere business.

He was doing nothing less now, he thought, than prescribing corrective lenses for Earthling souls. So many of those souls were lost and wretched, Billy believed, because they could not see as well as his little green friends on Tralfamadore.

'Don't lie to me, Father,' said Barbara. 'I know perfectly well you heard me when I called.' This was a fairly pretty girl, except that she had legs like an Edwardian grand piano. Now she raised hell with him about the letter in the paper. She said he was making a laughing stock of himself and everybody associated with him.

'Father, Father, Father – ' said Barbara, 'what are we going to *do* with you? Are you going to force us to put you where your mother is?' Billy's mother was still alive. She was in bed in an old people's home called Pine Knoll on the edge of Ilium.

'What is it about my letter that makes you so mad?' Billy wanted to know.

'It's all just crazy. None of it's true!'

'It's all true.' Billy's anger was not going to rise with hers. He never got mad at anything. He was wonderful that way.

'There is no such planet as Tralfamadore.'

'It can't be detected from Earth, if that's what you mean,' said Billy. 'Earth can't be detected from Tralfamadore, as far as that goes. They're both very small. They're very far apart.'

'Where did you get a crazy name like "Tralfamadore?"'

'That's what the creatures who live there *call* it.'

'Oh God,' said Barbara, and she turned her back on him. She celebrated frustration by clapping her hands. 'May I ask you a simple question?'

'Of course.'

'Why is it you never mentioned any of this before the airplane crash?'

'I didn't think the time was *ripe*.'

And so on. Billy says that he first came unstuck in time in 1944, long before his trip to Tralfamadore. The Tralfamadorians didn't have anything to do with his coming unstuck. They were simply able to give him insights into what was really going on.

Billy first came unstuck while World War Two was in progress. Billy was a chaplain's assistant in the war. A chaplain's assistant is customarily a figure of fun in the American Army. Billy was no exception. He was powerless to harm the enemy or to help his friends. In fact, he had no friends. He was a valet to a preacher, expected no promotions or medals, bore no arms, and had a meek faith in a loving Jesus which most soldiers found putrid.

While on maneuvers in South Carolina, Billy played hymns he knew from childhood, played them on a little black organ which was waterproof. It had thirty-nine keys and two stops – *vox humana* and *vox celeste*. Billy also had charge of a portable altar, an olive-drab attaché case with telescoping legs. It was lined with crimson plush, and nestled in that passionate plush were an anodized aluminum cross and a Bible.

The altar and the organ were made by a vacuum-cleaner company in Camden, New Jersey – and said so.

One time on maneuvers Billy was playing 'A Mighty Fortress Is Our God,' with music by Johann Sebastian Bach and words by Martin Luther. It was Sunday morning. Billy and his chaplain had gathered a congregation of about fifty soldiers on a Carolina hillside. An umpire appeared. There were umpires everywhere, men who said who was winning or losing the theoretical battle, who was alive and who was dead.

The umpire had comical news. The congregation had been theoretically spotted from the air by a theoretical enemy. They were all theoretically dead now. The theoretical corpses laughed and ate a hearty noontime meal.

Remembering this incident years later, Billy was struck by what a Tralfamadorian adventure with death that had been, to be dead and to eat at the same time.

Toward the end of maneuvers, Billy was given an emergency furlough home because his father, a barber in Ilium, New York, was shot dead by a friend while they were out hunting deer. So it goes.

When Billy got back from his furlough, there were orders for him to go overseas. He was needed in the headquarters company of an infantry regiment fighting in Luxembourg. The regimental chaplain's assistant had been killed in action. So it goes.

When Billy joined the regiment, it was in the process of being destroyed by the Germans in the famous Battle of the Bulge. Billy never even got to meet the chaplain he was supposed to assist, was never even issued a steel helmet and combat boots. This was in December of 1944, during the last mighty German attack of the war.

Billy survived, but he was a dazed wanderer far behind the new German lines. Three other wanderers, not quite so dazed, allowed Billy to tag along. Two of them were scouts, and one was an antitank gunner. They were without food or maps. Avoiding Germans, they were delivering themselves into rural silences ever more profound. They ate snow.

They went Indian file. First came the scouts, clever, graceful, quiet. They had rifles. Next came the antitank gunner, clumsy and dense, warning Germans away with a Colt .45 automatic in one hand and a trench knife in the other.

Last came Billy Pilgrim, empty-handed, bleakly ready for death. Billy was preposterous – six feet and three inches tall, with a chest and shoulders like a box of kitchen matches. He had no helmet, no overcoat, no weapon, and no boots. On his feet were cheap, low-cut civilian shoes which he had bought for his father's funeral. Billy had lost a heel, which made him bob up-and-down, up-and-down. The involuntary dancing, up and down, up and down, made his hip joints sore.

Billy was wearing a thin field jacket, a shirt and trousers of scratchy wool, and long underwear that was soaked with sweat. He was the only one of the four who had a beard. It was a random, bristly beard, and some of the bristles were white, even though Billy was only twenty-one years old. He was also going bald. Wind and cold and violent exercise had turned his face crimson.

He didn't look like a soldier at all. He looked like a filthy flamingo.

And on the third day of wandering, somebody shot at the four from far away – shot four times as they crossed a narrow brick road. One shot was for the scouts. The next one was for the antitank gunner, whose name was Roland Weary.

The third bullet was for the filthy flamingo, who stopped dead center in the road when the lethal bee buzzed past his ear. Billy stood there politely, giving the marksman another chance. It was his addled understanding of the rules of warfare that the marksman *should* be given a second chance. The next shot missed Billy's kneecaps by inches, going end-on-end, from the sound of it.

Roland Weary and the scouts were safe in a ditch, and Weary growled at Billy, 'Get out of the road, you dumb motherfucker.' The last word was still a novelty in the speech of white people in 1944. It

was fresh and astonishing to Billy, who had never fucked anybody –
and it did its job. It woke him up and got him off the road.

'Saved your life again, you dumb bastard,' Weary said to Billy in the
ditch. He had been saving Billy's life for days cursing him, kicking
him, slapping him, making him move. It was absolutely necessary
that cruelty be used, because Billy wouldn't do anything to save
himself. Billy wanted to quit. He was cold, hungry, embarrassed,
incompetent. He could scarcely distinguish between sleep and wake-
fulness now, on the third day, found no important differences, either,
between walking and standing still.

He wished everybody would leave him alone. 'You guys go on
without me,' he said again and again.

Weary was as new to war as Billy. He was a replacement, too. As a
part of a gun crew, he had helped to fire one shot in anger – from a
57-millimeter antitank gun. The gun made a ripping sound like the
opening of the zipper on the fly of God Almighty. The gun lapped up
snow and vegetation with a blowtorch thirty feet long. The flame left
a black arrow on the ground, showing the Germans exactly where the
gun was hidden. The shot was a miss.

What had been missed was a Tiger tank. It swiveled its 88-
millimeter snout around sniffingly, saw the arrow on the ground. It
fired. It killed everybody on the gun crew but Weary. So it goes.

Roland Weary was only eighteen, was at the end of an unhappy
childhood spent mostly in Pittsburgh, Pennsylvania. He had been
unpopular in Pittsburgh. He had been unpopular because he was
stupid and fat and mean, and smelled like bacon no matter how
much he washed. He was always being ditched in Pittsburgh by
people who did not want him with them.

It made Weary sick to be ditched. When Weary was ditched, he
would find somebody who was even more unpopular than himself,
and he would horse around with that person for a while, pretending
to be friendly. And then he would find some pretext for beating the
shit out of him.

It was a pattern. It was a crazy, sexy, murderous relationship
Weary entered into with people he eventually beat up. He told them

about his father's collection of guns and swords and torture instruments and leg irons and so on. Weary's father, who was a plumber, actually did collect such things, and his collection was insured for four thousand dollars. He wasn't alone. He belonged to a big club composed of people who collected things like that.

Weary's father once gave Weary's mother a Spanish thumbscrew in working condition – for a kitchen paperweight. Another time he gave her a table lamp whose base was a model one foot high of the famous 'Iron Maiden of Nuremburg.' The real Iron Maiden was a medieval torture instrument, a sort of boiler which was shaped like a woman on the outside – and lined with spikes. The front of the woman was composed of two hinged doors. The idea was to put a crininal inside and then close the doors slowly. There were two special spikes where his eyes would be. There was a drain in the bottom to let out all the blood.

So it goes.

Weary had told Billy Pilgrim about the Iron Maiden, about the drain in her bottom – and what that was for. He had talked to Billy about dumdums. He told him about his father's Derringer pistol, which could be carried in a vest pocket, which was yet capable of making a hole in a man 'which a bull bat could fly through without touching either wing.'

Weary scornfully bet Billy one time that he didn't even know what a blood gutter was. Billy guessed that it was the drain in the bottom of the Iron Maiden, but that was wrong. A blood gutter, Billy learned, was the shallow groove in the side of the blade of a sword or bayonet.

Weary told Billy about neat tortures he'd read about or seen in the movies or heard on the radio – about other neat tortures he himself had invented. One of the inventions was sticking a dentist's drill into a guy's ear. He asked Billy what he thought the worst form of execution was. Billy had no opinion. The correct answer turned out to be this: 'You stake a guy out on an anthill in the desert – see? He's facing upward, and you put honey all over his balls and pecker, and you cut off his eyelids so he has to stare at the sun till he dies.' So it goes.

*   *   *

Now, lying in the ditch with Billy and the scouts after having been
shot at, Weary made Billy take a very close look at his trench knife.
It wasn't government issue. It was a present from his father. It had a
ten-inch blade that was triangular in cross section. Its grip consisted
of brass knuckles, was a chain of rings through which Weary slipped
his stubby fingers. The rings weren't simple. They bristled with
spikes.

Weary laid the spikes along Billy's cheek, roweled the cheek with
savagely affectionate restraint. 'How'd you like to be hit with this –
hm? Hmmmmmmmmmm?' he wanted to know.

'I wouldn't,' said Billy.

'Know why the blade's triangular?'

'No.'

'Makes a wound that won't close up.'

'Oh.'

'Makes a three-sided hole in a guy. You stick an ordinary knife in
a guy – makes a slit. Right? A slit closes right up. Right?'

'Right.'

'Shit. What do you know? What the hell they teach in college?'

'I wasn't there very long,' said Billy, which was true. He had had
only six months of college, and the college hadn't been a regular
college, either. It had been the night school of the Ilium School of
Optometry.

'Joe College,' said Weary scathingly.

Billy shrugged.

'There's more to life than what you read in books,' said Weary.
'You'll find that out.'

Billy made no reply to this, either, there in the ditch, since he
didn't want the conversation to go on any longer than necessary. He
was dimly tempted to say, though, that he knew a thing or two about
gore. Billy, after all, had contemplated torture and hideous wounds
at the beginning and the end of nearly every day of his childhood.
Billy had an extremely gruesome crucifix hanging on the wall of his
little bedroom in Ilium. A military surgeon would have admired the
clinical fidelity of the artist's rendition of all Christ's wounds – the
spear wound, the thorn wounds, the holes that were made by the iron
spikes. Billy's Christ died horribly. He was pitiful.

So it goes.

*   *   *

Billy wasn't a Catholic, even though he grew up with a ghastly crucifix on the wall. His father had no religion. His mother was a substitute organist for several churches around town. She took Billy with her whenever she played, taught him to play a little, too. She said she was going to join a church as soon as she decided which one was right.

She never *did* decide. She did develop a terrific hankering for a crucifix, though. And she bought one from a Santa Fe gift shop during a trip the little family made out West during the Great Depression. Like so many Americans, she was trying to construct a life that made sense from things she found in gift shops.

And the crucifix went up on the wall of Billy Pilgrim.

The two scouts, loving the walnut stocks of their rifles in the ditch, whispered that it was time to move out again. Ten minutes had gone by without anybody's coming to see if they were hit or not, to finish them off. Whoever had shot was evidently far away and all alone.

And the four crawled out of the ditch without drawing any more fire. They crawled into a forest like the big, unlucky mammals they were. Then they stood up and began to walk quickly. The forest was dark and old. The pines were planted in ranks and files. There was no undergrowth. Four inches of unmarked snow blanketed the ground. The Americans had no choice but to leave trails in the snow as unambiguous as diagrams in a book on ballroom dancing – *step, slide, rest – step, slide, rest*.

'Close it up and keep it closed!' Roland Weary warned Billy Pilgrim as they moved out. Weary looked like Tweedledum or Tweedledee, all bundled up for battle. He was short and thick.

He had every piece of equipment he had ever been issued, every present he'd received from home: helmet, helmet liner, wool cap, scarf, gloves, cotton undershirt, woolen undershirt, wool shirt, sweater, blouse, jacket, overcoat, cotton underpants, woolen underpants, woolen trousers, cotton socks, woolen socks, combat boots, gas mask, canteen, mess kit, first-aid kit, trench knife, blanket, shelter-half, raincoat, bullet-proof Bible, a pamphlet entitled 'Know Your Enemy,' another pamphlet entitled 'Why We Fight,' and another pamphlet of German phrases rendered in English phonetics, which would enable Weary to ask Germans questions such as 'Where is

your headquarters?' and 'How many howitzers have you?' or to tell
them, 'Surrender. Your situation is hopeless,' and so on.

Weary had a block of balsa wood which was supposed to be a
foxhole pillow. He had a prophylactic kit containing two tough
condoms 'For the Prevention of Disease Only!' He had a whistle he
wasn't going to show anybody until he got promoted to corporal. He
had a dirty picture of a woman attempting sexual intercourse with a
Shetland pony. He had made Billy Pilgrim admire that picture
several times.

The woman and the pony were posed before velvet draperies which
were fringed with deedlee-balls. They were flanked by Doric columns.
In front of one column was a potted palm. The picture that Weary
had was a print of the first dirty photograph in history. The word
photography was first used in 1839, and it was in that year, too, that
Louis J. M. Daguerre revealed to the French Academy that an image
formed on a silvered metal plate covered with a thin film of silver
iodide could be developed in the presence of mercury vapor.

In 1841, only two years later, an assistant to Daguerre, André Le
Fèvre, was arrested in the Tuileries Gardens for attempting to sell a
gentleman a picture of the woman and the pony. That was where
Weary bought his picture, too – in the Tuileries. Le Fèvre argued
that the picture was fine art, and that his intention was to make
Greek mythology come alive. He said the columns and the potted
palm proved that.

When asked which myth he meant to represent, Le Fèvre replied
that there were thousands of myths like that, with the woman a
mortal and the pony a god.

He was sentenced to six months in prison. He died there of
pneumonia. So it goes.

Billy and the scouts were skinny people. Roland Weary had fat to
burn. He was a roaring furnace under all his layers of wool and straps
and canvas. He had so much energy that he bustled back and forth
between Billy and the scouts, delivering dumb messages which
nobody had sent and which nobody was pleased to receive. He also
began to suspect, since he was so much busier than anybody else,
that he was the leader.

He was so hot and bundled up, in fact, that he had no sense of danger. His vision of the outside world was limited to what he could see through a narrow slit between the rim of his helmet and his scarf from home, which concealed his baby face from the bridge of his nose on down. He was so snug in there that he was able to pretend that he was safe at home, having survived the war, and that he was telling his parents and his sister a true war story — whereas the true war story was still going on.

Weary's version of the true war story went like this: There was a big German attack, and Weary and his antitank buddies fought like hell until everybody was killed but Weary. So it goes. And then Weary tied in with two scouts, and they became close friends immediately, and they decided to fight their way back to their own lines. They were going to travel fast. They were damned if they'd surrender. They shook hands all around. They called themselves 'The Three Musketeers.'

But then this damn college kid, who was so weak he shouldn't even have been in the army, asked if he could come along. He didn't even have a gun or a knife. He didn't even have a helmet or a cap. He couldn't even walk right — kept bobbing up-and-down, up-and-down, driving everybody crazy, giving their position away. He was pitiful. The Three Musketeers pushed and carried and dragged the college kid all the way back to their own lines, Weary's story went. They saved his God-damned hide for him.

In real life, Weary was retracing his steps, trying to find out what had happened to Billy. He had told the scouts to wait while he went back for the college bastard. He passed under a low branch now. It hit the top of his helmet with a *clonk*. Weary didn't hear it. Somewhere a big dog was barking. Weary didn't hear that, either. His war story was at a very exciting point. An officer was congratulating the Three Musketeers, telling them that he was going to put them in for Bronze Stars.

'Anything else I can do for you boys?' said the officer.

'Yes, sir,' said one of the scouts. 'We'd like to stick together for the rest of the war, sir. Is there some way you can fix it so nobody will ever break up the Three Musketeers?'

Billy Pilgrim had stopped in the forest. He was leaning against a tree with his eyes closed. His head was tilted back and his nostrils were flaring. He was like a poet in the Parthenon.

This was when Billy first came unstuck in time. His attention
began to swing grandly through the full arc of his life, passing into
death, which was violet light. There wasn't anybody else there, or
any thing. There was just violet light – and a hum.

And then Billy swung into life again, going backwards until he was
in pre-birth, which was red light and bubbling sounds. And then he
swung into life again and stopped. He was a little boy taking a shower
with his hairy father at the Ilium Y.M.C.A. He smelled chlorine from
the swimming pool next door, heard the springboard boom.

Little Billy was terrified, because his father had said Billy was
going to learn to swim by the method of sink-or-swim. His father was
going to throw Billy into the deep end, and Billy was going to damn
well swim.

It was like an execution. Billy was numb as his father carried him
from the shower room to the pool. His eyes were closed. When he
opened his eyes, he was on the bottom of the pool and there was
beautiful music everywhere. He lost consciousness, but the music
went on. He dimly sensed that somebody was rescuing him. Billy
resented that.

From there he traveled in time to 1965. He was forty-one years old,
and he was visiting his decrepit mother at Pine Knoll, an old people's
home he had put her in only a month before. She had caught
pneumonia, and wasn't expected to live. She did live, though, for
years after that.

Her voice was nearly gone, so, in order to hear her, Billy had to
put his ear right next to her papery lips. She evidently had something
very important to say.

'How . . .?' she began, and she stopped. She was too tired. She
hoped that she wouldn't have to say the rest of the sentence, that
Billy would finish it for her.

But Billy had no idea what was on her mind. 'How *what*, Mother?'
he prompted.

She swallowed hard, shed some tears. Then she gathered energy
from all over her ruined body, even from her toes and fingertips. At
last she had accumulated enough to whisper this complete sentence:

'How did I get so *old*?'

*   *   *

Billy's antique mother passed out, and Billy was led from the room by a pretty nurse. The body of an old man covered by a sheet was wheeled by just as Billy entered the corridor. The man had been a famous marathon runner in his day. So it goes. This was before Billy had his head broken in an airplane crash, by the way – before he became so vocal about flying saucers and traveling in time.

Billy sat down in a waiting room. He wasn't a widower yet. He sensed something hard under the cushion of his overstuffed chair. He dug it out, discovered that it was a book, *The Execution of Private Slovik*, by William Bradford Huie. It was a true account of the death before an American firing squad of Private Eddie D. Slovik, 36896415, the only American soldier to be shot for cowardice since the Civil War. So it goes.

Billy read the opinion of a staff judge advocate who reviewed Slovik's case, which ended like this: *He has directly challenged the authority of the government, and future discipline depends upon a resolute reply to this challenge. If the death penalty is ever to be imposed for desertion, it should be imposed in this case, not as a punitive measure nor as retribution, but to maintain that discipline upon which alone an army can succeed against the enemy. There was no recommendation for clemency in the case and none is here recommended.* So it goes.

Billy blinked in 1965, traveled in time to 1958. He was at a banquet in honor of a Little League team of which his son Robert was a member. The coach, who had never been married, was speaking. He was all choked up. 'Honest to God,' he was saying, 'I'd consider it an honor just to be *water* boy for these kids.'

Billy blinked in 1958, traveled in time to 1961. It was New Year's Eve, and Billy was disgracefully drunk at a party where everybody was in optometry or married to an optometrist.

Billy usually didn't drink much, because the war had ruined his stomach, but he certainly had a snootful now, and he was being unfaithful to his wife Valencia for the first and only time. He had somehow persuaded a woman to come into the laundry room of the house, and then sit up on the gas dryer, which was running.

The woman was very drunk herself, and she helped Billy get her girdle off. 'What was it you wanted to talk about?' she said.

'It's all right,' said Billy. He honestly thought it was all right. He couldn't remember the name of the woman.

'How come they call you Billy instead of William?'

'Business reasons,' said Billy. That was true. His father-in-law, who owned the Ilium School of Optometry, who had set Billy up in practice, was a genius in his field. He told Billy to encourage people to call him Billy – because it would stick in their memories. It would also make him seem slightly magical, since there weren't any other grown Billys around. It also compelled people to think of him as a friend right away.

Somewhere in there was an awful scene, with people expressing disgust for Billy and the woman, and Billy found himself out in his automobile, trying to find the steering wheel.

The main thing now was to find the steering wheel. At first, Billy windmilled his arms, hoping to find it by luck. When that didn't work, he became methodical, working in such a way that the wheel could not possibly escape him. He placed himself hard against the left-hand door, searched every square inch of the area before him. When he failed to find the wheel, he moved over six inches, and searched again. Amazingly, he was eventually hard against the right-hand door, without having found the wheel. He concluded that somebody had stolen it. This angered him as he passed out.

He was in the back seat of his car, which was why he couldn't find the steering wheel.

Now somebody was shaking Billy awake. Billy still felt drunk, was still angered by the stolen steering wheel. He was back in World War Two again, behind the German lines. The person who was shaking him was Roland Weary. Weary had gathered the front of Billy's field jacket into his hands. He banged Billy against a tree, then pulled him away from it, flung him in the direction he was supposed to take under his own power.

Billy stopped, shook his head. 'You go on,' he said.

'What?'

'You guys go on without me. I'm all right.'

'You're what?'

'I'm O.K.'

'Jesus – I'd hate to see somebody *sick*,' said Weary, through five layers of humid scarf from home. Billy had never seen Weary's face. He had tried to imagine it one time, had imagined a toad in a fishbowl.

Weary kicked and shoved Billy for a quarter of a mile. The scouts were waiting between the banks of a frozen creek. They had heard the dog. They had heard men calling back and forth, too – calling like hunters who had a pretty good idea of where their quarry was.

The banks of the creek were high enough to allow the scouts to stand without being seen. Billy staggered down the bank ridiculously. After him came Weary, clanking and clinking and tinkling and hot.

'Here he is, boys,' said Weary. 'He don't want to live, but he's gonna live anyway. When he gets out of this, by God, he's gonna owe his life to the Three Musketeers.' This was the first the scouts had heard that Weary thought of himself and them as the Three Musketeers.

Billy Pilgrim, there in the creekbed, thought he, Billy Pilgrim, was turning to steam painlessly. If everybody would leave him alone for just a little while, he thought, he wouldn't cause anybody any more trouble. He would turn to steam and float up among the treetops.

Somewhere the big dog barked again. With the help of fear and echoes and winter silences, that dog had a voice like a big bronze gong.

Roland Weary, eighteen years old, insinuated himself between the scouts, draped a heavy arm around the shoulder of each. 'So what do the Three Musketeers do now?' he said.

Billy Pilgrim was having a delightful hallucination. He was wearing dry, warm, white sweatsocks, and he was skating on a ballroom floor. Thousands cheered. This wasn't time-travel. It had never happened, never would happen. It was the craziness of a dying young man with his shoes full of snow.

One scout hung his head, let spit fall from his lips. The other did the same. They studied the infinitesimal effects of spit on snow and history. They were small, graceful people. They had been behind German lines before many times – living like woods creatures, living from moment to moment in useful terror, thinking brainlessly with their spinal cords.

Now they twisted out from under Weary's loving arms. They told

Weary that he and Billy had better find somebody to surrender to. The scouts weren't going to wait for them any more.

And they ditched Weary and Billy in the creekbed.

Billy Pilgrim went on skating, doing tricks in sweatsocks, tricks that most people would consider impossible – making turns, stopping on a dime and so on. The cheering went on, but its tone was altered as the hallucination gave way to time-travel.

Billy stopped skating, found himself at a lectern in a Chinese restaurant in Ilium, New York, on an early afternoon in the autumn of 1957. He was receiving a standing ovation from the Lions Club. He had just been elected President, and it was necessary that he speak. He was scared stiff, thought a ghastly mistake had been made. All those prosperous, solid men out there would discover now that they had elected a ludicrous waif. They would hear his reedy voice, the one he'd had in the war. He swallowed, knew that all he had for a voice box was a little whistle cut from a willow switch. Worse – he had nothing to say. The crowd quieted down. Everybody was pink and beaming.

Billy opened his mouth, and out came a deep, resonant tone. His voice was a gorgeous instrument. It told jokes which brought down the house. It grew serious, told jokes again, and ended on a note of humility. The explanation of the miracle was this: Billy had taken a course in public speaking.

And then he was back in the bed of the frozen creek again. Roland Weary was about to beat the living shit out of him.

Weary was filled with a tragic wrath. He had been ditched again. He stuffed his pistol into its holster. He slipped his knife into its scabbard. Its triangular blade and blood gutters on all three faces. And then he shook Billy hard, rattled his skeleton, slammed him against a bank.

Weary barked and whimpered through his layers of scarf from home. He spoke unintelligibly of the sacrifices he had made on Billy's behalf. He dilated upon the piety and heroism of 'The Three Musketeers,' portrayed, in the most glowing and impassioned hues, their virtue and magnanimity, the imperishable honor they acquired for themselves, and the great services they rendered to Christianity.

It was entirely Billy's fault that this fighting organization no longer existed, Weary felt, and Billy was going to pay. Weary socked Billy a good one on the side of his jaw, knocked Billy away from the bank and onto the snow-covered ice of the creek. Billy was down on all fours on the ice, and Weary kicked him in the ribs, rolled him over on his side. Billy tried to form himself into a ball.

'You shouldn't even *be* in the Army,' said Weary.

Billy was involuntarily making convulsive sounds that were a lot like laughter. 'You think it's funny, huh?' Weary inquired. He walked around to Billy's back. Billy's jacket and shirt and undershirt had been hauled up around his shoulders by the violence, so his back was naked. There, inches from the tips of Weary's combat boots, were the pitiful buttons of Billy's spine.

Weary drew back his right boot, aimed a kick at the spine, at the tube which had so many of Billy's important wires in it. Weary was going to break that tube.

But then Weary saw that he had an audience. Five German soldiers and a police dog on a leash were looking down into the bed of the creek. The soldiers' blue eyes were filled with a bleary civilian curiosity as to why one American would try to murder another one so far from home, and why the victim should laugh.

Battalion in Defence

Evelyn Waugh

Guy was weary, hungry and thirsty, but he had fared better than
Fido in the last four days and, compared with him, was in good heart,
almost buoyant, as he tramped alone, eased at last of the lead weight
of human company. He had paddled in this lustral freedom on the
preceding morning when he caught X Commando among the slit
trenches and olive trees. Now he wallowed.

Soon the road ran out and round the face of a rocky spur – the
place where Fido had found no cover – and here he met a straggling
platoon of infantry coming fast towards him, a wan young officer well
ahead.

'Have you seen anything of Hookforce?'

'Never heard of them.'

The breathless officer paused as his men caught up with him and
formed column. They still had their weapons and equipment.

'Or the Halberdiers?'

'Cut off. Surrounded. Surrendered.'

'Are you sure?'

'Sure? For Christ's sake, there are parachutists everywhere. We've
just been fired on coming round that corner. You can't get up the
road. A machine-gun, the other side of the valley.'

'Where exactly?'

'Any casualties?'

'I didn't wait to see. Can't wait now. I wouldn't try that road if
you know what's healthy.'

The platoon scuffled on. Guy looked down the empty exposed road
and then studied his map. There was a track over the hill which
rejoined the road at a village two miles on. Guy did not greatly
believe in the machine-gun but he chose the short cut and painfully
climbed until he found himself on the top of the spur. He could see
the whole empty, silent valley. Nothing moved anywhere except the

bees. He might have been standing in the hills behind Santa Dulcina
any holiday morning of his lonely boyhood.

Then he descended to the village. Some of the cottage doors and
windows were barred and shuttered, some rudely broken down. At
first he met no one. A well stood before the church, built about with
marble steps and a rutted plinth. He approached thirstily but found
the rope hanging loose and short from its bronze staple. The bucket
was gone and leaning over he saw far below a little shaving-glass of
light and his own mocking head, dark and diminished.

He entered an open house and found an earthenware jar of classic
shape. As he removed the straw stopper he heard and felt a hum and,
tilting it to the light, found it full of bees and a residue of honey.
Then looking about in the gloom he saw an old woman gazing at
him. He smiled, showed his empty water-bottle, made signs of
drinking. Still she gazed, quite blind. He searched his mind for
vestiges of Greek and tried: '*Hudor. Hydro. Dipsa.*' Still she gazed,
quite deaf, quite alone. Guy turned back into the sunlight. There a
young girl, ruddy, bare-footed and in tears, approached him frankly
and took him by the sleeve. He showed her his empty bottle, but she
shook her head, made little inarticulate noises and drew him resolutely towards a small yard on the edge of the village, which had once
held live-stock but was now deserted except by a second, similar girl,
a sister perhaps, and a young English soldier who lay on a stretcher
motionless. The girls pointed helplessly towards this figure. Guy
could not help. The young man was dead, undamaged it seemed. He
lay as though at rest. The few corpses which Guy had seen in Crete
had sprawled awkwardly. This soldier lay like an effigy on a tomb –
like Sir Roger in his shadowy shrine at Santa Dulcina. Only the
bluebottles that clustered round his lips and eyes proclaimed that he
was flesh. Why was he lying here? Who were these girls? Had a weary
stretcher-party left him in their care and had they watched him die?
Had they closed his eyes and composed his limbs? Guy would never
know. It remained one of the countless unexplained incidents of war.
Meanwhile, lacking words the three of them stood by the body, stiff
and mute as figures in a sculptured Deposition.

To bury the dead is one of the corporal works of charity. There
were no tools here to break the stony ground. Later, perhaps, the
enemy would scavenge the island and tip this body with others into a
common pit and the boy's family would get no news of him and wait

and hope month after month, year after year. A precept came to
Guy's mind from his military education: 'The officer in command of
a burial party is responsible for collecting the red identity discs and
forwarding them to Records. The green disc remains on the body. If
in doubt, gentlemen, remember that green is the colour of
putrefaction.'

Guy knelt and took the disc from the cold breast. He read a
number, a name, a designation, *RC*. 'May his soul and the souls of
all the faithful departed, in the mercy of God, rest in peace.'

Guy stood. The bluebottles returned to the peaceful young face.
Guy saluted and passed on.

The country opened and soon Guy came to another village. Toiling
beside Fido in the darkness, he had barely noticed it. Now he found
a place of some size, other roads and tracks converged on a market
square; the houses had large barns behind them; a domed church
stood open. Of the original inhabitants there was no sign; instead,
English soldiers were posted in doorways – Halberdiers – and at the
cross-roads sat Sarum-Smith, smoking a pipe.

'Hullo, uncle. The CO said you were about.'

'I'm glad to find you. I met a windy officer on the road who said
you were all in the bag.'

'It doesn't look like it, does it? There was something of a schemozzle
last night but we weren't in that.'

Since Guy last saw him in West Africa, Sarum-Smith had matured.
He was not a particularly attractive man, but man he was. 'The CO's
out with the Adj, going round the companies. You'll find the second-
in-command at battalion headquarters, over there.'

Guy went where he was directed, to a farm-house beside the
church. Everything was in order. One notice pointed to the regimental aid post, another to the battalion-office. Guy passed the R S M
and the clerks and in the further room of the house found Major
Erskine. An army blanket had been spread on the kitchen table. It
was, in replica, the orderly room at Penkirk.

Guy saluted.

'Hullo, uncle, you could do with a shave.'

'I could do with some breakfast, sir.'

'Lunch will be coming up as soon as the CO gets back. Brought us
some more orders?'

'No, sir.'

'Information?'

'None, sir.'

'What's headquarters up to then?'

'Not functioning much at the moment. I came to get information from you.'

'We don't know much.'

He put Guy in the picture. The Commandos had lost two troops somehow during the night. An enemy patrol had wandered in from the flank during the morning and hurriedly retired. The Commandos were due to come through them soon and take up positions at Imbros. They had motor transport and should not have much difficulty in disengaging. The Second Halberdiers were to hold their present line till midnight and then fall back behind Hookforce to the beach perimeter. 'After that we're in the hands of the navy. Those are the orders as I understand them. I don't know how they'll work out.'

A Halberdier brought Guy a cup of tea.

'Crock,' said Guy, 'I hope you remember me?'

'Sir.'

'Rather different from our last meeting.'

'Sir,' said Crock.

'The enemy aren't attacking in any strength yet,' Major Erskine continued. 'They're just pushing out patrols. As soon as they bump into anything, they stop and try working round. All quite elementary. We could hold them for ever if those blasted Q fellows would do their job. What are we running away for? It's not soldiering as I was taught it.'

A vehicle stopped outside and Guy recognized Colonel Tickeridge's large commanding voice. He went out and found the Colonel and the Adjutant. They were directing the unloading from a lorry of three wounded men, two of them groggily walking, the third lying on a stretcher. As this man was carried past him he turned his white face and Guy recognized one of his former company. The man lay under a blanket. His wound was fresh and he was not yet in much pain. He smiled up quite cheerfully.

'Shanks,' said Guy. 'What have you been doing to yourself?'

'Must have been a mortar bomb, sir. Took us all by surprise, bursting right in the trench. I am lucky, considering. Chap next to me caught a packet.'

This was Halberdier Shanks who, Guy remembered, used to win

prizes for the Slow Valse. In the days of Dunkirk he had asked for compassionate leave in order to compete at Blackpool.

'I'll come and talk when the MO's had a look at you.'

'Thank you, sir. Nice to have you back with us.'

The other two men had limped off to the RAP. They must be from D Company too, Guy supposed. He did not remember them; only Halberdier Shanks, because of his Slow Valse.

'Well, uncle, come along in and tell me what I can do for you.'

'I was wondering if there was anything *I* could do for *you*, Colonel.'

'Yes, certainly. You will lay on hot dinners for the battalion, a bath for me, artillery support and a few squadrons of fighter aircraft. That's about all we want this morning, I think.' Colonel Tickeridge was in high good humour. As he entered his headquarters he called: 'Hi, there. Bring on the dancing-girls. Where's Halberdier Gold?'

'Just coming up, sir.'

Halberdier Gold was an old friend, since the evening at Matchet when he had carried Guy's bag from the station, before the question even arose of Guy's joining the corps. He smiled broadly.

'Good morning, Gold; remember me?'

'Good morning, sir. Welcome back to the battalion.'

'Vino,' called Colonel Tickeridge. 'Wine for our guest from the higher formation.'

It was said with the utmost geniality but it struck a slight chill after the men's warmer greeting.

Gold laid a jug of wine on the table with the biscuits and bully beef. While they ate and drank, Colonel Tickeridge told Major Erskine:

'Quite a bit of excitement on the left flank. We were up with D Company and I was just warning Brent to expect fireworks in half an hour or so when the Commandos pull out, when I'm blessed if the blighters didn't start pooping off at us with a heavy mortar from the other side of the rocks. De Souza's platoon caught it pretty hot. Lucky we had the truck there to bring back the pieces. We just stopped to watch Brent winkle the mortar out. Then we came straight home. I've made some nice friends out there – a company of New Zealanders who rolled up and said please might they join in our battle – first-class fellows.'

This seemed the moment for Guy to say what had been in his mind since meeting Shanks.

'That's exactly what I want to do, Colonel,' he said. 'Isn't there a platoon you could let me take over?'

Colonel Tickeridge regarded him benevolently. 'No, uncle, of course there isn't.'

'But later in the day, when you get casualties?'

'My good uncle, you aren't under my command. You can't start putting in for a cross-posting in the middle of a battle. That's not how the army works, you know that. You're a Hookforce body.'

'But, Colonel, those New Zealanders – '

'Sorry, uncle. No can do.'

And that, Guy knew from of old, was final.

Colonel Tickeridge began to explain the details of the rear-guard to Major Erskine. Sarum-Smith came to announce that the Commandos were coming through and Guy followed him out into the village and saw a line of dust and the back of the last Hookforce lorry disappearing to the south. There was a little firing, rifles and light machine-guns, and an occasional mortar bomb three-quarters of a mile to the north where the Halberdiers held their line. Guy stood between his friends, isolated.

A few hours earlier he had exulted in his loneliness. Now the case was altered. He was a 'guest from the higher formation', a 'Hookforce body', without place or function, a spectator. And all the deep sense of desolation which he had sought to cure, which from time to time momentarily seemed to be cured, overwhelmed him as of old. His heart sank. It seemed to him as though literally an organ of his body were displaced, subsiding, falling heavily like a feather in a vacuum jar; Philoctetes set apart from his fellows by an old festering wound; Philoctetes without his bow. Sir Roger without his sword.

Presently Colonel Tickeridge cheerfully intruded on his despondency.

'Well, uncle, nice to have seen you. I expect you want to get back to your own people. You'll have to walk, I'm afraid. The Adj and I are going round the companies again.'

'Can I come too?'

Colonel Tickeridge hesitated, then said: 'The more the merrier.'

As they went forward he asked news of Matchet. 'You staff wallahs get all the luck. We've had no mail since we went into Greece.'

The Second Halberdiers and the New Zealanders lay across the main road, their flanks resting on the steep scree that enclosed the

valley. D Company were on the far right flank, strung out along a
water-course. To reach them there was open ground to be crossed.
As Colonel Tickeridge and his party emerged from cover a burst of
fire met them.

'Hullo,' he said, 'the Jerries are a lot nearer than they were this
morning.'

They ran for some rocks and approached cautiously and circui-
tously. When they finally dropped into the ditch they found Brent
and Sergeant-Major Rawkes. Both were preoccupied and rather
grim. They acknowledged Guy's greeting and then turned at once to
their CO.

'They've brought up another mortar.'

'Can you pin-point it?'

'They keep moving. They're going easy with their ammunition at
present but they've got the range.'

Colonel Tickeridge stood and searched the land ahead through his
field-glasses. A bomb burst ten yards behind; all crouched low while
a shower of stone and metal rang overhead.

'We haven't anything to spare for a counter-attack,' said Colonel
Tickeridge. 'You'll have to give a bit of ground.'

In training Guy had often wondered whether the exercises at
Penkirk bore any semblance to real warfare. Here they did. This was
no Armageddon, no torrent of uniformed migration, no clash of
mechanical monsters; it was the conventional 'battalion in defence',
opposed by lightly armed, equally weary small forces. Ritchie-Hook
had done little to inculcate the arts of withdrawal, but the present
action conformed to pattern. While Colonel Tickeridge gave his
orders, Guy moved down the bank. He found de Souza and his
depleted platoon. He had a picturesque bandage round his head.
Under it has sallow face was grave.

'Lost a bit of my ear,' he said. 'It doesn't hurt. But I'll be glad
when today is over.'

'You're retiring at midnight, I gather.'

'"Retiring" is good. It sounds like a maiden aunt going to bed.'

'I dare say you'll be in Alexandria before me,' said Guy. 'Hookforce
is last out, covering the embarkation. I don't get the impression that
the Germans are anxious to attack.'

'D'you know what I think, uncle? I think they want to escort us quietly into the ships. Then they can sink us at their leisure from the air. A much tidier way of doing things.'

A bomb exploded short of them.

'I wish I could spot that damned mortar,' said de Souza.

Then an orderly summoned him to company headquarters. Guy went with him and rejoined Colonel Tickeridge.

It took little time to mount the withdrawal on the flank. Guy watched the battalion adjust itself to its new line. Everything was done correctly. Colonel Tickeridge gave his orders for the hours of darkness and for the final retreat. Guy made notes of times and lines of march in which the Halberdiers and New Zealanders would pass through Hookforce. Then he took his leave.

'If you run across any blue jobs,' said Colonel Tickeridge, 'tell them to wait for us.'

For the third time Guy followed the road south. Night fell. The road filled with many men. Guy found the remnants of his headquarters where he had left them. He did not inquire for Major Hound. Sergeant Smiley offered no information. They fell in and set out into the darkness. They marched all night, one silent component of the procession of lagging, staggering men.

Another day; another night.

Anopopei

Norman Mailer

At 0400, a few minutes after the false dawn had lapsed, the naval bombardment of Anopopei began. All the guns of the invasion fleet went off within two seconds of each other and the night rocked and shuddered like a great log foundering in the surf. The ships snapped and rolled from the discharge, lashing the water furiously. For one instant the night was jagged and immense, demoniac in its convulsion.

Then, after the first salvos the firing became irregular, and the storm almost subsided into darkness again. The great clanging noises of the guns became isolated once more, sounded like immense freight trains jerking and tugging up a grade. And afterward it was possible to hear the sighing wistful murmur of shells passing overhead. On Anopopei the few scattered campfires were snubbed out.

The first shells landed in the sea, throwing up remote playful spurts of water, but then a string of them snapped along the beach, and Anopopei came to life and glowed like an ember. Here and there little fires started where the jungle met the beach, and occasionally a shell which carried too far would light up a few hundred feet of brush. The line of beach became defined and twinkled like a seaport seen from a great distance at night.

An ammunition dump began to burn, spreading a rose-colored flush over a portion of the beach. When several shells landed in its midst, the flames sprouted fantastically high, and soared away in angry brown clouds of smoke. The shells continued to raze the beach and then began to shift inland. The firing had eased already into a steady, almost casual, pattern. A few ships at a time would discharge their volleys and then turn out to sea again while a new file attacked. The ammo dump still blazed, but most of the fires on the beach had smoldered down, and in the light which came with the first lifting of the dawn there was not nearly enough scud to hide the shore. About a mile inland, something had caught fire on the summit of a hill, and back of it, far away, Mount Anaka rose out of a base of maroon-colored smoke. Implacably, despite the new purple robes at its feet, the mountain sat on the island, and gazed out to sea. The bombardment was insignificant before it.

In the troop holds the sounds were duller and more persistent; they grated and rumbled like a subway train. The hold electric lights, a wan yellow, had been turned on after breakfast, and they flickered dully, throwing many shadows over the hatches and through the tiers of bunks, lighting up the faces of the men assembled in the aisles and clustered around the ladder leading up to the top deck.

Martinez listened to the noises anxiously. He would not have been surprised if the hatch on which he was sitting had slid away from under him. He blinked his bloodshot eyes against the weary glare of the bulbs, tried to numb himself to everything. But his legs would twitch unconsciously every time a louder rumble beat against the steel bulkheads. For no apparent reason he kept repeating to himself the last line from an old joke, 'I don't care if I do die, do die, do dy.' Sitting there, his skin looked brown under the jaundiced light. He was a small, slim and handsome Mexican with neat wavy hair, small sharp features. His body, even now, had the poise and grace of a deer. No matter how quickly he might move the motion was always continuous and effortless. And like a deer his head was never quite still, his brown liquid eyes never completely at rest.

Above the steady droning of the guns, Martinez could hear voices separating for an instant and then being lost again. Separate babels of sound came from each platoon; the voice of a platoon leader would buzz against his ear like a passing insect, undefined and rather annoying. 'Now, I don't want any of you to get lost when we hit the beach. Stick together, that's very important.' He drew his knees up tighter, rolled back farther on his haunches until his hipbones grated against the tight flesh of his buttocks.

The men in recon looked small and lost in comparison to the other platoons. Croft was talking now about the landing craft embarkation, and Martinez listened dully, his attention wavering. 'All right,' Croft said softly, 'it's gonna be the same as the last time we practised it. They ain't a reason why anything should go wrong, and it ain't goin' to.'

Red guffawed scornfully. 'Yeah, we'll all be up there,' he said. 'But sure as hell, some dumb sonofabitch is going to run up, and tell us to get back in the hold again.'

'You think I'll piss if we have to stay here for the rest of the war?' Sergeant Brown said.

'Let's cut it out,' Croft told them. 'If you know what's going on better than I do, *you* can stand up here and talk.' He frowned and then continued. 'We're on boat-deck station twenty-eight. You all know where it is, but we're goin' up together just the same. If they's a man here suddenly discovers he's left anythin' behind, that'll be just t.s. We ain't gonna come back.'

'Yeah, boys, don't forget to take your rubbers,' Red suggested, and that drew a laugh. Croft looked angry for a second, but then he drawled, 'I know Wilson ain't gonna forget his,' and they laughed again. 'You're fuggin ay,' Gallagher snorted.

Wilson giggled infectiously. 'Ah tell ya,' he said, 'Ah'd sooner leave my M-one behind, 'cause if they was to be a piece of pussy settin' up on that beach, and Ah didn't have a rubber, Ah'd just shoot myself anyway.'

Martinez grinned, but their laughter, irritated him. 'What's the matter, Japbait?' Croft asked quietly. Their eyes met with the intimate look of old friends. 'Aaah, goddam stomach, she's no good,' Martinez said. He spoke clearly, but in a low and hesitant voice as if he were translating from Spanish as he went along. Croft looked again at him, and then continued talking.

Martinez gazed about the hold. The aisles between the bunks were wide and unfamiliar now that the hammocks were lashed up, and it made him vaguely uneasy. He thought they looked like the stalls in a bit library in San Antonio and he remembered there was something unpleasant about it, some girl had spoken to him harshly. 'I don't care if I do die, do die,' went through his head. He shook himself. There was something terrible going to happen to him today. God always let you know things out of His goodness, and you had to . . . to watch out, to look out for yourself. He said the last part to himself in English.

The girl was a librarian and she had thought he was trying to steal a book. He was very little then, and he had got scared and answered in Spanish, and she had scolded him. Martinez's leg twitched. She had made him cry, he could remember that. Goddam girl. Today, he could screw with her. The idea fed him with a pleasurable malice. Little-tit librarian, he would spit on her now. But the library stalls were still a troop hold, and his fear returned.

A whistle blew, startling him. 'Men for boat-deck fifteen,' a voice shouted down, and one of the platoons started going up the ladder. Martinez could feel the tension in everyone around him, the way their voices had become quiet. Why could they not go first? he asked himself, hating the added tension which would come from waiting. Something was going to happen to him. He knew that now.

After an hour their signal came, and they jogged up the ladder, and stood milling outside the hatchway for almost a minute before they were told to move to their boat. The decks were very slippery in the dawn and they stumbled and cursed as they plodded along the deck. When they reached the davits which held their landing boat, they drew up in a rough file and began waiting again. Red shivered in the cold morning air. It was not yet six a.m., and the day had already the depressing quality which early mornings always had in the Army. It meant they were moving, it meant something new, something unpleasant.

All over the ship the debarkation activities were in different stages. A few landing craft were down in the water already, filled with troops and circling around the ship like puppies on a leash. The men in them waved at the ship the flesh color of their faces unreal against the gray paint of the landing craft, the dawn blue of the sea. The calm water looked like oil. Nearer the platoon, some men were boarding a landing craft, and another one, just loaded, was beginning its descent into the water, the davit pulleys creaking from time to time. But over most of the ship men were still waiting like themselves.

Red's shoulders were beginning to numb under the weight of his full pack, and his rifle muzzle kept clanging against his helmet. He was feeling irritable. 'No matter how many times you wear a goddam pack, you never get used to it,' he said.

'Have you got it adjusted right?' Hennessey asked. His voice was stiff and quivered a little.

'Fug the adjustments,' Red said. 'It just makes me ache somewhere else. I ain't built for a pack, I got too many bones.' He kept on talking, glancing at Hennessey every now and then to see whether he was less nervous. The air was chill, and the sun at his left was still low and quiet without any heat. He stamped his feet, breathing the curious odor of a ship's deck, oil and tar and the fish smell of the water.

'When do we get into the boats?' Hennessey asked.

The shelling was still going on over the beach, and the island looked pale green in the dawn. A thin wispy line of smoke trailed along the shore.

Red laughed. 'What! Do ya think this is gonna be any different today? I figure we'll be on deck all morning.' But as he spoke, he noticed a group of landing craft circling about a mile from them in the water. 'The first wave's still farting round,' he reassured Hennessey. For an instant he thought again of the Motome invasion, and felt a trace of that panic catching him again. His fingertips still remembered the texture of the sides of the rubber boat as he had clung to it in the water. At the back of his throat he tasted salt water again, felt the dumb whimpering terror of ducking underwater when he was exhausted and the Jap guns would not stop. He looked out again, his shaggy face quite bleak for a moment.

In the distance the jungle near the beach had assumed the naked broken look which a shelling always gave it. The palm trees would be standing like pillars now, stripped of their leaves, and blackened if there had been a fire. Off the horizon Mount Anaka was almost invisible in the haze, a pale gray-blue color almost a compromise between the hues of the water and the sky. As he watched, a big shell landed on the shore and threw up a larger puff of smoke than the two to three that had preceded it. This was going to be an easy landing, Red told himself, but he was still thinking about the rubber boats. 'I wish to hell they'd save some of that country for us,' he said to Hennessey. 'We're gonna have to live there.' The morning had a raw expectant quality about it, and he drew a breath, and squatted on his heels.

Gallagher began to curse. 'How fugging long we got to wait up here?'

'Hold your water,' Croft told him. 'Half the commo platoon is coming with us, and they ain't even up yet.'

'Well, why ain't they?' Gallagher asked. He pushed his helmet farther back on his head. 'It's just like the bastards to have us wait up on deck where we can have our fuggin heads blown off.'

'You hear any artillery?' Croft asked.

'That don't mean they ain't got any,' Gallagher said. He lit a cigarette and smoked moodily, his hand cupped over the butt as though he expected it to be snatched away from him any moment.

A shell sighed overhead, and unconsciously Martinez drew back against a gunhousing. He felt naked.

The davit machinery was complicated, and a portion of it hung over the water. When a man was harnessed into a pack and web belt and carried a rifle and two bandoliers and several grenades, a bayonet and a helmet, he felt as if he had a tourniquet over both shoulders and across his chest. It was hard to breathe and his limbs kept falling asleep. Climbing along the beam which led out to the landing craft became an adventure not unlike walking a tightrope while wearing a suit of armor.

When recon was given the signal to get into its landing boat, Sergeant Brown wet his mouth nervously. 'They could've designed these better,' he grumbled to Stanley as they inched out along the beam. The trick was not to look at the water. 'You know, Gallagher ain't a bad guy, but he's a sorehead,' Stanley was confiding.

'Yeah,' Brown said abstractedly. He was thinking it would be a hell of a note if he, a noncom, were to fall in the water. My God, you'd sink, he realized. 'I always hate this part,' he said aloud.

He reached the lip of the landing craft, and jumped into it, the weight of his pack almost spilling him, jarring his ankle. Everyone was suddenly very merry in the little boat which was swaying gently under the davits. 'Here comes old Red,' Wilson yelled, and everybody laughed as Red worked gingerly along the beam, his face puckered like a prune. When he reached the side he looked over scornfully at them and said, 'Goddam, got the wrong boat. They ain't no one stupid-looking enough here to be recon.'

'C'mon in, y'old billygoat,' Wilson chuckled, his laughter easy and phlegmy, 'the water's nice and cold.'

Red grinned. 'I know one place on you that ain't cold. Right now it's red-hot.'

Brown found himself laughing and laughing. What a bunch of good old boys they were in the platoon, he told himself. It seemed as if the worst part were over already.

'How's the General get into these boats?' Hennessey asked. 'He ain't young like us.'

Brown giggled. 'They got two privates to carry him over.' He basked in the laughter which greeted this.

Gallagher dropped into the boat. 'The fuggin Army,' he said, 'I bet they get more fuggin casualties out of guys getting into boats.' Brown roared. Gallagher probably looked mad even when he was screwing his wife. For an instant he was tempted to say so, and it made him laugh even more. In the middle of his snickering he had a sudden image of his own wife in bed with another man at this exact moment, and there was a long empty second in his laughter when he felt nothing at all. 'Hey, Gallagher,' he said furiously, 'I bet you even look pissed-off when you're with your wife.'

Gallagher looked sullen and then unexpectedly began to laugh too. 'Aaah, fug you,' he said, and that made everyone roar even more.

The little assault craft with their blunt bows looked like hippopotami as they bulled and snorted through the water. They were perhaps forty feet long, ten feet wide, shaped like open shoe boxes with a motor at the rear. In the troop well, the waves made a loud jarring sound beating against the bow ramp, and already an inch or two of water had squeezed through the crevices and was sloshing around the bottom. Red gave up the effort to keep his feet dry. Their boat had been circling for over an hour and he was getting dizzy. Occasionally a cold fan of spray would drop on them, shocking and abrupt and a trifle painful.

The first wave of soldiers had landed about fifteen minutes ago, and the battle taking place on the beach crackled faintly in the distance like a bonfire. It seemed remote and insignificant. To relieve the monotony Red would peer over the side wall and scan the shore. It still looked untenanted from three miles out, but the ornament of battle was there – a thin foggy smoke drifted along the water. Occasionally a flight of three dive bombers would buzz overhead and lance towards shore, the sound of their motors filtering back in a subdued gentle rumble. When they dove on the beach it was difficult to follow them, for they were almost in visible, appearing as flecks of pure brilliant sunlight. The puff their bombs threw up looked small and harmless and the planes would be almost out of sight when the noise of the explosions came back over the water.

Red tried to ease the weight of his pack by compressing it against the bulkhead of the boat. The constant circling was annoying. As he looked at the thirty men squeezed in with him, and saw how unnaturally green their uniforms looked against the blue-gray of the troop well, he had to breathe deeply a few times and sit motionless. Sweat was breaking out along his back.

'How long is this gonna take?' Gallagher wanted to know. 'The goddam Army, hurry up and wait, hurry up and wait.'

Red had started to light a cigarette, his fifth since their boat had been lowered in the water, and it tasted flat and unpleasant. 'What do you think?' Red asked. 'I bet we don't go in till ten.' Gallagher swore. It was not yet eight o'clock.

'Listen,' Red went on, 'if they really knew how to work these kind of things, we woulda been eating breakfast now, and we woulda got into these crates about two hours from now.' He rubbed off the tiny ash which had formed on his cigarette. 'But, naw, some sonofabitchin' looey, who's sleeping right now, wanted us to get off the goddam ship so he could stop worrying about us.' Purposely, he spoke loud enough for the Lieutenant from the communications platoon to hear him and grinned as the officer turned his back.

Corporal Toglio, who was squatting next to Gallagher, looked at Red. 'We're a lot safer out in the water,' Toglio explained eagerly. 'This is a pretty small target compared to a ship, and when we're moving like this it's a lot harder to hit us than you think.'

Red grunted. 'Balls.'

'Listen,' Brown said, 'they ain't a time when I wouldn't rather be on that ship. I think it's a hell of a lot safer.'

'I looked into this,' Toglio protested. 'The statistics prove you're a lot safer here than any other place during an invasion.'

Red hated statistics. 'Don't give me any of those figures,' he told Corporal Toglio. 'If you listen to them you give up taking a bath 'cause it's too dangerous.'

'No, I'm serious,' Toglio said. He was a heavy-set Italian of about middle height with a pear-shaped head which was broader in the jaw than in the temple. Although he had shaved the night before, his beard darkened all of his face under his eyes except for his mouth, which was wide and friendly. 'I'm serious,' he insisted, 'I saw the statistics.'

'You know what you can do with them,' Red said.

Toglio smiled, but he was a little annoyed. Red was a pretty good guy, he was thinking, but too independent. Where would you be if everybody was like him? You'd get nowhere. It took co-operation in everything. Something like this invasion was planned, it was efficient, down to a timetable. You couldn't run trains if the engineer took off when he felt like it.

The idea impressed him, and he pointed one of his thick powerful fingers to tell Red when suddenly a Jap shell, the first in half an hour, threw up a column of water a few hundred yards from them. The sound was unexpectedly loud, and they all winced for a moment. In the complete silence that followed, Red yelled loud enough for the whole boat to hear, 'Hey, Toglio, if I had to depend on you for my safety, I'd a been in hell a year ago.' The laughter was loud enough to embarrass Toglio, who forced himself to grin. Wilson capped it by saying in his high soft voice, 'Toglio, you can figger out more ways to make a man do something, and then it turns out all screwed up anyway. Ah never saw a man who was so particular over nothin'.'

That wasn't true, Toglio said to himself. He liked to get things done right, and these fellows just didn't seem to appreciate it. Somebody like Red was always ruining your work by making everybody laugh.

The assault boat's motor grew louder suddenly, began to roar, and after completing a circle, the boat headed in toward shore. Immediately the waves began to pound against the forward ramp, and a long cascade of spray poured over the troops. There was a surprised groan and then a silence settled over the men. Croft unslung his rifle and held one finger over the muzzle to prevent any water from getting into the barrel. For an instant he felt as though he were riding a horse at a gallop. 'Goddam, we're going in,' someone said.

'I hope it's cleaned up at least,' Brown murmured.

Croft felt superior and dejected. He had been disappointed when he had learned weeks before that recon was to be assigned to the beach detail for the first week. And he had felt a silent contempt when the men in the platoon had shown their pleasure at the news. 'Chickenshit,' he muttered to himself now. A man who was afraid to put his neck out on the line was no damn good. Leading the men was a responsibility he craved; he felt powerful and certain at such moments. He longed to be in the battle that was taking place inland from the beach, and he resented the decision which left the platoon on an unloading detail. He passed his hand along his gaunt hard cheek and looked silently about him.

Hennessey was standing near the stern. As Croft watched his white silent face, he decided that Hennessey was frightened and it amused him. The boy found it hard to be still; he kept bobbing about in his place, and once or twice he flinched noticeably at a sudden noise; his leg began to itch and he scratched it violently. Then, as Croft watched, Hennessey pulled his left trouser out of his legging, rolled it up to expose his knee, and with a great deal of care rubbed a little spittle over the irritated red spot on his knee. Croft gazed at the white flesh with its blond hairs, noticed the pains with which Hennessey replaced his trouser in the legging, and felt an odd excitement as if the motions were important. That boy is too careful, Croft told himself.

And then with a passionate certainty he thought, 'Hennessey's going to get killed today.' He felt like laughing to release the ferment in him. This time he was sure.

But, abruptly, Croft remembered the poker game the preceding night when he had failed to draw his full house, and he was confused and then disgusted. You figure you're getting a little too smart for yourself, he thought. His disgust came because he felt he could not trust such emotions, rather than from any conviction that they had no meaning at all. He shook his head and sat back on his haunches, feeling the assault boat race in toward land, his mind empty, waiting for what events would bring.

Martinez had his worst minute just before they landed. All the agonies of the previous night, all the fears he had experienced early that morning had reached their climax in him. He dreaded the moment when the ramp would go down and he would have to get out of the boat. He felt as if a shell would swallow all of them, or a machine-gun would be set up before the bow, would begin firing the moment they were exposed. None of the men was talking, and when Martinez closed his eyes, the sound of the water lashing past their craft seemed overwhelming as though he were sinking beneath it. He opened his eyes, pressed his nails desperately into his palms. 'Buenos Dios,' he muttered. The sweat was dripping from his brow into his eyes, and he wiped it out roughly. Why no sounds? he asked himself. And indeed there were none. The men were silent, and a hush had come over the beach; the lone machine-gun rapping in the distance sounded hollow and unreal.

A plane suddenly wailed past them, then roared over the jungle

firing its guns. Martinez almost screamed at the noise. He felt his
legs twitching again. Why didn't they land? By now he was almost
ready to welcome the disaster that would meet him when the ramp
went down.

In a high piping voice, Hennessey asked, 'Do you think we'll be
getting mail soon?' and his question was lost in a sudden roar of
laughter. Martinez laughed and laughed, subsided into weak giggles,
and then began laughing again.

'That fuggin Hennessey,' he heard Gallagher say.

Suddenly Martinez realized that the boat had ground to a stop.
The sound of its motors had altered, had become louder and a little
uncertain, as if the propeller were no longer biting the water. After a
moment he understood that they had landed.

For several long seconds, they remained motionless. Then the ramp
clanked down, and Martinez trudged dumbly into the surf, almost
stumbling when a knee-high wave broke behind him. He walked with
his head down, looking at the water, and it was only when he was on
shore that he realized nothing had happened to him. He looked
about. Five other craft had landed at the same time, and then men
were stringing over the beach. He saw an officer coming toward him,
heard him ask Croft, 'What platoon is this?'

'Intelligence and reconnaissance, sir, we're on beach detail,' and
then the instructions to wait over by a grove of coconut trees near the
beach. Martinez fell into line, and stumbled along behind Red, as the
platoon walked heavily through the soft sand. He was feeling nothing
at all except a conviction that his judgment had been delayed.

The platoon marched about two hundred yards and then halted at
the coconut grove. It was hot already, and most of the men threw off
their packs and sprawled in the sand. There had been men here
before them. Units of the first wave had assembled nearby, for the
flat caked sand was trodden by many feet, and there was the
inevitable minor refuse of empty cigarette packs and a discarded
ration or two. But now these men were inland, moving somewhere
through the jungle, and there was hardly anyone in sight. They could
see for a distance of about two hundred yards in either direction
before the beach curved out of view, and it was all quiet, relatively
empty. Around either bend there might be a great deal of activity,
but they could not tell this. It was still too early for the supplies to be
brought in, and all the troops that had landed with them had been

quickly dispersed. Over a hundred yards away to their right, the Navy had set up a command post which consisted merely of an officer at a small folding desk, and a jeep parked in the defilade where the jungle met the beach. To their left, just around the bend an eighth of a mile away, the Task Force Headquarters was beginning to function. A few orderlies were digging fox-holes for the General's staff, and two men were staggering down the beach in the opposite direction, unwinding an eighty-pound reel of telephone wire. A jeep motored by in the firm wet sand near the water's edge and disappeared beyond the Navy's CP. The landing boats which had beached near the colored pennants on the other side of Task Force Headquarters had backed off by now and were cruising out toward the invasion fleet. The water looked very blue and the ships seemed to quiver a little in the mid-morning haze. Occasionally one of the destroyers would fire a volley or two, and half a minute later the men would hear the soft whisper of the shell as it arched overhead into the jungle. Once in a while a machine-gun would start racketing in the jungle, and might be answered soon after with the shrill riveting sound of a Japanese light automatic.

Sergeant Brown looked at the coconut trees which were shorn at the top from the shelling. Farther down, another grove had remained untouched, and he shook his head. Plenty of men could have lived through that bombardment, he told himself. 'This ain't such a bad shelling, compared to what they did to Motome,' he said.

Red looked bitter. 'Yeah, Motome.' He turned over on his stomach in the sand, and lit a cigarette. 'The beach stinks already,' he announced.

'How can it stink?' Stanley asked. 'It's too early.'

'It just stinks,' Red answered. He didn't like Stanley, and although he had exaggerated the faint brackish odor that came from the jungle, he was ready to defend his statement. He felt an old familiar depression seeping through him; he was bored and irritable, it was too early to eat, and he had smoked too many cigarettes. 'There ain't any invasion going on,' he said, 'this is practice, amphibious maneuvers.' He spat bitterly.

Croft hooked his cartridge belt about his waist, and slung his rifle. 'I'm going to hunt for S-four,' he told Brown. 'You keep the men here till I get back.'

'They forgot us,' Red said. 'We might as well go to sleep.'

'That's why I'm going to get them,' Croft said.

Red groaned. 'Aaah, why don't you let us sit on our butts for the day?'

'Listen, Valsen,' Croft said, 'you can cut all the pissin' from here on.'

Red looked at him warily. 'What's the matter?' he asked. 'You want to win the war all by yourself?' They stared tensely at each other for a few seconds, and then Croft strode off.

'You're picking the wrong boy to mess with,' Sergeant Brown told him.

Red spat again. 'I won't take no crap from nobody.' He could feel his heart beating quickly. There were a few bodies lying in the surf about a hundred yards from them, and as Red looked a soldier from Task Force Headquarters began dragging them out of the water. A plane patrolled overhead.

'It's pretty fuggin quiet,' Gallagher said.

Toglio nodded. 'I'm going to dig a hole.' He unstrapped his entrenching tool, and Wilson snickered. 'You just better save your energy, boy,' he told him.

Toglio ignored him and started digging. 'I'm going to make one too,' Hennessey piped, and began to work about twenty yards from Toglio. For a few seconds the scraping of their shovels against the sand was the only sound.

Oscar Ridges sighed. 'Shoot,' he said, 'Ah might as well make one too.' He guffawed with embarrassment after he spoke, and bent over his pack. His laughter had been loud and braying.

Stanley imitated him. 'Waa-a-aaah!'

Ridges looked up and said mildly, 'Well, shoot, Ah just cain't help the way Ah laugh. It's good enough, Ah reckon.' He guffawed again to show his good will, but the laughter was much more chastened this time. When there was no answer, he began to dig. He had a short powerful body which was shaped like a squat pillar, for it tapered at neither end. His face was round and dumpy with a long slack jaw that made his mouth gape. His eyes goggled placidly to increase the impression he gave of dull-wittedness and good temper. As he dug, his motions were aggravatingly slow; he dumped each shovelful in exactly the same place, and paused every time to look about before he bent down again. There was a certain wariness about

him, as though he were accustomed to practical jokes, expected them
to be played on him.

Stanley watched him impatiently. 'Hey, Ridges,' he said, looking
at Sergeant Brown for approbation, 'if you were sitting on a fire, I
guess you'd be too lazy to piss and put it out.'

Ridges smiled vaguely. 'Reckon so,' he said quietly, watching
Stanley walk toward him, and stand over the hole to examine his
progress. Stanley was a tall youth of average build with a long face
which looked vain usually and scornful and a little uncertain. He
would have been handsome if it had not been for his long nose and
sparse black mustache. He was only nineteen.

'Christ, you'll be digging all day,' Stanley said with disgust. His
voice was artificially rough like that of an actor who fumbles for a
conception of how soldiers talk.

Ridges made no answer. Patiently he continued digging. Stanley
watched him for another minute, trying to think of something clever
to say. He was beginning to feel ridiculous just standing there, and
on an impulse kicked some sand into Ridges's foxhole. Silently,
Ridges shoveled it out, not breaking his rhythm. Stanley could feel
the men in the platoon watching him. He was a little sorry he had
started for he wasn't certain whether the men sided with him. But he
had gone too far to renege. He kicked in quite a bit of sand.

Ridges laid down his shovel and looked at him. His face was
patient but there was some concern in it. 'What you trying to do,
Stanley?' he asked.

'You don't like it?' Stanley sneered.

'No, sir, Ah don't.'

Stanley grinned slowly. 'You know what you can do.'

Red had been watching with anger. He liked Ridges. 'Listen,
Stanley,' Red shouted, 'wipe your nose and start acting like a man.'

Stanley swung round and glared at Red. The whole thing had gone
wrong. He was afraid of Red, but he couldn't retreat.

'Red, you can blow it out,' he said.

'Speaking of blowing it out,' Red drawled, 'will you tell me why
you bother cultivating that weed under your nose when it grows wild
in your ass-hole?' He spoke with a heavy sarcastic brogue which had
the men laughing before he even finished. 'Good ol' Red,' Wilson
chuckled.

Stanley flushed, took a step towards Red. 'You ain't going to talk to me that way.'

Red was angry, eager for a fight. He knew he could whip Stanley. There was something which he was not ready to face, and he let his anger ride over it. 'Boy, I could break you in half,' he warned Stanley.

Brown got to his feet. 'Listen, Red,' he interrupted, 'you weren't spoiling that damn hard to have a fight with Croft.'

Red paused, and was disgusted with himself. That was it. He stood there indecisively. 'No, I wasn't,' he said, 'but there ain't any man I won't fight.' He wondered if he had been afraid of Croft. 'Aaah, fug it,' he said, turning away.

But Stanley realized that Red would not fight, and he walked after him. 'This ain't settled for me,' he said.

Red looked at him. 'Go blow, will ya.'

To his amazement, Stanley heard himself saying, 'What's the matter, you going chickenshit?' He was positive he had said too much.

'Stanley,' Red told him, 'I could knock your head off, but I ain't gonna fight today.' His anger was returning, and he tried to force it back. 'Let's cut out this crap.'

Stanley watched him, and then spat in the sand. He was tempted to say something more, but he knew the victory was with him. He sat down by Brown.

Wilson turned to Gallagher and shook his head. 'Ah never thought old Red would back down,' he murmured.

Ridges, seeing he was unmolested, went back to his digging. He was brooding a little over the incident, but the satisfying heft of the shovel in his hand soothed him. Just a little-bitty tool, he told himself. Pa would git a laugh out of seein' something like that. He became lost in his work, feeling a comfortable familiarity in the labor. They ain't nothin' like work for bringin' a man round, he told himself. The hole was almost finished, and he began to tamp the bottom with his feet, setting them down heavily and evenly.

The men heard a vicious slapping sound like a fly-swatter being struck against a table. They looked around uneasily. 'That's a Jap mortar,' Brown muttered.

'He's very near,' Martinez muttered. It was the first thing he had said since they had landed.

The men at Task Force Headquarters had dropped to the ground.

Brown listened, heard an accelerating whine, and buried his face in the sand. The mortar exploded about a hundred and fifty yards away, and he lay motionless, listening to the clear terrifying sound of shrapnel cutting through the air, whipping the foliage in the jungle. Brown stifled a moan. The shell had landed a decent distance away, but . . . He was suffering an unreasonable panic. Whenever some combat started there was always a minute when he was completely unable to function, and did the first thing that occurred to him. Now, as the echo of the explosion damped itself in the air, he sprung excitedly to his feet. 'Come on, let's get the hell out of here,' he shouted.

'What about Croft?' Toglio asked.

Brown tried to think. He felt a desperate urgency to get away from this stretch of beach. An idea came to him, and he grasped it without deliberation. 'Look, you got a hole, you stay here. We're gonna head down about half a mile, and when Croft comes back, you meet us there.' He started gathering his equipment, dropped it suddenly, muttered, 'Fug it, get it later,' and began to jog down the beach. The other men looked at him in surprise, shrugged, and then Gallagher, Wilson, Red, Stanley and Martinez followed him, spread out in a long file. Hennessey watched them go, and looked over at Toglio and Ridges. He had dug his hole only a few yards away from the periphery of the coconut grove and he tried to peer into the grove now, but it was too thick to be able to see for more than fifty feet. Toglio's foxhole on his left was about twenty yards away but it seemed much farther. Ridges, who was on the other side of Toglio, seemed a very great distance away. 'What shall I do?' he whispered to Toglio. He wished he had gone with the others, but he had been afraid to ask for fear they would laugh at him. Toglio took a look around, and then, crouching, ran over to Hennessey's hole. His broad dark face was sweating now. 'I think it's a very serious situation,' he said dramatically, and then looked into the jungle.

'What's up?' Hennessey asked. He felt a swelling in his throat which was impossible to define as pleasant or unpleasant.

'I think some Japs sneaked a mortar in near the beach, and maybe they're going to attack us.' Toglio mopped his face. 'I wish the fellows had dug holes here,' he said.

'It was a dirty trick to run off,' Hennessey said. He was surprised to hear his voice sound natural.

'I don't know,' Toglio said. 'Brown's got more experience than I
have. You got to trust your noncoms.' He sifted some sand through
his fingers. 'I'm getting back in my hole. You just sit tight and wait.
If any Japs come, we've got to stop them.' Toglio's voice was
portentous, and Hennessey nodded eagerly. This was like a movie,
he thought. Vague images overlapped in his mind. He saw himself
standing up and repelling a charge. 'Okay, kid,' Toglio said, and
clapped him on the back. Crouching again, Toglio ran past his own
hole to talk to Ridges. Hennessey remembered Red's telling him that
Toglio had come to the platoon after the worst of the Motome
campaign. He wondered if he could trust him.

Hennessey squatted in his hole and watched the jungle. His mouth
was dry and he kept wetting his lips; every time there seemed to be a
movement in the bushes, his heart constricted. The beach was very
quiet. A minute went by, and he began to get bored. He could hear a
truck grinding its gears down the beach, and when he took a chance
and turned around, he could see another wave of landing craft
coming in about a mile from shore. Reinforcements for us, he told
himself, and realized it was absurd.

The harsh slapping sound came out of the jungle and was followed
by another discharge and another and another. That's the mortars,
he thought, and decided he was catching on fast. And then he heard
a screaming piercing sound almost overhead like the tearing squeals
of a car braking to avert a crash. Instinctively he curled flat in his
hole. The next instants were lost to him. He heard an awful exploding
sound which seemed to fill every corner of his mind, and the earth
shook and quivered underneath him in the hole. Numbly he felt dirt
flying over him, and his body being pounded by some blast. The
explosion came again, and the dirt and the shock, and then another
and another blast. He found himself sobbing in the hole, terrified and
resentful. When another mortar landed, he screamed out like a child,
'That's enough, *That's enough*!' He lay there trembling for almost a
minute after the shells had stopped. His thighs felt hot and wet, and
at first he thought, I'm wounded. It was pleasant and peaceful, and
he had a misty picture of a hospital bed. He moved his hand back,
and realized with both revulsion and mirth that he had emptied his
bowels.

Hennessey froze his body. If I don't move, I won't get any dirtier,
he thought. He remembered Red and Wilson talking about 'keeping

a tight ass-hole,' and now he understood what they meant. He began to get the giggles. The sides of his foxhole were crumbling, and he had a momentary pang of anxiety at the thought that they would collapse in the next shelling. He was beginning to smell himself and he felt a little sick. Should he change his pants? he wondered. There was only one other pair in his pack, and he might have to wear them for a month. If he threw these away, they might make him pay for them.

But no, that wasn't true, he told himself; you didn't have to pay for lost equipment overseas. He was beginning to get the giggles again. What a story this would make to tell Pop. He saw his father's face for a moment. A part of him was trying to needle his courage to look over the edge of his hole. He raised himself cautiously, as much from the fear of further soiling his pants as from an enemy he might see.

Toglio and Ridges were still beneath the surface of their slit-trenches. Hennessey began to suspect he had been left alone. 'Toglio, Corporal Toglio,' he called, but it came out in a hoarse croaking whisper. There was no answer; he didn't ask himself whether they had heard him. He was alone, all alone, he told himself, and he felt an awful dread at being so isolated. He wondered where the others were. He had never seen combat before, and it was unfair to leave him alone; Hennessey began to feel bitter at being deserted. The jungle looked dark and ominous like a sky blacking over with thunderclouds. Suddenly, he knew he couldn't stay here any longer. He got out of his hole, clutched his rifle, and started to crawl away from the hole.

'Hennessey, where are you going?' Toglio shouted. His head had suddenly appeared from the hole.

Hennessey started, and then began to babble, 'I'm going to get the others. It's important, I got my pants dirty.' He began to laugh.

'Come back,' Toglio shouted.

The boy looked at his foxhole and knew it was impossible to return to it. The beach seemed so pure and open. 'No, I got to go,' he said, and began to run. He heard Toglio shout once more, and then he was conscious only of the sound of his breathing. Abruptly, he realized that something was sliding about in the pocket his pants made as they bellied over his leggings. In a little frenzy, he pulled his trouser loose, let the stool fall out, and then began to run again.

Hennessey passed by the place where the flags were put up for the boats to come in, and saw the Navy officer lying prone in a little hollow near the jungle. Abruptly, he heard the mortars again, and then right after it a machine-gun firing nearby. A couple of grenades exploded with a loud empty sound that paper bags make when they burst. He thought for an instant, There's some soldiers after them Japs with the mortar. Then he heard the terrible siren of the mortar shell coming down on him. He pirouetted in a little circle, and threw himself to the ground. Perhaps he felt the explosion before a piece of shrapnel tore his brain in half.

Red found him when the platoon was coming back to meet Toglio. They had waited out the shelling in a long zigzag trench which had been dug by a company of reserve troops farther along the beach. After word had come that the Jap mortar crew had been wiped out, Brown decided to go back. Red didn't feel like talking to anybody, and unconsciously he assumed the lead. He came around a bend in the beach and saw Hennessey lying facedown in the sand with a deep rent in his helmet and a small circle of blood about his head. One of his hands was turned palm upward, and his fingers clenched as though he were trying to hold something. Red felt sick. He had liked Hennessey, but it had been the kind of fondness he had for many of the men in the platoon – it included the possibility that it might be ended like this. What bothered Red was the memory of the night they had sat on deck during the air raid when Hennessey had inflated his life belt. It gave Red a moment of awe and panic as if someone, *something*, had been watching over their shoulders that night and laughing. There was a pattern where there shouldn't be one.

Brown came up behind him, and gazed at the body with a troubled look. 'Should I have left him behind?' he asked. He tried not to consider whether he were responsible.

'Who takes care of the bodies?'

'Graves Registration.'

'Well, I'm going to find them so they can carry him away,' Red said.

Brown scowled. 'We're supposed to stick together.' He stopped, and then went on angrily, 'Goddam, Red, you're acting awful chicken today, picking fights and then backing out of them, throwing a fit over . . .' He looked at Hennessey and didn't finish.

Red was walking on already. For the rest of this day, that was one part of the beach he was going to keep away from. He spat, trying to exorcise the image of Hennessey's helmet, and the blood that had still been flowing through the rent in the metal.

The platoon followed him, and when they reached the place where they had left Toglio, the men began digging holes in the sand. Toglio walked around nervously, repeating continually that he had yelled for Hennessey to come back. Martinez tried to reassure him. 'Okay, nothing you can do,' Martinez said several times. He was digging quickly and easily in the soft sand, feeling calm for the first time that day. His terror had withered with Hennessey's death. Nothing would happen now.

When Croft came back he made no comment on the news Brown gave him. Brown was relieved and decided he did not have to blame himself. He stopped thinking about it.

But Croft brooded over the event all day. Later, as they worked on the beach unloading supplies, he caught himself thinking of it many times. His reaction was similar to the one he had felt at the moment he discovered his wife was unfaithful. At that instant, before his rage and pain had begun to operate, he had felt only a numb throbbing excitement and the knowledge that his life was changed to some degree and certain things would never be the same. He knew that again now. Hennessey's death had opened to Croft vistas of such omnipotence that he was afraid to consider it directly. All day the fact hovered about his head, tantalizing him with odd dreams and portents of power.

'Plane Land Here'

Charles J. Rolo

When Jefferies reached Brigade Headquarters on Marsh 25 he found Wingate pacing up and down the bed of a dry *chaung*, analysing the position. A large force was now concentrated under the Brigadier: his own column, Jefferies' party, and the three columns commanded by Ferguson, Scott, and Gilkes. The Japs had by this time drawn a tight net round the Chindits. In fact, one of Wingate's patrols had just reported that the enemy knew to within a few miles what area the force was in. Wingate realized that getting out of Burma was going to make the march in seem like a stroll through St James's Park.

'Just put yourself in the position of the Jap commander,' he said to Jefferies. 'Your one aim will be to prevent anyone from getting out alive. You've been made to look very stupid. Your superior officers are storming, "Are you going to let these appalling conditions continue?" There's only one way you can save face, and that's by annihilating the whole expedition. Yes, we can take it for granted that from now on the Jap commander is going to do everything in his power to wipe us out. And the first thing he'll do is make a very strong effort to prevent us from recrossing the Irrawaddy.'

After dusk Wingate summoned his senior officers and explained his plan of retreat. He would make a forced march to Inywa, where the Shweli river runs into the Irrawaddy. The Japanese commander would probably have commandeered all boats on the Irrawaddy, but they might find boats on the Shweli. For the sake of speed they would shoot and eat their few remaining bullocks, and would ditch half of their bedding, keeping one blanket and one ground-sheet for every two men. They started off at 1 a.m. And covered the forty miles of vile jungle in two nights' marching. At one of their rest halts on the way a Japanese patrol attacked the tail of the force with mortars, and Wingate detailed Major Fergusson's column to lead off the enemy.

Fergusson headed north-east, making his tracks as conspicuous as possible. In the jungle near Hintha he laid a dummy bivouac and abandoned various tempting articles of equipment with booby traps attached. The Japs did not put in an appearance. Next Day Fergusson led two platoons towards Hintha, which seemed a likely place for a Japanese garrison. He reckoned that a battle in this area would draw the enemy away from the Brigadier's force.

'On the edge of the village [Hintha],' Fergusson afterwards related,

sitting round a fire as it might be round a bridge table, were four men talking. They looked up incuriously as I approached. I addressed them in one of my rare Burmese sentences: 'What is the name of this village?' (to which I knew the answer, but I was just making conversation). They didn't respond, and the truth flashed upon me at the same moment as the man beside me gasped 'Japs!' Not only were they more surprised than I was, they were petrified and unable to move. They gazed fascinated at me as I struggled with the pin of the grenade which I had been carrying in my right hand for the last twenty-four hours. They still sat on while there followed a neat lob (though I say it myself) into the middle of the fire, and a most entrancing bang. Then they all fell over outward on to their backs with perfect symmetry.

Fergusson was right in his guess that Hintha would be heavily garrisoned. The fight which followed lasted nearly two hours. Fergusson suffered eleven casualties – four killed, including one of his senior officers, Captain Alec MacDonald, and seven wounded. He himself was hit in the leg by two mortar fragments. The enemy's losses were at least thirty. The fact remained that the Japs were in too great strength for the column to get past Hintha. Fergusson decided to break up into dispersal groups, and gave the order to proceed to a rendezvous twenty miles to the north. One of the groups later saw the Japanese attack the false bivouac and heard the bangs of booby traps exploding. The bulk of the column reached the rendezvous within the appointed twenty-four hours – a tribute to the training of Wingate's junior officers and NCO's – and Fergusson's men resumed their march towards the Irrawaddy in search of Brigade Headquarters.

All Fergusson's efforts to pick up Wingate's trail were unsuccessful, and his column had unfortunately lost its wireless set in a river. He finally gave up the chase, led his men across the Shweh, and set a northerly course for the Chindwin, dividing his column into three large dispersal groups. Their supplies consisted of three days' rations per man and a large stock of tobacco. When the rations ran out they lived off the jungle and what food they could buy from the natives.

For jungle reading Fergusson had taken along with him a copy of one of Trollope's lesser-known novels, *Ayala's Angel*. One by one of leaves were torn out to make cigarettes. Fergusson's men 'smoked' all six hundred pages.

At the end of April the group commanded by Fergusson reached India with twenty-two casualties out of seventy-four officers and men. Fergusson himself, limping badly from two leg-wounds, marched out under his own steam with his monocle neatly fixed in his right eye.

The remainder of the force under Wingate reached the Irrawaddy at a point immediately south of its confluence with the Shweli between one and two in the morning on March 29. The Brigadier learned from villagers that the enemy had established strong points all along the two rivers and was patrolling between these points. As Wingate had predicted, the Japs had taken all boats off the Irrawaddy. Some had been holed and were lying in the shallow water near the bank. The Chindits did, however, find a few boats on the Shweli and carried them down to the Irrawaddy.

Just before dawn they assembled for the crossing. Quickly and silently they began to unload the mules. Every now and then a man would glance anxiously up and down the river or pause for an instant to listen to a sound from the jungle. A zero-hour mood hung over the column. The men realized that this was a crucial point in the get-out. No one dared to hope for an easy crossing.

The sun rose blood-red in a very pale blue sky. The morning air was almost cold. A swift current was running and the Irrawaddy looked wider than when they had crossed it the first time. The whole scene seemed to Jefferies unnaturally peaceful.

Jefferies had been ordered to supervise the crossing. 'After nine years in the Navy,' Wingate remarked lightly, 'you ought to be able to get us across the Irrawaddy.' Nine years on a destroyer, Jefferies reflected gloomily, weren't much help when it came to commanding a flotilla of dugouts. He was fighting down an ominous feeling that something would go wrong. Up until now his hunches had usually been right.

The first dugout had pushed off and Wingate's men were tensely waiting their turn to cross when an incongruous thing happened. A boatload of natives popped up seemingly from nowhere and swarmed ashore to peddle their cargo of *jagri* balls and cheroots. Wingate quickly bought up the cargo, borrowed the boat, and the crossing continued.

An RAF rubber dinghy, carrying one of the precious wireless sets, bobbed slowly into mid-stream. Jefferies was standing on the beach. He was in a daze after the long march on half rations and the extra work of organizing the crossing. Every action required a conscious effort. Half in a dream he wondered hazily why the sand on the beach was spitting into the air. It was several seconds before he realized machine-gun bullets were biting into the ground just in front of him. He flattened behind a sandbank and whipped out his field-glasses. On the west bank he saw a large party of Japs, then a mortar shell landed with a splash a few feet away from the RAF dinghy. He suddenly felt slightly sick. It wasn't fear, just a tightening at the pit of the stomach. What he knew would happen had happened.

The enemy seemed to be in fairly large numbers on the west bank, but most of his machine-gun and small-arms fire was falling short. Wingate quickly put his mortars into action, and the second burst found the range. The Japs raised their sights, too far this time, and started shooting over the Chindits' heads. Wingate could have forced a crossing with heavy losses, but orders from India were to bring the men out alive. He made a split-second decision. Standing on a sandbank in the Irrawaddy, looking like some minor prophet with his huge beard and a blanket wrapped around his shoulders, he ordered the beach to be cleared. There was only one casualty. A signalman, bending over to lift a wireless set, had been hit in the head in the first volley.

Jefferies stood beside Wingate on the beach with bullets flying around them, hoping that the Brigadier would break into an undignified double. He did nothing of the kind. Walking slowly towards the jungle, he said to Jefferies, 'They are in some strength just behind us to the east; in what strength we don't know, but they may be down on us at any moment. They are in considerable strength on the other

side. We've got to make ourselves scarce, and pretty quickly. Get all
the officers into that dip over there and I'll give them instructions.'

Wingate's plan was for the columns to part company, move back
into the jungle to the east until they had given the Japanese the slip,
then make their way separately out of Burma by whatever route
seemed safest.

Major Kenneth Gilkes, a former Sussex paint manufacturer, decided
to head for China. His men climbed a broad belt of mountains ten
thousand feet high, and linked up with Chinese irregulars. The
inhabitants of the first Chinese village they reached provided rice for
the whole column and refused any payment. 'You have fought the
enemies of China,' one of them explained. 'The least we can do is
feed you.' With Gilkes was Captain Petersen, the Free Dane who had
helped Calvert rout the Japs in the battle at Nankan on the railway.
After crossing the Irrawaddy Petersen had been seriously wounded
in the head and could not sit his horse without help. He was
supported in the saddle by relays of men for a march of several
hundred miles until he was sufficiently recovered to walk and fight
with the rest of them. Eventually Gilkes' men reached the Salween
valley front, where the Japanese had been pressing forward when
Wingate's columns crossed into Burma. Here they watched a seven-
day battle in which the Chinese routed the Japs, who had transferred
a full division to Burma to deal with Wingate's raiders. Then they
crossed the Salween and later the Mekong, with guides supplied by
the regular Chinese Army, and eventually reaching Kunming. They
had marched fifteen hundred miles since leaving Imphal. The
Chinese Commander-in-Chief at Kunming had been notified of their
arrival and greeted them with flags flying and a band playing military
marches. He gave them new clothes, hot baths, and haircuts all
round, and lodged them in the best building in town. Their life
became a round of sumptuous meals capped by a banquet that cost
twenty thousand Chinese dollars. The hospitable Chinese General
even advanced Gilkes enough money to pay his men. Eventually the
column was flown back to India from Kunming in planes of the 10th
US Air Force.

After leaving the Brigadier Major Scott's men marched due north
in the direction of Fort Hertz. They bumped into a Japanese patrol,
fought a sharp engagement, and pushed on to the Irrawaddy. They

came out on to the river at a point between Katha and Bhamo, and lay for two days in the jungle by the bank watching Japanese patrol boats go by guarding all traffic. On the third morning a native boat, unescorted, ran aground in the mudbanks below where Scott's men were hiding. The raiders swarmed out, seized the boat, and crossed the river without interference. Two days later the mule carrying their wireless set, the only mule they had left, died. They wirelessed for a last supply-drop, then smashed the set and buried it.

The rendezvous for the dropping was a clearing near Bhamo, a large town one hundred and fifty miles behind the Japanese lines and not far from the China frontier. On the way to the rendezvous they ran out of rations. They dared not venture into the villages as the whole area was now heavily patrolled by the enemy. With nothing to eat but bamboo shoots and jungle palms, they began to drop like flies from hunger and disease.

Marching along through dark jungle shuttered from the sky with creepers, Major Scott noticed that the track ahead of him was growing lighter, as though he were nearing the end of a tunnel. Quite suddenly he was standing on the edge of the jungle, looking out on to what was probably the only large patch of grassland in Northern Burma. This was the rendezvous. Next day, with luck, the RAF would drop them food and new equipment.

There remained the problem of the sick and wounded. Sheer guts had carried them this far, but Scott knew that not one of them could ever make the long trek to Blighty. There was Colonel Cooke, one of Wingate's senior officers, weakened with dysentery and covered with deep, festering jungle sores; Corporal Jimmy Walker, who had dropped out of line two days before with dysentery and an infected hip, and had somehow dragged himself along behind them; and Lance-Corporal Fred Nightingale, worn to a skeleton by ulcers. Private Robert Hulse had ruptured himself carrying a machine-gun through the hills, and every few hours was seized with violent fits of vomiting. Private Jim Suddery had been shot in the back, and the bullet had gone right through him, leaving a purplish hole in his abdomen; somehow he was still marching. A Burma Rifle was shivering and sweating with malignant malaria. These and a dozen others had fought long and well. They must not be left to Japanese bayonets.

Scott knew they had only one hope – rescue from the air. He stared

out at the clearing. It was bumpy and badly pitted, but a good pilot
would have a sporting chance of landing. He sent for the Sergeant-
Major. 'Tell the men to tear some parachutes into strips and spell
out the words: PLANE LAND HERE.'

On Sunday, April 11, the planes came over and dropped supplies.
Circling low, they picked out the message, and one of them pointed
its nose to the ground. It skimmed the jagged field and roared up
again. The Chindits watched, breathless. Inside the plane Flying
Officer 'Lumme' Lord yelled at the crew, 'Hold tight, boys, we'll try
again.' Teeth clenched, drenched with sweat, he put the plane down.
The field jumped up at them. Rough turf scarred with potholes
flashed past the windows. Lord cursed savagely into the roar of the
engines. Not a hope. He swung his machine into a wide arc and
headed for home.

Back at base he reported to Wing Commander Burbury: 'It can be
done – if they mark out a runway.' Off went another plane with a
message to the Chindits. 'Mark out 1200-yard landing-ground to hold
12-ton transport.' On Tuesday at dawn the rescue plane took off,
rocketing into the rising run with Flying Officer Michael Vlasto at
the controls. Before it left the supply officer handed each crew
member a pair of army boots. 'You may need these,' he explained
cheerily, 'to walk home in.'

The crew was a mixed lot, catapulted by war from the corners of
Empire into a late-model. American aircraft just out of a California
factory. Vlasto – dark, going bald, hatchet-faced – had sandwiched
twelve hundred hours' flying time between civilian life in Calcutta's
jute mills and this April morning. His second, Pilot-Sergeant Frank
Murray, had left high school in Kingston, Jamaica, to be trained as a
flier in the New World. The Empire Air Training Scheme had given
him his wings, and chance had picked him out of thousands for duty
on the India-Burma front. Vlasto's radio operator, Sergeant Jack
Reeves, hailed from Bradford, Ontario. There was no sounder man
in the squadron. His mates called him 'Happy.' They'd never seen
him smile. The flight rigger, Sergeant Charles Alfred May, was a
mechanic in a garage in Leeds when Hitler invaded Poland. He had
worked his way to India by way of the Libyan desert, but close
contact with Stukas had not jarred his good humour.

The huge plane picked up fighter escort and stabbed into Burma,
cruising easily at 160 mph. 'She's a hot crate,' Vlasto thought. 'But

she can't be too hot for this job.' Smoke fires pointed the way to the clearing. Vlasto dipped and spotted a white line across the field. Dropping low, he read the message: 'Land on white line. Ground there VG.'

First the plane circled, releasing more supplies for the column. Then Vlasto skimmed the landing strip, weighing his chances. It was about eight hundred yards long – four hundred yards too short for comfort. A strong wind was blowing up the runway towards the tall teak forest, two hundred yards beyond where the white line ended. Vlasto knew that if anything went wrong they'd be past needing boots. 'What about it?' he asked the co-pilot. 'Here's hoping,' Murray said fervently. 'Plane landing,' Vlasto yelled to the crew, and they braced themselves in the rear. The big transport hit ground and touched down easily. Vlasto braked hard. They pulled up just at the end of the strip and taxied back slowly.

A band of hill-billy assassins tumbled out of the jungle and crowded happily around the plane. Mortar and Bren-gun crews remained at their posts. The Japs might attack any minute; it was a miracle they had not discovered the landing-ground days ago. The eighteen sick and wounded filed out from under cover and hobbled towards the plane. Some had to be supported, but they all wore their packs. For every one of them it was a reprieve from certain death. At the steps of the plane the eighteenth man halted and turned to Major Scott. 'I'm all right, sir. I came in on my feet, and I'd like to go out the same way.' Scott smiled. 'Good man,' he said, and No. 18 joined the group posing for a farewell picture. As the crew scrambled into the plane the Chindits waved their hats three times and cheered silently through closed lips.

The motors hummed and the door slammed to. Twelve minutes after landing the plane took off with seventeen walking hospital cases. She lifted slowly, labouring heavily. In the cockpit Vlasto and Murray sat, dead white, with their eyes glued on the teak-trees rushing towards the wind-shield. The runway was too short and the plane overloaded. Sweat poured down their faces; they were heading straight into the top branches. Vlasto was listening for the crash when the plane heaved and bounced upward. A frantic lift and over she went. Tree-tops flashed below the wing-tips. Murray grinned at Vlasto: 'Six inches to spare.' Vlasto brushed the sweat off his forehead: 'God bless No. 18.'

Three weeks later No. 18 and the rest of Scott's column fought their way through to Fort Hertz and were flown back to India.

MULE FOR BREAKFAST

When the columns commanded by Scott and Gilkes parted from Brigade Headquarters on the east bank of the Irrawaddy Jefferies' group remained with Wingate. On March 31, in a small jungle clearing ten miles east of the river, the Brigadier's force took a last supply-drop – eight days' hard rations per man for the hundred-and-fifty-mile homeward journey and paddles for the Irrawaddy crossing. For Jefferies there was a special item – a copy of his will, which he had deposited with his bank in India and had forgotten to sign. A bank official with a macabre sense of duty had sent him another copy for signature, thoughtfully suggesting that one of his fellow-officers could bring it back if anything happened to him.

Wingate now decided to break up the force remaining under him into small parties, each about forty strong. On the old military principle of 'scatter to live,' these groups were to fade into the jungle, cross the Irrawaddy at widely separated points, and make their way singly back to India. Before they dispersed Wingate ordered the whole of the force to fall in and gave the men a brief farewell talk. He explained what they had accomplished and summed up the situation in Burma, carefully pointing out Japanese concentration points on the homeward route. He thanked them all for their conduct, and confessed that it was a hard blow not to be able to lead them back to India as a force. He made no bones about the trek to the Chindwin being the most difficult portion of the campaign. 'Whatever you do,' he counselled, 'keep on the move. You'll be hungry and thirsty and tired. Don't get slack. Keep your wits about you, and I'm sure you'll make it. Good luck to you all.' The column split up, and each party struck off separately into the jungle to the east.

Wingate led his own group off in search of a safe bivouac, where they could rest and feed up for the return journey. He planned to lie low for a week to make the Japs believe they had cleared out of the area. The enemy, Wingate hoped, would eventually go hunting for them elsewhere, and leave them a clear passage across the Irrawaddy.

They soon came to a clearing by a dried-up *chaung* where, after some digging, they hit water and were able to drink, wash, and relax. After supper that night, resting in the bed of the *chaung*, Wingate sent for Jefferies and the Brigade-Major – Jim Anderson, a former Glasgow solicitor – and explained his plans for the withdrawal. He talked in a low murmur, running his fingers through his shaggy hair: 'Every man's experience is invaluable, and my orders are to save as many as possible. The only way of doing that is to keep dodging the enemy. There are forty of us; if we're caught by a battalion or even by a company we're done for. Speed is our only defence. Ergo – everything has to be sacrificed to speed. We'll have to kill the mules and eat them, scrap the wireless sets, and ditch the heavy equipment. That will mean no more supplies, no mortars, no machine-guns. We'll be foxes hunted every inch of the way. We're going to have to redouble our security measures. Every officer and man, irrespective of rank, will do his share of scouting, patrol work, and sentry duty. Anyone who is slack will be severely punished. See to it that it is understood by every one in the force.'

On April 1 Wingate sent off his final wireless message to India. The batteries for the wireless sets were almost exhausted; there was just enough power left to pick up a broadcast from New Delhi. The wireless operator then handed round the last news bulletin they would see until they got back. The war news cheered them up considerably. The Russians had made spectacular gains on the southern part of the front. The Allied aerial offensive in Western Europe was gaining momentum. In Yannan Province the Chinese were pushing back the Japs, and Japanese positions in New Guinea were being hammered from the air. Cairo reported that the Axis was concentrating ships to evacuate its troops from North Africa. This last item meant that the sequel to the Wingate expedition might not be long deferred. The Mediterranean would soon be opened up to Allied shipping and there would be more supplies for the India front. Next year might see the big offensive in Burma. After reading the news Wingate quoted: 'As cold waters to a thirsty soul, so is good news from a far country' (Proverbs xxv. 25).

That same day the slaughter of the mules began. Wingate himself, acting as executioner, showed how to kill them without a tell-tale pistol shot. It was a grisly business. The first mule was dragged forward and given bamboo-leaves to keep him quiet while a rope was

tied round his front and back legs. Four men lifted the mule and
threw him heavily to the ground. Then one man, stripped completely
naked, sat on the animal's head to keep him still while Wingate deftly
cut the carotid artery, explaining each detail of the operation like a
surgeon lecturing to students. There was an appalling surge of blood.
The naked man stood up – a monstrous figure drenched in blood
from head to foot. Veterans of three years of war slipped off,
nauseated, into the jungle.

The mule was immediately skinned and cut up, and portions were
dealt out to each man. Chops and steaks were cut out of the carcass.
They were tough and sweet, but gave the men new energy. The heart,
liver, tongue, and kidneys made excellent eating, skewered on the end
of a piece of bamboo and grilled over an open fire. Best of all was
mule soup. That, in the opinion of Wingate's Yorkshiremen, was
'really champion.' For six days they ate mule for breakfast, mule for
lunch, mule for dinner. On the seventh day they ate the horses.

The Brigadier enforced rigid security measures. Fires were lit only
for half an hour before dawn and half an hour after dusk because
smoke, hanging over the tree-tops, might give them away in the
daylight, whereas flames could be seen only a short distance through
the jungle and could be extinguished in a few seconds. Wingate
instructed the men who were chopping bamboo for more paddles to
disguise what they were doing by breaking up the regularity of their
strokes, which echoed through the jungle. He taught them to give one
mighty wallop, then a lot of quick strokes, then to stop. It was a slow
and tedious business. To keep the mules quiet while they were
waiting their turn for slaughter, Wingate saw to it that they had
bamboo-leaves to chew on all day long, and ordered an enormous
supply of leaves to be piled up every morning.

One mule-leader begged to have three of his pets spared. He
promised they would give no trouble and swore that he could bring
them out alive. The Brigadier explained patiently that even one mule
would endanger the whole party. With a mournful 'Very good,
Sahib,' the muleteer padded away to join his animals, who were to
be killed the next morning. All night he talked to them, caressed their
heads, and prayed in a low monotone. At dawn he vanished into the
jungle until it was all over. Afterwards he wept for three days.

Wingate's men did not dare to move out of the bivouac area – they might at any moment be discovered and attacked – and the seven-day rest period dragged by painfully slowly. There was not much to do except daydream, and the fact that they were now heading for home brought back thoughts banished during the months of training and action. The colour of the teak-leaves reminded Jefferies of a green jacket his best girl had worn in London. A noise in the jungle recalled the sound of a well-hit tennis ball. He would fall asleep dreaming of peace-time England, and wake up with the unbearable stench of dead mule in his nostrils.

Lying in the *chaung* bed, the officers rested, dozing, reading, or listening to Wingate talking. With the most dangerous part of the campaign still ahead, Wingate was incapable of relaxing. In those seven days he talked like a man possessed, rather as if he were striving to set in order the sum-total of his beliefs. The survivors in the party remembered fragments of what he said, but none could recapture the flavour of his language. Wingate talked of books, painting, music, and the future of mankind. He lectured them on the painting of the eighteenth century. He argued heatedly with Jefferies that the symphony and not – as Jefferies held – the piano concerto was the highest form of art. There were great possibilities in the cinema, he said, but they had never been fully exploited, except perhaps by Walt Disney, for whom he had a great admiration. He analysed the art of detective fiction, quoted Leonardo da Vinci, and recited in a whisper Gray's *Elegy written in a Country Churchyard* – one of his favourite poems. He talked a great deal about the good in various religions. He dissected the characters in the comic strips. His favourites were 'Jane,' of the *Daily Mirror*, and J. Wellington Wimpy, whose lack of courage, Wingate argued, was more human than Popeye's impossible feats of bravery. He would make whimsical plans of what he was going to do after the war. He had become very fond of the Burmese, and one day remarked, 'I've half a mind to settle down here when it's all over.' Next day he was talking of retiring to an oyster farm on the East Coast.

Only once did Wingate bring up the subject of war. 'A really good commander,' he said, 'leaves nothing to chance. But you can't completely rule out the element of luck in war-time. If a general is consistently unlucky, however good a general he may be, there's only one thing to do: sack him.'

Wingate talked a great deal about a league of nations, plans for a world federation, and the future of the world. A way would have to be found, he declared, to restore the white man's individuality and powers of initiative. 'European civilization,' he declared, 'prevents men from thinking and acting for themselves. Civilized man is like a white ant in a mound; he is entirely dependent on a complex social organization.' Then he discussed ways and means of enforcing the peace: 'This time, a league of nations or some federation of nations must be made to work. Any nation which breaks the law must be dealt with immediately.'

Between bouts of talking Wingate would bury his head in a book. He had brought with him Xenophon, Plato's *Dialogues*, Mark Twain's *Innocents Abroad*, and a *Pocket Oxford Dictionary*. When he spotted the life of Bernard Shaw that had been parachuted to Jefferies a few days before he asked if he could borrow it. 'Most English writers are sterile,' he complained to Jefferies. 'There is virtually nobody writing to-day of any importance – except Shaw and Wells.'

The Brigadier's vitality was quite a trial to his officers, who were completely exhausted and wanted to make the most of their seven days of rest. At night Wingate would call softly to Jefferies, and, if he was awake, confront him with some philosophical question. That usually led to a discussion which went on until Wingate was satisfied that the problem had been thoroughly polished off. One morning the Brigadier sent a man to tell Jefferies to join him in a hurry. When he saw the Major doubling over he put a finger to his lips and hissed 'Quiet.' Jefferies concluded they were in trouble. He found Wingate staring enraptured at an exquisitely coloured butterfly.

On April 7 Wingate decided to make a second try at crossing the Irrawaddy. If all went well the homeward march would take fourteen days; his party now had five days' paratroop rations apiece. Wingate jotted down in his notebook exactly what he would eat at each meal. On the way back he kept on consulting this notebook, and would remark aloud, 'Now I can have some chocolate. . . time for two biscuits.'

Before leaving the bivouac the men smashed and buried the wireless sets, mortars, and machine-guns, keeping Tommy-guns, rifles, and grenades. From now on all equipment would have to be manhandled every foot of the way. Smashing the wireless sets was the hardest blow of all. It gave the men a ghastly feeling to stand by

watching the RAF sergeant wrecking their last link with the outside
world.

They marched rapidly to the Irrawaddy, coming out on to the
stream between Tigyaing and Tagaung, twenty-five miles south of
where they had first attempted to cross. Every boat in sight had been
wrecked by the Japanese. Wingate's men collected three of them and
worked all day to make them floatable. The Japs had been too
thorough. The Chindits went back into the jungle, lay low for twenty-
four hours, and the following night tried crossing at another place.
This time there were no boats at all, and Wingate, through his field-
glasses, spotted Japs on the west bank. Again they marched back into
the jungle, tired and in very low spirits. It began to look as if they
would never get across. They spent that night and the following
morning in a sort of petrified forest of small stunted trees that
provided no shelter from the heat, and puzzled over ways and means
of getting back. Just before noon a patrol at last found a heavy dugout
on a lake near the Irrawaddy. They quickly carried it down to the
river. Wingate, Jefferies, and Anderson ran their field-glasses very
carefully up and down the opposite bank. There were no Japanese in
sight.

Eight men had crossed in the dugout when, to every one's
amazement, the Chindits saw a boat heading upstream. Wingate
hailed it, and it pulled in to the shore. The boatman, a Burmese
peasant, explained that the Japanese had allowed him on the river
because he was moving a corpse that had died of dysentery. He then
slyly lifted the floorboards and disclosed, under the corpse, a cargo of
tomatoes and salt. The corpse smelled very high, but Wingate
cheerfully bought and divided up the tomatoes. He was in no position
to be particular. More silver rupees changed hands and the boatman
was persuaded to dump the corpse and the salt and ferry them across.

Three-quarters of the party had safely reached the west bank when
a Japanese patrol spotted the boat heading eastward to collect the
remainder, and opened fire. The boatman paddled off at top speed
upstream, and the nine men on the east bank faded into the jungle.
Later, Wingate learned, the boatman calmly returned to pick up his
corpse and cargo of salt, and ferried the nine remaining men across.
Five of them eventually got back alive.

Wingate's force was now on the island on which Calvert's column
had fought a battle with the Japs on the way in. Jefferies felt that the

worst was behind them, and remarked jubilantly to Wingate, 'I can just see myself sitting down to a bottle of champagne in Calcutta.'

This remark enraged the Brigadier. 'You'd better realize, John,' he said angrily, 'that the rest of this trip is going to be no picnic. You'd be much wiser to concentrate on getting out of Burma alive. In any case, your stomach won't be able to stand up to that sort of thing.'

At this point villagers informed them that the Japanese were in great strength three miles to the north.

After crossing the channel between the island and the mainland Wingate's men set off along a rough jungle track pitted with great holes five or six feet deep. They had not gone very far when Wingate saw a burning torch coming towards them. It was no more than thirty yards away. In a flash they dived into fire positions at the side of the track and waited tensely. The ghostly torch crept forward unbearably slowly. It turned out to be a party of natives. Those Burmese had no idea how near they came to being riddled with bullets. Every one of Wingate's men had taken first pressure on his rifle.

The Chindits re-formed and moved off along the jungle track. They could find no water and eventually bivouacked in dry jungle by the side of the trail. It was a ghastly night. The rainy season was approaching, and clouds of mosquitoes made sleep impossible. Most of the men had by now lost their mosquito veils, and Wingate had given orders that anti-mosquito cream must be used only to grease their rifles – they had run out of rifle oil. Jefferies managed to keep off the mosquitoes for an hour or so by smoking four very strong Burmese cigarettes which the boatman with the corpse had given him during the Irrawaddy crossing.

At dawn they pushed off again, leaving the beaten track and hacking a path through the jungle. Another two days' march brought them to the next great hazard – the railway. By now it was heavily patrolled. The enemy had planted troops in every station, and every bridge and culvert was closely guarded. Wingate's men approached the line through teak forest thickly carpeted with fallen leaves, which made a loud crackling sound under their feet. After dark the Brigadier carried out a test to see how far away they could be heard. The result was discouraging. The crackling of the leaves could be picked up three hundred yards away. Next he tried to advance with one man leading the way on his hands and knees, clearing a path through the leaves. This proved hopelessly slow. Wingate decided to trust to luck.

Thick jungle extended to within ten yards of the railway on either side. Scouts reported that the Japs were stationed four hundred yards to their right and to their left. Somehow they would have to cover twenty yards of open ground across the railway without being spotted. Fortunately the teak-leaves petered out a hundred yards from the line and the going became noiseless underfoot. At the edge of the jungle they halted. Again it was like getting set to go over the top. The railway was the second critical lap in the withdrawal. Beyond it lay one more river – the Chindwin – then home. Wingate whispered softly, 'Here we go.' Bunched closely together they stole swiftly across the gap and disappeared into the jungle on the other side. The railway was behind them.

The Brigadier urged them forward at top speed, and did not say a word until they had put five miles between themselves and the line. Then he halted for a breather.

'Well, we can thank the Japanese for something,' he remarked to Jefferies. 'That was disgustingly bad patrol work. We should never have got through.'

Wingate was quick to check any tendency towards wishful thinking. Jefferies had acquired an inexplicable craving for mince-pies, and had been amusing himself by debating the wording of the telegram he would sent to Firpos in Calcutta when he got back.

'I'm going to order exactly six dozen,' he now confided to Wingate, 'and have them sent up to me somewhere in the hills. If the first lot are really good I'll order some more. I mean to have mince-pies at breakfast, lunch, and dinner.' Wingate cut him short.

'We're still a long way from Firpos,' he said severely, 'and crossing the Chindwin is going to be the toughest hurdle of all.'

'ONE MORE RIVER'

The Chindits now marched for several days through the Mingin mountains between the railway and the escarpment. At one point they had to make ropes of their rifle slings to get down a twenty-foot drop. They were so tired they stumbled over stones and boulders, and most of them were badly bruised. Their boots were in a shocking condition, cracked by the scorching sun and torn to shreds by sharp rocks. The only respite from mosquitoes was when they could lie beside the smoke of a camp-fire. Yet somehow their sense of humour came to the rescue at the hardest moments. One sweltering morning Wingate was leading the way up an almost perpendicular rock face strewn with loose boulders. It was a back-breaking climb, and the party was hungry, thirsty, and dead-beat. One man accidentally dislodged a large stone which hit the man behind him right in the face. 'What the hell do you think you're doing?' said the angry victim. 'Looking for edelweiss, you bloody fool,' a voice called back cheerily. 'And I mean to get the first one.'

By now all their paratroop rations were exhausted, and they had nothing left but rice. The Burma Rifles picked jungle roots, which they chewed or made into soup. One of the roots had a delicious flavour, a cross between chicken and mushrooms, but it was poor stuff to march on. Two of the British troopers killed and ate a scavenging hawk. All of them ate snakes. Pythons were best. Cut up into steaks and grilled, they tasted rather like fish. When there was no time for cooking they picnicked off strips of python hastily dipped in the camp-fire. Banana-leaves, when they could find them, made a good dessert. They had run out of cigarettes and made their own out of coarse native tobacco wrapped in the leaves of the books they had brought with them. Even matches had become very precious; they were needed to light fires to cook the rice, and their small supply would have to last Wingate's men until they crossed the Chindwin. The officers carried the few remaining boxes in waterproof anti-gas wallets.

Diarrhœa, dysentery, and jungle sores began to take a heavy toll. There was one British lance-corporal whose legs were infected with deep, spetic jungle sores. Several times Wingate had halted to do what he could for the man. The lance-corporal decided he would not slow up the column any longer. He casually told the man in front of them that he was slipping out of line – it was only diarrhœa, he said – and he would catch up with them later. When Wingate heard what had happened he went back to look for the lance-corporal. They never found him.

Every man was haunted with the fear of falling sick; the slightest suspicion of diarrhœa produced secret panic. Usually the sick just crumpled up in their tracks, aned there was the grim business of making them as comfortable as possible and leaving them behind to die. One British lieutenant, a signal officer and a key man, worn out with dysentery, just couldn't march another step and dropped to the side of the track muttering, 'Well, I've had it.' Wingate halted and talked to him gently for four or five minutes. When he turned to go the lieutenant rose shakily to his feet and saluted with a cheery smile. He might have been saying good-bye to his girlfriend at the Savoy on the eve of a big 'do.' Then he lay down at the foot of a tall teak-tree, and the dust settled over him as the column marched on.

The Chindits had set out strong, hearty, well-muscled. Now, with a few exceptions, their bodies were a shocking sight. Muscles had become stringy tendons; arms and legs were as emaciated as a Hindu ascetic's; stomachs caved inward; ribs stuck out above horrible cavities. In some cases starvation had affected speech and hearing; two or three of the men were unable to articulate properly or grasp orders. All were so exhausted that every time they lay down to sleep they felt they would never have the energy to get up again, and had to fight down the dangerous thoughts of how pleasant it would be just to lie here and give in. Wingate himself miraculously showed no physical signs of fatigue. He drove his men on with a cold, unrelenting ferocity – and probably saved half of them from throwing in the sponge. He gave orders that no one was to drop out of line, even for diarrhœa. By doing so they slowed down the whole column and weakened their own will to carry on. 'Don't worry about your trousers,' he told them. 'Just keep marching.'

The ability to go on marching was not so much a question of toughness and wind as of mental outlook. At this stage they kept going only by sheer will-power and faith in Wingate. All the way back, conscious only of hunger, thirst, and overpowering fatigue, the men repeated to themselves the slogan that had carried them confidently into Burma: 'The Brigadier will pull us through.'

Wingate watched over his men like a guardian angel. At dawn, before anyone else was awake, he would pad silently off into the jungle on a solitary scouting patrol. On the march he led the way himself. Knowing that their only security lay in speed, he set a merciless pace and would keep looking back over his shoulder to see that every man was in line. They marched in single file, and if anyone lagged a few yards behind the man in front of him Wingate would growl, 'Keep closed up. Keep closed up.' Lack of water was their worst hardship, and he allowed the men to drink from their water-bottles only when ordered or after obtaining his permission. One morning the party passed an enormous lime-tree, heavy with ripe fruit. For days they had had nothing to drink but a few mouthfuls of water drained out of hollow bamboos. Wingate refused to call a halt. Next day friendly natives told them that the Japs had been combing the jungle less than a mile from the lime-tree.

At the top of a ridge on the west side of the Mingin range Wingate's men heard the sound of British planes bombing Pinlebu in the Mu valley below them. They were so weak from hunger that the Brigadier decided to risk lighting big marker fires to attract the attention of the planes, and with the white backs of their maps they spelled out a recognition signal. The pilots failed to spot them.

The next dangerous stretch was a twenty-mile strip in the Mu river valley between Pinbon and Pinlebu, two main Japanese garrison villages connected by a motor road. On the march in Major Brom-head's column had been sent to engage the Japs at Pinbon, and Scott's men had tackled the garrison at Pinlebu. Now Wingate's small force had to slip through unnoticed. Luck was with them. They crossed the valley at night unobserved, and reached the foot of the escarpment without incident.

Before them rose a sheer wall of rock fifteen hundred feet high. There were few tracks across it, and it was probable that the Japs would be patrolling all of them. The need for food had now become desperate, and Wingate decided to venture into a village to buy some. All that the villagers had for sale were papayas. As they were leaving a small Burmese came running after them and offered to guide them over a little-known track across the escarpment. He also brought depressing news: the British patrols which Wingate was expecting to meet up with on the east bank of the Chindwin had recrossed the river some days before and the Japs were combing the countryside for Wingate's party. But Buddha, he announced solemnly, had sent him to save them from destruction. Wingate hesitated. It was quite possible that not Buddha but the Japanese had sent him – to lead them into a trap. But the situation called for desperate risks, and the little Burmese, with his dirty white *longyi*, cadaverous body, and pinched ascetic face, did look like one of Buddha's disciples. The Brigadier decided to take a chance.

Their tiny guide led them over the escarpment in half the time they had expected. At noon on April 23 with his men gathered round him Wingate – holding in his hand a long bamboo stave – stood on the crest of a ridge like Moses on Mount Nebo, and pointed to the Chindwin valley below bathed in a lovely blue haze. 'This is our last lap,' he said. 'There in that blue mist lies Jordan, and beyond it the Promised Land.'

The march to the river was the worst part of the whole campaign. For the first eight miles they waded waist-deep in water along a fast-flowing *chaung*, stumbling painfully against sharp rocks and repeatedly sinking up to their necks in deep holes on the bed of the *chaung*. It took them three days to cover the short stretch to the river, and there the situation was even blacker than their Burmese guide had indicated. One by one Wingate's scouts came back with grim reports that every village and likely crossing-place was occupied by the enemy. Two or three weeks before the British had sent strong patrols over to the east bank, but these had fallen back. All boats had been commandeered by the Japs. However, Buddha's messenger miraculously reappeared with a friend. He volunteered to buy food from the villagers and said that he knew where boats were to be found. Wingate, having trusted the man so far, decided he must trust him all the way. A few hours later the Burmese returned with rice and vegetables. He also brought alarming news: the enemy knew that Wingate's party was in the vicinity. Then he went on to describe very precisely the area which the enemy had combed the day before.

The strain was now becoming unbearable. When the Chindits left Imphal each man had mentally signed away his life, and during the campaign there had been no time to think beyond the next meal. But now they were within sight of home; on the other side of the Chindwin were the British lines – and safety. One thought was in every man's mind: 'It would be dirty luck to get pipped on the post.'

Wingate decided that the safest course would be to make for the river, advancing through the area patrolled by the Japs the day before. The two courageous Burmese guides went off in search of boats. Wingate's men never saw them again; they must have been captured and killed by the Japanese.

The Chindits marched and countermarched until dusk, laboriously covering up their tracks. That night they bivouacked in thick jungle, deliberately avoiding water for fear of an ambush. No one could sleep, and the Brigadier read Plato to them in a whisper by the light of the moon. Just before dawn Wingate closed the book wearily and muttered to Jefferies, 'Most soothing.'

Again Wingate and his officers pored over maps, and finally charted a course which would bring them on to the river at a point where British patrols were reported to be stationed on the west bank. There was considerable danger that they would be fired on by their own side, but they would have to trust to their recognition signals. They had not gone far along the planned course when they came to the worst tract of elephant-grass they had encountered in Burma. The blades were stiff and sharp – more like wire than grass – and rose to a height of fifteen feet. At the bottom they were inextricably tangled and matted together. The Chindits tried for three hours that night to push through the elephant-grass, but made virtually no headway. Reluctantly Wingate altered his plan, pulled back into the jungle, and the party flopped down utterly exhausted.

Wingate did not sleep. He paced noiselessly up and down, his head sunk forward, his hands clasped behind his back, thinking over every possible way of making the crossing. By dawn he had worked out a new plan. He himself and the four best swimmers would swim the river, contact the British on the west bank, and send out a patrol with boats to bring the rest of the party across. He fixed a rendezvous on the west bank, and agreed upon recognition signals. Then he picked four men to go with him – Major Jefferies, Captain Aung Thin, an RAF wireless operator (Sergeant Wilshaw), and Private Boardman. The remaining senior officer, Major Jim Anderson, was to take the rest of the party back into the jungle and lie low until nightfall.

At 5.30 a.m. Wingate's party of five pushed off. They examined the nearest jungle track, and found it heavily marked with Japanese footprints. This left them then the choice of two alternatives: to march boldly down the track, which might lead them straight into a Japanese ambush, or to make a superhuman effort to fight their way through the elephant-grass.

Wingate said to Jefferies, 'Well, John, which shall it be?'

'We have a fifty-fifty chance on the track,' Jefferies replied. 'In the elephant-grass we're sure of evading the Japs. I don't know if we can get through it; it'll be damned hard work. But I think it's worth trying.' Wingate nodded.

'Come on,' he said. 'We'll tear it apart blade by blade.'

That was exactly what they did. It was a pitched battle – man versus jungle. Marching in single file, they took turns at leading. The sharp-edged elephant-grass had to be forced aside or bent backward with bare hands. Within a few minutes blood was trickling from the palms of their hands and from long scratches on their arms and foreheads. Wingate fought the jungle like a man possessed, magically conjuring up hidden reserves of energy. He led the way longer than anyone else, and when he was not leading he carried the rifle of the man out in front.

After four hours of marching they had covered no more than five hundred yards. Wingate decided to halt for a few mouthfuls of rice. They found a buffalo track leading down to a swamp, and out of the stinking black slime squeezed enough moisture to cook their rice. They took care to use very dry tinder and waved their hats over the flame to disperse the smoke.

After eating they battered their way through another appalling stretch. Now it was a nightmarish game they were playing: each blade of elephant-grass was a Jap that had to be grabbed by the throat, shaken and bent and pummelled and trampled underfoot. Bleeding, sweating, panting, cursing, they pushed forward, yard by yard.

According to the map the elephant-grass ended several hundred yards short of the river, and a track – which the Japs would surely be patrolling – led down to the Chindwin. Wingate, who was leading, suddenly let out a grunt of surprise. 'Take a look at this, John,' he whispered to Jefferies, who was marching just behind him. Jefferies squeezed forward beside the Brigadier. There, almost at their feet, lay the Chindwin. Mercifully the map-maker had slipped. No track. No Japs.

It ws 3 p.m. Wingate made another of his lightning decisions. 'We won't wait until dusk,' he said. 'We'll swim the river now. In thirty minutes we can be behind our own lines.' His words braced the men, exhausted as they were, for a last spurt. They cut their slacks into shorts, took off their boots and tied them to their packs, and discarded their heavy equipment. Their rifles they kept. It was a point of honour to get back with pack and rifle, if it was humanly possible.

Wingate turned to them and said: 'As soon as we come out on to the bank we may expect to be fired upon. There must be no hesitation.

When I give the word run down the bank. Don't fight the current.
When you get to the other side take cover. Is every one ready?' The
men nodded. 'Good luck,' said the Brigadier. 'This is our last
obstacle.'

Wingate bent low and doubled down the bank into the stream with
Jefferies, Aung Thin, Wilshaw, and Boardman at his heels. After
swimming thirty or forty yards Jefferies was forced to let go of his
rifle and boots. About one hundred yards from the bank the tattered
shreds of his shirt-sleeves wound themselves tightly around his arms
and completely imprisoned them. He kicked out furiously with his
legs and drifted slowly into mid-stream. Then a small wave hit him
in the face and he swallowed several mouthfuls of muddy water. He
began to sink. Desperately he twisted round to look for help. Several
hundred yards downstream Wilshaw was floating along cosily in a
Mae West jacket which he had lugged through the whole of the
campaign. Wingate appeared to be in difficulties himself. Far behind
Boardman was helping Aung Thin, who had hurt his knee rather
badly in a rocky *chaung* a week before. None of them could possibly
come to his rescue. It seemed silly to give up and die a few hundred
yards from the post. The idea of dying at this point enraged him. He
kicked out savagely again and forged ahead slowly towards the bank.
Then he began to lose consciousness. His legs stiffened and the kicks
grew feebler. The rage was all gone. He felt only an enormous
weariness and thought to himself, 'Oh, well, at least it's going to be a
pleasant way of dying.' Just then his feet touched bottom.

He stumbled in a daze through the shallow water and collapsed on
the beach. A few minutes later Wingate was shaking him by the
shoulder. 'Come on. The Japs may be here. Run to cover.' Jefferies
struggled to his feet and lazily watched the Brigadier doubling up the
beach in his bare feet. Wingate had gone about eighty yards when he
let out a fiendish yell, spun round, and sprinted back into the water.
Wilshaw, Aung Thin, and Boardman, who were still in the river,
thought that this was the end: Japs on the west bank! Jefferies alone
realized what was the matter. The red-hot sand had roasted the soles
of the Brigadier's bare feet.

Wingate whipped off his shorts and wound them around his feet
bedouin-style. Then, crowned with the old pith helmet which he had
worn throughout the campaign, he started hobbling up the beach to

look for the British, clad only in a tattered bush shirt, its tails flapping in the breeze.

Near the bank Wingate's party found a small cultivator's hut. The owner gave them cheroots and pints of the juice of green coconuts, and offered to guide them to the nearest British front-line post, five miles away. It was the first time for many months that they had been able to relax. Wingate shook hands with each man. For weeks they had been dreaming of this moment. They were too played out to say a word.

Two hours later five scarecrows, barefooted, heavily bearded, wearing foul-smelling rags and (except for the Brigadier) enormous coolie hats, stumbled into a tidy little jungle outpost where a group of spruce-looking British officers were sitting on ration tins around a trestle-table drinking tea. The officer in charge, Major White, sat the Chindits down and gave them hot, sweet tea with condensed milk, a bully-beef stew, rum, and cigarettes. With the tension gone, dead weariness set in. Starved as they were, it was an effort to eat and to lift a mug of tea. Major White meanwhile had arranged for a patrol to cross the Chindwin with enough boats to pick up Major Anderson and the rest of Wingate's party. When the patrol was ready Wingate stood up and said quietly, 'I'm going along with them.' It was a five-mile march to the Chindwin and he had just marched fully two hundred. Jefferies, Aung Thin, and the others feebly volunteered to go with him. 'There's no need for that,' said Wingate. 'You stay here.' Gratefully they stretched out on blankets in the corner of the hut and the next moment were asleep.

Wingate trekked to the river and settled down at the rendezvous to wait for a signal from Major Anderson's party. He waited all night. No signal came.

After the Brigadier's group of five had pushed off at dawn to swim the Chindwin Anderson's scouts brought word that they had seen Japanese patrols near by, hunting for their tracks. Anderson's party marched and countermarched all day to give the enemy the slip, and at night went down to the river to contact the British on the west bank. They did not know whether or not Wingate's group had got across alive. To make matters worse, they were obliged to choose a crossing-point a mile south of the rendezvous as the Japanese were patrolling the bank higher up.

At this stage they had no torches and fell back on a primitive

method of signalling. They lined a large native cooking-pot with
white paper and held a lighted match inside it; by moving a bush hat
over and then away from the flame they managed to spell out shakily
a message in crude dots and dashes. That message Wingate, waiting
on the west bank a mile to the north, failed to detect. Anderson's
men, worn out and downhearted, pulled back into the jungle.

The next morning Captain Motilal Katju volunteered to venture
into a native village to look for boats. In peace-time Katju had edited
a newspaper in India. He had won a fine Military Cross for gallantry
in Libya, and was accompanying the expedition as official observer.
For several days he had had a premonition that he would not get out
alive, and had asked Jefferies to carry his diary, which contained a
day-by-day account of the campaign. To cheer him up Jefferies had
lightly replied, 'Nonsense. We all get to feeling that way,' and had
refused to take the diary. Katju never returned from that last patrol.

In the course of the day five of Anderson's men tried to swim the
Chindwin. One was drowned, but the others made it. They eventually
found Wingate and Major White's party – now joined by Jefferies,
Aung Thin, Wilshaw, and Boardman – and gave the Brigadier a
message from Anderson fixing a new rendezvous for the crossing that
night.

At dusk Wingate and the others moved to the rendezvous. As the
time for Anderson's signal drew near Wingate glanced at his watch.
Just then they heard the sound of a Japanese patrol pushing through
the elephant-grass on the east bank. A moment later Anderson's
signal flickered across the river.

Wingate's torch flashed an answer, and Major White's party shot
down into the boats. The Japs opened up with a mortar, but White
got across safely. Anderson's men piled swiftly into the boats, and the
tiny flotilla started back. When they were in mid-stream the Japanese
mortar again went into action, but its fire was very wide of the mark.
From the west bank a familiar sound welcomed them home – the
sharp, sustained rattle of Bren-guns raking the enemy on the east
bank. Then the mortar was silent. Out of the shadows a bearded
figure in an old pith helmet rose from the sandbanks to greet them.
It was Wingate, waiting on the edge of the river he had called
'Jordan' to lead them back into the Promised Land.

Mission Asymptote

Bruce Marshall

Once again he was travelling third-class, and he was to parachute. Because of the necessity for rescuing Brossolette before his identity was discovered Tommy had elected to jumpt in the dark rather than wait for the next moon period. He was accompanied by a saboteur whose code name was Trieur and whose first trip this was.

They were to be dropped near Clermont-Ferrand, about two hundred and fifty miles south of Paris, and had a long way to fly. There was the usual flak over the French coast, but the rest of the journey passed without incident.

The procedure was the same as on his first mission with Passy and Brossolette: when they were nearly over the pin-point the despatcher hooked up their static lines and opened up the hole. Trieur looked nervous and Yeo-Thomas, who was to jump first, tried to cheer him up by giving him the thumbs-up sign as he swung his legs into the trap. Below it was inky black and it was some time before Tommy could see the twinkling light of the reception committee. Then he felt the despatcher's hand on his shoulders, the red light went on, the aircraft made a wide turn and ran in over the ground; the green light went on, he pushed himself out through the hole, whirled round in the slipstream, floated and, because of the lack of moonlight, began to count. Dropped from a height of 500 feet he had been told that he would touch the ground when he reached twenty; instead his head hit it with a bang at thirteen, and he was knocked unconscious for two or three minutes. He was still dizzy and shaken when he unfastened his parachute; getting up with difficulty, he found that he had sprained his left ankle.

His discomfiture was increased when the aircraft made its second run overhead and he had to dodge its dropped containers as they came hurtling down. He was helped to cover by the Air Operations Officer, Evêque, whom he had already met in London. Trieur had landed safe and sound in the next field. Fortunately, the farmhouse where they were to spend the night was only half a mile distant, and Yeo-Thomas was able to hobble there painfully.

Next morning, although his ankle was still swollen, he determined to leave for Paris that afternoon: not until he was there could he get in touch with Abeille and Archer, who were in charge of the Britanny region, and with whom he hoped to be able to arrange a means of helping Bollaert and Brossolette. The farmer drove him and Trieur over rutty tracks covered with ice and put them in a bus which took them at a breakneck speed over even more slippery roads to Clermont-Ferrand. There they met and dined with Alain Bernay, the Regional Military Officer. Because of his hurry to get to Paris Yeo-Thomas refused Bernay's invitation to remain with him for a few days and visit the local groups, and Trieur and he caught the half-past eleven train to the capital.

It is a favourite device of unoriginal film producers to translate to the chant of revolving railway train wheels the not particularly profound problems of their puppets: 'CAN I BE A BUSINESS GAL AND STILL BE A GOOD WIFE TO AL?' By the rules of such facile onomatopoeia Tommy ought to have heard the train wheels singing: 'BROSSOLETTE, BROSSOLETTE, BROSSOLETTE'. He heard nothing of the sort, nor did he require to: indeed, he sought relief from thinking about Brosselette in tipping off to the as yet untried Trieur some of the dodges which the saboteur would have to employ if he were to remain for long undetected in Paris.

As soon as he arrived in Paris he handed Trieur over to Maud, who passed the saboteur on to Jacqueline Devaux, who found him a flat. From Maud Tommy learned that Bollaert and Brossolette were still in Rennes prison, and that the latter was still believed to be a M. Pierre Boutet. Maud had established contact with some of the German officials and, by bribing the guards and passing herself off to them as Boutet's mistress, had managed to send him food, wine and clothing in which were hidden messages to which Boutet had replied when sending out his linen to the laundry; by this means she had ascertained that Bollaert and Brossolette were relatively unmolested and that the latter's lock of white hair had not yet begun to show.

His first night in Paris Tommy spent with the Peyronnets, whose flat in the Avenue des Ternes was again considered to be comparatively safe.

The next day while waiting to contact Abeille and Archer, he got in touch, through the ever faithful José Dupuis, with Pichard and with Clouet des Pesruches, who, under the slightly less Boulevard St Germain pseudonym of Galilée, was Air Operations Officer for the Touraine. From them he was able to obtain a clear idea of the situation in the Paris, Seine et Marne, Tours and western France areas. Partly because the recently stepped up parachutings had not yet been going on long enough for their impact to be felt throughout the country, the morale of Resistance was low. There were four main reasons for this: the weariness of constantly waiting and constantly disappointed reception committees; lack of arms; a growing belief that the Allies had no real intention of ever invading the Continent; and the increased vigilance of the Gestapo, now aided more and more by Darnand's Militia and the Lafont Organization. It was the old story, with a few new drop scenes, and Tommy told his new version of the other old story to contradict it: parachuting operations were being formidably increased; Jérôme was now in London demonstrating the great potentiality of the Maquis; and the invasion *would* take place.

Not wishing too greatly to inconvenience the Peyronnets, whose flat had already been watched by the Gestapo, Tommy spent his second night in Paris in Jeanne Helbling's flat in the rue Casimir Pinel in Neuilly. Through his hostess he was able to contact Abeille and Archer. Abeille, who before the war had been a Prefect, immediately placed the whole of the Brittany organization at Tommy's disposal for the rescue of Bollaert and Brossolette. But before determining upon a given course of action Yeo-Thomas decided to go to Rennes and conduct a preliminary investigation on the spot.

He left for Rennes on 1 March, taking Maud with him. With a local lawyer, who was a member of the Resistance, he discussed the possibility of getting Brossolette transferred on a trumped-up charge from Rennes prison to another prison in the south of France where he would be forgotten about by the Rennes authorities and whence they could ultimately secure his release on the basis of wrongful arrest. In the end they abandoned this plan which failed to take into account Bollaert and which would be a lengthy process involving the suborning of at least two Gestapo officers and the manufacture of an imaginary but convincing misdeed. Because of the danger of Boutet's real identity being discovered time was the essence of the problem which could, therefore, be solved only by force.

He then went to reconnoitre the prison and its precincts. Almost opposite the main entrance, there was a grocer's shop, whose owner was a member of one of the Resistance groups and who numbered among his customers most of the French and some of the German prison officials. From the grocer Yeo-Thomas learned that the greater part of the prison had been handed over to the Germans and only a few cells left free for the French; the main entrance was heavily guarded; all the gates were closed and at each gate was posted a sentry with a light machine gun which could be trained on every avenue of approach; a direct telephone line connected the guard room of the prison with that of an SS barracks not more than 600 yards distant. Tommy made a careful reconnaissance, found where the telephone line ran and where it could most easily be cut.

He saw at once that a frontal attack would be foredoomed to failure, but he soon hit upon a plan which he thought would stand a chance of success. When the telephone wire connecting the two guard rooms had been cut ten men from the local Resistance groups would keep watch from points of vantage situated in houses opposite the prison and would cover all approaches to the main gate. Three other men, of whom one would speak German perfectly and the other two fluently, would present themselves in German uniform with Sicher-heitsdienst badges to the sentry at the main entrance; to him they would show forged instructions, supposedly emanating from the Paris or the Rennes Gestapo Headquarters and ordering the prison author-ities to free Bollaert and Brossolette for transfer. Once in the guard room, where it was the custom for those in charge to verify such documents by telephoning to the Headquarters from which they purported to have been issued, the three disguised men would overpower the guards who, when not on sentry duty, so the grocer had said, always removed their belts and hung their weapons on the wall. The man who spoke perfect German would then return to the sentry at the main entrance, tell him that all was in order and ask him to open the gate so that a car, which would be waiting outside, could be brought into the yard in order that the prisoners might be picked up without attracting the attention of passers-by; the driver would back in and stop the car in such a position as to prevent the sentry from closing the gates again. Meanwhile the two other men would proceed into the prison proper, taking with them the corporal of the guard whom they would threaten to shoot immediately if he did not obey their orders. Bollaert and Brossolette would be brought out of their cells, put in the car and driven to a second car which would be waiting round the corner from the grocer's shop. While the second car took them to a safe hiding place in the centre of the town, the first car would continue south leaving an obvious trail behind it.

The plan seemed a good one, but it could not be put into action immediately: three German-speaking Resistance members, two cars and petrol had to be found; and, owing to a recent lack of parachuting operations in Brittany, Sten guns, pistols, hand grenades and ammunition would have to be brought to Rennes from a remote region.

Full of energy and confidence Yeo-Thomas returned to Paris and put the preparations in train. In the meantime he carried on with his official work: he held conferences with Sapeur and Commandant Palaud who were responsible for the paramilitary organization of Paris, with 'Z' and with the leaders of Front National, Franc-Tireurs et Partisans, Ceux de la Libération, Ceux de la Résistance, and Organisation Civile et Militaire. Because of the repeated hold-ups by German police in the métro, and because vélo-taxis were rare, he had to do a great deal of walking: seven or eight contacts a day in places as widely separated as the Porte Maillot, the Boulevard St Michel, the Trocadéro, the Porte de St Cloud, the Parc Monceau and the Place de la Nation laid a considerable strain on his as yet imperfectly healed left ankle. He had also to take the usual precautions against being followed and to make sure that his contacts were not being trailed when he met them. For the Gestapo was more than ever alert. Pichard and Clouet des Pesruches were being hotly chased and José Dupuis had become so blown that she had had to be sent into the country for a months' rest. In view of this constant danger Tommy kept changing residences; but wherever he passed the night there was also a radio and once a week a cryptic message came over the BBC to assure him that Barbara had not been a casualty in the little blitz to which London was then being subjected.

He was staying in Suni Sandöe's flat in the rue Claude when he was informed that all was now in readiness for the attempt to rescue Bollaert and Brossolette from Rennes prison. Deciding to go to Rennes on the night of 21 March, and anxious to assure himself before he left that the air operations in the Touraine were running satisfactorily, he made an appointment for that morning with Antonin, a new agent-de-liaison lent to him by Pichard; Antonin was to bring him any messages he might have received from a girl called Brigitte who was Clouet des Pesruches' go-between, and to be prepared to pass on to Brigitte any instructions which Yeo-Thomas had for Clouet des Pesruches. The appointment had been fixed for eleven o'clock at the Passy métro station, situated, unlike most others, on a bridge above ground; Antonin was to walk down the steps on the left and Tommy was to come up them on the right; they were to cross in front of the newspaper kiosk next to the ticket office and to feign surprise when they met.

At eleven o'clock precisely Yeo-Thomas passed the kiosk, but Antonin was not there. Ordinarily Yeo-Thomas would not have broken his security rule of never waiting for an unpunctual contact, but it was imperative that instructions should be passed to Clouet des Pesruches at once in case he was detained in Rennes longer than he anticipated. He therefore went down the steps on the other side of the station and came up again, using the same steps as before. Having ascended the first flight and still seeing no sign of Antonin coming towards him he hesitated as to whether to pay a surprise visit to his father, whose flat was only a hundred yards distant. Deciding to put duty before pleasure, he continued up the steps, meeting a crowd of people coming down from the train which had just arrived and feeling fairly safe in the other crowd which was climbing the steps towards the station. As he drew level with the last flight leading up to the ticket office five men in civilian clothes pounced on him, hand-cuffed him and began scientifically to search his pockets. Just then Antonin, escorted by another two Gestapo men in civilian clothes, passed by on the other side of the steps, looked at Tommy and was led away.

'*Wir haben Shelley*,'* Tommy's captors shouted with glee.

HE WAS NOT WONDERFUL BY MISTAKE

As soon as Yeo-Thomas had been handcuffed two of the Gestapo men set about pushing back the excited crowd: they forbade access

* 'We've got Shelley.'

to the station and threatened to shoot anybody attempting to approach their prisoner. For a few minutes Tommy, tightly gripped by his captors, stood in a small arena of steps, hemmed in by a throng twenty yards above him and twenty yards below him, and reading on the spectators' faces fear or pity or the shamefaced loathing with which men contemplate misfortunes which they try to believe can never happen to themselves. This tableau however was of brief duration: he was quickly hustled up the steps, through the crowd and propelled into a Citroën with a uniformed driver which had been waiting at the corner of the Boulevard Delessert. He was made to sit in the back with two policemen on either side of him. As soon as the car started these two men began to take it in turn to punch him in the face. 'Shelley,' they cried, '*Wir haben Shelley. Englischer Offizier. Terrorist. Schweinhund. Scheisskerl.*'

This horrible little litany of imprecation continued until they reached the Gestapo Headquarters in the rue des Saussaies, and so did the cruel blows. Tommy's head felt twice its normal size and the blood from his lacerated face was pouring down over his shirt and suit. He says that he was surprised to find himself 'thinking in a completely impersonal manner just as though it were another person being beaten up and it was a very extraordinary feeling'. It must have been. What was even more extraordinary was that during this painful passage to prison he was able to wonder whether the attempt to rescue Bollaert and Brossolette would still be made and to think out what he was going to say when he was interrogated.

It was clear that the Dodkin story would no longer serve in its entirety: the fact that the Gestapo men had greeted him as Shelley seemed to indicate that Antonin had talked. (He learned later that the agent-de-liaison had been arrested while carrying in his pocket, contrary to all regulations, a piece of paper marked: SHELLEY PASSY 11.) It was obvious, therefore that the Germans would know that the otherwise unimpeachable identity papers in the name of Gaonach which he was carrying were false. The Gestapo knew and had long known that Shelley was a British officer, but they did *not* know the name of the British officer. If they discovered his real identity and failed by normal methods to make him speak they would certainly arrest his father and torture the old man in his presence. Dodkin then he would have to be and not a baled-out Dodkin: the absence of the identity discus stamped with his name and hidden beneath the floorboards of Suni Sandöe's flat would perhaps add to rather than detract from the credibility of the tale, as a British officer would be unlikely to carry such compromising property on his person while actually engaged in the field. All this he thought out while his face was being battered in the car.

When they reached their destination he was yanked violently out of the car and, with a pistol at his back, was propelled into the lift. His abrupt arrival in an office on the third floor astonished the three men sitting there. *'Wir haben Shelley,'* the leading policeman shouted as Tommy was pushed into the room. At this the three men rose from their chairs and began to punch him and kick him, knocking him against desks and cupboards and walls. They stopped only when he had been beaten into semi-insensibility. Then they locked the door, stripped him naked and made him stand on a telephone directory. Enraged by the discovery of his tear gas pen and revolver in a special holster strapped to his thigh they started in on him again. *'Schweinehund, Scheisskerl,'* the thugs shouted as they slapped his face and kicked him in his bare groin with their heavy boots. They tore from his neck the small brown canvas sachet which the Countess Grabbe had given him at the beginning of the war and laid it on a desk beside the other objects which they had removed from his pockets: among these were his identity papers, the keys of four of his apartments of which he had been intending to return three to the owners before he left Rennes, and two monocles which he had worn to disguise himself. The discovery of the last particularly infuriated his tormentors for they flung them on the floor and trampled on them. The spectacle was so ridiculous that Tommy laughed aloud in spite of his pain; this earned him another beating up.

This new battering was scientifically administered to him as he stood heels together, arms handcuffed behind his back, naked on the telephone directory: as a blow made him sway sideways, a punch on the jaw, the nose or the ear or a kick in the stomach restored his equilibrium. 'I don't know how long I was kept in this position,' Yeo-Thomas says. 'To me it seemed hours, but in all probability it was only an hour and a half.' Although so dazed that the room was swimming before his eyes, he was still able to think fairly clearly. Two desires were in mind: to avoid betraying his friends and to escape from his agony. He could do both if only he could get at the signet-ring containing the poison tablet which the thugs had omitted to remove from his left hand. Sooner or later, he felt, they would be bound to unhandcuff him and then he could slide open the top of the ring, swallow the tablet and put himself beyond treachery and pain.

Fraternizing With the Enemy?

Paul Brickhill

Dawn brought new strength to Bader. In the light he saw many things more clearly; knew where he was and what it meant and accepted it unwistfully. First things first and to hell with the rest. He must get legs and must get word to Thelma.

The door opened and in came two young Luftwaffe pilots, dark young men in tight short tunics pinned with badges, shapely breeches and black riding boots.

'Hallo,' brightly said the leader, who was Count von Someone-or-other. 'How are you?' His English was good.

'All right, thanks.'

Bader was fairly monosyllabic but the Germans chatted amiably. Would he like some books? They'd just come over from St Omer airfield to yarn as one pilot to another. Spitfires were jolly good aeroplanes.

'Yes,' Bader said. 'So are yours.'

After a while the Count said politely: 'I understand you have no legs?' He was looking at the foreshortened form under the bedclothes.

'That's right.'

They asked what it was like flying without legs. An elderly administrative officer came in and listened, looked at the left leg leaning against the wall and observed heavily: 'Of course it would never be allowed in Germany.'

Later they left and the next visitor was a baldheaded Luftwaffe engineering officer, who asked more boring questions about legs. Bader cut him short: 'Look, can you radio England and ask them to send me another leg?' He did not know how they would do it, but if they did Thelma would know he was alive.

The German thought it was a good idea.

'And while you're about it,' Bader followed up, 'could you send someone to look at the wreckage of my aeroplane. The other leg might still be in it.'

The German promised to do what he could.

A nurse brought in a basin of water. She was German and not talkative, making signs that he was to wash himself. He did so, moving painfully, and when he got to his legs was shocked to find a great dark swelling high up on his right stump. It looked as big as a cricket ball and was terribly sore. For ten years since the agony at Greenlands Hospital he had flinched at the thought of anything going wrong with his stumps, and now it loomed large and ugly in his mind.

Later, yesterday's doctor came in, looking precise behind the rimless glasses. Bader showed him the swelling, and the doctor looked grave and prodded it. After a while he said hesitantly: 'We will have to cut this.'

Bader burst out, 'By God, you don't,' panicky at the thought of an experimental knife. They argued violently about it till the doctor grudgingly agreed to leave it for a while.

A dark, plump girl came in, put a tray on his bed, smiled and went out. He realised he was hungry till he tasted the bowl of potato water-soup, two thin slices of black bread smeared with margarine and the cup of tepid ersatz coffee. It left a sour taste in his mouth.

Later it was the doctor again, with orderlies. 'We are going to put you in another room,' he said. 'With friend.'

Friends?

The orderlies carried him along a corridor into a larger room with five beds and dumped him on one of them. A fresh-faced young man in another bed said cheerfully in an American accent: 'Hallo, sir. Welcome. My name's Bill Hall. Eagle Squadron. We heard you were here.' He had a cradle over one leg which was in traction, the foot pulled by a weight on a rope. His kneecap had been shot off. In the next bed was a Pole with a burnt face, and beyond him Willie, a young Londoner who had been shot through the mouth. All Spitfire pilots. They chatted cheerfully till well after dusk. Willie and the Pole had been trying to think of some way of escaping, but the Germans had taken their clothes and they had only the nightshirts, which made it rather hopeless.

Bader asked: 'Isn't there any way out of here?'

'Yes,' Willie answered a little bitterly. 'Soon as you can stagger

they whip you off to Germany.' Apparently he and the Pole were due
to go at any moment.

'If you had clothes,' Bader persisted, 'how would you get out?'

'Out the bloody window on a rope,' Willie said. 'The gates are
always open and no guards on them.' He jerked his head at the door
of the room. 'They put the guards outside that door.'

'How would you get a rope?'

Willie said there were French girls working in the hospital who
might smuggle one in.

Bader slipped off to sleep thinking grimly about that, but he slept
well and in the morning did not feel so stiff and sore.

The plump girl came in early with more black bread and acorn
coffee, and Bill Hall introduced her to Bader as Lucille, a local
French girl. He tried to joke with her but she barely understood his
schoolboy French, though she coloured nicely and smiled at him
again. She did not say anything: a German guard stood in the
doorway.

The doctor came in to see his stumps but the swelling was visibly
less, which was an enormous relief. In his blunt way Bader told the
doctor that the food was 'bloody awful,' and the doctor bridled.
Bader waved a piece of black bread in his face and they had a
shouting match till the doctor stormed out. Lucille came back with
lunch – more potato water and black bread.

Later a tall, smart Luftwaffe officer of about forty came in. He
wore the red tabs of the Flak, clicked his heels, saluted Bader and
said: 'Herr Ving Commander, ve haf found your leg.' Like a star
making his entrance, a jack-booted soldier marched through the door
and jerked magnificently to attention by the bed, holding one arm
stiffly out. Hanging from it was the missing right leg, covered in mud,
the broken piece of leather belt still hanging from it. Bader delighted,
said, 'I say, thanks,' then saw that the foot still ludicrously clad in
sock and shoe stuck up almost parallel to the shin.

'Hell, it's been smashed.'

'Not so badly as your aeroplane,' said the officer. 'Ve found it in
the area of the other pieces.'

The soldier took two smart paces forward, clicked to a halt again,
and Bader took the leg. He unpeeled the sock and saw, as he feared,
that the instep had been stove in.

'I say,' he said, turning on the charm, 'd'you think your chaps at the aerodrome could repair this for me?'

The officer pondered. 'Perhaps,' he said. 'Ve vill take it and see.' After a mutual exchange of compliments the officer clicked his heels, saluted, swung smartly and disappeared.

Next it was a new girl, fair-haired and with glasses, carrying a tray. She was Hélène, and everyone goggled to see that she carried real tea on the tray and some greyish-white bread. Apparently the shouting match had been worth while.

In the morning the swelling on the stump had deflated with amazing speed and that was a great relief.

Later the officer with the red tabs marched crisply in, saluted, and as he said 'Herr Ving Commander, ve haf brought back your leg,' the jackbooted stooge made another dramatic entrance behind and came to a crashing halt by the bed, not flicking an eyelid, holding out a rigid arm with the leg suspended from it: a transformed leg, cleaned and polished and with the foot pointing firmly where a foot should be. Bader took it and saw they had done an amazing job on it; the body belt was beautifully repaired with a new section of intricately-worked, good quality leather and all the little straps that went with it. The dent in the shin had been carefully hammered out, so that apart from a patch bare of paint it looked normal. A dent in the knee had been hammered out, and even the rubbers correctly set in the ankle so there was resilient movement in the foot.

'It is OK?' the officer asked anxiously.

Bader, impressed and rather touched, said: 'It's really magnificent. It is very good of you to have done this. Will you please thank the men who did it very much indeed.'

He strapped both legs on, eased off the bed, feeling unsteady for a moment, and went stumping round the room, a ludicrous figure in nightshirt with the shoe-clad metal legs underneath. Without a stump sock (lost in the parachute descent), the right leg felt strange, and it gave forth loud clanks and thumps as he swung it. The others looked on fascinated. Beaming with pleasure, the Germans finally left. Bader lurched over to the window and looked thoughtfully at the ground three floors and forty feet below. To the left of the grass courtyard he could see the open gates, unguarded.

They became aware of a drone that began to swell and fade and swell again. The Pole and Willie joined him at the window, and high above they saw the twisting, pale scribble of vapour trails against blue sky; obviously a sweep and some 109's were having a shambles over St Omer. Tensely they watched but the battling aircraft were too high to see. Shortly a parachute floated down. A German, he hoped, and hoped there were more coming down without parachutes. He looked up at the contrails, at the parachute and down at the courtyard and the gates, his mind a fierce maelstrom.

A Luftwaffe Feldwebel came in and told Willie and the Pole to be ready to leave for Germany after lunch. He would bring their clothes later.

When he had gone Willie, depressed, said: 'Once they get you behind the wire you haven't got much chance.' Bader began worrying that it would be his turn next. He *must* stay in France as long as possible.

Lucille came in with soup and bread for lunch. The guard looked morosely in the doorway, and then turned back into the corridor. Bader whispered to the Pole: 'Ask her if she can help me get out or put me in touch with friends outside.'

In a low voice the Pole started talking to Lucille in fluent French. She darted a look at Douglas and whispered an answer to the Pole. They went on talking in fast, urgent whispers, each with an eye watching the door. Bader listened eagerly but the words were too fast. They heard the guard's boots clump in the corridor, and Lucille, with a quick, nervous smile at Douglas, went out.

The Pole came across and sat on his bed. 'She says you're "*bien connu*" and she admires you tremendously and will help if she can, but she can't get a rope because the Germans would guess how you got it. She doesn't know whether she can get clothes, but she has a day off next Sunday and will go to a village down the line called Aire, or something. She says there are "*agents Anglais*" there.'

English agents? It sounded too good. But she was going to try, and hope welled strongly. Sunday! This was only Wednesday. Hell, they mustn't take him. The uncertainty of fear gnawed. Better try and act weak from now on.

They took Willie and the Pole that afternoon. Now he had to rely on his schoolboy French.

In the morning Lucille came in with the usual bread and acorn coffee. The sentry lounged in the doorway. She put the tray on Bader's bed, leaning over so that her plump body hid him from the sentry. He grinned a cheerful '*Bon jour*' at her as she squeezed his hand and then the grin nearly slipped as he felt her pressing a piece of paper into his palm. He closed his fingers round it and slid the clenched fist under the bedclothes. It was very quick. She said nothing, but her mouth lifted in a pale smile as she went out of the room. The door closed behind the sentry.

Half under the clothes, Bader unfolded the paper and read, written in French in a clear, child-like hand: '*My son will be waiting outside the hospital gates every night from midnight until 2 am. He will be smoking a cigarette. We wish to help a friend of France.*'

It was signed 'J. Hiècque.'

Bill Hall looked curiously across the top of his suspended leg and asked: 'What's that?'

'Oh, just a message of good cheer.' Bader spoke casually, tingling inside with excitement. He tucked the note in the breast pocket of the nightshirt and stuffed a handkerchief on top. It was red hot. Somehow he must get rid of it. Destroy it. He knew that the person who bravely signed a name to it was liable to death. Lucille, too.

Now how the hell to get out of the hospital? And he *must* get his clothes back! Couldn't walk round the town in a white nightshirt. (And Bill Hall had said there was a curfew at ten o'clock.) Pretend he was walking in his sleep! With tin legs sticking out under his nightshirt! Silly thoughts chased their tails in his head. *Must* get clothes and *must* destroy the note.

He had his pipe and matches.

Reaching out, he picked up his tin legs from the wall, lifted his nightshirt, strapped them on and walked out of the door. The sentry stood in his way. He pointed to the lavatory and the sentry nodded.

Inside the lavatory he closed the door, struck a match and burnt the note, holding it by one corner till it was all wrinkled and charred, then dropped the ashes into the pan and flushed it.

Walking back up the corridor, the sentry gaped at him all the way and he knew angrily and self-consciously how ridiculous he looked in the nightshirt with the legs underneath. It was then that the idea struck him. It was a chance.

When the doctor came in later to inspect the stump again, Bader said in a voice of sweet reason: 'Look, I've got my legs back now but I just can't walk around in them with this nightshirt on. It's terribly embarrassing.' He explained about the gaping sentry. 'I'm sure you'll understand,' he went on winningly. 'I must have some clothes to wear. Even in bed this nightshirt's a damn' nuisance. It gets tangled up in my stumps.'

The doctor looked professionally thoughtful and then smiled. 'Oh, well, I suppose it is all right in your case. I will have your clothes brought to you.'

Quite a moment! God, how easy.

Half an hour later a German nurse came in with his clothes, put them in a neat pile beside his bed, smiled briefly at him and went out.

Hall said wryly: 'I wouldn't mind losing this damn' leg of mine just to get my pants back. I feel so stupid in this nightshirt.'

How to get out of hospital! He lay there fiercely thinking about it. It was the last problem. The toughest! No good trying to walk down the corridors and stairs. The guards were on at midnight and all night. They'd frogmarch him back and he'd lose his clothes again, too. He walked over to the window and stood looking down into the court-yard. Perhaps Lucille's 'agents Anglais' could help.

He was still there when the immaculate young count, the fighter pilot with the Knight's Cross, came in with his comrade. 'Ha,' he said, 'it is good to see you on your legs again. Look, we haf brought you two bottles of champagne. Will you come and drink them with us?'

They took him down a flight of stairs to the doctor's room, but the doctor was not there, just the three of them. The first cork popped. It was the first time he had drunk champagne since his second wedding to Thelma, and it developed into a cheerful little party.

The Count had obviously shot down some British aircraft but was too polite to mention that or to ask how many Bader had shot down. In fact, neither he nor his comrade asked any dangerous questions, but both chatted gaily about their own tactics and aeroplanes. The Count said they always sat in their cockpits at readiness – he always read a book. Bader liked them both; they were 'types' after his own heart and he would have liked to have had them in his wing. What a damn' silly war it was.

'Soon you may haf three legs,' the Count said. 'With the permission of Reichsmarshal Goering, the Luftwaffe has radioed to England on international waveband. They offer to give a British aeroplane unrestricted passage to fly your leg. We have given them a height and a course and a time to drop it over St Omer.' He shrugged, looking philosophical. 'They have not answered. I think they will.'

Bader gave a rich belly-chuckle. 'I bet they drop it with bombs,' he said. 'They don't need any unrestricted passage.'

The Count grinned amiably and raised his glass. 'We will be ready,' he promised. 'Let us hope the next leg will not be shot down.'

There was another thing he said. The Oberstleutnant Galland, who commanded at their airfield, Wissant, near St Omer, sent his compliments to Oberstleutnant Bader and would like him to come and have tea with them.

'We do not try to get information from you,' he added quite sincerely. 'He would like to meet you. We are comrades, as you say, on the wrong sides.'

Bader was intrigued. It would be churlish to refuse, and in any case he would love to meet Galland (probably they had already met in the air). It brought a breath of the chivalry lost from modern war. And it was a chance to spy out the country, to see the other side, life on an enemy fighter station, to weigh it up and compare it. Might get back home with a 109!

'I'd be delighted to come,' he said.

'Good,' beamed the Count. 'A car will come for you.'

Agreeably they finished the second bottle.

The car came bearing the bald little engineering officer, who sat by him all the fifteen miles to Wissant. It was a sunny day and it felt good to be out. They drew up in front of an attractive country farmhouse of red brick. German officers stood outside – it was the officers' mess. As Bader got out a good-looking man about his own age, dark-haired and with a little moustache, stepped forward. He had burn marks round the eyes and a lot of medals on his tunic. The Knight's Cross with Oak Leaves and Swords – almost Germany's highest decoration – hung round his neck. He put out his hand and said 'Galland.'

Bader put out his own hand. 'Oh, how d'you do. My name is Douglas Bader.' Galland did not speak English, and the engineering officer interpreted. A lot of others stepped forward in turn, clicking their heels as they were introduced. Galland led him off, trailed by the others, down a garden path lined with shrubs. Quiet and pleasant, Galland said: 'I am glad to see you are all right and getting about again. How did you get on bailing out?'

'Don't remember much about it.'

'One never does,' Galland said. 'One of your pilots shot me down the other day and I had to jump out. I landed very hard. It must be unpleasant landing with only one leg.'

Bader asked: 'Is that when you burnt your eyes?' and Galland nodded.

He led the way into a long, low arbour, and Bader was surprised to see it filled with an elaborate model railway on a big raised platform. Galland pressed a button and little trains whirred past little stations, rattling over points, past signals, through tunnels and model cuttings. Eyes sparkling, Galland turned to Bader, looking like a small boy having fun. The interpreter said: 'This is the Herr Oberstleutnant's favourite place when he is not flying. It is a replica of Reichsmarshal Goering's railway, but of course the Reichsmarshal's is much bigger.'

After playing a little while with that, Galland led him and the others several hundred yards along hedge-lined paths, through a copse of trees to the low, three-sided blast walls of an aircraft pen. In it stood an Me. 109.

Bader looked at it fascinated, and Galland made a polite gesture for him to climb in. He surprised them by the way he hauled himself on to the wing-root, grabbed his right leg and swung it into the cockpit and climbed in unaided. As he cast a glinting professional eye over the cockpit lay-out Galland leaned in and pointed things out. Mad thoughts about starting up and slamming the throttle on for a reckless take-off surged through Bader's mind.*

Lifting his head, he could see no signs of the aerodrome. He turned

---

* After the war Galland sent Bader a snapshot of the scene, and only then did he discover that a German officer beside the cockpit had been pointing a heavy pistol at him all the time he sat there.

to the interpreter. 'Would you ask the Herr Obserstleutnant if I can take off and try a little trip in this thing?'

Galland chuckled and answered. The interpreter grinned at Bader. 'He says that if you do he'll be taking off right after you.'

'All right,' Bader said, looking a little too eagerly at Galland. 'Let's have a go.'

Galland chuckled again and said that he was off duty at the moment.

As he stepped out of the 109, Bader looked across country and saw the sea. Far beyond he thought he could glimpse the white cliffs of Dover and for a moment felt quite sick. It brought it all home to him. And the future. England could be no more than forty miles away. Longingly he thought if only they'd leave him for a moment he could get off with the 109 and be back in the mess for tea.

They had tea in the farmhouse mess, waiters in white coats bringing sandwiches and real English tea (probably captured). It could have been an RAF mess except that all the other uniforms were wrong. The atmosphere was wrong too, which was understandable. Everyone smiled, exuding goodwill, but it was a little strained and formal and the talk was stilted. With Galland there no one seemed to speak much. No one tried to pump him for information. The little interpreter told him that the day he was shot down the Luftwaffe had got twenty-six Spitfires for no loss, which was such obvious nonsense that it put Bader in a very cheerful mood, because it confirmed RAF views on extravagant German claims.* He himself had got two that day, and possibly three, counting the mysterious man who had hit him.†

Later they showed him some camera-gun films – a Blenheim which did not seem to be shot down, a Spitfire which shovelled out black smoke and obviously *was* shot down, and then an odd film of a 109 strafing a British ship and 'sinking' it. The last few frames showed the half-submerged ship, but it was all too obviously a different ship.

Galland gave him a tin of English tobacco, and when he took him out to the car said: 'It has been good to meet you. I'm afraid you will

---

* In the Western Desert in 1942 the German 'ace,' Marseille, claimed personally to have shot down sixteen British aircraft in one day. That day the Desert Air Force lost two aeroplanes.

† Much later Bader found that his wing had got eight that day for two lost.

find it different in prison camp, but if there is ever anything I can do, please let me know.'

He smiled warmly, shook hands, clicked his heels and bowed. At a discreet distance behind, everyone else clicked heels and bowed. Bader got in the car with the little engineer and they drove back to the hospital. He would have liked to have had Galland in his wing. Rumour said he had over seventy victories, but of course he had been fighting in the Spanish Civil War and in Poland too.

The engineer officer took him back up to the ward, shook hands, clicked his heels and bowed himself out. More black bread stood by his bed. Lucille had evidently been in with 'dinner.' After his tea with Galland he regarded it distastefully.

'How'd you get on?' Bill Hall asked.

'Fine,' he said. 'Jolly fine. They're a good bunch. Got some loot too.' He held up the tobacco.

A comatose form lay in the bed by the window and the room stank disagreeably of ether. Bader looked across. 'Who's that?'

'New boy came in while you were out,' Hall said. 'Sergeant pilot. Shot down yesterday. They've just taken his arm off. He's still under the dope.'

The door opened and a German soldier wearing a coal-scuttle helmet came in. It was the first of the fabled helmets that Bader had seen. The soldier, who must have been awaiting his return, saluted and said in atrocious English: 'Herr Ving Commander to-morrow at eight o'clock you vill be pleased to be ready because you go to Chermany.'

The words seemed to hit Bader right in the stomach. The German clicked his heels, saluted and clumped out. He sat on his bed, stunned. Then, with deep feeling, uttered an eloquent word.

Hall murmured: 'Tough luck, sir. Looks like you've had it.'

Bader roused and said crisply: 'Well, I've got to get out to-night, that's all.'

He lurched over to the window and pushed it open. It seemed a long way down, and immediately below were flagstones. After the parachute affair he did not feel like jumping. He turned back and scowled round the room, austere with its board floor and five prim beds.

My God! Sheets! Knotted sheets!

One learned something from school!

Each bed had an undersheet and a double, bag-type sheet stuffed in the Continental style. He stumbled over to his bed and ripped the sheets from under the blanket. Need a damn' sight more than that! He clumped noisily to the two empty beds and stripped them the same way. With a sudden idea he began ripping the bag sheets along the seams to get two out of each one. The tearing seemed to scream a warning to the Germans.

'Make a noise,' he hissed to Hall, and Hall started on a monologue in a loud American voice, talking nonsense, saying anything that came into his head and laughing loud and humourlessly. Both were acutely conscious of the guard just outside the door. Once they heard the rasp of a boot on the boards and then a couple of clumps. Bader looked up like an animal. Then a creak as the guard sat in the wicker-chair out there.

'Know anything about knots?' Bader whispered to Hall.

'Not a sausage.'

He started knotting the corners together in an unskilled double 'granny' with three hitches, jerking tightly to make them fast and hoping they would stay so when the test came.

'What about the curfew?' Hall asked.

He said: ' – the curfew!'

The knots took up a lot of length, and when he had finished the 'rope' was clearly not long enough.

'Here, take mine,' Hall said.

Gently he eased the sheet from under Hall and took off the top one. When he had added them the rope still did not look long enough.

'You'll be up the creek if you're left hanging,' Hall warned. 'Won't be able to climb back and won't be able to drop without bisecting yourself.'

Bader went over to the bed of the sergeant pilot, who was breathing stertorously under the ether. Gently working the sheet from under him, he said: 'This is frightful, but I've just got to.'

'He won't mind,' reassured Hall. 'I'll tell him when he wakes up.'

Soon he had fifteen sheets knotted together, littered around the room, and prayed that no one would come in. He pushed the sergeant pilot's bed to the window, wincing at the noise, knotted one end of the rope round the leg and stuffed the rest under the bed (it still looked pretty obvious). Then he straightened the white blankets on all the beds and climbed back into his own, sweating, heart thumping, praying that darkness would come before the guard.

Time dragged dreadfully while dusk slowly gathered in the room. He and Hall tried to talk in low tones, but his mind kept jumping away from the words. It was not quite dark when the door handle rattled, the door opened and a German soldier struck his head in and looked round. Bader could not breathe. The guard muttered '*Gut Nacht*,' and the door closed behind him.

Three hours to go. As long as no nurse came to see the sergeant pilot!

That evening Thelma, who had eaten nothing for three days, braced herself and asked Stan Turner: 'Well, what do you really think?'

Turner said with simple directness: 'You'll have to face it. We should have heard something by this. I guess he's had it.'

In London the Luftwaffe's radio message had arrived saying that a spare leg could be flown across in a Lysander communications aircraft. Spitfires could escort it part of the way and then Messerschmitts would take over. The Lysander could land at St Omer, hand over the leg and then it could take off again.

From Leigh-Mallory and Sholto Douglas the reaction was prompt, definite and identical. No free passage or German escort (with its lump of propaganda plum cake for Goebbels). They would send the spare leg in a Blenheim on a normal bombing raid.

Dundas, Johnny Johnson and Crowley-Milling had gone across to the Bay House to do what they could for Thelma. She sat quietly, a sphinx-like stoic, and only roused when the phone rang. It was Woodhall for her. The others could only hear her saying: 'Yes . . . yes . . . yes . . . yes, Woody.' She said 'Thank you very much, Woody,' hung up and came back to the room. In the silence she sat down and lit a cigarette, trembling a little. Then she blew out smoke and said quietly: 'D. B.'s a prisoner.' Shouts of jubilation filled the room but she hardly heard, feeling sick with astonishment and delight and with emotions ploughing over her.

Weary aeons of time seemed to have passed before a clock somewhere in the darkness of St Omer chimed midnight. The night was breathlessly still. He eased on to the edge of the bed, vainly trying to stop the creaks, and strapped his legs on. Then his clothes. Praying that the guard was asleep in his chair, he took a step towards the window; the boards creaked and the right leg squeaked and thumped with a terrifying noise. Hall started coughing to cover it up as, unable to tiptoe, he stumbled blindly across the floor. One or the other was bound to wake the guard. At the window he quietly pushed it open and leaned out, but the night was coal black and he could not see the ground. Picking up the sheet rope, he lowered it out, hoping desperately that it was long enough, but could not tell if it reached the ground. It must have roused the sergeant pilot: coming out of the twilight of ether, the boy was groaning.

Hall whispered: 'We'll have a nurse here in a moment.'

Holding the rope, Bader leaned his chest on the window-sill and tried to winkle his legs out sideways. They seemed fantastically clumsy, more than ever before, huge, disjointed and swollen. Uncontrollable. Sweating, he took a hand off the rope to grab his right shin and bend the knee. Then somehow he was through, legs dangling, hands clutching the rope on the sill. The terrible pain pierced his ribs again, making him gasp.

Hall whispered: 'Good luck!' It sounded like a pistol shot.

He hissed: 'Shut up.' And then, 'Thanks.' Then he started easing himself down.

It was simple. The legs rasping against the wall were useless, but the arms that had developed such muscles since the long-ago crash at Reading took his weight easily. He lowered himself, hand under hand, under sure control. Holding the sheets was no trouble and the knots were holding – so far. In a few seconds he came to a window and knew it was the room where he had drunk champagne with the Luftwaffe. He was horrified to feel that it was open, but inside it was dark and he eased his rump on to the ledge for a breather, hoping the doctor was not sleeping inside. Sitting there, breathing quietly, he looked down but still could not see the ground or whether the rope reached it. (Only later he realised he should have counted the knots.) Too late to go back now; he eased himself off the ledge and went on down.

Very gently his feet touched the flagstones and he was standing, dimly seeing that yards of sheet seemed to be lying on the ground.

'Piece of cake,' he thought, and moved a couple of yards on to the grass, cursing the noise from his legs. Warily he steered across the grass towards where the gates should be, having no plan, only hoping the mysterious Frenchman would be there.

Something loomed darker even than the night. The gates! Good show. Then a shock – they were closed. He got his fingers in a crack between and one gate opened easily a foot. He squeezed through on to the cobbled *pavé* of the road and instantly, immediately opposite, saw the glowing end of a cigarette. He stumped diagonally across the road and the cigarette moved, converging on him. It came to his side with a dark shadow behind it that whispered urgently 'Dooglass!' in a strong French accent.

'*Oui*,' he said, and the shape took his right arm and they moved off along the *pavé*. The town was like a tomb in which his legs were making an unholy clatter, echoing in the darkness. He could not see, but the silent shape seemed to know by instinct. A pressure on the arm and they turned right and stumbled on.

The Frenchman began muttered to him: '*C'est bon. C'est magnifique. Ah, les sales Boches.*'

After a while Bader thought how funny it was, walking through the curfew in enemy-occupied St Omer arm-in-arm with a stranger he would not even recognise by day. He began to giggle. The Frenchman said 'Ssh! Ssh!' but that only made him giggle more. He tried to stop but couldn't, and the more he tried the more he giggled as the strained nerves took control. The Frenchman started to giggle and then it was so grotesque, the two of them giggling and clattering down the street, that it grew into loud laughter mingled with the terror inside him that the Germans would hear. Slowly the pent-up emotion washed away and the laughter subsided into suppressed sniggers that he was at last able to stop.

They walked on – and on – and on. Five minutes, ten – twenty. His right stump without the stump sock began to chafe. Thirty minutes . . . it was sore and starting to hurt. On and on they walked. He was limping badly and the Frenchman made soothing noises that sounded in inflection like 'Not far now' in French. Forty minutes must have passed. The steel leg had rubbed the skin off his groin and every step was searing agony. Stumbling and exhausted, he had both arms hanging on to the Frenchman's shoulders. At last the man took his arms round his neck, picked him up, dangling on his back, and staggered along. In a hundred yards or so he stopped and put him down, breathing in a rasping way. Bader leaned against a stone wall and the man pushed open a gate in the wall beside him.

He led the way and Bader stumbled after him up a garden path. A doorway showed ahead, framing soft light, and then he was in a little, low-ceilinged room with flowered wallpaper, and a tin oil-lamp on the table. An old man and a woman in a black shawl got up from the chairs and the woman put her arms round him and kissed him. She was over sixty, Madame Hiècque, plump and with a lined, patient face. Her husband, spare and stooping, brushed his cheeks with a wisp of grey moustache. Fleetingly he saw his guide, remembering mostly the lamplight sheen on the glossy peak of a cap drawn low over the face and the glint of smiling teeth. The young man shook his hand and was off out the door.

The old woman said gently: '*Vous êtes fatigúe?*'

Holding on to the table, he said, '*Oui*' and she led him with a candle up some cottage stairs into a room with a huge double bed. He flopped on it. She put the candle on the table, smiled and went out. He unstrapped his legs with enormous relief, stripped to his underclothes and slid under the bedclothes into a gloriously soft feather bed, thinking: 'That's foxed the bloody Huns. I'll be seeing Thelma in a couple of days.' Then he was asleep.

A hand on his shoulder woke him about 7 am. The old man was looking down, smiling with tobacco-stained teeth. He left a razor, hot water and towel. Bader freshened up and examined his stump, which was raw and bloodstained, terribly sore. No help for it. Just have to bear the pain. Done it before. He strapped his legs on and went wincingly downstairs. Madame had coffee and bread and jam waiting, and while he ate she planted an old straw hat squarely on her head and went out. Bader sat for a couple of hours in a red plush chair trying to talk to the old man, a stilted, fumbling conversation of invincible goodwill.

Madame came back in great glee. '*Les Boches*,' it seemed, '*sont très stupides.*' He gathered she had walked to the hospital and stood watching mobs of Germans running around searching the area. Great joke! In halting French he tried to make her understand that his presence was very dangerous to them. If they found him he, himself, would only be put in cells and then sent to prison camp, but the Hiècques were liable to be shot. He should leave them and hide somewhere.

Madame said, '*Non, non, non, non . . .*' The Germans would never find him here. That evening her son-in-law, who spoke English, would come and they would discuss things and get him to the Underground. She examined his right stump and produced a pair of long woollen underpants. Cutting one of the legs off, she sewed up the end and there was a perfectly good stump-sock. After she powdered the stump he put the sock on under the leg and felt much better.

At noon the familiar drone came overhead and they took him out into the shelter of the walled back garden. Yearningly he watched the tangled con-trails and saw tiny glints as twisting aircraft caught the sun. Out from the windows of houses all round leaned the women waving mops and towels, and shrilling: '*Vive les Tommies. Vive les Tommies.*' It was moving and delightful. Soon he'd be back up there among the con-trails, thinking differently about the sweeps, knowing what they meant.

At 15,000 feet, just south of St Omer, the Tangmere wing jockeyed round the Blenheim. Crowley-Milling, close escort, saw the bomb-bays open and a long thin box with the spare leg drop out. It looked like a little coffin. A parachute blossomed above it and it floated down, swaying gently, surrounded by the black stains of flak-bursts from the puzzled gunners far below.

The quiet, loyal and gallant Stokoe had asked to be dropped by parachute with it to look after the wing commander in prison, but permission had been refused. He had to content himself in helping Thelma stuff the leg with stump-socks, powder, tobacco and chocolate.

Madame gave Bader cold pork for lunch and went out again to the scene of the crime. She came back hugging herself with delight. Convinced that Bader could not walk far, the Germans had cordoned off an area round the hospital and were running about like ants, searching every house. But nowhere in this area.

He felt like twiddling his thumbs as the afternoon dragged. Madame went out again to see the fun. Sitting in shirt-sleeves in the plush chair, he thought: Roll on that English-speaking chap. About half-past five there came a sudden terrifying banging on the front door and a chill swept him. The old man jumped as though he had

been shot, peered furtively through the curtain, turned and whispered
'*Les Boches!*'

He grabbed Bader's arm and led him towards the back door. Only
at the last moment Douglas thought to grab his battledress jacket.
Together they stumbled into the garden, moving as fast as the legs
would let him. Three yards from the back door, against a wall, stood
a rough shed, galvanised iron nailed on posts, covering some baskets,
garden tools and straw. The old man pulled the baskets and straw
away, laid him on his stomach, cheek pillowed on his hands, against
the corner of the wall and piled the straw and baskets on top. Lying
there, he heard the old man's footsteps hurrying inside.

There was not long to wait. Within a minute he heard voices and
then tramping feet by the back door. He knew the sound of jackboots.
A vague kind of twilight filtered through the straw but he could not
see anything. The boots clumped along the paved path to the shed.
He heard baskets being kicked about. The straw over him started
moving with a loud rustle. He lay still, thinking, 'Here we go!'

Miraculously the footsteps retreated, diminishing down the garden
path. Elation filled him.

The boots were coming back up the path. Suddenly they clumped
again into the shed, then stopped and rasped about a yard from his
head. From his heart outwards ice seemed to freeze his nerves.

The baskets were being thrown around, the boots rasped on the
paving, and then there was a metallic clang that mystified him. There
was a movement in the hay just above and another clang. His eyes,
turned sideways, saw a bayonet flash down an inch from his nose and
stab through the wrist of his battledress jacket to hit the stone floor.
He knew what the clang was and guessed that the next stroke would
go into his neck or back.

It was a lightning decision. He jerked up on his hands, heaving out
of the hay like a monster rising from the sea, straw cascading off his
back. A young German soldier, bayonet poised for the next jab, leapt
back in shock and stared pop-eyed at him, holding rifle and bayonet
on guard. He started yelling hoarsely in German. Boots pounded and

three German soldiers clattered under the iron roof, all armed. They stood round him in a semi-circle, bayonet poised about four feet from him. Slowly he raised his hands.

A little Stabsfeldwebel (staff sergeant) with a dark, thin moustache ran up and covered him with a pistol as he stood there feeling like King Lear, or perhaps an escaped lunatic at bay, with straw in his hair and all over his battledress.

Looking pleased and quite friendly, the Stabsfeldwebel said in perfect, unaccented English: 'Ah, Wing Commander, so we have caught you again.'

'Yes,' said Bader. 'Would you mind asking these soldiers to put their rifles down. As you can see, I'm unarmed.'

The Stabsfeldwebel rattled off some German, and the soldiers lowered the rifles.

Still with his hands up, Bader said. 'You speak English very well.'

'Thank you, Wing Commander,' relied the German. 'I lived at Streatham* for eleven years.'

'Did you really,' Bader said. 'I used to live near Croydon myself.'

(It struck him that the conversation was unreal.)

'Ah, I know Croydon well,' the German answered. 'Did you ever go to the Davis Cinema?'

'Yes. And I used to go to the Locarno at Streatham.'

'Did you?' said the German. 'Many Saturday evenings I have danced there.'

Bader never forgot a word of that dialogue. The German courteously invited him to follow, and he stumped out of the shed into the back door again feeling that the world might well be rid of politicians and that this was a perfect example of the fact that ordinary people never caused wars. He felt no rancour towards the soldiers who had winkled him out, and as far as he could see they felt no rancour for him. He was thinking it made Hitler and Mussolini look 'pretty bloody stupid' when he saw the old man and woman standing in the room. They looked pale and he stiffly walked past, showing no sign of recognition.

At the front door he nodded his head back and said to the Stabsfeldwebel: 'Those people did not know I was in their garden. I came in last night through that gate in the wall.'

* London suburb.

Quite pleasantly the German replied: 'Yes, I understand that.'

By the kerb stood the Germans' car, and as they led him to it the rear door opened and a blonde girl with glasses got out. Rather surprised, he recognised Hélène, from the hospital, and said automatically: 'Hallo, Hélène,' but she walked past him with her eyes down.

They drove him to Headquarters in St Omer, where a German officer questioned him and got no answers. Then into a room where he was surprised and delighted to see the box containing his spare right leg. They explained, smiling, that it had been dropped that afternoon, and took his photograph standing by it. Then, to his annoyance, they refused to give it to him and prodded him instead into an upstairs room. There, for the first time, they really infuriated him; as he sat on a cot an officer and a soldier stood over him with a pistol and a bayonet, and made him take his trousers down and unstrap his legs: then they took his legs away.

He snarled at them, but the officer said stiffly it was orders from above. Two guards stayed and the rest went out, leaving him on the bed helpless, humiliated and seething. All night two men in full battle order, coal-scuttle helmets and loaded rifles stood over him. It was hot and he asked for the windows to be opened, but the officer came back and refused, saying that 'orders from above' forbade that too. They were taking no chances!

He lay awake all night as the guards coughed and muttered ceaselessly. It was then that he realised that Hélène had betrayed him and that the Germans must know about Madame and the old man, and he grew sick with worrying about what the Germans would do to them and to Lucille. Somehow he could not feel much resentment about Hélène. He supposed they had threatened her.

In Fighter Command Headquarters in England next morning the telephone rang in the office of Sholto Douglas. He picked it up and recognised the voice of Winston Churchill saying: 'Douglas!'

'Yes, sir.'

'I see from the newspapers you've been fraternizing with the enemy, dropping a leg to a captured pilot.'

'Well, sir,' Sholto Douglas said, 'you may call it fraternising, but we managed to shoot down eleven of the enemy for the loss of six or seven of our own, so I hope you might feel it was worth it.'

There was a grunt, and then a click as the phone was hung up.

Shooting Party

Lieut. Col. Graham Brooks, MC (Late RA)

SHOOTING PARTY

Until he has seen his troops in battle, there is always one thing in the mind of every commander of whatever grade; the question of how his officers and men will react, collectively and individually under fire. He seldom has to worry about collective reaction. But in the case of individuals he may get surprises; he may find some he thought the best are not so outstanding in leadership as he expected, whereas some whom he regarded as lacking drive or personality find both in action. He watches them all closely during their baptism of fire.

Ours came early next morning, a lovely sunny morning in the form of a swoop of 'planes from the blue, dive-bombing, incendiaries, and machine-gunning.

I was shaving at the time, but got three distinct impressions. First was Jack Leaman's laug, followed by unprintable descriptions of the enemy. Second was fat old Peter Booth glaring angrily at an incendiary which had dropped between his legs, growling: 'What bloody sauce!' Third was a Lewis-gunner blazing away at a dive-bomber which seemed to be making straight for him.

Greenhouses in a neighbouring nursery-garden were destroyed, bushes set on fire, two bombs fell beside the command-post but failed to explode, one small house damaged, some tiles and windows on other houses shattered, a cow killed by machine-gun fire near our guns; military casualties – military damage – NIL.

The effect of the enemy's effort had been of threefold benefit to us. It had reassured me as to the calibre of my boys; it had given the men confidence in their officers; it had aroused their fighting spirit by stirring up hatred of the Hun, for the sole human casualty had been a little girl of twelve or so who, with other refugees, was trudging wearily along the road clutching a doll. Our chaps were soon to have satisfaction; for that very day our guns were to be the first in the BEF to open fire on the Boches in this war.

Our battery was at Smeisberg, a tiny pocket of cottages. When we arrived, there were a few civilians, but these soon fled, taking with them nothing but bedding and mattresses piled on wheelbarrows, prams and bicycles. The morning's bombing changed the minds of the three who had hitherto decided to remain. The sight of those panic-stricken human beings, abandoning everything they owned, everything they had worked for, their homes, their petty treasures, achieved more in a few seconds than all my efforts in nine months in making the boys hate the Hun and all his works. An old man on crutches; toothless old women, stumbling as they pushed creaking perambulators loaded with pillows and blankets; a child with staring eyes; all going, they knew not whither or to whom or to what. And then the 'planes, the machine-guns, the bombs – directed, not at the soldiers or the guns, but at these harmless creatures.

We had seen plenty of refugees on our way up through Belgium, but they had been different. First there had been the wealthy in Mercédès cars, loaded with suit-cases and luxuries, plentifully supplied with money, womenfolk bedecked with jewels, speeding for safety and good living in France; secondly, families with carts and wagons laden with furniture and possessions, running away it is true, but more or less calmly, having taken time to choose what they would salve, journeying to the homes of friends or relatives. But these new sights were different. The former had been sad, some of it contemptible. This was sheer horror, savagery of the vilest kind.

It is the deliberate policy of the Hun to create his refugee problem. Fifth Column agents spread panic; Fifth Column agents, disguised as soldiers or civilian officials, advise the folk to get out quick; terrorism from the air adds its spur. Out on the roads scramble the wretched people. Roads are blocked, fields on either side are blocked, with men, women, children, horses, carts, cars, perambulators, bicycles, even cows and goats, all laden with bedding, and the sick, the dying, the infirm. You see some cripple carried on a stretcher improvised from a door; a woman with babe at breast. Some crying, some calm, some just stupefied. They block the roads for the army, but the army must get up to fight, so the army must harden its heart and push them off the road into the ditches and fields – and then they glare at you, you foreign cads, as if you were the hated enemy. It hurts. And it makes you hate the Hun still more.

The Hun works hard to keep this refugee problem acute, to keep the roads blocked against the army. Over and over again his 'planes have flown just above our heads on the march, and every minute we have expected the bombs to come crashing down on us; but no – the 'planes have left us alone, to unload death and panic on the mass of refugees in the villages and fields ahead.

If he ever invades this country, one of his first objects will be to create that same refugee problem here; and by that time, if it ever comes, he may decide to use gas as well. Adequate control by the civilian authorities could prevent a repetition of the trouble with which the army was faced in Belgium.

At Smeisberg, A and B Troops were in the open on the forward slope behind the road, C Troop a mile forward to the left in the front edge of a wood on high ground. Front edges of woods were then considered good gun positions; now we know the Boche sprays them with incendiaries and machine-gun bullets habitually. Our wagon lines were some miles in rear, hidden in woods near a cigar factory. You will hear about those cigars later.

Digging was the order of the day. First, slit trenches; then dugouts; gun-pits; trenches for ammunition; command-posts; pits for machine-guns and posts for the men manning anti-tank rifles. But could we get those men to dig? They just would *not* dig. The moment you turned your back, they stopped. I raved and stormed, for I knew how vital was this work, how speed was vital, too. Then came bombing, shelling, machine-gunning. After that, you couldn't stop the men digging. For the rest of our time overseas, we never had to tell the men to dig again.

Now let me take you where you can see the line. The position taken up by the BEF is a strong one. You can see the divisional front from our observation posts on the high ground behind Rhode Saint Agathe. Below is the river Dyle. Normally it is not a wide river, but has two forks and the Belgian authorities have flooded the area in between, so that it is a wide expanse of water that you look down upon. No tank could get across that, you think – but it is very shallow – and the Boche has amphibian tanks. On the far side the ground rises steadily back, so that the forward areas of what will be enemy country are well exposed to view, though there are numerous woods providing cover. At the moment our outposts are still across the Dyle, but will be withdrawn soon, and the main line of our defences stretches about half a mile in front of us. There is a fine battalion here – the Duke's; behind and around us the Guards, in reserve; a lot of digging is going on everywhere; deserted houses are being fortified or pulled to pieces so that doors, timber and masonry can be used for defence works elsewhere.

We were with the First Division. Until I read Lord Gort's published dispatches, I had not realised that only two Divisions besides ours moved up beyond Brussels. The rest of the BEF did not get so far.

It is a curious feeling watching the country beyond the river, knowing that somewhere behind it are the Boches. How far away are they now? How long before you get a glimpse of them? How long before you will hear the crack of the guns behind you and watch for the shell to burst among the Boches? Every now and then your signallers beside you test the line and the wireless to satisfy themselves that when that moment comes you will be able to control the fire of your guns by telephone or over the air without hitch.

Sad for me that when that moment came I was not there myself to see, but was busy at the command-post. Luck fell to Dennis Clarke, and good use he made of it. The first hint Dennis had was movement of animals. Away on high ground beyond the river, two or three miles away, he noticed moving herds of cows. They were not panic-stricken, but were moving as though they had been disturbed, away from the road, obliquely in our direction. Animal movement is most helpful to the artillery observer. Sure enough, motor-cyclists soon came into view, then an armoured car or two; these passed out of sight, down towards the river. Dennis now knew the spot on which to lay his guns. Down the p'hone went his orders.

The rattle of machine-guns from below told that the cyclists had come under fire from our infantry. This warning must have been heard by the Boche columns, too; if mechanized, they must have debussed on hearing machine-gun fire ahead; at any rate, the next to appear were marching infantry. Over the crest they came, a glorious target. Dennis waited until at least two hundred were in sight on the forward slope.

I was in the command post when I heard C Troop's guns open fire. 'What are you shooting at?' I inquired by telephone, expecting the reply that they were just registering some feature we might want to shoot at in the future. 'BOCHES!' came the proud response.

In some ways the Hun infantryman has not changed. Though our shells were dropping among them, men were falling and others running for safety, more infantry kept appearing over the crest, just as they used to come doggedly on in the last war without using any intelligence. This continued for some time before they changed their plan. In the meantime we had done useful execution.

Those were the first shells fired in anger on the Dyle. Altogether we were there four days. I propose to give just a brief general impression of that phase.

One of our greatest difficulties was the question of animals. It was a heart-rending business. Civilians, in their panic, had left their animals behind; cows, pigs, dogs, cats, even birds in cages. Some of these animals were left shut up, others roaming about. No attempt had been made by the civilian authorities to meet this problem.

First trouble came with the cows. The poor brutes needed milking; as their udders became distended and sore, they raced about the place, bellowing pitifully. Our chaps did their best to milk them, but we were all busy digging and fighting, and the cows were legion, so it was an impossible task. It seemed cruel to shut them up; on the otherhand, we could not let them run about, because they were fast becoming maddened with pain, and madness was hastened by fright from the bombs. They were becoming savage and really dangerous; and their movement attracted attention from the air. I therefore decided to shut up the few we could manage to milk, and shoot the rest of the poor creatures. What finally decided me was the sight of a little calf dying in agony. We shot it at once.

Next came the dogs. It was pathetic, searching deserted houses, to find dogs chained up, locked up, going mad for want of food and water, terrified by bombing and the noise of our guns. One dog, quite mad, flew at us when we entered, and we had to shoot in self-defence. Finally we deputed Sergeant Watts, himself a dog-lover, to go round and put them out of their misery. You would see him, pipe in mouth, rifle in hand, stroll into a house. Then you would hear a crack. Out would come Watts, pipe still in mouth, jerk his thumb towards the house and say to a gunner: 'Bury that poor dog, son!'

The chickens we ate. The goats we milked; we thought of taking them with us when we moved, but as things turned out that was impossible. The pigs were the least trouble, and the most phlegmatic of creatures. They wandered about as they pleased. Cliff Hackett, returning from a tour of duty at the observation post, went for a lie-down in an empty house. When I went to wake him, I found an old sow in the act of climbing on the bed where he was asleep. Eventually when orders came to retreat we shot the pigs as well and soaked the carcasses of all dead animals with petrol, for nothing must be left of use to the Boches.

Don't imagine we spent most of our time shooting animals. Our 18-pounder guns were busy day and night. It was like those days on the Somme in '16, especially at night, and our boys were having no mean introduction to artillery work in action. It was not all one-way stuff, either; we were getting some back at us. In fact the Boche let us know quite definitely that he had spotted the position of all three troops; if the boys had not dug so heartily, we should have had many casualties; even as things were it was decided to move some guns, so I went looking for new positions.

That morning we had received a document about Fifth Column activities which described an instance where a clover field had been cut so as to leave a sign in the form of an arrow visible from the air and pointing to a vital spot in our defences. When, therefore, in reconnoitring new gun positions, I looked down from a ridge at a clover field in which had been mown a large and distinct arrow pointing towards 25-pounder guns some three hundred yards away, I naturally thought this was the case referred to in that document. Horrified that it was allowed to remain there, we hurried to the officer on the guns. He was shaken to the core, obviously ignorant of the sign's existence; clearly this was not the same case. Armed with spades, we soon had that clover field so knocked about that the sign was no longer visible, but the area was heavily shelled that afternoon.

There was Fifth Column activity in other ways. Our telephone cables were cut over and over again; not by shell-fire or traffic, but the clean cut of shears. I was suspicious of a civilian who had stayed on for no apparent reason in a small house on the hill above us, but we could never catch him out. There was no control of evacuation by the civilian authorities; civilians went or stayed as they pleased; and why did some remain behind, we wondered?

One clever enemy agent, at least, managed to score. Dressed as a senior British staff officer, he went to a battery position, declared there was a general retirement, and ordered the guns to get out of action quick. He succeeded in getting the battery away – Here indeed was bad intelligence discipline! – but fortunately this was rectified before harm resulted. Rumour said that the man was later caught red-handed, trying to get another battery to move, and was shot.

It may have been this same man who tackled Cliff Hackett. One night Cliff, having been relieved at his observation post, came back with the story that the French had retreated on our flank, that the Boches were across the Dyle, and that all observation posts were being called in. He had been told this by a British officer down the lane leading from our command-post. We rushed after the 'British officer', but could find no trace of him in the dark.

This happened in the middle of a night when things were very jumpy. . . .We had had a false gas alarm, given by infantry who had seen the mist which creeps up the valley at night there. We had had several SOS calls for fire, some of which were undoubtedly a Boche ruse. We had had a party out searching for parachutists reported to have been dropped in the vicinity – another *canard*, I am sure. And then something else suspicious happened.

We had made our command-post in a sunken track between two high banks. The track itself was sandy. We had torn doors and walls from the sheds of neighbouring houses with which we completely roofed the track; then spread sand over this roof, so that from above it looked like the track itself, enabling us to work underneath well camouflaged.

During that night we smelt something burning. On searching, we found a tiny bonfire of twigs smouldering on the roof over our command-post. Nobody had heard or seen any one about, and a vigorous search failed to find anyone.

That same night the Boches got troops over the Dyle in rubber boats but they were eventually killed, captured, or driven back.

Soon after dawn next day Peter Booth and I stood on top of the sunken track, watching a hedge-hopping Lysander with Belgian markings. It was only about fifty feet up and we were just going to wave to the pilot when the 'plane skimmed towards us and opened up with its machine-gun from about two hundred yards away. Peter and I dived head first into the sunken track like pearl-fishers into the ocean. Flying the other chap's colours is, of course, a typical Boche trick. We were not caught napping again. In fact, orders were subsequently received to open fire on any 'plane flying below a certain height, whatever its markings.

The Hun is clever at legitimate ruses, too. He is particularly good at inducing you to waste ammunition on places where there is nothing to hurt. It was on the Dyle that we saw a Boche officer ride out ostentatiously from the front of a wood, look about him, then ride back into the wood. Although repeated, this little trick did not succeed, for in that particular light we could see into the wood through a telescope – there was nothing there; but in a wood some way to the right some guns *were* being brought into action – you could just make them out through the trees.

Presumably the officer had wanted to distract attention from the second wood by focusing it on the first.

On the evening of 16 May we received orders to retreat. Rumours that the French had not come up on our right must be true after all. Yet to leave this magnificent position on the Dyle – when the BEf had its tail right up – it couldn't be true!

We watched sappers preparing the bridge behind us for demolition. They were to blow it up at midnight. We must get our guns across it first, but at the last possible moment.

That night our little 18-pounders fired 1,200 rounds, a real farewell party. Now and then we got some back.

We spent some time smashing things up, so as to leave nothing of value to the Boches. We found a civilian motor-bike and some push-bikes to augment our own transport. Bombardier (now Second-Lieutenant) Thomas discovered a French dress sword which he annexed; riding his motor-bike, with the sword clattering against the back wheel, he looked a comic sight.

Indeed, many of the men began to look comic sights, for one advantage of battle is that you can dress for comfort instead of appearance. Battle dress is a loathsome invention; bitterly cold in the winter, because it gives no protection to the small of your back or or your buttocks; gruelling hvot in summer with its tight wrists and waistband; you miss the use of the big side pockets a tunic has. It cannot compare for utility or comfort with the old service dress. When not in battle you must bow to the whims of Brass Hats, so I have had to wear battle dress on occasion in this country myself, but once the battle started I could say goodbye to all that, and went about in comfort in breeches, tunic, and red and blue forage-cap. In the end I was glad of this for another reason; when all we could get away from Dunkirk was what we stood up in, it meant that I salved a good tunic, a good pair of breeches and a pair of field boots, instead of just a lousy suit of battle dress.

About midnight we pulled out and made the first step towards the long retreat. None of us could understand why. Every one on the Dyle had got the impression that the BEf was top dog over the Hun, who once again had shown his traditional dislike of the bayonet. 'Still,' we thought, 'we'll be back here again very soon.'

As we moved off without lights in the pitch dark; the Hun gave a parting salute. Again we were lucky – not one casualty. We had been the first guns to open fire; in that sector, we were the last guns to leave.

H-Hour

Cornelius Ryan

By now the long, bobbing lines of assault craft were less than a mile from Omaha and Utah beaches. For the three thousand Americans in the first wave H-Hour was just fifteen minutes away.

The noise was deafening as the boats, long white wakes streaming out behind them, churned steadily for the shore. In the slopping, bouncing craft the men had to shout to be heard over the roar of the diesels. Overhead, like a great steel umbrella, the shells of the fleet still thundered. And rolling out from the coast came the booming explosions of the Allied air forces' carpet bombing. Strangely, the guns of the Atlantic Wall were silent. Troops saw the coastline stretching ahead and wondered about the absence of enemy fire. Maybe, many thought, it would be an easy landing after all.

The great square-faced ramps of the assault craft butted into every wave, and chilling, frothing green water sloshed over everyone. There were no heroes in these boats – just cold, miserable, anxious men, so jam-packed together, so weighed down by equipment that often there was no place to be seasick except over one another. Newsweek's Kenneth Crawford, in the first Utah wave, saw a young 4th Division soldier, covered in his own vomit, slowly shaking his head in abject misery and disgust. 'That guy Higgins,' he said, 'ain't got nothin' to be proud of about inventin' this goddamned boat.'

Some men had no time to think about their miseries – they were bailing for their lives. Almost from the moment the assault craft left the mother ships, many boats had begun to fill with water. At first men had paid little attention to the sea slopping about their legs; it was just another misery to be endured. Lieutenant George Kerchner of the Rangers watched the water slowly rise in his craft and wondered if it was serious. He had been told that the LCA was unsinkable. But then over the radio Kerchner's soldiers heard a call for help: 'This is LCA 860! ... LCA 860! ... We're sinking! ...

We're sinking!' There was a final exclamation: 'My God, we're sunk!' Immediately Kerchner and his men began bailing.

Directly behind Kerchner's boat, Sergeant Regis McCloskey, also of the Rangers, had his own troubles. McCloskey and his men had been bailing for more than an hour. Their boat carried ammunition for the Pointe du Hoc attack and all the Rangers' packs. The boat was so waterlogged McCloskey was sure it would sink. His only hope lay in lightening the wallowing craft. McCloskey ordered his men to toss all unnecessary equipment overboard. Rations, extra clothing and packs went over the side. McCloskey heaved them all into the swell. In one pack was $1,200 which Private Chuck Vella had won in a crap game; in another was First Sergeant Charles Frederick's false teeth.

Landing-craft began to sink in both the Omaha and Utah areas — ten off Omaha, seven off Utah. Some men were picked up by rescue boats coming up behind, others would float around for hours before being rescued. And some soldiers, their yells and screams unheard, were dragged down by their equipment and ammunition. They drowned within sight of the beaches, without having fired a shot.

In an instant the war had become personal. Troops heading for Utah Beach saw a control boat leading one of the waves suddenly rear up out of the water and explode. Seconds later heads bobbed up and survivors tried to save themselves by clinging to the wreckage. Another explosion followed almost immediately. The crew of a landing-barge trying to launch four of the thirty-two amphibious tanks bound for Utah had dropped the ramp right on to a submerged sea mine. The front of the craft shot up and Sergeant Orris Johnson on a nearby LCT watched in frozen horror as a tank 'soared more than a hundred feet into the air, tumbled slowly end over end, plunged back into the water and disappeared.' Among the many dead, Johnson learned later, was his buddy. Tanker Don Neill.

Scores of Utah-bound men saw the dead bodies and heard the yells and screams of the drowning. One man, Lieutenant Francis X. Riley of the Coast Guard, remembers the scene vividly. The twenty-four-year-old officer, commanding an LCI, could only listen 'to the anguished cries for help from wounded and shocked soldiers and sailors as they pleaded with us to pull them out of the water.' But Riley's orders were to 'disembark the troops on time regardless of casualties.' Trying to close his mind to the screams, Riley ordered his craft on past the drowning men. There was nothing else he could do. The assault waves sped by, and as one boat carrying Lieutenant-Colonel James Batte and the 4th Division's 8th Infantry Regiment troops threaded its way through the dead bodies, Batte heard one of his grey-faced men say, 'Them lucky bastards – they ain't seasick no more.'

The sight of the bodies in the water, the strain of the long trip in from the transport ships and now the ominous nearness of the flat sands and the dunes of Utah Beach jerked men out of their lethargy. Corporal Lee Cason, who had just turned twenty, suddenly found himself 'cursing to high heaven against Hitler and Mussolini for getting us into this mess.' His companions were startled at his vehemence – Cason had never before been known to swear. In many boats now soldiers nervously checked and rechecked their weapons. Men became so possessive of their ammunition that Colonel Eugene Caffey could not get a single man in his boat to give him a clip of bullets for his rifle. Caffey, who was not supposed to land until 9 a.m., had smuggled himself aboard an 8th Infantry craft in an effort to catch up with his veteran 1st Engineer Brigade. He had no equipment and although all the men in the boat were overloaded with ammunition, they were 'hanging on to it for dear life.' Caffey was finally able to load the rifle by taking up a collection of one bullet from each of eight men.

In the waters off Omaha Beach there had been a disaster. Nearly half the amphibious tank force scheduled to support the assault troops had foundered. The plan was for sixty-four of these tanks to be launched two to three miles offshore. From there they were to swim in to the beach. Thirty-two of them had been allotted to the 1st Division's area – Easy Red, Fox Green and Fox Red. The landing-barges carrying them reached their positions, the ramps were dropped and twenty-nine tanks were launched into the heaving swell. The weird-looking amphibious vehicles, their great balloon-like canvas skirts supporting them in the water, began breasting the waves, driving towards the shore. Then tragedy overtook the men of the 741st Tank Battalion. Under the pounding of the waves the canvas water-wings ripped, supports broke, engines were flooded – and, one after another, twenty-seven tanks foundered and sank. Men came clawing up out of the hatches, inflating their lifebelts, plunging into the sea. Some succeeded in launching survival rafts. Others went down in the steel coffins.

Two tanks, battered and almost awash, were still heading for the shore. The crews of three others had the good fortune to be on a landing-barge whose ramp jammed. They were put ashore later. The remaining thirty-two tanks – for the 29th Division's half of the beach – were safe. Officers in charge of the craft carrying them, overwhelmed by the disaster they had seen, wisely decided to take their force directly on to the beach. But the loss of the 1st Division tanks would cost hundreds of casualties within the next few minutes.

From two miles out the assault troops began to see the living and the dead in the water. The dead floated gently, moving with the tide towards the beach, as though determined to join their fellow Americans. The living bobbed up and down in the swells, savagely pleading for the help the assault boats could not tender. Sergeant Regis McCloskey, his ammunition boat again safely under way, saw the screaming men in the water, 'yelling for help, begging us to stop – and we couldn't. Not for anything or anyone.' Gritting his teeth, McCloskey looked away as his boat sped past, and then, seconds later, he vomited over the side. Captain Robert Cunningham and his men saw survivors struggling, too. Instinctively their Navy crew swung the boat towards the men in the water. A fast launch cut them off. Over its loudspeaker came the grim words, 'You are not a rescue ship! Get on shore!' In another boat near by, Sergeant Noel Dube of an engineer battalion said the Act of Contrition.

Now the deadly martial music of the bombardment seemed to grow and swell as the thin wavy lines of assault craft closed in on Omaha Beach. Landing-ships lying about one thousand yards offshore joined in the shelling; and then thousands of flashing rockets whooshed over the heads of the men. To the troops it seemed inconveivable that anything could survive the massive weight of fire-power that flayed the German defences. The beach was wreathed in haze, and plumes of smoke from grass fires drifted lazily down from the bluffs. Still the German guns remained silent. The boats bored in. In the thrashing surf and running back up the beach men could now see the lethal jungles of steel-and-concrete obstacles. They were strewn everywhere, draped with barbed wire and capped with mines. They were as cruel and ugly as the men had expected. Behind the defences the beach itself was deserted; nothing and no one moved upon it. Closer and

closer the boats pressed in . . . five hundred yards . . . four hundred
and fifty yards. Still no enemy fire. Through waves that were four to
five feet high the assault craft surged forward, and now the great
bombardment began to lift, shifting to targets farther inland. The
first boats were barely four hundred yards from the shore when the
German guns – the guns that few believed could have survived the
raging Allied air and sea bombardment – opened up.

Through the din and clamour one sound was nearer, deadlier than
all the rest – the sound of machine-gun bullets clanging across the
steel, snoutlike noses of the boats. Artillery roared. Mortar shells
rained down. All along the four miles of Omaha Beach German guns
flayed the assault craft.

It was H-Hour.

They came ashore on Omaha Beach, the slogging, unglamorous
men that no one envied. No battle ensigns flew for them, no horn or
bugles sounded. But they had history on their side. They came from
regiments that had bivouacked at places like Valley Forge, Stoney
Creek, Antietam, Gettsburg, that had fought in the Argonne. They
had crossed the beaches of North Africa, Sicily and Salerno. Now
they had one more beach to cross. They would call this one 'Bloody
Omaha.'

The most intense fire came from the cliffs and high bluffs at either
end of the crescent-shaped beach – in the 29th Division's Dog Green
area to the west and the 1st Division's Fox Green sector to the east.
Here the Germans had concentrated their heaviest defences to hold
two of the principal exits leading off the beach at Vierville and
towards Colleville. Everywhere along the beach men encountered
heavy fire as their boats came in, but the troops landing at Dog
Green and Fox Green hadn't a chance. German gunners on the cliffs
looked almost directly down on the waterlogged assault craft that
heaved and pitched towards these sectors of the beach. Awkward and
slow, the assault boats were nearly stationary in the water. They were
sitting ducks. Coxswains at the tillers, trying desperately to
manoeuvre their unwieldy craft through the forest of mined obstacles,
now had to run the gauntlet of fire from the cliffs.

Some boats, unable to find a way through the maze of obstacles
and the withering cliff fire, were driven off and wandered aimlessly
along the beach seeking a less heavily defended spot to land. Others,
doggedly trying to come in at their assigned sectors, were shelled so

badly that men plunged over the sides into deep water, where they were immediately picked off by machine-gun fire. Some landing craft were blown apart as they came in. Second Lieutenant Edward Gearing's assault boat, filled with thirty men of the 29th Division, disintegrated in one blinding moment three hundred yards from the Vierville exit at Dog Green. Gearing and his men were blown out of the boat and strewn over the water. Shocked and half-drowned, the nineteen-year-old lieutenant came to the surface yards away from where his boat had gone down. Other survivors began to bob up, too. Their weapons, helmets and equipment were gone. The coxswain had disappeared and near by one of Gearing's men, struggling beneath the weight of a heavy radio set strapped to his back, screamed out, 'For God's sake, I'm drowning!' Nobody could get to the radioman before he went under. For Gearing and the remnants of his section the ordeal was just beginning. It would be three hours before they got on the beach. Then Gearing would learn that he was the only surviving officer of his company. The others were dead or seriously wounded.

All along Omaha Beach, the dropping of the ramps seemed to be the signal for renewed, more concentrated machine-gun fire, and again the most murderous fire was in the Dog Green and Fox Green sectors. Boats of the 29th Division, coming into Dog Green, grounded on the sand-bars. The ramps came down and men stepped out into water three to six feet deep. They had but one object in mind – to get through the water, cross two hundred yards of the obstacle-strewn sand, climb the gradually rising shingle and then take cover in the doubtful shelter of a sea wall. But, weighed down by their equipment, unable to run in the deep water and without cover of any kind, men were caught in criss-crossing machine-gun and small-arms fire.

Seasick men, already exhausted by the long hours spent on the transports and in the assault boats, found themselves fighting for their lives in water which was often over their heads. Private David Silva saw the men in front of him being mowed down as they stepped off the ramp. When his turn came, he jumped into chest-high water and, bogged down by his equipment, watched spellbound as bullets flicked the surface all around him. Within seconds machine-gun fire had riddled his pack, his clothing, and his canteen. Silva felt like a 'pigeon at a trap shoot.' He thought he spotted the German machine-gunner who was firing at him, but he could not fire back. His rifle was clogged with sand. Silva waded on, determined to make the sands ahead. He finally pulled himself up on the beach and dashed for the shelter of the sea wall, completely unaware that he had been wounded twice – once in the back, and once in the right leg.

Men fell all along the water's edge. Some were killed instantly, others called pitifully for help as the incoming tide slowly engulfed them. Among the dead was Captain Sherman Burroughs. His friend, Captain Charles Cawthon, saw the body washing back and forth in the surf. Cawthon wondered if Burroughs had recited 'The Shooting of Dan McGrew' to his men on the run-in as he had planned. And when Captain Carroll Smith passed by, he could not help but think that Burroughs 'would no longer suffer from his constant migraine headaches.' Burroughs had been shot through the head.

Within the first few minutes of the carnage at Dog Green one entire company was put out of action. Less than a third of the men survived the bloody walk from the boats to the edge of the beach. Their officers were killed, severely wounded or missing, and the men, weaponless and shocked, huddled at the base of the cliffs all day. Another company in the same sector suffered even higher casualties. Company C of the 2nd Ranger Battalion had been ordered to knock out enemy strongpoints at Pointe de la Percée, slightly west of Vierville. The Rangers landed in two assault craft with the first wave on Dog Green. They were decimated. The leading craft was sunk almost immediately by artillery fire, and twelve men were killed outright. The moment the ramp of the second craft dropped down machine-gun fire sprayed the disembarking Rangers, killing and wounding fifteen. The remainder set out for the cliffs. Men fell one after another. PFC Nelson Noyes, staggering under the weight of a bazooka, made a hundred yards before he was forced to hit the ground. A few moments later he got up and ran forward again. When he reached the shingle he was machine-gunned in the leg. As he lay there Noyes saw the two Germans who had fired looking down on him from the cliff. Propping himself on his elbows he opened up with his Tommy gun and brought both of them down. By the time Captain Ralph E. Goranson, the company commander, reached the base of the cliff, he had only thirty-five Rangers left out of his seventy-man team. By nightfall these thirty-five would be cut down to twelve.

Misfortune piled upon misfortune for the men of Omaha Beach. Soldiers now discovered that they had been landed in the wrong sectors. Some came in almost two miles away from their original landing areas. Boat sections from the 29th Division found themselves intermingled with men of the 1st Division. For example, units scheduled to land on Easy Green and fight towards an exit at Les Moulins discovered themselves at the eastern end of the beach in the hell of Fox Green. Nearly all the landing-craft came in slightly east of their touch-down points. A control boat drifting off-station, a strong current running eastward along the beach, the baze and smoke from grass fires which obscured landmarks – all these contributed to the wrong landings. Companies that had been trained to capture certain objectives never got near them. Small groups found themselves pinned down by German fire and isolated in unrecognisable terrain, often without officers or communications.

The special Army-Navy demolition engineers who had the job of blowing paths through the beach obstacles were not only widely scattered, they were brought in crucial minutes behind schedule. These frustrated men set to work wherever they found themselves. But they fought a losing battle. In the few minutes they had before the following waves of troops bore down on the beaches, the engineers cleared only five and a half paths instead of the sixteen planned. Working with desperate haste, the demolition parties were impeded at every turn – infantrymen waded in among them, soldiers took shelter behind the obstacles they were about to blow, and landing-craft, buffeted by the swells, came in almost on top of them. Sergeant Barton A. Davis of the 299th Engineer Combat Battalion saw an assault boat bearing down on him. It was filled with 1st Division men and was coming straight in through the obstacles. There was a tremendous explosion and the boat disintegrated. It seemed to Davis that everyone in it was thrown into the air all at once. Bodies and parts of bodies landed all around the flaming wreckage. 'I saw black dots of men trying to swim through the gasoline that had spread on the water and as we wondered what to do a headless torso flew a good fifty feet through the air and landed with a sickening thud near us.' Davis did not see how anyone could have lived through the explosion, but two men did. They were pulled out of the water, badly burned but alive.

But the disaster that Davis had seen was no greater than that which had overtaken the heroic men of his own unit, the Army-Navy

Special Engineer Task Force. The landing-boats carrying their explosives had been shelled, and the hulks of these craft lay blazing at the edge of the beach. Engineers with small rubber boats loaded with plastic charges and detonators were blown apart in the water when enemy fire touched off the explosives. The Germans, seeing the engineers working among the obstacles, seemed to single them out for special attention. As the teams tied on their charges, snipers took careful aim at the mines on the obstacles. At other times they seemed to wait until the engineers had prepared whole lines of steel trestles and tetrahedral obstacles for blowing. Then the Germans themselves would detonate the obstacles with mortar fire – before the engineers could get out of the area. By the end of the day casualties would be almost fifty per cent. Sergeant Davis himself would be one. Nightfall would find him aboard a hospital ship with a wounded leg, heading back for England.

It was 7 a.m. The second wave of troops arrived on the shambles that was Omaha Beach. Men splashed ashore under the saturating fire of the enemy. Landing-craft joined the ever-growing graveyard of wrecked, blazing hulks. Each wave of boats gave up its own bloody contribution to the incoming tide, and all along the crescent-shaped strip of beach dead Americans gently nudged each other in the water.

Piling up along the shore was the flotsam and jetsam of the invasion. Heavy equipment and supplies, boxes of ammunition, smashed radios, field telephones, gas masks, entrenching tools, canteens, steel helmets and life-preservers were strewn everywhere. Great reels of wire, ropes, ration boxes, mine detectors and scores of weapons, from broken rifles to stove-in bazookas littered the sand. The twisted wrecks of landing craft canted up crazily out of the water. Burning tanks threw great spirals of black smoke into the air. Bulldozers lay on their sides among the obstacles. Off Easy Red, floating in and out among all the cast-off materials of war, men saw a guitar.

Small islands of wounded men dotted the sand. Passing troops noticed that those who could sat bolt upright as though now immune to any further hurt. They were quiet men, seemingly oblivious to the sights and sounds around them. Staff Sergeant Alfred Eigenberg, a medical orderly attached to the 6th Engineers Special Brigade, remembers 'a terrible politeness among the more seriously injured.' In his first few minutes on the beach, Eigenberg found so many

wounded that he did not know 'where to start or with whom.' On
Dog Red he came across a young soldier sitting in the sand with his
leg 'laid open from the knee to the pelvis as neatly as though a
surgeon had done it with a scalpel.' The wound was so deep that
Eigenberg could clearly see the femoral artery pulsing. The soldier
was in deep shock. Calmly he informed Eigenberg, 'I've taken all my
sulphur pills and I've shaken all my sulphur powder into the wound.
I'll be all right, won't I?' The nineteen-year-old Eigenberg didn't
know quite what to say. He gave the soldier a shot of morphine and
told him, 'Sure, you'll be all right.' Then folding the neatly sliced
halves of the man's leg together, Eigenberg did the only thing he
could think of – he carefully closed the wound with safety pins.

Into the chaos, confusion and death on the beach poured the men
of the third wave – and stopped. Minutes later the fourth wave came
in – and they stopped. Men lay shoulder to shoulder on the sands,
stones and shale. They crouched down behind obstacles; they sheltered among the bodies of the dead. Pinned down by the enemy fire
which they had expected to be neutralised, confused by their landings
in the wrong sectors, bewildered by the absence of the sheltering
craters they had expected from the air force bombing, and shocked
by the devastation and death all around them, the men froze on the
beaches. They seemed in the grip of a strange paralysis. Overwhelmed by it all, some men believed the day was lost. Technical
Sergeant William McClintock of the 741st Tank Battalion came upon
a man sitting at the edge of the water, seemingly unaware of the
machine-gun fire which rippled all over the area. He sat there
'throwing stones into the water and softly crying as if his heart would
break.'

The shock would not last long. Even now a few men here and
there, realising that to stay on the beach meant certain death, were
on their feet and moving.

Ten miles away on Utah Beach the men of the 4th Division were
swarming ashore and driving inland fast. The third wave of assault
boats were coming in and still there was virtually no opposition. A
few shells fell on the beach, some scattered machine-gun and rifle fire
rattled along it, but there was none of the fierce infighting that the
tense, keyed-up men of the 4th had expected. To many of the men
the landing was almost routine. PFC Donald N. Jones in the second

wave felt as though it was 'just another practice invasion.' Other men thought the assault was an anticlimax; the long months of training at Slapton Sands in England had been tougher. PFC Ray Mann felt a little 'let down' because 'the landing just wasn't a big deal after all.' Even the obstacles were not as bad as everyone had feared. Only a few concrete cones and triangles and hedgehogs of steel cluttered the beach. Few of these were mined and all of them were lying exposed, easy for the engineers to get at. Demolition teams were already at work. They had blown one fifty-yard gap through the defences and had breached the sea wall, and within the hour they would have the entire beach cleared.

Strung out along the mile of beach, their canvas skirts hanging limply down, were the amphibious tanks – one of the big reasons why the assault had been so successful. Lumbering out of the water with the first waves, they had given a roaring support to the troops as they dashed across the beach. The tanks and the pre-assault bombardment seemed to have shattered and demoralised the German troops holding positions behind this beach. Still, the assault had not been without its share of misery and death. Almost as soon as he got ashore, PFC Rudolph Mozgo saw his first dead man. A tank had received a direct hit and Mozgo found 'one of the crew lying half in and half out of the hatch.' Second Lieutenant Herbert Taylor of the 1st Engineer Special Brigade was numbed by the sight of a man 'decapitated by an artillery burst just twenty feet away.' and PFC Edward Wolfe passed a dead American 'who was sitting on the beach, his back resting against a post, as though asleep.' So natural and peaceful did he seem that Wolfe 'had an urge to reach over and shake him awake.'

Stomping up and down the sands, occasionally massaging his arthritic shoulder, was Brigadier-General Theodore Roosevelt. The fifty-seven-year-old officer – the only general to land with first-wave troops – had insisted on this assignment. His first request had been turned down, but Roosevelt had promptly countered with another. In a hand-written note to the 4th's commanding officer, Major-General Raymond O. Barton, Roosevelt pleaded his case on the ground that 'it will steady the boys to know I am with them.' Barton reluctantly agreed, but the decision preyed on his mind. 'When I said good-bye to Ted in England,' he recalls, 'I never expected to see him alive again.' The determined Roosevelt was very much alive. Sergeant Harry Brown of the 8th Infantry saw him 'with a cane in one hand, a map in the other, walking around as if he was looking over some real estate.' Every now and then a mortar burst on the beach, sending showers of sand into the air. It seemed to annoy Roosevelt; impatiently he would brush himself off.

As the third-wave boats beached and men began to wade ashore, there was the sudden whine of German 88 fire and shells burst among the incoming troops. A dozen men went down. Seconds later, a lone figure emerged from the smoke of the artillery burst. His face was black, his helmet and equipment were gone. He came walking up the beach in complete shock, eyes staring. Yelling for an orderly, Roosevelt ran over to the man. He put his arm round the soldier. 'Son,' he said gently, 'I think we'll get you back on a boat.'

As yet only Roosevelt and a few of his officers knew that the Utah landings had been made in the wrong place. It had been a fortunate error; heavy batteries that could have decimated the troops were still intact, sited along the planned assault area. There had been a number of reasons for the mistake. Confused by smoke from the naval bombardment which had obscured landmarks, caught by a strong current moving down the coast, a solitary control boat had guided the first wave into a landing more than a mile south of the original beach. Instead of invading the beach opposite Exits 3 and 4 – two of the vital five causeways towards which the 101st Airborne was driving – the entire beach-head had slipped almost two thousand yards and was now astride Exit 2. Ironically, at this moment Lieutenant-Colonel Robert G. Cole and a miscellaneous band of seventy-five 101st and 82nd troopers had just reached the western end of Exit 3. They were the first paratroopers to get to a causeway. Cole and his men concealed themselves in the swamps and settled down to wait; he expected the men of the 4th Division along at any moment.

On the beach, near the approach to Exit 2, Roosevelt was about to make an important decision. Every few minutes from now on wave after wave of men and vehicles were due to land – thirty thousand men and 3,500 vehicles. Roosevelt had to decide whether to bring succeeding waves into this new, relatively quiet area with only one causeway, or to divert all assault troops and take their equipment to the original Utah Beach with its two causeways. If the single exit could not be opened and held, a nightmarish jumble of men and vehicles would be trapped on the beach. The General huddled with his battalion commanders. The decision was made. Instead of fighting for the planned objectives which lay back on the original beach, the 4th would drive inland on the single causeway and engage German positions when and where they found them. Everything now depended on moving as fast as possible before the enemy recovered from the initial shock of the landings. Resistance was light and the men of the 4th were moving off the beach fast. Roosevelt turned to Colonel Eugene Caffey of the 1st Engineer Special Brigade. 'I'm going ahead with the troops,' he told Caffey. 'You get word to the Navy to bring them in. We're going to start the war from here.'

Off Utah the USS *Corry's* guns were red-hot. They were firing so fast that sailors stood on the turrets playing hoses on the barrels. Almost from the moment Lieutenant-Commander George Hoffman had manœuvred his destroyer into firing position and dropped anchor, the *Corry's* guns had been slamming shells inland at the rate of eight five-inchers a minute. One German battery would never bother anyone again; the *Corry* had ripped it open with 110 well-placed rounds. The Germans had been firing back – and hard. The *Corry* was the one destroyer the enemy spotters could see. Smoke-laying planes had been assigned to protect the 'inshore close support' bombarding group, but the *Corry's* plane had been shot down. One battery in particular, on the bluffs overlooking the coast above Utah – the gun-flashes located it near the village of St Marcouf – seemed to be concentrating all its fury on the exposed destroyer. Hoffman decided to move back before it was too late. 'We swung around,' recalls Radioman Third Class Bennie Glisson, 'and showed them our fantail like an old maid to a Marine.'

But the *Corry* was in shallow water, close to a number of knife-edge reefs. Her skipper could not make the dash for safety until he was clear. For a few minutes he was forced to play a tense cat-and-mouse game with the German gunners. Trying to anticipate their salvoes, Hoffman put the *Corry* through a series of jolting manœuvres. He shot forward, went astern, swung to port, then to starboard, stopped dead, went forward again. All the while his guns engaged the battery. Near by, the destroyer USS *Fitch* saw his predicament and began firing on the St Marcouf guns too. But there was no let-up from the sharpshooting Germans. Almost bracketed by their shells, Hoffman inched the *Corry* out. Finally, satisfied that he was far away from the reefs he ordered, 'Hard right rudder! Full speed ahead!' and the *Corry* leaped forward. Hoffman looked behind him. Salvoes were smacking into their wake, throwing up great plumes of spray. He breathed easier; he had made it. It was at that instant that his luck ran out. Tearing through the water at more than twenty-eight knots the *Corry* ran headlong on to a submerged mine.

There was a great rending explosion that seemed to throw the destroyer sideways out of the water. The shock was so great that Hoffman was stunned. It seemed to him 'that the ship had been lifted by an earthquake.' In his wireless room Bennie Glisson, who had been looking out of a porthole, suddenly felt that he had been 'dropped into a concrete-mixer.' Jerked off his feet, he was hurled upwards against the ceiling, and then he crashed down and smashed his knee.

The mine had cut the *Corry* almost in half. Running across the main deck was a rip more than a foot in width. The bow and the stern pointed crazily upwards; about all that held the destroyer together was the deck superstructure. The fireroom and engine-room were flooded. There were few survivors in the number two boiler-room – the men were almost instantly scalded to death when the boiler blew up. The rudder was jammed. There was no power, yet somehow in the steam and fire of her death agonies the *Corry* continued to charge crazily through the water. Hoffman became suddenly aware that some of his guns were still firing – his gunners, without power, continued to load and fire manually.

The twisted pile of steel that had once been the *Corry* thrashed through the sea for more than a thousand yards before finally coming to a halt. Then the German batteries zeroed in. 'Abandon ship!' Hoffman ordered. Within the next few minutes at least nine shells ploughed into the wreck. One blew up the forty-millimetre ammunition. Another set off the smoke generator on the fantail, almost asphyxiating the crew as they struggled into boats and rafts.

The sea was two feet above the main deck when Hoffman, taking one last look round, dived overboard and swam towards a raft. Behind him the *Corry* settled on the bottom, her masts and part of her superstructure remaining above the waves – the US Navy's only major D-Day loss. Of Hoffman's 294-man crew thirteen were dead or missing and thirty-three injured, more casualties than had been suffered in the Utah Beach landings up to this time.

Hoffman thought he was the last to leave the *Corry*. But he wasn't.

Nobody knows now who the last man was, but as the boats and rafts pulled away, men on the other ships saw a sailor climb the *Corry's* stern. He removed the ensign, which had been shot down, and then, swimming and climbing over the wreckage, he reached the mainmast. From the USS *Butler* Coxswain Dick Scrimshaw watched in amazement and admiration as the sailor, shells still falling about him, calmly tied on the flag and ran it up the mast. Then he swam away. Above the wreck of the *Corry* Scrimshaw saw the flag hang limp for a moment. Then it stretched out and fluttered in the breeze.

Rockets trailing ropes shot up towards the hundred-foot-high cliff at Pointe du Hoc. Between Utah and Omaha beaches the third American seaborne attack was going in. Small-arms fire poured down on Lieutenant-Colonel James E. Rudder's three Ranger companies as they began the assault to silence the massive coastal batteries which intelligence said menaced the American beaches on either side. The nine LCAs carrying the 225 men of the 2nd Ranger Battalion clustered along the little strip of beach beneath the cliff overhang. It afforded some protection from the machine-gun fire and from the grenades that the Germans were now rolling down on them – but not much. Offshore the British destroyer *Talybont* and the US destroyer *Satterlee* lobbed in shell after shell on to the cliff top.

Rudder's Rangers were supposed to touch down at the base of the cliff at H-Hour. But the lead boat had strayed and led the little flotilla straight towards Pointe de la Percée, three miles east. Rudder had spotted the mistake, but by the time he got the assault craft back on course precious time had been lost. The delay would cost him his five-hundred-man support force – the rest of the 2nd Rangers and Lieutenant-Colonel Max Schneider's 5th Ranger Battalion. The plan had been for Rudder to fire flares as soon as his men had scaled the cliff, as a signal for the other Rangers waiting in their boats some miles offshore to follow in. If no signal was received by 7 a.m. Colonel Schneider was to assume that the Pointe du Hoc assault had failed and head for Omaha Beach four miles away. There, following in behind the 29th Division, his Rangers would swing west and drive for the Pointe to take the guns from the rear. It was now 7.10 a.m. No signal had been given, so Schneider's force was already heading for Omaha. Rudder and his 225 Rangers were on their own.

It was a wild, frenzied scene. Again and again the rockets roared, shooting the ropes and rope ladders with grapnels attached. Shells and forty-millimetre machine-guns raked the cliff top, shaking down great chunks of earth on the Rangers. Men spurted across the narrow, cratered beach trailing scaling ladders, ropes and hand rockets. Here and there at the cliff top Germans bobbed up, throwing down 'potato masher' hand grenades or firing Schmeissers. Somehow the Rangers dodged from cover to cover, unloaded their boats and fired up the cliff – all at the same time. And off the Pointe, two DUKWS – amphibious vehicles – with tall, extending ladders, borrowed for the occasion from the London Fire Brigade, tried to manœuvre closer in. From the tops of the ladders Rangers blasted the headlands with Browning automatic rifles and Tommy guns.

The assault was furious. Some men didn't wait for the ropes to catch. Weapons slung over their shoulders, they cut hand-holds with their knives and started up the nine-storey-high cliff like flies. Some of the grapnels now began to catch and men swarmed up the ropes. Then there were wild yells as the Germans cut the ropes and Rangers hurtled back down the cliff. PFC Harry Robert's rope was cut twice. On his third try he finally got to a cratered niche just under the edge of the cliff. Sergeant Bill 'L-Rod' Petty tried going up hand over hand on a plain rope but, although he was an expert free climber, the rope was so wet and muddy he couldn't make it. Then Petty tried a ladder, got thirty feet up and slid back when it was cut. He started back up again. Sergeant Herman Stein climbing another ladder was almost pushed off the cliff face when he accidentally inflated his Mae West. He 'struggled for an eternity' with the life preserver but there were men ahead and behind him on the ladder. Somehow Stein kept on going.

Now men were scrambling up a score of ropes that twisted and snaked down from the top of the cliff. Suddenly Sergeant Petty, on his way up for the third time, was peppered by chunks of earth flying out all around him. The Germans were leaning out over the edge of the cliff, machine-gunning the Rangers as they climbed. The Germans fought desperately, despite the fire that was still raining on them from the Rangers on the fire ladders and from the destroyers offshore. Petty saw the climber next to him stiffen and swing out from the cliff. Stein saw him, too. So did twenty-year-old PFC Carl Bombardier. As they watched, horrified, the man slid down the rope and fell, bouncing from ledges and rock outcroppings, and it seemed to Petty 'a lifetime before his body hit the beach.' Petty froze on the rope. He could not make his hand move up to the next rung. He remembers saying to himself, 'This is just too hard to climb.' But the German machine-guns got him going again. As they began to spray the cliff dangerously near him, Petty 'unfroze real fast.' Desperately he hauled himself up the last few yards.

Everywhere men were throwing themselves over the top and into shell-holes. To Sergeant Regis McCloskey, who had successfully brought his half-sinking ammunition boat in to the beach, the high plateau of Pointe du Hoc presented a weird, incredible sight. The ground was so pitted by the shells and bombs of the pre-H-Hour naval and air bombardment that it looked like 'the craters of the moon.' There was an eerie silence now as men pulled themselves up and into the protective craters. The fire had stopped for the moment, there was not a German to be seen, and everywhere men looked the yawning craters stretched back towards the mainland – a violent, terrible no-man's land.

Colonel Rudder had already established his first command post, a niche at the edge of the cliff. From it his signals officer, Lieutenant James Eikner, sent out the message 'Praise the Lord.' It meant 'All men up cliff.' But it was not quite true. At the base of the cliff the Rangers' medical officer, a pediatrician in private practice, was tending the dead and the dying on the beach – perhaps twenty-five men. Minute by minute the valiant Ranger force was being chipped away. By the end of the day there would only be ninety of the original 225 still able to bear arms. Worse, it had been a heroic and futile effort – to silence guns which were not there. The information which Jean Marion, the French underground sector chief, had tried to send to London was true. The battered bunkers atop Pointe du Hoc were empty – the guns had never been mounted.*

In his bomb crater at the top of the cliff, Sergeant Petty and his four-man BAR team sat exhausted after the climb. A little haze drifted over the churned, pitted earth and the smell of cordite was heavy in the air. Petty stared almost dreamily around him. Then on

---

* Some two hours later a Ranger patrol found a deserted five-gun battery in a camouflaged position more than a mile inland. Stacks of shells surrounded each gun and they were ready to fire, but the Rangers could find no evidence that they had ever been manned. Presumably these were the guns for the Pointe du Hoc emplacements.

the edge of the crater he saw two sparrows eating worms. 'Look,' said Petty to the others, 'they're having breakfast.'

Now on this great and awful morning the last phase of the assault from the sea began. Along the eastern half of the Normandy invasion coast, Lieutenant-General Dempsey's British Second Army was coming ashore, with grimness and gaiety, with pomp and ceremony, with all the studied nonchalance the British traditionally assume in moments of great emotion. They had waited four long years for this day. They were assaulting not just beaches but bitter memories – memories of Munich and Dunkirk, of one hateful and humiliating retreat after another, of countless devastating bombing raids, of dark days when they had stood alone. With them were the Canadians with a score of their own to settle for the bloody losses at Dieppe. And with them, too, were the French, fierce and eager on this homecoming morning.

There was a curious jubilance in the air. As the troops headed towards the beaches the loudspeaker in a rescue launch off Sword roared out 'Roll Out the Barrel.' From a rocket-firing barge off Gold came the strains of 'We Don't Know Where We're Going.' Canadians going to Juno heard the rasping notes of a bugle blaring across the water. Some men were even singing. Marine Denie Lovell remembers that 'the boys were standing up, singing all the usual Army and Navy songs.' And Lord Lovat's 1st Special Service Brigade commandos, spruce and resplendent in their green berets (the commandos refused to wear tin helmets), were serenaded into battle by the eerie wailing of the bagpipes. As their landing-boats drew abreast of Admiral Vian's flagship HMS *Scylla*, the commandos gave the 'thumbs-up' salute. Looking down on them, eighteen-year-old Able Seaman Ronald Northwood thought they were 'the finest set of chaps I ever came across.'

Even the obstacles and the enemy fire now lacing out at the boats were viewed with a certain detachment by many men. On one LCT, Telegraphist John Webber watched a Royal Marine captain study the maze of mined obstacles clotting the coastline, then remark casually to the skipper, 'I say, old man, you really must get my chaps on shore, there's a good fellow.' Aboard another landing-craft a 50th Division major stared thoughtfully at the round Teller mines clearly visible on top of the obstacles and said to the coxswain, 'For Christ's sake, don't knock those bloody coconuts down or we'll all get a free trip to hell.' One boatload of 48th Royal Marine commandos were met by heavy machine-gun fire off Juno and men dived for cover behind the deck superstructure. Not the adjutant, Captain Daniel Flunder. He tucked his swagger stick under his arm and calmly paraded up and down the foredeck. 'I thought,' he explained later, 'it was the thing to do.' (While he was doing it, a bullet ploughed through his map case.) And in a landing-craft charging for Sword Major C. K. 'Banger' King, just as he had promised, was reading *Henry V*. Amid the roar of the diesels, the hissing of the spray and the sound of gunfire, King spoke into the loud-hailer, 'And gentlemen in England now a-bed/Shall think themselves accurs'd they were not here . . .'

Some men could hardly wait for the fighting to begin. Two Irish sergeants, James Percival 'Paddy' de Lacy, who had toasted De Valera hours before for 'keepin' us out of the war,' and his buddy, Paddy McQuaid, stood at the ramps of an LST and, fortified by good Royal Navy rum, solemnly contemplated the troops. 'De Lacy,' said McQuaid, staring hard at the Englishmen all around them, 'don't you think now that some of these boys seem a wee bit timid?' As the beaches neared, de Lacy called out to his men, 'All right, now! Here we go! At the run!' The LST ground to a halt. As the men ran out, McQuaid yelled at the shell-smoked shore-line, 'Come out, ye bastards, and fight us now!' Then he disappeared under water. An instant later he came up sluttering. 'Oh, the evil of it!' he bellowed. 'Tryin' to drown me before I even get up on the beach!'

Off Sword, Private Hubert Victor Baxter of the British 3rd Division revved up his Bren gun carrier and, peering over the top of the armoured plating, plunged into the water. Sitting exposed on the raised seat above him was his bitter enemy, Sergeant 'Dinger' Bell, with whom Baxter had been fighting for months. Bell yelled, 'Baxter, wind up that seat so you can see where you're going!' Baxter shouted back, 'Not bloody likely! I can see!' Then, as they swept up the beach, the sergeant, caught up in the excitement of the moment, resorted to the very thing that had begun the feud in the first place. He slammed down his fist again and again on Baxter's helmet and roared, 'Bash on! Bash on!'

As the commandos touched down on Sword, Lord Lovat's piper, William Millin, plunged off his landing-craft into water up to his armpits. He could see smoke piling up from the beach ahead and hear the crump of exploding mortar shells. As Millin floundered towards the shore, Lovat shouted at him, 'Give us "Highland Laddie," man!' Waist-deep in the water, Millin put the mouthpiece to his lips and splashed on through the surf, the pipes keening crazily. At the water's edge, oblivious to the gunfire, he halted and, parading up and down along the beach, piped the commandos ashore. The men streamed past him, and mingling with the whine of bullets and the screams of shells came the wild skirl of the pipes as Millin now played 'The Road to the Isles.' 'That's the stuff, Jock,' yelled a commando. Said another, 'Get down, you mad bugger.'

All along Sword, Juno and Gold – for almost twenty miles, from Ouistreham near the mouth of the Orne to the village of Le Hamel on the west – the British swarmed ashore. The beaches were choked with landing-craft disgorging troops, and nearly everywhere along the assault area the high seas and underwater obstacles were causing more trouble than the enemy.

The first men in had been the frogmen – 120 underwater demolition experts whose job it was to cut thirty-yard gaps through the obstacles. They had only twenty minutes to work before the first waves bore down upon them. The obstacles were formidable – at places more densely sown than in any other part of the Normandy invasion area. Sergeant Peter Henry Jones of the Royal Marines swam into a maze of steel pylons, gates and hedgehogs and concrete cones. In the thirty-yard gap Jones had to blow he found twelve major obstacles, some of them fourteen feet long. When another frogman, Lieutenant John B. Taylor of the Royal Navy, saw the fantastic array of underwater defences surrounding him, he yelled out to his unit leader that 'this bloody job is impossible.' But he did not give it up. Working under fire, Taylor, like the other frogmen, methodically set to work. They blew the obstacles singly, because they were too large to blow up in groups. Even as they worked, amphibious tanks came swimming in among them, followed almost immediately by first-wave troops. Frogmen rushing out of the water saw landing-craft, turned sideways by the heavy seas, crash into the obstacles. Mines exploded, steel spikes and hedgehogs ripped along the hulls, and up and down the beaches landing-craft began to flounder. The waters offshore became a junkyard as boats piled up almost on top of one another. Telegraphist Webber remembers thinking that 'the beaching is a tragedy.' As his craft came in Webber saw 'LCTs' stranded and ablaze, twisted masses of metal on the shore, burning tanks and bulldozers.' And as one LCT passed them, heading for the open sea, Webber was horrified to see 'its well deck engulfed in a terrifying fire.'

On Gold Beach, where frogman Jones was now working with the Royal Engineers trying to clear the obstacles, he saw an LCI approach with troops standing on the deck ready to disembark. Caught by a sudden swell, the craft swerved sideways, lifted and crashed down on a series of mined steel triangles. Jones saw it explode with a shattering blast. It reminded him of a 'slow-motion cartoon — the men, standing to attention, shot up into the air as though lifted by a water spout . . . at the top of the spout bodies and parts of bodies spread like drops of water.'

Boat after boat got hung up on the obstacles. Of the sixteen landing-craft carrying the 47th Royal Marine commandos in to Gold Beach, four boats were lost, eleven were damaged and beached and only one made it back to the parent ship. Sergeant Donald Gardner of the 47th and his men were dumped into the water about fifty yards from shore. They lost all their equipment and had to swim in under machine-gun fire. As they struggled in the water, Gardner heard someone say, 'Perhaps we're intruding, this seems to be a private beach.' Going into Juno the 48th Royal Marine commandos not only ran afoul of the obstacles, they also came under intense mortar fire. Lieutenant Michael Aldworth and about forty of his men crouched down in the forward hold of their LCI as shells exploded all about them. Aldworth shoved his head up to see what was happening and saw men from the after hold running along the deck. Aldworth's men yelled out, 'How soon do we get out of here?' Aldworth called back, 'Wait a minute, chaps. It's not our turn.' There was a moment's pause and then someone inquired, 'Well, just how long do you think it will be, old man? The ruddy hold is filling full of water.'

The men from the sinking LCI were quickly picked up by a variety of craft. There were so many boats around, Aldworth recalls, that 'it was rather like hailing a taxi in Bond Street.' Some men were delivered safely on to the beaches; others were taken out to a Canadian destroyer, but fifty commandos discovered themselves on an LCT which had unloaded its tanks and was under instructions to proceed directly back to England. Nothing the infuriated men could say or do would persuade the skipper to change his course. One officer, Major de Stackpoole, had been wounded in the thigh on the run-in, but on hearing the LCT's destination he roared, 'Nonsense! You're all bloody well mad!' With that he dived overboard and swam for shore.

For most men the obstacles proved to be the toughest part of the assault. Once they were through these defences, troops found the enemy opposition along the three beaches spotty – fierce in some sectors, light and even non-existent in others. On the western half of Gold men of the 1st Hampshire Regiment were almost decimated as they waded through water that was at places three to six feet deep. Struggling through the heaving sea line abreast, they were caught by heavy mortar bursts and criss-crossing machine-gun fire that poured out from the village of Le Hamel, a stronghold occupied by the tough German 352nd Division. Men went down one after another. Private Charles Wilson heard a surprised voice say, 'I've bought it, mates!' Turning, Wilson saw the man, a strange look of disbelief on his face, slide beneath the water without another word. Wilson ploughed on. He had been machine-gunned in the water before – except that at Dunkirk he had been going the other way. Private George Stunell saw men going down all around him too. He came across a Bren gun carrier standing in about three feet of water, its motor running and the driver 'frozen at the wheel, too terrified to drive the machine on to the shore.' Stunell pushed him to one side and with machine-gun bullets whipping all around drove up on to the beach. Stunell was elated to have made it. Then he suddenly pitched headlong to the ground; a bullet had slammed into a tin of cigarettes in his tunic pocket with terrific impact. Minutes later he discovered that he was bleeding from wounds in his back and ribs. The same bullet had passed cleanly through his body.

It would take the Hampshires almost eight hours to knock out the Le Hamel defences, and at the end of D-Day their casualties would total almost two hundred. Strangely, apart from the obstacles, troops landing on either side encountered little trouble. There were casualties, but they were fewer than had been anticipated. On the left of the Hampshire, men of the 1st Dorset Regiment were off the beach in forty minutes. Next to them the Green Howards landed with such dash and determination that they moved inland and captured their first objective in less than an hour. Company Sergeant-Major Stanley Hollis, killer of ninety Germans up to now, waded ashore and promptly captured a pillbox single-handed. The nerveless Hollis, using grenades and his Sten gun, killed two and captured twenty in the start of a day that would see him kill another ten.

On the beach to the right of Le Hamel it was so quiet that some men were disappointed. Geoffrey Leach of the RAMC saw troops and vehicles pouring ashore and found that there was nothing 'for the medicos to do but help unload ammunition.' To Marine Denis Lovell, the landing was like 'just another exercise back home.' His unit, the 47th Royal Marine commandos, moved quickly off the beach, avoided all enemy contact, turned west and set out on a seven-mile forced march to link up with the Americans near Port-en-Bessin. They expected to see the first Yanks from Omaha Beach around noon.

But this was not to be – unlike the Americans on Omaha, who were still pinned down by the rugged German 352nd Division, the British and the Canadians were more than a match for the tired and inferior 716th Division with its impressed Russian and Polish 'volunteers.' In addition, the British had made the fullest possible use of amphibious tanks and armoured vehicles. Some, like the 'flail' tanks, lashed the ground ahead of them with chains that detonated mines. Other armoured vehicles carried small bridges or great reels of steel matting which, when unrolled, made a temporary roadway over soft ground. One group even carried giant bundles of logs for use as stepping-stones over walls or to fill in anti-tank ditches. These inventions, and the extra-long period of bombardment that the British beaches had received, gave the assaulting troops additional protection.

Still some strong pockets of resistance were encountered. On one half of Juno Beach men of the Canadian 3rd Division fought through lines of pillboxes and trenches, through fortified houses, and from street to street in the town of Courseulles before finally breaking through and pushing inland. But all resistance there would be mopped up within two hours. In many places it was being done with quickness and dispatch. Able Seaman Edward Ashworth, off an LCT which had brought troops and tanks in to the Courseulles beach, saw Canadian soldiers march six German prisoners behind a dune some distance away. Ashworth thought that this was his chance to get a German helmet for a souvenir. He ran up the beach and in the dunes discovered the six Germans 'all lying crumpled up.' Ashworth bent over one of the bodies, still determined to get a helmet. But he found 'the man's throat was cut – every one of them had had his throat cut,' and Ashworth 'turned away, sick as a parrot. I didn't get my tin hat.'

Sergeant Paddy de Lacy, also in the Courseulles area, had captured twelve Germans who had come almost eagerly out of a trench, their arms raised high above their heads. De Lacy stood staring at them for a moment; he had lost a brother in North Africa. Then he said to the soldier with him, 'Look at the super-blokes – just look at them. Here, take them out of my sight.' He walked away to make himself a cup of tea to soothe his anger. While he, was heating a canteen of water over a Sterno can a young officer 'with the down still on his chin' walked over and said sternly, 'Now look here, Sergeant, this is no time to be making tea.' De Lacy looked up and, as patiently as his twenty-one years of Army service would allow, replied, 'Sir, we are not playing at soldiers now – this is real war. Why don't you come back in five minutes and have a nice cup of tea?' The officer did.

Even as the fighting was going on in the Courseulles area, men, guns, tanks, vehicles and supplies were pouring ashore. The movement inland was smoothly and efficiently handled. The beachmaster, Captain Colin Maud, allowed no loiterers on Juno. Most men, like Sub-Lieutenant John Beynon, were a little taken aback at the sight of the tall, bearded officer with the imposing bearing and the booming voice who met each new contingent with the same greeting, 'I'm chairman of the reception committee and of this party, so get a move on.' Few men cared to argue with the custodian of Juno Beach; Beynon remembers he had a cudgel in one hand and the other held tight to the leash of a fierce-looking Alsatian dog. The effect was all he could have hoped for. INS correspondent Joseph Willicombe recalls a futile argument he had with the beachmaster. Willicombe, who had landed in the first wave of Canadians, had been assured that he would be allowed to send a twenty-five-word message via the beachmaster's two-way radio to the command ship for transmission to the US. Apparently no one had bothered to so inform Maud. Staring stonily at Willicombe, he growled, 'My dear chap, there's a bit of a war going on here.' Willicombe had to admit that the beachmaster had a point.* A few yards away, in the coarse beach

---

* Correspondents on Juno had no communications until Ronald Clark of United Press came ashore with two baskets of carrier pigeons. The correspondents quickly

grass, lay the mangled bodies of fifteen Canadians who had trodden
on mines as they dashed ashore.

All along Juno the Canadians suffered. Of the three British beaches
theirs was the bloodiest. Rough seas had delayed the landings. Razor-
edged reefs on the eastern half of the beach and barricades of obstacles
created havoc among the assault craft. Worse, the naval and air
bombardment had failed to knock out the coastal defences or had
missed them altogether, and in some sectors troops came ashore
without the protection of tanks. Opposite the towns of Berniéres and
St Aubin-sur-Mer men of the Canadian 8th Brigade and the 48th
Marine commandos came in under heavy fire. One company lost
nearly half its men in the dash up the beach. Artillery fire from St
Aubin-sur-Mer was so concentrated that it led to one particular
horror on the beach. A tank, buttoned up for protection and thrashing
wildly up the beach to get out of the line of fire, ran over the dead
and the dying. Captain Daniel Flunder of the commandos, looking
back from the sand dunes, saw what was happening and oblivious of
the bursting shells ran back down the beach shouting at the top of
his voice, 'They're my men!' The enraged Flunder beat on the tank's
hatch with his swagger stick, but the tank kept on going. Pulling the
pin on a grenade, Flunder blew one of the tank's tracks off. It wasn't
until the startled tankers opened the hatch that they realised what
had happened.

Although the fighting was bitter while it lasted, the Canadians and
the commandos got off the Berniéres-St Aubin beaches in less than
thirty minutes and plunged inland. Follow-up waves experienced
little difficulty and within an hour it was so quiet on the beaches that
Leading Aircraftman John Murphy of a barrage balloon unit found
that 'the worst enemy was the sand lice that drove us crazy as the
tide came in.' Behind the beaches street fighting would occupy troops
for nearly two hours, but this section of Juno, like the western half,
was now secure.

---

wrote brief stories, placed them in the plastic capsules attached to the pigeons' legs
and released the birds. Unfortunately the pigeons were so overloaded that most of
them fell back to earth. Some, however, circled overhead for a few moments – and
then headed towards the German lines. Charles Lynch of Reuter's stood on the
beach, waved his fist at the pigeons and roared, 'Traitors! Damned traitors!' Four
pigeons, Willicombe says, 'proved loyal.' They actually got to the Ministry of
Information in London within a few hours.

The 48th commandos fought their way through St Aubin-sur-Mer and, turning east, headed along the coast. They had a particularly tough assignment. Juno lay seven miles away from Sword Beach. To close this gap and link up the two beaches, the 48th was to make a forced march towards Sword. Another commando unit, the 41st, was to land at Lion-sur-Mer on the edge of Sword Beach, swing right and head west. Both forces were expected to join up within a few hours at a point roughly half-way between the two beach-heads. That was the plan, but almost simultaneously the commandos ran into trouble. At Langrune, about a mile east of Juno, men of the 48th found themselves in a fortified area of the town that defied penetration. Every house was a strongpoint. Mines, barbed wire and concrete walls – some of them six feet high and five feet thick – sealed off the streets. From these positions heavy fire greeted the invaders. Without tanks or artillery the 48th was stopped cold.

On Sword, six miles away, the 41st after a rough landing turned west and headed through Lion-sur-Mer. They were told by the French that the German garrison had pulled out. The information seemed correct – until the commandos reached the edge of town. There artillery fire knocked out three supporting tanks. Sniper and machine-gun fire came from innocent-looking villas that had been converted into blockhouses, and a rain of mortar shells fell among the commandos. Like the 48th the 41st came to a standstill.

Now, although no one in the Allied High Command knew about it yet, a vital gap six miles wide existed in the beach-head – a gap through which Rommel's tanks, if they moved fast enough, could reach the coast and, by attacking left and right along the shore, could roll up the British landings.

Lion-sur-Mer was one of the few real trouble-spots on Sword. Of the three British beaches, Sword was expected to be the most heavily defended. Troops had been briefed that casualties would be very high. Private John Gale of the 1st South Lancashire Regiment was 'cold-bloodedly told that all of us in the first wave would probably be wiped out.' The picture was painted in even blacker terms to the commandos. It was drilled into them that 'no matter what happens we must get on the beaches, for there will be no evacuation . . . no going back.' The 4th commandos expected to be 'written off on the beaches,' as Corporal James Colley and Private Stanley Stewart remember, for they were told their casualties would run as 'high as eighty-four per cent.' And the men who were to land ahead of the infantry in amphibious tanks were warned that 'even those of you who reach the beach can expect sixty per cent casualties.' Private Christopher Smith, driver of an amphibious tank, thought his chances of survival were slim. Rumour had increased the casualty figure to ninety per cent and Smith was inclined to believe it, for as his unit left England men saw canvas screens being set up on Gosport Beach and 'it was said that these were being erected to sort out the returned dead.'

For a while it looked as though the worst of the predictions might come true. In some sectors first-wave troops were heavily machine-gunned and mortared. In the Ouistreham half of Sword, men of the 22nd East Yorkshire Regiment lay dead and dying from the water's edge all the way up the beach. Although nobody would ever know how many men were lost in this bloody dash from the boats, it seems likely that the East Yorks suffered most of their two hundred D-Day casualties in these first few minutes. The shock of seeing these crumpled khaki forms seemed to confirm the most dreadful fears of follow-up troops. Some saw 'bodies stacked like cordwood' and counted 'more than 150 dead.' Private John Mason of the 4th commandos, who landed half an hour later, was shocked to find himself 'running through piles of dead infantry who had been knocked down like nine-pins.' And Corporal Fred Mears of Lord Lovat's commandos was 'aghast to see the East Yorks lying in bunches. . . . It would probably never have happened had they spread out.' As he charged up the beach determined to make 'Jesse Owens look like a turtle,' he remembers cynically thinking that 'they would know better the next time.'

Although bloody, the beach fight was brief.* Except for initial

---

* There will always be differences of opinion about the nature of the fighting on Sword. Men of the East Yorks disagree with their own history, which says that it was 'just like a training show, only easier.' The troops of the 4th commandos claim that when they landed at H-plus-30 they found the East Yorks still at the water's edge. According to Brigadier E. E. E. Cass, in command of the 8th Brigade that assaulted Sword, the East Yorks were off the beach by the time the 4th commandos landed. It is estimated that the 4th lost thirty men as they came ashore. On the western half of the beach, says Cass, 'opposition had been overcome by eight-thirty except for isolated snipers.' Men of the 1st South Lancashire Regiment landing there had light casualties and moved inland fast. The 1st Suffolks coming in behind them had just four casualties.

losses, the assault on Sword went forward speedily, meeting little sustained opposition. The landings were so successful that many men coming in minutes after the first wave were surprised to find only sniper fire. They saw the beaches shrouded in smoke, nursing orderlies working among the wounded, flail tanks detonating mines, burning tanks and vehicles littering the shore-line, and sand shooting up from occasional shell bursts, but nowhere was there the slaughter they had expected. To these tense troops, primed to expect a holocaust, the beaches were an anticlimax.

In many places along Sword there was even a bank holiday atmosphere. Here and there along the seafront little groups of elated French waved to the troops and yelled, '*Vive les Anglais!*' Royal Marine Signalman Leslie Ford noticed a Frenchman 'practically on the beach itself who appeared to be giving a running commentary on the battle to a group of townspeople.' Ford thought they were crazy, for the beaches and the foreshore were still infested with mines and under occasional fire. But it was happening everywhere. Men were hugged and kissed and embraced by the French, who seemed quite unaware of the dangers around them. Corporal Harry Norfield and Gunner Ronald Allen were astonished to see 'a person all dressed up in splendid regalia and wearing a bright brass helmet making his way down to the beaches.' he turned out to be the mayor of Colleville-sur-Orne, a small village about a mile inland, who had decided to come down and officially greet the invasion forces.

Some of the Germans seemed no less eager than the French to greet the troops. Sapper Henry Jennings had no sooner disembarked than he was 'confronted with a collection of Germans – most of them Russian and Polish "volunteers" – anxious to surrender.' But Captain Gerald Norton of a Royal Artillery unit got the biggest surprise of all: he was met 'by four Germans with their suitcases packed, who appeared to be awaiting the first available transportation out of France.'

Out of the confusion on Gold, Juno and Sword, the British and the Canadians swarmed inland. The advance was business-like and efficient and there was a kind of grandeur about it all. As troops fought into towns and villages examples of heroism and courage were all around them. Some remember a Royal Marine commando major, both arms gone, who urged his men along by shouting at them to 'get inland, chaps, before Fritz gets wise to this party.' Others remember the cocky cheerfulness and bright faith of the wounded as they waited for the field ambulance men to catch up with them. Some waved as the troops passed, others yelled, 'See you in Berlin, mates!' Gunner Ronald Allen would never forget one soldier who had been badly wounded in the stomach. He was propped up against a wall calmly reading a book.

Now speed was essential. From Gold troops headed for the cathedral town of Bayeux, roughly seven miles inland. From Juno the Canadians drove for the Bayeux – Caen highway and Carpiquet Airport, about ten miles away. And out of Sword the British headed for the city of Caen. They were so sure of capturing this objective that even correspondents, as the London *Daily Mail's* Noel Monks was later to recall, were told that a briefing would be held 'at point X in Caen at 4 p.m.' Lord Lovat's commandos marching out of the Sword area wasted no time. They were going to the relief of General Gale's embattled 6th Airborne troops holding the Orne and Caen bridges four miles away and 'Shimy' Lovat had promised Gale that he would be there 'sharp at noon.' Behind a tank at the head of the column Lord Lovat's piper Bill Millin played 'Blue Bonnets over the Border.'

For ten Britishers, the crews of the midget submarines X20 and X23, D-Day was over. Off Sword Beach Lieutenant George Honour's X23 threaded through waves of landing-craft streaming steadily in towards the shore. In the heavy seas, with her flat superstructure almost awash, all that could be seen of the X23 were her identifying flags whipping in the wind. Coxwain Charles Wilson on an LCT 'almost fell overboard with surprise' when he saw what appeared to be 'two large flags apparently unsupported' moving steadily towards him through the water. As the X23 passed, Wilson couldn't help wondering 'what the devil a midget sub had to do with the invasion.' Ploughing by, the X23 headed out into the transport area in search of her tow-ship, a trawler with the appropriate name of *En Avant.* Operation Gambit was over. Lieutenant Honour and his four-man crew were going home.

The men for whom they had marked the beaches marched into France. Everyone was optimistic. The Atlantic Wall had been breached. Now the big question was, how fast would the Germans recover from the shock?

Into Germany

R. J. Minney

Violette was taken by road to Fresnes, the vast prison just outside Paris. It was a journey of over two hundred miles. From the main entrance on the road a long drive down an avenue of tall and attractive trees takes one past a series of massive buildings on the right, each with large heavy gates. At the third of these the car pulled up. The gates were slowly swung back and, escorted by her armed and uniformed Gestapo guards, she was led through the yard into the section where the women prisoners were kept. There is accommodation here, and in the adjacent male block, for over 1,600 prisoners. In that summer of 1944 the prison was full to overflowing. The men far outnumbered the women and had five or even six prisoners in each cell, whereas the women for the most part had a cell each to themselves. Most of the prisoners were French, but others had been brought in by the Germans from Jersey and Guernsey on various charges and often on no charges at all but merely on suspicion. Many were held as hostages, so that the threat of their death might elicit information from relatives and friends who were in hiding. The number of British prisoners here was small and only a very few of these were secret agents.

What her fate here would be Violette had a fairly shrewd idea. She had already sampled the severities of detention, and it was clear to her that her arrest had not been effected merely to prevent her achieving a predesigned purpose, nor yet to punish her for what she may already have accomplished, but to extract from her certain vital information. At the Gestapo headquarters in Limoges, to which she was taken twice each day, the Colonel of the Gestapo, seated in his office at his large desk, desired to know the plans in hand for the effective use of the Maquis in preventing the free movement of the German forces through that region. A large map of the area was produced. He wanted her to indicate the points selected for the

blowing up of roads and railway lines, and for cutting communications. In view of the difficulties the Germans had already encountered
in policing the area, and the added difficulties at this juncture because
of the acute shortage of men, it was only by obtaining such information that time could be saved and much could be accomplished.
He wanted to know where the vast supplies of arms were stored, what
fields had been selected for parachute landings. He wanted to know
the identity of the principals in the organisation and where they could
be found (the Gestapo were, for example, aware of Anastasie's
activities and had for a long time been trying to find him). He asked
about the work on which she was herself engaged, the instructions
she was carrying, the code used by the wireless operator, for each
operator had his own individual code, and, as she had been taught to
use the radio, it was felt that the code would be known to her or
could be obtained by her. There was also the question of the expected
landings in the South of France, in readiness for which ten German
divisions had been kept in the south by Hitler. Had these landings
been abandoned – or where they to be made now that these divisions
were being moved to the north? It was a vital question and the
Gestapo were convinced that a secret agent, strategically placed
midway between north and south, must be able to supply the answer
and they were determined to prize the information out of her if in fact
she did possess it.

At first there was a show of affability and friendliness. She was told
by her Gestapo inquisitor that it was not their purpose to torture or
even to punish her. All they wanted were answers to a few simple
questions. She did not deny that she knew some at least of the
answers. She merely refused to answer any of the questions. There
then followed a protracted process of persuasion. It began quite
calmly with an endeavour to prove that the people for whom she
worked did not care what became of her, whether she survived or
was executed. Their one desire had been to use her and, if she failed,
to use in her place someone else. 'They will not lift a finger to save
you or help you. We, on the other hand, want to – and can.' She did
not know that at that moment plans were in hand for her rescue, nor
would it have mattered if she had. She realised that her work had
now taken on a completely new form. It was only by her silence now
that she could make her greatest contribution to the cause. No matter
what the pain and suffering she may be called upon to endure, that

silence would have to be maintained and she prayed that she would be strong enough for the ordeal when it came. 'I must not show any fear,' she said again and again to herself, and in her heart she knew none; for she had been aware all along of the price she might one day be called upon to pay. Her face was composed as she listened to the colonel's soft-voiced expressions of concern for her and his desire to help her. 'Of course you Germans always are most considerate and kind to your enemies,' she said with a mocking smile.

'Of course.'

It was then that she laughed.

This angered the colonel. He instantly ordered the guards to take her back to the jail.

Some hours later she was brought again before him and the persuasion went on.

'It is only a question of time,' he said, 'before we find out everything – yes, everything we want to know. I want you to save us this loss of time, and in return I will guarantee you your life and the lives of your friends. All those whose names you give me . . .'

She merely exploded with laughter. 'What do you take me for? A half-wit?'

A day or two later he appeared to have learned one or two things about her.

'You are really French,' he said, 'and you should give a thought to the fate of your own people. Your husband, who was also a Frenchman, very foolishly allowed himself to be used by the English. What good did it do him – or France? He lost his life, as you will lose yours if you persist in remaining silent. He could have lived in peace with us. There is peace between Marshal Pétain and ourselves. We arranged a most generous Peace. But your husband is dead – just one of many thousands who have been too blind to see things clearly. You have been very, very stupid. You have a child, I believe – haven't you? What do you think is going to become of your cbild if we shoot you? Mind you, I don't want to shoot you. I am anxious to help you. I want to see you get back to your home . . .'

'You do talk a lot of silly rot,' she interrupted. 'I'll tell you nothing – nothing. Can't you get that into your head? No matter what you do, it won't make any difference. I despise you – I despise the whole lot of you.' With the agility of a young animal she took a quick

menacing pace towards him, but the two guards sprang forward and
seized her to prevent whatever mischief she had in mind.

'Take her away,' said the colonel.

She had noticed that he had made no mention at all of her earlier
mission to Rouen and Le Havre. It seemed obvious that he did not
know of it. She was puzzled how he had learned of her marriage. Was
it just a shot in the dark?

The next morning at eleven she was brought in again. And so it
went on until in anger he ordered her removal to Fresnes. 'We shall
see if that will bring you to your senses,' he said.

'It isn't my senses you should be concerned about, but your own.
In a very short time the tables will be turned. Then you will be
standing here and one of our men will be seated in that chair.'

That indeed happened much sooner than she anticipated, though
not entirely as she foresaw it. She knew, of course, that Anastasie had
completed all his plans for harrying and impeding the movement of
German troops before they set out together on their fateful journey.
These plans were put into immediate operation. The messages she
was to deliver were taken on by others and the work was thus spread
out over the entire Maquis area. Railway lines were torn out. Bridges
were destroyed. The road was blown up at many points and as fast
as one section was reparied the Maquis speedily blew up another.
Ambushes were constantly operated. If the German troops survived
one, a little further on they ran into another. The Germans threatened
to shoot hostages, but that did not deter the Maquis. 'We piled up in
a deep cutting two kilometres north of Salon-la-Tour,' Staunton
states in his report, 'two successive passenger trains. This produced
an effective block for six weeks, the Germans being short of heavy
cranes.' At the same time the Maquis in the Correze piled several
tons of rock on the line between Uzerche and Brive. As a result of all
this the Das Reich SS Panzer division never reached Normandy. The
fighting there was over before it could get through.

Of all these operations Jean-Claude Guiet, the American wireless
operator attached to Staunton, kept London fully informed and,
through him, fresh directions were constantly being received with
regard to work that had still to be done.

These developments occurred for the most part while Violette was
at Fresnes; they brought about a complete reversal of the position at
Gestapo headquarters in Limoges, as will presently be revealed.

With her suit-case left in the car at Salon-la-Tour, she was without any change of clothing and not even her handbag – no comb or toothbrush, not a pair of stockings or a handkerchief. At the jail at Limoges they brought her two coarse garments to wear as under-clothes and for the rest she had to make do during the six days she was there with what she had on. On arrival at Fresnes, after her name had been entered in the office off the hall, she was led away by an SS wardress in grey, through a long underground passage, then up an iron staircase off which ran tier upon tier of corridors, caged in with iron bars, until they reached a cell on the fourth floor.

It was a small, dark cell, measuring about twelve feet by eight. The plaster was peeling off the walls, leaving horrible scars. On the wall opposite the door was a dirty window made up of small panes of frosted glass and heavily barred on the outside. The window could not be opened, for the handle had been wrenched off, but fortunately some of the panes had been smashed. The bed, a very rough and rusty iron frame, was folded against the wall. There was a lumpy palliasse to serve as mattress when the bed was let down. A rickety chair was the only other piece of furniture. There was a lavatory seat by the door with a cold water tap above it.

When she looked at the walls later Violette was able to discern numerous scratches, made with the fingernail or a hair-pin. They were mostly dates, a phrase or two from a prayer and a few angry words and curses. She had been brought up to believe that being sent to prison was a disgrace that one would never be able to live down; but here, as at Limoges, she felt a little proud that she could still make her personal contribution to the war. So far the Germans had extracted no information from her. Would she be able to hold out – and for how long, she wondered.

As night began to fall she heard raised voices, mostly the voices of the women in the cells around. In the gathering gloom of the unlighted cells, these voices seemed to bring an unseen companion-ship; for together, as one led and the others joined in, some voices cracked and tuneless, a few delightfully musical, they sang the old songs of France and of other countries. At intervals, rising above the singing, came harsh, defiant curses and cries of 'Courage, mon vieux' and 'Vive de Gaulle' and 'Vive Churchill'. Curses, vile and bitter curses, were heaped too upon the heads of Laval and Pétain, who were regarded as primarily responsible for the sufferings they were all enduring. Violette, who joined vehemently in these curses, would have derived some comfort had she known that in a very few months both Laval and Pétain would be occupying cells in this very prison.

A trolley trundling on rails along the corridor brought them their food. In the evenings it was cabbage soup with a few beans in it. This was brought in a wooden tub and, as the prison was very crowded and the wardresses did not want to waste time opening doors, they poured the soup through the peep-hole into a small rusty tin bowl on a ledge on the inside. Bread was restricted to 100 grammes a day. Sometimes a piece of cheese was served, usually it was unfit for human consumption. A thin finger of margarine appeared occasionally and even more rarely one got a solitary sausage, made, one found, of meat and bread salvaged from a bombed warehouse with bits of brick still in it. Not much nourishment could be obtained from such a diet and Violette, like the other prisoners here, was always very hungry.

For what purpose she had been brought to Fresnes was revealed a day later when the wardress opened the door and led her away. She was taken along the metalled corridor, down many flights of stairs, through the underground passage again, and out into the front yard. Here a Black Maria was waiting to take her into Paris.

As the van was windowless, save for a small grille in the back door, she caught only fleeting glimpses of the streets through which only a few weeks before she had roamed in freedom. She knew where she was being taken, for they had talked of it in England. It was to the house in the Avenue Foch where the Gestapo did their harsher questioning, aided by the persuasive refinements of torture. So it had come – the ordeal that had been constantly at the back of her mind. Urged by curiosity, and perhaps even awe, she had visited the Avenue Foch when she was last here and, with a swift glance at No. 84, she had walked quickly on.

Now, as the Black Maria swept along the Paris streets, she saw people seated in groups at the little round tables of the pavement cafés. The van turned into the Avenue Foch, one of the most attractive streets in all Paris, running from the Arc de Triomphe to the Bois. Gardens flanked it on both sides. The van coursed along an inner road which gave access to the houses and pulled up at No. 84. The guards swung back the gate, and she alighted in the sombre covered entrance to the house.

It was not at all like the Gestapo headquarters at Limoges. Once a private residence, it was almost palatial. A wide staircase led to five floors, each with many rooms that were used by the Gestapo for questioning and for torture. Her inquisitor was not in uniform. He was young, good looking and rather dandified. His manner was calm, polite, and assured. He had been carefully selected and trained for the work he was to do, just as she had been for hers. And he was determined to get the information he sought.

At that first interview he was unsuccessful. He was patient on this occasion, but when she was brought before him again the next day, after a bleak and uneasy night in her cell at Fresnes, with a short, sharp volley from a firing squad under her window early in the morning (staged possibly for her benefit), she realised that today he meant to get down to business. This was confirmed by the presence in the room of another man. The moment she sat down the man came up and stood by her chair. As the questioning proceeded and she still proved recalcitrant, implements of torture were produced and each was held up before her. The inquisitor said: 'Will you answer now?' and, just as defiantly as when she was a child, she replied: 'I won't. I *won't*.' The young German then gave the sign. There followed the most atrocious torture.

She winced and bit her lips. Her face was contorted in her horrible agony. But still, though hardly able to move her lips, her eyes unable now to flash their fire, she repeated, almost inaudibly: 'I won't. I *won't*.'

After a time the man said: 'All right, take her away.' Then, turning to her, he added: 'I have given you your chance. As you won't speak, there seems to be nothing left now but the firing squad.'

She refused to be assisted from the room. 'Don't touch me,' she said as, limping, she walked from the room.

She was in an agony for many days. Tossing amid constant discomfort and pain, her mind groped for precious memories from the past. The soothing hands of Etienne were on her brow, she heard again his whispered words of comfort, and she drew to her breast the warm, tender caresses of her child.

She did not know when she would be taken again to the Avenue Foch, or on which morning it would be her turn to face the firing squad. But, mingled with the dread and the suffering, was a feeling of elation. She had said nothing. By not one word had she betrayed what she knew. Mentally she felt invigorated, and she thanked God that she had been strong.

She wondered if her friends in Sussac knew where she was. They had, of course, heard that she had been taken to Fresnes and they were aware what the Fresnes prisoners had to undergo at the Avenue Bosche, as they called it. But Paris was too far away for any further attempt at rescue. Besides, they had important work in hand, which they had been undertaking with efficiency and dispatch. On 25 June, that is to say a fortnight after her capture and only a few days following her torture, the first parachute drop ever made by daylight during the war was made near Sussac. It was on a formidable scale. A force of 86 Flying Fortresses came over attended by many Lightnings and Mustangs. They dropped 864 containers filled with supplies – weapons, ammunition, hand grenades, explosives, stores, petrol and even money. It took 300 Maquis three days to carry these supplies away. Thirty lorries were used. All the roads on this journey were guarded by Maquis, who even put up road blocks at vital points to prevent the Germans getting in.

The effect of this vast daylight operation was electrifying. Seeing the planes come over in such great numbers, the entire countryside rushed into the fields to witness the unforgettable scene. As the hundreds of parachutes descended in successive waves, cheer upon cheer rose to greet them. There was the wildest jubilation. The people began to sing and sang while they loaded the trucks and took the supplies home. The few hundred Maquis of the Haute Vienne swelled overnight to well over 3,000.

Of all this Violette, of course, knew nothing. The Germans did not send for her again. At the Avenue Foch they were anxious and short tempered. Too much was happening in swift and startling succession in every direction. Much of Normandy was in Allied hands by the end of June. The Maquis were rising everywhere as fresh supplies reached them. In July an American assault group comprising thirty men, all of them in uniform, were dropped by night in the Sussac area. Bob Mortier, who was in charge of the reception committee, had met some of the parachuted men in London. They included two English officers, Captain Bisset and Captain Ted Fraser, who had been conducting officers for the French Section of SOE. Shortly afterwards, in the next parachuted batch, came Major de Guelis, who had been responsible for recruiting Bob Mortier in North Africa and sending him to Buckmaster in London; and young André Simon, son of the famous wine connoisseur. A third group followed composed entirely of French Special Air Service officers. Together they totalled just on a hundred. Arriving in such numbers, these highly trained officers both strengthened and hearted the Maquis. Staunton and Bob and Guiet unpacked the uniforms they had brought with them and wore than always thereafter. It was sad, they felt, that Violette's uniform had to remain in the suit-case she left behind above the grocer's shop at Sussac.

She spent her birthday in bed in the most acute pain. It was her twenty-third birthday and the last she was to know. Etienne had been dead for two years: it was three years since their last meeting. All through July she remained at Fresnes, the pain easing, her spirits rising, for, despite German efforts to withhold all news of these tremendous developments, some of it inevitably percolated through. Women tapped it out in the Morse code on the walls of their cells to tell their neighbours. In the evenings, as darkness fell, there was a greater lustiness in their singing. Violette led them in the singing of the British National Anthem. But only two voices joined hers, the others apparently did not know the words, but made a valiant effort at *la-la*-ing to give support. It suggested, of course, that there were only two other women from England in the prison at Fresnes.

The Allies landed in the South of France in the middle of August. They did not drive north in the direction of the Maquis of the Haute Viennes, but turned eastward and pursued the Germans up the Rhone Valley into Germany. Staunton and his group made their own swift moves. With what was now quite a large and well disciplined force they harried the Germans to right and to left, giving them no respite, and on 20 August they entered Limoges. General Gleiniger, commanding the German forces there, refused at first to surrender. On Staunton pointing out that the town was surrounded by a force of 20,000 strong, with reinforcements on the way, Gleiniger signed the surrender. His troops laid down their arms and were moved into a former prison camp for Jews.*

The next morning, Staunton, Bob and Guiet moved into the

---

* The Supreme Allied Commander, General Eisenhower has recorded: 'Thanks to the underground movement the liberation of France was accelerated by some six months.'

Gestapo headquarters. In the room in which Violette was so persistently questioned only two months before, Staunton now sat in the colonel's chair. The Gestapo, shirking the consequences of the altered situation, had already fled. Staunton was not, however, concerned with questioning and threatening. He had a bar set up at one end of the room, gaudily arrayed with bottles of whisky and the gay liqueurs of France. Here, while they planned their next moves, they were able in that blazing summer of 1944 to assuage their thirsts and to drink a toast to the courage, devotion and steadfastness of Violette.

Early in August there was bewilderment and alarm among the Germans in Paris, for the Third United States Army, under General Paton, and the Free French forces led by General Leclerc, were marching steadily on the capital. Nothing the Germans could do could stop them. Each day the panic grew. Orders came suddenly for the removal of certain specially selected prisoners from Fresnes to Germany as the Gestapo did not want 'to become available' to the advancing Allies.

On the morning of 8 August, that is to say seven and a half weeks after being brought to Fresnes, Violette was taken through the underground passage into the prison yard. There she saw three small coaches waiting. One of them was just moving off with a batch of male prisoners. The second, also containing men, was not yet full. She thought she saw in it someone she knew. He raised his hand in greeting and she realised that it was Harry Peulevé. For months she had been seeking him in London. It was strange that they should have been so near to each other in Fresnes. In the third coach there were fewer than a dozen girls. Harry called to her as his coach drove out. They could not speak, but there was the hope that they might meet if they happened to be travelling by the same train.

Harry was in London when the war broke out. He instantly joined the Territorials, served in France with the British Expeditionary Force and was evacuated at Dunkirk. He was a secret agent when he first met Violette at the Studio Club and had already been to France on a mission. She was working at the aircraft factory in Morden at the time. Etienne had been dead for nearly eight months, but Violette did not yet know it. A few weeks later, on learning the sad news about Etienne, Violette was herself to become a member of Harry's section of SOE and, though the girl who introduced them at the club that night had apparently a hand in getting Violette's name sent to the War Office, it was not until after the war that she revealed this to Harry. This girl, widow of a Battle of Britain pilot, who could not serve herself because she was an Italian by birth, wrote to say of Violette that she was 'an extremely suitable candidate for work in France as a secret agent'. At their next encounter in Piccadilly underground, Harry saw that Violette had on the uniform of a FANY. They went about a great deal together after that and some thought a romance might be developing. The last time they saw each other was early in 1944. They were with a large party at the Astor Club. Two nights later he left. He was dropped not far from where Violette was herself to come not many months later, for he was with the Maquis in the Correze area, only a few miles from Salon-la-Tour. Harry was arrested in March 1944, Violette in June; and both had been for many weeks in adjoining blocks at Fresnes.

As each coach left the prison yard parcels of food, enough to last for two days, were handed to the prisoners by the Red Cross. Those who had suit-cases were given them now. Violette had only a bundle containing the few garments given her in the prison at Limoges. No prisoner got back either jewellery or money, even their watches and rings were withheld. Etienne's engagement ring, which Violette had hoped to convert into cash when in a tight corner, she never saw again.

The men handcuffed in pairs, but the girls unfettered, they were taken to the Gare de l'Est and put into the train for Germany. It was not a long train. For the prisoners there was just one coach, which had been tacked on at the end. The other carriages were filled with German wounded. There was also an anti-aircraft gun in case of a raid.

The prisoners' coach had a lavatory and next to it a third-class compartment in which the girls were placed. Beyond that was what looked like two horse-boxes with stout iron doors that worked like lift gates and were kept shut to prevent access to the corridor. They had been formed by removing the seats from two compartments. Guards paraded the corridor and had a small compartment of their own to sit in just beyond the horse-boxes.

The girls were no sooner ushered into their compartment than they were chained by the ankles, in pairs. This was to prevent escape since there was no grille on their door.

After a wait at the station of many hours, during which, despite their efforts, Violette and Harry were unable to get to each other, the train started at last very late in the afternoon. It was obvious that the men would not be able to sleep, for there were nineteen of them in one section and eighteen in the other, with barely enough room to stand. Yeo-Thomas, known now as 'The White Rabbit', who was a director of Molyneux in Paris before the war, took charge, as the senior ranking officer among the prisoners. He arranged that they should take it in turn to lie down during the night, as only two pairs could do this at a time while the rest stood. It was a stiflingly hot August night and the men suffered the acutest discomfort. The women, though crowded closely together, at any rate had seats. Violette met now the two other Englishwomen at Fresnes. They were Denise Bloch and Lillian Rolfe; both had been wireless operators in the French Section of SOE. Lillian, who came from Horsell, near Woking, in Surrey, was tall and dark, with attractive brown eyes. She had a French mother and had been brought up in Brazil. Denise, broad-shouldered and blonde, had escaped from France during the Occupation. These three were to remain together through many ghastly and tragic developments.

In the morning, after a restless and exhausting night, the men were taken to the lavatory in pairs, still handcuffed together. The guard stood by the open door all the time. No further visits were allowed. As the day wore on the heat became increasingly intense. By the afternoon it was unbearable. The water, supplied in bottles by the Red Cross, had all been drunk during the night. The men kept clamouring for something to quench their raging thirst. They begged the guards to bring them just a glassful, but the guards ignored their pleas.

There were recurrent alarms that British planes had been seen overhead and there was a great fear that the train might be attacked. Near Chalons-sur-Marne, having come only eighty miles in twenty-two hours, these fears materialised. Two RAF planes bombed the train. There was a thundering explosion. Many windows were smashed. The train shuddered and came to a halt. In a panic the guards locked the doors of the coach and ran out into the fields where they took refuge in ditches. A machine-gun was mounted on a small mound and trained on the carriage so that none might try to escape. The anti-aircraft gun got into action. Flying very low, the RAF planes dropped more bombs and then opened fire with their machine-guns.

The roof of one of the carriages was split open and the prisoners heard the screams of the wounded and the dying.

The women had begun to cheer at the start of the attack, but the men, imprisoned in confined spaces behind the locked grilles, were possessed by the fear that, if an incendiary hit their coach, there could for them be no escape and they would all inevitably be burned to death. There were Belgians and Frenchmen among them and some of them got hysterical. Unable to throw themselves down on the floor, they threw themselves on top of each other. A few were frothing at the mouth. Yeo-Thomas says: 'We all felt deeply ashamed when we saw Violette Szabo, while the raid was still on, come crawling along the corridor towards us with a jug of water which she had filled in the lavatory. She handed it to us through the iron bars. With her, crawling too, came the girl to whose ankle she was chained.'

This act of mercy made an unforgettable impression on all. She spoke words of comfort, jested, went back with the jug to fill it again and again. 'My God that girl had guts,' says Yeo-Thomas. 'I shall never forget that moment,' says Harry Peulevé, 'I felt very proud that I knew her. She looked so pretty, despite her shabby clothes and her lack of make-up – and she was full of good cheer. I have never under any circumstances known her to be depressed or moody.'

When the planes departed and the guards returned, it was found that seventeen Germans had been killed. The raid was successful, says Yeo-Thomas. Either the engine or the track must have been damaged, for the train was unable to proceed. After a very long wait the prisoners were led out of their coach by the guards and put into two trucks requisitioned from farmers.

The trucks took them on to Metz, once regarded as a vital sector of the Maginot Line. Here they spent the night in the stables attached to the barracks. Straw had been spread out in the loose boxes. The men, also chained in pairs now, were given the stalls on the right, the women were separated from them by a narrow alleyway along which flowed the stable drain. The guards threatened to shoot if any attempt was made to cross from one side to the other. None the less, as the night advanced, some of the men and women crawled towards each other and talked across the drain until dawn. Peulevé says: 'Violette and I talked all through the night. Her voice, as always, was so sweet and soothing, one could listen to it for hours. We spoke of old times and we told each other our experiences in France. Bit by bit

everything was unfolded – her life in Fresnes, her interviews at the
Avenue Foch. But either through modesty or a sense of delicacy,
since some of the tortures were too intimate in their application; or
perhaps because she did not wish to live again through the pain of it,
she spoke hardly at all about the tortures she had been made to
suffer. She was in a cheerful mood. Her spirits were high. She was
confident of victory and was resolved on escaping no matter where
they took her.'

Thus, in the darkness, with each chained by the ankle to another,
and the drain between them, they had their last romantic inter-
changes, with their hopes and dreams unvoiced but no doubt shared.

The journey to the German frontier took the best part of a week.
They were taken from Metz to the Gestapo headquarters at Stras-
bourg and then northward to Saarbrücken. Here the women were
detached from the rest of the party and sent off to Ravensbruck.

Ironbottom Sound

Lindsay Baly

I was awakened by a sharp explosion; the whole ship seemed to jump sideways and bits of granulated cork showered down on me from the deckhead. Torpedoed! I sprang for the ladder but before my feet hit the bridge-grating a tongue of flame spewed out forty feet to port from the ship's side below the bridge and there was another ear-splitting explosion. B mounting was firing, both guns!

'CEASE FIRE, CEASE FIRE!' I yelled and jammed my thumb on the check fire bell. I saw Lachlan beside me, pressing the action alarm button. The two bells rang out discordantly through the ship.

'Who opened fire?'

'I am firing at a Japanese cruiser, sir.' It was Field. He was pointing over the port side into the pitch black night. I snatched binoculars but could see nothing and Field, frantic with frustration, cried: 'Now I've lost the bloody thing. It was out there, going like the clappers . . .' The implication that my intervention was the cause of this catastrophe was not lost on me. His angular frame whirled away from me, binoculars sweeping a wide arc.

'If you fired on friendly ships, I'll courtmartial you,' I said grimly and dived at the chart. 'Where is the northern patrol? If they are on their southern leg, they could be on that bearing.'

'I don't know. I haven't seen them all watch. All I know is, *Patterson* came up on TBS and said: 'Warning, warning, strange ships entering harbour.' Then I saw this Jap cruiser. B gun's in local control so the layer and trainer must have seen it too or they wouldn't have fired. It all happened in ten seconds; I didn't have time to call you.'

'You make time. I left orders to search for those ships and you're telling me no one's sighted them? Is everybody blind?'

No reply. But at least the pandemonium on the bridge had subsided.

It *had* to be a friendly ship or black was white, the sun would not rise, two admirals were fools and knaves and I was a criminal.

'Look!' shrieked the starboard look-out, forgetting all he had been taught. Then he added: 'Green 130.'

Three brilliant flares hung over Lunga Point bathing the shoreline in silver light and silhouetting *Canberra* and *Chicago*. Starshell?

'They're aircraft flares,' said Field. 'That's that thing that's been droning round for hours with navigation lights on. It's a Jap! A marker plane! They're amazing!'

Then all round *Canberra*, tall pillars of white water rose in seeming slow motion, hung as if frozen and gracefully subsided. I had seen these before; she was straddled by shell fire. From further astern there was a bellowing explosion and tongues of red flame.

'That's *Chicago*,' cried Field. 'Eight inch broadside. Thank Christ somebody's seen them.'

'Just hold everything! Something damned dangerous is going on here, but we're not going to make it worse . . .'

I searched out over the port side and then I saw a stab of orange flame again, but this time it was just forward of the beam.

'Get a bearing,' I shouted, but Lachlan was already bent over the pelorus, taking it. Good.

'Bearing 345, sir. Red 75,' he called.

'Alarm surface port, bearing red 75. Load, load, load,' boomed Field over the armament broadcast.

I turned on him in fury, but just then the *Canberra* was hit. There was an angry red flash and part of her super-structure seemed to subside like a landslide on a cliff face. Immediately she was hit again, on the forepart, a tremendous crash that heaved up the forecastle deck and dozens of flaming planks spun crazily upwards, like so many matches spilled from a box. She was smothered in splashes. She swung to starboard and slowed and then there was a third hit in the engine spaces, a great geyser of steam shot up and dark and white smoke mingled over her, screening red fires. Then she was lost to sight behind the smoke:

'Oh, my God.' It *had* happened, it must have – and yet there was no proof, I would not accept it until there was.

'Whoever they are, they've got be stopped. Full speed. Steer 045. Stand by torpedo tubes; bridge control. Tell the chief I want everything he's got. We'll get clear of this bloody mess and search.' I heard the clang of telegraphs repeating 'Full Ahead' and the rising whine of the turbines and I felt the screws bite deep and drag the ship's stern down as she moved off.

I took up the armament broadcast microphone myself.

'Do you hear there. This is the captain speaking,' I said. 'We are under attack by unidentified forces, presumed enemy. Wake up, settle down and get straight into action. Stand by.'

From the same direction as before, on the port beam, a searchlight flashed on. It groped towards us and away, found a target which from that distance seemed to be *Chicago* and switched off. A second later there was the orange flash of a broadside, fired from perhaps three miles away. This was no friendly ship. I was convinced.

'Target, a cruiser, bearing red 80. Open fire,' I screeched into the microphone.

Oh no! Oh no!

'I've got her. Get down to the plot,' I said to Field and shoved him aside at the binnacle.

If the Japanese ship was heading about north east, as seemed likely, we were on a good parallel course for a torpedo attack. Meanwhile, we could engage with gunfire.

I saw the back of our other sub-lieutenant, Hathaway just disappearing into the director control tower hatch. Oh, God, the gun crews were not closed up yet, we would be too late.

'Watch out for torpedo tracks. Weave,' I said, registering a flabbergasted Toby Marks beside me still struggling into his shirt, and sprinted for the control tower. I clung on to the outside of the hatch in the 30-odd knot wind of our passage in an agony of impatience while Hathaway talked into his headphones.

'Can you see anything?' I shouted.

'No, sir. We'll have to use starshell. X gun's ready.'

'Right, get going.' I half fell down the vertical director ladder, just as he ordered:

'Starshell fire spread!'

X gun cracked out three rounds in good time, but now I had lost my orientation on the bridge.

'What can you see, Pilot?' I gasped.

'*Canberra's* burning like a haystack back there sir, but apart from that, nothing. I can't see the target. There's nothing on TBS; there was a bit of gabble but I couldn't make anything out of it.'

'Where is the northern patrol?' I cried in anguish. 'We *must* be getting close to them.'

Marks muttered that he'd give his head for a radar set; only the newest American ships were fitted with this magic eye and the best equipped radar ship, *San Juan*, was patrolling off the Sealark Channel, far to the east, with *Hobart*.

The first starshell burst dead over the unmistakable pagoda-like superstructure of a *Kako* class heavy cruiser at 6000 yards. It showed a beam-on silhouette, a black shape surging forward with immense power and dreadful menace. The starshell should have burst to the right, but this was a fortunate, error. I took up the fire control phone to hear Hathaway saying:

'Inclination 100 right . . .

'Range 062, deflection 4 left.'

'Clock tuned, deflection set!' From the transmitting station down below. At last.'

'Spread line . . . *shoot*! From two stars right, starshell go on.'

The fire gong rang, there was a maddening three-second delay and our first 6-gun, 4.7 inch broadside was in the air, followed immediately by another starshell round. That was under way; now I could concentrate on the torpedo attack. I put the phone down but as I did so it was nearly snatched out of my hand by a bleary, cross-looking Tom Hughes, dragged from sleep. How long had he been there? I had forgotten all about him and I had been doing his job instead of my own. And why that ridiculous dash to the director? The phone I had just put down would have done just as well.

'Did you sight the northern patrol or didn't you?' I barked at him.

'No sir, I did not,' he shot back.

'Oh, Christ. This is it, Tom, it's bad. Good shooting,' I said and added 'Port Five,' down the voice pipe.

'Port Five. Five of port wheel on, sir.'

The ship started to swing in, rapidly at this speed. I could have fired torpedoes from where we were, but if I could get to 4000 or 3000 yards, I couldn't miss. But although we were going perhaps 10 knots faster than the Japanese cruiser, we were on converging courses and therefore keeping about steady relative to each other. The more I swung in, the more bearing I would lose and I risked slipping hopelessly astern if I was not careful.

'Midships.'

'Midships. Wheel's a-midships sir.'

The turn slowed up. Another starshell plopped over the cruiser and I saw our shell splashes rise around her; there should be hits in that. But God, she was close! 3,800 yards. If she shifted target to us, as soon she must . . . I gritted my teeth. In the next second, the searchlight flashed on and swept lazily across us.

We felt like bugs pinned on a board under that light; we wanted to squirm off the pin but had nowhere to go. I saw instant tableaux of guns' crews in motion; the very flash of our own broadside paled feebly in its glare, faces twisted in desperation on the bridge and the seething white cascade of wake distorted into a live thing, seeming to charge after us, about to swallow us up from behind. The light paused at the bridge, travelled insolently forward, swept aft, dwelt on the after part, and switched off. There were audible gasps of relief.

Now I hugged the shuddering binnacle to keep myself upright watching the target, instead of cowering for cover. I forced myself to read the target bearing: 265, 267, 270 . . . we were losing bearing pretty fast. Range? 3,400. It would have to do.

'Steady.'

'Steady. Course 342 sir.'

'Starboard ten.'

'Starboard ten. Ten of starboard wheel on.'

'Steer 010.'

It was the wrong way to turn for shell splashes but I had to fire torpedoes now or never.

'Check fire.'

'Check firing! Check check check check . . .' The check fire bells jangled and the guns stopped. A steady platform was needed for torpedoes.

'Set course. Bridge control. Fire on your sight,' I called to the torpedo officer, crouched over his sight on the port look-out sponson.

A deluge of dirty white water swamped the bridge, drenching everyone on it and out of the corner of my eye I saw another tall column collapsing to starboard. Straddled, first pop, but we were not hit. Somehow the terror lessened once the fall of shot could be seen.

What was happening on the torpedo sight? He should have given me thirty seconds to go. He had his hand on the sight, his body bent forward.

'How long to go? Torpedo control: you'll miss it, you bloody fool, what are you doing?'

Nothing happened. We passed the firing angle and no sleek warheads were streaking for the target. I stared in disbelief, from the black water to the control position.

A phone squealed and Lachlan answered it.

'It's the tubes, sir. They got no orders to prime! The torpedo gunner's mate says the fucking firing pistols aren't even shipped!'

I was speechless.

'But who – but I said – *why the hell not?*'

There was a loud explosion aft with an enormous sheet of flame, somewhere about the mainmast and more grey and white water cascaded all over us. Straddled again and hit this time. Was her back broken? I gave a wheel order and we swung rapidly through north east, heeling hard in the turn; she was still answering the wheel at least.

'Hard-a-starboard! 'I roared. 'Torpedo officer!' Through a red mist of rage I could see him, still hunched over his sight. He hadn't moved. 'Mr Morley!' I thundered. Lachlan scrambled over to him.

'Sir,' quavered Lachlan. 'He's dead. He . . . has no head.'

Oh, my Christ. Morley. No head?

'He's just standing there! Blood all down his front and he's . . . bits everywhere, I trod in it. It's all over me!'

He started scraping and scuffing his shoes frantically on the grating in a grotesque, shuffling dance.

'That will do, Sub!' I was ready to hit him.

He stood still.

'Sub, pull yourself together. If you don't want to go the same way, fight back. Do you know anything about torpedo control? Can you work that sight?'

'Sorry. Yes, sir, I can.' He was recovered now and reaching out for responsibility.

'Then get on the starboard sight and get the tubes ready. I am going to starboard and will fire to starboard this time.'

We drove hard round with full wheel on and those torpedoes got away straight and true. But, dear God, how could a 35 knot torpedo catch a 26 knot ship, end on and going away?

The First Bid for Freedom

P. R. Reid

We ate well on September 4th and prepared our kit, putting the final touches to our clothing. Maps – good survey maps which had been found, and others carefully traced on thin lavatory paper – were distributed. Our staple diet of raw oatmeal mixed with sugar provided at the expense of the German kitchen, was packed. My portion of staple diet went into two small sacks of strongly sewn canvas which were to be hung round my neck so as to fall over my chest and form a buxom bust, for I was to escape as a woman. I still possessed a large brown canvas pouch, which I had found in a caserne at Charleville. This I could carry by hand when dressed as a woman, and later on my back as a man. There was no room for my boots, so I made a brown paper parcel of them.

My female attire consisted of a large red spotted handkerchief for my head, a white sports-shirt as a blouse, and a skirt made of an old grey window-curtain, which I had also picked up during the trek into Germany. My legs were shaved and 'sunburnt' with iodine, and I wore black plimsolls.

Once clear of the camp, I would change into a man again, wearing a green-grey Tyrolean hat, cleverly made and dyed from khaki by a British sergeant (a former tailor), a heavy pullover to go over my shirt, a small mackintosh groundsheet for wet weather (also picked up during the journey to Germany), a pair of dark-blue shorts cut from a Belgian airman's breeches (obtained by barter), white Bavarian woollen stockings of the pattern common to the country, purchased at a shocking price in the German canteen, and my brown army boots dyed black.

The others had similar clothing, with minor individual differences. The tailor had devised enough Tyrolean hats to go round and had fashioned an Austrian cloak for Harry Elliott. Lockwood was also to make his exit disguised as a woman, and his costume was more or

less like mine. Rupert had an old grey blanket which he converted
into a cloak. We were a motley crowd and hardly fit to pass close
inspection by daylight, for we had not the experience required to
produce really finished garments from scratch. But the idea was that
we were young Austrian hikers, and we would only be seen at dusk
or dawn.

That night our room-mates made dummies in our beds, good
enough to pass the cursory glance of the German night patrol through
the room. We all slept in different rooms in the same buildings as the
tunnel, doubling up with other officers, and these arrangements were
made as secretly as possible to avoid any hubbub or infectious
atmosphere of excitement. The Senior Officers of the rooms in
question, who had to declare nightly to the German Officer on the
rounds the number of officers present, were not even aware of the
additions to or subtractions from their flock.

We were to rise at 4 am. None of us slept much, though we took
precautions against oversleeping by having a couple of 'knockers up'
in reserve. I remember banging my head on the pillow four times –
an old childhood habit which for some unaccountable reason usually
worked. It was hardly necessary on this occasion. I passed a most
unpleasant night with the cold sweat of nervous anticipation upon
me, and with that peculiar nausea of the stomach which accompanies
tense nerves and taut muscles. My mind turned over the pros and
cons a hundred times; the chances of success, immediate and later,
and the risks. If they shot, would they shoot to kill? If they caught us
sooner or later, what were our chances – to be liquidated or to
disappear into a Concentration Camp? At that period of the war,
nobody knew the answers. It was the first escape from this prison,
probably the first escape of British officers from any organized prison
in Germany. We were the guinea-pigs.

We undertook the experiment with our eyes open, choosing
between two alternatives: to attempt escape and risk the ultimate
price, or face up to the sentence of indefinite imprisonment. There
were many who resigned themselves from the beginning to the second
of these alternatives. They were brave, but their natures differed from
those of the men who escaped and failed, and escaped again; who
having once made the choice between escape and resignation, could
not give up, even if the war lasted the remainder of their lives. I am

sure that the majority of the men who sought to escape did it for self-preservation. Instinctively, unconsciously, they felt that resignation meant not physical but mental death – maybe lunacy. My own case was not exceptional. One awful fit of depression sufficed to determine my future course as a prisoner. One dose of morbidity in which the vista of emptiness stretched beyond the horizon of my mind was quite enough.

At 4 am, in a grisly darkness, I fastened my bossom in place, and put on my blouse and skirt. We crept downstairs to our collecting-point in the washroom beside the tunnel-room. A tap was turned on quietly to fill a water-bottle. It went on dripping. The sound of the drops was loud and exasperating. A sentry stood only thirty yards away by the courtyard gate. I felt he must hear it. . . . It was nerves. Captain Gilliat, one of the assistants, wore a gas-cape. Why he chose this garment for the occasion I never knew. It crackled loudly with every movement and nearly drove us mad. A watcher was by now at the end of the tunnel, waiting to pass the signal when the sentry near the tunnel exit went off duty. Other stooges were posted at vantage-points to give the alarm in case a patrol suddenly appeared in the buildings. We waited.

At 5.15 am the sentry outside the tunnel still remained at his post. It was probable now he would not leave till 6 am. There was nothing to do but wait quietly while our hearts pounded through our ribs with suppressed excitement.

There was a thundering crash and a reverberating clang as if fifty dinner-gongs had been struck hard with hammers all at once. There was a second crash and a third, diminishing in intensity, and, finally, some strident squeaks. This must be the end – but no one was allowed to move. We had our stooges and we had time after a warning to disappear. The men in the tunnel-room were safely locked in and could hide in the tunnel. A panic would have been dangerous.

Dick Howe and Peter Allan, tired of the long wait, had leant against one of the twelve-foot-long, solid cast-iron troughs which were used as communal washbasins, and finally they had sat on the edge of it. The next instant the whole trough collapsed on to the concrete floor. If I had tried for weeks I doubt if I could have thought of a better way of making the loudest noise possible with the least effort. The succeeding crashes and squeaks which kept our hair standing on end were caused by Dick and Peter who, having made a frantic attempt to save the crash, were extricating themselves from the wreckage and bringing the trough to rest quietly on the floor.

We waited for the signal to return. A minute passed, five minutes passed, and then – we began to breathe again. No Germans appeared. I never found out why they did not come. The noise woke up most of the officers in the building, which was a large one, and the sentry thirty yards away near the courtyard must have jumped out of his skin. Yet for some unaccountable reason he did not act.

Six o'clock chimed out from a distant steeple. We waited more anxiously as every minute passed. At last, at 6.15 am, the signal came through: 'All clear!' In a moment the door was unlocked and we hustled into the tunnel. I crawled quickly to the end, listened for a second, and then set to work like a demon. Down went the slats and I shovelled earth and cinders to my right and below me as fast as I could. As the hole enlarged I could see the various shed details. All the usual household cleaning equipment, piles of cardboard boxes at one end, clothes drying on a line, and then the slatted door and its lock – a large and formidable-looking padlock on a hasp. Once I tried to get through, but the opening was still too small. I enlarged it further and then squirmed upwards and into the shed. I pulled Rupert and then Peter through after me, telling Dick, who was next, to wait below while we found the way out. We searched quickly. The padlock would not open to a piece of wire which I inserted as a key. I climbed the cardboard boxes to reach a large opening in the slats near the roof and slipped, nearly bringing the boxes down on top of me. Peter held them and we readjusted the pile. We tried the door into the house; it was locked. Then in a flash I thought of the screwdriver. (I had asked Scarlet to lend me one – just in case.) I looked more closely at the hasp on which the padlock was bolted. What a fool I was!

The way was clear. With hands fumbling nervously, I unscrewed three large screws securing the hasp to the wood and the door swung open. I looked at my watch.

'Dick!' I whispered hoarsely down into the tunnel. 'You'd better come up quick, it's 6.30.'

As he started to worm himself up through the hole, there came the sound of an approaching horse and cart.

'Hold everything, Dick!' I said, 'don't move,' and to the others: 'Flatten yourselves against the walls!'

A moment later the cart appeared. Dick remained rigid like a truncated man at floor-level. The driver did not look our way and the cart passed on. We pulled Dick out of the hole. I repeated to him what he already knew.

'We're late. Our safe half-hour is already over and the woman may come in at any moment. Someone's got to replace this.' I pointed at the hasp and padlock. 'It will take five minutes. Add to this twenty minutes to clear the six of us.'

'It will take Scarlet fifteen minutes to close and camouflage the hole,' said Dick. 'It's now 6.35. That means. 7.15 before everything is clear.'

We looked at each other and I knew he read my thoughts. We had gone over the timetable so often together.

'I'm sorry, Dick! The graph has never shown the woman to be later than 7 o'clock, and she may arrive any minute. You'll have to lock up and follow tomorrow,' and I handed him the screwdriver.

'Make a good job of closing up our "Shovewood",' I added. 'Your escape depends on it.'

We quickly brushed each other down. I was worried about the back of my skirt, which had suffered in the exit as we had come out on our backs. I repeated nervously:

'Is my bottom clean? Is my bottom clean?'

For the sentry, about forty yards away on the trestle walkway, would see my back view and I did not want him to see a dirty skirt.

I tied my spotted handkerchief around my head, opened the door, and walked out into the sunlight. I turned the corner into the side street leading to the main road, and felt a gooseflesh sensation up my back and the sentry's stare burning through my shoulder-blades. I waited for the shot.

For thirty yards up the side street I walked with short steps imitating what I thought to be the gait of a middle-aged peasant woman, and thereby prolonging the agony of every yard. At last I reached the main road. There was no alarm and I turned the corner.

The road was almost deserted. A few people were cleaning their shop-windows, a restaurant manager was pinning up his menu, and a girl was brushing the pavement. A cyclist or two passed. The hush of dawn and of sleep still lay over the town. I received casual glances, but did not attract any stares.

After I had gone about two hundred yards I heard the heavy footsteps of two persons following me, marching in step. I turned into a square and crossed it diagonally towards the bridge over the river. The footsteps grew louder and nearer. I was being followed: a patrol had been sent after me by the suspicous sentry. They did not run for fear of making me run. I was finished – the game was up – but, I thought, I may as well play it to the end and I ambled along with my bundles across the bridge, not daring to turn round. How those footsteps echoed, first in the street, now on the bridge! The patrol came alongside and passed me without accosting me. I raised my head and to my relief saw two young hikers. They were Rupert and Peter, walking briskly away from me. I had never expected them so soon.

About a hundred yards past the bridge I turned right, following the other two. This route brought me alongisde a local railway line and towards the outskirts of the town. We could see the line from the camp, and it had been arranged we should follow the path beside it and rendezvous in the woods about a quarter of a mile out of the town.

As I turned the corner, a little girl, playing with a toy, looked up at me and caught my eye. Astonishment was written all over her face. I might take in a casual adult observer, but I could not pass the keen observation of a child. She continued to look wide-eyed at me as I passed and when I was a few yards farther on I heard her running into a house – no doubt to tell her parents to come and look at the extraordinary man dressed up as a woman. Nobody came, so I presumed they just did not believe her. Grown-ups always know better than their children!

It was a misty morning heralding a hot day. I followed the railway into the woods, where it swept to the left in a big curve. I heard a train approaching and made for cover among the trees. It passed and I continued a short distance, expecting to see the other two waiting for me. There was no sign of them and I began to worry. I whistled, but there was no answer. I continued slowly, whistling 'We're going to hang out our washing on the Siegfried Line. . . .' They must be close by the woods. Still no answer. Then I heard shots in the distance and dogs barking. I immediately dashed into the woods and decided to hide and change rapidly. I could not go on in my makeshift skirt. Maybe the child's parents had phoned the camp or the police. They might search for someone with a skirt on!

I found myself close to the river and was soon in among high reeds, where I started to change. It was about 7.15 am. Shots continued spasmodically and the barking of dogs increased. I was at my wits' end and sure the 'hunt was up', and I had lost the other two. Rupert had the only compass – a good army one given him by a fellow-officer, who had managed to conceal it through all searches. I could not travel without one.

I suddenly heard people approaching along a wood path close to the reeds. I crouched and waited until I saw them. Thank God, it was my two hikers once more!

'I thought I'd lost you for good,' I said, quickly completing my change and hiding my skirt in the reeds. 'I was already bothering about how I was going to reach Yugoslavia without a compass.'

'What's all the shooting about?' said Peter.

'I haven't the foggiest idea. I don't like it. They've probably discovered something and are shooting up the camp. They'll be after us in no time. We'll have to hide up.'

'It sounds to me like rifle-range shooting,' said Rupert.

'Well, why have we never heard it before, then?' I questioned, 'and how do you account for the dogs?'

'Probably the village dogs barking at the gunfire.'

'The fact is, Rupert, we've never heard shooting like this before, and besides, it's still misty in places. I believe they're after us and we'd better hide up quickly.

'I bet you five pounds it's range-shooting. Anyway, it's no use hiding here. We're much too close. Come on, let's make tracks!'

We made for the top of a high wooded hill which lay in our general direction southwards. From it we could see all the surrounding country. We crossed the railway, then a road and some open fields before entering the friendly cover of more woods. We simply scuttled across the fields, Rupert, who was the calmest, doing all he could to make us walk normally. In the woods we disturbed some chamois which fled away noisily, giving us the fright of our lives.

We had left tracks in the dew-laden grass of the fields and we were out of breath from the steep uphill going. We rested for a moment and smeared our boots with German mustard, which we had brought for the purpose of putting dogs off the scent, and then continued, climbing steeper and steeper. We heard woodcutters at work and kept clear of them. Eventually, at about 9 am, we reached the top of the hill.

The shooting and the barking of dogs had ceased. We gained confidence. Either the hunters had lost track of us or it had been a false alarm, as Rupert thought.

The camp *Appell*, that is, roll-call, was due and soon we should have an important matter decided. We had arranged that, from a window high up in the camp building, a sheet would be hung, as if to air; white for 'all clear', blue check if our absence had been discovered.

The Germans held two separate *Appells*, one for the Officers, and immediately afterwards one for the Other Ranks – in another courtyard. This gave us an opening of which we were not slow to avail ourselves. I had arranged with six 'good men and true' that they would stand in for the Officers' *Appell* and then do a rapid change in a lavatory into orderlies' attire and appear on the Other Ranks parade. Only three of them would be necessary today.

It was a glorious morning and I climbed a tree to look down into the valley, now clear of mist and bathed in luxurious sunshine. The view was beautiful, rich in September fruitfulness, with the river in the foreground rushing over its pebbly bed, a ribbon of sparkling light.

I could see our prison in the distance reflecting a warm golden colour from its walls. I had never thought that our Archbishop's Palace could be called beautiful, but from a distance it certainly was so. Then I realised why: I could not distinguish the windows in the walls. We were farther away than we had estimated, and the sunlight was at a bad angle. There was no hope of seeing a sheet of any colour. Later, when the sun had moved round, Peter climbed the tree, but he could scarcely distinguish the windows and, although his sight was keen, could see no sign of a sheet.

We hid the whole day in a copse of young fir-trees on the top of the hill. We were only disturbed once, by a woodman who passed close by but did not see us. We reconnoitred the southern slope of the hill along the route we were to take that night, but it was wooded for a long distance so we soon gave up, letting the darkness bring what it might. We were in very good hiding. I believe only dogs would ever have found us.

We lay in long grass in an open patch among the trees, dozing from time to time, scarcely ever talking. The sun shone in a cloudless sky. It was good to be alive, to breathe the air of freedom, the scent of pines and dry grass, to hear the murmur of flying insects around and the distant chopping of a woodman's axe, to listen to a lark above one's head – a fluttering speck against the infinity of the clear blue sky. We were free at last. A restful calm, a silent relish of this precious day spread over us. There was a hush on the sunbathed, pleasant countryside. We felt attuned to it. Our hearts were full of thanksgiving. Animals do not need to speak, I thought.

At meal-time we sat up and ate our meagre ration. We had worked it out to last us twelve days. We drank a mouthful of water each from a small bottle, exchanged a few remarks on the chances of Dick and the others the next day and then returned to our dreaming.

A beautiful autumnal evening set in, and with it came a chill in the air as the sun sank peacefully over the horizon. I have seldom in my life spent a happier day. The war did not seem to exist.

We clothed ourselves, put chalk in our socks and boots, and, as darkness approached, set off downhill through the woods – southwards to Yugoslavia. It was about one hundred and fifty miles away across the mountains of the Austrian Tyrol. We hoped to make it in ten days.

THE PRICE OF FAILURE

We had a large-scale map which covered the first sixty miles of our journey. It showed all the contours, and even tiny villages and mountain paths. Its acquisition deserves an explanation.

Our camp was formerly the depot of the 100th Gebirgsjäger Regiment – mountain troops. At the top of one of our buildings was a staircase leading up to an attic. The former was entirely shut off by a wood partition and a door made of slats which was heavily chained and padlocked. We could not see far up the staircase, but its situation was intriguing and invited inspection.

One day Scarlet O'Hara solved the problem of how to by-pass the door. The stair passed diagonally across a window, the springer being about eight inches away from the glass. The sill of this window could be reached from the flight of stairs below by climbing on a man's shoulder. A thin man could worm himself up through the eight-inch gap on to the forbidden staircase, and thus the secrets of the attic were revealed. A few doors with very simple locks were no barrier to Scarlet, and an old storeroom was found in which there were many copies of survey maps of the district around Laufen. Other useful things, such as small hatchets, screws and nails, pens and coloured inks, were found, and even badges of the mountain regiment. We took away a small portion of everything, hoping the stock had never been accurately counted.

Before we escaped, someone a little too fat had tried the window route and split the glass. The Jerries realized what was happening and barred off the window completely. There was not much left in the attic by that time. The Germans created a big fuss and searched the camp and prisoners individually. The search lasted a day, but nothing seriously incriminating was found, and our tunnel, being behind German locks, was not troubled.

Rupert's compass had survived many such searches by employing the following simple ruse. Before being searched, the owner of the compass demanded urgently to go to the lavatory, meeting there by arrangement a friend who had been searched already. Although the owner was accompanied by a sentry while carrying out this simple duty, a moment always arrived when it was possible to slip the article to the friend unobserved. The method required good synchronization and deft handling of an opportunity, or even the making of an opportunity by diverting the attention of the sentry.

There was no moon and it soon became pitch-dark in the woods. We were in thick undergrowth and brambles and made slow progress, so much so that we altered our compass bearing and headed southeast, trying to find easier going. After about two hours we cleared the woods and were able to trek across country at a good speed, aiming at a chosen star which we checked by the compass as being in our line. It was then only necessary to look at the compass every hour or so and change our guiding star as the constellations moved in the sky.

Walking at night straight across country is an eerie experience. Only the actual ground for a few yards around is real, be it long grass, corn stubble, potato field, or moorland. Beyond this island lies an ocean composed entirely of shadows, unreal and mysterious. Into this outer world one gropes with the eyes, peering and straining all the time, seeking to solve its mysteries. Shadows of every shape, some grotesque, some frightening, varying infinitesimally and subtly in depth from the deepest black, through blues and greens to the patchy greys and whiteness of the ground mist. One walks into the unknown; one might be walking on the moon. Shadows are deceptive things. A little copse seems like an impenetrable forest. A field of hay may turn into a discouraging reedy marsh. A stook of corn suddenly takes on a fantastic resemblance to a silent listening man. A sheet-white ghost looms out of the mist. It moves – a stray cow shies off, as frightened as ourselves by the encounter. Stately mansions turn into derelict barns, and a distant hedge becomes a deep cutting with a railway line at the bottom. On this unreal planet one walks with every sense alert to the 'sticking-point.'

We went in single file spaced as far apart as possible, taking turns at leading with a white handkerchief draped over our backs. We would follow the leader, listening for the muttered warnings: 'ware wire, brambles, a ditch, marsh and so on. We often stumbled. We avoided buildings, but even so, in the silence of the night, our progress would be heard by dogs and they would start barking as we hurried off into the shadows. We knew there was no big river in our path but we had to ford several streams, sometimes taking off boots and stockings and wading knee-deep to do so. We stopped to rest occasionally, and had a meal under a haystack at about 1 am.

As dawn approached, we searched for a hiding-place for the day and found one in a grove of trees far away from any buildings. We had done only thirteen miles, and were rather disappointed. We did not sleep much and were anxious to move on. The first part of our next night's march lay across a wide valley. Noting landmarks on our line, we set off a little before nightfall. Our feet were sore and blisters were appearing. Peter had borrowed a pair of suitable-looking boots which, however, did not fit him too well, and he developed enormous blisters on his heels. I had warned him what to expect. He stuck it well.

Later we found ourselves in mountainous country with occasional rushing torrents, waterfalls, and deep gorges, and mostly wooded.

Farms, surrounded by small patches of cultivation cleared out of the woods, were few and far between.

The weather held fine. On our third day of freedom we considered making a start in daylight. By the early afternoon our impatience got the better of us and we set off.

After some steep climbing, we found a sparkling stream where in the clearer pools basked mountain trout.

'Rupert,' I said, 'I can't resist this. My clothes are wringing wet; I'm perspiring like a pig. I'm going to have a bathe.'

I started to undress. Rupert bent over a rock to feel the water.

'Ye gods!' he shouted, withdrawing his hand as if he had been scalded. 'This water comes straight from the North Pole.'

'Just what you need to freshen you up.' I thought of my long walking tours as a student, when I learnt the benefit of bathing my feet frequently in cold water.

'Peter,' I added, 'it'll do your blisters no end of good. I insist we all sit with our feet dangling in a pool for at least ten minutes.'

We all had a lightning dip, while our damp and sweaty clothes lay drying in the sun, and then we dangled our feet until we could not feel them any more. When we set off again, we were walking on air.

The going soon became so difficult that we took to paths and cattle tracks, and for the first time met another human being. Previously we had narrowly escaped being seen by some Hitler youths and girls whom we heard singing and laughing on our path close behind us. The new intruder was a woodman – we passed him with a casual 'Heil Hitler!' He took no notice of us.

Later we came upon a small farm and Peter made so bold as to ask the farmer the way. Although our survey map could hardly have been better, our route was strewn with deep narrow valleys and we became confused as to which one we were in.

As evening drew on we found another gurgling stream and, piling up some stones on its bank, we made a fire. We had hot soup from cubes and roasted some potatoes, which we had collected earlier from a potato patch. It was a heavenly meal. After a good rest and a doze, we pushed on again as night fell.

We tried to maintain our direction on the small mountain paths, but found ourselves more and more frequently consulting our map with the aid of matches. This was an unwelcome necessity, for we did not want a light to give us away, and, even in woods, shielded the matches with our capes. Eventually we found a minor road and embarked on it. Soon it started to wind downhill and in a general direction at right angles to ours. At the same time we became hemmed in with impenetrable-looking forest which we dared not enter. We did not want to go downhill; it was out of our way and, in any case, it is always an advantage when walking across country to keep high up; then, with a map, one's position can be checked by bearings taken on the surrounding country. At the rate we were going we would be in the main Salzburg (Salzach) valley by morning. Even from our map we could not be certain which road we were on. In fact, we were lost.

We decided to wait till dawn and retrace our steps until our position could be checked up. Penetrating about fifty yards into the woods, we lay down to sleep in a leafy hollow. It was bitterly cold and we huddled together for warmth with our scanty coverings spread over all three of us. Our muscles ached and we spent a miserable few hours dozing fitfully. Just before daylight we could stand it no longer and were about to move off when Rupert suddenly declared in a horrified tone:

'The compass is gone, I can't find it!'

There was a long silence as we regarded each other. I broke the awkward spell.

'That's a nice kettle of fish! When do you last remember having it?'

'Miles away! Before we started coming downhill – the last time we lit those matches.'

We stared blankly at each other in the cold dawn, shivering miserably and depressed beyond description.

'Well! let's start searching,' I said. 'Be careful where we've been lying. Start from one end of the hollow and let's work on our hands and knees in line. Feel first for lumps and don't turn over more leaves than you can possibly help.'

We searched, carefully patting the leaves and moss, advancing slowly yard by yard over the whole area of our bivouac.

'I've got it!' said Peter in triumph suddenly, holding it up like a trophy.

We sighed our relief. In this country, without a compass we could not keep a consistent course for five minutes.

After about two hours' walking, as the dawn came up, we were able to locate ourselves and once more set off in the right direction across meadows and along the edges of woods, following a mountain ridge while it ran more or less parallel with our course.

This was our fourth day of freedom and we had had no rain. We met nobody all day. By evening we had reached the main road which heads south-east from Golling to Radstadt and across the mountain hump by way of the Radstädter Tauern pass. From now on it was apparent we should have to follow the road, because the mountains were high and the valley was a gorge. We set off along the road in the cool of the evening. Within ten minutes several people passed us on foot or on bicycles, and a Jerry soldier ambled by with a 'Heil Hitler!' to which we replied with gusto. Although he had not appeared to see anything unusual in our now ragged and dirty clothing, we decided to retire into the woods and continue only after dark. This we did, and during the night we walked fast and with few stops, for the cold was becoming intense.

Our feet were at last becoming hardened. We made good going and by dawn had gone about twenty-four miles. There were two incidents during the night. At about 11 pm a girl on a bicycle caught us up and insisted on talking to us.

'*Guten Abend! wo gehen Sie hin?*' she volunteered, dismounting and walking along beside us.

'Forward hussy, what?' murmured Rupert under his breath.

'Peter, you're a lady-killer,' I whispered; 'go on, do your stuff.'

Peter took over.

'We're going to Abtenau. We've got army leave and are hiking. And where might you be going?'

Peter's German was correct even to the Austrian accent. The girl was pleased.

'I live at Voglau. It's only two miles from here on the main road. You come from Salzburg?'

'No, from Saalfelden,' replied Peter, naming a place as far away from Salzburg as possible.

'I'll walk with you to my house. Father may offer you beer.'

I understood enough to know that the conversation was taking an unhappy turn. I promptly sat down as a grass bank at the edge of the road and, pulling Rupert by his sleeve, said in an undertone, hoping my indifferent German accent would not be noticed, '*Hans! Kommen Sie hier. Ich gehe nicht weiter.*' Rupert took the hint and sat beside me. Peter and the girl were alreayd some yards ahead. I heard her say:

'Your friends do not seem to like me. They will not speak. How rude they are.'

'They are not rude but very tired, *Fräulein*,' put in Peter. 'I am too tired to continue farther without a rest. *Auf Wiedersehen!* You must hurry home, for it is very late and your father will be worried. *Auf Wiedersehen!*'

With that Peter practically sat her on her bicycle and finally got rid of her. She left us a bit disgruntled and probably with some queer impression. I doubt if she suspected us, though she was capable of talking to someone in a village who might. This was an added reason for our making good headway during the night and moving out of the district.

Occasionally a car passed with headlights blazing – no thought of blackout! – which gave us enough warning to take cover. We did not take cover for pedestrians who passed or for cyclists who, in any case, were liable to catch us up, unheard above the roar of a mountain river which the road now followed. We walked together, feeling that if we were accosted there was always one of us who could reply.

Approaching a small village beyond the junction town called Abtenau, we saw several lights and torches flickering. We hastily took to a field. The lights persisted for a long time – about two hours – and garrulous voices could be heard. Finally the episode wound up when a very drunken man passed down the road reeling from side to side, throwing and kicking his bicycle along in front of him. He was shouting and swearing and could be heard a mile away. Loud crashes punctuated his tirade, indicating that the bicycle was the victim of his rage and presumably the cause of it!

The lights were ominous. We continued when all was quiet and shortly afterwards encountered a small house with an army motor-cycle standing outside. Dogs barked as we passed, so we hurried on.

We were about three thousand feet above sea-level. The valley became narrower than ever and it was out of the question to travel other than on the road. In daylight we would be conspicuous walking through the small villages.

We rested during the fifth day (a Monday) on a promontory overlooking the road. Towards late afternoon a cold drizzle began to fall. We became restless and argued about going on. One by one we gave in and agreed to move. With our odd-looking capes and blankets over our shoulders, we trudged uphill along the now muddy road –

passed a sawmill where a few men were working. They stared at us, and later a motor-lorry from the mill caught us up before we had time to take cover. As it passed, a youth leaned out and had a good stare at us.

This was disquieting. I insisted we should disappear again until nightfall. We found a resting-place beside the river among trees about fifteen yards from the road. The rain continued till nightfall and then ceased, leaving us cold, wet, and dispirited. I was nervous after the experience of the sawmill. We drank water copiously before starting. If a man drinks far more than he has the desire for, he can walk for eight hours without feeling unduly thirsty. We continued up the winding valley past straggling villages and small chalets. The night was pitch-dark and there were no stars. We were nearing the top of the pass and were only a few miles from Radstadt, which was the halfway point on our journey to Yugoslavia. We had walked about seventy-five miles.

We entered a small village at about 11.30 pm. It was called Lungötz. All was quiet. Suddenly the light of an electric torch was directed down at us from a window high above. After a few seconds it went out. Very suspicous! But there was nothing we could do about it in the middle of a village. We had been seen, so we had to bluff our way out. Coming to a fork in the road, we hesitated a moment while I peered at the signpost, and then took the left branch. After a couple of hundred yards we left the village behind and the road entered deep woods. We breathed more freely.

The next moment there was a loud crashing of branches and undergrowth. Beams from powerful torches flashed on us and we saw the gleam of rifle barrels. Men shouted '*Halt! Halt! Wer da?*' We stopped, and Peter, a few steps ahead, answered '*Gut Freund.*' Three men jumped down to the road from the banks on either side and approached, with their rifles aimed at us from the hip. At a few yards' distance they began shouting at Peter all together. I could see they were very nervous.

'Who are you? What are you doing in the woods at this hour? Where are you going? Produce your papers!'

'One at a time! One at a time!' shouted Peter. 'What is all this fuss? We are innocent people. We are soldiers on leave and we go to Radstadt.'

'Where are your papers? We do not believe you. Show us yo
papers.'

'We do not carry papers. We are on leave.'

One of them approached Rupert and me and knocked the sti
which we held out of our hands with his rifle, jabbering hysterica
at us. We could not have answered him if we had wanted to.

'So you have no papers. Why are your two companions silent?
think you are spies, enemies of the Reich!'

There was a moment when Rupert and I might have run for i
back down the road, zigzagging – leaving Peter. But the opportun
passed before we had time to pull our wits together. We might h
got away with it if there were no patrols behind us.

Then the men were all shouting, '*Hände hoch! Hände hock!*' and
put up our hands, Peter still protesting we were innocent and anxi
to get on to Radstadt. It was no use. If Peter had been alone he mi
have deceived them, but we two were just so much dead weight
our dumbness or sullenness was the last straw.

We were marched back at bayonet point to a small inn in
village. Several windows in a house opposite were lit up. I recogni
it as the house from which the torchlight had first been flashed at
The owner of the torch had probably been in touch with the amb
party by signal. In the *Gaststube* (dining-room) of the inn, we w
lined against a wall and ordered by one of the three policemen, m
ferocious and nervous than the rest, to keep our arms stretc
upwards. We were then left with two guards until about 1.30
when the third guard returned. We were marched out and put in
back of an open lorry, which I recognized as the one which
passed us, and were driven off down the road along which we
come. It was heartbreaking to see the landmarks we had passed
a few hours before as free men. The two guards sat facing us
their rifles at the ready. Since our capture there had not been
faintest chance of a getaway. The remainder of the night was spe
the police-station at Abtenau, then two hours' drive under ar
guard, and we were back in the German *Kommandantur* at Oflag
C, a depressed and sorry-looking trio.

A German under-officer approached us and we were 'for it'
was the one who checked numbers at *Appells*, and he knew Peter
since Peter had acted as camp interpreter on many occasions
roared at us, forcing us to stand rigidly to attention while he to

clothing. He shook Peter wildly by the shoulders,
o his face. It was a wonderful exhibition. He had
a bad time since our absence was discovered.

ng off his revenge he led us to the German Camp
took us one by one into his office and questioned us.
me.

ss to try to escape. You were warned. Now it is proved.
nate not to have been shot. When did you leave?'

ffference does it make? We know everything. Six of you
ft on Saturday, did you not?'

mann, you are an officer and I understand your point
en the whole matter is closed and finished, surely we
r freely?'

Herr Oberst, I understand. I did not know you had
e more officers.'

ding question. Please remember I am questioning you
are not here to question me. You had money, of

ve you travelled so far in such a short time?'
s of travelling, Herr Oberst.'
ble bicycles?'
ng involved. My 'No' to the question concerning
good answer. I fell back upon 'I cannot reply to

l me the day you escaped, I shall have to assume
cycles. This is a very serious charge.'

ealed your absence at one *Appel*. How did you do

t others did. You see, your absence was known at
aturday. Your escape was made at night. There-
Appell your absence was concealed. You admit it
not?'

. It was, of course, clever of you to hide in the

grass compound. We are building a guard ring of barbed wire two yards from the fences now. You will not be able to repeat your escape. Did you hide near the river or high up?'

'I just concealed myself.'

'But where?'

'I cannot say.'

'I know that soldiers concealed your *Appell*. Unless you tell me their names, I shall be compelled to have them all punished. That is not fair, to punish all for the offence of six. What were their names?'

'I do not know.'

'You know well. If you do not give the names, it will be bad for all. You can save much hardship by a simple answer.'

'I am sorry, Herr Oberst.'

'Well then! You have either stolen bicycles or you have had assistance from outside the camp. For a prisoner to steal a bicycle is punishable with death. If you have received help, you can say so. I shall not ask the names and shall not charge you with theft of German private property. Come now, that is fair.'

'Your answer is so fair, Herr Oberst, that I know you will understand my inability to answer you.'

'You are a fool,' he answered, becoming angry. 'I have given you enough chances. You will suffer for your silence. Do you like concentration camps? Do you like to starve? Do you like to die? I give you one more chance. Your obstinacy is madness – it has no reason. Did you receive any help?'

I did not answer.

'So you insult me. Very well. You will be punished for silent insolence as well. About turn! March!'

I left the room and the others were paraded in turn. The questioning and tactics were the same in each case, as I found out. Rupert and Peter gave nothing away. We had a pretty good idea by now of German bluff, and in our three months' imprisonment we were beginning to learn that even a POW had rights and that a document known as the 'Geneva Convention' existed.

I learnt in time to bless this International Convention for the treatment of Prisoners-of-War and must record here my gratitude to its authors. This product of the League of Nations stands as a testimony to our civilization. Its use in World War II demonstrated the force of that civilization amidst the threat of its ruin.

Our questioning ended, we were marched off to the town jail, which was close by, and each locked in a separate cell. For several days we languished in our dungeons like forgotten men. My cell was empty except for an unused heating stove, a bucket, and a jug of water. Wood floor, stone walls, and a tiny window just below a high ceiling made up my surroundings. There was no bed or bedding. At night the cold was intense, though it was only September.

During the day we walked our rooms or sat on the floor. We tried knocking to each other through the walls, which annoyed the guards, who cursed and threatened us if we continued. This depressing period was no doubt intended to demoralize us, for we were again taken individually and questioned, and when we refused to speak we were informed that we would be held for court martial.

When an officer is recaptured after an escape, the same principle holds good as when he is first taken prisoner – namely, that it is better to say nothing than tell lies. Lies may temporarily deceive the enemy in one direction, but they often lead him to unearth something which was never intended to be discovered. If I had replied to the question 'How did you escape.' by saying we escaped over the roofs, it was quite liable to upset a plan being prepared by other officers in the camp unknown to us.

If to the question 'When did you escape?' I gave a date several days before the actual event, I ran a good risk of being found out in a lie through a chance identification, or I might make the Germans so aghast at the length of my absence that the repercussion on future *Appell* precautions might be disastrous. If I named a date some time after the actual event, I immediately gave the Jerries false ideas as to how far I could travel in a given time and thereby enlarged the circumference of cordons for future escapers. I found also that Jerry quickly lost respect for an enemy who talked. He expects silence. It is in accord with his own rules.

We returned, to a languish in our jail. Every second day we were thrown a slab of brown bread in the morning and given a bowl of soup at midday.

On the fourth day there was a loud commotion and we heard the voices of Dick Howe, Harry Elliott, and Kenneth Lockwood! They were locked in neighbouring cells. Their arrival was further cause for depression.

We soon made complaints about the bucket sanitation and were eventually allowed to use a lavatory at the end of the corridor. Then we complained of lack of exercise and were allowed to walk for half an hour daily in single file at twenty-five paces from each other in a circle in the Oflag courtyard, the other officers being temporarily shut off from the area.

We established communications with the camp and among ourselves. With the aid of pencil butts dropped in the courtyard where we walked, notes were later written on pieces of lavatory paper, and left to be picked up by officers. The first Red Cross parcels had just arrived. We asked for food in our notes and were soon receiving it: chocolate, sugar, Ovo-sport, cheese!

We would enter the courtyard carrying our towels as sweat-rags. After a turn or two we would notice an inconspicuous pile of swept-up dust. This was the food done up in a small round parcel. A towel would be dropped carelessly in the corner over the rubbish and left until the end of the half-hour's exercise. The towel and the parcel would then be recovered in one movement and nonchalantly carried back to the cells to be divided later and left in the lavatory.

Gradually we learnt each other's stories. We found out also that no one else had escaped, and were aghast at this and extremely disappointed. Men could have been escaping every other day or so. We could not understand it.

Dick Howe, Harry Elliott, and Kenneth Lockwood had been recaught about sixty-three miles away, on the road to Switzerland, after eight days of freedom. Their escape worked to plan. Scarlet O'Hara closed up the hole. After two days' march the three of them jumped a goods train near Golling which took them to a place called Saalfelden. Although they gained about four days' march by this, they had to retrace their steps for some two days to regain their correct route. They had some bad going and bad weather, and had to lie up for a day or two in deserted mountain huts. Walking along a river bank close to a village, they were accosted by two women who appeared to suspect them. Harry's German passed. The women were looking for a man who had burgled their house. Farther on they were trapped by a policeman who conducted them to the village to question them concerning the burglary. Only when they were searched did the local bobby realize he had strained at a gnat and had narrowly missed swallowing a camel.

After ten days in the cells we were told that there would not be a court martial after all, but we were to await our sentences. In due course these were meted out, and to our surprise varied considerably. Peter got off with a fortnight, Rupert and I were the longest with a month each, without retroactive effect from our first day in cell. The differences were explained by minor offences, such as carrying a cut-up German blanket or being in possession of a compass or a map and so on. The sentences were 'bread and water and solitary'; that is to say, bread and water only and a board bed for three days out of every four. On the fourth day the prisoner was given a mattress and two meals of thick potato soup or other gruel. As sentences finished we were allowed to live together in one cell; a large one with mattresses, blankets, and German prison ration food. Thus it came to pass, after forty days, that all six of us were together again. We wondered what would happen to us next. We knew that escaped prisoners were usually moved to new camps.

One day a camp padre was allowed to visit us and give us spiritual comfort. We had complained repeatedly that we were not allowed to read books, not even a Bible. Padre Wynne Price Rees gave us the first news as to what had happened to our tunnel.

For some inexplicable reason Scarlet O'Hara and others had postponed using the tunnel, at first for a week and then, upon our recapture, indefinitely. Finally, questions having been asked in the town as to whether any suspicious individuals had been seen between certain dates, a little girl was brought by her mother to the Camp Commandant. She reported having seen one morning, in a woodshed near the camp walls, a man in pyjamas whom she did not recognize as being anyone belonging to the household of the woodshed owner. A stranger in pyjamas in the woodshed of a house in the early morning – wonderful food for gossip in Laufen! This event occurred about three weeks after our escape. Little notice was taken of the child's story by anyone except an elderly *Feldwebel* who had been a POW in England during the First World War and who had helped German officers to build a tunnel. He went 'snooping' in the part of the camp near the woodshed, sounding the walls and floors. Eventually he arrived at the little locked room, where he came upon the hidden piles of earth and finally our tunnel entrance in the darkest corner under a table. It was camouflaged against casual observation by a large piece of painted cardboard made to fit the hole.

We could pride ourselves on the fact that the camouflage of the tunnel exit had held out. I felt a little ashamed that our entrance had not been better finished. My excuse was that I had never meant it to last three weeks and, moreover, we found from later experience that it was difficult under any circumstances to keep an escape-hole concealed for long after prisoners were known to have escaped.

The figure in pyjamas turned out to be Scarlet O'Hara, who was feverishly screwing up the woodshed door-bolt when he looked up to see the face and startled eyes of the little girl peering at him through the slats of the door. She bolted in terror, and Scarlet, equally frightened, disappeared backwards down our rabbit burrows at high speed. Scarlet's face was at no time beautiful, and I am sure the little girl had nightmares for weeks afterwards.

A few days after the padre's visit we were summoned and, to our utter astonishment, sent back to the camp. We became once more normal prisoners-of-war. It was not to be for long. A week later we were given an hour's notice to assemble for departure to an unknown destination.

The six of us had profited by our week to pass on what information and experience we had gained to the others, and we could not understand why the Germans had given us the opportunity. They had no microphones in Laufen, of that we were certain. Before we departed, our Senior British Officer (always known as the SBO) insisted on being told our destination. I believe he also insisted on this information being cabled to the International Red Cross. We packed our meagre belongings and, with a large five-gallon drum filled with cooked potatoes which we took it in turn to carry, two at a time, we set off on foot for the station under heavy guard. Our destination was Oflag IV C, Colditz, Saxony.

Some Were Unlucky

Guy Gibson, VC

We had been flying for about an hour and ten minutes in complete silence, each one busy with his thoughts, while the waves were slopping by a few feet below with monotonous regularity. And the moon dancing in those waves had become almost a hypnotising crystal. As Terry spoke he jerked us into action. He said, 'Five minutes to go to the Dutch coast, skip.'

I said, 'Good,' and looked ahead. Pulford turned on the spotlights and told me to go down much lower; we were about 100 feet off the water. Jim Deering, in the front turret, began to swing it from either way, ready to deal with any flak ships, which might be watching for mine-layers off the coast. Hutch sat in his wireless cabin ready to send a flak warning to the rest of the boys who might run into trouble behind us. Trevor took off his Mae West and squeezed himself back into the rear turret. On either side the boys tucked their blunt-nosed Lancs in even closer than they were before, while the crews inside them were probably doing the same sort of thing as my own. Someone began whistling nervously over the intercom. Someone else said, 'Shut up.'

Then Spam said, 'There's the coast.'

I said, 'No, it's not; that's just low cloud and shadows on the sea from the moon.'

But he was right and I was wrong, and soon we could see the Dutch Islands approaching. They looked low and flat and evil in the full moon, squirting flak in many directions because their radar would now know we were coming. But we knew all about their defences, and as we drew near this squat and unfriendly expanse we began to look for the necessary landmarks which would indicate how to get through that barrage. We began to behave like a ship threading its way through a minefield, in danger of destruction on either side, but safe if we were lucky and on the right track. Terry came up beside me to check up on Spam. He opened the side windows and looked out to scan the coast with his night glasses. 'Can't see much,' he said. 'We're too low, but I reckon we must be on track because there's so little wind.'

'Hope so.'

'Stand by, front gunner; we're going over.'

'OK. All lights off. No talking. Here we go.'

With a roar we hurtled over the Western Wall, skirting the defences and turning this way and that to keep to our thin line of safety; for a moment we held our breath. Then I gave a sigh of relief; no one had fired a shot. We had taken them by surprise.

'Good effort, Terry. Next course.'

'105 degrees magnetic.'

We had not been on the new course for more than two minutes before we came to more sea again; we had obviously just passed over a small island, and this was wrong. Our proper track should have taken us between the two islands, as both were fairly heavily defended, but by the grace of God, the gunners on the one we had just passed over were apparently asleep. We pulled up high to about 300 feet to have a look and find out where we were, then scrammed down on the desk again as Terry said, 'OK – there's the windmill and those wireless masts. We must have drifted to starboard. Steer new course – 095 degrees magnetic, and be careful of a little town that is coming up straight ahead.'

'OK, Terry, I'll go around it.'

We were turning to the left now, and as we turned I noticed with satisfaction that Hoppy and Mickey were still flying there in perfect formation.

We were flying low. We were flying so low that more than once Spam yelled at me to pull up quickly to avoid high-tension wires and tall trees. Away on the right we could see the small town, its chimneys outlined against the night sky; we thought we saw someone flash us a 'V', but it may have been an innkeeper poking his head out of his bedroom window. The noise must have been terrific.

Our new course should have followed a very straight canal, which led to a T-shaped junction, and beyond that was the Dutch frontier and Germany. All eyes began looking out to see if we were right, because we could not afford to be wrong. Sure enough, the canal came up slowly from underneath the starboard wing and we began

to follow it carefully, straight above it, for now we were mighty close
to Eindhoven, which had the reputation of being very well defended.
Then, after a few minutes, that too had passed behind and we saw a
glint of silvery light straight ahead. This was the canal junction, the
second turning point.

It did not take Spam long to see where we were; now we were right
on track, and Terry again gave the new course for the River Rhine.
A few minutes later we crossed the German frontier, and Terry said,
in his matter-of-fact way: 'We'll be at the target in an hour and a
half. The next thing to see is the Rhine.'

But we did not all get through. One aircraft, P/O Rice, had already
hit the sea, bounced up, lost both its outboard engines and its
weapon, and had flown back on the inboard two. Les Munro had
been hit by flak a little later on, and his aircraft was so badly
damaged that he was forced to return to base. I imagined the feelings
of the crews of these aircraft who, after many weeks of intense practice
and expectation, at the last moment could only hobble home and
land with nothing accomplished. I felt very sorry for them. This left
sixteen aircraft going on; 112 men.

The journey into the Ruhr Valley was not without excitement.
They did not like our coming. And they knew we were coming. We
were the only aircraft operating that night; it was too bright for the
main forces. And so, deep down in their underground plotting-rooms,
the Hun controllers stayed awake to watch us as we moved steadily
on. We had a rough idea how they worked, these controllers, moving
fighter squadrons to orbit points in front of us, sounding air-raid
sirens here and there, tipping off the gun positions along our route
and generally trying to make it pretty uncomfortable for the men who
were bound for 'Happy Valley'. As yet they would not know where
we were going, because our route was planned to make feint attacks
and fox their control. Only the warning sirens would have sounded
in all the cities from Bremen southwards. As yet, the fighters would
be unable to get good plots on us because we were flying so low, but
once we were there the job would have to take quite a time, and they
would have their chance.

We flew on. Germany seemed dead. Not a sign of movement, of
light of a moving creature stirred the ground. There was no flak,
there was nothing. Just us.

And so we came to the Rhine. This is virtually the entrance to the

Ruhr Valley; the barrier our armies must cross before they march into the big towns of Essen and Dortmund. It looked white and calm and sinister in the moonlight. But it presented no difficulties to us. As it came up, Spam said, 'We are six miles south. Better turn right, skip. Duisburg is not far away.'

As soon as he mentioned Duisburg my hands acted before my brain, for they were more used to this sort of thing, and the Lanc banked steeply to follow the Rhine up to our crossing point. For Duisburg is not a healthy place to fly over at 100 feet. There are hundreds of guns there, both light and heavy, apart from all those searchlights, and the defences have had plenty of experience . . .

As we flew up – 'How did that happen?'

'Don't know, skip. Compass u/s?'

'Couldn't be.'

'Hold on, I will just check my figures.'

Later – 'I'm afraid I misread my writing, skip. The course I gave you should have been another ten degrees to port.'

'OK, Terry. That might have been an expensive mistake.'

During our steep turn the boys had lost contact, but now they were just beginning to form up again; it was my fault the turn had been too steep, but the name Duisburg or Essen, or any of the rest of them, always does that to me. As we flew along the Rhine there were barges on the river equipped with quick-firing guns and they shot at us as we flew over, but our gunners gave back as good as they got; then we found what we wanted, a sort of small inland harbour, and we turned slowly towards the east. Terry said monotonously, 'Thirty minutes to go and we are there.'

As we passed on into the Ruhr Valley we came to more and more trouble, for now we were in the outer light-flak defences, and these were very active, but by weaving and jinking we were able to escape most of them. Time and again searchlights would pick us up, but we were flying very low and, although it may sound foolish and untrue when I say so, we avoided a great number of them by dodging behind the trees. Once we went over a brand-new aerodrome which was very heavily defended and which had not been marked on our combat charts. Immediately all three of us in front were picked up by the searchlights and held. Suddenly Trevor, in the rear turret, began firing away trying to scare them enough to turn out their lights, then he shouted that they had gone behind some tall trees. At the same time Spam was yelling that he would soon be shaving himself by the tops of some corn in a field. Hutch immediately sent out a flak warning to all the boys behind so that they could avoid this unattractive area. On either side of me, Mickey and Hoppy, who were a little higher, were flying along brightly illuminated; I could see their letters quite clearly, 'TAJ' and 'MAJ', standing out like Broadway signs. Then a long string of tracer came out from Hoppy's rear turret and I lost him in the momentary darkness as the searchlights popped out. One of the pilots, a grand Englishman from Derbyshire, was not so lucky. He was flying well out to the left. He got blinded in the searchlights and, for a second, lost control. His aircraft reared up like a stricken horse, plunged on to the deck and burst into flames; five seconds later his mine blew up with a tremendous explosion. Bill Astell had gone.

The minutes passed slowly as we all sweated on this summer's night, sweated at working the controls and sweated with fear as we flew on. Every railway train, every hamlet and every bridge we passed was a potential danger, for our Lancasters were sitting targets at that height and speed. We fought our way past Dortmund, past Hamm – the well-known Hamm which has been bombed so many times; we could see it quite clearly now, its tall chimneys, factories and balloons capped by its umbrella of flak like a Christmas tree about five miles to our right; then we began turning to the right in between Hamm and the little town of Soest, where I nearly got shot down in 1940. Soest was sleepy now and did not open up, and out of the haze ahead appeared the Ruhr hills.

'We're there,' said Spam.

'Thank God,' said I, feelingly.

As we came over the hill, we saw the Möhne Lake. Then we saw the dam itself. In that light it looked squat and heavy and unconquerable; it looked grey and solid in the moonlight, as though it were part of the countryside itself and just as immovable. A structure like a battleship was showering out flak all along its length, but some came from the power-house below it and nearby. There were no searchlights. It was light flak, mostly green, yellow and red, and the colours of the tracer reflected upon the face of the water in the lake. The reflections on the dead calm of the black water made it seem there was twice as much as there really was.

'Did you say these gunners were out of practice?' asked Spam, sarcastically.

'They certainly seem awake now,' said Terry.

They were awake all right. No matter what people say, the Germans certainly have a good warning system. I scowled to myself as I remembered telling the boys an hour or so ago that they would probably only be the German equivalent of the Home Guard and in bed by the time we arrived.

It was hard to say exactly how many guns there were, but tracers seemed to be coming from about five positions, probably making twelve guns in all. It was hard at first to tell the calibre of the shells, but after one of the boys had been hit, we were informed over the RT that they were either 20-mm type or 37-mm, which, as everyone knows, are nasty little things.

We circled around stealthily, picking up the various landmarks upon which we had planned our method of attack, making use of some and avoiding others; every time we came within range of those bloody-minded flak-gunners they let us have it.

'Bit aggressive, aren't they?' said Trevor.

'Too right they are.'

I said to Terry, 'God, this light flak gives me the creeps.'

'Me, too,' someone answered.

For a time there was a general bind on the subject of light flak, and the only man who didn't say anything was Hutch, because he could not see it and because he never said anything about flak, anyway. But this was not the time for talking. I called up each member of our formation and found, to my relief, that they had all arrived, except, of course, Bill Astell. Away to the south, Joe McCarthy had just begun his diversionary attack on the Sorpe. But not all of them had been able to get there; both Byers and Barlow had been shot down by light flak after crossing the coast; these had been replaced by other aircraft of the rear formation. Bad luck, this being shot down after crossing the coast, because it could have happened to anybody; they must have been a mile or so off track and had got the hammer. This is the way things are in flying; you are either lucky or you aren't. We, too, had crossed the coast at the wrong place and had got away with it. We were lucky.

Down below, the Möhne Lake was silent and black and deep, and I spoke to my crew.

'Well, boys, I suppose we had better start the ball rolling.' This with no enthusiasm whatsoever. 'Hello, all Cooler aircraft. I am going to attack. Stand by to come in to attack in your order when I tell you.'

Then to Hoppy: 'Hello, "M Mother". Stand by to take over if anything happens.'

Hoppy's clear and casual voice came back. 'OK, Leader. Good luck.'

Then the boys dispersed to the pre-arranged hiding-spots in the hills, so that they should not be seen either from the ground or from the air, and we began to get into position for our approach. We circled wide and came around down moon, over the high hills at the eastern end of the lake. On straightening up we began to dive towards the flat, ominous water two miles away. Over the front turret was the dam silhouetted against the haze of the Ruhr Valley. We could see the towers. We could see the sluices. We could see everything. Spam, the bomb-aimer, said 'Good show. This is wizard.' He had been a bit worried, as all bomb-aimers are, in case they cannot see their aiming points, but as we came in over the tall fir trees his voice came up again rather quickly. 'You're going to hit them. You're going to hit those trees.'

'That's all right, Spam. I'm just getting my height.'

To Terry: 'Check height, Terry.'

To Pulford: 'Speed control, Flight-Engineer.'

To Trevor: 'All guns ready, gunners.'

To Spam: 'Coming up, Spam.'

Terry turned on the spotlights and began giving directions – 'Down – down – down. Steady – steady.' We were then exactly sixty feet.

Pulford began working the speed; first he put on a little flap to slow us down, then he opened the throttles to get the air-speed indicator exactly against the red mark. Spam began lining up his sights against the towers. He had turned the fusing switch to the 'ON' position. I began flying.

The gunners had seen us coming. They could see us coming with our spotlights on for over two miles away. Now they opened up and the tracers began swirling towards us; some were even bouncing off the smooth surface of the lake. This was a horrible moment: we were being dragged along at four miles in a minute, almost against our will, towards the things we were going to destroy. I think at that moment the boys did not want to go. I know I did not want to go. I thought to myself, 'In another minute we shall all be dead – so what?' I thought again, 'This is terrible – this feeling of fear – if it is fear.' By now we were a few hundred yards away, and I said quickly to Pulford, under my breath, 'Better leave the throttles open now and stand by to pull me out of the seat if I get hit.' As I glanced at him I thought he looked a little glum on hearing this.

The Lancaster was really moving and I began looking through the special sight on my windscreen. Spam had his eyes glued to the bombsight in front, his hand on his button; a special mechanism on board had already begun to work so that the mine would drop (we hoped) in the right spot. Terry was still checking the height. Joe and Trev began to raise their guns. The flak could see us quite clearly now. It was not exactly inferno. I have been through far worse flak fire than that; but we were very low. There was something sinister and slightly unnerving about the whole operation. My aircraft was so small and the dam was so large; it was thick and solid, and now it was angry. My aircraft was very small. We skimmed along the surface of the lake, and as we went my gunner was firing into the defences, and the defences were firing back with vigour, their shells whistling past us. For some reason, we were not being hit.

Spam said, 'Left – little more left – steady – steady – coming up.' Of the next few seconds I remember only a series of kaleidoscopic incidents.

The chatter from Joe's front guns pushing out tracers which bounced off the left-hand flak tower.

Pulford crouching beside me.

The smell of burnt cordite.

The cold sweat underneath my oxygen mask.

The tracers flashing past the windows – they all seemed the same colour now – and the inaccuracy of the gun positions near the power-station; they were firing in the wrong direction.

The closeness of the dam wall.

Spam's exultant, 'Mine gone.'

Hutch's red Very lights to blind the flak-gunners.

The speed of the whole thing.

Someone saying over the RT, 'Good show, leader. Nice work.'

Then it was all over, and at last we were out of range, and there came over us all, I think, an immense feeling of relief and confidence.

Trevor said, 'I will get those bastards,' and he began to spray the dam with bullets until at last he, too, was out of range. As we circled round we could see a great, 1,000–feet column of whiteness still hanging in the air where our mine had exploded. We could see with satisfaction that Spam had been good, and it had gone off in the right position. Then, as we came closer, we could see that the explosion of the mine had caused a great disturbance upon the surface of the lake and the water had become broken and furious, as though it were being lashed by a gale. At first we thought that the dam itself had broken, because great sheets of water were slopping over the top of the wall like a gigantic basin. This caused some delay, because our mines could only be dropped in calm water, and we would have to wait until all became still again.

We waited.

We waited about ten minutes, but it seemed hours to us. It must have seemed even longer to Hoppy, who was the next to attack. Meanwhile, all the fighters had now collected over our target. They knew our game by now, but we were flying too low for them; they could not see us and there were no attacks.

'At last – 'Hello, "M Mother". You may attack now. Good luck.'

'OK. Attacking.'

Hoppy, the Englishman, casual, but very efficient, keen now on only one thing, which was war. He began his attack.

He began going down over the trees where I had come from a few moments before. We could see his spotlights quite clearly, slowly closing together as he ran across the water. We saw him approach. The flak, by now, had got an idea from which direction the attack was coming, and they let him have it. When he was about 100 yards away someone said, hoarsely, over the RT: 'Hell! he has been hit.'

'M Mother' was on fire; an unlucky shot had got him in one of the inboard petrol tanks and a long jet of flame was beginning to stream out. I saw him drop his mine, but his bomb-aimer must have been wounded, because it fell straight on to the power-house on the other side of the dam. But Hoppy staggered on, trying to gain altitude so that his crew could bale out. When he had got up to 500 feet there was a vivid flash in the sky and one wing fell off; his aircraft disintegrated and fell to the ground in cascading, flaming fragments. There it began to burn quite gently and rather sinisterly in a field some three miles beyond the dam.

Someone said, 'Poor old Hoppy!'

Another said, 'We'll get those bastards for this.'

A furious rage surged up inside my own crew, and Trevor said, 'Let's go in and murder those gunners.' As he spoke, Hoppy's mine went up. It went up behind the power-house with a tremendous yellow explosion and left in the air a great ball of black smoke; again there was a long wait while we watched for this to clear. There was so little wind that it took a long time.

Many minutes later I told Mickey to attack; he seemed quite confident, and we ran in beside him and a little in front; as we turned, Trevor did his best to get those gunners as he promised.

Bob Hay, Mickey's bomb-aimer, did a good job, and his mine dropped in exactly the right place. There was again a gigantic explosion as the whole surface of the lake shook, then spewed forth its cascade of white water. Mickey was all right; he got through. But he had been hit several times and one wing-tank lost all its petrol. I could see the vicious tracer from his rear-gunner giving one gun position a hail of bullets as he swept over. Then he called up, 'OK. Attack completed.' It was then that I thought that the dam wall had moved. Of course we could not see anything, but if Jeff's theory had been correct, it should have cracked by now. If only we could go on pushing it by dropping more successful mines, it would surely move back on its axis and collapse.

Once again we watched for the water to calm down. Then in came Melvyn Young in 'D Dog'. I yelled to him, 'Be careful of the flak. It's pretty hot.'

He said, 'OK.'

I yelled again, 'Trevor's going to beat them up on the other side. He'll take most of it off you.'

Melvyn's voice again. 'OK. Thanks.' And so as 'D Dog' ran in we stayed at a fairly safe distance on the other side, firing with all guns at the defences, and the defences, like the stooges they were, firing back at us. We were both out of range of each other, but the ruse seemed to work, and we flicked on our identification lights to let them see us even more clearly. Melvyn's mine went in, again in exactly the right spot, and this time a colossal wall of water swept right over the dam and kept on going. Melvyn said, 'I think I've done it. I've broken it.' But we were in a better position to see than he, and it had not rolled down yet. We were all getting pretty excited by now, and I screamed like a schoolboy over the RT: 'Wizard show, Melvyn. I think it'll go on the next one.'

Now we had been over the Möhne for quite a long time, and all the while I had been in contact with Scampton Base. We were in close contact with the Air Officer Commanding and the Commander-in-Chief of Bomber Command, and with the scientist, observing his own greatest scientific experiment in Damology. He was sitting in the operations room, his head in his hands, listening to the reports as one after another the aircraft attacked. On the other side of the room the Commander-in-Chief paced up and down. In a way their job of waiting was worse than mine. The only difference was that they did not know that the structure was shifting as I knew, even though I could not see anything clearly.

When at last the water had all subsided I called up No. 5 – David Maltby – and told him to attack. He came in fast, and I saw his mine fall within feet of the right spot; once again the flak, the explosion and wall of water. But this time we were on the wrong side of the wall and could see what had happened. We watched for about five minutes, and it was rather hard to see anything, for by now the air was full of spray from these explosions, which had settled like mist on our windscreens. Time was getting short, so I called up Dave Shannon and told him to come in.

As I turned I got close to the dam wall and then saw what had happened. It had rolled over, but I could not believe my eyes. I heard someone shout, 'I think she has gone! I think she has gone!' Other voices took up the cry and quickly I said, 'Stand by until I make a recco.' I remembered that Dave was going in to attack and told him to turn away and not to approach the target. We had a closer look. Now there was no doubt about it; there was a great breach 100 yards across, and the water, looking like stirred porridge in the moonlight, was gushing out and rolling into the Ruhr Valley towards the industrial centres of Germany's Third Reich.

Nearly all the flak had now stopped, and the other boys came down from the hills to have a closer look to see what had been done. There was no doubt about it at all – the Möhne Dam had been breached and the gunners on top of the dam, except for one man, had all run for their lives towards the safety of solid ground; this remaining gunner was a brave man, but one of the boys quickly extinguished his flak with a burst of well-aimed tracer. Now it was all quiet, except for the roar of the water which steamed and hissed its way from its 150–foot head. Then we began to shout and scream and act like madmen over the RT, for this was a tremendous sight, a sight which probably no man will ever see again.

Quickly I told Hutch to tap out the message, 'Nigger', to my station, and when this was handed to the Air Officer Commanding there was (I heard afterwards) great excitement in the operations room. The scientist jumped up and danced round the room.

Then I looked again at the dam and at the water, while all around me the boys were doing the same. It was the most amazing sight. The whole valley was beginning to fill with fog from the steam of the gushing water, and down in the foggy valley we saw cars speeding along the roads in front of this great wave of water, which was chasing them and going faster than they could ever hope to go. I saw their headlights burning and I saw water overtake them, wave by wave, and then the colour of the headlights under the water changing from light blue to green, from green to dark purple, until there was no longer anything except the water bouncing down in great waves. The floods raced on, carrying with them as they went – viaducts, railways, bridges and everything that stood in their path. Three miles beyond the dam the remains of Hoppy's aircraft was still burning gently, a dull red glow on the ground. Hoppy had been avenged.

Then I felt a little remote and unreal sitting up there in the warm cockpit of my Lancaster, watching this mighty power which we had unleashed; then glad, because I knew that this was the heart of Germany, and the heart of her industries, the place which itself had unleashed so much misery upon the whole world.

We knew, as we watched, that this flood-water would not win the war; it would not do anything like that, but it was a catastrophe for Germany.

I circled round for about three minutes, then called up all aircraft and told Mickey and David Maltby to go home and the rest to follow me to Eder, where we would try to repeat the performance.

We set our course from the southern tip of the Möhne Lake, which was already fast emptying itself – we could see that even now – and flew on in the clear light of the early morning towards the south-east. We flew on over little towns tucked away in the valleys underneath the Ruhr Mountains. Little places, these, the Exeters and Baths of

Germany; they seemed quiet and undisturbed and picturesque as they lay sleeping there on the morning of May 17. The thought crossed my mind of the amazing mentality of German airmen, who went out of their way to bomb such defenceless districts. At the same time a bomb or two on board would not have been out of place to wake them up as a reprisal.

At the Sorpe Dam, Joe McCarthy and Joe Brown had already finished their work. They had both made twelve dummy runs and had dropped their mines along the lip of the concrete wall in the right spot. But they had not been able to see anything spectacular, for these earthen dams are difficult nuts to crack and would require a lot of explosive to shirt them. It looked as if we would not have enough aircraft to finish that job successfully because of our losses on the way in. However, the Sorpe was not a priority target, and only contributed a small amount of water to the Ruhr Valley Catchment Area.

After flying low across the treetops, up and down the valleys, we at last reached the Eder Lake and, by flying down it for some five minutes, we arrived over the Eder Dam. It took some finding because fog was already beginning to form in the valleys, and it was pretty hard to tell one part of the reservoir filled with water, from another valley filled with fog. We circled up for a few minutes waiting for Henry, Dave and Les to catch up; we had lost them on the way. Then I called up on the RT.

'Hello, Cooler aircraft – can you see the target?'

Dave answered faintly, 'I think I'm in the vicinity. I can't see anything. I cannot find the dam.'

'Stand by – I will fire a red Very light – right over the dam.' No sooner had Hutch fired his Very pistol than Dave called up again. 'OK – I was a bit south. I'm coming up.'

The other boys had seen the signal too, and after a few minutes we rendezvous'd in a left-hand orbit over the target. But time was getting short now; the glow in the north had begun to get brighter, heralding the coming dawn. Soon it would be daylight, and we did not want this in our ill-armed and unarmoured Lancasters.

I said, 'OK, Dave. You begin your attack.'

It was very hilly all round. The dam was situated, beautifully, I thought, in a deep valley with high hills all around densely covered with fir trees. At the far end, overlooking it, was rather a fine Gothic castle with magnificent grounds. In order to make a successful approach our aircraft would have to dive steeply over this castle, dropping down on to the water from 1,000 feet to 60 feet – level out – let go the mine – then do a steep climbing turn to starboard to avoid a rocky mountain about a mile on the other side of the dam. It was much more inaccessible than the Möhne Valley and called for a much higher degree of skill in flying. There did not seem to be any defences, though, probably because it was an out-of-the-way spot and the gunners would not have got the warning. Maybe they had just been warned and were now getting out of their beds in the nearby village before cycling up the steep hill to get to their gun emplacements. Dave circled wide and then turned to go in. He dived down rather too steeply and sparks came from his engine, as he had to pull out at full boost to avoid hitting the mountain on the north side. As he was doing so . . .

'Sorry, leader. I made a mess of that. I'll try again.'

He tried again. He tried five times, but each time he was not satisfied and would not allow his bomb-aimer to drop his mine. He spoke again on the RT 'I think I had better circle round a bit and try and get used to this place.'

'OK, Dave. You hang around for a bit, and I'll get another aircraft to have a crack – Hello, "Z Zebra"' (this was Henry). 'You can go in now.'

Henry made two attempts. He said he found it very difficult, and gave the other boys some advice on the best way to go about it. Then he called up and told us that he was going in to make his final run. We could see him running in. Suddenly he pulled away; something seemed to be wrong, but he turned quickly, climbed up over the mountain and put his nose right down, literally flinging his machine into the valley. This time he was running straight and true for the middle of the wall. We saw his spotlights together, so he must have been at 60 feet. We saw the red ball of his Very light shooting out behind his tail, and we knew he had dropped his weapon. A split second later we saw something else; Henry Maudsley had dropped his mine too late. It had hit the top of the parapet and had exploded immediately on impact with a slow, yellow, vivid flame which lit up the whole valley like daylight for just a few seconds. We could see him quite clearly banking steeply a few feet above it. Perhaps the blast was doing that. It all seemed so sudden and vicious and the flame seemed so very cruel. Someone said, 'He has blown himself up.'

Trevor said, 'Bomb-aimer must have been wounded.'

It looked as though Henry had been unlucky enough to do the thing we all might have done.

I spoke to him quickly, 'Henry – Henry. "Z Zebra" – "Z Zebra". Are you OK?' No answer. I called again. Then we all thought we heard a very faint, tired voice say, 'I think so – stand by'. It seemed as though he was dazed, and his voice did not sound natural. But Henry had disappeared. There was no burning wreckage on the ground; there was no aircraft on fire in the air. There was nothing. Henry had disappeared. He never came back.

Once more the smoke from his explosion filled the valley, and we all had to wait for a few minutes. The glow in the north was much brighter, and we would have to hurry up if we wanted to get back.

We waited patiently for it to clear away.

At last to Dave – 'OK. Attack now, David. Good luck.'

Dave went in and, after a good dummy run, managed to put his mine up against the wall, more or less in the middle. He turned on his landing light as he pulled away and we saw the spot of light climbing steeply over the mountain as he jerked his great Lancaster almost vertically over the top. Behind me there was that explosion which, by now, we had got used to, but the wall of the Eder Dam did not move.

Meanwhile, Les Knight had been circling very patiently, not saying a word. I told him to get ready, and when the water had calmed down he began his attack. Les, the Australian, had some difficulty too, and after a while Dave began to give him some advice on how to do it. We all joined in on the RT, and there was a continuous back-chat going on.

'Come on, Les. Come in down the moon; dive towards the point and then turn left.'

'OK, Digger. It's pretty difficult.'

'Not that way, Dig. This way.'

'Too right it's difficult. I'm climbing up to have another crack.'

After a while I called up rather impatiently and told them that a joke was a joke and that we would have to be getting back. Then Les dived in to make his final attack. His was the last weapon left in the squadron. If he did not succeed in breaching the Eder now, then it would never be breached; at least, not tonight.

I saw him run in. I crossed my fingers. But Les was a good pilot and he made as perfect a run as any seen that night. We were flying above him, and about 400 yards to the right, and saw his mine hit the water. We saw where it sank. We saw the tremendous earthquake which shook the base of the dam, and then, as if a gigantic hand had punched a hole through cardboard, the whole thing collapsed. A great mass of water began running down the valley into Kassel. Les was very excited. He kept his radio transmitter on by mistake for quite some time. His crew's remarks were something to be heard, but they couldn't be put into print here. Dave was very excited and said, 'Good show, Dig!' I called them up and told them to go home immediately. I would meet them in the Mess afterwards for the biggest party of all time.

The valley below the Eder was steeper than the Ruhr, and we followed the water down for some way. We watched it swirling and slopping in a 30–foot wall as it tore round the steep bends of the countryside. We saw it crash down in six great waves, swiping off power-stations and roads as it went. We saw it extinguish all the lights in the neighbourhood as though a great black shadow had been drawn across the earth. It all reminded us of a vast moving train. But we knew that a few miles farther on lay some of the Lutfwaffe's largest training bases. We knew that it was a modern field with every convenience, including underground hangars and underground sleeping quarters . . . We turned for home.

Dave and Les, still jabbering at each other on RT, had by now turned for home as well. Their voices died away in the distance as we set our course for the Möhne Lake to see how far it was empty. Hutch sent out a signal to Base using the code word, 'Dinghy', telling them the good news – and they asked us if we had anymore aircraft availabe to prang the third target. 'No, none,' I said. 'None,' tapped Hutch.

Now we were out of RT range of our base and were relying on WT for communication. Gradually, by code words, we were told of the movements of the other aircraft. Peter Townsend and Anderson of the rear formation had been sent out to make one attack against the

Sorpe. We heard Peter say that he had been successful, but heard nothing from Anderson.

'Let's tell Base we're coming home, and tell them to lay on a party,' suggested Spam.

We told them we were coming home.

We had reached the Möhne by now and circled twice. We looked at the level of the lake. Already bridges were beginning to stick up out of the lowering water. Already mudbanks with pleasure-boats sitting on their sides could be seen. Below the dam the torpedo nets had been washed to one side of the valley. The power-station had disappeared. The map had completely changed as a new silver lake had formed, a lake of no strict dimensions; a lake slowly moving down towards the west.

Base would probably be panicking a bit, so Hutch sent out another message telling them that there was no doubt about it. Then we took one final look at what we had done and afterwards turned north to the Zuider Zee.

Trevor asked a question – Trevor, who had fired nearly 12,000 rounds of ammunition in the past two hours. 'I am almost out of ammo,' he called, 'but I have got one or two incendiaries back here. Would you mind if Spam tells me when a village is coming up, so that I can drop one out? It might pay for Hoppy, Henry and Bill.'

I answered, 'Go ahead.'

We flew north in the silence of the morning, hugging the ground and wanting to get home. It was quite light now, and we could see things that we could not see on the way in – cattle in the fields, chickens getting airborne as we rushed over them. On the left someone flew over Hamm at 500 feet. He got the chop. No one knew who it was. Spam said he thought it was a German night-fighter which had been chasing us.

I suppose they were all after us. Now that we were being plotted on our retreat to the coast, the enemy fighter controllers would be working overtime. I could imagine the Führer himself giving orders to 'stop those air pirates at all costs'. After all, we had done something which no one else had ever done. Water when released can be one of the most powerful things in the world – similar to an earthquake – and the Ruhr Valley had never had an earthquake.

Someone on board pointed out that Duisburg had been pranged the night before and that our water might put the fires out there.

Someone else said – rather callously, I thought – 'If you can't burn 'em, drown 'em.' But we had not tried to do this; we had merely destroyed a legitimate industrial objective so as to hinder the Ruhr Valley output of war munitions. The fact that people were in the way was incidental. The fact that they might drown had not occurred to us. But we hoped that the dam wardens would warn those living below in time, even if they were Germans. No one likes mass slaughter, and we did not like being the authors of it. Besides, it brought us in line with Himmler and his boys.

Terry looked up from his chart-board. 'About an hour to the coast,' he said.

I turned to Pulford. 'Put her into maximum cruising. Don't worry about petrol consumption.' Then to Terry – 'I think we had better go the shortest way home, crossing the coast at Edmond – you know the gap there. We're the last one, and they'll probably try to get us if we lag behind.'

Terry smiled and watched the air-speed needle creep round. We were now doing a smooth 240 indicated, and the exhaust stubs glowed red hot with the power she was throwing out. Trevor's warning light came on the panel, then his voice – 'Unidentified enemy aircraft behind.'

'OK. I'll sink to the west – it's dark there.'

As we turned – 'OK. You've lost it.'

'Right. On course. Terry, we'd better fly really low.'

These fighters meant business, but they were hampered by the conditions of light during the early morning. We could see them before they saw us.

Down went the Lanc until we were a few feet off the ground, for this was the only way to survive. And we wanted to survive. Two hours before we had wanted to burst dams. Now we wanted to get home – quickly. Then we could have a party.

Some minutes later Terry spoke. 'Thirty minutes to the coast.'

'OK. More revs.'

The needle crept round. It got very noisy inside.

We were flying home – we knew that. We did not know whether we were safe. We did not know how the other boys had got on. Bill, Hoppy, Henry, Barlow, Byers and Ottley had all gone. They had all got the hammer. The light flak had given it to most of them, as it always will to low-flying aircraft – that is, the unlucky ones. They had all gone quickly, except perhaps for Henry. Henry, the born leader. A great loss, but he gave his life for a cause for which men should be proud. Boys like Henry are the cream of our youth. They die bravely and they die young.

And Burpee, the Canadian? His English wife about to have a baby. His father who kept a large store in Ottawa. He was not coming back because they had got him, too. They had got him somewhere between Hamm and the target. Burpee, slow of speech and slow of movement, but a good pilot. He was Terry's countryman and so were his crew. I like their ways and manners, their free-and-easy outlook, their openness. I was going to miss them a lot – even when they chewed gum.

I called up Melvyn on the RT. He had been with me all the way round as deputy-leader when Mickey had gone home with his leaking petrol tank. He was quite all right at the Eder. Now there was no reply. We wondered what had happened.

Terry said, 'Fifteen minutes to go.'

Fifteen minutes. Quite a way yet. A long way, and we might not make it. We were in the black territory. They had closed the gates of their fortress and were locked inside; but we knew the gap – the gap by those wireless masts at Edmond. If we could find that, we should get through safely.

Back at the base they would be waiting for us. We did not know that when they received the code word 'Dinghy' there was a scene in the operations room such as the WAAF Ops Clerks had never seen before. The Air Officer Commanding had jumped up and had shaken Jeff by the hand, almost embracing him. The Commander-in-Chief had picked up the phone and asked for Washington. At Washington another US-Great Britain conference was in progress. Sir Charles Portal, the CAS, was giving a dinner-party. He was called away to the telephone. Back at Scampton the C.-in-C. yelled, 'Downwood successful – yes'. At Washington, CAS was having difficulty in hearing. At last members of the dinner-party heard him say quietly, 'Good show'. From then on the dinner-party was a roaring success.

We did not know anything about the fuss, the Press, the publicity which would go round the world after this effort. Or of the honours to be given to the squadron or of trips to America and Canada, or of visits by important people. We did not care about anything like that. We only wanted to get home.

We did not know that we had started something new in the history of aviation, that our squadron was to become a byword throughout the RAF as a precision-bombing unit – a unit which could pick off anything from viaducts to gun emplacements, from low level or high level, by day or by night. A squadron consisting of crack crews using all the latest new equipment and the largest bombs, even earthquake bombs. A squadron flying new aeroplanes, and flying them as well as any in the world.

Terry was saying, 'Rotterdam's 20 miles on the port bow. We will be getting to the gap in five minutes.' Now they could see where we were going, the fighters would be streaking across Holland to close that gap. Then they could hack us down.

I called up Melvyn, but he never answered. I was not to know that Melvyn had crashed into the sea a few miles in front of me. He had come all the way from California to fight this war and had survived sixty trips at home and in the Middle East, including a double ditching. Now he had ditched for the last time. Melvyn had been responsible for a good deal of the training that made their raid possible. He had endeared himself to the boys, and now he had gone.

Of the sixteen aircraft which had crossed the coast to carry out this mission, eight had been shot down, including both Flight Commanders. Only two men escaped to become prisoners of war. Only two out of fifty-six, for there is not much chance at 50 feet.

They had gone. Had it been worth it? Or were their lives just thrown away on a spectacular mission? Militarily, it was cheap at the price. The damage done to the German war effort was substantial. But there is another side to the question. We would soon begin our fifth year of war – a war in which the casualties had been lighter than the last; nevertheless, in Bomber Command there have been some heavy losses. These fifty-five boys who had lost their lives were some of many. The scythe of war, and a very bloody one at that, had reaped a good harvest in Bomber Command. As we flew on over the low fields of Holland, past dykes and ditches, we could not help thinking, 'Why must we make war every twenty-five years? Why must men fight? How can we stop it? Can we make countries live normal lives in a peaceful way?' But no one knows the answer to that one.

The answer may lie in being strong. A powerful, strategic bomber force based so that it would control the vital waterways of the world,

could prevent and strangle the aggressor from the word 'Go'. But it
rests with the people themselves; for it is the people who forget. After
many years they will probably slip and ask for disarmament so that
they can do away with taxes and raise their standards of living. If the
people forget, they bring wars on themselves, and they can blame no
one but themselves.

Yes, the decent people of this world would have to remember war.
Movies and radio records should remind this and the future generations of what happened between 1936 and 1942. It should be possible
to keep this danger in everyone's mind so that we can never be caught
on the wrong foot again. So that our children will have a chance to
live. After all, that is why we are born. We aren't born to die.

But we ourselves must learn. We must learn to know and respect
our great Allies who have made the chance of victory possible. We
must learn to understand them, their ways and their customs. We
British are apt to consider ourselves the yardstick upon which
everything else should be based. We must not delude ourselves. We
have plenty to learn.

We must learn about politics. We must vote for the right things,
and not necessarily the traditional things. We want to see our country
remain as great as it is today – for ever. It all depends on the people,
their common-sense and their memory.

Can we hope for this? Can all this be done? Can we be certain that
we can find the answer to a peaceful world for generations to come?

'North Sea ahead, boys,' said Spam.

There it was. Beyond the gap, in the distance, lay the calm and
silvery sea, and freedom. It looked beautiful to us then – perhaps the
most wonderful thing in the world.

We climbed up a little to about 300 feet.

Then – 'Full revs and boost, Pulford.'

As he opened her right up, I shoved the nose down to get up extra
speed and we sat down on the deck at about 260 indicated.

'Keep to the left of this little lake,' said Terry, map in hand.

This was flying.

'Now over this railway bridge.'

More speed.

'Along this canal . . .' We flew along that canal as low as we had
flown that day. Our belly nearly scraped the water, our wings would
have knocked horses off the towpath.

'See those radio masts?'

'Yeah.'

'About 200 yards to the right.'

'OK.'

The sea came closer. It came closer quickly as we tore towards it. There was a sudden tenseness on board.

'Keep going; you're OK now.'

'Right. Stand by, front gunner.'

'Guns ready.'

Then we came to the Western Wall. We whistled over the anti-tank ditches and beach obstacles. We saw the yellow sand-dunes slide below us silently, yellow in the pale morning.

Then we were over the sea with the rollers breaking on the beaches and the moon casting its long reflections straight in front of us – and there was England.

We were free. We had got through the gap. It was a wonderful feeling of relief and safety. Now for the party.

'Nice work,' said Trevor from the back.

'Course home?' I asked.

Behind us lay the Dutch coast, squat, desolate and bleak, still squirting flak in many directions.

We would be coming back.

Nella Last's War

Nella Last

Friday night, 2 May, 1941

What with one thing and another, I've had a busy day, and it's a while since I've had such a thrill over anything like I have over my new chicks! I have been on the run all day with little saucers of food – brown bread-crumbs and hard-boiled eggs is their favourite, although they love cornflakes, and this week I'm giving them my packet from the grocer's.

Miss Mac's housekeeper called with some socks, and she says she fears for Miss Mac's reason if the war keeps on. Poor old soul, she is sixty-five and has so coddled Miss Mac all her life. Now, at forty-seven, Miss Mac is like a frightened child. Then she is ill, too, poor thing, and will *not* do as the doctor says and try to find outside interests to help her forget the war.

The garden is wakening rapidly, and I can see signs of blossom buds on my three little apple-trees. I put a lot of water round the roots as last year, in the drought, the blossom withered without setting. I'm keeping my rockery plants alive with constant watering for the sake of the bees, since I want them to come constantly now there are signs of blossom. A blackbird seems to be building nearby – she has been busy with straw all day today – and now the old tree at the bottom of the next-door garden shows buds against the blue sky.

My husband had a night off from work and said he really must get another row of peas and potatoes in, so I got some mending and ironing done, and two pierrot dolls cut out ready for machining up. The moon swam slim serene among the one-way pointing, silvered barrage balloons – I thought it dreadful when I once saw a Zeppelin against the moon. As I stood gazing up at the sky, I wondered if she had ever looked on so strange a sky occupant before. It was like a drawing illustration for one of Wells' books. I do so dread these next few nights till the full moon. Tonight, with a slim crescent, it was clear and bright. Some poor city will suffer.

Saturday, 3 May, 1941

Another disturbed night. The guns and bombs were so bad on Merseyside that our windows and doors rattled! I called in at the grocer's to see if any marmalade had come in. I prefer it to jam for my ration, and was so lucky – I got a tin of casserole steak, and I'll put it carefully by on a shelf. I could do a lot with it if I had to.

Sunday, 4 May, 1941

A night of terror, and there are few windows left in the district – or roof tiles! Land mines, incendiaries and explosives were dropped, and we cowered thankfully under our indoor shelter. I've been so dreadfully sick all day, and I'm sure it's sheer fright, for last night I really thought our end had come. By the time the boys come, I'll be able to laugh about it. Now I've a sick shadow over me as I look at my loved little house that will never be the same again. The windows are nearly all out, and metal frames strained, the ceilings down, the walls cracked and the garage roof showing four inches of daylight where it joins the wall. Doors are splintered and off – and there is the *dirt* from the blast that swept down the chimney. The house rocked, and then the kitchenette door careered down the hall and plaster showered on to the shelter. I'll never forget my odd sensations, one a calm acceptance of 'the end', the other a feeling of regret that I'd not opened a tin of fruit salad for tea – and now it was too late!

I'm so very frugal nowadays, and I look at a tin of fruit longingly sometimes, now that fruit is so scarce – but I put it back on the shelf, for I think we may need it more later. Looking back, I think the regret about the fruit salad was stronger than fear of all being over. Odd how things come back to one – we have been nearly five years in this house, and just after we had moved I went to Blackpool, where Arthur was in the Tax Office there. A gay party of us went into Olympia Fun City, and all the women went to have their fortunes told by a gypsy there called Madame Curl. I can recall every detail – and how she upset me and made me vow that I'd never go again, even in fun. She said, 'You have moved into a new house, but you will not end your days in it,' and went on to say that something would happen, and both the boys would leave home – the second in

a way that I would not expect – and then I'd be a widow and would
remarry a widower who looked in my direction often! The boys have
gone – Cliff in a very unexpected way; and my poor pretty house I
fear will not stand up to much more.

I've worked and worked, clearing glass and plaster and broken
china – all my loved old china plates from the oak panelling in the
hall. With no sleep at all last night, and little on Friday night, I've
no tiredness at all, no dread of the night, no regrets, just a feeling of
numbness. All the day, the tinkle of glass being swept up and dumped
in ash-bins has sounded like wind-bells in a temple, together with the
knock-knock as anything handy was tacked in place over gaping
windows. We have brought the good spring-bed down into the dining-
room, both for comfort and safety. My chicks are safe, and my cat,
who fled terrified as a splintered door crashed, has come home. The
sun shines brightly, although it's after tea and there is no sign of
kindly clouds to hide the rising moon.

All neighbours who have cars, and friends in the country, have fled
– a woman opposite brought her key and said, 'Keep an eye on things
please.' I said, '*No*, you must do it yourself. You have no right to
expect me or anyone else to do it for you. You are strong and well
and have no children to think of. I'd not put out an incendiary if I
saw it strike your house – unless I thought the flame would be a
danger to others.' I think I'm a little mad today. I'd never have
spoken so plainly until now. The damage to houses is very widespread
– and all round, there's the circle of hovering balloons. It's not saved
the Yard, though, for two shops have been destroyed – one, the
pattern shop, burned like a torch with its wood-fed flames.

The birds sang so sweetly at dawning today – just as the all-clear
sounded and people timidly went round looking at the damage. I
wonder if they will sing as sweetly in the morning – and if we all will
hear them. Little sparrows had died as they crouched – from blast
possibly. It looked as if they had bent their little heads in prayer, and
had died as they did so. I held one in my hand: 'He counteth the
sparrow and not one falleth that He does not see' – Poles, Czechs,
Greeks, all sparrows. There are a number of people round here killed,
and houses flat; and a dog whose master was killed, and whose
mistress was frantic with fear and grief, ran over half a mile, climbed
fourteen steps and crawled under a bed – and both its back legs were
broken, and it had internal injuries. A lady saw it and called a vet,

who gave it an injection and slept it away: it looked up gratefully and then rolled over.

It's funny how sick one can be, and not able to eat – just through fright and fear. I keep wondering and wondering how many killed and injured there are. It's only a little town, and does not need a big blitz to wipe it out. I'm glad Cliff did not come on leave. He will grieve when he sees all the ceilings and gapes in the skirtings, and the tiles in the bathroom; but we have a roof and a light, and have a lot to be thankful for. Our newspapers did not come till 3.30; there must have been a bomb on the line somewhere. Only Merseyside was mentioned on the wireless. We will not want them to know they have got to the Shipyard perhaps.

I've opened the tin of fruit salad, and put my best embroidered cloth on, and made an egg-whip instead of cream. My husband will be so tired. I'll not take my clothes off tonight, and I'll give the animals an aspirin. My face is clean and I've combed my hair and put powder and lipstick on. I'm too tired and spent to have a bath and then put my clothes on again. I could not settle at all if I'd to undress: we may have to fight incendiaries – a lot more were dropped in other parts of town. I thought Ruth and her aunt might be bombed out and be coming, and I got all cleaned up in case they did.

Bedtime

I hardened my heart to all who came asking where my husband could be found. I said I had not the slightest idea, and was glad I had done so when he came in absolutely whacked after working, from five in the morning till seven at night, on our own house and then on shops. There seems to be a lot of damage done, with whole districts roped off. My new neighbours say that nothing they had in London was so bad – poor things, they have so little furniture and all of it obviously second-hand bits. They were bombed out at Harrow, and then again at Liverpool. The little boy has such a stutter, and his mother said it came on after the raid on London. It must be nerves, for I had a bad 'hesitation' for weeks after the shock of war being declared – it seemed even to affect my thinking, as well as speaking.

Aunt Eliza is nervy and tedious, so wants my company and trails in and out, and Miss Mac's housekeeper came and asked me to go up and see her. I was lying down resting and I heard my husband say, 'Is it anything important?' and she said, 'No, not really, but Miss

Mac feels so low and Mrs Last is so bright and calm.' My husband's
reply somewhat staggered me, for he said, 'Mrs Last is resting – *must*
rest – for she has two jobs, you know. She may seem bright and calm,
but it's for other people's sake often, and I'm going to see she has not
to put on a show if I can help it – for me or anyone else in the future.'

My balloons swam like silver fish in a blue-grey bowl, and then, as
the sun sank, they turned to a faint blush-pink. So odd how one
changes: I have loved the crash and roar of waves all my life, but
now I never look at them if I can help it; they make me think of
shipwrecks and horror. Always I have loved the moon – tonight I felt
a detachment, a sense of menace. No 'peaceful', 'benign', 'serene',
'kindly' moon, as she rose to point the way for devil-bombers, but a
sneering, detached Puck who delighted in holding a burglar's lantern.

Monday, 5 May, 1941
To come through last night and keep calm was a good test of nerves
all right – *and* heart. Both must be stronger than I thought. Screaming
bombs, planes we did not hear until the bombs dropped, dog-fights
overhead, machine-gunning, rattling and spattering, so dreadful, so
frightening. The little dog and cat burrowing thankfully under the
eiderdown. I thought of little frightened children, and of desperate
frightened mothers, and marvelled at the thoughtlessness that could
and did keep children in bombed places. I felt so dreadfully sick and
ill, and sipped Lucozade at intervals: it's weakening to vomit so
much. I must go on a light, milky diet, and see what that does. I
must keep well – and cheerful: it's hard enough to keep 'gay and
saucy', without a sickness that saps me of energy and 'go'.

I'm so worried about Mrs Waite. Her house is in the Hawcoat
district, which is roped off, and where the water and gas have done.
Her big sandstone house is on the hill, and she has no shelter. She
kept putting off ordering it, saying her walls were built to endure.
Poor old lamb, she could *not* understand how wide a difference there
is between this war and any previous one. I'll have my breakfast and
then, after a tidy round, since everything is so thick with 'blast dirt'
again, I think I'll roll up my good hand-made rugs and cover the
suite in the lounge with dust-sheets. I hate futile repetition, and get
no satisfaction from doing the same thing twice. I'll go downtown
and take my grocery order: the walk may refresh my so tired head.

Bedtime

A wire came from Cliff to say he would arrive some time tonight, and I felt I'd rather he had not been coming. I've put the drop-end of the settee down, and blankets out, and I'll get him to sleep there, for the plaster in his bedroom is still dropping. Then, if a raid starts, he can squeeze into the shelter with us. My thoughts are with Arthur in Northern Ireland. I'm wondering and wondering how he got on in the raids last night.

I met Miss Ledgerwood: she looked so tired, and asked me to go along to the Rest Centre and help with food for the thousand evacuated to the Girls' Grammar School. There are unexploded bombs everywhere, and long detours have to be taken by all traffic. Loads of fresh soldiers, police and airmen were arriving – I wonder if they expect trouble again tonight. There was no meat in town, but my butcher said, 'Don't worry, I'll let you have a bit of something later in the week.' I soaked and cooked the ham shank I got last week, and there will be a good meal of soup and ham for Cliff when he gets in – if he *does* get in tonight.

Our Centre has got it again, but I don't know what damage has been done. Mrs Waite's good sandstone house is 'just hanging'. On the phone, she said *everything* that could be broken had been, and seemed so distressed. She said it would be better to close the Centre for a week, as just about all the Committee seemed to have enough to do – and so many have been evacuated. Mrs Finlay's house has gone: she was dug out badly shaken and has gone out of town. Mrs Boorman's house is flat, but she is out of town with her husband – he has had a bad nervous breakdown. Marks of 'put-out' incendiaries made me realize that, out of the four houses on our side and quite eight on the other side, only my husband and I are on the spot to put any fires out. The warden had left the communal tin hat with Mr Atkinson. I said firmly, 'You give it to us – with shrapnel falling like rain you cannot expect us to go out without one.'

I ground up some dog biscuits I had on the shelf – Sol prefers bits off the table, and eats his bits of dried scone and bread and butter. I pick out dried stuff I get given for the hens. I am wondering what to do about him, poor old pet. He has had a wonderfully kind and loving life, for a little dog friend, and I'm thinking I can best reward him by giving him sleep, sleep before he is too terrified. Today the siren went, and Margaret and Mrs Atkinson ran in to take cover under my shelter, but old Sol and Mr Murphy beat us to it, and were comfortably settled by the time we had slipped our shoes off to get on to the bed. My wild, free cat does not care tuppence for planes – he is very much the captain of his soul, and can take his chance. But today, when Mrs Helm took her beloved fox-terrier to the vet, I tried to make up my mind about Sol. My husband thinks it would be kinder – I do myself tonight – but in the morning when I see him so fond of his little doggy life, so happy and busy to trot round after me, and so pleased with so little in general, I shrink from ending his faithful life, his kind little life. He has never offended me by an action, and the crook of my finger brings him running. A quiet 'Good dog' is all he hopes for or expects to get. If he goes, I'll never have another dog. He shall always be my dog.

Tuesday, 6 May, 1941
A tap-tap in the night brought me quickly to the door, to see Cliff, who had got to Grange and been brought on by bus. I'd brought a bowl of soup and little ham into the dining-room in a few minutes, and he said, 'I was thinking all day that perhaps there would be soup waiting. I'd rather have it than a full-course meal on the train.'

We had an alert, and flames and guns over, but a comparatively quiet night. I suggested Cliff should settle to sleep under the shelter. It's really grand – five feet wide – and I extended the four-foot bed with pillows down the side. We slept comfortably, enough though 'three in a bed'.

I don't know what's the matter with me, or what my reactions really are. There are two distinct 'me's'. One says, 'Oh, *look* at that plaster off, and *look* at that crack in the wall – it's worse than yesterday.' The other me says, 'Um', and turns indifferently away. I wish the two of me would go together again, and think about things more, it's so *odd*. If anyone had told me *I* could feel so detached at my little treasured home ruined, I could never have believed it. Cliff and I were talking of evacuating into the country, and he says he wishes he could think we went out every night to sleep. I said firmly. 'NO, not while I've a roof and my nerves can possibly stand it. Do you think I'd feel shame before the women of London and Bristol who have stood it for so long? And who would look after Daddy and make his meals and keep him well for work if I ran away?'

Wednesday, 7 May, 1941

A busy morning, with Ruth in. Although I'd worked so hard on
Sunday and Monday getting the worst plaster and dirt away, there
were hidden 'deep' parts that she tackled, and we got the garage a
bit tidy. She made Cliff and me laugh with her description of her
registrations on Saturday. She was asked, 'Married?' and answered,
'No' – 'Any children?'! I wonder how often girls say 'Yes'.

   We decided to go out early after lunch – that I'd shop and then we
would go to the pictures. I've a real love and talent for shopping. I
am not a 'telephone shopper', and don't really like my butcher to
'send what he can'. I got veal and mutton for a pie. I'd have preferred
beef and mutton, but it should be all right: a veal jelly-bone, with
enough meat on it to make a little bowl of potted meat, and a shank-
end mutton bone for a stock-pot – all for 2s.1d., so I've still 11d. left
for when Cliff goes back. I had put 6d. worth of cress seeds on some
felt for my chicks, but it's been grand for salads – with chopped
carrots and beets – and our Cliff could eat salads at every meal.
There will be enough for the chicks too, and I've planted a little more
to come on later. Lettuce were from 1s.2d. to 1s.7d. Today, and not
as good value as my scrap of cress, costing 1d. At most. I'm *stubborn*
– I'll not buy things I think are too highly priced, or queue for them.
I firmly believe women are to blame for high prices. If they would
not buy, say, salmon at 8s.6d. a pound, next week it would be
cheaper. My butcher laugh at me – says I shop like a French woman
who demands the best even if it costs less. I understand what he
means for I'll order brisket in preference to sirloin, pot-roast it till it's
like chicken, or steam and press it and have good, soft, butter-like fat
for cooking – at half the price of sirloin which, after eating once hot,
is apt to be rather dreary.

   We went to one of the three picture-houses open now, to see James
Stewart in 'No time for Comedy' – and they hadn't! It irritated me. I
am not a 'picture fan', and only like to go if I'm interested or amused.
When we came out, a dirty tired man on a bicycle, with a broken but
once gay, cornflower blue hat-box under his arms, dismounted and
said, 'Hallo, Mrs Last. Poor Kathleen has gone – went the other
night in that direct hit in Hawcoat Lane.' Luckily Cliff put his arm
round me and held me for a second. I'm not a fainting woman, but I
felt for one split second that I'd melt and pour out of my clothes.
Kathie Thompson – the gayest, sweetest and most lovable of all the

nice young things that came and went when the boys were home –
the loveliest little bride I think I've ever seen, only three months ago,
and only twenty-one now. We are, indeed, all in the fighting-line. I
could only stammer feebly how sorry, how very sorry, I was to her
brother – what *can* we say now?

My husband's youngest sister is homeless, but luckily she and her
husband and two babies were in a good solid-built shelter. We went
down to offer to store her furniture, or part of it, for our front bedroom
has a lot of room now that the bed is downstairs. She is living with
her other sister, and I looked at the two of them – little prematurely
old women (as a family they age at forty). I looked at their greying
hair and weary faces and their rather frightened eyes, and felt a
friendship for them that I'd never felt before. Elsie, who has lost her
home, is about thirty-three or thirty-four, and her babies eighteen
months and two and a half years. I said, 'Elsie, my dear, I'm sure my
cousin Mary could take you in at Greenodd. Shall we run up and
see?' She said, 'No, certainly not, there is a good shelter here at Flo's,
and Stan needs me – needs us all. If things got too bad, I'd have to
take the kiddies and go, but I'm not quitting yet.' Flo said, 'Well, I
feel the same – I feel that, as long as the kiddies can eat and sleep
and are reasonably safe, it's no use running away. They will have to
learn to take it. It's getting a very funny world, and they had better
learn as they go on.' When I looked at their so tired faces – no clothes
off to sleep for several nights, 'blitz dirt' that seems to inbed itself,
their list of thermos flasks, hot water bottles, biscuits etc. which they
were busy checking over – I thought of all the women who were 'just
having to get out of Barrow to sleep at night'.

Ruth says there is trouble brewing in the Yard, for all the lights
are turned off when the alert goes, and the men *ordered* into the
shelter, and now they don't pay them as they formerly did: four to six
hours are knocked off a night's pay. As the men say, they cannot
afford it and think they should have tin hats, and shelters by their
machines to crowd under, as in other places. Here, they are even kept
in the shelter for half an hour after the all-clear. The damage is
unbelievable, considering we had no 'waves' of planes. Yet the loss of
life is slight, and due to direct hits on houses – the damage is more
by blast. Many people from the better houses have gone and left
them as they stand – such an invitation to looters from the poorer
end of town, who may have lost all.

I got through on the phone to Mrs Waite, who stays in her shattered home all day but cannot sleep in at nights. Her serene old voice floated over the phone, begging me to come and see her 'mess of a house', and I'll go tomorrow.

We open all the windows and leave them on the casement catch, and tonight my husband opened the dining-room window and said, 'Hush, hark – what's that?' Rather tremulously and with a hesitating note, a nightingale started to sing, and he sang as if deep in a mossy wood and not in a nearly urban district. We have lots of lovely wild birds still left, including missel-thrushes, but I've never heard a nightingale before. My husband said, 'No wonder they wrote "A Nightingale Sang in Berkeley Square" – I've never heard anything so beautiful.' I could see only a broken, blue hat-box, so dusty and crushed, and I remembered when it was new. Kathie was one of a gay party going to a dance, and went off in our car. She was radiant with excitement – her first 'grown-up' dance. She was eighteen and so bright – and gay in spite of a cross old father, who had forgotten his own youth. I hope where Kath has gone there are little silver dancing sandals and a little fun.

Thursday, 8 May, 1941
Another night of terror, and more damage and death – although the latter was not as heavy as it might have been. The Shipyard got a 'plastering' and there are to be no more night-shifts – only two day-shifts, from six to two and from two to ten at night. As it is, there will be several thousand out of work, I hear. I went up to Mrs Waite's, and felt sick with pity for her smashed and ruined home. After fifty-three years of marriage – prosperous years, always with plenty of money – her collection of old china and glass and silver was really worthwhile, and her furniture was all good. Now all is in a welter of destruction, with only a few oddments still whole. Bless her, she was as black as a gypsy, and picking up and salvaging here and there.

The Government Regional Commissioner came down and, after looking round, said, 'Barrow is blitzed as badly as any place in England – London or Bristol included – in relation to its size.' Because Barrow is not big, any bombs and blast are felt and heard by all. Cliff said, 'Thank god for one thing: when I picture you in the future, it's under your iron Morrison shelter and not under an outside brick one. It will be a great comfort to me to know you are reasonably

safe.' People seem bright – brittle bright – and I've *yet* to hear real
moans and grizzles. All the 'moaning Minnies', as Cliff calls them,
seem to go off at 4.30 by bus or on foot – even to sleep in the fields,
and it's bitterly cold at nights. Cliff said, 'Either my eyes deceive me,
or else I see you shrinking.' I said, 'Oh, I go up and down more with
loss of sleep than anything else, for then I'm so sickly I don't want
food.' Cliff is like Arthur – thinks a thing and *does* it! When we went
out, he drew up at a street corner and said to the traffic policeman at
the crossing, 'Can you tell me where Dr Millar is having his surgery?'
And I was taken off willy-nilly, without being asked. Dr Millar – a
dusty little figure in crumpled clothes and with such tired eyes – said,
'Don't worry, Cliff. I'm glad really, for it's a shock outlet. Your
mother has too good a control over her nerves for a highly-strung
woman – it would be more natural for her to have a crying fit, or
hysteria. This is nature's way of finding an outlet, and a damned
pleasanter way than some I've seen.' He says, 'Don't bother about
food at all. Nibble and sip whenever you can, have glucose to drink
or sweets to suck, chew gum and rest when you can.'

His home has gone from one road, and his dispensary out of
another, and the other things really clean about him are his hands
and a white coat that is clean on twice a day, and which he carries in
a pillow slip inside his bag. He said, 'Never thought there was so
much blasted muck about in the whole world' – and then we all
laughed at the weak little pun. He has sent his wife and two children
out of town and says, 'Oh well, there is *always* a bright side – I've
had peace at home for the first time in years.'

I must dream when I doze, for my husband says I crush up into a
little space, or push him to make room, and am helping all kinds of
people into a shelter and saying, 'There is plenty of room, press up
close and then we can all get in.' I don't know anything about it at
all. Dr Millar referred to something that had struck me: the rather
curious reaction to our bombings in most people's mind – the really
hurt anger that we are lightly dismissed as the 'North-West area and
Merseyside', or that only Liverpool is named. I said, 'Oh, it's
frightfully hush-hush – shows really how *very* important we are, being
done out of a little bit of glory in a very mean fashion by the BBC.'

Friday, 9 May, 1941
I never thought I'd be so thankful to see either of the boys leave as I

was to see Cliff go. The trains ran from the Central station in spite of the wreckage. Hundreds of people jostled and milled to get into the train, and the travellers to London and the south had to fight to get into it. The poor things with bundles and bedding were only going one or two stations out, and there should have been a 'local' – and a *free* one – even if only made up of wagons. It was so pitiful to see their looks of terror at being left, for so many lived round the Steel Works and the Yard. In all that crowd, I heard no whimper, no complaining – only 'Aye, we got a direct hit in our street,' or 'Blast made all our houses unfit to live in.'

The damage to the station was bad, but order was coming out of chaos, and tidy piles of planks and pieces of iron were about everywhere on the platform. All the railway people have known me for years – my Dad was an accountant with the old Furness Railway. I stopped to chat to one old man who remembered him. I said, 'Do you remember the red geraniums in the signal-box windows in the old days?' He said, 'Aye – and when a tip of tuppence got you a drink of beer if you wanted it. And now 2s. is no use for a drink or a smoke!' Cliff surprised me by telling me that, this week, most of the hotel bars in Barrow have been closed after tea – no draught beer and little bottled, and little or no spirits or wine. He said one double or two halves for the evening was the ration for all customers, and chance drinkers only got one – or none!

When we came home, I learned with pleasure that the buses were all running free after a certain hour, to take anyone out to nearby districts. People have been sleeping in hedges and fields all round the outside of town – no one has *any* faith in shelters. After the first small attack, when people died in bed and amid their ruined homes and the shelters stood up unharmed, practically all deaths have been in shelters when houses crashed on them. In the centre of town last night it was dreadful, for after the bombs started to fall and crash, the poor things rushed from the little box-like back street shelters into their houses, and then out into the street again – frantic with fear and not knowing where to go. We have no really decent public shelters. I don't think our Council ever really thought we would 'get it' – in fact, I don't think many people did.

There were public shelters in Barrow for only 3,500 people out of a

population of 70,000. As a direct result of the Blitz, 83 people were killed,
330 injured, and 10,000 houses were damaged.

Saturday, 10 May, 1941

Last night started off so terribly that, if it had gone on, there would
have been little of Barrow left. Pieces of railway rails and slates
seemed everywhere this morning, and the sky was red with fire.
There was a lull in the barrage, then we heard a plane or planes from
another direction and the raiders were chased out to sea. Ruth called
in to say there had been a lot of damage to streets and the Yard
again, and people were being dug out of shelters again. She spoke of
Thursday's damage to the Yard, when men were trapped for a while
in the deep shelters. She said Gerald – her sweetheart – had not
spoken all day, and then his mother had coaxed him to talk and get
it out of his system. Ruth said that the men took cover as usual, and
as usual played cards by torchlight and sat and talked – mostly
doubtful jokes and stories and, in the hardboiled way of Yard workers,
they cursed and blasphemed. After one frightful crash, when a large
crane came down, the foreman went to see the damage and came
back and said, 'I hope to God there is not another – it looks as if we
are trapped now.' As he spoke there was a worse crump, and then a
deathly silence. Gerald said torches dropped from nerveless fingers
on to the floor, and by their light he saw the 'round' of knees as men
instinctively dropped to kneel on playing cards or newspapers. He
saw clenched or clasped hands and a glimpse of grey hollowed cheeks,
and then a calm steady voice rose, 'Father, into thy hands we
commend our spirits,' and the Lord's Prayer started. Gerald recognized the voice as belonging to about the dirtiest-mouthed and
hardest-swearing man in the shop – a footballer. Above their heads,
the layer of concrete cracked and shifted with the weight of piling
machinery, flung in a heap by the blast; and then a wide crack
appeared on the side of the shelter, and light showed through. They
managed to scramble out and all were saved – as if by a miracle, for
the floor of the shop caved in on to their shelter shortly afterwardss.

Armour-piercing shells wrecked two streets near the docks, and
more general damage was done. What would have happened if
Spitfires had not come, one trembles to think. Barrow is so small that
we are 'all in it together', and it's so dreadful when people have no
confidence in their brick shelters. I bless the impulse that made my

husband decide, after weeks of consideration, to send for our iron
indoor shelter, where we can go to bed and feel reasonably safe.

Few seemed to be going to sleep in Barrow, if the cars and buses
were any guide, and a steady trek without break stretched for miles
as we came from Spark Bridge. Gone is all the weariness and age
from that little old Aunt of mine. Instead, there is a bustling busy
person, with grey hair like a last-year's bird's nest, sleeves rolled up
above the elbow, preparing soup and vegetables for tomorrow, getting
out every possible cover and pillow, and considering at every moment
the best course to pursue. My husband said, 'You're a queer lot –
you actually seem to *like* danger and upset. I've never seen you work
so hard, or seen you so cheerful for years – and on less food and sleep
at that!' It set me pondering, and while it would be *wrong* to say I'm
enjoying it, I've a queer feeling that at last I've ceased to be 'always
on the outside looking in' – as Flanagan and Allen sing.

Monday, 12 May, 1941

I've a content and happiness tonight, which I've not known since our
bombing started. For a week I've had a bewildered *shame* at the way
our W.V.S. officials have behaved. Mrs Burnett, Mrs Cummin and
Mrs Hamer got into uniform at the beginning of the war, and have
been *very* much W.V.S. And have that lot got in our hair at Hospital
Supply, with their prancings and parades! Poor old Mrs Waite has so
much to see to in her wrecked house, and Mrs Lord, who has always
been so jealously insistent that as 'organiser' she has been above Mrs
Waite (although we all considered Mrs W. to be our head), fled with
'shattered nerves'; and of all the Committee, only two remain beside
myself. I've felt frantic at the thought of things needed and not
getting done; and after sitting and having a good think, I went up
and put my idea before Mrs Waite. Mrs Waite thought it a good,
constructive one, so I'll carry it out. I will open the Centre myself
tomorrow – I've put a notice in tonight's 'Mail' that the Centre at
Christchurch will be open for War Savings and knitting to be handed
in.

National Savings were a feature of the war, as the government
pressed people to lend their money for the war effort. Special
'drives' and savings weeks were arranged, with exhibitions and

parades, and savings certificates were sold by all kinds of voluntary agencies.

Tuesday, 13 May, 1941

A busy morning, and a rush to get washed before lunch and ready to go out and down to the Centre for two o'clock.

My sister-in-law was so eager to start collecting her War Savings Certificates that she was there before I got to the Centre. We sat and looked at each other, wondering if anyone would come. We did not expect a lot, since I'd put the advert in so late in the day that it was only in the stop-press – too late for classification and not very noticeable. But we were surprised at the number who called, and Beat collected £38. A good few called who had 'heard in town' that the Centre was open, and who said they would come in on Thursday with extra contributions, with it being War Weapons Week.

I was quite busy, sorting wool and booking it carefully as I gave it out, and feeling pleased at the pile of returned work, when Mrs Lord swept in like an act of God! She was *furious* at my 'interference', and would *not* listen to anything I'd to say at all. That got my back up and I went 'all mischievous' – the best way I've found to deal with some people! I went 'big-eyed', and put my finger on my lips and said, 'Sh, sh, sh, *shush* – NOT in front of the children, dear,' and all the 'children' howled – women of fifty to sixty who had come in and sat down for a chat. Mrs Wilkins looked ghastly, but she laughed till she cried, and then said, 'That's settled it – we will get a couple of tables up on Thursday and start. It's the only place crazy enough nowadays to get a laugh – pictures seem a waste of time and the wireless bores me.' Mrs Lord said grandly, 'So *little* amuses us these hysterical times,' and her pursed mouth and prim look of disapproval set us off again like a pack of silly kids.

Tonight I was a bit tired perhaps, but I got *really* cross with my husband and told him a few things for the good of his soul. Each week since the war, I've always steadily saved a tin or two of meat, fish or soup and jam, syrup etc. I was so dreadully short in the last war – not only money but food – when I lived in the New Forest near Southampton. A little while back, my husband said, 'How splendid of you!', 'How you must have planned and contrived!', 'What a sacrifice it must have been!', and so on and so on. Now, when there is more than a chance we will be bombed out, he *whines*, 'If you had only had *sense*, and saved the money instead of getting a dozen tins of meat' – forgetting that he has never given me a sliding-scale of housekeeping, and I've had to stretch and *stretch* it always. I find I'm 'short-sighted' and a 'silly hoarder', and that I may never use what I've saved, and so on. On reflection, I think I was more than a bit *bitchy*, to say the least of it. I did a bit of resurrecting of old history and a bit of 'yes and *anyway*'; and I can remember clearly saying that I was tired of always having to do all the thinking and planning for the house, and that it was time he grew up. So undignified and tiresome to be so tired and edgy as to lose control of a temper schooled for thirty years.

This war seems to have no end – it's like a stone dropped in a lake where waves and surges are felt as unknown or unsuspected edges and shores.

Wednesday, 14 May, 1941
I called up at Mrs Waite's. As I stood on her terrace, I looked across at the wreckage of the once gay little housing estate and felt a cold sadness. Kathie Thompson's house and the one next-door had only party-walls standing, and from the wrecked windows fluttered pennons of torn silk – scraps of the blue that Kathie loved – and below, a bank of lovely forget-me-nots blazed like a summer sky. In the flower-beds, ranks of May-flowering tulips were opening, and I *never* saw such a glory of aubrietia and saxifrage in rockeries – so tidy and well kept in front of shattered homes. Furniture in splinters and burst beds and chairs were being dragged from ruins, while overhead a lark shrilled and from the trees behind the Waite's house blackbirds and thrushes sang. It seemed so heartbreakingly wrong, all nature at peace, so busy in the sun after the rain, so constructive in marching forward – yet with destruction, wanton *useless* destruction, everywhere.

I was far away in my thoughts, and did not realize the door had opened and Mr Waite was looking at me very concerned. He said, 'What is it, my dear? You look upset.' I said, 'Nothing – just thoughts,' and I waved towards the little wrecked houses. He said, 'Odd how furious we were to see that land sold for building, and how we hated the idea of small houses on our good road. It seems so pretty and little to look back on now.' Mrs Waite had brought a little order out of chaos – she is the right one to do it – but looked so very tired. She said, 'I'm coming down to the Centre tomorrow, my dear,' and I began to say, 'Don't worry, we will manage this week, you rest a little,' when I could see by signs from Mr Waite that I should hush. She went on to say, 'I'll not have Mrs Lord saying things to you and hurting you – she is as mad as a hatter over you *daring* to go above her head and open the Centre.' I said, 'Don't worry, I know I did right, and if I know that, I'll fight more than Mrs Lord.'

Thursday, 15 May, 1941

I got in latish and had rather a rush to make tea. As I was going to sit down, there was a ring at the door. It was a W.V.S. Canteen leader I know slightly. She said, 'I've come to ask you a favour – I hear you have been upset because you could not find a way to help. I would be so thankful if you would take a turn with the mobile canteen – can you drive?' I said, 'No, I've not even driven the car for several years.' She said, 'Never mind, you can serve tea and then cut sandwiches for the night trays.' So it looks as if I have found another job to help someone, who needs it. I'm not clear where we will go, or whom we will feed, but that's all right – I'll hear tomorrow.'

Wednesday, 28 May, 1941

I got all my odds and ends of tidying up done this afternoon and then lay down for an hour, for I felt very sleepy and tired. My husband said, 'Have you any worry on your mind? You have wakened me these last two nights sobbing so bitterly.' I cannot think what it can be that I worry over when I'm asleep, unless it's been the loss of the Hood and the thought of all those men drowned. Or perhaps, deep down, I fret more than I'll admit over the scattering of Hospital Supply, and knowing valuable time is being lost. A thing built up slowly has been given a shattering blow, if not a mortal one, by our blitz.

Major Major Major Major

Joseph Heller

Major Major Major Major had had a difficult time from the start.

Like Minniver Cheevy, he had been born too late – exactly thirty-six hours too late for the physical well-being of his mother, a gentle, ailing woman who, after a full day and a half's agony in the rigors of childbirth, was depleted of all resolve to pursue further the argument over the new child's name. In the hospital corridor, her huband moved ahead with the unsmiling determination of someone who knew what he was about. Major Major's father was a towering, gaunt man in heavy shoes and a black woolen suit. He filled out the birth certificate without faltering, betraying no emotion at all as he handed the completed form to the floor nurse. The nurse took it from him without comment and padded out of sight. He watched her go, wondering what she had on underneath.

Back in the ward, he found his wife lying vanquished beneath the blankets like a desiccated old vegetable, wrinkled, dry and white, her enfeebled tissues absolutely still. Her bed was at the very end of the ward, near a cracked window thickened with grime. Rain splashed from a moiling sky and the day was dreary and cold. In other parts of the hospital chalky people with aged, blue lips were dying on time. The man stood erect beside the bed and gazed down at the woman a long time.

'I have named the boy Caleb,' he announced to her finally in a soft voice. 'In accordance with your wishes.' The woman made no answer, and slowly the man smiled. He had planned it all perfectly, for his wife was asleep and would never know that he had lied to her as she lay on her sickbed in the poor ward of the country hospital.

From this meager beginning had sprung the ineffectual squadron commander who was now spending the better part of each working day in Pianosa forging Washington Irving's name to official documents. Major Major forged diligently with his left hand to elude identification, insulated against intrusion by his own undesired authority and camouflaged in his false mustache and dark glasses as an additional safeguard against detection by anyone chancing to peer in through the dowdy celluloid window from which some thief had carved out a slice. In between these two low points of his birth and his success lay thirty-one dismal years of loneliness and frustration.

Major Major had been born too late and too mediocre. Some men are born mediocre, some men achieve mediocrity, and some men have mediocrity thrust upon them. With Major Major it had been all three. Even among men lacking all distinction he inevitably stood out as a man lacking more distinction than all the rest, and people who met him were always impressed by how unimpressive he was.

Major Major had three strikes on him from the beginning – his mother, his father and Henry Fonda, to whom he bore a sickly resemblance almost from the moment of his birth. Long before he even suspected who Henry Fonda was, he found himself the subject of unflattering comparisons everywhere he went. Total strangers saw fit to deprecate him, with the result that he was stricken early with a guilty fear of people and an obsequious impulse to apologize to society for the fact that he was *not* Henry Fonda. It was not an easy task for him to go through life looking something like Henry Fonda, but he never once thought of quitting, having inherited his persever-ance from his father, a lanky man with a good sense of humour.

Major Major's father was a sober God-fearing man whose idea of a good joke was to lie about his age. He was a long-limbed farmer, a God-fearing, freedom-loving, law-abiding rugged individualist who held that federal aid to anyone but farmers was creeping socialism. He advocated thrift and hard work and disapproved of loose women who turned him down. His speciality was alfalfa, and he made a good thing out of not growing any. The government paid him well for every bushel of alfalfa he did not grow. The more alfalfa he did not grow, the more money the government gave him, and he spent every penny he didn't earn on new land to increase the amount of alfalfa he did not produce. Major Major's father worked without rest at not growing alfalfa. On long winter evenings he remained indoors and did not mend harness, and he sprang out of bed at the crack of noon every day just to make certain that the chores would not be done. He invested in land wisely and soon was not growing more alfalfa than any other man in the country. Neighbors sought him out for advice on all subjects, for he had made much money and was therefore wise. 'As ye sow, so shall ye reap,' he counseled one and all, and everyone said, 'Amen.'

Major Major's father was an outspoken champion of economy in government, provided it did not interfere with the sacred duty of government to pay farmers as much as they could get for all the alfalfa they produced that no one else wanted or for not producing any alfalfa at all. He was a proud and independent man who was opposed to unemployment insurance and never hesitated to whine, whimper, wheedle, and extort for as much as he could get from whomever he could. He was a devout man whose pulpit was everywhere.

'The Lord gave us good farmers two strong hands so that we could take as much as we could grab with both of them,' he preached with ardor on the courthouse steps or in front of the A & P as he waited for the bad-tempered gum-chewing young cashier he was after to step outside and give him a nasty look. 'If the Lord didn't want us to take as much as we could get,' he preached, 'He wouldn't have given us too good hands to take it with.' And the others murmured, 'Amen.'

Major Major's father had a Calvinist's faith in predestination and could perceive distinctly how everyone's misfortunes but his own were expressions of God's will. He smoked cigarettes and drank whiskey, and he thrived on good wit and stimulating intellectual conversation, particularly his own when he was lying about his age or telling that good one about God and his wife's difficulties in delivering Major Major. The good one about God and his wife's difficulties had to do with the fact that it had taken God only six days to produce the whole world, whereas his wife had spent a full day and a half in labor just to produce Major Major. A lesser man might have wavered that day in the hospital corridor, a weaker man might have compromised on such excellent substitutes as Drum Major, Minor Major, Sergeant Major, or C. Sharp Major, but Major Major's father had waited fourteen years for just such an opportunity, and he was not a person to waste it. Major Major's father had a good joke about opportunity. 'Opportunity only knocks once in this world,' he would say. Major Major's father repeated his good joke at every opportunity.

Being born with a sickly resemblance to Henry Fonda was the first of a long series of practical jokes of which destiny was to make Major

Major the unhappy victim throughout his joyless life. Being born Major Major Major was the second. The fact that he had been born Major Major Major was a secret known only to his father. Not until Major Major was enrolling in kindergarten was the discovery of his real name made, and then the effects were disastrous. The news killed his mother, who just lost her will to live and wasted away and died, which was just fine with his father, who had decided to marry the bad-tempered girl at the A & P if he had to and who had not been optimistic about his chances of getting his wife off the land without paying her some money or flogging her.

On Major Major himself the consequences were only slightly less severe. It was a harsh and stunning realization that was forced upon him at so tender an age, the realization that he was not, as he had always been led to believe, Caleb Major, but instead was some total stranger named Major Major Major about whom he knew absolutely nothing and about whom nobody else had ever heard before. What playmates he had withdrew from him and never returned, disposed, as they were, to distrust all strangers, especially one who had already deceived them by pretending to be someone they had known for years. Nobody would have anything to do with him. He began to drop things and to trip. He had a shy and hopeful manner in each new contact, and he was always disappointed. Because he needed a friend so desperately, he never found one. He grew awkwardly into a tall, strange, dreamy boy with fragile eyes and a very delicate mouth whose tentative, groping smile collapsed instantly into hurt disorder at every fresh rebuff.

He was polite to his elders, who disliked him. Whatever his elders told him to do, he did. They told him to look before he leaped, and he always looked before he leaped. They told him never to put off until the next day what he could do the day before, and he never did. He was told to honor his father and his mother, and he honored his father and his mother. He was told that he should not kill, and he did not kill, until he got into the Army. Then he was told to kill, and he killed. He turned the other cheek on every occasion and always did unto others exactly as he would have had others do unto him. When he gave to charity, his left hand never knew what his right hand was doing. He never once took the name of the Lord his God in vain, committed adultery or coveted his neighbor's ass. In fact, he loved his neighbor and never even bore false witness against him. Major

Major's elders disliked him because he was such a flagrant nonconformist.

Since he had nothing better to do well in, he did well in school. At the state university he took his studies so seriously that he was suspected by the homosexuals of being a Communist and suspected by the Communists of being a homosexual. He majored in English history, which was a mistake.

'*English* history!' roared the silver-maned senior Senator from his state indignantly. 'What's the matter with American history? American history is as good as any history in the world!'

Major Major switched immediately to American literature, but not before the FBI had opened a file on him. There were six people and a Scotch terrier inhabiting the remote farmhouse Major Major called home, and five of them and the Scotch terrier turned out to be agents for the FBI. Soon they had enough derogatory information on Major Major to do whatever they wanted to with him. The only thing they could find to do with him, however, was take him into the Army as a private and make him a major four days later so that Congressmen with nothing else on their minds could go trotting back and forth through the streets of Washington, DC, chanting, 'Who promoted Major Major? Who promoted Major Major?'

Actually, Major Major had been promoted by an IBM machine with a sense of humor almost as keen as his father's. When war broke out, he was still docile and compliant. They told him to enlist, and he enlisted. They told him to apply for aviation cadet training, and he applied for aviation cadet training, and the very next night found himself standing barefoot in icy mud at three o'clock in the morning before a tough and belligerent sergeant from the Southwest who told them he could beat hell out of any man in his outfit and was ready to prove it. The recruits in his squadron had all been shaken roughly awake only minutes before by the sergeant's corporals and told to assemble in front of the administration tent. It was still raining on Major Major. They fell into ranks in the civilian clothes they had brought into the Army with them three days before. Those who had lingered to put shoes and socks on were sent back to their cold, wet, dark tents to remove them, and they were all barefoot in the mud as the sergeant ran his stony eyes over their faces and told them he could beat hell out of any man in his outfit. No one was inclined to dispute him.

Major Major's unexpected promotion to major the next day plunged the belligerent sergeant into a bottomless gloom, for he was no longer able to boast that he could beat hell out of any man in his outfit. He brooded for hours in his tent like Saul, receiving no visitors, while his elite guard of corporals stood discouraged watch outside. At three o'clock in the morning he found his solution, and Major Major and the other recruits were again shaken roughly awake and ordered to assemble barefoot in the drizzly glare at the administration tent, where the sergeant was already waiting, his fists clenched on his hips cockily, so eager to speak that he could hardly wait for them to arrive.

'Me and Major Major,' he boasted, in the same tough, clipped tones of the night before, 'can beat hell out of any man in my outfit.'

The officers on the base took action on the Major Major problem later that same day. How could they cope with a major like Major Major? To demean him personally would be to demean all other officers of equal or lesser rank. To treat him with courtesy, on the other hand, was unthinkable. Fortunately, Major Major had applied for aviation cadet training. Orders transferring him away were sent to the mimeograph room late in the afternoon, and at three o'clock in the morning Major Major was again shaken roughly awake, bidden Godspeed by the sergeant and placed aboard a plane heading west.

Lieutenant Scheisskopf turned white as a sheet when Major Major reported to him in California with bare feet and mud-caked toes. Major Major had taken it for granted that he was being shaken roughly awake again to stand barefoot in the mud and had left his shoes and socks in the tent. The civilian clothing in which he reported for duty to Lieutenant Scheisskopf was rumpled and dirty. Lieutenant Scheisskopf, who had not yet made his reputation as a parader, shuddered violently at the picture Major Major would make marching barefoot in his squadron that coming Sunday.

'Go to the hospital quickly,' he mumbled, when he had recovered sufficiently to speak, 'and tell them you're sick. Stay there until your allowance for uniforms catches up with you and you have some money to buy some clothes. And some shoes. Buy some shoes.'

'Yes, sir.'

'I don't think you have to call me "sir", sir,' Lieutenant Scheisskopf pointed out. 'You outrank me.'

'Yes, sir. I may outrank you, sir, but you're still my commanding officer.'

'Yes, sir, that's right,' Lieutenant Scheisskopf agreed. 'You may outrank me, sir, but I'm still your commanding officer. So you better do what I tell you, sir, or you'll get into trouble. Go to the hospital and tell them you're sick, sir. Stay there until your uniform allowance catches up with you and you have some money to buy some uniforms.'

'Yes, sir.'

'And some shoes, sir. Buy some shoes the first chance you get, sir.'

'Yes, sir. I will, sir.'

'Thank you, sir.'

Life in cadet school for Major Major was no different than life had been for him all along. Whoever he was with always wanted him to be with someone else. His instructors gave him preferred treatment at every stage in order to push him along quickly and be rid of him. In almost no time he had his pilot's wings and found himself overseas, where things began suddenly to improve. All his life, Major Major had longed for but one thing, to be absorbed, and in Pianosa, for a while, he finally was. Rank meant little to the men on combat duty, and relations between officers and enlisted men were relaxed and informal. Men whose names he didn't even know said 'Hi' and invited him to go swimming or play basketball. His ripest hours were spent in the day-long basketball games no one gave a damn about winning. Score was never kept, and the number of players might vary from one to thirty-five. Major Major had never played basketball or any other game before, but his great, bobbing height and rapturous enthusiasm helped make up for his innate clumsiness and lack of experience. Major Major found true happiness there on the lopsided basketball court with the officers and enlisted men who were almost his friends. If there were no winners, there were no losers, and Major Major enjoyed every gamboling moment right up till the day Colonel Cathcart roared up in his jeep after Major Duluth was killed and made it impossible for him ever to enjoy playing basketball there again.

'You're the new squadron commander,' Colonel Cathcart had shouted rudely across the railroad ditch to him. 'But don't think it means anything, because it doesn't. All it means is that you're the new squadron commander.'

Colonel Cathcart had nursed an implacable grudge against Major Major for a long time. A superfluous major on his rolls meant an untidy table of organization and gave ammunition to the men at

Twenty-seventh Air Force Headquarters who Colonel Cathcart was positive were his enemies and rivals. Colonel Cathcart had been praying for just some stroke of good luck like Major Duluth's death. He had been plagued by one extra major; he now had an opening for one major. He appointed Major Major squadron commander and roared away in his jeep as abruptly as he had come.

For Major Major, it meant the end of the game. His face flushed with discomfort, and he was rooted to the spot in disbelief as the rain clouds gathered above him again. When he turned to his teammates, he encountered a reef of curious, reflective faces all gazing at him woodenly with morose and inscrutable animosity. He shivered with shame. When the game resumed, it was not good any longer. When he dribbled, no one tried to stop him; when he called for a pass, whoever had the ball passed it; and when he missed a basket, no one raced him for the rebound. The only voice was his own. The next day was the same, and the day after that he did not come back.

Almost on cue, everyone in the squadron stopped talking to him and started staring at him. He walked through life self-consciously with downcast eyes and burning cheeks, the object of contempt, envy, suspicion, resentment and malicious innuendo everywhere he went. People who had hardly noticed his resemblance to Henry Fonda before now never ceased discussing it, and there were even those who hinted sinisterly that Major Major had been elevated to squadron commander *because* he resembled Henry Fonda. Captain Black, who had aspired to the position himself, maintained that Major Major really *was* Henry Fonda but was too chickenshit to admit it.

Major Major floundered bewilderedly from one embarrassing catastrophe to another. Without consulting him, Sergeant Towser had his belongings moved into the roomy trailer Major Duluth had occupied alone, and when Major Major came rushing breathlessly into the orderly room to report the theft of his things, the young corporal there scared him half out of his wits by leaping to his feet and shouting '*Attention!*' the moment he appeared. Major Major snapped to attention with all the rest in the orderly room, wondering what important personage had entered behind him. Minutes passed in rigid silence, and the whole lot of them might have stood there at attention till doomsday if Major Danby had not dropped by from Group to congratulate Major Major twenty minutes later and put them all at ease.

Major Major fared even more lamentably at the mess hall, where Milo, his face fluttery with smiles, was waiting to usher him proudly to a small table he had set up in front and decorated with an embroidered tablecloth and a nosegay of posies in a pink cut-glass vase. Major Major hung back with horror, but he was not bold enough to resist with all the others watching. Even Havermeyer had lifted his head from his plate to gape at him with his heavy, pendulous jaw. Major Major submitted meekly to Milo's tugging and cowered in disgrace at his private table throughout the whole meal. The food was ashes in his mouth, but he swallowed every mouthful rather than risk offending any of the men connected with its preparation. Alone with Milo later, Major Major felt protest stir for the first time and said he would prefer to continue eating with the other officers. Milo told him it wouldn't work.

'I don't see what there is to work,' Major Major argued. 'Nothing ever happened before.'

'You were never the squadron commander before.'

'Major Duluth was the squadron commander and he always ate at the same table with the rest of the men.'

'It was different with Major Duluth, sir.'

'In what way was it different with Major Duluth?'

'I wish you wouldn't ask me that, sir,' said Milo.

'Is it because I look like Henry Fonda?' Major Major mustered the courage to demand.

'Some people say you *are* Henry Fonda,' Milo answered.

'Well, I'm not Henry Fonda,' Major Major exclaimed, in a voice quavering with exasperation. 'And I don't look the least bit like him. And even if I do look like Henry Fonda, what difference does that make?'

'It doesn't make any difference. That's what I'm trying to tell you, sir. It's just not the same with you as it was with Major Duluth.'

And it just wasn't the same, for when Major Major, at the next meal, stepped from the food counter to sit with the others at the regular tables, he was frozen in his tracks by the impenetrable wall of antagonism thrown up by their faces and stood petrified with his tray quivering in his hands until Milo glided forward wordlessly to rescue him, by leading him tamely to his private table. Major Major gave up after that and always ate at his table alone with his back to the others. He was certain they resented him because he seemed too good to eat with them now that he was squadron commander. There was never any conversation in the mess tent when Major Major was present. He was conscious that other officers tried to avoid eating at the same time, and everyone was greatly relieved when he stopped coming there altogether and began taking his meals in his trailer.

Major Major began forging Washington Irving's name to official documents the day after the first CID man showed up to interrogate him about somebody at the hospital who had been doing it and gave him the idea. He had been bored and dissatisfied in his new position. He had been made squadron commander but had no idea what he was supposed to *do* as squadron commander, unless all he was supposed to do was forge Washington Irving's name to official documents and listen to the isolated clinks and thumps of Major — de Coverley's horseshoes falling to the ground outside the window of his small office in the rear of the orderly-room tent. He was hounded incessantly by an impression of vital duties left unfulfilled and waited in vain for his responsibilities to overtake him. He seldom went out unless it was absolutely necessary, for he could not get used to being stared at. Occasionally, the monotony was broken by some officer or enlisted man Sergeant Towser referred to him on some matter that Major Major was unable to cope with and referred right back to Sergeant Towser for sensible disposition. Whatever he was supposed to get done as squadron commander apparently was getting done without any assistance from him. He grew moody and depressed. At times he thought seriously of going with all his sorrows to see the chaplain, but the chaplain seemed so overburdened with miseries of his own that Major Major shrank from adding to his troubles. Besides, he was not quite sure if chaplains were for squadron commanders.

He had never been quite sure about Major — de Coverley, either, who, when he was not away renting apartments or kidnapping foreign laborers, had nothing more pressing to do than pitch horseshoes. Major Major often paid strict attention to the horseshoes falling softly against the earth or riding down around the small steel pegs in the ground. He peeked out at Major — de Coverley for hours and marveled that someone so august had nothing more important to do. He was often tempted to join Major — de Coverley, but pitching horseshoes all day long seemed almost as dull as signing 'Major Major Major' to official documents, and Major — de Coverley's countenance was so forbidding that Major Major was in awe of approaching him.

Major Major wondered about his relationship to Major — de Coverley and about Major — de Coverley's relationship to him. He knew that Major — de Coverley was his executive officer, but he did not know what that meant, and he could not decide whether in Major — de Coverley he was blessed with a lenient superior or cursed with a delinquent subordinate. He did not want to ask Sergeant Towser, of whom he was secretly afraid, and there was no one else he could ask, least of all Major — de Coverley. Few people ever dared approach Major — de Coverley about anything and the only officer foolish enough to pitch one of his horseshoes was stricken the very next day with the worst case of Pianosan crud that Gus or Wes or even Doc Daneeka had ever seen or even heard about. Everyone was positive the disease had been inflicted upon the poor officer in retribution by Major — de Coverley, although no one was sure how.

Most of the official documents that came to Major Major's desk did not concern him at all. The vast majority consisted of allusions to prior communications which Major Major had never seen or heard of. There was never any need to look them up, for the instructions were invariably to disregard. In the space of a single productive minute, therefore, he might endorse twenty separate documents each advising him to pay absolutely no attention to any of the others. From General Peckem's office on the mainland came prolix bulletins each day headed by such cheery homilies as 'Procrastination is the Thief of Time' and 'Cleanliness is Next to Godliness.'

General Peckem's communications about cleanliness and procrastination made Major Major feel like a filthy procrastinator, and he always got those out of the way as quickly as he could. The only official documents that interested him were those occasional ones pertaining to the unfortunate second lieutenant who had been killed on the mission over Orvieto less than two hours after he arrived on Pianosa and whose partly unpacked belongings were still in Yossarian's tent. Since the unfortunate lieutenant had reported to the operations tent instead of to the orderly room, Sergeant Towser had decided that it would be safest to report him as never having reported to the squadron at all, and the occasional documents relating to him dealt with the fact that he seemed to have vanished into thin air, which, in one way, was exactly what did happen to him. In the long

run, Major Major was grateful for the official documents that came
to his desk, for sitting in his office signing them all day long was a lot
better than sitting in his office all day long not signing them. They
gave him something to do.

Inevitably, every document he signed came back with a fresh page
added for a new signature by him after intervals of from two to ten
days. They were always much thicker than formerly, for in between
the sheet bearing his last endorsement and the sheet added for his
new endorsement were the sheets bearing the most recent endorsements of all the other officers in scattered locations who were also
occupied in signing their names to that same official document. Major
Major grew despondent as he watched simple communications swell
prodigiously into huge manuscripts. No matter how many times he
signed one, it always came back for still another signature, and he
began to despair of ever being free of any of them. One day – it was
the day after the CID man's first visit – Major Major signed
Washington Irving's name to one of the documents instead of his
own, just to see how it would feel. He liked it. He liked it so much
that for the rest of the afternoon he did the same with all the official
documents. It was an act of impulsive frivolity and rebellion for
which he knew afterward he would be punished severely. The next
morning he entered his office in trepidation and waited to see what
would happen. Nothing happened.

He had sinned, and it was good, for none of the documents to
which he had signed Washington Irving's name ever came back!
Here, at last, was progress, and Major Major threw himself into his
new career with uninhibited gusto. Signing Washington Irving's
name to official documents was not much of a career, perhaps, but it
was less monotonous than signing 'Major Major Major.' When
Washington Irving did grow monotonous, he could reverse the order
and sign Irving Washington until that grew monotonous. And he *was*
getting something done, for none of the documents signed with either
of these names ever came back to the squadron.

What did come back, eventually, was a *second* CID man, masquer-
ading as a pilot. The men knew he was a CID man because he
confided to them he was and urged each of them not to reveal his
true identity to any of the other men to whom he had already confided
that he was a CID man.

'You're the only one in the squadron who knows I'm a CID man,' he confided to Major Major, 'and it's absolutely essential that it remain a secret so that my efficiency won't be impaired. Do you understand?'

'Sergeant Towser knows.'

'Yes, I know. I had to tell him in order to get in to see you. But I know he won't tell a soul under any circumstances.'

'He told me,' said Major Major. 'He told me there was a CID man outside to see me.'

'That bastard. I'll have to throw a security check on him. I wouldn't leave any top-secret documents lying around here if I were you. At least not until I make my report.'

'I don't get any top-secret documents,' said Major Major.

'That's the kind I mean. Lock them in your cabinets where Sergeant Towser can't get his hands on them.'

'Sergeant Towser has the only key to the cabinet.'

'I'm afraid we're wasting time,' said the second CID man rather stiffly. He was a brisk, pudgy, high-strung person whose movements were swift and certain. He took a number of photostats out of a large red expansion envelope he had been hiding conspicuously beneath a leather flying jacket painted garishly with pictures of airplanes flying through orange bursts of flak and with orderly rows of little bombs signifying fifty-five combat missions flown. 'Have you ever seen any of these?'

Major Major looked with a blank expression at copies of personal correspondence from the hospital on which the censoring officer had written 'Washington Irving' or 'Irving Washington.'

'No.'

'How about these?'

Major Major gazed next at copies of official documents addressed to him to which he had been signing the same signatures.

'No.'

'Is the man who signed these names in your squadron?'

'Which one? There are two names here.'

'Either one. We figure that Washington Irving and Irving Washington are one man and that he's using two names just to throw us off the track. That's done very often you know.'

'I don't think there's a man with either of those names in my squadron.'

A look of disappointment crossed the second CID man's face. 'He's a lot cleverer than we thought,' he observed. 'He's using a third name and posing as someone else. And I think . . . yes, I think I know what that third name is.' With excitement and inspiration, he held another photostat out for Major Major to study. 'How about this?'

Major Major bent forward slightly and saw a copy of the piece of V mail from which Yossarian had blacked out everything but the name Mary and on which he had written, 'I yearn for you tragically. R. O. Shipman, Chaplain, US Army.' Major Major shook his head.

'I've never seen it before.'

'Do you know who R. O. Shipman is?'

'He's the group chaplain.'

'That locks it up,' said the second CID man. 'Washington Irving is the group chaplain.'

Major Major felt a twinge of alarm. 'R. O. Shipman is the group chaplain,' he corrected.

'Are you sure?'

'Yes.'

'Why should the group chaplain write this on a letter?'

'Perhaps somebody else wrote it and forged his name.'

'Why should somebody want to forge the group chaplain's name?'

'To escape detection.'

'You may be right,' the second CID man decided after an instant's hesitation, and smacked his lips crisply. 'Maybe we're confronted with a gang, with two men working together who just happen to have opposite names. Yes, I'm sure that's it. One of them here in the squadron, one of them up at the hospital and one of them with the chaplain. That makes three men, doesn't it? Are you absolutely sure you never saw any of these official documents before?'

'I would have signed them if I had.'

'With whose name?' asked the second CID man cunningly. 'Yours or Washington Irving's?'

'With my own name,' Major Major told him. 'I don't even know Washington Irving's name.'

The second CID man broke into a smile.

'Major, I'm glad you're in the clear. It means we'll be able to work together, and I'm going to need every man I can get. Somewhere in the European theater of operations is a man who's getting his hands on communications addressed to you. Have you any idea who it can be?'

'No.'

'Well, I have a pretty good idea,' said the second CID man, and leaned forward to whisper confidentially. 'That bastard Towser. Why else would he go around shooting his mouth off about me? Now, you keep your eyes open and let me know the minute you hear anyone even talking about Washington Irving. I'll throw a security check on the chaplain and everyone else around here.'

The moment he was gone, the first CID man jumped into Major Major's office through the window and wanted to know who the second CID man was. Major Major barely recognized him.

'He was a CID man,' Major Major told him.

'Like hell he was,' said the first CID man. 'I'm the CID man around here.'

Major Major barely recognized him because he was wearing a faded maroon corduroy bathrobe with open seams under both arms, linty flannel pajamas, and worn house slippers with one flapping sole. This was regulation hospital dress, Major Major recalled. The man had added about twenty pounds and seemed bursting with good health.

'I'm really a very sick man,' he whined. 'I caught cold in the hospital from a fighter pilot and came down with a very serious case of pneumonia.'

'I'm very sorry,' Major Major said.

'A lot of good that does me,' the CID man sniveled. 'I don't want your sympathy. I just want you to know what I'm going through. I came down to warn you that Washington Irving seems to have shifted his base of operations from the hospital to your squadron. You haven't heard anyone around here talking about Washington Irving, have you?'

'As a matter of fact, I have,' Major Major answered. 'That man who was just in here. He was talking about Washington Irving.'

'Was he really?' the first CID man cried with delight. 'This might be just what we needed to crack the case wide open! You keep him under surveillance twenty-four hours while I rush back to the hospital and write my superiors for further instructions.' The CID man jumped out of Major Major's office through the window and was gone.

A minute later, the flap separating Major Major's office from the orderly room flew open and the second CID man was back, puffing frantically in haste. Gasping for breath, he shouted. 'I just saw a man in red pajamas jumping out of your window and go running up the road! Didn't you see him?'

'He was here talking to me,' Major Major answered.

'I thought that looked mighty suspicious, a man jumping out the window in red pajamas.' The man paced about the small office in vigorous circles. 'At first I thought it was you, hightailing it for Mexico. But now I see it wasn't you. He didn't say anything about Washington Irving, did he?'

'As a matter of fact,' said Major Major, 'he did.'

'He did?' cried the second CID man. 'That's fine! This might be just the break we needed to crack the case wide open. Do you know where we can find him?'

'At the hospital. He's really a very sick man.'

'That's great!' exclaimed the second CID man. 'I'll go right up there after him. It would be best if I went incognito. I'll go explain the situation at the medical tent and have them send me there as a patient.'

'They won't send me to the hospital as a patient unless I'm sick,' he reported back to Major Major. 'Actually, I am pretty sick. I've been meaning to turn myself in for a checkup, and this will be a good opportunity. I'll go back to the medical tent and tell them I'm sick, and I'll get sent to the hospital that way.'

'Look what they did to me,' he reported back to Major Major with purple gums. His distress was inconsolable. He carried his shoes and socks in his hands, and his toes had been painted with gentian-violet solution, too. 'Who ever heard of a CID man with purple gums?' he moaned.

He walked away from the orderly room with his head down and tumbled into a slit trench and broke his nose. His temperature was still normal, but Gus and Wes made an exception of him and sent him to the hospital in an ambulance.

Major Major had lied, and it was good. He was not really surprised that it was good, for he had observed that people who did lie were, on the whole, more resourceful and ambitious and successful than people who did not lie. Had he told the truth to the second CID man, he would have found himself in trouble. Instead he had lied and he was free to continue his work.

He became more circumspect in his work as a result of the visit from the second CID man. He did all his signing with his left hand and only while wearing the dark glasses and false mustache he had used unsuccessfully to help him begin playing basketball again. As an additional precaution, he made a happy switch from Washington Irving to John Milton. John Milton was supple and concise. Like Washington Irving, he could be reversed with good effect whenever he grew monotonous. Furthermore, he enabled Major Major to double his output, for John Milton was so much shorter than either his own name or Washington Irving's and took so much less time to write. John Milton proved fruitful in still one more respect. He was versatile, and Major Major soon found himself incorporating the signature in fragments of imaginary dialogues. Thus, typical endorsements on the official documents might read, 'John, Milton is a sadist' or 'Have you seen Milton, John?' One signature of which he was especially proud read, 'Is anybody in the John, Milton?' John Milton threw open whole new vistas filled with charming, inexhaustible possibilities that promised to ward off monotony forever. Major Major went back to Washington Irving when John Milton grew monotonous.

Major Major had bought the dark glasses and false mustache in Rome in a final, futile attempt to save himself from the swampy degradation into which he was steadily sinking. First there had been the awful humiliation of the Great Loyalty Oath Crusade, when not one of the thirty or forty people circulating competitive loyalty oaths would even allow him to sign. Then, just when that was blowing over, there was the matter of Clevinger's plane disappearing so mysteriously in thin air with every member of the crew, and blame for the strange mishap centering balefully on him because he had never signed any of the loyalty oaths.

The dark glasses had large magenta rims. The false black mustache was a flamboyant organ grinder's, and he wore them both to the basketball game one day when he felt he could endure his loneliness no longer. He affected an air of jaunty familiarity as he sauntered to the court and prayed silently that he would not be recognized. The others pretended not to recognize him, and he began to have fun. Just as he finished congratulating himself on his innocent ruse he was bumped hard by one of his opponents and knocked to his knees. Soon he was bumped hard again, and it dawned on him that they did recognize him and that they were using his disguise as a license to elbow, trip and maul him. They did not want him at all. And just as he did realize this, the players on his team fused instinctively with the players on the other team into a single, howling, bloodthirsty mob that descended upon him from all sides with foul curses and swinging fists. They knocked him to the ground, kicked him while he was on the ground, attacked him again after he had struggled blindly to his feet. He covered his face with his hands and could not see. They swarmed all over each other in their frenzied compulsion to bludgeon him, kick him, gouge him, trample him. He was pummeled spinning to the edge of the ditch and sent slithering down on his head and shoulders. At the bottom he found his footing, clambered up the other wall and staggered away beneath the hail of hoots and stones with which they pelted him until he lurched into shelter around a corner of the orderly room tent. His paramount concern throughout the entire assault was to keep his dark glasses and false mustache in place so that he might continue pretending he was somebody else and be spared the dreaded necessity of having to confront them with his authority.

Back in his office, he wept; and when he finished weeping he washed the blood from his mouth and nose, scrubbed the dirt from the abrasions on his cheek and forehead, and summoned Sergeant Towser.

'From now on,' he said, 'I don't want anyone to come in to see me while I'm here. Is that clear?'

'Yes, sir,' said Sergeant Towser. 'Does that include me?'

'Yes.'

'I see. Will that be all?'

'Yes.'

'What shall I say to the people who do come to see you while you're here?'

'Tell them I'm in and ask them to wait.'

'Yes, sir. For how long?'

'Until I've left.'

'And then what shall I do with them?'

'I don't care.'

'May I send them in to see you after you've left?'

'Yes.'

'But you won't be here then, will you?'

'No.'

'Yes, sir. Will that be all?'

'Yes.'

'Yes, sir.'

'From now on,' Major Major said to the middle-aged enlisted man who took care of his trailer, 'I don't want you to come here while I'm here to ask me if there's anything you can do for me. Is that clear?'

'Yes, sir,' said the orderly. 'When should I come here to find out if there's anything you want me to do for you?'

'When I'm not here.'

'Yes, sir. And what should I do?'

'Whatever I tell you to.'

'But you won't be here to tell me. Will you?'

'No.'

'Then what should I do?'

'Whatever has to be done.'

'Yes, sir.'

'That will be all,' said Major Major.

'Yes, sir,' said the orderly. 'Will that be all?'

'No,' said Major Major. 'Don't come in to clean, either. Don't come in for anything unless you're sure I'm not here.'

'Yes, sir. But how can I always be sure?'

'If you're not sure, just assume that I am here and go away until you are sure. Is that clear?'

'Yes, sir.'

'I'm sorry to have to talk to you in this way, but I have to. Goodbye.'

'Goodbye, sir.'

'And thank you. For everything.'

'Yes, sir.'

'From now on,' Major Major said to Milo Minderbinder, 'I'm not going to come to the mess hall any more. I'll have all my meals brought to me in my trailer.'

'I think that's a good idea, sir,' Milo answered. 'Now I'll be able to serve you special dishes that the others will never know about. I'm sure you'll enjoy them. Colonel Cathcart always does.'

'I don't want any special dishes. I want exactly what you serve all the other officers. Just have whoever brings it knock once on my door and leave the tray on the step. Is that clear?'

'Yes, sir,' said Milo. 'That's very clear. I've got some live Maine lobsters hidden away that I can serve you tonight with an excellent Roquefort salad and two frozen éclairs that were smuggled out of Paris only yesterday together with an important member of the French underground. Will that do for a start?'

'No.'

'Yes, sir. I understand.'

For dinner that night Milo served him broiled Maine lobster with excellent Roquefort salad and two frozen éclairs. Major Major was annoyed. If he sent it back, though, it would only go to waste or to somebody else, and Major Major had a weakness for broiled lobster. He ate with a guilty conscience. The next day for lunch there was terrapin Maryland with a whole quart of Dom Pérignon 1937, and Major Major gulped it down without a thought.

After Milo, there remained only the men in the orderly room, and Major Major avoided them by entering and leaving every time through the dingy celluloid window of his office. The window unbuttoned and was low and large and easy to jump through from either side. He managed the distance between the orderly room and his trailer by darting around the corner of the tent when the coast was clear, leaping down into the railroad ditch and dashing along with his head bowed until he attained the sanctuary of the forest. Abreast of his trailer, he left the ditch and wove his way speedily toward home through the dense underbrush, in which the only person he ever encountered was Captain Flume, who, drawn and ghostly, frightened him half to death one twilight by materializing without warning out of a patch of dewberry bushes to complain that Chief White Halfoat had threatened to slit his throat open from ear to ear.

'If you ever frighten me like that again,' Major Major told him. '*I'll* slit your throat open from ear to ear.'

Captain Flume gasped and dissolved right back into the patch of dewberry bushes, and Major Major never set eyes on him again.

When Major Major looked back on what he had accomplished, he was pleased. In the midst of a few foreign acres teeming with more than two hundred people, he had succeeded in becoming a recluse. With a little ingenuity and vision, he had made it all but impossible for anyone in the squadron to talk to him, which was just fine with everyone, he noticed, since no one wanted to talk to him anyway. No one, it turned out, but that madman Yossarian, who brought him down with a flying tackle one day as he was scooting along the bottom of the ditch to his trailer for lunch.

The last person in the squadron Major Major wanted to be brought down with a flying tackle by was Yossarian. There was something inherently disreputable about Yossarian, always carrying on so disgracefully about that dead man in his tent who wasn't even there and then taking off all his clothes after the Avignon mission and going around without them right up to the day General Dreedle stepped up to pin a medal on him for his heroism over Ferrara and found him standing in formation stark naked. No one in the world had the power to remove the dead man's disorganized effects from Yossarian's tent. Major Major had forfeited the authority when he permitted Sergeant Towser to report the lieutenant who had been killed over Orvieto less than two hours after he arrived in the squadron as never having arrived in the squadron at all. The only one with any right to remove his belongings from Yossarian's tent, it seemed to Major Major, was Yossarian himself, and Yossarian, it seemed to Major Major, had no right.

Major Major groaned after Yossarian brought him down with a flying tackle, and tried to wiggle to his feet. Yossarian wouldn't let him.

'Captain Yossarian,' Yossarian said, 'requests permission to speak to the major at once about a matter of life or death.'

'Let me up, please,' Major Major bid him in cranky discomfort. 'I can't return your salute while I'm lying on my arm.'

Yossarian released him. They stood up slowly. Yossarian saluted again and repeated his request.

'Let's go to my office,' Major Major said. 'I don't think this is the best place to talk.'

'Yes, sir,' answered Yossarian.

They smacked the gravel from their clothing and walked in constrained silence to the entrance of the orderly room.

'Give me a minute or two to put some mercurochrome on these cuts. Then have Sergeant Towser send you in.'

'Yes, sir.'

Major Major strode with dignity to the rear of the orderly room without glancing at any of the clerks and typists working at the desks and filing cabinets. He let the flap leading to his office fall closed behind him. As soon as he was alone in his office, he raced across the room to the window and jumped outside to dash away. He found Yossarian blocking his path. Yossarian was waiting at attention and saluted again.

'Captain Yossarian requests permission to speak to the major at once about a matter of life or death,' he repeated determinedly.

'Permission denied,' Major Major snapped.

'That won't do it.'

Major Major gave in. 'All right,' he conceded wearily. 'I'll talk to you. Please jump inside my office.'

'After you.'

They jumped inside the office. Major Major sat down, and Yossarian moved around in front of his desk and told him that he did not want to fly any more combat missions. What *could he do*? Major Major asked himself. All he could do was what he had been instructed to do by Colonel Korn and hope for the best.

'Why not?' he asked.

'I'm afraid.'

'That's nothing to be ashamed of,' Major Major counseled him kindly. 'We're all afraid.'

'I'm not ashamed,' Yossarian said. 'I'm just afraid.'

'You wouldn't be normal if you were never afraid. Even the bravest men experience fear. One of the biggest jobs we all face in combat is to overcome our fear.'

'Oh, come on, Major. Can't we do without that horseshit?'

Major Major lowered his gaze sheepishly and fiddled with his fingers. 'What do you want me to tell you?'

'That I've flown enough missions and can go home.'

'How many have you flown?'

'Fifty-one.'

'You've only got four more to fly.'

'He'll raise them. Every time I get close he raises them.'

'Perhaps he won't this time.'

'He never sends anyone home, anyway. He just keeps them around waiting for rotation orders until he doesn't have enough men left for the crews, and then raises the number of missions and throws them all back on combat status. He's been doing that ever since he got here.'

'You mustn't blame Colonel Cathcart for any delay with the orders,' Major Major advised. 'It's Twenty-seventh Air Force's responsiblity to process the orders promptly once they get them from us.'

'He could still ask for replacements and send us home when the orders did come back. Anyway, I've been told that Twenty-seventh Air Force wants only forty missions and that it's only his own idea to get us to fly fifty-five.'

'I wouldn't know anything about that,' Major Major answered. 'Colonel Cathcart is our commanding officer and we must obey him. Why don't you fly the four more missions and see what happens?'

'I don't want to.'

What could you do? Major Major asked himself again. What could you do with a man who looked you squarely in the eye and said he would rather die than be killed in combat, a man who was at least as mature and intelligent as you were and who you had to pretend was not? What could you say to him?

'Suppose we let you pick your missions and fly milk runs,' Major Major said. 'That way you can fly the four missions and not run any risks.'

'I don't want to fly milk runs. I don't want to be in the war any more.'

'Would you like to see our country lose?' Major Major asked.

'We won't lose. We've got more men, more money and more material. There are ten million men in uniform who could replace me. Some people are getting killed and a lot more are making money and having fun. Let somebody else get killed.'

'But suppose everybody on our side felt that way.'

'Then I'd certainly be a damned fool to feel any other way. Wouldn't I?'

What could you possibly say to him? Major Major wondered forlornly. One thing he could not say was that there was nothing he could do. To say there was nothing he could do would suggest he *would* do something if he could and imply the existence of an error or injustice in Colonel Korn's policy. Colonel Korn had been most explicit about that. He must never say there was nothing he could do.

'I'm sorry,' he said. 'But there's nothing I can do.'

The Battle of the Bulge

Martha Gellhorn

January 1945

They all said it was wonderful Kraut-killing country. What it looked like was scenery for a Christmas card: smooth white snow hills and bands of dark forest and villages that actually nestled. The snow made everything serene, from a distance. At sunrise and sunset the snow was pink and the forests grew smoky and soft. During the day the sky was covered with ski tracks, the vapor trails of planes, and the roads were dangerous iced strips, crowded with all the usual vehicles of war, and the artillery made a great deal of noise, as did the bombs from the Thunderbolts. The nestling villages, upon closer view, were mainly rubble and there were indeed plenty of dead Krauts. This was during the German counteroffensive which drove through Luxembourg and Belgium and is now driven back. At this time the Germans were being 'contained,' as the communiqué said. The situation was 'fluid' – again the communiqué. For the sake of the record, here is a little of what containing a fluid situation in Kraut-killing country looks like.

The road to Bastogne had been worked over by the Ninth Air Force Thunderbolts before the Third Army tanks finally cleared the way. A narrow alley was free now, and two or three secondary roads leading from Bastogne back to our lines. 'Lines' is a most inaccurate word and one should really say 'leading back through where the Germans weren't to where the Americans were scattered about the snowscape.' The Germans remained on both sides of this alley and from time to time attempted to push inward and again cut off Bastogne.

A colleague and I drove up to Bastogne on a secondary road through breath-taking scenery . The Thunderbolts had created this scenery. You can say the words 'death and destruction' and they don't mean anything. But they are awful words when you are looking at what they mean. There were some German staff cars along the side of the road; they had not merely been hit by machine-gun bullets, they had been mashed into the ground. There were half-tracks and tanks literally wrenched apart, and a gun position directly hit by bombs. All around these lacerated or flattened objects of steel there was the usual riffraff: papers, tin cans, cartridge belts, helmets, an odd shoe, clothing. There were also, ignored and completely inhuman, the hard-frozen corpses of Germans. Then there was a clump of houses, burned and gutted, with only a few walls standing, and around them the enormous bloated bodies of cattle.

The road passed through a curtain of pine forest and came out on a flat, rolling snow field. In this field the sprawled or bunched bodies of Germans lay thick, like some dark shapeless vegetable.

We had watched the Thunderbolts working for several days. They flew in small packs and streaked in to the attack in single file. They passed quickly through the sky and when they dived you held your breath and waited; it seemed impossible that the plane would be able to pull itself up to safety. They were diving to within sixty feet of the ground. The snub-nosed Thunderbolt is more feared by the German troops than any other plane.

You have seen Bastogne and a thousand other Bastognes in the newsreels. These dead towns and villages spread over Europe and one forgets the human misery and fear and despair that the cracked and caved-in buildings represent. Bastogne was a German job of death and destruction and it was beautifully thorough. The 101st Airborne Division, which held Bastogne, was still there, though the day before the wounded had been taken out as soon as the first road was open. The survivors of the 101st Airborne Division, after being entirely surrounded, uninterruptedly shelled and bombed, after having fought off four times their strength in Germans, look – for some unknown reason – cheerful and lively. A young lieutenant remarked, 'The tactical situation was always good.' He was very surprised when we shouted with laughter. The front, north of Bastogne, was just up the road and the peril was far from past.

At Warnach, on the other side of the main Bastogne road, some soldiers who had taken, lost and retaken this miserable village were now sightseeing the battlefield. They were also inspecting the blown-out equipment of two German tanks and a German self-propelled gun which had been destroyed here. Warnach smelled of the dead; in subzero weather the smell of death has an acrid burning odor. The soldiers poked through the German equipment to see if there was anything useful or desirable. They unearthed a pair of good bedroom slippers alongside the tank, but as no one in the infantry has any chance to wear bedroom slippers these were left. There was a German Bible but no one could read German. Someone had found a German machine pistol in working order and rapidly salted it away; they hoped to find other equally valuable loot.

The American dead had been moved inside the smashed houses and covered over; the dead horses and cows lay where they were, as did a few dead Germans. An old civilian was hopelessly shovelling grain from some burned and burst sacks into a wheelbarrow; and farther down the ruined street a woman was talking French in a high angry voice to the chaplain, who was trying to pacify her. We moved down this way to watch the goings-on. Her house was in fairly good shape; that is to say, it had no windows or door and there was a shell hole through the second-floor wall, but it was standing and the roof looked rainproof. Outside her palor window were some German mines, marked with a white tape. She stood in her front hall and said bitterly that it was a terrible thing, she had left her house for a few moments that morning, and upon returning she found her sheets had been stolen.

'What's she saying?' asked an enormous soldier with red-rimmed blue eyes and a stubble of red beard. Everyone seems about the same age, as if weariness and strain and the unceasing cold leveled all life. I translated the woman's complaint.

Another soldier said, 'What does a sheet look like?'

The huge red-bearded man drawled out, 'My goodness,' a delicious expression coming from that face in that street. 'If she'd of been here when the fighting was going on, she'd act different.'

Farther down the street a command car dragged a trailer; the bodies of Germans were piled on the trailer like so much ghastly firewood.

We had come up this main road two days before. First there had been a quick tempestuous scene in a battalion headquarters when two planes strafed us, roaring in to attack three times and putting machine-gun bullets neatly through the second-story windows of the house. The official attitude has always been that no Germans were flying reclaimed Thunderbolts, so that is that. No one was wounded or killed during this brief muck-up. One of the battalion machine-gunners, who had been firing at the Thunderbolts, said, 'For God's sake, which side are those guys fighting on?' We jumped into our jeep and drove up nearer the front, feeling that the front was probably safer.

A solitary tank was parked close to a bombed house near the main road. The crew sat on top of the tank, watching a village just over the hill which was being shelled, as well as bombed by the Thunderbolts. The village was burning and the smoke made a close package of fog around it, but the flames shot up and reddened the snow in the foreground. The armed forces on this piece of front consisted, at the moment, of this tank, and out ahead a few more tanks, and somewhere invisibly to the left a squadron of tanks. We did not know where our infantry was. (This is what a fluid situation means.) The attacked village would soon be entered by the tanks, including the solitary watchdog now guarding this road.

We inquired of the tank crew how everything went. 'The war's over,' said one of the soldiers, sitting on the turret. 'Don't you know that? I heard it on the radio, a week ago. The Germans haven't any gasoline. They haven't any planes. Their tanks are no good. They haven't any shells for their guns. Hell, it's all over. I ask myself what I'm doing here,' the tankist went on. 'I say to myself, boy, you're crazy, sitting out here in the snow. Those ain't Germans, I say to myself, didn't they tell you on the radio the Germans are finished?'

As for the situation, someone else on the tank said that they would gratefully appreciate it if we could tell them what was going on.

'The wood's full of dead Krauts,' said another, pointing across the road. 'We came up here and sprayed it just in case there was any around and seems the place was full of them, so it's a good thing we sprayed it all right. But where they are right now, I wouldn't know.'

'How's your hen?' asked the Captain, who had come from Battalion HQ to show us the way. 'He's got a hen,' the Captain explained. 'He's been sweating that hen out for three days, running around after it with his helmet.'

'My hen's worthless,' said a soldier. 'Finished, no good, got no fight in her.'

'Just like the Germans,' said the one who listened to the radio.

Now two days later the road was open much farther and there was even a rumor that it was open all the way to Bastogne. That would mean avoiding the secondary roads, a quicker journey, but it seemed a good idea to inquire at a blasted German gun position. At this spot there were ten Americans, two sergeants and eight enlisted men; also two smashed German bodies, two dead cows and a gutted house.

'I wouldn't go up that road if I was you,' one of the sergeants said. 'It's cut with small-arms fire about a quarter of a mile farther on. We took about seventeen Heinies out of there just a while back, but some others must of got in.'

That seemed to settle the road.

'Anyhow,' the sergeant went on, 'They're making a counter-attack. They got about thirty tanks, we heard, coming this way.'

The situation was getting very fluid again.

'What are you going to do?' I said.

'Stay here,' said one of the soldiers.

'We got a gun,' said another.

War is lonely and individual work; it is hard to realize how small it can get. Finally it can boil down to ten unshaven gaunt-looking young men, from anywhere in America, stationed on a vital road with German tanks coming in.

'You better take that side road if you're going to Bastogne,' the second sergeant said.

It seemed shameful to leave them. 'Good luck,' I said, not knowing what to say.

'Sure, sure,' they said soothingly. And later on they got a tank and the road was never cut and now if they are still alive they are somewhere in Germany doing the same work, as undramatically and casually – just any ten young men from anywhere in America.

About a mile from this place, and therefore about a mile and a half from the oncoming German tanks, the General in command of this tank outfit had his headquarters in a farmhouse. You could not easily enter his office through the front door, because a dead horse with spattered entrails blocked the way. A shell had landed in the farmyard a few minutes before and killed one cow and wounded a second, which was making sad sounds in a passageway between the house and the barn.

The air-ground-support officer was here with his van, checking up on the Thunderbolts who were attacking the oncoming German tanks. 'Argue Leader,' he said, calling on the radio-phone to the flight leader. 'Beagle here. Did you do any good on that one?'

'Can't say yet,' answered the voice from the air.

Then over the loud-speaker a new voice came from the air, talkiing clearly and loudly and calmly. 'Three Tigers down there with people around them.'

Also from the air the voice of Argue Leader replied rather peevishly, 'Go in and get them. Don't stand there talking about it.' They were both moving at an approximate speed of three hundred miles an hour.

From the radio in another van came the voice of the Colonel commanding the forward tank unit, which was stopping this counter-attack on the ground. 'We got ten and two more coming,' said the Colonel's voice. 'Just wanted to keep you posted on the German tanks burning up here. It's a beautiful sight, a beautiful sight, over.'

'What a lovely headquarters,' said a solider who was making himself a toasted cheese sandwich over a small fire that served everyone for warmth and cookstove. He had opened the cheese can in his K ration and was doing an excellent job, using a German bayonet as a kitchen utensil.

'Furthermore,' said a lieutenant, 'they're attacking on the other side. They got about thirty tanks coming in from the west too.'

'See if I care,' remarked the soldier, turning his bread carefully so as to toast it both ways. A shell landed, but it was farther up the road. There had been a vaguely sketched general ducking, a quick reflex action, but no one of course remarked it.

Then Argue Leader's voice came exultantly from the air. 'Got those three. Going home now. Over.'

'Good boys,' said the ground officer. 'Best there is. My squadron.'

'Listen to him,' said an artillery officer who had come over to report. 'You'd think the Thunderbolts did everything. Well, I got to get back to work.'

The cow went on moaning softly in the passageway. Our driver, who had made no previous comment during the day, said bitterly, 'What I hate to see is a bunch of livestock all beat up this way. Goddammit, what they got to do with it? It's not their fault.'

Christmas had passed almost unnoticed. All those who could, and that would mean no farther forward than Battalion Headquarters, had shaved and eaten turkey. The others did not shave and ate cold K rations. That was Christmas. There was little celebration on New Year's Eve, because everyone was occupied, and there was nothing to drink. Now on New Year's Day we were going up to visit the front, east of Luxembourg City. The front was quiet in the early afternoon, except for artillery, and a beautiful fat-flaked snowstorm had started. We decided, like millions of other people, that we were most heartily sick of war; what we really wanted to do was borrow a sled and go coasting. We borrowed a homemade wooden sled from an obliging little boy and found a steep slick hill near an abandoned stone quarry. It was evidently a well-known hill, because a dozen Luxembourg children were already there, with unsteerable sleds like ours. The sky had cleared and the ever present Thunderbolts returned and were working over the front less than four kilometers away. They made a lot of noise, and the artillery was pounding away too. The children paid no attention to this; they did not watch the Thunderbolts, or listen to the artillery. Screaming with joy, fear, and good spirits, they continued to slide down the hill.

Our soldier driver stood with me at the top of the hill and watched the children. 'Children aren't so dumb,' he said. I said nothing. 'Children are pretty smart,' he said. I said nothing again. 'What I mean is, children got the right idea. What people ought to do is go coasting.'

When he dropped us that night he said, 'I sure got to thank you folks. I haven't had so much fun since I left home.'

On the night of New Year's Day, I thought of a wonderful New Year's resolution for the men who run the world: get to know the people who only live in it.

There were many dead and many wounded, but the survivors contained the fluid situation and slowly turned it into a retreat, and finally, as the communiqué said, the bulge was ironed out. This was not done fast or easily; and it was not done by those anonymous things, armies, divisions, regiments. It was done by men, one by one – your men.

The Invasion of Papua

Raymond Paull

Lieutenant Kienzle set out from Uberi on 6th July, intending to inspect the track through to Kokoda, and by preceding Captain Templeton and his troops, organize their stages on the march. However, Templeton joined him at Uberi on the following day, and they went on together with 120 carriers on the morning of the 8th. The Australians enjoyed the rare luxury of travelling light across the Kokoda Trail. The natives carried their packs and rations, while the lugger *Gili Gili* carried their bulk supplies and equipment. Templeton was instructed to meet and discharge the lugger on arrival at Buna.

An alert and capable leader, Templeton had seen active service as Leading Seaman (Gunner) in the Royal Naval Reserve during the First World War. He was a man of great physical and mental stamina, but his age excluded him from the Second A.I.F. His men knew him as 'Uncle Sam' – a somewhat gruff, kindly Company Commander who shirked nothing, and they were unreservedly devoted to him. At Iorabaiwa, having struggled to the top of the ridge after the first day's march, Templeton walked back for two hours along the track, and returned with six rifles and two packs taken from footsore men.

From Iorabaiwa next morning, the Australians and natives reached Nauro after four and a half hours. Although not greatly encumbered, the troops were sorely taxed by the steep descents and equally stiff climbing, so Templeton, out of consideration for their aching muscles, rested them on the 10th, and they pushed on through Menari to Efogi on the 11th. Lieutenant Peter Brewer awaited them at Kagi with 186 carriers from Kokoda, so Kienzle sent back the carriers brought from Ilolo, with instructions to build up the depots established at the intermediate stages. He believed that he would obtain the best results if he confined the carriers' work to one stage. Accustomed mainly to

the milder coastal climate, the chill air and the rigours of their tasks
in the mountains easily distressed them.

The Australians left Kagi after breakfast on 13 July with the
Kokoda carriers. It was a miserable journey. They marched in a
heavy, continuous downpour, the track swirling with water. The men
fell through the thin, mossy carpet, or floundered on roots concealed
by the mud. The perpetual drip of the moss forest subdued them.
This was *keru gabuna*, the Cold Place. They were happier on the
descent into the upper reaches of Iora Creek, arriving at the first
crossing at noon, and after three hours more, at Iora Creek village.

Continuing next morning, Kienzle and Templeton left the troops
and carriers at Deniki and went down into Kokoda. Kienzle also took
this opportunity of visiting his own plantation at Yodda, and returned
to Deniki in the afternoon with fresh foodstuffs and five homestead
natives.

While the carriers rested on the 16th, he sorted stores for the
southward journey, and at Kokoda next day, bade farewell to
Templeton and B Company before going back along the roadway
through the plantation on the long march to Port Moresby. Arriving
at Kagi on the afternoon of the 19th, Kienzle checked over the
supplies delivered in the wake of the advance party. They consisted
of 42 tins of biscuits, 42 loads of rations and 2,700 lb. of rice.

An 'old hand', experienced in the use of native labour, Kienzle
realized that to maintain a supply line over such a long, difficult
route was not a simple matter of porterage. Not only did the limited
number of carriers available aggravate the problem; on such a route
too many natives were laden with supplies to sustain themselves and
their fellow carriers. The longer the journey, the greater the aggregate
weight of the carrier line's own rations, and the smaller the weight of
supplies – Australian rations, ammunition, equipment, medical stores
and the many other items needed by the troops – delivered at their
destination. In proportion to the number of carriers employed, the
quantity of supplies of all kinds delivered at Kokoda would be
negligible.

The supply problem would be simplified if, on the other hand, the
carriers' loads were flown from Port Moresby to a convenient
dropping place sufficiently far forward. Kienzle considered that Kagi
fulfilled this qualification. It did not provide an extensive dropping
area, and it might often be obscured by cloud, but deliveries to Kagi

by aircraft would reduce the number of carrying stages forward to
Kokoda, and have the effect of increasing the supply of native labour.
He decided to discuss this proposal fully on his return to New Guinea
Force Headquarters.

The *Gili Gili*, a Thursday Island lugger, sailed from Port Moresby
on 4th July with 20 tons of Templeton's stores, equipment and
ammunition. Staff-Sergeant A. L. Collyer and three other men of the
39th Battalion travelled in the ship, and directed the discharge of her
cargo at Buna. When it had been cleared from the beach, they
followed the laden carriers along the Kokoda road. At Awala three
days later, Collyer reported to Templeton, proceeding with Pte. John
McBride from Kokoda to Buna. They returned to Awala on 21st
July. As they rested there from the heat, they heard but disregarded
a distant rumbling noise which seemed to emanate from the massive
banks of cloud, the seat of tropical thunder, in the direction of the
coast. The same rumbling noise went unheeded by the troops
Templeton had left at Kokoda.

In the Buna Government Station, Lieutenant Alan Champion and
Sergeant Harper were studying a newly arrived cypher at 3.30 p.m.
on 21st July when a police-boy burst in. He said warningly, 'Airplane, taubada'. As they accompanied him on to the beach, they saw
a Kawanisi float-plane approaching over Holnicote Bay. It passed
the station building and flew along the coast, turned back, and strafed
the station as it crossed the clearing.

Half an hour after the plane's appearance, the police-boy called
again from beneath the coconut palms above the beach, 'Ssip i kom
taubada'. The ship he indicated lay six miles off to the north-west,
and there were more silhouetted beyond her. Champion and Harper
identified the foremost as a cruiser, which opened fire as they
watched. They saw the flashes of her gunfire clearly from the Buna
beach, but when no shells fell around them, the two men assumed
her target to be Gona or Sanananda Point.

Harper ran quickly to the radio hut. He tuned his transmitter to
the emergency frequency, and in plain language reported what he
had seen: 'A Japanese warship is shelling off Buna, apparently to
cover a landing at Gona or Sanananda. Acknowledge, Moresby.

Over. . . .' He listened for Port Morseby's reponse. The receiver was silent.

Harper repeated his message again and again, while the boom of the cruiser's gunfire echoed across the bay.

The legendary figure of the Kokoda Trail was Doctor Geoffrey Hamden Vernon. A tall, elderly Australian, Vernon cheerfully took upon himself the care of the native carriers toiling over the trail beneath loads of supplies and equipment and returning with stretcher casualties. The Australian people, who generously extolled the praises of the 'Fuzzy Wuzzy Angels' in the months ahead, failed to realize that the carriers' patience, tenderness and fortitude with wounded Australians rewarded, in part, Vernon's unsparing services on their behalf.

A son of a Sydney city architect, Vernon graduated in medicine and surgery from the University of Sydney to a practice in the distant Queensland town of Winton. He relinquished this to serve in the First A.I.F. As Regimental Medical Officer in the 11th Light Horse Regiment, and returned to Australia with the Military Cross and a deafness caused by a bursting shell on Gallipoli in 1915. During his Kokoda days, unable to hear normal speech, Vernon remarked wryly that his deafness was an advantage, because he heard none of the wild rumours that circulated with the stamp of gospel truth among the troops around him.

The outbreak of the Second World War found him at Misima. Knowing that his age and disability excluded him from active service, he volunteered to substitute anywhere in the Territory for a younger man. A walker on a marathon scale, he combined duty with enjoyment in the next two years on patrols for the Medical Service. When the Australian Government evacuated the women, children and older men from Papua in December, 1941, Vernon flatly refused to go. The authorities threatened him with arrest and compulsory explusion. He ignored them, determined to find his own useful niche.

Towards the end of June, 1942, after serving as medical officer at the native hospital at Sapphire Creek, below Rouna Pass, Vernon transferred to Ilolo and there became responsible for the carrier lines on the Kokoda Trail. One of his first decisions gave two days' rest to a carrier line which, having just arrived from Kagi, had been ordered to make another outward journey next morning. Vernon went himself, to inspect conditions and medical posts along the track.

On the heights above Nauro, the morning was clear and pleasant, the air fresh and invigorating. A breeze stirred the trees, and the grass had a dewiness and fragrance. The little outpost at Iorabaiwa, separated from the ridge by the deep valley of the Ofi River, seemed far below. Vernon stopped on the ridge for a pannikin of hot soup. As he sat there, relishing the peace and remoteness of this upland place, Kienzle halted on his journey back from Kokoda. The two men exchanged views while they shared the soup.

During the late afternoon, Vernon scrambled over the boulders on the river crossing and climbed up to Efogi. Weary from the day's march, he saw much still to be done, especially in the native hospital, where a single, busy orderly treated injured feet, abraded shoulders, respiratory infections and other ailments. Nearly every patient showed positive evidence of hard work and exposure.

Vernon stayed at Efogi on the following day to supervise the treatment of these natives. He noted also a shortage of blankets. Although a biting mountain cold prevailed at these altitudes, Efogi did not possess enough blankets to issue one to each man.

Resuming his journey on 25th July with Sergeant Jarrett, of Angau, a police-boy carrying a note overtook them at the foot of the hill below the village. Jarrett read and passed the note without comment to Vernon. It related that Japanese troops had landed at Gona, and were advancing inland towards Kokoda.

'I'll go on,' said Vernon. 'There's no M.O. with those 39th youngsters.' He continued on his way, while Jarrett returned to improve the staging conditions at Efogi.

The blue-print for the first stage of the Japanese campaign to capture Port Moresby gave a major part to the 15th Independent Engineer Regiment. Its role combined the construction of roads and bridges during the advance inland with that of strengthening the fighting potential of the striking force. The regiment embarked at Talamo on 29th June in the transports *Ryoyo Maru* and *Ayatozan Maru* to join the Nankia Shitai at Rabaul.

The Commander of this regiment, Colonel Yokoyama, issued a remarkable document on 14 July towards the end of the voyage:

'From today, we are entering an area subject to air attack. Hereafter, there will be no more exercises; any attack will be the real thing. Get out on deck before the enemy's arrival. Those who are slow will be regarded as cowards. When sinking, remain calm until the water touches the feet, and when in the water, take the necessary precautions. Those who hurriedly jump into the sea will drown. When in the water, sections or platoons should gather together and sing military songs. All must be calm, even when awaiting rescue for perhaps two days and night.' Yokoyama was unduly pessimistic. Both ships entered Rabaul harbour unmolested early next morning.

From the units available there, and en route, the Japanese Command chose a highly mobile advance force, known as the Yokoyama Advance Butai, its commander being the author of the homily on air attacks at sea.

Documents captured at a later stage of the Owen Stanley campaign showed the composition of the Yokoyama Advance Butai as:

Unit	Commander
15th Indep. Engr. Regt.	Colonel Yokoyama
1st. Bn. 144th Inf. Regt.	Lieut.-Colonel Tsukamoto
No. 5 Coy. 2nd Bn. 144th Inf. Regt.	1st. Lieut. Kamimura
No. 7 Coy. 2nd Bn. 41st Inf. Regt.	1st Lieut. Kamida
No. 2 Bty. 47th Fd. A/A Bn.	1st Lieut. Nakashima
No. 1 Bty. 55th Mtn. Arty. Bn.	1st Lieut. Hamada
Two Coys. Sasebo No. 5 Special Naval Landing Party (Marines)	Commander Tsukioka
Part of 15th Naval Pnr. Unit.	
2 Pl. No. 2 Coy. and Eqpt. Pl. No. 3 Coy. Indep. Engrs.	
2 Sec. 144th Regt. Sig. Unit.	

A separate document calculated, for provisioning purposes, the strength of the Yokoyama Advance Butai at 7,000 troops, with 1,200 natives and 2,630 horses. These figures included 1,700 infantry and attached personnel, and 1,000 personnel of the 15th Independent Engineer Regiment. The provisioning plan envisaged ration supplies for thirty days, together with emergency rations for twelve days, and additional rations for ten days to be sent to the battlefield.

Beneath these calculations, however, were more figures purporting to show the combined strength of the advance force, including its supply column:

	Strength	Horses
Main Force...............................	3,800	330
Waggon Transport, 1 Coy..................	400	300
Packhorse Transport, 4 Coys..............	2,800	
	2,000	
Total	7,000	2,630

Against the figures, 3,800, shown for 'main force', was a pencilled amendment, 2,700. From this document, therefore, it would appear that the combined strength of the Yokoyama Advance Butai was not less than 2,700 combat troops, 3,200 supply and base troops – a total of 5,900 Japanese – and 1,200 natives for porterage and other menial tasks.

The Yokoyama Advance Butai embarked in the transports *Ryoyo Maru* and *Ayatozan Maru* at Rabaul on 19th July, and sailed on the 20th with an escort of two cruisers and two destroyers for Basabua, about 1,000 yards east of the Gona Mission. The convoy passed through St George's Channel and down the east coast of New Britain without incident, and made its landfall on the Papuan coast in clear, warm weather, on the afternoon of 21st July.

The naval bombardment seen from Buna by Champion and Harper lifted at 4 o'clock, and the Japanese landed from barges on the empty beach. The landing went on uninterrupted all night long; not until the coming dawn was the first offensive action taken against it. Dispatched from Port Moresby in the early morning of the 22nd to reconnoitre the enemy's strength, Flight Lieutenant L. W. Manning, of 32 (Hudson) Squadron, RAAF, flew for some miles beyond the north coast, doubled back, and approached Gona from the direction of Rabaul. His bomb-racks held four 250 lb. bombs.

Manning first sighted a destroyer. He passed over the ship at 1,000 feet, and examined another ship which proved to be a cruiser. Circling, Manning found another destroyer and cruiser and the two transports. The *Ryoyo Maru* and *Ayatozan Maru* lay 500 yards from the beach, and the cruisers about two miles out. The destroyers steamed slowly a little farther off. Hearing the Hudson's approach from the north, the Japanese apparently believed it to be one of their own aircraft. The two transports and one of the cruisers were motionless; the second cruiser scarcely moved in the water. None challenged the solitary aircraft flying overhead in the darkness.

Seeing only the six ships, Manning headed out to sea to make his radio report to Port Moresby. Then, in the half dark that precedes the day, he turned for his attack run, choosing one of the transports as his target. He dived from 1,500 feet. This was the moment Manning and his crew had dreamed about, yet when the opportunity presented itself, tension and eagerness conspired to spoil their judgement. The four bombs fell into the sea, the nearest drenching the ship from a distance of 40 yards. Manning pulled the Hudson's nose up and climbed away over the coast, eluding the enemy's angry fire, and leaving the bombers from Port Moresby to find their prey.

The crew of the *Ryoyo Maru*, probably the ship Manning attacked, soon had her under way. The horses had not yet been put ashore, and cargo lay in her open holds. She escaped unscathed. The *Ayatozan Maru*, not so fortunate, received a direct bombing hit and began to burn, although the survivors of the attack turned her head towards the beach and ran her aground. The *Ayatozan Maru* afterwards assumed the familiarity of a landmark, known to troops and air crew as the 'Gona wreck'.

A communiqué issued on 23rd July from General Douglas Mac-Arthur's headquarters* conceded the fresh Japanese gains: 'The enemy effected a landing at Gona Mission, on the north coast of Papua, a point not occupied by the Allied Forces. The enemy convoy was discovered by reconnaissance, and our Air Forces executed a series of bombing attacks throughout the day on enemy shipping, landing barges and personnel on shore. One large transport and one barge were sunk, and heavy casualties were inflicted on debarking troops. An enemy float-plane was shot down in combat. Two of our fighters are missing.'

In spite of air attacks, the Japanese established and consolidated their beachhead. The vanguard – marines, infantry and engineers – had already set out, some on foot, some on bicycles, to reconnoitre the road to Kokoda. The main strength of the Yokoyama Butai followed.

The strip of country between the north coast and the foothills of the Owen Stanley Range is flat and perpetually swampy. It is subject to widespread inundation with each daily deluge. From its spongy

---

* MacArthur, escaping from the Philippines to Australia, had been appointed Supreme Allied Commander, South-West Pacific Area.

ground rises a dense jungle, dank and foetid, broken occasionally by patches of kunai, and intersected by the native pads connecting the villages and crossing the Buna-Kokoda road. In July, 1942, the Kokoda road was no more than a narrow muddy vehicle track extending to the Kumusi River, which was spanned by a stout suspension footbridge, the crossing-place being known as Wairopi, or Wire Rope.

The Kumusi at this point is a stream about eighty yards wide, its depth varying from hour to hour according to the rains falling over its vast headwaters to the east of the Kokoda Trail. Normally, the flow of its current is between eight and ten knots, but it can change in a few minutes to a roaring torrent. Beyond the river, the track follows the course of Oivi Creek, crossing its tributaries, passing Ilimo and Gorari villages, and climbing 800 feet to the summit of the steep Oivi spur, which protrudes from the base of the Owen Stanleys to separate the Kumusi and Mambare waters. The spur is clothed with a dense rain forest of tangled undergrowth, trees and vines. The Oivi rest huts stood then in a clearing on the crest of the slope, providing shelter for the passing traveller. The track passes through the clearing, falls gradually with an even grade to the crossing on Iora Creek, and ascends the escarpment above the Mambare into Kokoda.

In the advance to Kokoda, the Japanese vanguard wore green uniforms, and steel helmets garnished with leaves. Some wore scarlet helmets. They carried abundant supplies of ammunition, mess tins of cooked rice, and equipment which included a light shovel slung across the back, and a machete for cutting a pathway through the jungle.

Their tactics appeared to follow a definite pattern. A mobile spearhead advanced rapidly until opposing forces barred further progress. While the spearhead deployed and engaged the opposition, support troops would site a machine-gun, and might also bring up one or more mortars. Feint or deliberate attacks disclosed the width and strength of the defensive position by drawing the enemy's fire. For this purpose, advance scouts often risked and forfeited their lives. The stronger support elements, coming forward, cut their way round their opponents' flanks, either to force a withdrawal or to annihilate the defenders in a surprise attack from the rear.

Out-flanking tactics were sometimes varied to confuse, bluff or

frighten the opposition. If the Japanese thought that a threatened
encirclement would compel their adversaries to retire without fighting, they indulged in shouting, noisy scrub-cutting and wasteful fire.
They employed some badly chosen English phrases and scraps of
pidgin to entrap an unwary enemy. A bird-like whistle or a single
rifle-shot sometimes signalled the attack. In a frontal attack, the
Japanese were dogged and persistent, probing ceaselessly for weak
spots in the enemy's defences.

Communiqués issued from GHQ on 24th and 25th July contained
brief references to attacks made by bombers, dive-bombers and
strafing aircraft against the Japanese beachhead. On the 27th the
communiqué reported that 'our patrols engaged the enemy in light
skirmishes at Awala'. It chronicled, on the 28th, the bare fact of
contact between 'Australian patrols' and the enemy in the vicinity of
Oivi.

In Sydney on the same day, the veteran Australian politician,
William Morris Hughes, inquired how and why the enemy had
succeeded so easily in gaining their foothold in Papua. 'We must
wake up to the fact,' said Mr Hughes, 'that we are fighting an enemy
who is not afraid to die; an enemy who is on the offensive everywhere.
To reach Buna, the Japanese had to come in a convoy, with barges
and troopships. We have an Air Force on duty there, day and night.
The Japanese ought not to have got there. Every day, they are
creeping nearer and nearer. Soon, they may have established sufficient bases to make a major attack on Australia itself. . . .'

Kokoda was lost while the newspapers reporting Mr Hughes'
words tumbled from the presses in Australia early next morning.

RETREAT TO OIVI

Port Moresby never picked up the message sent by Sergeant Harper
from Buna on 21st July, but heard a simultaneous warning from
Sergeant Hanna at Ambasi, forty miles to the north-west. In the
absence of any response to his call on the emergency frequency,
Harper dispatched a police-boy to Awala with a written message,
instructing him not to stop until he had delivered it. Lieutenant
Champion and Harper then considered their own means of escape

before the enemy isolated and captured them. They left the Government Station just before 6 o'clock. They were barely out of the clearing when enemy bombers attacked the building.

Champion and Harper dined that evening at Higaturu with Captain Austin, but in spite of their persuasions, he declined to accompany them, saying the journey would too greatly tax his strength, whereas he would be safe enough in his well-stocked refuge in the hills. They left him collecting the few personal belongings and treasures he was loath to leave for the Japanese. At Awala on the following morning, having travelled throughout the night, Champion and Harper reported to Captain Grahamslaw.

The unexpected appearance of the Japanese, and their rapid advance inland, trapped many of the Europeans at the hospitals, missions and plantations on the Buna coast. Few succeeded in eluding the enemy and crossing the mountains to the south coast. Lieutenant Louis Austin and an Anglican mission party – Miss Margaret Branchley, Miss Lilian Lashman, the Reverend Henry Holland, the Reverend Vivian Hedlich, Mr John Duffill, two half-caste mission workers, Louise Artango and Anthony Gore, and Gore's six-year-old son – travelling from Ioma to Tufi, were betrayed to the Japanese by the natives of Perembata village. At Buna on 12th August, outside the headquarters of the Sasebo No. 5 Special Naval Landing Party, the entire party were beheaded one by one with the sword – the boy last of all.

The self-appointed executioner responsible for this inhuman massacre of Christian mission workers was Sub-Lieutenant Komai,* a Company Commander of this Marine Butai.

A traitorous guide betrayed Miss Hayman and Miss Parkinson from the Gona Mission. After a night under guard in the coffee-house at Popondetta, the Japanese took the two women to a spot where graves had been dug, and repeatedly bayoneted their prisoners until death mercifully ended their agonies. Their bodies, recovered some

---

* Komai was identified also as the executioner of Flight-Lieutenant William Ellis Newton, v.c., at Salamaua on 29th March, 1943. The Marine Commander, Torashige Tsukioka, and his Adjutant, Lieutenant Kagahito Okabayashi, were both killed during a bombing attack on Salamaua three months after the callous 'Bushido' murder of Newton. An Australian War Crimes Investigation team traced Komai to the point where his death was established beyond doubt. The natives responsible for the betrayal of the mission party were hanged.

months later by Sergeant-Major Arek, a Wanigela native, received Christian burial at Sangara Mission. Father Benson alone survived captivity.

Near Popondetta also, the Japanese captured and killed Hanna and a small band of American Airacobra pilots forced down on various missions over the north coast.

The advancing Japanese encountered their first resistance near the Isivita-Sangara track junction, 1,000 yards east of Awala, on 22nd July. Against them, the Australians mustered the 39th Battalion's 11 Platoon, under Lieutant H. E. Mortimore, and Major Watson's handful of Papuan Infantry. They possessed no better weapons than rifles, a few revolvers and Thompson sub-marchine guns, and a single Lewis gun with one drum of ammunition.

An urgent message from Templeton on the previous day had instructed Mortimore to proceed from Kokoda with his men. Mean-while, Watson had disposed the PIB in defensive positions covering Awala. Mortimore and his platoon, arriving at 11 o'clock after marching all night, had barely shed their packs when the Japanese scouts appeared. With the exchange of the first shots, the enemy threw out flanking patrols and brought up machine-guns, a mortar and an infantry support gun, like a well rehearsed exercise. The Australians attempted to provide covering fire for the withdrawal, to find that the speed of the enemy's attack had dispersed the PIB. Watson, with the remnants of his patrol and the Australians extri-cated themselves and fell back across the Kumusi, where Sergeant Collyer and Private McBride attacked the bridge. Unable to cut the cables, they broke up the footplates and loosened the lock-nuts with which the cables were secured. The bridge collapsed into the river's broad channel.

Templeton left a section of 11 Platoon at Wairopi to delay the enemy's crossing while the remainder of the force withdrew to Gorari Creek, a stream with a channel twenty yards wide flowing through a deep defile into Oivi Creek. A wire suspension bridge also spanned Gorari Creek, but the Australians left it untouched for ambush purposes, and sited two Lewis guns at the side of the track covering the bridge. Templeton placed a section of the platoon on either side, and kept a third in reserve. He also brought 12 Platoon forward from Kokoda.

Lieutenant-Colonel Owen joined Templeton at Gorari, having flown across to Kokoda in the late afternoon of the 24th (the pilot had turned back on the first attempt on the previous day), and gone forward immediately. New Guinea Force on the 18th had instructed Owen to send his rifle companies across the range, and on the 22nd, extended his command to that of Maroubra Force, the name given to the combined Australian and Papuan force on the northern side of the Owen Stanleys. Captain A. C. Dean and C Company, the first of the troops to follow Templeton, left Ilolo on the same day.

The oncoming Japanese soon crossed the Kumusi's wide channel under a barrage of mortar and machine-gun fire, and on the 25th ran into the Gorari trap. The Australians succeeded at first in holding them on the far side of the creek, and thwarted their customary encircling tactics on the steep, open crossing. Japanese snipers finally broke the deadlock by climbing high up into the foliage of the jungle trees and pouring an accurate fire on to the Australians.

Returning to Kokoda late that night, Owen dispatched a signal to Port Moresby saying: 'Clashed at Gorari and inflicted approximately 15 casualties at noon. At 5 p.m., our position was heavily engaged, and two tired platoons are now at Oivi. Third platoon now at Kokoda is moving to Oivi at 6 a.m. Must have more troops, otherwise there is nobody between Oivi and Dean, who is three days out from Ilolo. Will have drome open for landing. Must have two fresh companies to avoid being outflanked at Oivi. Advise me before 3 a.m. if air-borne troops not available.'

Owen received thirty-two reinforcements next day – Lieutenant D. I. H. McClean and 16 Platoon of D Company. The other platoons of this company made the journey over the mountain and back with pilots reluctant to risk landing at Kokoda. These troops, returning to the 7-Mile, set out on the long overland journey in the wake of C Company.

McClean and fourteen of his men made the first crossing in a civilian Douglas airliner devoid of camouflage, preceding Sergeant E. J. Morrison with sixteen men and the platoon's two Bren guns still immersed in the original protective layer of grease in their boxes.

As the plane approached the Mambare, McClean and his men saw the Kokoda airfield bestrewn with obstacles. The Douglas circled,

pitching in the valley's turbulence, while the troops vomited despond-
ently into their tin hats, and 10 Platoon and a few natives removed
the obstacles.

McClean's troops were still shaky from their air-sickness when the
plane landed and taxied to the end of the runway where Owen
awaited them. As they emerged from the cabin, Owen said, 'Sorry I
can't give you a spell Mac. B Company is in trouble at Oivi, and I'll
have to send you off right away. It's half a day's march.' The new
arrivals picked up their packs and rifles, stumbled across the Kokoda
plateau, and in the early afternoon toiled up the spur into Oivi. B
Company, resting there, were hollow-eyed and exhausted, having
had little sleep or food in four days.

Nobody could suggest that Oivi provided a good defensive position.
The troops manned a perimeter along the edge of the high jungle
wall, and positions overlooking the track from Gorari. A standing
patrol of one section, under Corporal R. Stent, lay in the jungle across
the track below the clearing, until the Japanese set up a heavy
machine-gun, the Juki, nearby, and two scouts flushed the Australians. They retaliated by shooting the two Japanese, and returned
unharmed into the perimeter, with the enemy vanguard of Marines
close behind.

By three o'clock, Templeton could not conceal his anxiety about
the prospects of holding the Japanese. He had learned from McClean
that the balance of 16 Platoon expected to join him at Oivi, as well
as the main strength of D Company. Templeton reasoned that if the
Japanese overwhelmed his small force there, Garland's platoon at
Kokoda could not hope to survive, and the enemy then might march
unchecked to the top of the main range before they encountered
Dean. Before the full weight of the attack developed, Templeton
decided to go back along the track towards Kokoda with the object
of bringing up the reinforcements. Ten minutes after his departure,
Collyer heard the single, sharp crack of a rifle. Templeton did not
return, nor did a small patrol sent out to find him. A burst of
machine-gun fire, falling suddenly around Collyer and Stent on the
Kokoda side of the clearing, warned the Australians that the enemy
had penetrated along the flank. The Japanese launched their attack
in the late afternoon, but when it failed to dislodge the Australians, it
subsided at dusk.

Every man at Oivi felt Templeton's loss keenly, for he was a courageous and efficient officer. They cursed their easy acquiescence in allowing him to go unescorted. The sole evidence of his fate discovered much later in the campaign suggests that the Japanese ambushed and captured Templeton, badly wounded him, and killed him to rid themselves of an unwanted encumbrance.

At Oivi, the remaining officers agreed at nightfall that to continue the battle there invited annihilation. The noise of scrub-cutting on all sides, and the discovery of a Juki, newly sited on the north-western flank for a dawn attack, lent strength to this decision. Lance-Corporal Sinopa, a tall, reliable police-boy, suggested the means of escape, by volunteering to guide the Australians by a circuitous route back to Kokoda. Sinopa's success earned him promotion and the Military Medal.

The Australians struck out into the jungle on the north-eastern side of the clearing at 10 o'clock. They descended a steep bank into Oivi Creek, and travelled along the course of the stream, sometimes waist deep in its icy waters, until Sinopa led them up the right-hand bank into dense jungle. The men groped their way blindly in the intense darkness, clutching the bayonet scabbard or webbing straps of the man immediately ahead, yet even this journey provided its sample of the Australian soldier's irrepressible humour, in the advice addressed to the column by a man who had seized a handful of phosphorescent fungus: 'Grab yourself some headlights, fellas.'

The weary column emerged just before dawn on to the foothills track between Gebara and Sangai. Sitting there on the narrow pathway, the men had broken open their emergency rations when from the direction of Oivi, a distant din proclaimed the Japanese attack on the empty clearing.

By an unfortunate accident of omission, five Australians still manned a section of the perimeter when the withdrawal occurred. Finding themselves alone in the clearing at some undetermined hour of the night, they departed with considerable haste, skirted the enemy's positions safely, and returned to the main track to meet Morrison's party. Unable to break through the Japanese lines into Oivi, Morrison had disposed his men defensively across the track forward of Kokoda, awaiting fresh instructions or an opportunity of assisting B Company by attacking the Japanese from the rear. Morrison also had gathered up several men of the patrol sent out from Oivi in search of Templeton.

Another lad of this patrol whom Morrison failed to intercept
stumbled into Kokoda with grave news – Oivi surrounded and
Templeton missing. Owen proceeded at once to mobilize his meagre
resources for the defence of the Kokoda Trail. This he regarded as
the task of paramount importance. Having barely fifty men on hand,
he knew that he could not hope to hold the Kokoda plateau, airfield
and track against the enemy, and he saw no likelihood of relief for
some days. After consulting Garland, Owen sent a police-boy with a
message for Morrison. It is a gem among military orders: 'Withdraw
patrol through me at Kokoda at 10 a.m. Be careful that enemy do
not catch up to you unexpectedly on bicycles.' The police-boy also
carried a bunch of bananas which served as lunch for Morrison and
his men.

Meanwhile, the Australians at Kokoda buried in the rubber
plantation the grenades and ammunition they were unable to carry,
and set out up the Deniki hill after midnight to positions above a
waterfall, which offered the nearest perimeter defences.

Travelling westward along the foothills track, the column from Oivi
reached the outskirts of Kokoda to find the plateau silent and
deserted. Watson and Captain Stevenson, who had been Templeton's
Second-in-Command, and now commanded B Company, could
understand Owen's withdrawal, but the absence of the Japanese
puzzled them. Suspecting a trap, they retired warily, followed Iora
Creek upstream, and climbed the Deniki hill, where Owen welcomed
them heartily.

Vernon, going forward on his voluntary mission, reported to Owen
on the same day, saying he would remain to assist until Captain J. A.
McK. Shera, the 39th Battalion's Medical Officer, arrived from Port
Moresby.

The night was cheerless and cold. Vernon did not have the comfort
of a single blanket for his shake-down in the improvised Aid Post.
The wind blew a chill draught through the gaping fissures in the
floor, and a miniature shower-bath fell through the roof. At 10 o'clock
next morning, when a reconnaissance of Kokoda showed it still to be
unoccupied, the Australians descended the hill and again took up the
defence of the plateau. Vernon also began packing his few belongings

until Owen, misled by the doctor's grey hairs and gaunt figure, interrupted him.

'I think you should remain here at Deniki, doctor,' he said.

Vernon shook his head. 'Sorry, I'm rather deaf. I didn't hear you.'

'I suggest that you should remain here at Deniki,' Owen shouted.

'Nonsense,' said Vernon scornfully. 'Where do you think the wounded will be – here, or down at Kokoda?' He followed the troops early in the afternoon.

At 11.30 a.m., Owen signalled Port Moresby, saying, 'Reoccupied Kokoda. Fly in reinforcements, including 2 Platoon and four detachments of mortars. Drome opened.'

The opportunity afforded by his advice to reinforce Kokoda was lost that day. At dusk, the Japanese attacked in strength.

KOKODA – THE FIRST BATTLE

Lieutenant-Colonel Owen anticipated correctly that the Japanese would attack along the Mambare River and the Oivi track, so he prepared his main defensive positions on the plateau at the northern end, where the plateau narrows to an abrupt point, with steep slopes falling to the river. He protected his rear with a trench dug along the line of the rubber trees.

Approaching cautiously in the failing light, the enemy attacked with an estimated strength of 400 troops, but withdrew under the steady rifle-fire from the men along the top of the escarpment. Returning again after nightfall, the Japanese tried to climb the escarpment on to the point of the plateau, without gaining ground. Their mortars, emplanted across the Mambare, bombarded the plateau, and they renewed the attack under the covering fire of their Jukis.

The grenades and savage fire pouring down from the plateau halted the Japanese momentarily, before they pressed forward again, clinging precariously to the slope, winning a piecemeal yard of cover, and falling back. The Japanese commander committed more troops and added an infantry support gun to the bombardment.

A chance enemy bullet at this stage of the battle hastened the end. It mortally wounded Owen as he threw a grenade from a trench at the point of the plateau where the fighting was heaviest. Owen fell back into the trench. He died while the Japanese swarmed over the plateau and the Australians withdrew up the hill-side. Owen's command of the 39th Battalion lasted no more than twenty-two days, yet he left with his men an indelible impression of courage and determination that inspired them in their ordeal by battle until Papua was won again for Australia.

The most graphic description of this first Battle of Kokoda lies in the pages of Doctor Vernon's personal diary. Acute deafness and advancing years never impaired his sharp impressions and keen memory.

'The night of the 28th and the early morning of the 29th of July will not easily fade from my memory,' he wrote.

'Kokoda is approached from a range through a grove of rubber trees about three-quarters of a mile in depth. The rubber trees, as deeply shaded as a natural forest, suddenly give way to the grass and gardens of the station. . . .

'On arrival, I reported to the 39th Battalion and then inspected and arranged the police house, which had been converted into the RAP. In front of this was a large scorched area, where a quantity of Army and Canteen stores had been burnt before the withdrawal on the 26th. Our Angau OC took me at dusk into the HQ kitchen and gave me a very solid meal. I was tired after the forced march from Efogi, and want of sleep the night before at Deniki, and I said I would have a rest in Graham's house near the RAP, arranging to be called for the first casualty. I selected a lounge and lay down, in company with a fine ginger cat whose acquaintance I had already made when visiting the Grahams eight months previously. I fed the cat with pieces of scone. He seemed hungry and grateful for the snack, and nestling up against me, we both fell asleep. I hung my last few remaining treasures on a hook, where I could grab them in an emergency, but eventually I had to leave them there. When the time came to retrieve them, it was too late to enter the house, as it was being riddled with bullets from a Jap machine-gun, posted just below it on the upper slope of the escarpment.

'Dusk fell early, a grey, misty, cheerless evening though the moon was at the full. Jap scouts had already been reported, and about 7.30, cat-calls and a stray mortar shot or so came ringing across the Mambare. Thereafter, there was increasing noise and salvoes of firing, mostly I think, from the Japs, who had a big mortar with them, at shorter and shorter intervals. By midnight, the firing on both sides had become almost continuous. It was warm and comfortable in the lounge, and I slept secure in the knowledge that I would be called when wanted.

'About one o'clock on the 29th a hand touched my shoulder. It was Brewer, with news that Colonel Owen had been wounded. The moon was now in full strength, and shone brightly through the white mountain mist as I hurried with Brewer past the old magistrate's house, now the HQ, where we picked up a stretcher and several bearers.

'We crept down a shallow communication trench leading forward to a firing pit at the very edge of the escarpment. The CO was propped up in the narrow space, struggling violently yet more than semi-conscious, quite unable to realize where he was, or to help us get him out. Removal was difficult, but we got him on to the stretcher at last and carried him to the RAP where Wilkinson* was waiting with a lantern, and the instruments laid out for operating. Lieutenant-Colonel Owen had received a single GSW† at the outer edge of the right frontal bone just above the eyebrows. There appeared to be no wound of exit, and a little bleeding was controlled by gauze packing. Skull and brain had, of course, been penetrated. He was now quite unconscious, with occasional convulsive seizures which lessened as he grew weaker. At the time of our withdrawal he had become quite still, and was on the point of death. He probably did not survive another fifteen minutes.

'Major Watson came in to see him, and then we had four or five casualties in rapid succession who, when dressed, were told to get back to Deniki as soon as they could. Wilkinson held the lantern for me, and every time he raised it, a salvo of machine-gun bullets was fired at the building. This particular enemy machine-gun was as yet a little below the edge of the escarpment, probably just behind Graham's back premises, so its range was bound to be too high, and while the roof was riddled, those working below could feel reasonably safe. I was very glad to have Jack Wilkinson with me. He had been an old friend on Misima, and thanks to his experience in Greece and

* WO John Wilkinson.
† Gun-shot wound.

Crete, I felt every confidence in him. There are many Angau men who treated me with the utmost kindness and consideration during the whole campaign, always ready to shield me from any personal danger or discomfort, and I am glad to be able to acknowledge their care.

'We had now evacuated our walking wounded, and there was a lull in our work. Presently, Wilkinson came bursting into the RAP and said that an order for all to retreat at once had been given. I spoke of returning to Graham's house for my bag, but already it was a death-trap, and I was advised to let the Japs have my things. Before leaving, I spent some five or ten minutes in the RAP during which we fixed up Colonel Owen, who was now dying as comfortably as possible – moistening his mouth and cleaning him up. Then I stuffed our operating instruments and a few dressings into my pocket, seized the lantern, and went out towards the rubber. The rest of the medical equipment had to be abandoned, but it was not very extensive, and I think we saved all the instruments.

Outside, the mist had grown very dense, but the moonlight allowed me to see where I was going. Thick white streams of vapour stole between the rubber trees, and changed the whole scene into a weird combination of light and shadow. The mist was greatly to our advantage; our own line of retreat remained perfectly plain, but it must have slowed down the enemy's advance considerably, another chance factor that helped to save the Kokoda force. After a hasty look round the almost deserted plateau, I walked into the rubber. The firing was still heavy, coming, I suppose, from the Japs, as many of our men had left. I stayed awhile on the edge of the rubber, hoping to strike someone in authority, but as all the men were hurrying out to Deniki, I slowly followed them.

'I had not gone far before I felt uneasy at leaving the combat area while any troops who might have been wounded remained there. In the 1914–18 Sinai campaign, it was dinned into me that the place of the MO was at the tail of a retreating column, in company with the Second-in-Command. I had many a scramble over the sandhills with two or three AMC men, and no one else between us and the Turks, and usually found such hurried escapes somewhat exhilerating. Hence, at Kokoda, where my orders had been second-hand, I thought on reflection that I should remain for a while, at least till I had met some responsible officer, and I called to several withdrawing parties to ask if there were any officers amongst them. The men seemed neither to know, or greatly to care; their orders to leave had been definite enough, and they were carrying them out. By now, I had gone nearly half a mile through the rubber, and I turned back and hid behind the trunk of a tree just at the edge of the Kokoda clearing, in sight of the RAP and the station garden. The firing had almost died down, and the parties making for the hills were smaller and came less frequently. Finally, after a long period, during which no one passed and I was beginning to think I had better leave too, Major Watson, in company with Lieutenant Brewer and a couple of officers of the 39th passed along the track. I felt considerably relieved, and leaving my hiding place, called to Watson, who said, 'Come on, we are the last out'. Actually, two men followed us a little later. I heard afterwards that the station was then full of Japs, but in the mist, I recognized none, nor was I molested in any way.

'The Major sent Brewer on ahead, and walked very leisurely through the plantation. At the time, his dawdling walk rather mystified me, but I put it down to his being very tired. This was not the case. Later, he explained that he had dallied purposely to see that all the men got out, and his subsequent good spirits as we got well away from the battle area showed me he had not turned a hair over the night's events. A mile and a half along the track, we passed Skinner's signal post. This had been hurriedly evacuated, and several boxes of soldiers' treasures lay open and abandoned. I was told to help myself, and thus only an hour or two later, I more or less made up my involuntary gift to some Jap or other in Kokoda.

'Dawn on the 29th found us approaching the foothills and when it was full daylight, we passed a detachment acting as rearguard. This party, I believe, was unmolested for two or three days, and then fell back on Deniki. At 9 a.m., we reached our assembly point at Deniki. On arrival, I checked off our wounded from Kokoda, finding several who had not gone through the RAP. One man had a bullet lying superficially over the knee, so we laid him down on the track and removed it under a local anaesthetic. Then we had a meal and a rest, and thus ended the retreat from Kokoda. Apparently everyone was accounted for, as regards the Army, but I still had one worry on my mind – what had become of my pal, the ginger cat?

'Looking back on the Japanese assault on Kokoda, I can now see that by withdrawing, we took the wisest course. That we were

considerably out-manned by the enemy was only too certain; we had
but about ninety combatants, not counting a detachment of the PIB,
whereas the Japanese force was variably estimated at from three
hundred to five hundred men. Besides this advantage in numbers,
they had others, particularly in that our line of retreat was practically
undefended, and open to them had they worked around to our rear.
In that case, the entire force would have been surrounded, and
capture or death the fate of every individual. By withdrawing in good
time, we saved men who later held up the Japs till reinforcements
arrived, a very good example of the military axiom that the only
conclusive victory consists in the complete annihilation of enemy
forces.

'Our casualties amounted to one killed; one, I believe, missing – a
man named Maloney posted on the right flank – and about seven or
eight wounded. This trifling loss may indicate a somewhat brief
resistance, but there was no reason to wait till more were killed. The
result must have been the same in any case – retreat, and when that
was cut off, annihilation.

'I was told that the Japs fell freely as they stormed the escarpment,
but that there were too many of them to account for all. Their
casualties must have been far heavier than ours – this was the case
throughout the Owen Stanley campaign – and I was given different
accounts of thirty to seventy killed during the assault.

'Taking it all round, though our early retreat prevented full
resistance, the results could hardly have been bettered.

'Setting aside small clashes around Sangara, and the more extensive delaying actions at Wire Rope and Oivi, the assault on Kokoda
can be called the first pitched battle on Papuan soil. It was an
experience I would not have cared to miss, and among the impressions of that exciting night, none stands out more clearly than the
weirdness of the natural conditions – the thick white mist dimming
the moonlight, the mysterious veiling of trees, houses and men, the
drip of moisture from the foliage, and at the last, the almost complete
silence, as if the rubber groves of Kokoda were sleeping as usual in
the depths of the night, and men had not brought disturbance.'

The two men mentioned by Vernon who overtook the officers in the
plantation were Pte. 'Snowy' Parr, a Brenn-gunner in 16 Platoon,

and Pte. 'Rusty' Hollow, a lad acting as Parr's, 'offsider'. Parr bestowed his respect in the battalion on a limited field – Owen, Sergeant Morrison, and his Bren-gun.

From his position alongside Owen, Parr swept the escarpment with bursts of fire during the worst of the fighting, and a cold rage moved him when Owen fell back, mortally wounded, into the trench. Until the withdrawal began, the fighting was too close and too general for Parr to particularize in his vengeance. Then, retiring slowly with Hollow as the enemy came over the far side of the escarpment, he crossed the plateau unnoticed, to find a group of perhaps fifteen Japanese celebrating their victory on what once had been Brewer's lawn. From a range of less than sixty yards, he expended a full Bren magazine on the group, keeping his trigger finger hard against the metal, directing the muzzle accurately on to the Japanese so that none would survive, nor any round be wasted.

When the muzzle spat out the last round, Parr turned and spoke, 'Come on, Rusty'. Without haste, almost satisfied, he walked into the shelter of the rubber plantation, with Hollow silent at his side.

Vernon's estimate of Australian casualties is short of the true figure. Apart from Owen, the official record shows six men missing and presumed dead; one who died of wounds, and five wounded. Fourteen others originally reported missing were eventually recovered. This one inaccuracy in Vernon's moving narrative of the Battle of Kokoda may perhaps be attributed to his deafness.

Until Dean arrived with C Company, the 39th Battalion had five officers and 67 other ranks to hold Deniki. At 7 a.m. on 29th July, Captain Stevenson reported by signal to Port Moresby: 'Kokoda lost from this morning. Blow the drome and road east of Oivi. Owen mortally wounded and captured. Templeton missing.' Two hours after Stevenson sent this message, the GHQ communiqué issued in Brisbane announced: 'Gona – Allied ground patrols attacked and drove back the enemy from his advance outpost positions.' Twenty-four hours later, such were the intricacies of military censorship, the only reference to North-Eastern Papua in the communiqué stated: 'Kokoda – Allied and enemy forward elements engaged in skirmishes in this area,' and correspondents, still unaware of the loss of Kokoda, were permitted to speculate on its strategic importance.

Two Japanese documents, captured some months later, provide other glimpses of the battle. A 'Report from the Front Line' declared that 'No. 1 Company Commander – 1st Lieutenant Yukio Ogawa – was killed in action. The Australians left forty dead.' A methodical officer of the 3rd (Kuwada) Battalion, 144th Regiment, 2nd Lieutenant Hidetaka Noda, after noting the weather, 'Overcast, occasionally fine,' quotes a report received at Rabaul: 'In the Kokoda area, our Advance Force has been engaged in battle with 1,200 Australians, and has suffered unexpectedly heavy casualties. . . .'

No Trouble at All

Flying Officer 'X' (H. E. Bates)

The day was to be great in the history of the Station; it was just my luck that I didn't come back from leave until late afternoon. All day the sunlight had been a soft orange colour and the sky a clear wintry blue, without mist or cloud. There was no one in the mess ante-room except a few of the night-staff dozing before the fire, and no one I could talk to except the little WAAF who sits by the telephone.

So I asked her about the show. 'Do you know how many have gone?' I said.

'Ten, sir,' she said.

'Any back yet?'

'Seven were back a little while ago,' she said. 'They should all be back very soon.'

'When did they go? This morning?'

'Yes, sir. About ten o'clock.' She was not young; but her face was pleasant and eager and, as at the moment, could become alight. 'They looked marvellous as they went, sir,' she said. 'You should have seen them, sir. Shining in the sun.'

'Who isn't back? You don't know?'

But she did know.

'K for Kitty and L for London aren't back,' she said. 'But I don't know the other.'

'It must be Brest again?' I said.

'Yes, sir,' she said. 'I think it's Brest.'

I didn't say anything, and she said, 'They are putting you in Room 20 this time, sir.'

'Thank you. I'll go up,' I said.

As I went upstairs and as I bathed and changed I made calculations. It was half-past three in the afternoon and the winter sun was already growing crimson above the blue edges of flat ploughed land beyond the Station buildings. I reckoned up how far it was to Brest.

If you allowed half an hour over the target and a little trouble getting away, even the stragglers should be back by four. It seemed, too, as if fog might come down very suddenly; the sun was too red and the rim of the earth too blue. I realized that if they were not back soon they wouldn't be back at all. They always looked very beautiful in the sun, as the little WAAF said, but they looked still more beautiful on the ground. I didn't know who the pilot of L for London was; but I knew, and was remembering, that K for Kitty was my friend.

By the time I went downstairs again the lights were burning in the ante-room but the curtains were not drawn and the evening, sunless now, was a vivid electric blue beyond the windows. The little WAAF still sat by the telephone and as I went past she looked up and said:

'L for London is back, sir.'

I went into the ante-room. The fire was bright and the first crews, back from interrogation, were warming their hands. Their faces looked raw and cold. They still wore sweaters and flying-boots and their eyes were glassy.

'Hallo,' they said. 'You're back. Good leave?' They spoke as if it was I, not they, who had been 300 miles away.

'Hallo, Max,' I said. 'Hallo, Ed. Hallo, J.B.'

I had been away for five days. For a minute I felt remote; I couldn't touch them.

I was glad when someone else came in.

'Hallo. Good trip?'

'Quite a picnic.'

'Good. See anything?'

'Everything.'

'Good show, good show. Prang them?'

'Think so. Fires burning when we got there.'

'Good show.'

I looked at their faces. They were tired and hollow. In their eyes neither relief nor exhilaration had begun to filter through the glassiness of long strain. They talked laconically, reluctantly, as if their lips were frozen.

'Many fighters?'

'Hordes.'

'Any trouble?'

'The whole bloody crew were yelling fighters. Came up from everywhere.'

'Any Spits?'

'Plenty. Had five Me.'s on my tail. Then suddenly wham! Three Spits came up from nowhere. Never saw anything like those Me.'s going home to tea.'

'Good show. Good show.'

The evening was darkening rapidly and the mess-steward came in to draw the curtains. I remembered K for Kitty and suddenly I went out of the ante-room and stood for a moment in the blue damp twilight, listening and looking at the sky. The first few evening stars were shining and I could feel that later the night would be frosty. But there was no sound of a plane.

I went back into the ante-room at last and for a moment, in the bright and now crowded room, I could not believe my eyes. Rubbing his cold hands together, his eyes remote and chilled, his sweater hanging loose below his battledress, the pilot of K for Kitty was standing by the fireplace. There was a cross of flesh-pink elastic bandage on his forehead and I knew that something had happened.

'Hallo,' I said.

'Hallo,' he said. 'You're back.'

For a minute I didn't say anything else. I wanted to shake his hand and tell him I was glad he was back. I knew that if he had been in a train wreck or a car crash I should have shaken his hand and told him I was glad. Now somebody had shot him up and all I said was:

'When did you get in?'

'About an hour ago.'

'Everything OK?'

'Wrapped her up.'

'Well,' I said. 'Just like that?'

'Just like that,' he said.

I looked at his eyes. They were bleared and wet and excited. He had made a crash landing; he was safe; he was almost the best pilot in the outfit.

'Anyone see me come in?' he said.

'Saw you from Control,' someone said.

'How did it look?'

'Perfect until the bloody airscrew fell off.'

Everyone laughed: as if airscrews falling off were a great joke. Nobody said anything about anybody being lucky to be back, but only:

'Have an argument?'

'Flak blew bloody great bit out of the wing. The intercom went and then both turrets.'

'Many fighters?'

'Ten at a time.'

'Get one?'

'One certain. Just dissolved. One probable.'

'Good show. What about the ships?'

'I think we pranged them.'

'Good show,' we said. 'Good show.'

We went on talking for a little longer about the trip: beautiful weather, sea very blue, landscape very green in the sun. And then he came back to the old subject.

'How did I land? What did it look like?'

'Beautiful.'

'I couldn't get the tail down. Both tyres were punctured.'

'Perfect all the same.'

He looked quite happy. It was his point of pride, the good landing; all he cared about now. With turrets gone, fuselage like a colander, wings holed, and one airscrew fallen off, he had nevertheless brought her down. And though we all knew it must have been hell no one said a word.

Presently his second dicky came into the ante-room. He was very young, about nineteen, with a smooth aristocratic face and smooth aristocratic hair. He looked too young to be part of a war and he was very excited.

'Went through my sleeve.'

He held up a cannon shell. Then he held up his arm. There was a neat tear in the sleeve of his battledress. He was very proud.

'And look at this.'

Across the knuckles of his right hand there was a thread line of dried blood, neat, fine, barely visible. He wetted his other forefinger and rubbed across it, as if to be sure it wouldn't wash away.

'Came in on the starboard side and out the other.'

'Good show,' said somebody quite automatically. 'Good show.'

'Anybody hurt?' I asked.

'Engineer.'

'Very bad?'

'Very bad. I bandaged him and gave him a shot coming home.'

As he went on talking I looked down at his knees. There were dark patches on them, where blood had soaked through his flying-suit. But all that anyone said was:

'Think you pranged them?'

'Oh! sure enough. They've had it this time.'

'Good show,' we said. 'Good show.'

Now and then, as we talked, the little WAAF would come in from the telephone to tell someone he was wanted. With her quiet voice she would break for a moment the rhythm of excitement that was now rising through outbursts of laughter or exhilaration. She would hear for a second or two a snatch of the now boisterous but still laconic jargon of flight, 'Think we may have pranged in, old boy. Good show. Piece of cake. No trouble at all,' but there would be no sign on her calm and rather ordinary face that it conveyed anything to her at all. Nor did the crews, excited by the afternoon, the warmth and the relief of return, take any notice of her. She was an automaton, negative, outside of them, coming and going and doing her duty.

Outside of them, too, I listened and gathered together and finally pieced together the picture of the raid; and then soon afterwards the first real pictures of operations were brought in for the Wing Commander to see, and for a moment there was a flare of excitement. We could see bomb-bursts across the battleships and the quays and then smoke over the area of town and docks. 'You think we pranged them, sir?' we said.

'Pranged them? Like hell we did.'

'Good show. Bloody good show.'

'Slap across the Gluckstein.'

'No doubt this time?'

'No doubt.'

'Good show,' we said. 'Good show.'

At last, when the photographs had been taken away again, I went out of the ante-room into the hall. As I walked across it the little WAAF, sitting by the telephone, looked up at me.

'A wonderful show, sir,' she said.

I paused and looked at her in astonishment. I wondered for a moment how she could possibly know. There had been no time for her to hear the stories of the crews; she had not seen the photographs; she did not know that K for Kitty had been wrapped up and that it must have been hell to land on two dud tyres and with a broken

airscrew; she did not know that the ships had been hit or that over
Brest, on that bright calm afternoon, it had been partly magnificent
and partly hell.

'How did you know?' I said.

She smiled a little and lifted her face and looked through the glass
door of the ante-room.

'You can tell by their faces, sir,' she said.

I turned and looked too. In the morning we should read about it
in the papers; we should hear the flat bulletins; we should see the
pictures. But now we were looking at something that could be read
nowhere except in their eyes and expressed in no language but their
own.

'Pretty good show,' I said.

'Yes, sir,' she said. 'No trouble at all.'

Stalingrad – the Story of the Battle

Ronald Seth

When Hitler had marched into Poland, Vyacheslav Mikhailovich Molotov had made a speech which was broadcast throughout the length and breadth of the Union of Soviet Socialist Republics. In Stalingrad the people had gathered in the Square of 9th January to listen to it. Russia, they had heard him say, had no intention of going to war with anyone. If any assurance were needed the Non-Aggression Pact just signed with National-Socialist Germany, Russia's greatest ideological enemy, gave ample proof of the Soviet Union's peaceful intentions. The people of Stalingrad, like the people of the rest of Russia, had believed him, and had settled down to their own peaceful lives, from time to time indulging a new pastime – that of standing on the side-lines watching the German fascists and the western bourgeoisies trying to cut each other's throats. Even when it looked as if the detested Hitler was winning easily, no one was greatly perturbed, for not even Hitler would be mad enough to attack mighty Mother Russia.

So when, without warning, on 22nd June, 1941, Hitler did prove that he was certifiably insane, all the Russian people were taken by surprise, and none more so than the inhabitants of Stalingrad. But surprise was quickly translated into apprehension as the German armies penetrated one hundred, two hundred, three hundred miles towards the heart of Russia in an unbelievably few short weeks, rolling back the Red Army before them as though it were a roll of carpet, repeating the pattern of German invincibility first fashioned in the west.

However, not merely the Red Army was involved. Every Russian – man, woman and child old enough to walk – was involved. It was not a way of life that was at stake, nor fear of a foreign master, nor the Constitution, nor what the Kremlin stood for, that inspired the resistance of two hundred million Russians. The source of their inspiration was the fact that the very soil of Holy Russia, the actual physical soil, had been desecrated by alien feet, who trod it not in peace but in enmity.

It is difficult for the western mind to apprehend exactly the motives which impelled the Russians to defend their country as they did. We in the west gave everything we could to help our country ward off the same invader, not because we loved just this side idolatry the lakes of Cumberland, the Downs of Sussex, the Highlands of Scotland, the rich black earth of the Fens, the Yorkshire Moors, the plot of land behind our house we call our garden, the geraniums in our window-boxes. We joined the Services, we worked at unaccustomed factory benches, we parted from homes and families, we offered and gave our lives, because we valued freedom of conscience, freedom of religion, freedom of thought, liberty of action within certain well-defined limits, in fact, all the nebulous indefinable things which make up our way of life and to which we have given the name democracy. We fought to preserve institutions rather than some physical concrete object which we could touch and see. It is not to be denied that something of the same motives activated the Russians, but these primary sources of inspiration with us were secondary considerations with them. Not even the houses that stood on the land, nor the crops that grew out of the land, nor the ore that was dug out of the land, nor the machinery made out of the ore were so precious that they could not be destroyed, if need be, without a qualm; but the soil of Mother Russia must remain inviolate.

That, of course, meant fighting, ruthless fighting with no quarter given and none expected; and it meant that every soldier must be supported by every man, woman and child who did not bear arms. The soldiers must be given food, they must be clothed, they must be given arms.

To the people of Stalingrad it meant tanks to protect the soldiers and to destroy the enemy, and lorries to carry them to the front and to take them food and clothing and ammunition. The Tractor Factory began modifications on 25th June, 1941, to transform the tractor-producing assembly lines into tank-producing lines. Work was carried out at such speed that by mid-July a steady stream of tanks was leaving the factory for the fronts. The motor-car factory had made a similarly rapid change-over and soon heavy army lorries and other essential vehicles were being added to the contribution of tanks.

But as yet, despite the rate of the German advances on all sectors of the front, the battle itself was hundreds of miles from Stalingrad. Proud and defiant by the broad waters of the Volga, on the very frontier between Europe and Asia, the city felt itself secure. The armchair strategists explained away the speed of the German advances in the only terms patriots might use without being accused of creating alarm and despondency.

'It's plain enough what the High Command are doing,' they said. 'They are falling back like this to entice the Germans on, until their lines of communication are stretched to breaking point. Stalin's scorched-earth policy is all part of the plan. By destroying everything in the path of the oncoming armies our men force them to rely on their own supplies which have to be brought up all the way from Germany. There aren't half enough railways to provide all the supplies and reinforcements such armies need, and when autumn comes the roads will be out of commission, too, on account of the mud. By the time the mud freezes with the winter frosts our people will have regrouped, and before the Germans can bring up what they need our men will attack and destroy them wherever they can find them.'

It was comforting talk, even if one did wonder why the Germans did not see that they were being led into a trap. Even when Leningrad was surrounded and when the German armies advanced with frightening speed on Moscow, and Field-Marshal von Rundstedt's panzers took Rostov, there was still no need for alarm. And when Marshal Timoshenko's armies in the centre suddenly turned on von Bock in September and forced the Germans on to the defensive, the pundits could say: 'We told you, so!' though, since they did not know the true position, they could not explain that the Marshal's strategy was not identical with theirs.

Even when German aircraft made their first bombing attack on the city in October 1941, the Stalingraders were not unduly perturbed. In fact, it gave them a kind of inner warmth – they were now actively involved in the fighting. Their factories were making a contribution to the Russian war effort which was hardly bettered by any other city with identical resources, so it was perfectly natural that the Germans should try to destroy the factories and kill the people. Besides, if what they achieved on this first raid was the best they could do, clearly they had been grossly overrated, for not a single factory was hit.

Dwelling-houses and a kindergarten were destroyed, though no airman had ever wished for bigger and better targets than the Dzerzhinsky Tractor Factory, the Red October Factory and the oil refinery, conspicuous with its squat rotund storage-tanks reflected in the very waters of the Volga. 'Prestige raid,' the armchair pundits called it. 'They want to make their people think they have got to the boundary of Asia.'

It was the coldest winter Leningrad and Moscow had experienced for a long time. Even down in Stalingrad it was colder than usual. But the production lines in the factories did not falter; non-stop, manned by men and women for twenty-four hours a day, seven days a week – how many days a month? why bother to count? – they turned out the tanks and the lorries, the weapons and the ammunition and sent them off to the front.

But when the spring came the Germans started coming forward again. No one could tell exactly where they were eventually making for yet. It might be the south, where the oil was, though Hitler would gain much greater prestige if he succeeded in doing what Napoleon had failed to do – capture Moscow.

In May 1942 German aircraft began to visit Stalingrad again. The raids were not exceptionally heavy and though they did some damage it was not critically serious, but they were frequent now. At first the people hurried to the shelters as soon as the sirens of the Volga ferries gave the warning. But this slowed down production, which was what the Germans wanted as the next best thing to destroying plant. Somehow a way had to be found which would protect the bulk of the people and at the same time not stop the machines.

The men of the Tractor Factory found the answer. They set aside temporarily one of the smaller shops and soon were producing reinforced steel pill-boxes large enough to take one man. A heavy steel door swung to when the man had stepped inside, and through a narrow hooded slit in it he would watch the machines which were now left running instead of being turned off. One of these pill-boxes was placed at all strategic points throughout the factory, and men were detailed to stay with them when the bombs began to fall on the factory itself, for now the workers remained at the benches and by the machines until the danger warning was given. In this way much time was saved, and though some production was still lost, it was only a fraction of what the losses had formerly been; and this procedure was adopted in all factories producing war materials.

Then when the Germans started their offensive in June the people of Stalingrad still did not expect to see anything of them except their aircraft. The fighting was still 125 miles away to the east, and was not the Don, almost as mighty a river as the Volga and a defence barrier that would take some breaching, between the fighting and the city, and was not the general direction of the German advance north-eastwards towards Moscow?

Then quite suddenly even the armchair strategists changed their tune. Whichever way the Germans went now, Stalingrad must be threatened, for they could never leave such a strong-point on one or other of their flanks.

By mid-July the German intention had become a certainty. The German Fourth Panzer Army had crossed the Don and reached the heights of Kotelnikovo, and its spearhead, instead of pointing south, as though to protect the flank of First Panzer Army, was pointing north, and obviously coming up towards Stalingrad. Not only that, German activity in the great bend of the Don seemed to indicate the probability of a drive being made across the river, and that could only be interpreted to mean one thing – a full attack on Stalingrad.

Once it became obvious that the city might soon be in dire danger, the Soviet Government lost no time in preparing it and its people to withstand any assault which might be launched against it. What was called the Stalingrad Front was formed, with the Russian Sixty-second, Sixty-fourth and Fifty-seventh Armies under the command of General Yeryomenko.

At the same time a City Defence Council was set up under the leadership of Chuyanov, chairman of the Party Committee. This Council organised the civilians of Stalingrad, and liaised closely with the Military Council of the Commander-in-Chief. In the Red Army, in units above division level, authority had always been vested in a Military Council which was normally composed of three men: one, the Commanding General; two, his Chief of Staff; and three, a gentleman always referred to in Russian as 'The Member of the Military Council'. Before the War, the Member of the Military Council was always a highly trusted member of the Communist Party, and he stood in relation to the Commanding General as the Political Commissar stood to the C.O. in lower units. This form of dual control gradually tended to disappear during the War, and the Member of the Military Council more often than not filled the rôle of Deputy to the Commanding General dealing mainly with political and strategic questions rather than being involved with tactics.

With regard to the Member of the Military Council in Stalingrad, history repeated itself once more. In 1918, no one, even those in the inner conclaves of the Party, had an inkling that Stalin, who had filled this position in this place then, would rise to the supreme position in Russia after the death of Lenin; in 1942, no one could have guessed that the Member of the Military Council, Nikita Kruschev, would succeed Stalin on the same pinnacle of power.

Marshal Timoshenko, who had so successfully brought pressure to bear on Field-Marshal von Bock's armies in the September and October of the previous year, was no longer able to hold the greatly reinforced Germans. Fighting fierce delaying actions with comparatively small forces, he withdrew the bulk of his men across the Don, across the steppes and across the Volga, there to reorganise and re-equip them. The longer he delayed the German advance, the more men would he save for another day, and the longer would Stalingrad be safe.

But it could not be long before the attack was launched, and everything that could be done for the defence of the city must be done with all speed. It was decided that an anti-tank trench must be dug, and at first workers in non-essential industries, those, that is, not engaged in war production, and office workers were organised into labour battalions under the direction of military commanders. Such soldiers of Yeryomenko's city defence as could be spared were also set to work digging; but they were slow at the work, protesting they would rather fight any day than dig. So the colleges and schools were closed and all students, boys and girls above the age of twelve, and all men and women who could be released from their normal work, whatever it was, were given spades and forks and picks and buckets and asked to dig.

The response of the civilian population was one of the many miraculous factors which contributed to the Russian defence of Stalingrad. The main anti-tank trench, fifteen feet deep and twelve feet wide, was to stretch from the Tractor Factory in the extreme northern suburb, along the western boundary of the city, to the ravine at Beketovskaya in the south. From the Tractor Factory to

Beketovskaya is twenty-five miles; only the ten southernmost miles of the city's entire length were not protected by the great ditch!

In itself the digging of this trench was a wonder. The people of Stalingrad, from young boys and girls to old men and ancient crones, dug with pick and fork and shovel, dug deep and piled up the earth on the westward edge of the trench.

There were not enough tools to go round, but that did not matter. The organisation was such that as soon as a worker paused for a second to wipe the sweat from his brow or ease an aching back his tool was snatched from him and a fresh digger took his place. In two weeks the great ditch was completed.

While this main work was going on, other much shorter stretches of trenches were being dug at salient points, and barricades were being erected across the western mouths of streets. In the central and northern sectors of the city, that is, in the new city, which had sprung up over the old Tsaritsyn since 1927, the lay-out had been as regular as the planning of Manhattan's financial section. By that I mean that though many of the streets were set obliquely to the river – contrary to the layout of the post-war Stalingrad – they were straight and broad. At the western limit old carts and sandbags and above all the precious proud trees of the streets and the courtyards were piled across the entrances, and by the time all were closed in this way the city was sealed off against all normal intruders from the west. Other barricades were also erected in the depths of the city, so that if the first line were breached there could be no forward surge of the enemy which would press back the defenders by the sheer weight of its impetus.

Behind these defence works were posted the men of General Chuikov's understrength Sixty-second Army. (Shumilov with the Sixty-fourth and Tolbukhin with the Fifty-seventh were away to the south-western approaches.) Their backs were to the Volga, over which there has never been and still is not a bridge of any sort by which they might retreat. They had one order: to prevent the Germans from capturing the city. If they could not do that they must die where they stood or throw themselves into the river.

Behind Sixty-second Army stood all the men of Stalingrad and many of the women, too. In late June all the healthy males of the city from fifteen to fifty years of age had been registered, called up and organised into military units. Some were given uniforms, but the

majority of them had only armbands. Even before the digging of the
trenches began and the barricades were erected, the men who had
been organised started work on other types of defences. These were
mostly dug-in tanks, that is to say, tanks buried in holes in the
ground with only their turrets and guns exposed. Sometimes they
would be covered with a shell of concrete before the earth was
replaced over them, though even just a covering of earth made them
extremely effective strong-points if their siting had been expertly
done.

During this period of making preparations, apart from the strange
work they were called upon to do, the people of Stalingrad began to
experience a totally new way of life. The men already allotted their
units, and the units given their tasks to perform, assumed at once the
separation from their families and homes which is normally caused
by military service. They were fed by the authorities and they slept
wherever they happened to find themselves when the time came for
sleeping. In the northern and central sectors more often than not it
was in the streets or in the courtyards of the flats. Fortunately it was
summer time with even the night-temperatures well above a hundred
degrees Fahrenheit, and the likelihood of rain extremely remote. In
the south, where the wooden one-storey houses of the old Tsaritsyn
still stood in apparent disorder among a maze of deep-rutted, dirt-
surfaced lanes, the surrounding fields were thicker with men than
with grass during the dark hours. Nor was it merely the husbands
whom the wives and mothers did not see for days at a time. Their
sons and daughters might be digging or building the crazy-looking
defence walls in some alien part of the city and they, too, getting food
wherever it was obtainable, slept at night wherever they happened to
be when sleep overtook them. Many of the younger ones were taken
into nearby flats and given mattresses and cushions or a space on the
bare floors of sitting-room or kitchen, but the majority slept in the
courts under the trees and in the squares under the stars.

The atmosphere in which all this was carried out was unreal, tense
and very brittle. Those in authority urged all to their work with
words of encouragement and patriotic slogans. Perhaps one of the
reasons why revolutions have been so few among the English-
speaking peoples is because English is so matter-of-fact, so uninflam-
matory that the words needed to suspend the reason of rabbles are
entirely lacking. The Romance languages, on the other hand, have

not this disability, and the Slavonic languages seem to have been invented for the purpose of expressing or arousing the most intimate emotions without embarrassing either oneself or ones hearers. The constant exhortations of the leaders added to the natural national and civic patriotism of the Stalingraders was more than enough to stimulate to tremendous physical efforts every man, woman and child in the city, and to raise their morale and imbue them with a determination to resist the enemy when he came at all costs, even of life itself.

Outwardly, then, there was confidence and defiance, though the excitement, which was inevitable among adults and young alike, tended to undermine the eventual degree of effectiveness. But underneath the outward courage there was also fear and a shaken morale which had affected the soldiers as well as the civilians. Indeed, it has been expressed to me recently in Stalingrad by people who went through the battle that the morale of the soldiers was much lower than that of the civilians at the beginning.

'It was natural that this should be so, I think,' Andrei Galishev said to me. 'You see, the soldiers knew what the advances of the Germans really meant; that the Germans had better and more numerous weapons than we had, and that their soldiers were much more highly trained. Our armies had *fallen back*, had been pushed back, a very long way; and the enemy armies had *advanced* just that same distance. When you go on retreating for hundreds and hundreds of miles you must sometime begin to get despondent. Lots of our soldiers in Stalingrad, though they were prepared to fight until they had given their last drop of blood, believed that they would never be able to hold the city. Well, if you think those things, whether you whisper them to your bosom friend or keep them strictly to yourself, some of your potential as a soldier is taken away. There was another thing, too, which disturbed many secretly, and it applied to civilians as well as soldiers. This was the terrible brutality with which the Germans treated prisoners of war and our civilians. Soldiers who had come from the west, where we had retreated first and then advanced a little and retreated again, brought terrible stories of men beaten up until they died, little twelve-year-old girls raped, young men sexually mutilated – this was a form of sport for the German soldiers – and multiple gallows by the roadsides bearing our men and our women hanging side by side, young and old alike. Now and again, too, a prisoner of war had escaped and the stories they had to tell of the treatment they received from the Germans were so horrible that they turned your stomach upside down. These stories were true, but even had they not been, the best they could have been in the minds of the people were exaggerations. Once stories like this begin to circulate, though they may be so wild as to seem patently untrue, something of them lingers in the mind. Courage is unsettled then, and it takes longer to get used to being brave.'

But whatever happened, whether schools or offices or shops were closed, or ditches were dug or barricades raised, or you slept on the kitchen floor of somebody else's house or a strange courtyard under the stars, you worked to the limit of your powers to defend the city, and if you were making tanks or heavy lorries or guns or ammunition, you doubled your efforts, and at the same time prepared for the future.

In the Tractor Factory, for example, the workers were organised into armoured battalions, and raised a complete regiment. When they were not making tanks they were learning to drive the tanks they made and to fire the guns and to know the tactics of mobile warfare. What they did in the Tractor Factory they did elsewhere. In the Red October Factory the women workers formed themselves into a so-called brigade under the command of Sergeant Kovalova, who was to meet her death at the head of her 'men' when she led them out to the defence of her factory.

By the end of July it was clear that the German offensive against the city could not be long in coming. The very old, it was decided, and the very young, where the mother could be spared by the rest of her family to go with them, should be evacuated from the city across the Volga. This was not easy to propose nor to accomplish, for the old people were strongly attached to their city, and the mothers of the very young were afraid that if they were separated from the rest of their families they might never find one another again; and the authorities were hard put to it to know what to do with them once they were across the great river. On the east bank of the Volga just here the naked steppe looks like the edge of the world. For miles upon miles there are no rivers, no towns, nothing; and to get them away from this void, nothing could be spared them but their own old and tired legs to carry them under the scorching summer sun to the nearest little town many miles away to the north-east out of the way of the bombs and from under the feet of the defenders.

This first evacuation was a limited movement. It had to be. So as the days of August slipped by, and the tension mounted, and the life of the city changed every hour, you began to wish something would happen; either that Tomoshenko and his men would hold the Germans on the other side of the Don, though you knew that could not happen without a miracle, or that the German would come to your city so that he could be sent staggering back.

But then news reached the city that a German tank army had come up to within eighteen miles in the south. The city authorities called the people together in the afternoon of 22nd August to tell them and to urge them to remain calm. The attack would come very soon now. Exactly when, it was difficult to say. It might be tomorrow; it might be the day after, or the day after that. But whenever it came, let them not panic whatever happened; both the Army and the city had everything in hand.

The exhortation came not a day too soon, for the day the Germans had chosen was tomorrow. Almost before it was light on 23rd August, high above the city, so high that the eastern rising sun made them look like a cloud of silver dust no bigger than a man's hand, Junkers of German VIII Air Corps came over the city and before you could turn your eyes away to shade them, the earth seemed to be leaping up to the sky, and the noise in your ears threatened to burst open your skull.

THE ASSAULT BEGINS

No one in Stalingrad could say with certainty how many German aeroplanes came over the city and dropped their bombs that day. They came with the first morning light, and with hardly a pause they droned over the city until nightfall, and after nightfall, still they came. Some of the Russian air-observer corps insist that on 23rd August, 1942, the Germans flew over two thousand sorties to the city in the hours of daylight alone.

As the sun came up over the eastern steppes of Asia on the other side of the river, the stifling night gave way to a burnished, breathless

day, and through the shimmering heat, with a whistling rush of
terrified air, the bombs rained down and shook the earth to the skies.
Never before had so many German aircraft come to the city at one
time, nor had so many bombs been dropped. In the same way that
the artillery barrage in the Kaiser's War had heralded an imminent
attack, so this attack from the air was the signal that the assault on
the city had begun. At least, so the Russians believed; and they were
to be proved right.

The air-attack on Stalingrad on this and the two following days is
in some way comparable with the destruction of Rotterdam on 14th
May, 1940, but with this difference – only the centre of the Dutch
city was razed, whereas scarcely a single quarter of Stalingrad
escaped. The German's chief aim was to create panic among the
civilian population and by so doing impede all the attempts of the
military to function effectively. Though from the ground it appeared
at the time as if the Richthofen squadron – Colonel-General Baron
von Richthofen, the most outstanding Luftwaffe leader of the War,
was commanding Fourth Air Fleet, whose VIII Air Corps was
supporting Sixth Army – were dropping their bombs haphazardly,
when the damage was plotted on a map it could be seen that
Stalingrad was being annihilated according to a plan. The main point
of effort was directed initially at the residential and administrative
sectors. There was little sense in attacking those industries you hoped
to turn to your own good account when you had captured the city.
Nevertheless, despite the intention, the human element varied the
results. If at first bombs fell on factories and other industrial
undertakings by mistake, in a week or two there would be no
discrimination, for by then the city had to be taken even if it were
only a heap of rubble and stinking, grotesquely maimed corpses.

On the shore of the river almost exactly opposite the centre stood a
field of oil-storage tanks, and it was not long before German bombs
had hit the tanks. The city was already burning, but now the dense
black smoke of oil was adding its pall to the thick canopy of smoke
and dust and quivering heat haze which hung over the city. This
smoke and dust blotted the sun for the most part completely from
sight, though here and there, if you glanced up, you could see a
strange extinguished moon of a sun which seemed to be cowering in
pale stature behind the veil of awfulness. But beneath the smoke and
through it fierce flames shot up so high that it seemed as if they were

trying to escape by taking to the air. And the oil was running away, too, with a fat man's agility which surprises by its speed. The ground about the tanks sloped down to the river so gently that you scarcely noticed it. But the oil found the slope and let itself slip irresistibly down and into the river. Yet the water could not quench its flames. As more and more oil forced its way into the river it pushed the first rim farther and farther out into the middle stream, in a great blazing mass of flame which was carried by the currents here almost across the kilometre-wide Volga until it seemed that the Volga itself was on fire.

A small river-barge, one of the many which plied between city and city, bringing grain from Yenotaevsk to the people of Saratov and Kuibyshev, and taking back manufactured goods, had been damaged by a near-missing bomb which fell into the river and exploded not far from it. The engine had died of the shock and nothing that Andrei Parfenov could do would restore it to life. The boat meant livelihood to Andrei and for many years now he and it had worked together and become attached to one another. They had come to Stalingrad as soon as they had heard that the city was threatened because Andrei thought that they could be useful in such jobs as helping the old and the children across the river, thus relieving the ferries.

As he bent over the engine he could see nothing wrong, and yet it would not go. Cursing softly at it and then with increasing vigour, he unscrewed this and that, looked at it closely, blew on it and put it back, and tried again. But without result.

'Andrei! Andrei!' a voice almost shrill with scarcely controlled fear shouted down to him.

'What is it?' he called back impatiently.

Since he had come down to look at the engine he had left behind the pandemonium of whistling and exploding bombs, the crash of buildings and the cries of anxious men. Only now and again did a near or excessively loud noise impinge on his pre-occupation with the engine.

'What is it?'

'It's the river, Andrei,' the voice shouted back. 'The river's on fire.'

'Talk sense, Matsve!' Andrei called. 'I've worries enough without your lunacy.'

'But it's true, Andrei!' Matsve insisted. 'The oil is on fire and it's spread on to the river and the flames are coming this way.'

'What's that?' Andrei looked up at the white face peering down at him, white even against the black and white picture framed in the hatch.

'The flames are coming this way quickly, I tell you.'

Andrei, spanner still in hand, came quickly up the companion-way on to the deck. He looked across to the city and could not see it, only the great blanket of smoke and the tossing sheets of flame. The boy was right! The river was on fire, and the fire was spreading rapidly across the river to where he had moored his barge, a little east of mid-stream, until he could repair the engine.

'Can't you mend the engine?' Matsve asked.

'No . . . not yet. Can you swim?'

The boy nodded.

'It's a long way,' Andrei pointed out.

'I can do it. But what about you?'

'It will be some time before the fire reaches here. I shall stay . . .'

'Then so shall I!'

Andrei made a little gesture of annoyance.

'Listen to what I've got to say, will you?' he snapped. 'Swim ashore as quickly as you can and ask anyone who has a dinghy to lend it to you to come and fetch me off. I can't swim. Understand?'

'Yes, Andrei.' Already the boy was pulling his shirt over his head.

'Will you listen?' Andrei repeated. 'If no one will lend you one, take the first you find. Be as quick as you can.'

The boy stripped off his trousers, paused for a brief moment on the edge of the barge, then drawing in his breath he plunged head-first into the river. Andrei watched his slick, sun-darkened body sliding through the water for a dozen yards or so. The boy could swim like an eel. They all could these days; yet here he was, he'd lived on the river fifty years and by the river five before that and hadn't learned to swim. He wasn't the only one who made a living off the river who couldn't swim, but they were all born before the Revolution, when nobody took much notice of teaching children anything except how to work. It was a good thing he'd taken the boy aboard, and just as well that Vassiliev and Mosha were in the city, because they couldn't swim either. But what was he thinking? If anyone survived what was going on in the city, it would be a miracle!

He turned back and looked towards the great wall of flame and pall of smoke. The oil on the water was spreading out slowly, with the relentless forward creeping of lava. You could not see it move, and yet you could divine the perpetual motion of the flames.

He hoped the boy would waste no time. He swung round and looked towards the sandy east bank. The smoke from the burning oil was being driven across the river to the east by the light breeze which had been blowing almost constantly these last three weeks. Fortunately it was billowing obliquely across the wide water, and just on the clear northern edge of it he saw the shining body of Matsve wading ashore. The boy stood at the water's edge for a moment, looking back towards the barge and waving. Andrei waved back; the boy answered and then went scrambling up the bank on all fours and out of sight.

The difficulty which was facing Andrei derived in great part from the currents, which here flowed right into the path of the burning oil and carried it downstream and across the river. Now that he was without any means of motivation, if he pulled up his anchor, before he would know where he was he would be running right among the flames, which, in their turn, while being carried down-river were also spreading outwards with ever-extending perimeter like a grease-spot on flannel; so even if he stayed where he was it would not be long before they crept up on him.

The barge was empty and riding high in the water, for since he had only come down the river from Nikolayevskij, intending to take a shipment of cured hides on board at Stalingrad, it had not been worth while taking on ballast. If he had had a pole long enough he would have tried poling the barge to the other side of the river, provided the lightness of it had not allowed the stream to carry it too quickly down into the flames. The thought had occurred to him when he had sent the boy to fetch the dinghy that they might be able to tow the barge to safety – but, again, only if the stream were not too strong and the barge too light.

He glanced round to the east bank, but there was no sight of the boy. The heat from the leaping flames was now added to the heat of the smoke-hidden sun; but it was a particular heat, for he could feel the scorch of it on his cheeks. Supposing the boy couldn't find a dinghy? Then it would be all up, not only with the barge but with him, too. He was fond of the barge and would hate to lose her, she had been more than a good friend; but he wasn't going to let a silly sort of sentimentality make him take foolish risks. He was keen to go on living, even though he was over sixty. He liked being alive, and besides he could do his bit against – what did they call them? – the fascist barbarians, and if they went on behaving like this, Mother Russia would be wanting the help of every man she could lay hands on, whether boys like Matsve or ancients like himself. It had been a wonderful and beautiful city, and now, in the three or four hours since daybreak and the first enemy bombs had fallen, the fine, tall buildings had come tumbling down, filling the streets with debris, and under the smoke heavens knew what was happening. Now the enemy bombers were coming back again. You could hear them above the crackle of burning and the distance-muted shouts of men and the thunder-crackle of anti-aircraft guns. What were the Germans hoping to do? Destroy the city utterly and its people?

On the top of the east bank Matsve heard the dull drone of the German bombers, too, and paused in his scrambling, the soles of his feet tingling with the branding heat of the soft sand into which they sank over the ankles, to look across the river at the city. Into his mind came the same question as the one Andrei had asked himself. Yet, what good would a ruined city be to them? Not that they were ever going to capture the city. The people and the soldiers would see to that, and when he had rescued Andrei from the barge he was going to cross the river and go into the city and help them.

He looked at the near-edge of the river to the north, searching for a dinghy, but could not see one. There were two or three long-boats, used chiefly for ferry work on short distances, capable of carrying half a dozen people and their sacks and baskets and parcels, but requiring a small motor to propel them, or two or three men with oars. These were packed now with old people, women and children and the few pitiful belongings they had been able to snatch up in their flight from the city. One was already on its way back to the west bank, to fetch another load, Matsve supposed. They were going to save several lives. He could not ask one of them to go and rescue Andrei from his barge.

At that moment he heard a shrill woman's voice on the other side of him, to the south, and on the edge of the smoke-cloud he saw two women with four or five children, one of whom was coughing and being sick and crying all at the same time, while the others were carrying bundles and baskets up the bank from a rowing-boat. With a private cry of joy he ran obliquely down the bank to where one of the women and an older girl were unloading the boat.

'Is that your boat?' he asked.

Without stopping, the woman said: 'It is ours. Why?'

'Please could you lend it to me?' he pleaded. 'You see that barge out there in the middle of the river, near the buring oil? The engine's broken down, my friend is on board, an old man, but in any case he can't swim, and every minute the flames are getting nearer.'

The woman looked out across the river, then turned her head back.

'Yes,' she said simply. 'You may have the boat, but it is too heavy for you to row on your own against the river. Anya will take an oar with you. Help us with these things, otherwise you will be too late to save your friend.'

Within two or three minutes the last of the bundles had been removed from the boat.

'I can manage on my own,' Matsve said to the fifteen- or sixteen-year-old girl.

'We shall get there quicker if I help you,' the girl answered, sitting down and taking an oar.

Matsve pushed the boat off the sand and as it floated jumped in. Sitting in front of the girl, he took up the other oar.

'Now, together – pull!' he called over his shoulder, as they came out into the stream. 'You'll have to keep us on course.'

On the barge Andrei had lost sight of the boy after answering his wave. There was nothing he could do, only hope that the burning oil would stay away from the barge until Matsve could get back. They would make an attempt to tow the barge to the east bank, but if the current was too strong, well – it would just have to take whatever came to it.

While he was waiting, he prepared a rope. One end he fixed to a cleat in the stern, and coiled the rest and put it down beside the cleat ready to throw into the dinghy. Another shorter length he fixed to a second cleat, and threw the running end over the side of the barge into the river. Down this rope he would slide into the dinghy – if Matsve could find one and if he arrived in time.

Over the city droned the German bombers, though you could not hear this noise now; it was drowned by the barking of the A-A guns and the whistle of bombs falling and the tremendous blasts of exploding bombs. The heat from the blazing oil was beginning to burn one's eyeballs; that was how near it was now. Matsve had to come soon or not at all.

Andrei turned away from the city and looked towards the east and his heart turned over.

'Row, boy! Row, daughter! You're doing fine!' he yelled.

Less than fifty strokes away was the big dinghy. He was saved! But only just, for as he shouted a billowing, acrid darkness swirled over him, and when it had cleared he saw flames dancing over the point of the bows. He ran to the side and looked down. The oil had come up to the barge now and the flames were lapping at it. It would be useless to try to save it. He heard Matsve calling out to him.

'The barge is alight!' the boy shouted.

'I know,' Andrei shouted back. 'Come under the stern; under this rope!'

The boy and girl manoeuvred the boat under the stern, and in no time at all the old man had lowered himself over the side of the barge and into it. Almost before he had righted himself Matsve and the girl were pulling away, and not until they were thirty or forty yards from the barge did they pause and sit looking at it as it blazed from end to end.

'Well-seasoned timber and many coats of pitch,' Andrei commented. 'That's why she burns so well.'

'I read once in a book at school,' Anya said, 'that in the old times in one of the northern countries where the people were great sailors and sailed across the seas and conquered many countries . . .'

'I've read about them, too,' Matsve said. 'You mean the . . . the . . . Oh, I can't remember! But when their great chiefs died they put them in one of their long-boats and set fire to the boat. Why do you remember that?'

'The barge looks like such a boat, I imagine,' the girl said. 'I'm sorry for you, Comrade.'

'She's been a good friend,' Andrei said. 'I shall miss her.'

'Perhaps, when the war is over and the Germans have gone, they will give you another barge,' the girl suggested.

'Perhaps. . . .Well, let's get to the bank,' Andrei said.

One of the women was with the children on top of the bank, but the other came down to the water's edge and held the bow steady while Anya, Matsve and old Andrei got out. When they had pulled the dinghy up on to the sand, she held out a pair of trousers to Matsve.

'You'll need these,' she said. 'I suppose you've left all your things in the barge.'

For the first time Matsve realised that ever since he had gone into the water he had been naked. Under the skin of his cheeks the blood which rushed there heightened his tan. Turning to Anya he said: 'I'm sorry. I was so anxious . . .'

'It's of no consequence,' the woman said. 'She has brothers. They're in the city. They would not come with us.'

'I must go to the city, too,' Matsve said. 'They will need all the help we can give them.'

'I shall come with you,' Andrei said.

'I will row you over,' Anya offered.

'No. It's not safe. Up there they are bringing people over in the little ferries and then going back to the city. We shall go back with them,' Matsve answered.

'What will you do?' Andrei asked the woman.

'Try to find somewhere to live not too far away,' the woman with the sick child said. 'But what shall we do to find our husbands and our sons? Do you think we shall ever see them again?'

'Of course you will see them again,' Andrei answered. 'My advice is, go and join those people down there. If there is a crowd of people they must do something for them. Let us all go to them together.'

Anya took the sick child from its mother, and Matsve walked beside her carrying a heavy bundle of belongings.

'Thank you for helping me,' he said. 'I hope we shall meet again some day.'

'Yes,' she replied. 'I hope so.'

But as their homes over the river buckled and burned under the enemy bombs their hopes could be little more than politenesses. Yet they did meet again and fifteen years later were telling their story to an Englishman in the sitting-room of their brand-new flat in the brand-new city of Stalingrad.

When Matsve and Andrei at last got back to the city, they found a strange and terrible confusion. Though the Germans had not created the panic they had planned, the weight and length of the bombing attacks had knocked the authorities off balance. They had not expected that the main attacks would be directed on the women and children in the residential quarters of the city, but rather in the northern suburbs. It was there that the majority of the anti-aircraft artillery had been sited. Though even then the A-A defences were nothing like so strong as they ought to have been; but if equipment just is not available, you have to make the best of what you have.

The people had been taken unawares by the first bombs. Most had believed that the first raid was merely a repetition of the raids on the industrial sector which the Germans had been making since the previous February, and scarcely anyone had bothered to go to the shelters. But as the second wave came in something seemed to tell the people that they were the chosen targets, and there was a scurrying rush for the cellars. Nevertheless, hundreds of women and children were killed and maimed before the survivors went underground for safety.

One of the great difficulties facing the military and civil authorities in Stalingrad was the almost complete absence of any air-warning system. The Germans were operating from airfields one hundred and two hundred miles away, and they were routed across almost empty steppe. There had been no time to erect forward warning stations, and, in any case, the military situation out in the steppe was extremely fluid, the Russian forces either fighting delaying actions or retreating. In such conditions it was not possible to plot aircraft and send back information. Almost the first news of the Germans' approach, therefore, was the sound of their engines followed by the quick sight of them.

In the circumstances the most satisfactory procedure would have been to keep the city under constant alert, since, though you knew the aircraft had gone when you could not hear them any more, you could not know when the next wave would come over. But how can you keep a city under constant alert, down in cellars which were never intended to be in any degree comfortable, nor equipped with any kind of conveniences? The people had to feed themselves and relieve themselves. In any case, so many were trapped and killed and injured, so many houses were heaps of rubble above the cellars, so many had lost all their belongings, including their food, that to have kept them shut up would have denied assistance to the helpless and suffering and those who could help themselves.

By the afternoon of the first day it was clear to the civilian authorities that all women and children and old men who could not be of any help would have to be evacuated. Where they would go no one had any idea, but the main thing was to get them out of the city and across the Volga. Once there it would be time enough to decide on the next step. Fortunately the city organisation for peacetime purposes was so good that very soon a plan had been worked out, and arrangements made for the first contingents to be shipped across the river before dawn next day.

Happily, though a large section of the city telephone network had been destroyed in the bombing, there was a telephone link with all of the local administrative centres. The word was passed to these, and the rest was done orally by the local officials. As a piece of *ad hoc* organisation it possessed that quality of native genius which was to stamp so much that the Russians did in their struggle against the Germans, not only here in Stalingrad – though here it was extremely marked – but everywhere else where Russians met Germans, and which very largely enabled the Russians to turn disaster into ultimate victory. When the Russo-German campaign opened stories trickled through to us of German hilarity caused by the matchboard characteristics of Russian armour-plating and the primitive nature of Russian tanks. It is true that, compared with the German, or British, or French, Russian armour-plating was of inferior quality and their tanks were merely mobile engines mounted with guns lacking the thousand and one refinements which adorned Western tanks, most of which on the battle-field proved useless, and often an impediment. But the Russians had no time for refinements. They wanted tanks able to carry out the simple functions of tanks in modern warfare without any of the frills, and they built tanks which performed these functions. Many Russian tanks were knocked out but they also knocked out many of the enemy; and if many were knocked out the Russians did not mind all that much, for their production was more than double the German production, simply because the finish was less polished and the gadgets less numerous, though neither lack of polish nor gadgets detracted from the functions of the tank as the Russian experts saw the rôle of these machines. We English, too, pride ourselves on our ability to extemporise in times of crisis. We are justifiably proud of this knack – we may look upon Dunkirk as one of the supreme examples of this ability – but we shall delude ourselves if we believe that we are unique in our achievements in this field. Again and again on every sector of the Eastern Front the

Russians proved they were our equals and often our masters in extemporisation, and here in Stalingrad they were to save their city very largely by the ability to adapt themselves to a kind of fighting quite unknown to them and by making use of every conceivable advantage that presented itself on the spur of the moment.

The heaviest raid of this first day came between two and three in the afternoon. The smoke of the burning buildings and the smoke from the oil-storage tanks still drew its veil across the blue of the sky. The fire-fighters were hampered by streets blocked by fallen houses and by lack of water, particularly in those parts of the city farthest from the river. In most cases there was little that could be done except let the burning buildings burn themselves out. But even when water was available in satisfactory quantities, the appliances were often inadequate to deal with the fierce intensity of the fires.

This was what happened when the dockyards caught fire during this raid. The yards were built chiefly of wood, and though the Volga lapped at the jetties and stocks and at the walls of dry-docks, it could do nothing to quell the fire, for the wood was old and seasoned and dry, and when it was attacked by flames it went up like the driest tinder, despite the efforts of the men there to pump up the river to quench the swiftly destroying flames. The men were standing by the pumps and the hoses when the bombs fell. Many of them were killed by the same bombs which set fire to the docks, and before their surviving companions could shake the dust out of their eyes and grasp their heads to stop the vibrations of the brain-cells which the noise and the blast had set up, the flames had taken such hold that the men were helpless.

All day long the voluntary evacuations, mostly of mothers with young children, had been going on, and since midday the larger ferries had been brought into use for this. Several naval monitors had also joined the few which had been at Stalingrad when the raids began. By chance entirely, for the German aircraft stayed high up above the city, a number of the ferries and the monitors received damage from bomb splinters and the blast from near-misses; and two monitors and three civilian boats were sunk by freak direct hits.

While this raid was going on news reached the military command of the situation out in the steppe, and word was sent to the northern sector, where the factories had been working more or less at the wartime normal, of the threat that was coming up on their northern flank. The main weight of the Russian defence was concentrated to the south, where the Fifty-seventh and Sixty-fourth Armies had gone out to meet the German Fourth Panzer Army, leaving General Chuikov and his Sixty-second Army to guard the city and the northern flank. There could be no possible doubt now that this was the beginning of the assault on the city, and it looked as if the German plan was to come into Stalingrad from the north, where the General would have to rely for the most part upon the workers in the factories to defend the factories and the streets while he moved his soldiers out into the steppe to ward off the blow as long as they could.

So in the mid-afternoon the first phase of defence was put into effect. The specified formations of civilians were instructed to report to their depots, where they were issued with rifles, ammunition and armbands.

It is not possible to appreciate the state of mind in which the men of Stalingrad went to the barricades that night. Duty demanded that they should not go to their homes to allay apprehensions concerning their families, but should stay at their posts conscious of other men's wives and children, brothers and sisters, fathers and mothers lying dead all round them and not knowing whether they themselves might not now be alone in the world. True, the bombs had begun to fall while they were on their way to work; but who was to tell them that this was not a raid like all the others, despite the unusual timing? And once at their bench or by their machine they could not go rushing home as the raid developed, to make sure their families were safe or to die with them. But the fate of their families and the ruin of their homes instilled in them an even greater determination to frustrate the fascist plans. Already men were saying: 'We can build the city again, but we cannot refurbish honour' – wisely they did not say, 'We can make other families to replace the old' – and every man vowed in his heart that if ever the city were taken it would be over his lifeless body.

Gone now, dispersed by the brutal destruction of this one day, was the belief that the Germans were so superior as to be invincible. By attempting to destroy morale Hitler had restored it to full vigour.

As the afternoon light flickered into the indeterminate half-light of dusk the General's soldiers sent back the news that the Germans had reached the Volga to the north of the city. They were only mobile columns, however, and neither so numerous nor so strong that they could not be held out of the city should they attempt to attack before reinforcements of tanks or infantry arrived.

The news was both surprising and reassuring: surprising that these forces should have crossed the steppe so easily, and reassuring because any imminent attack by these forces could be decisively in their favour. But in getting where they had, the Germans had not had it entirely their own way. The General's men had stood in their way and his tanks had given battle. Many of those tanks would never fight again, nor would their crews; but many were crippled, yet still had fight in them. When the light had failed to such an extent that it was dangerous trying to distinguish friend from enemy, the crippled hobbled back to the city and to the factory from which they had emerged in shining eagerness only a day or two before. From this first day they formed a habit in which they were to persist so long as the Tractor Factor could offer them shelter; a habit which they transferred to the workers in the factory. By day they went out and fought, both tanks and workers; by night they returned to the factory to have their wounds patched and their damage repaired.

And if the senseless destruction of helpless life that day had not hardened the determinations of the men of Stalingrad, these stories which the tank-crews told them as they worked on through the night could not have failed to stir them by example. If youngsters still in their teens could conquer their misgivings, forget the dangers and fight with complete disregard for their lives so that the soil of the city might not be fouled by German possession, then men of experience in life and love of Russia could no longer have wavering doubts.

Such a story they were telling about Ivan Khvastantsev, a Sergeant in charge of an anti-tank gun squad. About eleven miles to the south and three to the east of Kotleban, Sergeant Khvastantsev established his squad in a small farm-house and the surrounding out-buildings. Khvastantsev's little group was one of the most advanced elements of the Sixty-second Army which had gone to the city.

'This farm where you are to go,' said his battalion* commander, who was with his company commander when he went to receive his orders, 'this farm where you are to go lies almost directly in the path of the German XIVth Panzer Corps which is advancing from

---

* In the Red Army four companies = one battalion, four battalions = one regiment, four regiments = one division.

Vartiachii. Your orders are simple. You will engage and destroy as many enemy tanks as you can. That is all. You do not retreat until you have no ammunition left. Do you understand, Comrade Sergeant?'

'Yes, Comrade Captain, I understand,' Sergeant Khvastantsev answered, and without another word had returned to his men and told them just as economically what was expected of them.

With all the speed they could get out of their vehicles they had dashed across the steppe to the farm. The farmer was young, his wife younger and they had four small children, the oldest of whom was six.

'You must take your wife and children to safety,' the Sergeant had said, when he had explained to the farmer why he and his men had come.

'But when will it be safe?' the young man had asked.

'Go towards the city, but to the south,' the Sergeant suggested, almost unable to answer the man's question. 'In that way, you will not be in the way of our soldiers who are coming out of the city. In the city you can be of some help, and they will send your wife and the children across the river to safety.'

'Very well,' the farmer replied, and while Sergeant Khvastantsev deposed his men, the strongest horse was harnessed to the cart, and clothes and cushions and other precious belongings were loaded into it, and finally the children, frightened by the soldiers and excited at the same time, were placed on the cushions with their mother beside them, the youngest at her breast.

'Go as quickly as you can,' Khvastantsev urged the mn. 'It may be difficult in the city, but there will be many there to help you and to tell you what to do. Goodbye, and don't worry about your farm or your house. Whatever you lose will be made up to you again when we've beaten the Germans. But now the chief thing is to defeat the enemy.'

He stood watching them until they had turned into the roadway, and then he went back to the house. There his men had almost completed their arrangements. Overhead an aircraft engine could be heard throbbing, but the machine must have been in the sun, for wherever you could look in the sky unblinded, you could see nothing. It could be either Russian or German, for it was obviously on a reconnaissance mission, since it was going on a circular route – round

and round over the steppe, searching no doubt for signs of dust or
columns of lorries or lumbering tanks which would tell the advance
of one side or another.

He had detailed a look-out to sit on the gable of the barn with
field-glasses to keep a constant watch to the west. The first he knew
of the advance of the enemy, therefore, was from him.

'What are they?' Khvastantsev called up to the man.

'MGs they look like,' the man shouted down, peering all the time
through the glasses.

Khvastantsev climbed up on to an upturned cart and through his
own glasses searched the steppe. But all he could distinguish was the
bow of the leading tank and the dust which the column was sending
up into the air.

'Can you see how many there are?' he asked the look-out.

'Not properly, but five or six, I think, all fairly close together. Then
there's quite a gap, and way back more dust. . . .Yes, the second lot
are armoured lorries.'

'No infantry?'

'No, Comrade Sergeant, no infantry.'

'Right! Keep out of sight,' Khvastantsev told the man. 'And let me
know what happens. How far are they away now?'

'Half a mile perhaps, but advancing quickly.'

Khvastantsev's men knew what to do. Between them they were
armed with two Soviet-type bazookas, three anti-tank rifles and
several dozen hand grenades. They would not open fire until they got
the word from him, and then they would fire at their own discretion
until the enemy retreated or were destroyed, or they themselves were
killed.

From his point of vantage, standing in the rickety cart, the Sergeant
was soon able to pick out the leading tank. Not until it was level with
the entrance to the farm would he give the order to fire. His look-out
was well enough hidden by the low chimney behind which he
sprawled on his belly on the farmhouse thatch. It was not essential
that the German should be unaware of his squad's presence at the
farm, but the element of surprise was always a valuable ally in any
encounter. If he judged his time well the first four or five tanks could
be knocked out before they knew from which direction the attack was
coming or their companies could come to their assistance. If they

could be stopped in the roadway they could prove quite an obstacle to the following column, until they were cleared out of the way.

'The leader is only three hundred yards off,' the look-out called down.

'Yes, I can see him,' Khvastantsev called back. 'Now, don't move, anybody – especially you up there on the roof. Take aim!'

Khvastantsev lowered his glasses. The leading German tanks were near enough now to be seen quite clearly without them. Under his breath, the Sergeant began to count softly to himself, and as the first tank appeared by the entrance he shouted: 'Fire!'

The pandemonium, which cut short the single-syllabled cry, made a shiver of excitement course down his backbone. It always had done from the first time in front of Moscow; a hundred, two hundred times and more he must have given the order, but it was an order you could never become accustomed to, for every time it was a challenge both to your enemy and yourself.

The shell from a bazooka hit the leading enemy tank amid-ship. With a violent stagger it turned across the road obliquely and came to a stop, completely blocking the way. While the second tank was concentrating on taking avoiding action, the second bazooka found its mark, and almost at once the third came into range of the first bazooka, whose rocket carried away part of the tank's track; its momentum sent it hurtling forward into the rear of the tank in front.

By this time the two rear tanks had realised that they had run into an ambush, and had also determined the source of the attack. They turned off the road and came hurtling like awkward automatons across the field towards Khvastantsev and his man, their guns blazing.

The Germans always reacted in this way. Whenever they ran into this kind of trap, those tanks which were not immobilised at once made a head-on attack on the attackers. It had happened to Khvastantsev and his men again and again. But they had camouflaged their positions so well that the Germans could not draw accurate aim and were firing blind. Holding their fire, without any order from their leader, until the German tanks were within most effective range, the bazookas then let fly and within seconds the two tanks were smoking, motionless wrecks.

Khvastantsev called up to the look-out to ask what was happening farther away. The column had stopped, the man said, and more tanks were coming up.

'What sort of a force is it? Can you see?' the Sergeant shouted.

'Light tanks, MGs like these and lorries of infantry, they look like,' came the answer.

'Then they'll have to clear the road before they can go on,' the Sergeant muttered. 'The lorries would get bogged down if they left the road. That means they'll have to push us out of here.'

He knew at once what that meant. There had been no mention of reinforcements coming up. His orders had been simple: stop the enemy as long as you can. He said nothing to his men. They would fight until the enemy retreated or they themselves were killed. They would not run away whatever happened; but it was as well that they should be able to concentrate on the battle, for knowledge of certain death can deflect even the most courageous from singleness of purpose.

'Another five tanks are advancing, Comrade Sergeant,' the look-out called down. 'It looks as if they're going to try and surround us.'

But the look-out was wrong. The tanks advanced in a semi-circle, and it needed only the slightest variation of his disposition to meet this threat. Half an hour later four more German tanks lay smoking and silent in the fields to the west of the house, and the fifth was retreating lamely to out-of-range safety.

It was an hour before the Germans made their next move. This time eight tanks came forward; but this time the aim of the Russians faltered, and when once again the enemy withdrew, leaving another four casualties on the field, they had taken their toll of the Sergeant's force. Out of fifteen men, six were dead and three so seriously wounded that they could take no further part in the battle. But still the three first tanks blocked the advance.

In the next attack one of the bazookas was put out of action and three of the six still unharmed men were killed. Taking over the remaining bazooka and somehow performing the almost miraculous feat of loading and firing himself, Khvastantsev was presently by himself and must have known that it would not be long now before he joined his companions.

A splinter from a shell struck his left arm and the arm fell to his side limp and useless. Now, with only one hand, he could not load and fire the bazooka.

Two tanks, realising from the now very intermittent fire that the opposition was broken, came rumbling forward to administer the coup de grâce. With his still usable right hand Khvastantsev fumbled at his belt and somehow managed to free one of the grenades attached to it. Drawing the pin with his teeth, he waited until the nearer tank was almost upon him, then raising himself on one knee he lobbed the grenade at it, in the same moment getting to his feet. Almost before the grenade exploded he had seized another and drawn the pin, and with it still in his hand he ran at the tank and deliberately threw himself beneath it, and as he died claimed his last victim. Now, and only now, when all firing had stopped did the Germans come forward to clear the road, and when they went on, as a result of the courage and outstanding bravery of Sergeant Khvastantsev and his men they were weaker by no fewer than twenty tanks.

Only one of all Khvastantsev's little band survived – Philip Sharupov, radio-operator, who, through the entire engagement, had sent a running report of all that was happening. The last words that came from Sharupov's radio was his simple description of his leader's final act. Then the transmitter went dead, and Sharupov has never been seen or heard of since. But the story which he told, as the battle in the farmhouse raged, reached not only those who awarded Khvastantsev the honour of Hero of the Soviet Union, but the men, the ordinary men, of Stalingrad, and gave them heart as they themselves prepared to meet the enemy.

The speed with which the Germans advanced on the northern flank was bewildering. By mid-afternoon it became clear to the defenders that the enemy would reach the Volga by nightfall. Steps had been taken to contain them within a fairly narrow corridor by troops pressing down from the north and by elements of Sixty-second Army sent out from the city pressing up from the south, and, in fact, the German front along the Volga eventually extended for only three miles. Nevertheless, the Russians expected next day to receive the full weight of a determined attack on the northern sector of the city.

But the attack did not come. As usual the German van had outrun not only the main body, but supplies and reinforcements through the totally unexpected absence of fierce opposition. Instead, they continued the systematic bombing of the city, street by street, block by block, dropping an estimated two thousand bombs on every square kilometre. From the east bank of the Volga and from the western steppe, it appeared that the whole city was ablaze.

From first-light the official evacuation of the civilian population who were not bearing arms was speeded up. A constant stream of women and children were led down to the river and put upon ferries and any kind of boat that was at hand. Stukas were now accompanying the German bombers, and seeing the ceaseless to-and-fro trans-river traffic they swooped down and bombed and machine-gunned the helpless refugees, killing and maiming, and frightening the women and children into near panic. When news of what was happening on the river reached other parts of the city, an unofficial evacuation began. Soon old men, women and children were leaving the city, their pitiful belongings in sacks and hand-carts. They passed through the defences and made towards the west. There was no attempt to stop them. In the city they were a liability as well as a responsibility, and the steppe was vastly wide.

On this and the following days the exodus in both directions continued, and by the end of the month fewer than ten thousand civilians remained in the city. These included a few children whose mothers refused to leave the one place in the world they knew – home. If they were to die, they said, they would prefer to die there than on the road to the Don or across the river in the strange east. But mostly they were women prepared to act as nurses, or to look after the men, or even to bear arms as soldiers.

These events made even an attempt at orderly life and living no longer possible, and on 25th August the authorities declared martial law. Already the form that the battle was ultimately to take had begun to emerge, for the majority of all who remained in the city were forced into the cellars and basements which, they discovered now for the first time, offered shelter against the German terror and a strange security. In these underground fastnesses they were already beginning to acquire the determination to defy the enemy when, logically, they should have caved in and cried *Kamerad*.

In the north the hedgehog formed by the forward German troops came under relentless Russian pressure from the Don army, striking southwards against it. For a time, until reinforcements and supplies of ammunition were brought up, the situation looked critical for the 16th Panzer Division. The pressure from the south by the Russian Sixty-second Army gradually weakened, however, as the advance of

the main forces of Sixth Army on the central sector compelled it to
retire within the city's defences. In the south, too, the Fourth Panzer
Army was slowly but surely pushing back the Russian south-western
armies.

Taken all in all, the future of Lieutenant-General Paulus and his
men looked rosy indeed. The main danger seemed to come from the
speed of their own advance; the forward elements were outstripping
their supplies. However, the Army High Command were jubilant,
and began to calculate the days until Stalingrad would be in German
hands. Then, imperceptibly at first, and dangerously on that account
but with increasing certainty, it began to dawn on them that Sixth
Army's future was not so assured as that.

As the Germans approached nearer the city the Russian resistance
began to stiffen. On the airfield of Gumrak, a long, fierce battle was
waged, an augury, if only the Germans had been able to read it, of
what was to come. Soon, however, it became apparent to their
Commanders at all levels that the strength of the divisions was being
whittled away with the same attritional inevitability as water wears
out a stone. Losses could not entirely be avoided; in fact, they were
to be expected. But equally to be expected was that the losses would
be made good. But they were not. Reinforcements and replacements
were coming up irregularly and when they did arrive they were, more
often than not, totally inadequate.

The Russians, on the other hand, were strengthening their forces
all the time on the northern sector, and they were bringing up men,
too, opposite the city, on the east bank of the Volga. So far, however,
the latter were only in such numbers as to provide encouragement for
the men in the city, who were gradually being crushed between vastly
superior enemy odds – despite the increasingly heavy German losses
– and the river.

By the end of the first week of September the German Sixth Army
had come up to the western limits of the city almost along the whole
of its length, with the Fourth Panzer Army at the southern limits.
Now the battle proper for the city began.

Ditches and barricades proved no lasting barriers to the weight of
German pressure; only men could hold the enemy back. The air-
attacks had stopped, for only a freak building here and there stood
practically untouched among the vast devastation. The great blocks

of flats, the fine public buildings were now crazy, hollow shells. Only the basements were peopled.

It was for this crazy shell of a city that the fiercest of all city-battles of the Second World War was joined. For the Russians its factories could no longer contribute to the Soviet war-effort; for the Germans it was useless as a shelter. Even its strategic value either to Germans or Russians was now extremely doubtful. For Hitler, as we shall see, it was to become the object of a Führer-prestige obsession; for Stalin, it was to become the symbol of the ultimate in Russian defiance. For the Germans it was to achieve synonymity with final defeat; for the Russians it was to mark the beginning of final victory.

So, under Hitler's direct and personal orders, with everything they possessed the Germans attacked, street by street, house by house. The Russians fell back and the Germans came on. As they fell back the Russians mined the streets and set booby traps in every nook and cranny, and these claimed almost as many victims as the rifles and grenades.

By the middle of September, Fourth Panzer Army had reached the Tsaritsa and occupied the southern suburbs of the city. But the area they were occupying needed a great deal of mopping up, and at Beketovka the Russians held a deep, bell-shaped bridgehead on the west bank of the Volga, which extended seven miles along the shore of the river, having a width of two miles, and including the important industrial districts of Krasno and Sarepta up to Beketovka. From this bridgehead Fourth Panzer Army could not dislodge them without reinforcements, and these were not forthcoming.

On 15th September, Fourth Panzer Army withdrew its northern boundary from the Tsaritsa to the south side of the railway line, and at the same time Lieutenant-General Paulus took over control of all German operations in the city north of the railway. That is to say, while Fourth Panzer Army held the unimportant southern districts right up to the Volga, as far as the railway, Sixth Army had to contend with the gradual, and terrifyingly bloody, wearing-down conflict in the central sector.

But by now, besides losses of men, the Russians were beginning to be faced with a particularly difficult problem of food supplies. Such supplies as had been in the city when the battle began were rapidly running down, and it had not yet been possible to organise a regular system of replacements from across the river. It would appear, however, by a strange incident which took place on 15th September on the boundary of Fourth Panzer Army and the Russian Sixty-second Army, that the Germans were, surprisingly, in equally straitened circumstances.

A vast elevator stuffed with several thousand tons of grain was set on fire during operations that day and neither side could do anything to put out the flames, which very soon spread from the actual building to its contents. Fighting for the time-being forgotten, Russians from the north and Germans from the south strove long and hard to save the precious grain, but the combined amounts rescued by both sides added up to only a fraction of the whole. At the time the loss of so much food constituted a real tragedy for the Russians, but before the battle was concluded the rations of the garrison would be overflowing plenty compared with the terrible privations which the Germans were to suffer.

When the Luftwaffe decided that it had done enough and withdrew, both sides began to rely more and more on artillery. The Russians were helped in this by monitors of the Soviet navy, small shallow-draught ships with extremely heavy gun-power which presented difficult problems for the Germans, for, unlike their own fixed heavy artillery they could be constantly moved, and their positions could not be pin-pointed to allow eliminating attacks to be made on them. The guns of both sides carried on the destruction of the city where the Luftwaffe had left off, the Germans using theirs to attack the derelict houses whose crazy roofs and shattered upper stories harboured nests of snipers; their deadly aim took heavy toll of advancing troops and their defences could not be reached except by well-directed artillery fire.

The Russian defence grew more and more tenacious as each day passed, and though the Germans advanced yard by yard, their losses were fantastically high. By the beginning of October it was clear to Lieutenant-General Paulus that the date of the capture of Stalingrad was no longer predictable. Each street, each house in each street, even each room in each house, would have to be fought for; and as the Russians were pushed ever nearer to the river, so did their resistance increase, and soon it took a day to take a house where formerly it had taken half a day to take a street.

With each day that passed Hitler became more and more insistent that not one free Russian should be left in the ruins of Stalingrad.

But he did not know how fanatically the Russians were defending their ruins. Nor did he know, nor did the Commander-in-Chief of his Sixty Army know, how hard pressed these same fanatical Russians were.

'Stalingrad must be taken!' Hitler commanded, and in anticipation announced the fall of the city in his communiqués.

'If the city falls, you will die with it!' Stalin bluntly told the defenders of his city.

So a quarter of a million men pressed hard upon a force less than one quarter of their own strength, and by sheer disregard for losses they pushed the Russians back until all the city was in their hands except for a few pockets of resistance here and there in the factories and in the north and except for the main area, six square miles in extent, in the central sector, known by the Germans as *Der Tennisschläger*, the Tennis Racquet.

The railway system of Stalingrad is industrially strategic; that is to say, it has been planned to meet the requirements of the factories rather than the citizens, who are more inclined to use the river as their chief highway for moving from one part of the city to another. One line runs from Kuibyshev, some six hundred miles north of Stalingrad, right through the city and out at the southern end to Krasnodar, not far from the north-eastern Black Sea coast. Two other links enter the city from the north-west and south-west coming respectively from Moscow and Rostov. The former meets the Kuibyshev-Krasnodar line in the central sector of the city, and at the time of the battle in the new city this feature has been eliminated – the main marshalling yards were situated here. The Central Station was connected by a loop to the marshalling yards, which were much nearer to the river. The loop began to the north of the station, curved east and south-east and rejoined the main line south of the station, and the shape of the area enclosed by the loop was exactly that of a tennis-racquet's head.

This area, together with the larger portion of the Mamai heights to the north-west of it, and the streets and squares lying between it and the river, the Soviet Sixty-second Army resolutely refused to surrender. We shall see later that what is generally called the Battle of Stalingrad was, for the greater part of its later stages, really two battles which were waged simultaneously – the battle for German survival fought in the steppes to the west from the Volga to the Don, and the battle for the city itself, fought, with even greater intensity, in this area of the Tennis Racquet. Out in the steppes the Russians were triumphantly on the offensive, the Germans surrounded and in as grave a situation as can face any army completely encircled by vastly superior forces. In the city, in the basements and ruins of the Tennis Racquet, the Germans struggled to satisfy a personal whim of their Führer, and the Russians struggled to thwart that whim.

It was this concentration on the battle of the Tennis Racquet, where alone victory could allow Hitler to proclaim: 'I have captured Stalin's own city,' which was to prove the undoing of Lieutenant-General Paulus and his Sixth Army, and was to be the proving of Russian arms. Judged by any standard, it was a strange battle, as we shall see.

The Soldier Looks for his Family

John Prebble

The first bomb fell as the soldier got off the train. It fell just outside the station and the blast picked up the soldier and flung him against the wall. From the roof, a semicircle of glass and steel, long splinters spun through the air. There was shouting outside, and people were running. Then the sirens began to sound all over the city.

The soldier was in a hurry to get home to his family. He knew his wife would be frightened by the guns, and they might be starting at any moment now. He walked past the deserted ticket gate and into the street. There was no moon and the city was black and quiet. Even the noise of the explosion and the frantic haste of hurrying feet had gone. It was on the wide pavement, where his feet crunched splintered glass, that the military policeman stopped him.

'Where are you going?'

The soldier looked up at the sky. He had hardly heard the question. It was still very quiet, and as yet there was no sound of the planes above.

'Where are you going?'

'Home,' said the soldier. He was listening for the plane, quite intently. It seemed that nothing was so important as the syncopated noise of the engines at that moment. The policeman was listening too, and there was a pause before he spoke again.

'Have you got a pass?'

The questions were asked and answered automatically. Indifferent actors hurrying through their lines with an eye on the vast darkness of the auditorium. The policeman held out his hand and the soldier put his inside his blouse, and then the guns began. They had not found the plane but were feeling in the sky for it. First, the rippling flash beyond the silhouettes of dark houses, and then the heaving belching noise of the discharge. It went on intermittently, flash, thunder, darkness, the leaping shadows of the houses with their chimneys darting up like derisive fingers. And policeman and soldier watched it, heads turned towards it, one with a hand thrust out and the other with a hand inside his blouse. The soldier felt suddenly a great sadness as he thought of his wife and what the noise of these guns must be doing to her.

The policeman said, 'Let me see the pass. Hurry up, soldier, it's getting hot!' And as he said it the guns roared again in agreement.

The soldier looked at the man who had stopped him. Red light from the gun flashes caught the chiaroscuro of his features. He was very tall, the visor of his cap down over his nose, and the deep eye-holes behind it. The cap-badge shone from the sullen glow of his scarlet cap. He did not look human, thought the soldier. His belt shone on the bend of his chest, and the flap of his pistol-holster had been loosened. His hand was still held out and the soldier gave it the pass.

The policeman could not read it. He turned it to the gun flashes and held it up to his face. His lips parted with tense concentration and seemed to snarl, but his voice was friendly.

'I can't see the blasted thing. It's all right.'

The soldier looked up. Craned his neck. In a short silence he had heard the enemy plane.

The second bomb fell and exploded on the station.

It was all noise, suffocation and an irresistible weakness. The soldier was forced back against the station wall. He did not know whether the policeman had quickly thrust him there or the bomb had tossed him against it. It was like a strong, a very strong hand on his chest, pressing hard, convexing his ribs, and behind him the stones heaved. His knees gave way and he didn't know that he rolled over and over into the gutter because he was unconscious when that happened . . .

The liquid spurting violently into his face was hot. It hit him regularly and he struggled away from it for it had a disgusting taste. He tried to stand up but he was too weak. The air was thick and dusty, and behind him the rolling angry rustle of falling debris. His mouth fell open and he tried to breathe. He did not think he had been hurt, but as the station behind him burst into fire he saw that his hands and clothes, white with dust, were patched here and there with red. And his face was wet. He wiped it with his hand and saw that it was blood. He struggled to his knees and was sick in the gutter because he thought that he was seriously hurt and it frightened him.

Other bombs were falling. They hit the city regularly and it recoiled beneath them and answered from the flame-lips of its guns. The soldier held his head between his hands and felt that he wanted to cry because he had come home and been bombed. If he could get to his feet he would be able to walk home and find his wife; and she would have a cup of tea for him, and perhaps they could shut out the noise of the bombs, and the waterfall of falling rubble. But then more bombs fell, *one* . . . *two* . . . *three* . . . and the soldier was sick again.

'Soldier!'

The cry was faint, but he recognized the military policeman's voice, and he looked about him until he saw the man lying on his back about ten yards away. The red cap had rolled from his head and what hair he had was close-cropped and insignificant. His eyes were frightened and he was clutching at his groin.

He had only one leg now. The other had gone it seemed and the blood pounded regularly from what was left of the thigh. A man can't last more than seven minutes when the femoral artery has been severed. Life jets away as regularly as from a pump, and the military policeman knew that. He was trying to force a fist down on the pressure-point. But it wasn't enough. The blood spurted its liberation through his fingers. He must have been holding his hand there for over two minutes to judge by his face.

'*Soldier!*'

There were many fires in the city now. The noise they made, and of people's voices, was clamorous, but in this courtyard of the station there were only two soldiers, and the one who was sick looked at the one who was dying very rapidly.

The policeman was too weak to call again, but he opened his mouth and looked at the soldier. The soldier got up and stumbled across. He did not like looking at the blood but he fumbled along the mangled thigh and tried to put pressure on the critical point with both his thumbs. He could feel the blood knocking steadily, gently, and he pressed harder. The policeman groaned. The blood would not stop its flow, and the soldier raised himself on his toes until his body was arched, and he leant on the man's groin. His respirator slipped round from his back and hung beneath him. His cap fell over the other man's face. And he tried to press harder. The concentration left him quite weak and he trembled.

He must have leant on the groin for more than five minutes after the man died. There was a lot of blood and the bombs were still falling.

And then the soldier got up and went to find his family. He walked down the main street to a turning beyond the cupola which surrounded the obese equanimity of the old queen. She sat there in bronze silence, only the flames lighting up her indifference and the Bible on her knees. Beneath the stone fountain at her feet three Medical Corps men were sheltering, and they shouted to the soldier to come under there with them, but he did not answer and went on down the turning. He had put on his steel helmet and he was anxious to get home to his family.

It was a short turning, and should have led to the street in which he lived. But the street was not there, or rather its skeleton watched him eyeless. The bombs had matched its length precisely and the soldier did not recognize it now. He stood and looked at it. Flames lit one end where there were people and the quarrelling tangle of fire hoses. The wind brought moisture to his face, and it clung there like tears. Now and then a bomb fell within a half a mile or so and it stirred up the dust until it was mud that the hoses flung on his cheeks. Everything had happened so quickly, so violently, in the midst of so much noise, that it made little impression upon him. An invisible hand, as if flung in front of his face to ward off a blow, shut out of sight what was happening.

His house was to the right, should have been to the right. On the other side of the road, down by the flames. He walked in the gutter toward it, for the pavement was crowded with masonry and the gesticulating caricatures of iron railings. Water from the playing hoses caracoled toward the drains over his boots. He was looking among the shells of houses for his own.

He recognized the doorsteps. They were all that was to be recognized. Five of them, undamaged, that went up into nothingness and hung over the gap where his house had been. He recognized them because he had painted them green, dark green with white black-out lines. And there they were still. But the white black-out lines weren't necessary tonight for the public house, burning at the end of the road, gave a brilliant light. There was plenty of dust and people were coughing. The soldier could hear them coughing, even above the noise of the fire and the bombs still falling.

He took off his respirator and steel helmet and sat down on his doorstep. It bent beneath his weight and mortar fell from it to the pit below. He felt as if nothing could touch him. He did not want to look behind him to the house in case there was something to be seen there that might make this tragedy real. So he sat hoping that he might be sick again.

Firemen were running out fresh hose. They passed and repassed him but none of them looked at him. They were trying hard to put out the fire and they were not noticing the bombs. They were very busy, and the soldier, forgetting that something terrible had happened to him, something so terrible that it had as yet made no impression on him, envied these firemen.

He sat there a long time alone. It was a warden who spoke to him first and advised him to take shelter, because anyway the rescue party would be along shortly to get out the bodies below him. It had been a direct hit, he said, and the soldier realized what had happened. He looked at the warden quite calmly and began to cry. At first it didn't hurt as badly as being told that his leave, his precious leave, had been cancelled, and then he looked at the warden calmly and began to cry. His big face became stupid with the tears tracing dusty lines down it, and the long hands dropping between his knees. And the warden, thinking that perhaps he had shock, ordered him away roughly. But the soldier went on crying quietly because this was his second leave and he had made a lot of plans. He told the warden about them, but the warden hurried away to the fire, and, in his place, the wind brought the dust and smoke, the water and smell of beer from the burning public house. The soldier went on talking and he talked to the darkness between the doorsteps at his feet.

Even as he talked he remembered that the military policeman had been holding his leave pass when the second bomb fell. He wondered where it was, whether he ought to go back and look for it. It would be a pity if he were picked up without a pass. It would spoil his leave.

It was silly to sit there, and he stopped crying because that was silly too. He ought to try and find Lil. Perhaps she hadn't been in, although she was expecting him, perhaps she hadn't been in, just the same. Or the children.

The raid was getting worse – even worse. If he sat there long enough perhaps another bomb would hit him. Third time lucky. It might be best. There wasn't much sense in anything else. Camp, war, being away from home, and not being able to say in letters what you were feeling.

Dear darling Lil,
I hope I will be home on leave soon. It will be nice to see you and the kids again for us older men don't get so used to the army quickly like the young ones do. And when I come home I can get that bit of yard dug up and perhaps you can keep some hens there so the kids will have an egg now and then. We are having route marches and we get lectures but I'm always thinking about you . . .

'Dear darling Lil' and 'Your ever-loving husband, Sid.' He'd try to write something better next time, so that Lil could know how much he liked being her husband, and what he had in mind for the children's future. He'd write more next time to take her mind off the war. She was a good girl, was Lil, and she was pretty too. People didn't seem to see things like that. The films were wrong there. In films only the officers had pretty girls, and the soldiers had fat wives who nagged. He'd tell Lil that in his next letter.

But, it's funny, you can't write letters to corpses. Though, if they delivered the letters here, and the postman pushed them down through the bricks and the plaster and the window glass, maybe Lil would reach up a hand sometime and get the letters and read them out to the children, if she could see down there in the dark.

The third bomb shouldn't be long now. Maybe it would come before the warden returned to move him on. But although the bombs fell and fires blossomed out into poppy flowers all over the city, the raiders had exhausted themselves as far as this street was concerned, and the soldier sat untouched on his doorstep while the firemen tried to put out the fire in the public house.

Down to his left, away from the fire, there was a mobile canteen. It had been driven on to a pile of rubble and left there, tilted drunkenly, with its mudguards bent and its headlamps on. It wasn't far from the soldier, a matter of a few yards, and he could see the red triangle on its side. One of the windows in the offside door was broken, all the

glass gone but for a spear-headed piece that stuck up and reflected
the ruddy fire-glow.

There was someone in the cab. A white face. It might have been a
woman there was so much hair. But the face seemed shapeless. There
were no eyes, no nose, nothing familiar like that, and he looked at it
for some time before he realized that the woman had covered her face
with her hands, and was sitting there quite still. The clefts between
her fingers were dark shadows and her fingernails were scarlet almost.
She didn't move, although he watched her closely for some time.

Curiously he got up and walked over to the car. She was a young
girl. He could tell that by the softness of her hands, the lustre of her
hair, dusty though it was beneath the grey steel of the civilian helmet.
He could smell perfume, and he thought of how Lil had looked when
he married her. He reached over the broken glass and touched her
shoulder.

'Miss!'

She dropped her hands and shrank away from him. She was very
frightened and he smelt of blood.

'Don't touch me!'

He looked hurt and dropped his hand. They stared at each other.
She was very pretty and very young, and he wondered if she was an
officer's girl, although Lil was as pretty. She was alone in the cab and
he noticed that the windscreen was splintered and patterned like hoar
frost.

He had not moved but she said again. 'Don't *touch* me!'

'What's the matter, miss?'

She didn't answer. She was looking at the blood on his blouse, the
blood caked on his face, and he asked her again.

'Are you frightened?'

She wouldn't answer, but trembled.

'It's not safe here, miss. You'd better go home. There's a raid on.'
And neither of them saw how funny it was for him to say a thing like
that.

'I've got to serve tea to the firemen.'

'That's all right, miss. You serve tea, there's nothing much to be
frightened of.'

'The bombs . . .'

'They make a lot of noise, that's all. Them chaps want some tea.'
He placed one foot on the running board, and when he put his weight

on it he heard the shifting of broken crockery inside the van. 'Shall we go down? Move over, miss, I can drive a truck. Let's go down and give them firemen some tea.'

Automatically she pulled her steel helmet down over her eyes. She didn't look at him. The soldier climbed into the cab and put it into reverse. It argued with him and would not move. He felt the old familiar friendliness of the wheel, the pedals beneath his feet, and he tried again. It was obedient this time. In an old gesture he raised a thumb silently before his face and pressed some invisible object with satisfaction.

He drove off the rubble and pointed the car towards a fire. The first floor of the public house fell into the flames and a shower of climbing sparks sped up to the shell-bursts. The soldier sat back and turned to the girl.

'I could do with a cup of tea myself,' he said.

The White Mouse and the Maquis D'Auvergne

Nancy Wake

Hubert and I were parachuted into France near Montluçon, and were taken to the nearby village of Cosne-d'Allier, where I did my meet-the-people in the village square.

I did not meet the farmer on whose property we had landed. Had the Germans made any enquiries regarding the activity so close to his farmhouse on the night in question, he wanted to be able to say he had gone to bed early and had not heard any strange noises.

Although we would have been happier and felt safer away from Cosne-d'Allier, we were waiting for someone called Hector to contact us, as he was our only link to Gaspard, the leader of the Maquis d'Auvergne. This was the group we were to work with, but we had to be taken to them by an intermediary.

By now I had given Hubert a watered-down version of my social début in the village and he was even more anxious to find another place to live. We discussed the pros and cons fully and agreed we would wait another day, but miraculously Hector arrived the next morning. Trouble in his own area had been the cause of his delay.

There was no bathroom in this old house and I had been washing myself from neck to knee in a tiny *cabinet de toilette*. I was tired of standing up in the cramped roomette, so I got a big basin, filled it with water, took it back to the bedroom, sat down and started to wash my feet, at the same time discussing our immediate plans with Hubert. My revolver was by my side.

In walked Hector, who took one look at me, my feet and my revolver and laughed for at least two minutes. Actually neither of us thought it was very amusing but perhaps the long delay we had experienced had made us lose our sense of humour. Every time he recounts this tale my feet get bigger and the basin gets smaller, and the last time I heard the story I had a Bren gun by my side!

We were greatly relieved to see him in spite of the fact that he did not have the information or addresses we required, but as he promised to send them with his courier in two days' time we were both happy to think our troubles were over.

Our happiness was short-lived as the courier did not arrive. And we did not see Hector again until after the war. He was arrested, survived Buchenwald and now lives on the outskirts of Paris. Sadly we had to face the cold truth. For the time being we were up the proverbial creek without a paddle. Hubert and I both decided we would have to forget all about security and confide to a certain extent in our host Jean and his wife. This done, he thought he might be able to find Laurent's hideout. Laurent was one of the leaders of a local Maquis group, and he would be able to take us to Gaspard, who was in charge of all the separate groups of the Maquis in the area.

We started out early in the morning in Jean's *gazogène* (a charcoal-fuelled car). He seemed to know all the secondary roads extremely well and assured us there was not much danger of running into the Germans. We looked at each other in silence as we had been briefed in London only to travel by bicycle or train, or better still on foot. Hubert was white in the face; as for me, once again I decided I was going to play it by ear.

Jean drove from one contact to another until, when it was late evening, we found Laurent. I was always grateful to Jean and his wife for delivering us into the safe hands of Laurent, who was a tall, handsome man. When I knew him better we became great friends. I respected him, too, because he was a man who knew no fear. He conducted us to an old château near Saint-Flour in the Cantal and went to inform Gaspard of our arrival.

The purpose of our mission was to meet Gaspard, who was believed to have three to four thousand men hiding in the departments of the Allier, Puy-de-Dôme, Haute Loire and Cantal. We were to make our own assessment not only of the leader Gaspard, but also of the manner in which his considerable army had been formed and was now being operated and controlled. If we felt reasonably sure that he and his Maquis would be an asset to the Allies when and after they landed on D-day, then the French Section of SOE, commanded by Colonel Buckmaster in England would assist them with finance and arms.

Laurent had been gone for days before Gaspard arrived at the château and our meeting was not a happy one. He maintained he had no knowledge of Hector and had therefore not been expecting any assistance from SOE. He did not inform us that he was hoping for the support of an Inter-Allied team, a fact that London, for reasons of their own, had failed to mention in our briefings.

If Hubert and I had possessed all the cards in the pack we would not have wasted the time we did when we first landed. It was also unfortunate that, owing to the arrest of Hector, we had not received the detailed local information promised to us in London. The fact that our wireless operator chose to spend some time with a friend before joining us did not diminish our problems.

Hubert and I had the good fortune to overhear the group discussing us while they were sitting in the big kitchen where they congregated all the time. They seemed sure we had some money and they were plotting to relieve me of it and get rid of me at the same time. At a later period when Gaspard and I had more respect for each other he assured me the men had been joking. That could be true, but when I am stranded in an old, empty château, many kilometres from civilization, surrounded by a gang of unshaven, disreputable-looking men, I tend to be cautious and take things seriously.

Without any radio contact with London we were not in an enviable position, so when Gaspard suggested he would send us to Chaudes-Aigues in the Cantal, where a man called Henri Fournier was in charge of the local Maquis, we readily agreed.

In retrospect I can guess why Gaspard adopted the attitude he did. He was banking on the support of the Inter-Allied group but in the event it did not materialize he did not want to antagonize us irreparably. We were of no use to him without a radio and the money, which we said (quite untruthfully) we did not possess. He would kill two birds with one stone. He would dispatch us to a man he disliked who would have us on his hands if we failed to become functional. When many years had passed, after reading information that was gradually coming to light, I concluded that Gaspard had been under the misapprehension that an elaborate military scheme involving a French airborne force being dropped in the Massif Central area before D-day would become operational. It did not materialize, probably another case of the left hand not letting the right hand know what it was doing.

In normal times Henri Fournier was an executive in hotel management. He detested the Germans and he and his wife had come to live in Chaudes-Aigues for the duration of the Occupation. He was puzzled by our arrival but when we explained the situation I think the mystery was clarified because, when we became friends, he admitted to me in confidence that he heartily disliked Gaspard.

Fournier arranged accommodation for us in a funny little hotel high up in the hills, in a village called Lieutades. It was freezing cold, both inside the hotel and outside, and there was little to eat. We had absolutely nothing to do and we were both beginning to worry as our radio operator, Denis Rake, was long overdue.

Denis (or Denden, as he was called) had been one of our instructors at SOE school, the one arguing with the French-woman. Even in those days when homosexuality was illegal he had never concealed the fact that he was queer. Indeed it was always the first thing he mentioned, especially to women, who often found him too attractive for his liking. We were both fond of him but knew he could be completely unreliable.

Denden arrived by car just as we were beginning to give up hope. He found me sitting on the wall of the local cemetery and wanted to know if I was picking a suitable grave! He realized that his late arrival had caused us needless anxiety and in true Denden fashion he told us a cock-and-bull story which neither of us believed. However, a radio operator is an important person in the field, and we were not going to give him a reason to leave us and go straight back to his lover, which was exactly where he had been. On landing in France by Lysander he had met the man he had been having an affair with several weeks before in London, and they had decided to have a last fling.

Nevertheless, we were absolutely delighted to see him for now we could put our plans into action. While waiting for Denden we had decided that if he did arrive we would help Fournier first of all. We had been impressed by what we had seen of his group. We respected him and knew that he had spent a lot of his savings on the Resistance. We packed our bags and left for Chaudes-Aigues.

Fournier was overwhelmed with joy when told that we would shortly be in radio contact with London and that his group would be the first to receive our report. He and Hubert were busy making out the lists of weapons and explosives they hoped would be sent from

England, and Denden and I were busy coding the messages to be transmitted.

When the day and hour of the transmission arrived the room was full of Maquisards anxious to witness this exciting event. They appeared to be making Denden nervous so I asked them to leave the room. Reluctantly they filed out, all except Fournier, who refused to budge. Denden looked more nervous than before. He told me why. He was transmitting on the wrong schedule. He was twenty-four hours too soon. The three of us managed to restrain our laughter and started the proceedings all over again the following day. There were no more hitches and soon we were preparing for our first operation.

The plateaux on top of the mountains which surround Chaudes-Aigues were ideal of air-drops. Fournier and his group had surveyed the whole area and were of the opinion that we could receive, unpack and distribute the contents of the containers on the field and return to our homes without any interference. As soon as London had received our messages and we were all organized we received air-drops on six consecutive nights. It continued to be a roaring success until later on when Gaspard arrived with his men and was followed almost immediately by the Germans.

We manned the fields from ten at night until four in the morning, unless the planes arrived beforehand. We would unpack the containers immediately. The weapons had to be cleaned and all the protective grease removed before we handed them over to the leaders of the individual groups. Every available man assisted. Nevertheless, sometimes it would be noon before we finished and after lunch before we could snatch a few hours' sleep. It was a strenuous time for everyone; we were kept on the go continuously, but it was also rewarding to witness the enthusiasm of Fornier and his Maquis.

Every now and then Hubert, Denis and I would receive parcels from London which would arrive in a special container. Words cannot describe the thrill it gave me to open mine, stamped all over with 'Personal for Hélène'. Here we were, in the middle of a war, high up in the mountains of Central France, yet because of the thoughtfulness of SOE Headquarters we felt close to London.

My parcel always contained personal items unobtainable in France during the Occupation, plus supplies of Lizzie Arden's products, Brooke Bond tea, chocolates or confectionery. Without fail there'd be a note and a small gift from Claire Wolf, the only girl I'd been friendly with at headquarters. We remained staunch friends, and when she died at her home on the Isle of Man in 1984 I was grief-stricken.

Once, to my delight, I received a letter from my old pal, Richard Broad. I remember jumping up and down shouting, 'I've got a letter from R.B.!' Hubert and Denis weren't a bit interested – they'd never heard of him! But I kissed every page as I read the letter. I still have it – and it's still covered in lipstick.

I was thankful that Hubert and I had arranged the tasks we would perform to our mutual satisfaction. He would deal with all matters of a military nature and meet Gaspard whenever necessary and possible. I would be in charge of finance and its distribution to the group leaders. I would visit the groups, assess the merit of their demands and arrange for their air-drops, which we would both attend if possible. The tables had turned. After being regarded as a bloody nuisance by Gaspard when I first arrived, I now carried a lot of weight. *I* was the one who decided which groups were to get arms and money. Denden was in charge of coding and decoding the messages he transmitted and received. German detectors looking for illegal transmitters had to be evaded, and when we were expecting a message from London about a drop of arms, we listened to the five BBC news broadcasts a day. It was time-consuming, exacting work.

For my part, I had found a different attitude in France when I returned and joined the Maquis. By the spring of 1944 anyone with a brain could see that the Allies would beat the Germans and consequently some French people were already preparing to play politics. This exasperated me as the memory of the colossal harm caused by politics in the thirties still rankled. The majority of the men wanted to kick the Germans out of their country, return to their homes and pick up the threads of their lives. Liberation was on the horizon; now it was no longer a battle between 'cops and robbers', it was becoming a battle of wits.

When Fournier told me Colonel Gaspard was promoted to general, I snorted and Fournier laughed. Hubert was inclined to be impressed and a little in awe of rank. I was not. Not that I did not respect genuine rank, but in the Resistance, especially in the Maquis, some of them upgraded themselves in such a fashion that the chap you met one week as a solider or civilian suddenly appeared as a colonel a few days later. If you enquired about such a rapid promotion you would be given the name of someone you had never heard of, or the initials of some secret organization equally unknown to you. Furthermore, the alleged promotion would be promulgated after the Liberation. Some of the newly promoted officers tried to pull rank with me.

Fournier laughed when I told him what I wanted to do. In view of the importance of my department – finance and air-drops – I promoted myself to the rank of field marshal, to be promulgated after the war! No one would pull rank on me and get away with it. I continued to arm and assist, to the best of my ability, the worthwhile and dedicated groups in the Maquis, irrespective of the rank of their leaders.

During May, as a direct outcome of the large concentration of men in the mountains, a continuity of pitched battles were being fought between the Germans and our Maquis d'Auvergne. The Maquisards defended themselves brilliantly. Although they were always outnumbered by the enemy, sometimes comprising crack SS troops, the losses inflicted on the Germans were staggering. A few days before the Allies landed in Normandy the Germans attacked Gaspard's group in Mont Mouchet. They were stopped by the Maquis and driven back in defeat.

It was soon clear that the Germans were becoming concerned about the steadily increasing strength and actions of the Maquis. It was either just before or after this battle that the traitor Roger the Légionnaire was in our region. He and another German agent had managed to infiltrate Gaspard's Maquis, stating they wished to join his group. Their story and their odd behaviour aroused suspicions almost immediately, and in the cross-firing which subsequently took place, one Maquisard was killed and both German agents were seriously wounded. Roger received three bullets in the chest from a Colt .45 but as he was wearing a bullet-proof vest he did not die immediately. Interrogated under extreme pressure, he confessed to having been responsible for initiating a series of unbelievably inhuman punishments inflicted on captured members of the Resistance. He also stated that he had been directly responsible for the arrest of O'Leary at Toulouse on 2 March 1943. His confessions were taken down and I was given a copy to forward to London. Shortly afterwards Roger and the other German agent were shot and buried on Mont Mouchet.

I shivered when I read the report. One of the Resistance members

Roger was seeking was the person who obtained the arms from England. Little did he know that he had passed me as he drove along the narrow mountain track. It was unbelievable that I had missed him in Toulouse and been so close to him on this mountain.

I left the area as soon as possible. I could understand the hatred the Maquisards had for the Germans who behaved like crazed wild animals in their dealings with the Resistance. I hated and loathed them too but personally I favoured an accurate bullet and a quick death. Nevertheless there is a lot to be said for the proverb 'an eye for an eye', and when all is said and done Roger was only paying for some of the abominable treatment meted out to his victims. Torture is horrible. But before any outsiders form an opinion they should study both sides of the story closely.

On 4 June 1944 I received a special message from London stating that 'Anselm' was being dropped that night in the Montluçon area, in the *départment* of the Allier, and I was ordered to collect him. That was easier said that done. Hector had been arrested before he had time to give us details of safe houses, contacts and passwords. I knew that a Madame Renard was one of the contacts and I thought I had heard that she had been the housekeeper of an ambassador in Paris and also that she made good cakes.

Fourner gave me his best car and driver plus a bicycle which we put on the roof. The area between Chaudes-Aigues and Montluçon was swarming with Germans and Maquis each thirsting for revenge. In those days the only petrol-driven cars belonged to either the Germans or the Resistance. We were inclined to be more afraid of the Maquis than we were of the Germans because some Maquisards had been known to shoot first and ask questions afterwards. We didn't want them to mistake us for the enemy.

However, all went well. We enquired at each village along our route as to the whereabouts of Germans and Maquisards and, thanks to the help and information given us, we reached Montluçon safely. We hid the car in some bushes and my driver concealed himself a little distance away so he could observe anyone who discovered our vehicle.

I had promised one of the men in my group that I would call on his wife who was pregnant. She was happy to have news of her husband but had never heard of a Madame Renard. She did give me the name and address of a friend who, she said, might be able to

help. I cycled to her home. Although the name Renard did not ring a
bell, when I mentioned the fact that she had been in the employ of
an ambassador she was able to help me trace her. The town was full
of Germans and there were patrols and road-blocks everywhere.

Madame Renard opened the door when I rang. I tried to explain
as best I could the predicament I was in and how I had found her.
She just stood there staring at me intently. Suddenly I could smell
rum baba and I told her I knew all about her cakes. She laughed and
led me into the kitchen. She called to 'Anselm', who came out of a
cupboard pointing a Colt .45 clutched in his hand. We looked at each
other in astonishment. It was René Dusacq, whom I had met during
my training in England. He was also one of the men who had kissed
me goodbye when I left on my mission. He was to become known as
Bazooka.

Dusacq nearly passed out when I said we would be going by car to
Chaudes-Aigues. He sat in the back with his Colt at the ready, while
I was in the front with the driver, a couple of Sten guns and half a
dozen grenades. It was a smooth trip back to our headquarters where,
to my bitter disappointment, I learnt that during my absence the
Allies had landed and I had missed all the fun of blowing up our
targets.

On 10 June the Germans attacked Mont Mouchet, this time
supported by other 11,000 troops, with artillery, tanks and armoured
cars, as against Gaspard's 3,000 Maquisards with light arms. Incre-
dibly, they captured an armoured car and two cannons. During the
night the Germans withdrew which gave the Maquis the opportunity
to remove some of their vehicles, food and clothing over to our region.
The attack recommenced at dawn. The Maquis were ordered to pull
out at nightfall but in the meantime they fought like tigers. They
were magnificent. The German losses were always anything from 4
to 10 per cent more than the casualties of the Maquis. Is it any
wonder that the next time they attacked the Maquis d'Auvergne,
they doubled their strength? I was destined to find myself in the
centre of their mighty battle array. The wonder is that I was not
captured or killed.

From our headquarters we could hear the sound of the battle
raging. Alas, we could offer no assistance to our colleagues in arms.
The nature of the terrain between our position and the Maquis under
attack made it impossible. All through the day our scouts kept us

informed of the fighting going on. All we could do was get on with
our work.

It was unfortunate that hundreds of new recruits were streaming
into our area, ready to be armed. Hubert and Fournier and his
lieutenants had no time to worry about the conflict going on over the
mountain. They were trying desperately to interview, however briefly,
and arm the new recruits. It was a fantastic sight. The men were
coming into Chaudes-Aigues from all directions. Not even the sound
of the fighting nearby dampened their enthusiasm.

Denden was forever coding and decoding; not only for the night
operation but for the daylight parachutage from 150 planes we had
been promised. I had been designated to the footwear department!
Every man had to be fitted with one pair of British army boots and
two pairs of socks. When the supplies in the village ran out I went up
to the plateau and opened more containers. As soon as they had been
fitted with boots they were passed on to Bazooka, who all day long
and far into the night would be instructing them on how to use our
weapons.

Gaspard and his men arrived soon after their battle with the
Germans and installed themselves on top of one of the plateaux
surrounding Chaudes-Aigues. Hubert tried diplomatically to get him
to form his men into smaller groups but Gaspard waved aside the
suggestion. He was rightly proud of the way he and his men had
faced up to the German attack but he was a stubborn man and very
self opinionated.

We were receiving more and more air-drops. Night after night the
planes would fly over our plateau and drop our precious containers.
We were so occupied unpacking them, degreasing and assembling
the weapons before distributing them we had little time for sleep, but
the atmosphere of the Maquisards with whom we were in daily
contact was so exhilarating and gratifying that we never worried. I
don't think any of the reception committees ever got over the thrill of
seeing the parachutes drop from the planes. Least of all Fournier,
who never missed a drop and who made sure that his men were in
position at the correct time. It was bitterly cold on the plateau and
from ten at night the ground would be soaking wet with the heavy
dew. We used to soak loaf sugar in *eau de vie* (plum brandy) and suck
them to try to keep warm.

Now that Gaspard was a 'General' he proceeded to turn the little village of Saint-Martial (I seem to remember it had been deserted by its inhabitants) into a pukka headquarters. He had a colonel from the regular Army with him on his staff, who had brought his wife with him. The colonel obviously had not forgotten the regular eating hours in the officers' mess and he introduced the same system in their headquarters. We had been used to eating when it was convenient and thought this was a bit of a joke. I kept out of the way and continued to eat in Chaudes-Aigues if possible.

Hubert attended the 'mess meals' on several days and begged me to at least put in an appearance. For the sake of peace I agreed to accompany him the next day. The 'general' sat at one end of the table, the colonel at the other end next to his wife, and the British and American members with the other French leaders were seated in between. I thought I heard someone address the colonel's wife as 'Madame la Colonel' and decided I must be mistaken, but after a while I realized they really were addressing her in this manner. That was enough for me. The Maquis and the way we were forced to live did not merit such French Army formality. Denden, Bazooka and I always found excuses to be too occupied at noon to join the 'High Command', as we called them, and soon Hubert followed suit whenever he could. He knew that with us at least he would have a laugh.

In spite of the danger and hard work we were enjoying working together with Fournier and his men. We all pulled together and there was never any friction between us. We could not say the same about Gaspard. We agreed unanimously that he was an extremely difficult man to get along with. I must admit that I personally never had any trouble with him after the first meeting. He may not have liked to admit it but he had met his match with me. And I intended to keep it that way.

I was glad to have René Dusacq with us. Although we had not yet received any bazookas, they were his favourite weapon after his Colt .45, which never left his side; hence his nickname. Also he helped me keep Denden under control. When I returned from visiting other groups an irate farmer came to see me, stating that his son had complained about an alleged advance from Denden. I managed to calm him down but it was embarrassing for our team. We had to be so careful the way we handled Denden because we knew he was just itching for an excuse to go and join his current lover further north.

Bazooka, like us, was fond of him, but we could not close our eyes to the problems which would arise if we let him run wild amongst the good-looking young men in the Maquis. The trouble with Denden was that he actually believed most men were homosexual and if they were not, then they should be!

It always amuses me when I look back on those days with Denden. I often wonder why London decided to send him with us. Did they think our mission so hopeless it did not matter whom they sent? Did they think I was some kind of 'Den Mother'? This much I do know. Not many heterosexual men from SOE headquarters would have cared to go into the midst of 7.000 full-blooded Maquisards with a self-proclaimed homosexual. They owe us a special debt of gratitude that, because of our understanding and handling of the affair, there were no court cases after the war, and that Denden was not torn to pieces or, alternatively, shot to death by an irate father.

Apart from that particular problem we were a happy team with Fournier, when he could get away from his nagging wife. We would laugh about the antics of the would-be politicians and others seeking power after the Liberation. For my part I always admired the men, so many of whom had been forced to leave their families unprovided for, either to escape the *relève* or the Germans. To me they will always represent the true spirit of the Resistance.

More and more recruits were joining Gaspard on the plateaux. The numbers of men assembling within the one area was getting completely out of control and our team felt it was courting trouble. Readily we agreed with Hubert's suggestion that we move further north. Unfortunately we had an air-drop that night and the next, plus our first daylight parachutage, in which we had been promised 150 planes. It had been so hard to organize and the arms would mean such a lot to the Maquis that we decided to postpone our departure for a few more days.

We came down from the plateau just before dawn, we were all exhausted and suffering from lack of sleep. Chaudes-Aigues has natural hot water springs so I went over to the public baths and soaked myself before popping into bed to snatch a few hours' sleep. It was not to be. The sound of gunfire made me leap out of bed. Hurriedly I dressed myself and raced down to the hall of the hotel where we lived.

The Germans were attacking us. Our look-outs came into the

village to report. The whole area surrounding the mountains was literally swarming with Germans. When it was all over we learnt that they had been 22,000 strong, supported by over 1,000 vehicles, including tanks and armoured cars, trench mortars, artillery to back up the infantry, plus ten planes.

Several weeks previously I'd met Graham Buchanan, an Australian who'd been shot down near Nevers and rescued by a Maquis group. He was just as surprised as I was to meet another Australian in the French mountains.

From Nevers he and several other Allied airmen had been sent to Chaudes-Aigues where they were billeted in our hotel. I assured them there was nothing to worry about as I wished them goodnight. But a few hours later I had to tell them there was lots to worry about, that we were being attacked and would have to withdraw. Despite the panic and confusion which followed, all of this group eventually got back to England safely. (Graham Buchanan now lives near Murwillumbah in New South Wales, where he's a farmer.)

We packed as much as we could in our cars and raced up to Fridfont on the plateau to join the Maquis, which was 7,000 strong by now. Hubert left to confer with Gaspard who was on the other end of the plateau. He refused to consider withdrawal and stated he would fight to the death with his own group. I coded the message while Denden tried to contact London, not an easy thing to do when an operator's call is not expected. He persevered for hours and eventually received an instruction to transmit in one hour's time. Our message cancelled all our drops and requested Gaspard be ordered to withdraw.

Many of the containers had not been opened the night before as the planes had arrived late. I went along to the dropping zone and finished unpacking and putting the weapons in working order. Then I drove to all the positions where I could see our men, and once the arms and ammunition had been distributed I went back to Denden. We were the only two people not fighting. The men were holding back the onslaught and displaying outstanding bravery and enthusiasm as they defended the plateaux.

By now I was so exhausted I could hardly move. I was thirsty, hungry, sleepy and every bone in my body ached. As I could not help Denden until he received the final message from London I told him I was going to have a little kip and to wake me when I was needed.

I went to bed in a farmhouse where we had been authorized to take refuge. Just as I was dropping off to sleep Fournier came in and made me get up as he said it was too dangerous to stay inside. I was so sleepy I didn't care what happened. The only thing that would have wakened me completely was if I had come face to face with a German. I slept for a couple of hours under a tree which I thought was just as dangerous and less comfortable than in the bed.

Finally, the message came through. We were all ordered to withdraw and a personal message for Gaspard ordered him to follow suit. Knowing how stubborn he could be, I asked Denden to sign the message as if coming from Konig, de Gaulle's General who led the Free French Forces of the Interior. I think the signature of a genuine General did the trick as Gaspard was as meek as a lamb when he took delivery of the signal.

Several planes bombed Saint-Martial as I left the village, and as my car became visible on the road to Fridfont one pilot of a Henschel left his group and started to chase my car. I could see his helmet and goggles as he banked to continue the pursuit, and I could hear the bullets whizzing as his aim got closer and closer. Suddenly a young Maquisard who was hiding in some bushes signalled me, shouting at the same time to jump. We flung ourselves into a culvert by the roadside as the plane flew overhead. The young man explained that Fridfont was being evacuated and that Bazooka was waiting for me further down the mountain. We dashed from cover to cover as the German pilot kept up the chase.

By the time I regained Fridfont everyone had been evacuated. Denden had already left with a group, Hubert with another. A young man who had waited for me conducted me to where my group was hiding and where I was delighted to find Bazooka. He always looked after me when he was around.

The withdrawal from the plateaux was a credit to the leaders of the Maquis. When the Germans arrived there was not a soul left. They must have felt very frustrated when, after the fierce fighting and their huge losses of life, they reached the top of the mountain only to find the entire Maquis had evaporated.

We had been formed into groups of fifty to 100, each one being led by one or two men familiar with the terrain we would be covering. Our leader had been a non-commissioned officer in the French Army. He originated from Alsace but although he was not a local man he was an experienced tracker so we had no qualms about getting lost in the tough mountains we would have to cross.

The Germans were patrolling all the bridges over the river Truyére which was deep, rapid and dangerous in most parts. They were also guarding closely any part of the river they thought we might attempt to cross. Thanks to Fournier and his men, we were able to cross the river in all the most dangerous places.

When Hubert and I first went to Chaudes-Aigues we were a little dubious about Fournier's suggestion that we use the plateaux as dropping zones, mainly because we were afraid we could get trapped by the Germans, without an escape route. It was then he showed us the ingenious scheme they had devised for crossing the river well away from bridges and secluded by heavy foliage.

They had installed layer after layer of heavy slabs of local stone on the river-bed and covered them by secured dead tree-trunks. They were not visible from above as they were at least 45 cm below the level of the water. All we had to do was remove our footwear, release the logs, balance ourselves with a walking stick or the branch of a tree, and cross in absolute safety. It worked perfectly.

Our destination was Saint-Santin, north-west of our present position. We headed south, crossed more mountains and gradually proceeded north in a round-about fashion. All the groups were taking different routes and we aimed to keep well away from each other whenever possible.

It took us about four days to reach Saint-Santin. It was tough going all the way. We were miles from the German infantry but their planes circled the entire region for days. They criss-crossed the area where we had been, dropping bombs, then systematically bombed all the surrounding mountains and forests hoping, presumably, to flush out the Maquisards, who luckily were not there.

After two days we were all thirsty and starving. We were out of immediate danger so we approached a prosperous-looking farm asking for water and a little food. They offered milk and food to 'L'anglaise', which I did not accept as they treated the bedraggled-looking men as if they were lepers. The poorer farmers and their wives gave as much food as they could spare and let us sleep in their barns overnight. I could not help thinking of the old saying, 'The rich get richer and the poor get poorer'.

At last we reached our destination. We ran into Gaspard and his group. I will always remember this meeting with him. He looked at me and said, 'Alors, Andrée', took my arm and walked the rest of the way with me and Bazooka. I do not know what he was thinking at that moment but for my part it was something special, as if from then on we would understand each other. He was a man of few words, and I knew from those two that he respected me as a comrade-in-arms.

From the information London had been able to give us at our briefings we got the impression that the German garrisons in the Auvergne were manned by elderly men and puny boys. I don't know what happened to them, perhaps they were too tired or too weak to take part in the conflict. We only saw crack German troops plus some mighty tough Mongol warriors who cared for little else but slaughter and plundering. Some of them were found lying on the battlefields with their pockets full of watches and human fingers with gold wedding-rings still on them. Nevertheless, hundreds and hundreds of the enemy lay wounded and over 1,400 were dead. The Maquis lost over a hundred and about the same number were wounded. What a glorious victory for Gaspard and his Maquis d'Auvergne, but from then on the Germans would be all out for revenge.

About thirty of us installed ourselves in an unfinished house on the outskirts of Saint-Santin. It belonged to the parents of a good-looking young man in our group on whom Denden had designs. Therefore, Bazooka, who was never without his Colt .45, was detailed to watch over this young man's honour.

For several days groups of men kept arriving with exciting tales of their long cross-country hike. Denden turned up, footsore and weary, without his transmitter, which he had buried, or his codes, which he had destroyed. We were back to square one, out of contact with London and useless to everyone. From that day on until the end of the Occupation I don't think I ever stopped for more than two or three hours. If I wasn't walking or riding a bicycle, or fighting, or being chased by the Germans, or the Vichyites, it just wasn't a normal day.

Fortunately, through contacts I learnt of the whereabouts of a Free French radio operator living just over the adjacent mountain. It was hoped that he would co-operate if I mentioned the name of our mutual acquaintance. Someone lent me a man's bicycle which I half pushed and carried up the mountain but literally flew down the other side. The bike was getting up such speed that the brakes were useless, and I fell off several times. I pedalled about twenty kilometres only to find that because of all the German activity in the region, the Frenchman had left the day before. The mountain lying between me and Saint-Santin did little to lift the disappointment I felt.

Denden knew there was an SOE operator in Châteauroux because that is where he had spent his idyllic week while we were waiting for him in the Auvergne. He gave me as much information as he could remember and it was decided I would leave as soon as I could make myself presentable, even though it was 200 kilometres away.

We had been given the address of a friendly tailor in Aurillac but I had to wash and mend my slacks and blouse before I could appear anywhere without raising suspicion. Just then Laurent drove up in a car of all things; he had driven right around the Germans without any trouble. We were so happy to see him but livid when we thought of his comfortable trip, whereas we were all exhausted.

Laurent wouldn't give me a car to drive to Châteauroux as he said that since our battle the Germans had tightened up all regulations, and road-blocks had been installed all over the entire region. Further-more any identity cards issued in the Cantal were suspect and by law had to be exchanged at the local police stations under the supervison of the Germans. As my identity card was from the Cantal I would have to travel without any papers. Added to which I doubted that I would get to Châteauroux on a bicycle, let alone return, and he strongly counselled Hubert to prevent me from continuing with my plan. Laurent thought that quite apart from the problems with identity cards, papers and tighter regulations, 200 kilometres was just too far to cycle. But, as I pointed out, we were useless without our radio, and this was our only immediate hope.

Once Laurent accepted the fact that I would make the trip irrespective of all the obstacles he put in my way, he lost no time in doing everything he could to make my journey less dangerous. Men were sent in all directions to collect local information about German movements and then when he had studied all the details he mapped out the route he advised me to take. I would have to cycle about 200 kilometres of the roundabout route, without an identity card or a licence for the beautiful new ladies' bicycle a Maquisard had been able to purchase for me 'under the counter'. If I reached Châteauroux safely I would have to return by the best way I could.

While all these preparations were going on I was busy trying to get my wardrobe together. I needed an entire new outfit plus some walking shoes. I cycled into Aurillac where the tailor agreed to make me a costume in twenty-four hours, with one fitting in two hours' time. He also gave me the name and address of a cobbler who could supply me with shoes without a coupon. When I arrived at the cobbler's shop I was dismayed to hear the tailor had phoned to warn me not to return for the fitting as the Milice who were next door to his shop had already been enquiring about the woman in slacks.

The Germans had, meantime, placed road-blocks on all the main roads leading into town. I escaped by crossing several fields and heading north between two main roads until I could cross one of them and regain Saint-Santin, which lay to the west. All the way back I had been trying to think of a way to go back for my fitting. I had to find a disguise. But what? Then I had an idea.

The parents of the handsome young man in whose house we were hiding lived in the village. I went to see them and asked if they had any old clothes I could borrow. His grandmother had an old trunk with an amazing array. I borrowed a long white piqué dress which must have been fashionable before World War I. They introduced me to a farmer who was taking his horse and cart to the market in Aurillac early the next morning. I became secretive about my plans as I knew Hubert, and Denden in particular, would rag me if they saw me in my disguise. I crept out of the house early and waited for the farmer. Unfortunately, just as I had installed myself in the front of the cart beside the farmer with a pair of his trousers on my lap, which was my reason for the visit to the tailor, Denden appeared and alerted everyone else. Of course they had a good hearty laugh at my expense. Who wouldn't? There I was sitting up in the cart surrounded by fruit and vegetables looking like a real country bumpkin, wet hair pulled back tight, no make-up, an old-fashioned dress, and wearing a pair of the farmer's old boots.

Our cart and the produce were inspected several times by the Germans as we entered Aurillac; they did not give me a second look, even their first glance was rather disdainful. I did not blame them. I did not look very fetching. The only thing that boosted my morale that day was when the tailor failed to recognize me as I entered his shop. My costume was delivered the following day, and I set off for Châteauroux the day after.

On the eve of my departure Laurent sent several men on ahead to warn as many villages as they could in the Cantal and the Puy-de-Dôme to look out for me and to warn me if trouble lay ahead. In the Allier he had not been able to make any contacts so I just had to trust to luck. I had company as far as Montluçon. A Maquisard was going to visit his wife, who was ill. When we had to take the National Route we pushed our bikes instead of riding them in case any Germans approached, in which event we would have time to dive into the culverts by the side of the road until they passed.

I by-passed Montluçon and was heading for Saint-Amand. It was getting dark and I wanted to make a few enquiries. I went into a bistro and had a simple meal and a glass of wine. Listening to the conversation of the other customers, I gathered that the Germans in the area were quiet for the time being. I found a barn not far away, removed my costume and slept until the sound of an air raid awakened me.

At Saint-Amand I stopped for a coffee and overheard that Bourges had been raided the day before. When I arrived there I thought the place was quiet — not a soul in the streets and all the shutters were closed. It was only afterwards I found out that the Germans had shot some hostages that morning. I passed two groups of Germans but they made no attempt to stop me.

At Issoudon I stopped for a black-market meal, cleaned myself up and entered into conversation with the owner of the restaurant, who shared some of my wine and brandy. The dangerous part was yet to come and I needed all the local information I could obtain. There is nothing like brandy to loosen the tongue! I cycled to the local markets and filled my string bag with all the fruit and vegetables I could buy without food coupons, hoping that I would pass for a housewife out shopping. I was still making good time although my legs were beginning to ache because of the mountainous terrain I had crossed. I had cycled 200 kilometres.

There were continuous streams of German vehicles leaving Issoudon for Châteauroux so I cycled west to Brion then south-west to Villedieu-sur-Indre, and entered the city without any trouble. One German patrol was checking on the opposite side of the road but they waved me on when they saw me hesitate. I pedalled round and round the town and was just about to give in, with much despair, when I came across the bistro I was looking for. It was exactly as Denden had described it. But when I called at the SOE house they refused to help me; they refused to send a message to London. Actually their performance was completely stupid because if I had been a German or one of their agents, they would have been arrested on the spot. I left the house in disgust and returned to the bistro.

They must have been saying prayers for me back in the Auvergne because as I was pedalling around Châteauroux I had run into a Maquisard I had met several weeks before in the Corrèze. He was looking for a Free French radio operator as their operator had been killed in action. We had both agreed to help each other if one of us found our contacts and I had left him at the bistro where he was waiting when I returned with the bad news.

Off we pedalled to find his contact, who was also a patron of a bistro which was situated opposite the home of the radio operator. He warned us that the Germans had not caught the radio operator but they were in the house waiting to trap any callers.

The town was literally swarming with Germans. They were completely surrounding areas and checking the houses systematically, so we decided to leave immediately. We separated and arranged to meet outside the town. Both of us were able to by-pass the road-blocks and, wasting no time, we headed for a Maquis group my companion knew in the Creuse. The leader belonged to the Free French and had come from Algiers, where his headquarters were. He was understanding when I told him the trouble I was in and said that if his radio operator did not object to sending my message, neither would he. The operator agreed to my request to send a message to Colonel Buckmaster in London via the Free French in Algiers. I wished my travelling companion good luck and was on my way.

By now I was so tired I resolved to take the quickest route home. Every kilometre I pedalled was sheer agony. I knew that if I ever got off the bike, I could never get on it again, so I kept pedalling. Halfway across the Allier the companion I had left in Montluçon was looking out for me. He had guessed the road I would take if all went well. His wife had presented him with a baby son and they were both well, so he was happy. I arrived back in Saint-Santin twenty-four hours before the time they had anticipated I would, even though they were well aware I might never return. I had pedalled 500 kilometres in seventy-two hours.

They greeted me with open arms and shouts of joy. All I could do was cry. When I got off that damned bike I felt as if I had a fire between my legs and the inside of my thighs were raw. I couldn't stand up, I couldn't sit down, I couldn't walk and I didn't sleep for days. But thanks to all the help I had been given by one and all, I had succeeded and all we had to do now was to wait and see if Algiers sent our signal on to Colonel Buckmaster. They did. As I said to Hubert, Denden and Bazooka, I never wanted to be told any more that the Free French agents in the field would not help the British ones, because I knew better. I never heard of that group in the Creuse after that so I have never been able to say 'thank you' in peacetime.

It took me a few days to recover. The doctor from the village had dressed my thighs which were in a horrible state but there was little else anyone could do. My three close colleagues looked in frequently to see how I was faring, but I just wanted to be left alone. When I'm asked what I'm most proud of doing during the war, I say 'the bike ride'.

Finally the day came when I could move without experiencing too much pain, and I dressed and went out to lunch. To my surprise a strange Frenchman, to whom I was not introduced, was sitting at my table. He had arrived during my absence, stating that he was a full Colonel in the regular French Army and that he was going to take over our outfit and run it on correct military lines. Hubert had not been game to tell me that this man had been our uninvited guest for days.

Normally one could ask for identity papers but in those days it was pointless to do so as everybody's papers in the Resistance were false. Perhaps he was a Colonel. I neither knew or cared. All I could see was that now victory was so close too many people wanted to jump on the bandwagon and play that ugly game of politics. I had been a budding journalist in the thirties and witnessed the havoc caused by politicians and other power-hungry individuals, so I was not impressed by this 'Colonel's' speech.

When he had finished his pep-talk, obviously for my ears as the others had heard it before, I asked him what he was going to do for money and arms, because I certainly was not going to give him any of ours. Hubert looked embarrassed but Bazooka, Denden and the rest of our group did not try to conceal their joy. The four of us discussed this new situation later and they agreed with my suggestion

that we all move further north towards Tardivat, the gallant Frenchman who greeted me when I dropped into France. Tardivat was not
a politician. From then on until the end of the Occupation we never
looked back.

When Hubert and I drove up north to the *département* of the Allier
and towards Tardivat, Bazooka was left in charge, with Denden
detailed to listen to all the BBC personal messages in the event we
received a signal from London acknowledging our SOS and perhaps
confirming the parachutage we requested.

Tardivat was delighted to see us. Immediately he found a suitable
site for our group not far from Ygrande and near a field we had been
using for air-drops. Hubert remained with him to prepare the camp,
while I returned to Saint-Santin to fetch our belongings and the men,
who were 200 strong.

Not only did I find London had received our signal, they had
already sent me my own radio operator, who would share his codes
with Denden. Roger was a good-looking American Marine, aged
nineteen. He spoke very little French but they all liked him and he
fitted into our life-style smoothly. Unhappily for us all, Bazooka had
been ordered to the Clermont-Ferrand area to instruct another
Maquis group.

Hubert had been working hard setting up our camp and we all
settled in straightaway. The men were still part of the Maquis
d'Auvergne but they were more or less our own special group
attached to our Allied team. We were lucky to have them with us;
they were all good men, we knew them personally and, like the
Americans and British, they had no political aspirations. They only
wanted to get rid of the enemy and return to their families. That
night we were joined by thirty young Frenchmen, all evaders from
the *relève* – the German compulsory labour force. They were enthusiastic but as yet untrained.

I was heartily sick of sleeping on the damp ground and when one
day Tarvidat asked me for an extra quantity of Bren guns which were
in short supply, I bribed him by promising Brens for a bus. However,
I stipulated a bus with two long seats in the rear, facing each other,
so I could balance the big mattress (also procured by Tardivat) on
top of them. He took a few men down to a main road and set up a
road-block. As each bus reached the barriers he made all the

passengers alight while he inspected the rear. This procedure continued until a suitable bus arrived. The poor passengers must have been
petrified by the sight of the Maquisards, all armed to the teeth and
looking fierce. The passengers in the unsuitable buses must have
been mystified also when they were allowed to continue their journey.
Naturally he received his Bren guns. He was going to get them
anyway. So I used to sleep in the back of the bus, on a beautiful soft
mattress with nylon parachutes for sheets, and entertain in the front.

Somehow or other I'd managed to have with me a couple of pretty
nighties, leftovers from another life. No matter how tired I was, after
a day in a male world, wearing trousers, I'd change into a frilly
nightie to sleep in my bus.

Our immediate plan at Ygrande was to increase the level of
security which had been impossible when we were attached to the
oversized groups further south. We had a conference with our men
and it was decided unanimously that we would never remain in one
spot more than three or four days. If the site happened to be in a
particularly favourable position we could stay one week, but no
longer. As soon as we moved to one place we would agree on the next
one and the leaders would be informed. In the case of a sudden attack
my bus would be loaded immediately with wireless equipment, the
operators themselves and my bicycle, and proceed to our rendezvous
point. A driver and one man were detailed to enforce this rule.

We had not been in Ygrande two days when our lookouts warned
us that a large body of Germans were approaching. Our withdrawal
went like clockwork. Three thousand Huns wasted all their ammunition to capture one empty farmhouse. We were all delighted, as can
well be imagined.

Two American weapons instructors were to be dropped at a field
nearby that same night. Remembering the complete lack of security
when I had been introduced to the entire village of Cosne-d'Allier, I
determined that things would be different when these two arrived.
And they were different, almost unique, in fact.

They arrived safely, although one of them had lost his suitcase and
we took them straight back to our camp, where we entertained them
in the bus. Naturally we greeted these two Americans, John Alsop
and Reeve Schley, with French champagne. They did not speak
much French but we didn't mind as long as they could instruct the
Maquis groups in the use of our weapons. They gave us news from

London and we carried on talking and drinking until about four in the morning.

They looked smart in their uniforms, especially Schley who had on beautiful leather cavalry boots. I knew that when our men saw how well dressed they were they would start moaning again about our uniforms. All we could give them were socks, boots, khaki trousers and shirts, and they were dying to have decent uniforms. We took them to their simple quarters which Denden and I had cleaned up; we had even put some wildflowers in a jamjar next to their beds. As we left, one of them asked quite casually if we ever got attacked, and quite casually I replied that we had just been attacked the day before but I didn't think the Germans would be back that day. That proved to be the understatement of the year. They were already at our back door.

I woke up when the Germans started firing and yelled out to the Americans who were close by to get up – we were being attacked. We couldn't find Hubert; he had disappeared. As we learned much later, he had got up early to find the missing suitcase before anyone else did. Schley must have been in such a hurry to get dressed that he put on his cavalry boots first and couldn't get his trousers on, so reckoning he didn't have time to start all over again, he cut his trousers with a knife and appeared in front of me in short scalloped trousers. I wasn't much better – I hadn't time to take my pink satin nightdress off and it was showing under my shirt.

Our 200 men had disappeared to fight and our 'High Command', consisting only of Denden and me, were packing everything into my bus which had started to leave when I noticed the bicycle was left behind. Denden raced over and threw it on top of the bus, and immediately started screaming blue murder. He had got caught on some electric wires! Roger and the driver were laughing their heads off. I was doubled up, tears running down my face. All this time the Americans were standing there surveying the scene amidst the sound of machine-gun fire, grenades and what have you.

Thank goodness they didn't understand much French, as the scouts soon came back with the news that we were being attacked by 6,000 Germans. We were 200 plus two in the High Command, two newly arrived Americans and thirty new recruits. We were definitely outnumbered. For a while we hoped Hubert would arrive with some reinforcements, but he was trapped, kilometres away.

Then some of our defenders came back and said the Germans were well entrenched but why couldn't we try the bazookas that had been dropped the previous night and which they were obviously dying to try out. The problem was that the two instructors were the only ones who knew how to use them, and they couldn't speak French. But our men insisted they could knock out a few German posts if only someone would show them what to do. Those poor Americans! It was like a scene from a comic opera.

The wounded were being brought in so I put the other member of the High Command, Denden, in charge of them, irrespective of his plea that he didn't like the sight of blood. I gave him plenty of bandages and a gallon of pure alcohol. I didn't issue him with any arms as he didn't like them either.

We collected all the bazookas and prepared to face the enemy, the two non-French-speaking instructors, the interpreter (me), and two men for each bazooka. I think our new recruits must have thought it was going to be a piece of cake because twenty of them volunteered to carry some of our material. I warned them to stick to the woods but they unfortunately disobeyed my orders and took a short-cut. Seven of them were killed immediately by the German machine-guns. The other thirteen fled back to our camp.

The rest of us carried on regardless. Everything was put in place, the Americans instructed on bazookas, firing off. I ran from one crew to another translating. They knocked out several German posts and when we had exhausted our supply of ammunition (some had not been unpacked) we withdrew. This may have been a first for the Americans but it was also a first for me. I had never been on a battlefield translating from English into French on how to fire a bazooka.

We returned to our camp to find Denden with a loaded carbine slung over his shoulder, a row of grenades fastened on to his belt, and a Colt. The man who was afraid of guns! He was also very, very drunk. He had been drinking the pure alcohol as he tended the wounded, and it had given him Dutch courage. I removed the grenades as he could have not only killed himself, he could have killed us too, and I had enough trouble on my plate.

I kept my fingers crossed as I told Alsop and Schley that everything would be all right and asked one of our scouts to show me the way to the Spaniards' camp. We crawled across several fields and when I reached one of their outposts I asked the sentry on duty to ask his Colonel to send my SOS to Tardivat.

When I returned to our camp Schley said he didn't want the Germans to smoke the Havana cigars his father had given him back in New York, so the three of us sat down and puffed away as if we didn't have a care in the world. Suddenly we heard the sound of Bren guns and mortars to the rear of the Germans. I yelled out to everyone: 'Tardivat, let's go!' He gave us time to retreat, then retreated himself, leaving the Germans to conquer a deserted campsite.

Tardivat and his men had been sitting down to lunch when he received my SOS. I was amazed that Frenchmen would leave their meal, and said so flippantly. All he said was, 'Aren't you glad you gave me all those Bren guns?' However, he had saved our lives. We had smoked those cigars for nothing! All this happened during the first twelve hours after the Americans' arrival, and I had planned such a pleasant and relaxed day for them, a day they would remember. They would certainly remember it, but for entirely different reasons.

We found Hubert hiding in a barn. Having retrieved Schley's suitcase he had been cut off from us when the fighting had begun and had therefore been unable to assist in any way.

Several of our badly wounded men were smuggled into a private hospital run by a religious order. The seven reckless young men who had died so tragically were laid to rest in a nearby cemetery. They were buried with all the military honours possible considering the danger of conducting such a service.

We stayed near the Spanish camp for a couple of days and moved onto a good site in the Forêt de Tronçais. It was well concealed, protected by Tardivat's groups and, to our delight, near a large pond where we were able to enjoy the pleasure of bathing ourselves, instead of having to carry out our ablutions from a small bucket of water. If we were bathing during the daytime we either dived under the water or made a dash for the forest when German planes flew overhead.

We were receiving new recruits every day. Alsop and Schley were kept busy all day long instructing them on the use of weapons and explosives, fortunately within the peace of our forest and not on the battlefield!

The Americans had brought their cameras with them and they had, unknown to me, taken a snap of me getting out of my pink satin nightdress. Denden had told them of my famous satin nightdresses, one pink and one blue. However mannish I looked by day, I always slept in satin.

I determined to get even. I waited until Schley went into bathe one morning. He undressed and left his clothes and camera by a tree. I took the camera and sat by the water's edge, waiting for him to emerge. After being in the icy cold water for thirty minutes he was blue in the face but he would not admit defeat. The German planes appeared on the horizon and he was forced to reassess his predicament. We always found time to play jokes on one another and enjoy a good laugh. It became a battle of wits between the sexes.

There had been nothing violent about my nature before the war yet the years would see a great change. But in spite of my virulent attitude to the enemy I could not condone torture and brutality on our part, although I was not foolish enough to believe they would extend me the same courtesy. Consequently the day I was informed confidentially by a man in our Maquis that a group nearby were holding three females, one of whom was a German spy. I threatened to disarm them if they did not release the poor unfortunate women into my custody. All three had been ill-treated and used as if they were prostitutes.

The leader of the group concerned was a married man. I had accepted his hospitality before he had joined the Maquis. When I learnt his wife had been aware of the brutality meted out to the women I was horrified to think I had been friendly with them both.

The two French girls were no problem, but the German girl could not be set free. I interrogated her and she admitted she had been sent to spy on the Maquis and then to report back to the Gestapo. She hated the French and the British as much as I hated her people. Reluctantly I informed her she would have to be shot as there was no alternative under the circumstances.

At first the men refused to shoot a woman and agreed to form a firing squad only after I had announced I would undertake the task myself. She spat at me as she passed and shouted 'Heil Hitler' before she died.

For my part I showed absolutely no emotion as she walked to her death. How had this been possible? How had I become so aggressive? It was simple. I remembered Vienna, Berlin and the Jews. I remembered seeing a poor French woman, seven months pregnant, tied to a stake and bayonetted, criss-cross, in the stomach by a German soldier. Her screaming two-year-old held her hand and she was left to die with her unborn child. A German officer stood by and watched the soldier carry out his orders. I remembered my friend in the escape-route network who was beheaded with an axe after he had been captured by the Gestapo. The enemy had made me tough. I had no pity for them nor would I expect any in return.

I have returned to Germany many times since their defeat. They have worked hard to rebuild their Fatherland. It is a lovely country to visit and although I am quite happy to be friendly with some young Germans I keep well away from the older generation in case I become involved with some ex-Nazi. I will never be able to forget the misery and death they caused to so many millions of innocent people; the savage brutality, the sadism, the unnecessary bloodshed, the slaughter and inhuman acts they performed on other human beings. I am inclined to feel sorry for the young Germans of today, knowing how utterly miserable I would be if I was descended from a Nazi.

War is a calamity. It is destructive and brings great sorrow and loss of life. But at least it is, or should be, a clear-cut manoeuvre between two opposing nations fighting each other until one side admits defeat. Civil war is disastrous because it means two or more parts of a nation fighting for supremacy. Although I did not go to Spain during the Civil War I was always in close touch with people who did.

By July 1944 there were so many branches of the Resistance it was difficult to keep track of them. They were right-wingers, left-wingers, red-hot Communists, government officials, civil servants, ex-Vichyites, ex-Milicians, secret army, regular army and dozens more, besides masses of individuals trying to get on the bandwagon. We kept our distance from the would-be politicians, concentrating on arming the Maquisards as efficiently and rapidly as possible.

Hubert was fully occupied with the leaders of the adjacent groups, discussing and executing plans that would frustrate the Germans wherever and whenever the opportunity arose. They attacked the enemy convoys on the road, they intercepted and stole hundreds of wagon-loads of food being transported to Germany, they set up ambushes in the most unlikely places and generally made the existence of the Germans in the area a perilous one. Apart from these activities they manned the dropping zones at night and in their spare

time they prepared the explosives needed to destroy the targets we
had been assigned.

Laurent had provided me with a new car and a driver who knew
the Allier and the Puy-de-Dôme like the back of his hand. I would
contact dozens and dozens of groups of men hiding in forests. After
meeting their leaders I would assess their groups, most of whom
impressed me, and would promise to arm their men and also
contribute a certain amount of money towards their subsistence.

Sometimes Roger accompanied me. He was not as good or experienced an operator as Denden but he was more relaxed and never
complained about the conditions under which he worked. If he had
to transmit or receive messages while we were travelling by car we
would pull into the side of the road, he would throw the aerial over a
tree, sit on the wheel or bumper bar, balance his set on his knee and
tap away in Morse code. If we ran out of distilled water he never
made a fuss like Denden did, he would simply substitute ordinary
water.

I had to find new fields where we could organize our air-drops.
This was becoming more and more difficult as the Germans were
attacking Maquis groups every day in retaliation. Roger and I had to
shoot our way out of a road-block on two occasions and we were
extremely fortunate to escape capture.

One day I was obliged to go to Vichy. When my business there
was concluded I decided to treat myself to a good meal in an
expensive black-market restaurant before returning to the forest. A
member of an unruly group of men (whom, incidentally, I had
refused to arm) had apparently been informed of my extravagance
and decided I had been spending money to which his so-called
'Resistance' group was entitled. He was quite wrong as Hubert,
Denden and I always received our own personal allowances from
London. This ignorant and uncouth individual was airing his views
about our British team in a café in a little village where I was due at
midday. My visit had obviously been discussed there. He became
very, very inebriated and announced he was going to kill me. He then
opened a case and displayed several grenades. The patron of the café
became alarmed and was going to dispatch someone to warn me as
soon as I arrived on the outskirts of the village.

This village was old, with narrow streets. The only way a motorist
could drive through it was to take a blind alleyway where a reflecting

mirror warned of the traffic ahead. The café was only a few metres away.

I was early, and blissfully unaware of the drama about to unfold. When the would-be assassin heard a car approaching he took a grenade out of the case, removed the pin and held it in his hand. When he saw a woman in the car he went to throw it but he was so drunk he had forgotten the pin was out and it blew up in his hand. I saw the explosion and bits of human flesh all over the place, but it was a few minutes before I heard the story. I could not feel sorry for him. He and his men were the types who pretended to be members of the Resistance and at times gave it a bad name.

This story reached the forest via 'bush wireless' before I returned. It was decided there and then that I would have a bodyguard whenever I travelled by car. Tardivat suggested we approach the Spanish group and their colonel immediately delegated six of his best men to protect me.

We must have made an impressive sight as our three cars sped along the roads. They had installed a Bren machine-gun in the windscreen of each car and another one at the rear. Whenever possible we remained on the secondary roads, which were covered in red dust. As I always travelled in the second car I arrived at our destination looking like a Red Indian, so after the first trip I transferred to the first car. I tried to explain in Spanish that it was because of vanity and not bravery but I don't think it convinced them.

These six Spaniards became devoted to me and I never had any worries when I was with them, even though at times we were obliged to use the National Routes. If we stopped at a village for a meal and anyone dared to look sideways at me they would stand there looking fierce with their Sten guns at the ready. They would inspect the kitchens and one day they forced two men to show their identity cards simply because they were staring at me during lunch. They were experienced fighters, having gone through the Spanish Civil War. I must have covered thousands of kilometres with my bodyguard. To me it was all very theatrical but the Spaniards took it seriously. I often wondered what the people thought of our little convoy as we passed through the villages.

In the latter part of July and during August I was travelling continuously. Every night hundreds of containers filled with weapons

and explosives were being parachuted on to our fields in anticipation
of the Allied landings, which ultimately took place in the south of
France on 15 August.

The arrival of the Americans – especially as they were officers
wearing such splendid uniforms – had boosted the morale of the
Maquisards in the area to such an extent that we had intended to
hold a banquet in their honour. The battle the morning after their
arrival and several subsequent mishaps had forced us to abandon all
major social activities. However, as Tardivat pointed out, we now
had two important events to celebrate: firstly, the arrival of our
American instructors and secondly, my lucky escape. We chose a
night when the moon was low as we would be unlikely to receive an
air-drop.

Tardivat was in charge of all the catering arrangements. He
conferred with a chef in a nearby town who prepared most of the food
in his hotel. The morning of the banquet he was 'kidnapped' at gun-
point and taken to our forest. The alleged kidnapping was to protect
him in case he was interrogated by the Germans or the Milicians at a
later date.

Denden, assisted by several experts, installed an elaborate row of
lights overhead which could be turned off immediately if our sentries
warned us of enemy planes approaching. Our tables consisted of long
logs covered by white sheets borrowed from friendly villagers. The
chef served a magnificent eight-course meal, accompanied by some
superb French wines. He hovered around looking impressive wearing
his snow-white chef's hat and apron, assisted by several volunteers
from our group, suitably dressed for the occasion.

It was a banquet I will never forget, and most certainly one that
could never be repeated. Several hundred men attended and every
single one had been spending hours trying to make his clothes look as
smart as possible. The lighting system was a huge success – our part
of the forest looked like a fairyland. Tardivat greeted the guests with
typical French formality and the foreign guests responded with great
dignity! We toasted everyone and everything. We swore our eternal
allegiance and love to France, Great Britain and the United States of
America. When we couldn't think of anything else to toast we swayed
to our feet and toasted the Germans and the Allied Forces for not
having interrupted our gala dinner.

Half-way through this extraordinary banquet a serious French

Maquisard was escorted to my table by a sentry. He was delivering a message from his leader. Naturally we invited him to join our party. He looked at all the food on the tables and the piles of empty bottles on the ground and the full ones in the process of being consumed, and asked me if this was the style in which we dined every night. We managed to keep a serious face and everyone who had heard his question replied, 'Yes, of course, don't you?'

In the early hours of the morning a violent thunder and lightning storm forced us to scurry back to our respective camps in a disorderly fashion. The bright and almost continuous flashes of lightning made it easy for me to find my way to my bus, but the ground had become like a bog and I was soaking wet and covered with mud by the time I reached it. Furthermore, I was feeling sorry for myself and for the unceremonious manner in which our banquet had been terminated.

Soon after installing ourselves in the forest we had bought a horse, especially for Roger as sometimes he got bored, although Schley exercised it if he had the time. As I was trying to clean my clothes I heard the horse neighing. I looked through the window and there he was in the pouring rain making a terrible noise. Immediately I stopped feeling sorry for myself and proceeded to lavish all my love and sympathy on the poor unfortunate horse. We had a galvanised iron lean-to attached to my bus which we used as a makeshift bathroom and where we kept our toilet necessities. I dragged the horse in, talking to him all the time, telling him not to worry about the storm as I would look after him. Then I fell asleep.

I woke up several hours later. The horse and the galvanised-iron roof had disappeared. Actually he was foolish to run away as, with the meat shortage, he could not have gone far before ending up in some hungry person's saucepan. We found the roof some distance away. The contents of our bathroom were ruined as they were all mixed up with horse manure. Alsop had been sleeping under a yellow parachute. The rain had soaked through it, so he appeared looking as if he had jaundice. Denden took one look at him and went back to bed. That night our personal message to the BBC was 'Andrée had a horse in the bathroom.'

Thank goodness the Germans did not attack that night.

Without doubt, Tardivat was the man I most admired then. He was intelligent, disciplined, reliable, honest and very brave. He also had a fantastic sense of fun, which I appreciated. When I was not on the road he would invite me to take part in some of his escapades. We carried out several ambushes together and blew up a few small bridges. If any German convoys were foolish enough to pass through his area he always managed to do some damage to their vehicles. In suitable terrain we loved using what we called a 'trip wire'. It was attached to a tree on each side of the road and the first vehicle in the convoy would blow up. We liked to be concealed on a nearby hill so we could watch the confusion before withdrawing to a safer spot.

The most exciting sortie I ever made with Tardivat was an attack on the German headquarters in Montluçon. He and his men organised this raid from beginning to end. All the weapons and explosives used were hidden in a house near the headquarters, ready to be picked up just after noon when the Germans would be enjoying their pre-lunch drinks. Each one of us had received specific orders. I entered the building by the back door, raced up the stairs, opened the first door along the passage way and threw in my grenades, closed the door and ran like hell back to my car which was ready to make a quick getaway. The headquarters was completely wrecked inside the building, and several dozen Germans did not lunch that day, nor any other day for that matter. The hardest part of the raid was to convince the nearby residents that the Allies had not landed and that they should return immediately to their homes and remain indoors.

In the early hours of the morning of 15 August, the long-awaited invasion of the south of France became a reality. Nearly 300,000 troops, comprised of Americans, British, Canadians and French, disembarked between Toulon and Cannes. The Resistance movements all over France had been anxiously awaiting the landings, as it would mean the beginning of the end for the Germans.

The numerous Maquis groups in the Allier set about destroying the targets they had been assigned for the second D-day. I'd brought the plans for these raids from England in that handbag – the bridges, roads, cable lines, railways, factories – anything that could be of use to the Germans. They destroyed them all except one which was a synthetic petrol plant at Saint-Hilaire. Tardivat, who had seized the entire output of fuel two months previously, said it would be a shame to destroy the plant as another supply of fuel would soon be available. London gave us permission to leave the plant intact as long as we could be certain the fuel would not fall into German hands.

Tardivat, plus the Anglo-American team, backed by several of our most bloodthirsty-looking Maquisards, called to see the plant manager at his home. He was not a bit co-operative when we informed him we were going to run his plant for the Allies. However, he was taken by force to the distillery and then to the boardroom, where he was interrogated by the male members of our team. He was warned that his failure to comply with their orders would have drastic consequences and that as he had traded with the enemy he would be put under arrest and placed under the charge of the Maquis.

He was white in the face and trembling by this time and assured us he would reserve the total output of fuel for the Maquis, mentioning the amount we could expect. I had not been included in this particular conversation, I was just standing by, armed to the teeth and trying to look as fierce as possible. Nevertheless, I did not want to be left out of the proceedings so I piped up and said that according to the figures I had, the amount of fuel he promised was not the entire output. To everyone's surprise, including my own, he agreed that perhaps it could be a little more. Tardivat left several men to protect our interests and keep an eye on the manager, but he was so scared of the Maquis he did not put a foot wrong after that day. Now we were all oil kings we made for the nearest bistro to celebrate our success.

All our operations were not as comical as our Saint-Hilaire one had been, but as the weeks sped by and the Germans were on the run, both from the Allied Forces and the French Resistance, it was often possible to enjoy a little light relief as we carried on with our duties.

At long last the Germans were paying a high price for the suffering they had inflicted on the French people. They knew the Resistance was lurking everywhere, just waiting to pounce. Too often the enemy had behaved like savages and now they were afraid for their own lives.

We trooped over to Cosne-d'Allier, the little village where Hubert and I had stayed when we first arrived. As we had been introduced to the entire village, they all came out of their houses when they saw me and followed us around when we laid our charges on the bridges and road junctions. It was the most enthusiastic audience we had ever seen or heard. They jumped up and down as each was detonated, and clapped and cheered as we withdrew. The difficult part of the operation had been to keep the villagers at a safe distance.

Tardivat decided, after his success with the German headquarters, that he would like to attack their garrison at Montluçon, where the force had been reduced to about 3,000. He set off with about 300 men and Alsop, Schley and Hubert. All the leaders were armed with bazookas – a popular weapon during World War II and especially suitable for the Maquis. Alsop and Schley led their groups while Hubert returned to our camp with a message from Tardivat inviting me to join in the fun. I had just finished coding my signals for London so I grabbed a bazooka, my carbine and several grenades, and set off for Montluçon in Hubert's car. When we reached the town and made enquiries as to Tardivat's position we were informed that he had captured half the garrison and we would have to cross a certain bridge in order to reach him. The only trouble was that as we began crossing the bridge someone opened fire with machine-guns. I got out of the car and started waving to Tardivat up in the garrison. It wasn't Tardivat, it was a German, and we were on the wrong bridge. We did a quick about-turn but the others teased us for days.

The fort was held for several days but the Germans sent over strong reinforcements from the east and the Maquis withdrew back to the forest. However, the whole town and the temporary victors could not conceal the satisfaction the event had given them.

It had rained for days, and the forest was like a quagmire. We were soaked to the skin and thoroughly miserable. Now that the Germans had troubles of their own they no longer presented a great threat to the Maquis and we determined to find more comfortable quarters. We were told of Fragne, an empty château a few kilometres from Montluçon. The owner had inherited it from an aunt but as he had not been able to install electricity and running water it had never attracted the attention of the Germans. Hubert and I talked to the caretaker, and through her the owner gave us permission to occupy the château for as long as we wished.

It was a huge place with spacious rooms. We slept on mattresses or in sleeping-bags and it was absolute bliss to be out of the rain. There was a lovely old clock-tower and a deep well at the rear of the château where we fetched our water for washing purposes, but for cooking the caretaker allowed us to fill our buckets from her kitchen tap. We moved in about one week before my birthday, which was on 30 August. As the men were all walking around looking secretive I guessed they were planning some kind of celebration.

We were occupied day and night. Alsop and Schley were instructing men on the use of the weapons and explosives we were receiving; Hubert was conferring with the other leaders; and I was receiving air-drops every night of the moon period. I had about twenty fields scattered all over the area but I decided that in future we would use the grounds of the château for any air-drops intended for our own use.

The men laughed when I announced this but realising I was serious they immediately volunteered to assist me to try to make the plan functional. They prepared an elaborate lighting system, using every available battery, and after a trial run we were convinced we could retire to our beds if the planes were delayed or cancelled. Should we hear them coming while we were in bed, we could switch on the lights which were already in position, hop out of bed and be on the field in time for the reception. London was informed immediately of our latest dropping zone.

At the headquarters of the Special Operations Executive, a Canadian ready to be parachuted on our new field found the château was marked on the Michelin map and wanted to know what idiot was using it. They informed him. Apparently all he said was, 'Oh, Nancy.' He was the chap who blew up the condom at Beaulieu. He and his travelling companions dropped quite safely on our field. We ushered them into our château with great pride and extended our usual hospitality.

Paris was liberated on 25 August 1944, and the whole country rejoiced; it would be hard to describe the excitement in the air. After defeat and years of humiliation their beautiful capital was free. The aggressors were now the hunted. The Germans were on the run and the French people were overcome with joy. My men were organizing a surprise for my birthday and at the same time we were going to celebrate the Liberation of Paris.

It was a wonderful party, which happily the Germans did not interrupt. All our colleagues were invited and so was our landlord. If anyone was unable to attend the luncheon, they came along afterwards. Everyone we knew helped us obtain the food and wine. It was amazing to see how many bottles of wine and champagne some farmers had been able to bury in their fields. Madame Renard and her daughter were guests. We supplied the ingredients for the marvellous dessert tarts and cakes she made for our party.

When all the guests had arrived we were escorted to the steps of the terrace leading into the rear entrance of the château. It was a secluded spot and could not be seen from the main road, which the Germans were still using. I was presented with a magnificent bouquet of flowers and told at the same time to be ready to take the salute. That was the surprise they had been planning. I was amazed to see we had so many smart, well-trained men. There were hundreds and hundreds of them. Then suddenly I recognised a man I had already seen marching by. The penny dropped. Once they had marched past our steps they ran like the devil right around the château and rejoined the men ahead. Without doubt they were the finest and fittest body of fighters I have ever had the honour and privilege to salute.

We gathered in the immense hall where rows of makeshift tables had been erected. Beautiful floral decorations surrounded the tables so that the emptiness of the vast room was not noticed. The speeches were endless and became more and more sentimental as we consumed bottle after bottle of the best wines and champagne France could offer.

There was only one sad note. Madame Renard's daughter announced at the table that Alex, Denden's boyfriend, had been killed. She had not known of the relationship between the two. We had to console him the best way we could but I'm afraid we were all too busy to be able to sympathise with appropriate dignity.

Everyone brought me some little gift. They must have been searching in the village for ages as at that time everything was in short supply. My Spaniards, who had absolutely no money, had gathered all the wildflowers they could find in the forest and wrapped them in a Spanish flag, and one of the bodyguard had written me a poem. It was all very touching. The party continued until the early hours of the morning. It was a great success and the talk of the Allier for some time.

When the Germans evacuated Montluçon, we were lucky. The château had been empty for so long and still, from the outside, looked deserted. The whole German convoy passed by without disturbing our Allied team hiding inside.

In September 1944 the Germans evacuated Vichy. Gaspard and Hubert had prearranged to join forces and enter the town at the same time. But Gaspard had stolen a march on us and gone on ahead. We gathered our team together and hurried after him. Vichy represented

everything we had been fighting against, and we were determined to
be a part of its liberation.

The collaborators seemed to have vanished into thin air and the
crowds in the street went wild with joy. All through the night we
were fêted wherever we went.

A ceremony was organised the following morning at the Cenotaph.
All the assembled groups were to lay wreaths. I was nominated by
our Allied team to represent them. When the mayor had finished his
address, a woman emerged from the crowds and came towards me.
She had been a receptionist at the Hôtel du Louvre et Paix in
Marseille. Quite abruptly she informed me that Henri was dead. I
was stunned. I do not know whether I had decided it was unreasonable to let the nightmare I had had in London influence my feelings;
perhaps I had subconsciously put the dream at the back of my mind
and determined to carry on as if it had not happened. But I do know
that ever since my return to France I had been taking it for granted
that Henri was alive. I burst into tears. Denis took me away.

I wanted to go straight to Marseille to find out what had happened.
Laurent, who was a magician where vehicles were concerned, put our
car into perfect running order and the five of us raced down to
Marseille – Hubert, Denden, John Alsop, our doctor friend Pierre
Vellat and myself. It was a chaotic journey. The Allied Air Force had
destroyed all the major bridges and the Resistance had sabotaged the
targets they had been given for the landing in the south of France.
We were the only ones going in the opposite direction. Finally, we
arrived in Marseille.

I went straight to my butcher's shop, which was closed, so I went
around to the back entrance and tapped on the kitchen window.
They recognised me and I could see the look of alarm that passed
between them as they wondered whether I was aware of the bad
news. I put them at ease at once, then asked about Picon. The
Ficetoles had taken him when Henri had been arrested, but their
home had been destroyed in one of the air raids and no one knew if
they were dead or alive.

After spending hours searching for them we were directed to a little
place outside Marseille. There was no answer when I knocked on the
door but Picon was inside and started howling. After twenty months
he had recognised my voice. He was so excited when he was let out

after the Ficetoles returned that our doctor, Pierre, had to give him tranquillisers.

Henri had been arrested by the Gestapo in May 1943. He had been imprisoned until his death on 16 October, five months later. It was in the middle of October that I had had that nightmare in London.

We returned to the château. Picon, who would not let me out of his sight, came too. We found dozens of invitations waiting there for us from all the towns and villages where we had been known.

I think that somehow I'd been subconsciously mourning Henri since the dream in London nearly a year before. Nothing was going to bring him back, and in spite of my grief I could not be unhappy knowing I'd contributed to the Liberation of France.

Our group of men at the château was preparing to go home. The Americans returned to London. We left the château in good order, thanked the landlord and caretaker for their kindness, and the three of us dawdled back to Paris. All along the route the French were celebrating the Liberation and it seemed to be one glorious party after another. We thought we might be the last ones to report back to Paris, where SOE had opened a branch, but a few more stragglers were still enjoying French hospitality.

Paris had been liberated in August 1944, but it would be another nine months of fighting across France before the German surrender in May 1945. After Paris was freed, Tardivat joined the army and kept fighting. Tragically, after all his adventures as a Maquis leader, he lost a leg in the fighting at Belfort Gap.

As there was a long waiting list for seats on an Allied Transport plane, we proceeded to enjoy ourselves in Paris. Denden spent a whole day at the hairdresser and came out looking ten years younger. Hubert disappeared for days. It transpired he had been looking after his future and organised himself an interesting position in a government department. I tried to trace old friends. Some were dead — some, including Stephanie, had disappeared and others had not returned from the country areas where they had taken refuge.

Fear of Death

F. J. Salfeld

Why did I want to join the Navy and fight? Mostly I wished to test the unknown in myself. As a child I was once accidentally pushed into a park lake on Boxing Day. I must have been terrified, but I cannot recall my fear. All that remains is a memory, bright after thirty years, of lying on my back under the water, looking up as if into a frosted mirror and seeing a white shadow across the rippling grey when a swan paddled over me, in hopes that the disturbance meant bread crusts. I was too young to realize death. Later, a youth, I was trapped by the tide on a cliff-bound Devon shore. But I had time to seek ways of escape, and I did not believe I should die. So although I was alone, I was not afraid.

But when I was in the Mediterranean last summer . . . Rommel had crossed the Egyptian border. Alexandria was preparing to defend itself. No British ship expected, in those waters, to escape attack by aircraft, warship or submarine – or any two of these and sometimes all three.

The first day I tasted action was sunny, but a sharp wind blew, making stays and wires hiss. Coming off duty I paused on the gun deck to watch the ship swing through the creamy sea, to count the attending destroyers and the stolid merchantmen smoking along in line ahead like chaperoned dowagers.

Then I went down to my mess deck and began to darn a sock. Three of the relieved watch took their soap and towels to the bathroom. Others dragged the leather seats off the long stools, laid them on the deck and went to sleep. One wrote a letter. Some chatted, an odd mixture of Cockney, Liverpool, Glasgow, Yorkshire, Canadian and other accents.

I had finished the warp of my darn and started on the weft when the alarm sounded: a series of urgent longs on the buzzer. It was also the first time most of my messmates had gone into action – indeed the first time some of them had been to sea. I don't know what I expected our first reactions to be; but not something so entirely unheroic as bad temper. I was annoyed at having to put my sock away half-darned. The sleepers resented being wakened up. The letter-writer flung his pen down with an exclamation of anger. A formerly active service AB, recalled after serving his time, said: ' – it! Just like them bastards to wait till we're off watch.' There he spoke for all. He stood on the stool and made a short speech to the canary he had bought ashore and hung in its cage above the mess table. 'Yer've got yer seed,' he said, gravely, 'an' yer've got yer water. Fill yer belly till I comes back. So long, cock.' The bird hopped sharply on its perch.

Then the unanimous rush for gas masks, tin hats, anti-flash gear, oilskins and sea-boots, the clank of feet up the iron ladder, the crash of the hatch cover shutting off the empty deck, the milling of dozens of men in the narrow alleyways as they sought their stations, petty officers shouting 'Double away there!' in the detached, irritated tones of men already looking inward to their own fate, the steady shuffle-shuffle of rubber and leather on linoleum.

I remembered, as I pushed my way to my magazine, aft, how in war films of infantry advancing their paces seemed to slow as a dream. So with us, until the press thinned out, and we could run. Ahead of me, in the engine room flat, I heard a sudden yell of laughter. Two stokers, taking a shower when the buzzer went, had been caught naked. As they shoved frantically against the human stream their towels were snatched from around their waists and the alleyway resounded with the echo of flat hands against bare buttocks. The stokers were grinning. One hadn't had time to dry his body.

The hatchway to my magazine lay just aft the wardroom. I glanced in as I passed. It was empty. Periodicals sprawled on the padded benches and the carpeted deck. On the arm of a chair a book had been placed, covers up, so that the owner need not search for his place when he returned.

Down the vertical ladder to the flooding cabinet, down again to the magazine. The face of one of the damage control party peered at us from above. 'All down?' he shouted. 'All down', replied the corporal of maraines in charge, and the rating, like a dandyish racing motorist in his white anti-flash helmet and long white gloves, descended to the cabinet and closed the armoured, counter-weighted hatch, so heavy that it took his full strength to move. Then, as the weight balanced and started in his favour, it fell with a jar. A pause, as he climbed up again, and then the dropping of the top cover and snick of its clips.

So there we were, a dozen blue-overalled men in this chilly cavern stacked from deck to deckhead with cordite and shells – safe so long as no bomb struck or, if the magazine had to be flooded, we could get out before the water rose; and with some prospect of escape if the ship, supposing her torpedoed, did not sink too quickly. Either the armoured hatch might be raised by the pressure of shoulders, or we might follow each other up the ladder inside the turret. There was just enough room to squeeze in there and haul oneself up the iron rungs, wet with warm oil dripping down from the pump that moved the guns. The pump was pounding now like an excited heart, and the turret slowly swung to meet the bombers, German or Italian, that we knew were coming in. Shut off below in a clamour of sound – the pump, the rattle of steel shell and brass cartridges in the racks, the communicated vibration of the propeller shafts on either side – we should have to guess its progress from the way the turret swung, from the abrupt lift of the deck as the ship heeled in a quick evasive turn to dodge a stick of bombs, from the commander's voice through the loud speaker should a lull allow him to broadcast a commentary. But we could not hear his voice unless we climbed the ladder and held our faces to the speaker.

The telephone rang from above. The corporal pressed his answering buzzer and jammed his ear against the instrument, listened, yelled back a jest I could not catch and told us to stand by. I had unclipped a number of charges and the bar of the first shell rack had been taken down. The shell hoist was loaded and men stood by the cordite lifts, waiting for the automatic doors to open. I held a charge in my arms. We were all ready. There was time to think and I was unsure whether I liked my thought, which was not that I might die but that I wanted to live lest my death should bring sorrow to those who loved me. The idea fascinated. I was filled with a sorrow in which lay no regret for the stopping of my own breath; I felt what I imagined would be the ache and emptiness in *their* hearts.

Masochism or vanity, or both, the notion drew me further. How would A and B adjust their lives, when they could no longer share mine? Would C mind very much, or D and E remember me for long? From the desolation of this self-torture I was glad to be freed by what sounded, in the general din, like a couple of polite coughs. Our guns had opened fire. The hoists began to work.

The next hour gave us no time for thought. We were all too busy, lifting the 80 lb shells out of the racks, shovelling in the cordite whenever the doors opened, sliding on the greasy grating as the ship rolled, chipping flesh off knuckles and elbows, swearing, sweating and laughing when somebody lurched or fell. And all the time, the remote, irregular cough of the guns, and every now and then a curious thud against the ship's side that shook the magazine – the near misses of the unseen bombs, whistling down in the sunlight.

Then we had our first lull and I the glad relief of not having been too much afraid. The corporal rang up his friend the sergeant in the turret to find out what had happened. A boy of twenty, a clerk in civil life, who had told me once that his ambition was to find a cure for cancer, took out of his overalls a pamphlet on biochemistry. A stout, fat-cheeked youth, who had come into the Navy from a Thames barge, squatted down and began to read an oily, battered copy of *No Orchids for Miss Blandish*. Two others resumed an earlier, giggly wrestling bout. The rest I could not see; the charge cases hid them. I could hear their voices, casual to the point of anti-climax.

Was this all, then? Did the prospect of death mean no more than a check to a clerk's dream, the interruption of a book and the postponement of childish horseplay? I looked round at my companions, to divine if I could, behind this extrovert behaviour, some secret speculation. It was then that I noticed the man in the corner. I didn't know his name (it turned out later that none of us did) or anything about him. He might have been thirty; he could have been forty. He never chatted to anyone and seemed to have no friends or interests in the ship, but lived his own withdrawn life. He was sitting now on a sand-filled fire bucket, his hands laid inertly on his knees, his colourless face a stare of strain, as if death had spoken to him already and he knew he was lost. (Which might have been so, for the next day he was removed from the magazine and, at his own request, made an anti-aircraft lookout, and at his post a bullet from a Junkers killed him.)

I wanted to ask him what thoughts he had, to be thus paralysed. Or was his fear without form? Or was he afraid of fear, as most men are until they have tried themselves out. But these questions are not to be asked – and the telephone had rung again, the turret was turned. Again the discreet cough, the choking, the stumbling and the oaths. But this time the atmosphere was new. The constraints were gone. The question mark poised in every brain had vanished. For good or ill, we each had our answer. One man sang as he staggered from the racks with his shells; and I, who suddenly felt happy and free, knew why. He had passed his test; he was on good terms with his spirit.

We all, in more or less degree, shared this strange intoxication – except the corporal of marines, to whom action was ordinary, and the pale man in the corner, who sat on, not watching, seeing nothing. The corporal stumbled over the deck to him. 'Well strike me pink!' he exclaimed. 'What the hell do you think this is, mate? A make-and-mend? Come on then, stand easy's over.' Whereupon the man rose from his bucket, walked over to the turret and began to climb up the escape ladder – not with panic speed but deliberately, as if in obedience to an order. The corporal watched him with dropped jaw, charged after him and pulled him down again by his heels. 'You can't do that there 'ere,' he said, patiently.

The man stood where the corporal had pushed him, against an empty shell rack, his hands by his side, still silent, like a martyr with eyes of pain. And the corporal could find nothing more to say. He put his arms akimbo, then scratched the back of his head with his right hand. But it was beyond him to deal with a man in a trance. He could only point to the fire bucket, and the man returned there and stood like a statue. Thus he was when the second and final action of that day ended, the 'All clear' was broadcast, the armoured hatch was opened from above, and we were free. Nobody spoke to the man whose nerve was gone and nobody looked at him, except that the corporal, who always left the magazine last, said to him with a rough, puzzled gentleness: 'Up you go, mate.'

I found my mess-deck half-wrecked by a heavy bomb which had crashed through without exploding, fractured a water pipe, smashed table and hurled jags of metal through lockers, hammocks and fittings. Most of the lights were out. At the forward end, which was undamaged, grimy men clustered around the tables smoking, talking of the action and of friends who were wounded or dead, and of how they had died. At the end of the table a youngster sat crying openly like the child he had so recently been. He had seen his 'winger', his best friend, decapitated. Grief and shock joined in the tears that drew two pink lanes down his grease-stained cheeks. The old AB was searching among debris for the corpse of his canary. The place had the air of a cemetery chapel.

No consolation, no comfort, was offered. They were inarticulate men, unable to frame the smooth sympathies of a politer life. I think they were more instinctive than men of education, and out of their instinct knew that grief cannot be soothed by those it does not touch. So they talked and argued and boasted around the weeping boy as though he wasn't there.

The AB found his crushed and muddied bird and showed it to us. He leaned across the table, his mouth tight with anger. He had placed the bird in a dirty handkerchief. Somebody spoke the epitaph: 'Poor little bastard! 'E never done nobody no 'arm.' The AB laid a chunk of fractured piping beside the corpse, wrapped it up carefully and tied a reef knot in the handkerchief. Then he left the mess. We knew what he was going to do. Dead men over the side in weighted canvas, a canary in a knotted handkerchief – it seemed no parody. All were victims.

Nobody knew what to say next. We became embarrassed by our own silence. At last the leading hand of that mess stood up. 'Well, what about some eats?' he asked, nervously, uncertain whether the idea was fitting. We consented by moving away so that the table could be laid, with the boy still sobbing at the end of it, and none telling him he was in the way of the cooks as they lifted plates and mugs down from the rack above him.

The food was brought from the galley, the bread dumped on the white American cloth. I was astonished at my hunger. The old AB, the sobbing boy, whose tears had now become hiccups at which even he himself laughed, everybody ate an enormous meal.

The Invaders

John Steinbeck

Tonder sat down on his chair and put his hands to his temples and he said brokenly, 'I want a girl. I want to go home. I want a girl. There's a girl in this town, a pretty girl, I see her all the time. She has blonde hair. She lives beside the old-iron stove. I want that girl.'

Prackle said, 'Watch yourself. Watch your nerves.'

At that moment the lights went out again and the room was in darkness. Hunter spoke while the matches were being struck and an attempt was being made to light the lanterns; he said, 'I thought I had all of them. I must have missed one. But I can't be running down there all the time. I've got good men down there.'

Tonder lighted the first lantern and then he lighted the other, and Hunter spoke sternly to Tonder. 'Lieutenant, do your talking to us if you have to talk. Don't let the enemy hear you talk this way. There's nothing these people would like better than to know your nerves are getting thin. Don't let the enemy hear you.'

Tonder sat down again. The light was sharp on his face and the hissing filled the room. He said, 'That's it! The enemy's everywhere! Every man, every woman, even children! The enemy's everywhere. Their faces look out of doorways. The white faces behind the curtains, listening. We have beaten them, we have won everywhere, and they wait and obey, and they wait. Half the world is ours. Is it the same in other places, Major?'

And Hunter said, 'I don't know.'

'That's it,' Tonder said. 'We don't know. The reports – everything in hand. Conquered countries cheer our soldiers, cheer the new order.' His voice changed and grew soft and still softer. 'What do the reports say about us? Do they say we are cheered, loved, flowers in our paths? Oh, these horrible people waiting in the snow!'

And Hunter said, 'Now that's off your chest, do you feel better?'

Prackle had been beating the table softly with his good fist, and he said, 'He shouldn't talk that way. He should keep things to himself. He's a soldier, isn't he? Then let him be a soldier.'

The door opened quietly and Captain Loft came in, and there was snow on his helmet and snow on his shoulders. His nose was pinched and red and his overcoat collar was high about his ears. He took off his helmet and the snow fell on to the floor and he brushed his shoulders. 'What a job!' he said.

'More trouble?' Hunter asked.

'Always trouble. I see they've got your dynamo again. Well, I think I fixed the mine for a while.'

'What's your trouble?' Hunter asked.

'Oh, the usual thing with me – the slow-down and a wrecked dump car. I saw the wrecker, though. I shot him. I think I have a cure for it, Major, now. I just thought it up. I'll make each man take out a certain amount of coal. I can't starve the men or they can't work, but I've really got the answer. If the coal doesn't come out, no food for the families. We'll have the men eat at the mine, so there's no dividing at home. That ought to cure it. They work or their kids don't eat. I told them just now.'

'What did they say?'

Loft's eyes narrowed fiercely. 'Say? What do they ever say? Nothing! Nothing at all! But we'll see whether the coal comes out now.' He took off his coat and shook it, and his eyes fell on the entrance door and he saw that it was open a crack. He moved silently to the door, jerked it open, then closed it. 'I thought I had closed that door tight,' he said.

'You did,' said Hunter.

Prackle still turned the pages of his illustrated paper. His voice was normal again. 'Those are monster guns we're using in the east. I never saw one of them. Did you, Captain?'

'Oh, yes,' said Captain Loft. 'I've seen them fired. They're wonderful. Nothing can stand up against them.'

Tonder said, 'Captain, do you get much news from home?'

'A certain amount,' said Loft.

'Is everything well there?'

'Wonderful!' said Loft. 'The armies move ahead everywhere.'

'The British aren't defeated yet?'

'They are defeated in every engagement.'

'But they fight on?'

'A few air-raids, no more.'

'And the Russians?'

'It's all over.'

Tonder said insistently. 'But they fight on?'

'A little skirmishing, no more.'

'Then we have just about won, haven't we, Captain?' Tonder asked.

'Yes, we have.'

Tonder looked closely at him and said, 'You believe this, don't you, Captain?'

Prackle broke in, 'Don't let him start that again!'

Loft scowled at Tonder. 'I don't know what you mean.'

Tonder said, 'I mean this: we'll be going home before long, won't we?'

'Well, the reorganisation will take some time,' Hunter said. 'The new order can't be put into effect in a day, can it?'

Tonder said, 'All our lives, perhaps?'

And Prackle said, 'Don't let him start it again!'

Loft came very close to Tonder and he said, 'Lieutenant, I don't like the tone of your questions. I don't like the tone of doubt.'

Hunter looked up and said, 'Don't be hard on him, Loft. He's tired. We're all tired.'

'Well, I'm tired, too,' said Loft, 'but I don't let treasonable doubts get in.'

Hunter said, 'Don't bedevil him, I tell you! Where's the colonel, do you know?'

'He's making out his report. He's asking for reinforcements,' said Loft. 'It's a bigger job than we thought.'

Prackle asked excitedly, 'Will he get them – the reinforcements?'

'How would I know?'

Tonder smiled. 'Reinforcements!' he said softly. 'Or maybe replacements. Maybe we could go home for a while.' And he said, smiling, 'Maybe I could walk down the street and people would say "Hello", and they'd say, "There goes a soldier", and they'd be glad for me and they'd be glad of me. And there'd be friends about, and I could turn my back to a man without being afraid.'

Prackle said, 'Don't start that again! Don't let him get out of hand again!'

And Loft said disgustedly, 'We have enough trouble now without having the staff go crazy.'

But Tonder went on, 'You really think replacements will come, Captain?'

'I didn't say so.'

'But you said they might.'

'I said I didn't know. Look, Lieutenant, we've conquered half the world. We must police it for a while. You know that.'

'But the other half?' Tonder asked.

'They will fight on hopelessly for a while,' said Loft.

'Then we must spread out all over.'

'For a while,' said Loft.

Prackle said nervously, 'I wish you'd make him shut up. I wish you would shut him up. Make him stop it.'

Tonder got out his handkerchief and blew his nose, and he spoke a little like a man out of his head. He laughed embarrassedly. He said, 'I had a funny dream. I guess it was a dream. Maybe it was a thought. Maybe a thought or a dream.'

Prackle said, 'Make him stop it, Captain!'

Tonder said, 'Captain, is this place conquered?'

'Of course,' said Loft.

A little note of hysteria crept into Tonder's laughter. He said, 'Conquered and we're afraid; conquered and we're surrounded.' His laughter grew shrill. 'I had a dream – or a thought – out in the snow with the black shadows and the faces in the doorways, the cold faces behind curtains. I had a thought or a dream.'

Prackle said, 'Make him stop!'

Tonder said, 'I dreamed the Leader was crazy.'

And Loft and Hunter laughed together, and Loft said, 'The enemy have found out how crazy. I'll have to write that one home. The papers would print that one. The enemy have learned how crazy the Leader is.'

And Tonder went on laughing. 'Conquest after conquest, deeper and deeper into molasses.' His laughter choked him and he coughed into his handkerchief. 'Maybe the Leader is crazy. Flies conquer the flypaper! Flies captured two hundred miles of new flypaper!' His laughter was growing more hysterical now.

Prackle leaned over and shook him with his good hand. 'Stop it! You stop it! You have no right!'

And gradually Loft recognised that the laughter was hysterical and he stepped closer to Tonder and slapped him in the face. He said, 'Lieutenant, stop it!'

Tonder's laughter went on and Loft slapped him again in the face and he said, 'Stop it, Lieutenant! Do you hear me!'

Suddenly Tonder's laughter stopped and the room was quiet except for the hissing of the lanterns. Tonder looked in amazement at his hand and he felt his bruised face with his hand and he looked at his hand again and his head sank down towards the table. 'I want to go home,' he said.

There was a little street not far from the town square where small peaked roofs and little shops were mixed up together. The snow was beaten down on the walks and in the streets, but it piled up on the fences and it puffed on the roof peaks. It drifted against the shuttered windows of the little houses. And into the yards paths were shovelled. The night was dark and cold and no light showed from the windows to attract the bombers. And no one walked in the streets, for the curfew was strict. The houses were dark lumps against the snow. Every little while the patrol of six men walked down the street, peering about, and each man carried a long flashlight. The hushed tramp of their feet sounded in the street, the squeaks of their boots on the packed snow. They were muffled figures deep in thick coats; under their helmets were knitted caps which came down over their ears and covered their chins and mouths. A little snow fell, only a little, like rice.

The patrol talked as they walked, and they talked of things that they longed for – of meat and of hot soup and of the richness of butter, of the prettiness of girls and of their smiles and of their lips and their eyes. They talked of these things and sometimes they talked of their hatred of what they were doing and of their loneliness.

A small, peak-roofed house beside the iron shops was shaped like the others and wore its snow cap like the others. No light came from its shuttered windows and its storm doors were tightly closed. But inside a lamp burned in the small living-room and the door to the bedroom was open and the door to the kitchen was open. An iron stove was against the back wall with a little coal fire burning in it. It was a warm, poor, comfortable room, the floor covered with worn carpet, the walls papered in warm brown with an old-fashioned *fleur-de-lis* figure in gold. And on the back wall were two pictures, one of fish lying dead on a plate of ferns and the other of grouse lying dead on a fir bough. On the right wall there was a picture of Christ walking on the waves towards the despairing fishmen. Two straight chairs were in the room and a couch covered with a bright blanket. There was a little round table in the middle of the room, on which stood a kerosene lamp with a round flowered shade on it, and the light in the room was warm and soft.

The inner door, which led to the passage, which in turn led to the storm door, was beside the stove.

In a cushioned old rocking-chair beside the table Molly Morden sat alone. She was unravelling the wool from an old blue sweater and winding the yarn on a ball. She had quite a large ball of it. And on the table beside her was her knitting with the needles sticking in it, and a large pair of scissors. Her glasses lay on the table beside her, for she did not need them for knitting. She was pretty and young and neat. Her golden hair was done up on the top of her head and a blue bow was in her hair. Her hands worked quickly with the ravelling. As she worked, she glanced now and then at the door to the passage. The wind whistled in the chimney softly, but it was a quiet night, muffled with snow.

Suddenly she stopped her work. Her hands were still. She looked towards the door and listened. The tramping feet of the patrol went by in the street and the sound of their voices could be heard faintly. The sound faded away. Molly ripped out new yarn and wound it on the ball. And again she stopped. There was a rustle at the door and then three short knocks. Molly put down her work and went to the door.

'Yes?' she called.

She unlocked the door and opened it and a heavily cloaked figure came in. It was Annie, the cook, red-eyed and wrapped in mufflers. She slipped in quickly, as though practised at getting speedily through doors and getting them closed again behind her. She stood there red-nosed, sniffling and glancing quickly around the room.

Molly said, 'Good evening, Annie. I didn't expect you tonight. Take your things off and get warm. It's cold out.'

Annie said, 'The soldiers brought winter early. My father always

said a war brought bad weather, or bad weather brought a war. I
don't remember which.'

'Take off your things and come to the stove.'

'I can't,' said Annie importantly. 'They're coming.'

'Who are coming?' Molly said.

'His Excellency,' said Annie, 'and the doctor and the two Anders
boys.'

'Here?' Molly asked. 'What for?'

Annie held out her hand and there was a little package in it. 'Take
it,' she said. 'I stole it from the colonel's plate. It's meat.'

And Molly unwrapped the little cake of meat and put it in her
mouth and she spoke around her chewing. 'Did you get some?'

Annie said, 'I cook it, don't I? I always get some.'

'When are they coming?'

Annie sniffed. 'The Anders boys are sailing for England. They've
got to go. They're hiding now.'

'Are they?' Molly asked. 'What for?'

'Well, it was their brother Jack, was shot today for wrecking that
little car. The soldiers are looking for the rest of the family. You know
how they do.'

'Yes,' Molly said, 'I know how they do. Sit down, Annie.'

'No time,' said Annie. 'I've got to get back and tell His Excellency
it's all right here.'

Molly said, 'Did anybody see you come?'

Annie smiled proudly. 'No, I'm awful good at sneaking.'

'How will the Mayor get out?'

Annie laughed, 'Joseph is going to be in his bed in case they look
in, right in his night-shirt, right next to Madame!' And she laughed
again. She said, 'Joseph better lie pretty quiet.'

Molly said, 'It's an awful night to be sailing.'

'It's better than being shot.'

'Yes, so it is. Why is the Mayor coming here?'

'I don't know. He wants to talk to the Anders boys. I've got to go
now, but I came to tell you.'

Molly said, 'How soon are they coming?'

'Oh, maybe half, maybe three-quarters of an hour,' Annie said.
'I'll come in first. Nobody bothers with old cooks.' She started for the
door and she turned midway, and as though accusing Molly of saying

the last words she said truculently, 'I'm not so old!' And she slipped
out of the door and closed it behind her.

Molly went on knitting for a moment and then she got up and
went to the stove and lifted the lid. The glow of the fire lighted her
face. She stirred the fire and added a few lumps of coal and closed
the stove again. Before she could get to her chair, there was a
knocking on the outer door. She crossed the room and said to herself,
'I wonder what she forgot.' She went into the passage and she said,
'What do you want?'

A man's voice answered her. She opened the door and a man's
voice said, 'I don't mean any harm. I don't mean any harm.'

Molly backed into the room and Lieutenant Tonder followed her
in. Molly said, 'Who are you? What do you want? You can't come in
here. What do you want?'

Lieutenant Tonder was dressed in his great grey overcoat. He
entered the room and took off his helmet and he spoke pleadingly. 'I
don't mean any harm. Please let me come in.'

Molly said, 'What do you want?'

She shut the door behind him and he said, 'Miss, I only want to
talk, that's all. I want to hear you talk. That's all I want.'

'Are you forcing yourself on me?' Molly asked.

'No, Miss, just let me stay a little while and then I'll go.'

'What is it you want?'

Tonder tried to explain. 'Can you understand this – can you
believe this? Just for a little while, can't we forget this war? Just for a
little while. Just for a little while, can't we talk together like people –
together?'

Molly looked at him for a long time and then a smile came to her
lips. 'You don't know who I am, do you?'

Tonder said, 'I've seen you in the town. I know you're lovely. I
know I want to talk to you.'

And Molly still smiled. She said softly, 'You don't know who I
am.' She sat in her chair and Tonder stood like a child, looking very
clumsy. Molly continued, speaking quietly: 'Why, you're lonely. It's
as simple as that, isn't it?'

Tonder licked his lips and he spoke eagerly. 'That's it,' he said.
'You understand. I knew you would. I knew you'd have to.' His
words came tumbling out. 'I'm lonely to the point of illness. I'm

lonely in the quiet and the hatred.' And he said pleadingly, 'Can't we talk, just a little bit?'

Molly picked up her knitting. She looked quickly at the front door. 'You can stay not more than fifteen minutes. Sit down a little, Lieutenant.'

She looked at the door again. The house creaked. Tonder became tense and he said, 'Is someone here?'

'No, the snow is heavy on the roof. I have no man any more to push it down.'

Tonder said gently, 'Who did it? Was it something we did?'

And Molly nodded, looking far off. 'Yes.'

He sat down. 'I'm sorry.' After a moment he said, 'I wish I could do something. I'll have the snow pushed off the roof.'

'No,' said Molly, 'no.'

'Why not?'

'Because the people would think I had joined with you. They would expel me. I don't want to be expelled.'

Tonder said, 'Yes, I see how that would be. You all hate us. But I'll take care of you if you'll let me.'

Now Molly knew she was in control, and her eyes narrowed a little cruelly and she said, 'Why do you ask? You are the conqueror. Your men don't have to ask. They take what they want.'

'That's not what I want,' Tonder said. 'That's not the way I want it.'

And Molly laughed, still a little cruelly. 'You want me to like you, don't you, Lieutenant?'

He said simply, 'Yes,' and he raised his head and he said, 'You are so beautiful, so warm. Your hair is bright. Oh, I've seen no kindness in a woman's face for so long!'

'Do you see any in mine?' she asked.

He looked closely at her. 'I want to.'

She dropped her eyes at last. 'You're making love to me, aren't you, Lieutenant?'

He said clumsily, 'I want you to like me. Surely I want you to like me. Surely I want to see that in your eyes. I have seen you in the streets. I have watched you pass by. I've given orders that you mustn't be molested. Have you been molested?'

And Molly said quietly, 'Thank you; no, I've not been molested.'

His words rushed on. 'Why, I've even written a poem for you. Would you like to see my poem?'

And she said sardonically, 'Is it a long poem? You have to go very soon.'

He said, 'No, it's a little tiny poem. It's a little bit of a poem.' He reached inside his tunic and brought out a folded paper and handed it to her. She leaned close to the lamp and put on her glasses and she read quietly:

> Your eyes in their deep heavens
> Possess me and will not depart;
> A sea of blue thoughts rushing
> And pouring over my heart.

She folded the paper and put it in her lap. 'Did you write this, Lieutenant?'

'Yes.'

She said a little tauntingly, 'To me?'

And Tonder answered uneasily, 'Yes.'

She looked at him steadily, smiling. 'You didn't write it, Lieutenant, did you?'

He smiled back like a child caught in a lie. 'No.'

Molly asked him, 'Do you know who did?'

Tonder said, 'Yes, Heine wrote it. It's "*Mit deinen blauen Augen*". I've always loved it.' He laughed embarrassedly and Molly laughed with him, and suddenly they were laughing together. He stopped laughing just as suddenly and a bleakness came into his eyes. 'I haven't laughed like this since forever.' He said, 'They told us the people would like us, would admire us. They do not. They only hate us.' And then he changed the subject as though he worked against time. 'You are so beautiful. You are as beautiful as the laughter.'

Molly said, 'You're beginning to make love to me, Lieutenant. You must go in a moment.'

And Tonder said, 'Maybe I want to make love to you. A man needs love. A man dies without love. His insides shrivel and his chest feels like a dry chip. I'm lonely.'

Molly got up from her chair. She looked nervously at the door and she walked to the stove and, coming back, her face grew hard and her eyes grew punishing and she said, 'Do you want to go to bed with me, Lieutenant?'

'I didn't say that! Why do you talk that way?'

Molly said cruelly, 'Maybe I'm trying to disgust you. I was married once. My husband is dead now. You see, I'm not a virgin.' Her voice was bitter.

Tonder said, 'I only want you to like me.'

And Molly said, 'I know. You are a civilised man. You know that love-making is more full and whole and delightful if there is liking, too.'

Tonder said, 'Don't talk that way! Please don't talk that way!'

Molly glanced quickly at the door. She said, 'We are conquered people, Lieutenant. You have taken the food away. I'm hungry. I'll like you better if you feed me.'

Tonder said, 'What are you saying?'

'Do I disgust you, Lieutenant? Maybe I'm trying to. My price is two sausages.'

Tonder said, 'You can't talk this way!'

'What about your own girls, Lieutenant, after the last war? A man could choose among your girls for an egg or a slice of bread. Do you want me for nothing, Lieutenant? Is the price too high?'

He said, 'You fooled me for a moment. But you hate me, too, don't you? I thought maybe you wouldn't.'

'No, I don't hate you,' she said. 'I'm hungry and – I hate you!'

Tonder said, 'I'll give you anything you need, but – '

And she interrupted him. 'You want to call it something else? You don't want a whore. Is that what you mean?'

Tonder said, 'I don't know what I mean. You make it sound full of hatred.'

Molly laughed. She said, 'It's not nice to be hungry. Two sausages, two fine, fat sausages can be the most precious things in the world.'

'Don't say those things,' he said. 'Please don't!'

'Why not? They're true.'

'They aren't true! This can't be true!'

She looked at him for a moment and then she sat down and her eyes fell to her lap and she said, 'No, it's not true. I don't hate you. I'm lonely too. And the snow is heavy on the roof.'

Tonder got up and moved near to her. He took one of her hands in both of his and he said softly, 'Please don't hate me. I'm only a lieutenant. I didn't ask to come here. You didn't ask to be my enemy. I'm only a man, not a conquering man.'

Molly's fingers encircled his hands for a moment and she said softly, 'I know; yes, I know.'

And Tonder said, 'We have some right to life in all this death.'

She put her hand to his cheek for a moment and she said, 'Yes.'

'I'll take care of you,' he said. 'We have some right to life in all the killing.' His hand rested on her shoulder. Suddenly she grew rigid and her eyes were wide and staring as though she saw a vision. His hand released her and he asked, What's the matter? What is it?' Her eyes stared straight ahead and he repeated, 'What is it?'

Molly spoke in a haunted voice. 'I dressed him like a little boy for his first day in school. And he was afraid. I buttoned his shirt and tried to comfort him, but he was beyond comfort. And he was afraid.'

Tonder said, 'What are you saying?'

And Molly seemed to see what she described. 'I don't know why they let him come home. He was confused. He didn't know what was happening. He didn't even kiss me when he went away. He was afraid, and very brave, like a little boy on his first day of school.'

Tonder stood up. 'That was your husband.'

Molly said, 'Yes, my husband. I went to the Mayor, but he was helpless. And then he marched away – not very well, not steadily – and you took him out and you shot him. It was more strange than terrible then. I didn't quite believe it then.'

Tonder said, 'Your husband!'

'Yes; and now, in the quiet house, I believe it. Now, with the heavy snow on the roof, I believe it. And in the loneliness before daybreak, in the half-warmed bed, I know it then.'

Tonder stood in front of her. His face was full of misery. 'Good night,' he said. 'God keep you. May I come back?'

And Molly looked at the wall and at the memory; 'I don't know,' she said.

'I'll come back.'

'I don't know.'

He looked at her and then he quietly went out of the door, and Molly still stared at the wall. 'God keep me.' She stayed for a moment staring at the wall. The door opened silently and Annie came in. Molly did not even see her.

Annie said disapprovingly, 'The door was open.'

Molly looked slowly towards her, her eyes will wide open. 'Yes, oh yes, Annie.'

'The door was open. There was a man came out. I saw him. He looked like a soldier.'

And Molly said, 'Yes, Annie.'

'Was it a soldier here?'

'Yes, it was a soldier.'

And Annie asked suspiciously, 'What was he doing here?'

'He came to make love to me.'

Annie said, 'Miss, what are you doing? You haven't joined them, have you? You aren't with them, like that Corell?'

'No, I'm not with them, Annie.'

Annie said, 'If the Mayor's here and they come back, it'll be your fault if anything happens; it'll be your fault!'

'He won't come back. I won't let him come back.'

But the suspicion stayed with Annie. She said, 'Shall I tell them to come in now? Do you say it's safe?'

'Yes, it's safe. Where are they?'

'They're out behind the fence,' said Annie.

'Tell them to come in.'

And while Annie went out, Molly got up and smoothed her hair and she shook her head, trying to be alive again. There was a little sound in the passage. Two tall, blond young men entered. They were dressed in pea-jackets and dark turtle-neck sweaters. They wore stocking caps perched on their heads. They were wind-burned and strong and they looked almost like twins, Will Anders and Tom Anders, the fishermen.

'Good evening, Molly. You've heard?'

'Annie told me. It's a bad night to go.'

Tom said, 'It's better than a clear night. The planes see you on a clear night. What's the Mayor want, Molly?'

'I don't know. I heard about your brother. I'm sorry.'

The two were silent and they looked embarrassed. Tom said, 'You know how it is, better than most.'

'Yes; I know.'

Annie came in the door again and she said in a hoarse whisper, 'They're here!' And Mayor Orden and Doctor Winter came in. They took off their coats and caps and laid them on the couch. Orden went to Molly and kissed her on the forehead.

'Good evening, dear.'

He turned to Annie. 'Stand in the passage, Annie. Give us one knock for the patrol, one when it's gone, and two for danger. You can leave the outer door open a crack so that you can hear if anyone comes.'

Annie said, 'Yes, sir.' She went into the passage and shut the door behind her.

Doctor Winter was at the stove, warming his hands. 'We got word you boys were going tonight.'

'We've got to go,' Tom said.

Orden nodded. 'Yes, I know. We heard you were going to take Mr Corell with you.'

Tom laughed bitterly. 'We thought it would be only right. We're taking his boat. We can't leave him around. It isn't good to see him in the streets.'

Orden said sadly, 'I wish he had gone away. It's just a danger to you, taking him.'

'It isn't good to see him in the streets.' Will echoed his brother. 'It isn't good for the people to see him here.'

Winter asked, 'Can you take him? Isn't he cautious at all?'

'Oh, yes, he's cautious, in a way. At twelve o'clock, though, he walks to his house usually. We'll be behind the wall. I think we can get him through his lower garden to the water. His boat's tied up there. We were on her today getting her ready.'

Orden repeated, 'I wish you didn't have to. It's just an added danger. If he makes a noise, the patrol might come.'

Tom said, 'He won't make a noise, and it's better if he disappears at sea. Some of the town people might get him and then there would be too much killing. No, it's better if he goes to sea.'

Molly took up her knitting again. She said, 'Will you throw him overboard?'

Will blushed. 'He'll go to sea, ma'am.' He turned to the Mayor. 'You wanted to see us, sir?'

'Why, yes, I want to talk to you. Doctor Winter and I have tried to think – there's so much talk about justice, injustice, conquest. Our people are invaded, but I don't think they're conquered.'

There was a sharp knock on the door and the room was silent. Molly's needles stopped, and the Mayor's outstretched hand remained in the air. Tom, scratching his ear, left his hand there and stopped scratching. Everyone in the room was motionless. Every eye was turned towards the door. Then, first faintly and then growing louder, there came the tramp of the patrol, the squeak of their boots in the snow, and the sound of their talking as they went by. They passed the door and their footsteps disappeared in the distance. There was a second tap on the door. And in the room the people relaxed.

Orden said, 'It must be cold out there for Annie.' He took up his coat from the couch and opened the inner door and handed his coat through. 'Put this around your shoulders, Annie,' he said and closed the door.

'I don't know what I'd do without her,' he said. 'She gets everywhere, she sees and hears everything.'

Tom said, 'We should be going pretty soon, sir.'

And Winter said, 'I wish you'd forget about Mr Corell.'

'We can't. It isn't good to see him in the streets.' He looked inquiringly at Mayor Orden.

Orden began slowly. 'I want to speak simply. This is a little town. Justice and injustice are in terms of little things. Your brother's shot and Alex Morden's shot. Revenge against a traitor. The people are angry and they have no way to fight back. But it's all in little terms. It's people against people, not idea against idea.'

Winter said, 'It's funny for a doctor to think of destruction, but I think all invaded people want to resist. We are disarmed; our spirits and bodies aren't enough. The spirit of a disarmed man sinks.'

Will Anders asked, 'What's all this for, sir? What do you want of us?'

'We want to fight them and we can't,' Orden said. 'They're using hunger on the people now. Hunger brings weakness. You boys are sailing for England. Maybe nobody will listen to you, but tell them from us – from a small town – to give us weapons.'

Tom asked, 'You want guns?'

Again there was a quick knock on the door and the people froze where they were, and from outside there came the sound of the patrol, but a double step, running. Will moved quickly towards the door. The running steps came abreast with the house. There were muffled orders and the patrol ran by, and there was a second tap at the door.

Molly said, 'They must be after somebody. I wonder who, this time.'

'We should be going,' Tom said uneasily. 'Do you want guns, sir? Shall we ask for guns?'

'No, tell them how it is. We are watched. Any move we make calls for reprisals. If we could have simple, secret weapons, weapons of stealth, explosives, dynamite to blow up rails, grenades, if possible, even poison.' He spoke angrily. 'There is no honourable war. This is a war of treachery and murder. Let us use the methods that have been used on us! Let the British bombers drop their big bombs on the works, but let them also drop us little bombs to use, to hide, to slip under the rails, under tanks. Then we will be armed, secretly armed. Then the invader will never know which of us is armed. Let the bombers bring us simple weapons. We will know how to use them!'

Winter broke in. 'They'll never know where it will strike. The soldiers, the patrol, will never know which of us is armed.'

Tom wiped his forehead. 'If we get through, we'll tell them, sir, but – well, I've heard it said that in England there are still men in power who do not care to put weapons in the hands of common people.'

Orden stared at him. 'Oh! I hadn't thought of that. Well, we can only see. If such people still govern England and America, the world is lost, anyway. Tell them what we say, if they will listen. We must have help, but if we get it' – his face grew very hard – 'if we get it, we will help ourselves.'

Winter said, 'If they will even give us dynamite to hide, to bury in the ground to be ready against need, then the invader can never rest again, never! We will blow up his supplies.'

The room grew excited. Molly said fiercely, 'Yes, we could fight his rest, then. We could fight his sleep. We could fight his nerves and his certainties.'

Will asked quietly, 'Is that all, sir?'

'Yes,' Orden nodded. 'That's the core of it.'

'What if they won't listen?'

'You can only try, as you are trying the sea tonight.'

'Is that all, sir?'

The door opened and Annie came quietly in. Orden went on, 'That's all. If you have to go now, let me send Annie out to see that the way is clear.' He looked up and saw that Annie had come in. Annie said, 'There's a soldier coming up the path. He looks like the soldier that was here before. There was a soldier here with Molly before.'

The others looked at Molly. Annie said, 'I locked the door.'

'What does he want?' Molly asked. 'Why does he come back?'

There was a gentle knocking at the outside door. Orden went to Molly. 'What is this, Molly? Are you in trouble?'

'No,' she said, 'no! Go out the back way. You can get out through the back. Hurry, hurry out!'

The knocking continued on the front door. A man's voice called softly. Molly opened the door to the kitchen. She said, 'Hurry, hurry!'

The Mayor stood in front of her. 'Are you in trouble, Molly? You haven't done anything?'

Annie said coldly, 'It looks like the same soldier. There was a soldier here before.'

'Yes,' Molly said to the Mayor. 'Yes, there was a soldier here before.'

The Mayor said, 'What did he want?'

'He wanted to make love to me.'

'But he didn't?' Orden said.

'No,' she said, 'he didn't. Go now, and I'll take care.'

Orden said, 'Molly, if you're in trouble, let us help you.'

'The trouble I'm in no one can help me with,' she said. 'Go now,' and she pushed them out of the door.

Annie remained behind. She looked at Molly. 'Miss, what does this soldier want?'

'I don't know what he wants.'

'Are you going to tell him anything?'

'No.' Wonderingly, Molly repeated, 'No.' And then sharply she said, 'No, Annie, I'm not!'

Annie scowled at her. 'Miss, you'd better not tell him anything!' And she went out and closed the door behind her.

The tapping continued on the front door and a man's voice could be heard through the door.

Molly went to the centre lamp, and her burden was heavy on her. She looked down at the lamp. She looked at the table, and she saw the big scissors lying beside her knitting. She picked them up wonderingly by the blades. The blades slipped through her fingers until she held the long shears and she was holding them like a knife, and her eyes were horrified. She looked down into the lamp and the

light flooded up in her face. Slowly she raised the shears and placed
them inside her dress.

The tapping continued on the door. She heard the voice calling to
her. She leaned over the lamp for a moment and then suddenly she
blew out the light. The room was dark except for a spot of red that
came from the coal stove. She opened the door. Her voice was
strained and sweet. She called, 'I'm coming, Lieutenant. I'm coming!'

The Blooding of the *Compass Rose*

Nicholas Monsarrat

Dunkirk, as it was bound to, made a great difference to the balance of things in the Atlantic: the operation itself drew off many ships, destroyers and corvettes alike, from regular convoy-escort, and some of them were lost, others damaged, and still others had to remain in home waters when it was over, to be on hand in case of invasion. The shortage of escorts at this stage was ludicrous: even with the arrival of fifty obsolescent destroyers which America had now made available to the Allies, convoys sailed out into the Atlantic with only a thin token screen between them and the growing force of U-boats. When, after Dunkirk, the Royal Navy turned its attention to the major battle again, it was to find control of the battlefield threatened by a ruthless assault, which quickened and grew with every month that passed.

There was another factor in the altered account. The map now showed them a melancholy and menacing picture: with Norway gone, France gone, Ireland a dubious quantity on their doorstep, and Spain an equivocal neutral, nearly the whole European coast-line, from Narvik, to Bordeaux, was available to U-boats and, more important still, as air-bases for long-range aircraft. Aircraft could now trail a convoy far out into the Atlantic, calling up U-boats to the attack as they circled out of range: the liaison quickly showed a profit disastrous to the Allies. In the three months that followed Dunkirk, over two hundred ships were sent to the bottom by these two weapons in combination, and the losses continued at something like fifty ships a month till the end of the year. Help was on the way – new weapons, more escorts, more aircraft: but help did not come in time, for many ships and men, and for many convoys that made port with great gaps in their ranks.

It was on one of these bad convoys, homeward bound near Iceland, that *Compass Rose* was blooded.

* * *

When the alarm bell went, just before midnight, Ferraby left the bridge where he had been keeping the first watch with Baker, and made his way aft towards his depth-charges. It was he who had rung the bell, as soon as the noise of aircraft and a burst of tracer bullets from the far side of the convoy indicated an attack; but though he had been prepared for the violent clanging and the drumming of feet that followed it, he could not control a feeling of sick surprise at the urgency which now possessed the ship, in its first alarm for action. The night was calm, with a bright three-quarter moon which bathed the upper deck in a cold glow, and showed them the nearest ships of the convoy in hard revealing outline; it was a perfect night for what he *knew* was coming, and to hurry down the length of *Compass Rose* was like going swiftly to the scaffold. He knew that if he spoke now there would be a tremble in his voice, he knew that full daylight would have shown his face pale and his lips shaking; he knew that he was not really ready for this moment, in spite of the months of training and the gradually sharpening tension. But the moment was here, and somehow it had to be faced.

Wainwright, the young torpedo-man, was already on the quarter-deck, clearing away the release-gear on the depth-charges, and as soon as Wainwright spoke – even though it was only the three words 'Closed up, sir,' – Ferraby knew that he also was consumed by nervousness . . . He found the fact heartening, in a way he had not expected: if his own fear of action were the common lot, and not just a personal and shameful weakness, it might be easier to cure in company. He took a grip of his voice, said: 'Get the first pattern ready to drop,' and then, as he turned to check up on the depth-charge crews, his eye was caught by a brilliant firework display on their beam.

The attacking aircraft was now flying low over the centre of the convoy, pursued and harried by gun-fire from scores of ships at once. The plane could not be seen, but her swift progress could be followed by the glowing arcs of tracer-bullets which swept like a huge fan across the top of the convoy. The uproar was prodigious – the plane screaming through the darkness, hundreds of guns going at once, one or two ships sounding the alarm on their sirens: the centre of the convoy, with everyone blazing away at the low-flying plane and not worrying about what else was in the line of fire, must have been an inferno. Standing in their groups aft, close to the hurrying water, they watched and waited, wondering which way the plane would turn at the end of her run: on the platform above them the two-pounder gun's-crew, motionless and helmeted against the night sky, were keyed ready for their chance to fire. But the chance never came, the waiting belts of ammunition remained idle: something else forestalled them.

It was as if the monstrous noise from the convoy must have a climax, and the climax could only be violent. At the top of the centre column, near the end of her run, the aircraft dropped two bombs: one of them fell wide, raising a huge pluming spout of water which glittered in the moonlight, and the other found its mark. It dropped with an iron clang on some ship which they could not see – and they knew that now they would never see her: for after the first explosion there was a second one, a huge orange flash which lit the whole convoy and the whole sky at one ghastly stroke. The ship – whatever size she was – must have disintegrated on the instant; they were left with the evidence – the sickening succession of splashes as the torn pieces of the ship fell back into the sea, covering and fouling a mile-wide circle, and the noise of the aircraft disappearing into the darkness, a receding tail of sound to underline this fearful destruction.

'Must have been ammunition,' said someone in the darkness, breaking the awed and compassionate silence. 'Poor bastards.'

'Didn't know much about it. Best way to die.'

You fool, thought Ferraby, trembling uncontrollably: you fool, you fool, no one wants to die . . .

From the higher vantage-point of the bridge, Ericson had watched everything; he had seen the ship hit, the shower of sparks where the bomb fell, and then, a moment afterwards, the huge explosion that blew her into pieces. In the shocked silence that followed, his voice giving a routine helm-order was cool and normal: no one could have guessed the sadness and the anger that filled him, to see a whole crew of men like himself wiped out at one stroke. There was nothing to be done: the aircraft was gone, with its frightful credit, and if there were any men left alive – which was hardly conceivable – *Sorrel*, the stern escort, would do her best for them. It was so quick, it was so brutal . . . He might have thought more about it, he might have mourned a little longer, if a second strike had not followed swiftly; but even as he raised his binoculars to look at the convoy again, the ship they were stationed on, a hundred yards away, rocked to a sudden explosion and then, on the instant, heeled over at a desperate angle.

This time, a torpedo . . . Ericson heard it: and even as he jumped to the voice-pipe to increase their speed and start zig-zagging, he thought: if that one came from outside the convoy, it must have missed us by a few feet. Inside the Asdic-hut, Lockhard heard it, and started hunting on the danger-side, without further orders: that was a routine, and even at this moment of surprise and crisis, the routine still ruled them all. Morell, on the fo'c'sle, heard it, and closed up his gun's-crew again and loaded with star-shell: down in the wheel-house, Tallow heard it, and gripped the wheel tighter and called out to his quartermasters: 'Watch that telegraph, now!' and waited for the swift orders that might follow. Right aft, by the depth-charges, Ferraby heard it, and shivered: he glanced downwards at the black water rushing past them, and then at the stricken ship which he could see quite clearly, and he longed for some action in which he could lose himself and his fear. Deep down in the engine-room, Chief E. R. A. Watts heard it best of all: it came like a hammer-blow, hitting the ship's side a great splitting crack, and when, a few seconds afterwards, the telegraph rang for an increase of speed, his hand was on the steam-valve already. He knew what had happened, he knew what might happen next. But it was better not to think of what was going on outside: down here, encased below the water-line, they must wait, and hope, and keep their nerve.

Ericson took *Compass Rose* in a wide half-circle to starboard, away from the convoy, hunting for the U-boat down what he presumed had been the track of the torpedo; but they found nothing that looked like a contact, and presently he circled back again, towards the ship that had been hit. She had fallen out of line, like one winged bird in a flight of duck, letting the rest of the convoy go by: she was sinking fast, and already her screws were out of water and she was poised for the long plunge. The cries of men in fear came from her, and a thick smell of oil: at one moment, when they had her outlined against the moon, they could see a mass of men packed high in the towering stern, waving and shouting as they felt the ship under them begin to slide down to her grave. Ericson, trying for a cool decision in this moment of pity, was faced with a dilemma: if he stopped to pick up survivors, he would become a sitting target himself, and he would also lose all chance of hunting for the U-boat: if he went on with the

hunt, he would, with *Sorrel* busy elsewhere, be leaving these men to
their death. He decided on a compromise, a not-too-dangerous
compromise: they would drop a boat, and leave it to collect what
survivors it could while *Compass Rose* took another cast away to
starboard. But it must be done quickly.

Ferraby, summoned to the quarter-deck voice-pipe, put every effort
he knew into controlling his voice.

'Ferraby, sir.'

'We're going to drop a boat, Sub. Who's your leading hand?'

'Leading-Seaman Tonbridge, sir.'

'Tell him to pick a small crew – not more than four – and row over
towards the ship. Tell him to keep well clear until she goes down.
They may be able to get some boats away themselves, but if not, he'll
have to do the best he can. We'll come back for him when we've had
another look for the submarine.'

'Right, sir.'

'Quick as you can, Sub. I don't want to stop too long.'

Ferraby threw himself into the job with an energy which was a
drug for all other feeling: the boat was lowered so swiftly that when
Compass Rose drew away from it and left it to its critical errand the
torpedoed ship was still afloat. But she was only just afloat, balanced
between sea and sky before her last dive; and as Tonbridge took the
tiller and glanced in her direction to get his bearings, there was a
rending sound which carried clearly over the water, and she started
to go down. Tonbridge watched, in awe and fear: he had never seen
anything like this, and never had a job of this sort before, and it was
an effort to meet it properly. It had been bad enough to be lowered
into the darkness from *Compass Rose*, and to watch her fade away and
be left alone in a small boat under the stars, with the convoy also
fading and a vast unfriendly sea all round them; but now, with the
torpedoed ship disappearing before their eyes, and the men shouting
and crying as they splashed about in the water, and the smell of oil
coming across to them thick and choking, it was more like a
nightmare than anything else. Tonbridge was twenty-three years of
age, a product of the London slums conditioned by seven years'
Naval training; faced by this ordeal, the fact that he did not run away
from it, the fact that he remained effective, was beyond all normal
credit.

They did what they could: rowing about in the darkness, guided

by the shouting, appalled by the choking cries of men who drowned
before they could be reached, they tried their utmost to rescue and to
succour. They collected fourteen men: one was dead, one was dying,
eight were wounded, and the rest were shocked and prostrated to a
pitiful degree. It was very nearly fifteen men: Tonbridge actually had
hold of the fifteenth, who was gasping in the last stages of terror and
exhaustion, but the film of oil on his naked body made him impossible
to grasp, and he slipped away and sank before a rope could be got
round him. When there were no more shadows on the water, and no
more cries to follow, they rested on their oars, and waited; alone on
the enormous black waste of the Atlantic, alone with the settled
wreckage and the reek of oil; and so, presently, *Compass Rose* found
them.

Ferraby, standing in the waist of the ship as the boat was hooked
on, wondered what he would see when the survivors came over the
side: he was not prepared for the pity and horror of the appearance.
First came the ones who could climb aboard themselves – half a
dozen shivering, black-faced men, dressed in the filthy oil-soaked
clothes which they had snatched up when the ship was struck: one of
them with his scalp streaming with blood, another nursing an arm
flayed from wrist to shoulder by scalding steam. They looked about
them in wonder, dazed by the swiftness of disaster, by their rescue,
by the solid deck beneath their feet. Then, while they were led to the
warmth of the messdeck, a sling was rigged for the seriously wounded,
and they were lifted over the side on stretchers: some silent, some
moaning, some coughing up the fuel oil which was burning and
poisoning their intestines: laid side by side in the waist, they made a
carpet of pain and distress so naked in suffering that it seemed cruel
to watch them. And then, with the boat still bumping alongside in
the eerie darkness, came Tonbridge's voice: 'Go easy – there's a dead
man down here.' Ferraby had never seen a dead man before, and he
had to force himself to look at this pitiful relic of the sea – stone-cold,
stiffening already, its grey head jerking as it was bundled over the
side: an old sailor, unseamanlike and disgusting in death. He wanted
to run away, he wanted to be sick: he watched with shocked
amazement the two ratings who were carrying the corpse: how can
you bear what you are doing, he thought, how can you touch –
it . . . ? Behind him he heard Lockhart's voice saying: 'Bring the
whole lot into the fo'c'sle – I can't see anything here,' and then he

turned away and busied himself with the hoisting of the boat, not looking behind him as the procession of wrecked and brutalized men was borne off. When the boat was in-board, and secure, he turned back again, glad to have escaped some part of the horror. There was nothing left now but the acrid smell of oil, and the patches of blood and water on the deck: nothing, he saw with a gasp of fear and revulsion, but the dead man lying lashed against the rail, a yard from him, rolling as the ship rolled, waiting for daylight and burial. He turned and ran towards the stern, pursued by terror.

In the big seamen's messdeck, under the shaded lamps, Lockhart was doing things he had never imagined possible. Now and again he recalled, with a spark of pleasure, his previous doubts: there was plenty of blood here to faint at, but that wasn't the way things were working out . . . He had stitched up a gash in a man's head, from the nose to the line of the hair – as he took the catgut from its envelope he had thought: I wish they'd include some directions with this stuff. He had set a broken leg, using part of a bench as a splint. He bound up other cuts and gashes, he did what he could for the man with the burnt arm, who was now insensible with pain: he watched, doing nothing with a curious hurt detachment, as a man who had drenched his intestines and perhaps his lungs with fuel oil slowly died. Some of *Compass Rose*'s crew made a ring round him, looking at him, helping him when he asked for help: the two stewards brought tea for the cold and shocked survivors, other men offered dry clothing, and Tallow, after an hour or two, came down and gave him the largest tot of rum he had ever seen. It was not too large . . . Once, from outside, there was the sound of an explosion, and he looked up: by chance, across the smoky fo'c'sle, the bandaged rows of wounded, the other men still shivering, the twisted corpse, the whole squalid confusion of the night, he met the eye of Leading-Seaman Phillips. Involuntarily, both of them smiled, to mark a thought which could only be smiled at: if a torpedo hit them now, there would be little chance for any of them and all this bandaging would be wasted.

Then he bent down again, and went on probing a wound for the splinter of steel which must still be there, if the scream of pain which the movement produced was anything to go by. This was a moment to think only of the essentials, and they were all here with him, and in his care.

It was nearly daylight before he finished; and he went up to the bridge to report what he had done at a slow dragging walk, completely played out. He met Ericsoon at the top of the ladder: they had both been working throughout the night, and the two exhausted men looked at each other in silence, unable to put any expression into their stiff drawn faces, yet somehow acknowledging each other's competence. There was blood on Lockhart's hands, and on the sleeves of his duffle-coat: in the cold light it had a curious metallic sheen, and Ericson looked at it for some time before he realized what it was.

'You must have been busy, Number One,' he said quietly. 'What's the score down there?'

'Two dead, sir,' answered Lockhart. His voice was very hoarse, and he cleared his throat. 'One more to go, I think – he's been swimming and walking about with a badly-burned arm, and the shock is too much. Eleven others. They ought to be all right.'

'Fourteen . . . The crew was thirty-six altogether.'

Lockhart shrugged. There was no answer to that one, and if there had been he could not have found it in his present mood: the past few hours, spent watching and touching pain, seemed to have deadened all normal feeling. He looked round at the ships on their beam, just emerging as the light grew.

'How about things up here?' he asked.

'We lost another ship, over the other side of the convoy. That made three.'

'More than one submarine?'

'I shouldn't think so. She probably crossed over.'

'Good night's work.' Lockhart still could not express more than a formal regret. 'Do you want to turn in, sir? I can finish this watch.'

'No – you get some sleep. I'll wait for Ferraby and Baker.'

'Tonbridge did well.'

'Yes . . . So did you, Number One.'

Lockhart shook his head. 'It was pretty rough, most of it. I must get a little book on wounds. It's going to come in handy, if this sort of thing goes on.'

'There's no reason why it shouldn't,' said Ericson. 'No reason at all, that I can see. Three ships in three hours: probably a hundred men all told. Easy.'

'Yes,' said Lockhart, nodding. 'A very promising start. After the war, we must ask them how they do it.'

'After the war,' said Ericson levelly, 'I hope they'll be asking us.'

The Victorious *Compass Rose*

In the cold hour that stretched between two and three a.m., with the moon clouded and the water black and fathomless as sable, a step on the bridge ladder. But now it was a different sort of step: cheerful, quick-mounting, no longer stealthy. It was Chief E. R. A. Watts.

'Captain, sir!' he called to the vague figure hunched over the front of the bridge.

Ericson, stiff and cold with his long vigil, turned awkwardly towards him. 'Yes, Chief?'

'Ready to move, sir.'

So that was that, thought Ericson, standing up and stretching gratefully: they could get going, they could leave at last this hated corner, they could make their escape. The relief was enormous, flooding in till it seemed to reach every part of his body: he felt like shouting his congratulation, seizing Watts' hand and shaking it, giving way to his light-headed happiness. But all he said was: 'Thank you, Chief. Very well done.' And then, to the voice-pipe: 'Wheel-house!'

'Wheel-house, bridge, sir!' came the quartermaster's voice, startled from some dream of home.

'Ring "Stand by, main engines".'

Very soon they were off: steaming swiftly northward, chasing the convoy: the revolutions mounted, the whole ship grew warm and alive and full of hope again. There was no need to look back: they had, by all the luck in the world, left nothing of themselves behind and given nothing to the enemy.

At about six o'clock, with the first dawn lightening the sky to the eastwards, they 'got' the convoy on the very edge of the Radar-screen. Lockhart, who was Officer-of-the-Watch, looked at the blurred echo appreciatively: it was still many miles ahead, and they would not be

in direct touch till mid-morning, but it put them on the map again –
they were no longer alone on the waste of water that might have been
their grave. He woke the Captain to tell him the news, as he had
been ordered to: it seemed a shame to break into his sleep with so
straightforward an item, which might well have been kept till later in
the morning, but the orders had been explicit – and probably Ericson
would sleep the easier for hearing that they were in touch again.
Indeed, the sleepy grunt which came up the voice-pipe in answer to
Lockhart's information seemed to indicate that Ericson had only just
risen to the surface, like a trout to a fly, to take in the news, before
diving down fathoms deep to the luxury of sleep once more. Lockhart
smiled as he snapped the voice-pipe cover shut again. After such a
night, the Captain deserved his zizz.

The morning watch progressed; towards its ending at eight o'clock
the light grew to the eastward, blanching the dark water: Tomlinson,
the junior steward, foraging for the cups and sandwich plates of the
night's session, went soft-footed on the wet and dewy decks, like a
new character in a suddenly cheerful third act. The engine revolutions
were now set near their maximum: *Compass Rose*'s course was steady,
aiming for the centre of the convoy ahead: Lockhard had nothing to
do but stamp warmth into his feet and keep an appraising eye on the
Radar-screen as the range closed and the pattern of ships hardened
and took shape. It was good to see that compact blur of light, as
welcome and as familiar as the deck under his sea-boots, gaining
strength and edging nearer to them: they had been away from it too
long, they wanted, above all, an end to their loneliness, and here it
was at last, tangible and expectant, like a family waiting to greet
them at the finish of a journey . . . His thoughts wandered: he
responded automatically as the quartermaster and the look-outs
changed for the final half-hour of the watch: *Compass Rose*, breasting
the long Atlantic swell and shifting gently under his feet, might have
been a train rocking over the last set of points as it ran into Euston
station. At the end of the platform there would be – he jerked to
attention suddenly as the bell rang from the Radar-compartment.

'Radar – bridge!'

Lockhart bent to the voice-pipe. 'Bridge.'

The voice of the Radar operator, level, rather tired, not excited,
came up to him, 'I'm getting a small echo astern of the convoy, sir.
Can you see it on the repeater?'

Lockhart looked at the Radar-screen beside the voice-pipe, a replica of the one in the operator's compartment, and nodded to himself. It was true. Between the convoy and themselves there was now a single small echo, flickering and fading on the screen like a candle guttering in a gentle draught. He watched it for a half a minute before speaking. It was never more than a luminous pinpoint of light, but it always came up, it was persistently *there* all the time: it was a contact, and it had to be accounted for. He bent to the voice-pipe again.

'Yes, I've got it . . . What do you make of it?' Then, before the man could answer, he added: 'Who's that on the set?'

'Sellars, sir.'

Sellars, thought Lockhart: their Leading Radar Mechanic, a reliable operator, a man worth asking questions . . . He said again: 'What do you make of it?'

'Hard to tell, sir,' answered Sellars. 'It's small, but it's there all the time, keeping pace with the convoy.'

'Could it be a back-echo off the ships?'

'I don't think so, sir.' Sellars' voice was dubious. 'The angle's wrong, for a start.'

'Well, a straggler, then?'

'It's a bit small for a ship, sir . . . Do you see the ship right out to starboard – probably one of the escorts? That one's a lot bigger.'

Lockhart stared at the Radar-screen. That, again, was quite true. On the edge of the convoy-pattern, away to starboard, was a single detached echo which was probably a corvette; and it was appreciably bigger than the speck of light which they were querying. He found himself hesitating, on the verge of reporting the strange echo to the Captain, and yet not wanting to wake him up from his deserved sleep without good reason. It could be one of many things, all of them harmless: it could be a fault in the set, which was not yet clear of its teething-troubles; it could be a straggler from the convoy (though its size was against it): it could conceivably be a rain-storm. Or it could – it *could* – be something that they really wanted to see . . . After watching for a full two minutes, while the echo strengthened slightly, maintaining level pace with the convoy as before, he said to Sellars: 'Keep your eye on it,' and then, unwillingly, he crossed to the Captain's voice-pipe and pressed the bell.

When he came up to the bridge, knuckling his eyes and rubbing his stiff face, Ericson was not in the best of tempers. He had had a bare four hours' sleep, interrupted by the first convoy-report; and to have it broken into again, just because (as he phrased it to himself) there was a bloody seagull perched on the Radar-aerial and the First Lieutenant hadn't got the sense to shoo it away, did not seem to him the best way of greeting the happy dawn. He grunted as Lockhart pointed out the echo and explained how it had developed: then he looked up from the Radar-screen, and said briefly:

'Probably a straggler.'

'It's a lot smaller than the other ships, sir,' said Lockhart tentatively. He recognized the Captain's right to be short-tempered at this godforsaken hour of the morning, but he had taken that into account when he woke him up, and he wanted to justify the alarm. He pointed to the screen. 'That's the stern escort, I should say. This thing is at least ten miles behind that.'

'M'm,' grunted Ericson again. Then: 'Who's the Radar operator?' he asked, following Lockhart's own train of thought.

'Sellars, sir.'

Ericson bent to the voice-pipe, and cleared his throat with a growl. 'Radar!'

'Radar – bridge!' answered Sellars.

'What about this echo?'

'Still there, sir.' He gave the range and the bearing. 'That makes it about ten miles astern of the last ship of the convoy.'

'Nothing wrong with the set, is there?'

'No, sir,' said Sellars, with the brisk air of a man who, at ten minutes to eight on a cold morning, was disinclined for this sort of slur, even coming from a bad-tempered Captain. 'The set's on the top line.'

'Have you had an echo like this before?'

There was a pause below. Then: 'Not exactly, sir. It's about the size we'd get from a buoy or a small boat.'

'A trawler? A drifter?'

'Smaller than that, sir. Ship's boat, more like.'

'H'm . . .' Ericson looked at the Radar-screen again, while Lockhart, watching him, smiled to himself. It was clear that his bad temper was fighting a losing battle with his acknowledgement of Sellars' competence. Behind them, the rest of the bridge personnel, and Baker, who had just come up to take over the watch, were also eyeing the Captain speculatively, alert for any decision. But when it came, it was still a surprise.

'Sound "Action-Stations",' said Ericson, straightening up suddenly. And to the wheel-house, in the same sharp voice. 'Full ahead! Steer ten degrees to starboard.'

Lockhart opened his mouth to speak, and then snapped it shut again. Taken by surprise, he had been about to say something phenomenally silly, like 'Do you really think it's a submarine, sir?' The loud, endless shrilling of the alarm-bells all over the ship, and the thud of heavy boots along the decks and up the ladder, gave the best answer of all to this foolish speculation . . . He stood by the battery of voice-pipes, conscious of more than the usual excitement as the various positions were reported to him, and he acknowledged the reports: the pattern and the sequence of this were yawningly familiar, it was all old stuff, they had been doing it, in fun or in earnest, for two whole years: but this time, this time it really might have some point to it . . .

One by one the voices pricked his eagerness.

Ferraby from aft: 'Depth-charge crews closed up!'

Morell from the fo'c'sle: 'Gun's crew closed up!'

Baker from amidships: 'Two-pounded gun closed up!'

Chief E. R. A. Watts from far below: 'Action steaming-stations!'

Tallow from the wheel-house: 'Coxswain on the wheel, sir!'

Lockhart gave a swift glance round him, and fore and aft, a final check for his own satisfaction. The bridge look-outs were at their places on the Hotchkiss guns: Leading-Signalman Wells was ready by the big signal-lamp. Grouped round the four-inch gun just below the bridge, the steel-helmeted crew stood alert, with Morell staring ahead through his binoculars and then turning back to direct the loading: far aft, Ferraby was the centre of another group of men, clearing away the safety-lashings from the depth-charges and preparing them for firing. Satisfied, Lockhart turned to the Captain, presenting the completed pattern for whatever use he chose to make of it.

'Action-Stations closed up, sir!' he called out. Then he dropped back to his own charge, the Asdic-set: the killing instrument itself, if one were needed . . . Underneath them, as if conscious of her weight of tensed and ready men, *Compass Rose* began to tremble.

Ericson was watching the Radar-screen. His call for Action-Stations had been not much more than an impulse: he could even admit that it might have been prompted by irritation, by the feeling that, if he himself had to be awake, then no one else on board was going to go on sleeping. But certainly they had picked up an odd-looking echo, one of the most promising so far: it was possible that this time they were really onto something, and in that case the full readiness of *Compass Rose* was a solid comfort. Momentarily, he raised his binoculars, and peered ahead, but the morning mist lay all round the horizon and there was nothing to be seen. He looked down at the Radar-screen again, and then bent to the voice-pipe.

'Report your target.'

Sellars gave the range and the bearing of the contact. Whatever it was, it was still moving at the slow convoy speed, and they were overhauling it rapidly.

'It's gaining strength a bit, sir,' he concluded. 'Same size, but a firmer echo. Must be something pretty solid.'

That was what the picture on the Radar-screen showed. The whole convoy had emerged now: a compact square of ships, with the outlying escorts showing clearly, and the small stranger swimming along behind . . . Ericson had begun to believe in it; for the first time, he felt he was watching a U-boat behaving according to the book – trailing a convoy just out of sight, perhaps after an abortive night attack, and waiting for dusk to come again, before moving up for another attempt. But what this U-boat *didn't* know about was the straggling escort left behind, the ship outside the picture which was hurrying in to spoil it. If they could just get within range before they were spotted . . .

Compass Rose ran on; the whole ship was expectant, pointing towards her target, racing to find out what it was, hoping for the legal quarry. If it were a U-boat, then they were building up towards the best chance of the war so far: it was the thing they had been waiting for, the point of all their endurance; the next hour could make sense of everything. All over the upper deck, the men standing-to were cheerful in their hope: the word had gone round that they were chasing something definite, and a steady leakage of informatin from the Radar-room kept them up to date and fed their expectation. And on the bridge, every man who had a pair of glasses – the Captain,

Wells, the two look-outs – strained towards the horizon, and the promise that might break from it at any moment.

Compass Rose ran on: the bow-wave creamed under her forefoot, the boiling wake spread behind her, whipping against the wind with rough impatience as she drove towards her prey. The sun was over the horizon now, a pale sun which melted the mist and set the waves sparkling for ten and fifteen miles ahead: a pale sun, a strengthening sun, a cheerful sun which was on their side and had come up to help them. The rigging began to whine: the trembling of the bow-plating as it thrust and divided the water could be felt all over the upper deck: by the depth-charge rails, the pulse of the screw against the racing sea made the whole after-part vibrate, on a broad monotone singing-note like a statement of intention in some formidable work of music. Chief must be giving it stick, thought Ericson with a grin of satisfaction: that'll wake up those loafing stokers, that'll shake a bit of soot down the funnel . . . After last night's protracted helplessness, it was good to reverse the roles and to be launched on this swift stalking hunt.

Compass Rose ran on. 'Report your target!' said Ericson, for the fifth or sixth time: from below, Sellars' voice, excited and jubilant, confirmed the dwindling range, the certainty of a lively rendezvous. For Ericson, it was as if the whole ship were gathering itself together under his hand, getting wound up taut for the spring: it was a fanciful thought, such as he sometimes had when he was very tired or very tense: he felt the ship under him like the rider feels the horse, and he felt glad and proud of her ready response. It was for this they had waited so long and sweated so hard . . . He crossed to the compass platform, took an exact bearing from the last Radar report, raised his glasses, and stared along the line.

Almost immediately he saw it.

It was a square speck of black on the horizon: it was the conning-tower of a U-boat. Even as he looked at it, it lifted to the long swell, and he saw at its base a plume of white – the wash thrown off by the submerged hull. Far ahead of it, to complete the picture, there were some stray wisps of smoke, the tell-tale marks of the convoy which was betraying itself from over twenty miles away. Two targets, two hunters – he straightened up with a jerk, and whipped to the front of the bridge.

'Morell!' he snapped.

Morell looked up. 'Sir?'

'There's a U-boat on the surface, dead ahead. Far out of range at the moment. But be ready. We want to get a couple of shots in before she dives – if we can get near enough.' Ericson half-turned towards Lockhart: as he did so, Wells, who was standing by his side and staring through his binoculars, called out:

'I can see it, sir – dead ahead!' His voice was high with excitement, but almost immediately his professional sense pulled him back to normal again. 'Shall we send a sighting report, sir?'

'Yes. W/T signal. Warn the office.' He gathered his thoughts together. 'Take this down . . . "ADMIRALTY, REPEATED TO VIPEROUS. SUBMARINE ON SURFACE TEN MILES ASTERN OF CONVOY T.G. 104. COURSE 345, SPEED FIVE KNOTS, AM ENGAGING".' He turned round again, towards Lockhart in the Asdic-cabinet. 'Number One! There's a – '

Lockhart put his head out of the small window, smiling widely. 'I kind of overheard, sir,' he answered. 'Too far away for me, at the moment.'

Ericson smiled in answer. 'We'll need that damned box of tricks before very long. You can stand by for the quickest crash-dive in history, as soon as they see us.'

'Sir,' said Lockhart, 'let's make the most of it while their trousers are down.'

All over the ship, the next five minutes were intense and crowded. The warning of immediate action was passed to Ferraby on the depth-charges aft, and then to the engine-room. 'Crack it on, Chief!' said Ericson, crisply, down the voice-pipe: 'we've only got a certain amount of time to play with.' *Compass Rose* began to romp across the sea towards her target: under pressure from the last few pounds of steam, she seemed to be spurning the water in a desperate attempt to close the range before she was discovered. Through Ericson's glasses, the square speck of the conning-tower was bigger now: it had gained in detail, it had a variety of light and shade, it even had the head and shoulders of a man – a man silhouetted against the hard horizon, a man gazing stolidly ahead, ludicrously intent on his arc of duty. All unconscious of their fate, the little victims play, thought Lockhart, who could now see the U-boat with his naked eye, without effort: it was still too far away for an Asdic contact, but at this rate, by God, they could do a straightforward ramming job, without calling on the blessings of science . . . The distance shortened: Sellars' voice rose steadily up the scale as he reported the closing range: presently a totally unfamiliar bell rang on the bridge – the bell from the four-inch gun – and Morell, with the air of a man presenting his compliments on some purely speculative occasion, said:

'I think I could reach him now, sir.'

The range was four sea-miles: eight thousand yards. It was a long shot for a small gun, it might spoil the whole thing; but surely, thought Ericson, that stolid man in the conning-tower *must* turn round, and see them, and say either 'Donnerwetter!' or 'Gott in Himmel!' and take the U-boat in a steep dive down to safety . . . He delayed for a moment longer, weighing the chances of discovery against the limitation of the valiant pop-gun which was their main armament; then he leant over the front of the bridge, and nodded permission to Morell.

The roar of the gun could hardly have followed more swiftly: Morell's finger must have been hovering very near the trigger . . .

It was a good shot, even with the help of Radar to do the range-finding, but it was not good enough for their crucial circumstances; the spot of grey-white water which leapt skywards was thirty yards ahead of the U-boat – the best alarm-signal she could ever have had. The man in the conning-tower turned as if he could hardly credit his senses, like a lover who has been given positive guarantees that the husband is overseas and now hears his voice in the hall; then he ducked down, as if plucked from below, and the conning-tower was empty. In the expectant silence, their gun roared again: Ericson swore aloud as this time the shot fell short, and the tall column of water unsighted them. When it fell back into the sea, and their vision cleared, the U-boat was already going down, at a steep angle, in a fluster of disturbed water.

Whatever the state of her look-outs, she must have had her crash-diving routine worked out to perfection. In a matter of seconds, the hull and most of the conning-tower were submerged: Morell got in a third shot before the surface of the sea was blank, but in the flurry of her dive it was difficult to spot its exact fall. It seemed to land close alongside: it might have hit her. She was moving to the right as she disappeared.

Ericson shouted: 'She's down, Lockhart!'

Almost immediately, Lockhart's tense voice answered: 'In contact . . .'

The pinging echo of the Asdic contact was loud and clear, audible
all over the bridge: Lockhart watched in extreme nervous excitement
as the operator settled down to hold onto it: they could not lose it
now, when the U-boat had been right before their eyes a few seconds
ago . . . *Compass Rose* was moving very fast, and he had to prompt the
operator once as the U-boat seemed to be slipping out of the Asdic
beam; the man was sweating with excitement, pounding with his fist
on one edge of his chair. 'Moving quickly right, sir?' Lockhart called
out, and nodded to himself as Ericson laid a course to cut the corner
and intercept. He rang the warning-bell to the depth-charges aft:
they were now very near, and the sound of the contact was getting
blurred, merging with the noise of the transmission. This was the
moment when luck could take a hand: if the U-boat chose her
moment rightly, and made a violent alteration of her course, she
might slip out of the lethal area of the coming explosion. There were
a few more seconds of waiting, while they covered the last remaining
yards of the attack; then Lockhart pressed the firing-bell, and a
moment later the depth-charges were down.

The whole surface of the sea jumped as the pattern exploded:
Ferraby, busy over the re-loading and harassed by the knowledge
that there was a U-boat within a few yards of them, jumped with it,
startled out of his wits by the noise so close to him. The columns of
water shot high into the air: it seemed to all of them unfair – scarcely
believable, in fact – that the shattered U-boat did not shoot up at the
same time, so sure were they that they must have hit her . . . As
Compass Rose ran on, and the shocked sea subsided, they were left
staring, voiceless with expectation, at the great patch of discoloured
water that marked the explosion area: they were waiting for the U-
boat to break surface and surrender.

Nothing happened: the ripples began to subside, and with them
their foolish hopes: in anger and amazement they realized that the
attack had been a failure. 'But God damn it!' swore Lockhart,
speaking for the whole ship, 'we *must* have got her. The damned thing
was *there* . . .' 'Get back on that search,' said Ericson shortly. 'We
haven't finished yet.' Lockhart flushed at the rebuke, which could not
have been more public: he felt raw enough already, without the
Captain giving the wound an extra scrape. He said: 'Search sixty
degrees across the stern,' and bent to the Asdic-set again: almost

immediately, they regained the contact, fifty yards from where they had dropped the pattern of depth-charges.

Compass Rose turned under full helm, and raced for her second attack. This time it was simpler: perhaps they *had* done some damage after all, because the U-boat did not seem to be moving or making any attempt at evasion. 'Target stationary, sir!' reported Lockhart as they completed their turn, and he repeated the words, at intervals, right down to the very end of their run-in. Once more the depth-charges went down, once more the enormous crack of the explosion shook the whole ship, once more they waited for success or failure to crown their efforts.

Someone on the bridge said: 'Any minute now . . .'

The U-boat rose in their wake like a huge unwieldy fish, black and gleaming in the sunlight.

A great roar went up from the men on the upper deck, a howl of triumph. The U-boat came up bows first at an extraordinary angle, blown right out of her proper trim by the force of the explosion: clearly she was, for the moment, beyond control. The water sluiced and poured from her casings as she rose: great bubbles burst round her conning-tower: gouts of oil spread outwards from the crushed plating amidships. 'Open fire!' shouted Ericson – and for a few moments it was Baker's chance, and his alone: the two-pounder pom-pom, set just behind the funnel, was the only gun that could be brought to bear. The staccato force of its firing shook the still air, and with a noise and a chain of shock like the punch! punch! punch! of a trip-hammer the red glowing tracer-shells began to chase each other low across the water towards the U-boat. She had now fallen back on a level keel, and for the moment she rode at her proper trim: it was odd, and infinitely disgusting, suddenly to see this wicked object, the loathsome cause of a hundred nights of fear and disaster, so close to them, so innocently exposed. It was like seeing some criminal, who had outraged honour and society, and had long been shunned, taking his ease at one's own fireside.

The two-pounder was beginning to score hits: bright flashes came from the U-boat's bows, and small yellow mushrooms of cordite-smoke followed them: the shells were light, but the repeated blows were ripping through her pressure-hull and finding her vitals. As *Compass Rose* came round again, listing sharply under her full helm, the machine-guns on her bridge and her signal-deck joined in, with

an immense clatter. The U-boat settled a little lower, and men began
to clamber and pour out of her conning-tower. Most of them ran
forward, stumbling over the uneven deck, their hands above their
heads, waving and shouting at *Compass Rose*; but one man, more
angry or more valiant than the rest, opened fire with a small gun
from the shelter of the conning-tower, and a spatter of machine-gun
bullets hit *Compass Rose* amidships. Then the counter-firing ceased
suddenly, as the brave man with the gun slumped forward over the
edge of the conning-tower: the rest of the crew started jumping
overboard – or falling, for *Compass Rose*'s guns were still blazing away
and still scoring hits on men and steel. Blood overran the U-boat's
wet deck, and sluiced down through the scuppers, darkly and
agreeably red against the hated grey hull: she began to slide down,
stern first, in a great upheaval of oil and air-bubbles and the smoke
and smell of cordite. A man climbed halfway out of the conning-
tower, throwing a weighted sack into the water as he did so: for a
moment he wrestled to get his body clear, but the dead gunner must
have jammed the escape-hatch, for the U-boat disappeared before he
could free himself. A final explosion from below drove a cascade of
oily water upwards: then there was silence. 'Cease fire,' said Ericson,
when the sea began to close in again and the surface flattened under
a spreading film of oil. 'Wheel amidships. Stop engines. And stand
by with those scrambling nets.'

The wonderful moment was over.

The Diary of a Desert Rat

R. L. Crimp

9th November

One thing the Quartermaster makes sure of: that we have plenty of tea, milk and sugar for brews. These desert brews are an institution, the making being almost a ritual. Half a gallon of water is poured into the brewcan and set on the fire. The fire is built of scrubwood when there's any about, with a couple of stones to support the pot, but usually consists of a cut-down biscuit tin or petrol-can, gashed in the sides for ventilation, with a few inches of neat petrol or petrol-soaked sand in the bottom, which burns fiercely for several minutes. When the pot is boiling a couple of handfuls of tea are cast upon the seething water. Then the pot's removed and the brew allowed to strengthen up. Meanwhile the section mugs are marshalled on the ground, and spoonfuls of tinned milk and sugar put in each. Then they're filled with tea, straight out of the brew-can. The result is 'Desert Char'.

Heaven knows how much petrol is used on the Blue for brewing-up. The whole Battalion must burn the best part of a hundred gallons daily, besides using plenty for running the vehicles and washing clothes when water's scarce. Petrol, in fact, is nearly always more plentiful than water.

Our second main comfort is tobacco. We get a buckshee issue of fifty cigarettes every week, usually of rather poor quality (Indian 'V'), and can buy a hundred more decent ones whenever a canteen comes up.

As long as there's no lack of char or fags everyone's happy. When there's a shortage of either, morale slumps.

10th November

See a shufty-wallah* downed today. He comes over about mid-morning from the west, low enough for us to be able to discern clearly

---

* Shufty-wallah – literally 'look-see boy' – refers to an enemy spotter plane on a reconnaissance flight.

the features and markings of an Italian Savoia 4-engined bomber.
He's obviously out to photograph the new railway line which is being
extended by South African engineers (close by here) up from its
former terminus at Mersa Matruh towards the Libyan frontier in
preparation for the next push. The enemy's been making strenuous
efforts lately to recce the track, but even so, the appearance of this
slow and solitary bomber in broad daylight seems recklessly intrepid.
At first, however, it looks as though he's going to get away with it. As
usual on crucial occasions there's not a plane of ours in the sky. It's
only after he's made a leisurely turn and is headed westward for
home that five of our fighters swoop from the blue on his tail. For a
few minutes they gambol around, sparring and feinting, cat-and-
mouse fashion, each taking a turn at loosing a burst of fire, while the
Savoia forges undeviatingly onward, straining engines in a desperate
attempt to escape its tormentors. Then one of the Hurricanes slips in
behind to deliver the *coup-de-grâce*. There's a wrathful snarl of
machine-guns. The Savoia falters, loses altitude, veers off right, out
of its belly blob two white parachutes (soon pendant above) and with
a strident, deepening howl it dives nose-down to the ground. The
point of impact must be a couple of miles away, beyond a ridge. A
dull crash follows, and a dense pink-and-yellow mushroom blossom-
ing of smoke and flame and sand. Then silence.

A section of our chaps is detailed off to round up the parachutists
(who, however, float well out of our area) and the only human relics
they find in the wreckage are a few charred hands and feet.

11th November

On guard. What a curse having to ruin a good night's rest! One looks
forward so much to bed, the one blessing after the day's discomfort.
The six detailed men and the corporal i/c rendezvous after the 9
o'clock news by the CSM's truck, side-hats and overcoats on, collars
up, hands in pockets, bondhooks slung, – 'slouch order'. The formal-
ities are likewise simple. The men pair up, and the corporal, having
secreted in his palm three match-sticks of unequal length with the
tips protruding level, invites selection. Each pair picks a stick, and
that getting the longest has choice of tour on stag. Middle stick gives
second choice, and the shortest has to have what's left. Favourite tour
is the first, from nine to midnight, as its pair can get down to six
hours' kip as soon as it's over. Next choice is usually the last, which

allows six hours' sleep before starting, but entails the responsibility of rousing the Company at first light.

I'm on middle watch, and the hours seem endless as we pace round the leaguer, past the silent trucks with their sleeping crews on the ground beside them. My partner is Squirts Mulberry, from Cpl. Spandrell's section. He's an Old Soldier, but you wouldn't think so, as he is thoughtful and speaks earnestly as if seeking to inspire approval or sympathy. His experiences in war, however, have kindled in him a vast aversion to the seamy side, and the other Old Soldiers seem to have little time for him; but he doesn't mind. It's said he's bomb-happy (hence the Squirts) and Squirt's slit'uns are quite legendary. Certainly wherever we come to a halt, even for only an hour, he sets to with pick and shovel and digs himself a capacious trench. In fixed positions his hole is always a foot deeper than anyone else's. Another of his habits is the perpetual wearing of a topee. Everybody has one of these sun-helmets, which, in scorn of all concession to climate, is kept merely as an exhibit for kit inspections and is usually to be found, after much rummaging on the truck, wedged between the reserve watercans or crushed beneath the bren-gun box. But not so Squirts Mulberry's, an exceptionally large size, which he wears permanently over his ears, even in the cool of evening. (They say he even wears it in bed, though some aver he sports his tin one there.)

His main theme tonight is Communism, which he propounds earnestly as the only panacea against the evils of a capitalistic society whose avarice is responsible for the present war and for dragging millions of peace-loving chaps like himself and me into it. 'Capitalism:' he says, 'the creed of greed, smash-and-grab on the social plane, the economic cult of "Muck you, Jack, I'm in". The high priests: the blackhatted money barons of the big city, the usurers and monopolists, the conjurors of credit, the manipulators of paper. And the God: mammon unlimited, filthy lucre. Those who have it use it to get more (personal aggrandisement). Those who haven't any, get used up to make more for those who have it (exploitation). "To Him That Hath",' etc., etc.

'In a sense,' he says, 'it's only logical that the Germans, the arch-exponents of national capitalism, should be fighting the Russians, the champions of peace and Communism.' 'How comes it that we're with the Russkies fighting the Germans?', I asked. 'That's the fault of Herr Hitler,' he says, 'and of the contradictions inherent in the capitalist system.'

15th November

Arthur was stung by a scorpion last night. Before making his bed on the ground he'd kicked away a loose stone, and the scorpion, sheltering beneath as is its custom, must have crept into his blankets. Arthur leapt from his bed yelling. A large bump came up on his leg which, despite anointment by the MO, twinged intensely for several hours. This morning, after a winkless night, he's feeling better. Lucky it wasn't a black scorpion or a tarantula – big, pink, spidery brutes with an 'ace of spades' on their bulbous backs – whose poison is said to be fatal.

Scorpion-baiting is a minor sport. You sprinkle petrol in the sand around one, and then ignite it with a match. If he stayed put he'd be all right, but maybe the heat is too fierce. Again and again he tries charging out, but every time must draw back, baffled by the ring of fire. His tail lunges desperately the while till quite soon, all hope gone, down comes the tip to his own back, probing in between the scales. Then, all frenzy stilled, he convulses slowly, almost voluptu-ously, and sinks down, dead. They always kill themselves like this, bound *in extremis* to spend their prized weapon, even upon themselves. Perhaps there is a last ecstasy in their extinction.

16th November

It's obvious a push will be on very shortly indeed. The usual inertia of desert life has given way to a rarefied nervous alacrity. All kinds of inspections have been held – weapons, reserve rations, petrol, etc. – and anything faulty has been replaced. A lot of brand-new ammo has been issued for sorting out into tracer, armour-piercing and ordinary, then fitting into clips, bandoliers and bren-magazines. The platoon-sergeant has been round taking the names and addresses of everyone's next-of-kin, and checking up on identity discs. Most chaps seem pretty calm, resigned to the fact that there's no option but to accept the inevitable. Though some of the new hands, who've seen no real action, are inclined to be a bit jumpy. Percy Ruff, from Cpl. Spandrell's section, for instance, seems to be getting very worried. Every evening he comes over to our truck in leaguer (perhaps his own pals are browned off with his jittering) and asks all sorts of questions about what it's going to be like and how do we feel. Maybe it relieves him to vent his forebodings in conversation, or maybe he hopes to elicit something reassuring. He's a tough, rough, beefy kind of chap, but his eyes have a look of listless dismay.

Of course I don't feel too keen myself. After all, our traffic with the warlike Hun has so far been only child's play. But what's the use of anticipating trouble? It's easier to be just fatalistic over the whole issue.

17th November

Platoon pep-and-griff talk this afternoon. The balloon goes up tomorrow. Mr R., platoon-officer, gives us general details of the plan, dispositions and resources of the Eighth Army.

The first object will be to relieve Tobruk. Up in the coastal area at Halfaya an Indian division will contain the Hun in case of any retaliatory incursion into Egypt. South of the Indians a New Zealand division will cross the wire, outflank Halfaya and wheel north towards Bardia. Below them the South Africans will cross the wire opposite Bir Sheferzen. And further south still, our division will pass through at Maddalena and strike in a wider arc northwestwards to Tobruk. The garrison here will attempt to break out and join up with our relieving force at the appropriate moment. When this has been achieved, the Axis armies will be driven out of Cyrenaica once and for all. This time, Tripoli is to be the ultimate objective. The Eighth Army has vast supplies of new equipment. In men, tanks and guns we outnumbered the enemy. In the air we're on level terms. Our battalion moves forward into the concentration area tonight. The Companies are functioning separately, each with a different rôle.

This morning, a minor sensation. Squirts Mulberry has deserted! Two days ago he and another chap went in a truck to Mersa Matruh on an errand for the Company Commander. They were expected back the same night, but nothing's been seen of them since. Everyone's mildly surprised (it's an unheard of thing for an Old Soldier). 'Fancy Squirts bucking off! Didn't think he had the guts. Of course he was always ticking, but that was just natter. The other bloke must have put him up to it.' But no one seems to bear any rancour. 'Good luck to 'em both,' is the general sentiment.

18th November

The push is on. We moved up last night after dark and a few miles short of the wire went into a very shrouded leaguer – not even a cigarette was allowed to be lit. There must have been hundreds of other leaguers, pushed right forward like ours, ready for the word 'Go'.

This morning we rouse at four o'clock in pitch dark, and at first streak of dawn are off. And so apparently are all the other units of our armoured division, as though released in some gigantic race. In the gathering light there's something theatrical about the whole business, an air of pageantry. The breaking day itself seems apocalyptic, with its flashing golden splendour and eastward tiers of fringe-flaming cloud. As far as the eye can reach over the desert-face are dust-reeking lines of vehicles – pennanted tanks and armoured cars, guns and limbers, carriers, trucks and lorries – all speeding along in parallel course westwards to Libya.

At Maddalena the great concourse converges into double file on the track through the sand-silted dug-outs and derelict blockhouses of the old Italian outpost fort, and then spreads out into widely dispersed separate routes on the 'in' side of the wire. Very soon all the other units have disappeared and our Company continues alone northwestwards.

This evening we leaguer up after having covered about sixty miles. The journey has been almost leisurely, and quite uneventful. No sign of the enemy, not even a shufty-wallah over and no indication that we've been observed.

19th November

Continue in jerky stages, with several lengthy halts. Situation still very quiet. It seems ridiculous we haven't been spotted yet. There's an occasional rumble of gunfire over to the east, which may be the South Africans moving up the wire.

The Libyan side of the frontier seems rather nicer than the Egyptian. The mardam is firmer, a reddish sort of gravel in most parts, profusely covered with scrub. This evening it looks delightful, opposite the sun under an egg-blue sky, decked as far as the horizon with an unbroken mantle of silver-grey.

20th November

After another dozen miles, gunfire seems only a short way ahead. We reach a shallow depression with a line of sandhills in front. Mr R.

goes off on a recce with the Company Commander and other platoon-officers. While he's away we hang about by the truck. A feeling of flaccid enervation begins to distil into my limbs from the pit of my stomach. Our first taste of battle in earnest sounds just beyond the forward ridge. Arthur suggests putting a brew on, and preparing this eases the suspense. But before the water is boiling Mr R. arrives back at Platoon HQ and his driver climbs onto the bonnet of his truck to give the horizontal-flags signal for an NCO's conference. So Pedlar goes over to get the griff. Ten minutes later we watch him return, trying to gauge the portents by his gait and demeanour. He merely says we've got to dig a defensive position and our job is to guard Support Group HQ. So 'C' Company's clicked for another cushy job.

Having hastily swigged, we pack up and move ahead into the sandhills. Trucks are parked in one of the wadis and the platoon proceeds on foot with weapons and trenching-tools over the crest, down on to the forward slopes. Here Mr R. allocates section positions, about fifty yards apart.

Immediately in front is a broad flat valley. Beyond it, some two thousand yards away on an expanse of more elevated ground are a score or so black objects: airplanes. Pedlar, who has binoculars (picked up from a Wop colonello on a previous push) pronounces them Jerry. They stand strangely still and deserted. Nearer at hand, in the valley, are batteries of our 25-pounders, in lines facing half-left away from the airfield, towards the northwest. They're smiting hard, splitting the air with curt salvoes. The crews are stripped to the waist, and voices can be heard, fragile yet clear, calling the fire-orders. Limbers and auxiliary vehicles stand scattered behind the guns.

Retaliation soon comes. Shells begin sweeping the valley, bursting with horizontal flash, whiplash crack, and residue of black smoke. The auxiliary vehicles move back, and we judge it time to start digging our trench. By midday it's five feet deep, and the platoon-officer, on a tour of the positions, is quite impressed; never has he seen such keenness before. Bob Harris asks him about the planes in front. Apparently they're German Stukas, abandoned by the enemy when we overran the airfield. 'A' Company is dug in there now.

While we were having a lunch of biscuits and cheese, eight Stukas approach from the west, wheel right over our area, and proceed, in single file, to dip, dive and discharge strings of bombs which can be seen clearly falling. As the planes turn and climb away, like scraggy black carrion birds, their speed, despite the shrieking crescendo of engines, is agonisingly slow. Somewhere behind us follows a series of great, clattering, disintegrating crashes, and seconds later the ridge to our rear has a rolling mane of sand and smoke. Support HQ, very likely, is 'taking the can'. Shortly after, a squadron of Marylands passes over in close formation, flying back from a mission. Half a dozen Messerschmidts are warily harassing them. One of the Germans darts in behind a flanking bomber and delivers a brief burst. The Maryland falters, goes into a dive, catching fire as it does so. Two white specks blob out in the blue sky. The rest of the formation goes on.

By sunset our trench is deep enough. As night falls, everything becomes almost uncannily calm. None of us feel much inclined to sleep, in the warm air. Out in the darkness, Verey lights describe bright, silent, leisurely parabolas. A few glowing orange points beyond the valley betoken vehicles burning. Occasionally a graceful tracery of ack-ack founts up from the horizon above momentary patches of pallor. The northern sky is restless with silent flickering, and at intervals comes a remote rumbling, hardly noticeable. We argue quietly over the two latter phenomena, squatting on the trench-edge. Arthur is positive they emanate from fighting at Bardia and Tobruk. Pedlar and Ernie and Sam ascribe them to electrical storms over the Mediterranean, seasonal now. Eventually we turn in and sleep round the trench, doing ninety minutes stag apiece during the course of the night.

21st November

An attack goes in this morning. The 25-pounders are early putting down a barrage. From our position we get a good view of the start. At 8 o'clock two companies of infantry (our 'B' and one from another battalion in the Brigade) move off across the valley northwestwards with a dozen bren-carriers. Strung out in open order they look pathetically exposed on the wide, flat expanse. I don't envy those poor blighters, dwindling slowly into the distance.

At last the trudging and trundling specks disappear over the horizon ridge. Shortly afterwards a burst of machine-gun fire, like a peremptory challenge, suggests they're near their objective. Then following another burst – sustained, staccato, remorseless – brens stutter, small arms crackle, and mortar bombs crash in ragged succession like train doors slamming at Clapham Junction during the rush-hour. It all seems so remote and impersonal, but we can imagine the bitter intensity for the chaps over there in the thick of it.

Our guns in the valley now fire as fast as their crews can load them, the air is rent continuously by the blast, and, up above, the arching flight of the shells makes a wild mewing chorus. After ten minutes they slacken off, and sounds of strife over the ridge have also petered out. An hour later two carriers come back with casualties on board. They stop near us to enquire the whereabouts of the ADS. When we ask how the scrapping's gone, the sergeant says it's been tough, but the Jerry positions are in the bag. Then mentioning a pal of his, adds bitterly: 'Poor old Smudger got his lot. But I made sure of the sod that did him. Filled his guts with this bren, close range, the bastard!' (Smudger was a corporal, steady and serious, who came out on our draft.)

Midday: situation quiet. A column of men appears from over the ridge, approaching slowly across the valley. They march in good order, and after a while resolve themselves into German prisoners. They're escorted by a section of carriers, who halt near our position and hand them over to us. There are about 150 of them, looking pretty dishevelled, most of them wearing dusty grey jackets and trousers, brown boots and long-peaked 'engine-driver' caps. They behave quietly and seem pre-occupied. Half a dozen extra chaps from other sections are called in to keep them covered by bren-guns, while our section, on instructions from the platoon-officer, begins the business of counting, checking and searching them. The Germans seem to know the drill, and discard stuff wholesale, so that very soon quite a large pile of letters, photographs, diaries, pay-books, wallets, respirators and penknives lies on the ground. Then, with their officers segregated into a small, aloof group, and the mass of other ranks marshalled into a square, they sit or lie, silent or talking quietly together, making no effort to ingratiate themselves.

1400 hrs: Another column of prisoners comes in, this time all Italians. They, too, look dishevelled and dusty, but are in quite good spirits. Most appear to have brought their blankets with them, and with their ill-fitting bluish coats, voluminously sagging plus-four breeches and many extraneous bundles of personal belongings, look for all the world like a troop of touring cyclists, bereft of bicycles. The Germans show little interest in the arrival of their allies.

We immediately search the new lot, and out of the pile of discarded gear I reserve a penknife for myself. (Its body is fashioned of a dull metal in the form of a fascist lictoral-bundle, with an inset relief of Mussolini, steel-helmeted and jutting-jawed. On the single blade is inscribed '*Nelle mie vene scorre sangui autentici rurali*,' and on the butt '*Sendador Maniago*,' which suggests a momento of the Spanish Civil War.) But scarcely have these been checked than shells begin bursting sporadically in the valley. So, to get cover and to simplify the problem of watching over the multitude, we shepherd them into one of the wadis. Remaining in separate groups, they resume their squatting and reclining. One of the Italians has a small white dog, which frisks about with friend and foe alike.

Soon a new element becomes apparent in the shell-fall. Missiles of small calibre come whizzing and winging over and fall at random, some exploding, others not. Pedlar says there must be a tank battle going on, and these are stray solids. But whatever they are, it's very awkward keeping a careful watch on the prisoners and a suitable sang-froid. The Italians lie flat on their bellies, but the Germans appear unperturbed. One of the 25-pounder batteries in the valley quickly veers front ninety degrees, facing northeast. To the right of the abandoned airfield a score or so squat heavy vehicles are approaching. With barrels horizontal, over open sights, the guns fire furiously. After a pause of seeming indecision, during which one of the tanks appears to be hit, the rest turn tail and make a lumbering withdrawal.

1530 hrs: Situation quiet again. An ordnance sergeant comes along and spends a few minutes pottering about farther up the wadi, where there are three newly-made graves, small oblong mounds of sand and white rock-fragments. He bangs in at the head of each grave a rough cross, made of crate-wood and pencil-inscribed with particulars of the casualty beneath. Two of them are gunners from the valley, the 3rd Ack-ack.

Mr R., who's shifted Platoon HQ into the wadi now that our main job seems to be looking after prisoners, dishes out a spot of 'dope'. Everything's going satisfactorily. We've made important gains. The Tobruk garrison is in the process of breaking out, but the enemy, after having been caught on the wrong foot in the opening stages, has put in several counter-attacks, and is making desperate efforts to prevent our union. The name of this place is Sidi Rezegh. The biggest aerodrome in Cyreniaca – El Adem – is only a few miles from here, and Tobruk's about twenty.

2200 hrs: Tonight, after dark, the unheard-of happens: it rains heavily. The trucks, collecting casualties, haven't yet returned, and our bedding and overcoats are out with them. So things are pretty cheerless. The prisoners are better off in the way of covering than we are. The wadi is full of the noise of rustling waterproof capes, low conversation, coughing, shifting limbs, and spasmodic rain patter. Now and then the little white dog barks furiously, and an Italian voice, languid and melancholy, calls 'Moshka, Moshka – silencio!' The desert blackness all around is broken only by distant fire-specks, waxing and waning.

Soon after midnight comes the sound of vehicles approaching, whining in low gear, then shouts. I'm on stag with Bob Harris, so we go down to the wadi-entrance to challenge them. It proves to be a couple of our trucks, which have been milling for hours in the dark, trying to locate the position. Each is full of enemy wounded. The drivers want the ADS but that'll have to wait till morning. Much groaning comes from the people on board, one Italian keeps sobbing 'Maria!' Some call desperately for 'acqua'. There's a little Italian medical officer with them who wrings his hands hopelessly, because he's lost all his kit. He keeps muttering something like 'spritz' – German, I think, for morphia. Harris has a torch and screening the lens, probes aboard where the wounded are piled, one on top of another. The beam rests for a while on a young German, a big fellow with fair hair, broad pale face, purple-blue eyes and feline expression. His left sleeve from wrist to shoulder is saturated with blood, but he says nothing, only stares moodily, resenting the intrusion.

22nd November

Daybreak comes wet and cold, but welcome. The rain soon eases up, and the wounded-laden trucks move on. Mr R. is a little anxious about the prisoners. He thinks we ought to have deprived each man of his boots last night, to discourage escapes. But we check them over and the number seems to tally. Then the question of the little white dog comes up for deliberation. The officer doesn't want it here another night, because of the danger of our position being revealed by its barking. So he says it's got to be shot. Nobody relishes the job much, as it's a friendly little tike. Besides, shooting it is easier said than done; nobody fancies holding it out at arm's length for the *coup de grâce*, and on the ground it frisks continually. A chap from one of the other sections eventually takes a pot and misses. His next shot hits it somewhere near the base of its spine, so that the poor little beast can only drag its hindquarters and yelp in agony. The expression of reproach in its eyes upset everyone. Besides, such an exhibition of marksmanship makes us look ridiculous in front of all these Germans and Italians, who watch with ironic expressions. 'For God's sake, shoot it through the head at once,' shouts Mr R. vehemently. A couple more rounds do the trick. Then some Italians dig a hole and bury the carcass.

Our own truck turns up this morning, so we get a change of clothing off it, as well as rations for breakfast. It's awkward preparing and eating meals, though, in view of the prisoners. The Italians are already getting clamorous for food and drink, but orders are that nothing at all is to be given to them.

1000 hrs: Heavy thumping and buffeting out beyond the northwest ridge. Shells whizz over and crash disconcertingly. Everyone keeps his head low. The wadi doesn't afford much cover, and the Iteyes soon begin scooping out trenches feverishly with their fingernails. Most of the Germans still lie seemingly impervious. But the situation is most unpleasant for several minutes. When at last it cools down, there's a sudden scuffle among the Italians. One of their number is still prone on the ground, his face in the sand, and a couple of others drag him out of the ranks. The crown of his head is spurting blood. (So even now, 'safely' a prisoner, he gets his lot.) His comrades dig a grave up the wadi, along by the other three. The body is carefully put in, and someone covers the face with a green handkerchief. An Italian officer delivers a sort of formal valediction, to which at intervals the rest, standing round, give a concerted deep-throated response and the fascist salute. The Germans observe this rather theatrical climax coldly. Then the grave is filled in and bordered with pieces of rock.

1100 hrs: A heavy battle must be going on out west. Continuous thunder of guns.

1230 hrs: Orders come through for all prisoners to be evacuated. So they're formed up in threes and marched off under escort in a long

column back over the crest. Soon after they've gone a couple of
Messerschmidts strafe in the area behind us.

Now the wadi seems strangely empty. Its floor, where the Italians
were, is a honeycomb of shallow slit-trenches. Just after lunch, when
the missiles come hurtling over again, we take cover in them. A solid
falls near mine, nuzzles its way with murderous snarl over the edge
and drops into the corner, spins, then lies still. I touch it gingerly,
and it's quite warm. Mr R. wants to have a look, so I chuck it across
to him (silly thing to do). 'It's certainly got your number on it,' he
says. 'You ought to be bucked.' I suppose he refers to the old
superstition about predestined bullets, and the more cheerful corollary that if yours happens to not to get you, then what else can?

When our chaps come back from escorting the prisoners they say
it was they whom the Messerschmidts strafed – the pilots recognising
their compatriots, it was the guard on the flanks that got the muck.
It made them hop about and look silly.

1400 hrs: The officer is summoned by runner to Coy HQ for a
conference. Whatever he's told he keeps to himself. The afternoon
wears on rather unpleasantly. There's a lot of confused firing beyond
the horizon over to the northeast, as well as out west. The batteries
in the valley get plastered several times by enemy barrages. A Signals
vehicle happens to be passing by when shells crash down close to our
wadi, and one of the crew, running for cover, is hit by shrapnel. His
mates bring him in. The Battalion MO is with us, having called on
one of his flying visits. He examines the wound and says: 'It's in the
lung. He can't live,' then gives a large injection of morphia. The poor
chap, quite a youngster, is wrapped in a blanket. Our lads prepare
another grave, beside the other four. As they lower him in, his boots,
rough and sandy, dangle pathetically out of the blanket.

1530 hrs: A curious sort of sixes-and-sevens atmosphere has settled
in. Nobody seems to know what's happening. There's obviously
heavy fighting in progress all around, but our task of guarding HQ
appears to have been forgotten, or shelved. We merely hang about in
the wadi, keeping our heads down. Even though the thunder of guns
is intenser than ever, there's a feeling of anti-climax in the air. The
battle seems somehow decided; in whose favour we can't tell.
Instinctive optimism, of course, suggests ours.

But the mystery thickens when the abandoned airfield comes under
fire. For fifteen minutes it's plastered with what looks like incendiary

shells. Turgid growths of sand and smoke sprout up between the planes, some of which heel over and all, one after another, begin blazing. One of our companies is still dug in out there, and it must be pretty hot for them, poor blighters.

About half an hour before sunset, Mr R. gives orders to pack up. We hastily take our gear to the trucks, stow it on board, and within five minutes are away, back over the ridge. Travelling at speed we soon fall in with other platoons of the Company, and after several miles south reach most of the rest of the Battalion in temporary leaguer. A large number of lorries filled with South African infantry meet us on the way, moving north in some urgency. A sombre sunset scourges the western sky. Behind us, one or two guns bark distantly; a dismal sound, like doors slamming up in the attic of an empty house.

23rd November

We're just about to start breakfast when there's sudden agitation all around and somebody shouts: 'Tanks!' Sure enough, over the ridge not more than a mile away come rolling thirty or so German panzers, led by one which looks twice as big as any other, flying a huge swastika standard. One look, and everyone dashes for the trucks. Precious kit is slung on board, engines roar into action, and within less than a couple of minutes the whole Battalion's on the move. None of our own tanks are in the vicinity, so it's obviously suicidal for us to hang about. Our truck manages to get well off the mark, though we leave a good breakfast of bacon and burgoo behind on the mardam. The tanks fire a few shots after, but we're soon out of range, and keep moving at fair speed for ten miles, with hundreds of other vehicles streaming in concourse. It looks like a stampede, but everything's under control. Apparently these 'scarpers' are accepted desert technique; when there's no cover at all and no particular bit of ground is tactically worth much sacrifice, getting thrown up against heavily superior enemy forces leaves no option but to clear out, the quicker the better – discretion proving the better part of valour every time.

Red flag eventually goes up, and the vehicles do a bit or sorting out into respective companies. Then after an hour stationary, the Battalion moves on again, still southwards. Half an hour later there's another stop, then three more in a further five miles. The last of these is quite lengthy, but orders are circulated that we're to be ready to continue at a minute's notice, which precludes even putting a brew on. While waiting aimlessly we watch some Hurricanes strafing something beyond the horizon to the east – perhaps the enemy, or possibly our own supply-dumps, which in either case doesn't look too promising. They raise a tall column of smoke.

Eventually we get going again, at a wary pace and on a different bearing, more west. Our next halt is for almost two hours. Everyone's getting a bit perplexed at the queer progress, especially as no griff has been given. Pedlar describes it as a 'jildy move' – he's been in one or two already.

The next stretch, still very cautious and now more east again, is terminated just before sunset, which gives us the chance of making a quick brew and heating some tins of M. & V.

As soon as it's dark we go on, the vehicles nose to tail in double file. After a couple of hours, direction is changed ninety degrees, practically due west. Wrapped in our overcoats and blankets on the piled-up back of the truck, we try to get a bit of sleep. It may be any time later that coming out of a doze I find the column stopped again. Everything's quiet, all engines are off. The moon is shining brilliantly, right overhead. There's not a movement anywhere. Then comes a rumbling of powerful motors, with the unmistakable 'chafing-clink-ing' sound that can only mean tanks in motion. And a hundred yards across the desert, several grey masses are vaguely visible. They stop, and everything's tensely still again. Our vehicles stand, in their close ranks, motionless and spectral in the moonlight. We must be seen, and the question is: whose are the tanks? Ten minutes pass, utterly still, rigidly expectant. Arthur, lying next to me, begins to snore, and I feel impatient at the noise, as though it'll give the game away. Then suddenly: bang! and a red tracer shell from one of the tanks comes whistling over us. It must be a challenge, but our people don't know the answer, and silence follows, even more bated. Then, after another long pause: bang, bang, bang! – almost a relief as breaking the suspense – and three more tracers come chasing over, lower and closer and much more businesslike. Instantly, all is turmoil. Chaps leap off trucks, dodge about for a bit of cover. Orders are shouted to get moving, engines roar, everyone tries to scramble on again. Each truck veers away full left and charges off. Our truck must have jumped the gun, I can only clamber on one of Seven Platoon's.

Tracers whizz over plentifully now, in lurid red streaks; most of them, luckily, too high.

At length the trucks thin out, but the corporal sitting with the driver says: 'Foot down, keep moving!' A mist has developed, like cotton-wool, absorbing the moonlight. All's quiet. Then suddenly we think we see tanks again, just ahead. 'Bear off!' says Cpl. Cowl and we give them, if any there are, a wide berth. One of the chaps on board is a stranger to us, of an entirely different unit. Where he came from, and how we picked him up, lord knows. He keeps on suggesting we jag in, appealing to our common sense: What's the use of going on? The game's up. Better for us all to get put in the bag than be blown to bits by a dirty great panzer!

Soon we strike a large leaguer, wrapt still and silent in sleep and mist. But whether it's Jerry's or ours we can't tell, so pass right through, running the gauntlet of the scattered vehicles, without challenge or hindrance. After this we're alone, push on eastwards several miles, and a little before dawn get down for an hour's kip.

24th November
While we're cooking breakfast a truck appears on the southwest skyline and turns out to belong to an RE officer with his detachment of three sappers. He doesn't know where our Battalion is and suggests we accompany him to Army HQ, where we'll no doubt be able to get a precise location. But for a more immediate job he tells us to prepare to meet a small body of Germans he's heard is approaching in a couple of half-tracks from the west. So we dispose ourselves with his men in positions of as much cover and concealment as possible, and wait, bren mounted, rifles ready.

An hour passes and nothing happens. So we pack up and move off eastwards.

25th November
Reach Army Forward HQ – the Battalion's present position not known.

26th November
Through the wire at Sidi Omar, until recently a large German strongpoint. The sand here bears witness to intense vehicle activity, but there's no other sign now of human sojourning. Bir Sheferzen is

likewise deserted, but an Ack-ack Echelon we meet a few miles west speak of Support Group having recently been in the Bir Gibni region.

At Bir Gibni there are numerous supply-dumps, but no Support Group. Some resident Service Corps people, however, give us a likely location for Support Group HQ, a dozen miles off on a N.W. bearing. By nightfall we haven't found it.

27th November

Continue search. Jerry seems to have cleared right out of this area, so we roam at will. Various units are scattered about, most of them stationary. Eventually we find some gunners belonging to our division who direct us on to Div. HQ.

28th November

Primed with an exact map reference, at last find Support Group. Then Batt. HQ and the Company. No one seems much surprised at our return to the fold. 'Either we were in the bag, or would turn up peachy.'

29th November

The Battalion seems to have suffered no damage in the recent débâcle. On the morning after the 'nightmare' drive there was quite a bit of sorting-out to do, and several splinters were temporarily lost. Ours is the last to rejoin.

The whole battle was evidently rather a fiasco. The Tobruk garrison got out all right, but couldn't make contact with our relieving force, owing to a strong German wedge in between. The Germans then powerfully counter-attacked and forced us to withdraw from the Sidi Rezegh area. After that, chaos. With German panzers thrusting everywhere and our people on the wrong foot always, the whole thing was touch-and-go.

The main trouble appears to have been the disparity between our tanks and the Germans. We may have had the greater number, but most of them are 'Honeys' – lanky, lightweight, gangling cruisers, pretty fast, but mounted with feeble 2-pounder guns, no earthly good against the thicker armour and much more powerful 75mm armament of the German panzers. How many crews have been wasted in useless tanks, not being able to retaliate against the long-ranged enemy guns before having approached several hundred yards nearer their opponents over open desert and under fire? And only then with mere 'peashooters'! But the division is supposed to have acquitted itself quite creditably, and the General* is going to get a VC for leading his tanks into action standing up in an open staff-car.

The situation now seems to have taken a better turn, and the higher-ups a more optimistic view. Jerry's attempts to disorganise our supplies have failed. The enemy themselves have been split, with one portion cut off and besieged in the Bardia region, and the remainder roaming in open desert.

The Battalion, after a breather guarding supply dumps, is now about to become active again. Each Company has been allocated to a mobile column. These columns each consist of a bttery of 25-pounder field-guns, a troop of Ack-ack Bofors, a troop of mounted 2-pounder anti-tank guns, a Company of motorised infantry, some armoured cars, and a few odds-and-ends like sappers, Medicals (with ambulance), Signals and Service Corps – light and mobile and with plenty of sting. The main job will be harassing enemy lines of supply and communication. There are three columns functioning in concert: June, July and August. Our Company is in July.

30th November
The column gets its first assignment today. We start off after lunch, travelling north. Some sort of heavy enemy convoy out of the beleaguered Bardia area moving westward along the coast road is anticipated, and our job is to cut the road, lay a barrier of mines on either side, and see what else can be done in the way of an ambush. Our infantry trucks move on the fringe of the dispersed phalanx. Inside us drive the anti-tank and ack-ack guns, and the few column supply wagons. In the centre, the precious kernel, roll the dozen RA 'quads', each with its limber and 25-pounder, muzzled against the dust, bouncing and bumping on tow. Our slower carriers swan in the rear.

During the run I see my first dead German. Our truck passed almost over him. He's lying on his back in a patch of camelthorn, a stocky man of about forty, maybe a warrant-officer, in grey uniform. His face, purplish, has a full and stagnant look, and there's a coagulated trickle of dark blood from the corner of his mouth.

* General Jock Campbell, VC.

After three hours' travelling the column stops. Several miles ahead on the flat mardam a speck can be seen tearing through the scrub, churning up a huge wake of dust, obviously in such a hurry as to bother not at all about avoiding detection. Pedlar whips out his binoculars, and identifies it as a motor-cycle. Perhaps we've surprised a stray Jerry despatch-rider. More likely, though, it's a one-man observation post. As soon as he's scuttled over the north-eastern horizon, we continue our journey. Night falls shortly afterwards, and we have to move cautiously in pitch darkness. Eventually the column must remain stationary until moonrise, before it can descend a devious incline down the face of an escarpment. The scenery here is quite impressive, with the florid moonlight lending an aspect of veiled grandeur to the towering bluffs and cavernous recesses.

At the bottom of the declivity the track leads across another perfectly flat expanse, scattered about which is the wreckage of several German and Italian planes; the airfield of Gambut. A mile or so farther on we come to the brink of another escarpment, and just as one of our platoons is going forward to reconnoitre the way down, across the darkness in front speeds a string of white tracer, followed in a few seconds by peculiar double gun-reports: whoomph-bang! whoomph-bang! whoomph-bang! This is rather disconcerting, yet I can't believe it's actual opposition, meant for us. Very soon, however, another white flight, wings silently across, followed again by the inexorable: whoomph-bang! whoomph-bang! It's difficult to judge where the explosions come from, but they're obviously from not very far off.

A section of carriers is sent on to investigate, and while waiting in column behind the scarp-edge we discuss the identity of the importunate whoomph-bang. Pedlar and the two Old Soldiers, Ernie and Sam, eventually agree on recognising it as an Italian Breda. When the carriers return they report 'an enemy machine-gun in a wadi about half a mile off'. Hereupon transpires a brief conference among the column officers, the upshot of which is a decision to send out an infantry platoon on fighting patrol to clear the way. Mr R. primed with full instructions and a stiff whisky from the Company Commander, announced that our platoon has been chosen for the job. 'Gym shoes will be worn, for the sake of quietness. Tin hats will not be taken – they might fall off and make a noise. Every man to be sure he's got fifty rounds. Cpl. Gardner's section in front, the other behind

in diamond formation. Start off in ten minutes'. So that's that – one
of those moments you always knew would come, and here it is. But
with the knowledge that it's got to be met resignation sets in, and
even a certain expectant alacrity. Several chaps, turning out packs,
find their gym shoes missing, and an almost general epidemic of
coughing breaks forth. But eventually everyone's ready and we set off
silently on the zigzag path down the scarp, striking across a flat
stretch at the bottom.

By now the half-moon is well up in the eastern sky. Everything's
quiet, only our footfalls can be heard. For half a mile we pad along
over the desert, beginning to hope for a picnic after all. Then suddenly
somewhere in front, there's a series of explosions, and we fling
ourselves to the ground. Lying absolutely still, peer up from the
corner of my eye: strings of luminous yellow slots speed overhead,
like beads on a rod, hissing. My heart beats heavy hammerblows.
This is deadly! The missiles soon cease, however, and after several
minutes' silence we get up and move forward, very warily. But we've
only covered forty yards when: bang, bang bang! and again we have
to lie flat while a further instalment of vivid gashes pursues unerring
flight over us a few feet above the ground. Thank God for these small
scrub bushes! – mere bumps of sand with a few twigs sprouting, but
it's surprising how much happier you feel with one in front of your
nose.

When all's quiet once more, Mr R. passes word along to continue
forward, but almost immediately we have to dive again with the
tracers streaking and rasping over our heads. I now begin to realise
that this may really be IT; quite calmly, but objectively regretful. We
seem properly pinned down, and there doesn't seem much future in
it. After a while a different sort of report becomes audible: lighter,
single phuts, followed by the sound of things searing through high
air. Then seconds later, and from well behind us, comes a succession
of hollow crashes; obviously mortar bombs, plastering the track down
the scarp. But it's still impossible to pinpoint the enemy's positions.
When the tracers are ripping, we must keep our heads low, and
Jerry's crafty enough not to sling up flares. What makes it worse, the
moon is so bright and is still behind us. Overhead, and down to the
western horizon, the sky is obscured by a shawl of cloud, towards
which the moon is climbing, but how slowly! If only it would get a
move on.

For a long time we stay motionless, pressing our noses into the sand. A night breeze blows cold. Then Mr R. Signals the next move, and a stealthy mass-wriggling across to the left begins, everyone painfully and determinedly propelling himself horizontally over the ground by fin-movements of hand and feet, with any amount of rustling and scraping, hoping thus to remove ourselves from the direct line of fire. When at last the advance is resumed on foot, the platoon appears scattered and depleted. Pedlar is still with Mr R. in front. The sergeant has decided to cover the rear, 'to whip up stragglers'. Ernie and Sam, out on the flank, look like two of the Seven Dwarfs, crouching double and lifting their knees in exaggeratedly high strides as though they're playing musical chairs.

Our next stop is by some vehicles, deserted and probably derelict, about half a dozen, Jerry design. As we're scouting around, a machine-gun opens up, evidently ranged on them, as the bullets bounce uncomfortably close. First we crouch behind the wheels, then scramble down in the lee of a low sandbank near by. What strikes most disconcertingly about this new interruption is that it seems to come from a different direction, sixty degrees off the previous line of fire. And the gun sounds fairly near. So we have another lengthy pause, during which the moon at last sails into the cloud-screen, leaving the scene in comparative darkness.

Meanwhile Mr R. is getting very impatient. He keeps looking at his watch and peering strenuously ahead for signs of the enemy dispositions. He even crawls forward and disappears for ten minutes on a solo recce. On his return he says he thinks he knows where the enemy are and starts making plans for an attack. Pedlar, however, points out that the bulk of the platoon has melted away, and suggests it may be rash to try an assault with the few chaps that remain, against an enemy whose strength is still uncertain. All that are left of us, in fact, are Pedlar, Bob Harris, Ernie and Sam, five chaps from other sections, Arthur and myself. Mr R., fortunately, has enough sense to see the snags, but he's very disappointed at the way things have turned out. Obviously he doesn't at all relish having to report back to the Company Commander the failure of his first important mission. So we wait a bit longer, to give the stragglers a chance to catch up.

The situation is quiet again. We lie inert, alongside one another under cover of the sand-rampart. Arthur is next to me, and although the night strikes very cold, blissful snores soon reveal he's asleep. I even feel like that myself, the peace and quiet are so relaxing after our recent spell of tension. I rouse myself after a while, however, and glancing across his motionless back, can't discern any of the others. Arthur, unwillingly returning to consciousness, is as surprised as I am and can't account for their disappearance. No doubt his neighbour signalised an impending move-off by a prod in the ribs (to avoid the noise of speech) and Arthur, of course, was oblivious. So we creep forward together, very cautiously, in the hope of regaining contact. But not a trace do we find in the darkness. We might just as easily stumble across Jerry. In fact, a few yards farther on he's within earshot. We can hear voices speaking quite loudly in German. One chap is talking in rather dogmatic tones, probably giving orders. Others join in, on and off, and they all sound earnest and confident. Somebody is messing about with a gun – the click of the mechanism is clearly audible, and intermittently comes the tinny whining of their field telephone. As they obviously have no idea we're so close, we decide to stay put in case Mr R. and his little band start the attack. Every moment wew expect to hear a sudden uproar of shots and shouting. But nothing happens. The Jerries continue nattering unconstrainedly, and of our own boys there's never a sound. Then sometime later comes the rumble and rattle of a stream of heavy vehicles passing in the vicinity, which goes on for about ten minutes; presumably the convoy.

Our problem now is to keep awake. We can't risk dozing off together, else we'll find ourselves waking in broad daylight with Jerry pistols under our noses. So we try taking turns at keeping alert, but this isn't very successful, although the rumble of Arthur's snoring often brings me apprehensively to my senses again. Our plan is to hang on here till the earliest suspicion of dawn, and then in the growing light, which will still afford cover and also enable us to get a few bearings, return to the escarpment as quickly as possible. Luckily I'm awake when the first glow appears in the east, and we get moving immediately.

Half an hour's steady marching brings us back to the foot of the cud. It looks empty in the sour light, but we're challenged by a section of 12 Platoon who're dug in at the bottom of the path. From them we learn that Mr R. and his remnants arrived back two hours ago, having jagged in the twitch because of inadequate numbers.

Some of the other chaps have been back since soon after midnight, and nobody's missing.

Meanwhle daylight shows us the whole scene of the night's exploits, and we get a gallery-view from our eyrie on the scarp-edge. Two thousand yards across the flat expanse below, a black ribbon of road is visible, with the pale desert stretching away again beyond it. By the road there's a flat, white, rectangular building, a blockhouse, and a few hundred yards short of it, to the left, is the group of derelict vehicles. As for the enemy, he's nowhere apparent. But through Pedlar's binos it's possible to descry what may be trenches near the blockhouse.

Our 25-pounders, sited behind us on the airfield plateau, open up with a brisk morning salvo, which brings considerable animation into the panorama. Figures scramble out of the trenches and run back behind the blockhouse, probably going inside. The falling shells flash viciously, tearing gouts of smoke and sand from the desert surface. As the guns lay it on thicker, more figures appear, from places farther from the blockhouse, to which they run for dear life. In all, it looks as though there were at least half a dozen enemy posts out there last night, and fifty or sixty men with mortars and machine-guns. So it was perhaps fortunate that the attack didn't come off. But it's nice now to sit back and watch the Huns scuttling like rabbits under our fire, which the 25-pounders soon concentrate on the blockhouse itself. Here, however, the result is disappointing. Instead of the walls collapsing in rubble, they seem to withstand the shelling with no apparent effect.

A little later we pack up – somewhat hastily ourselves now, as it's reported German tanks are approaching. The column retires through Gambut airfield with occasional shells falling, and getting up the second scarp is a tricky job. But no enemy risks pursuit and we travel all morning at leisurely pace down into the southern 'lebensraum'.

2nd December

Postscript to the coast-road 'twitch': Percy Ruff is being sent back. The night's alarums jangled his nerves so badly that Mr R. has had him examined by the MO and certified as a menace to the morale of the platoon. Although Mr R. is careful not to betray his feelings, you can see he despises such conduct with the scorn of a young man to

whom danger is a part of war. It probably came as a shock to his preconceived theories to find how hard it is to keep control when bullets
are flying.

8th December
A big thing's happened, the Americans are in the war. The Japanese,
gone berserk, have struck them in the Pacific, joined up with the
Axis, declared war on us. So the Yanks are now our comrades in
arms, and the whole world's ablaze.

The Mannerheim Line

James Aldridge

Finland had become a world cause when Wolfe left England. He accepted the Finnish war negatively. He had developed enough cynicism to doubt anything that became such an official cause; and he landed in the snow at Helsinki airport without feeling the necessity for quick sympathy or particular distress.

When the days passed and the Finns let him go to the front, he went with Jack Ladd. Lieutenant Gripenburg collected them at the Kamp Hotel in a 1938 Chrysler. They walked across the road and a Shutzguard saluted them as they got in.

'Use your lights,' Gripenburg told the Shutzguard.

'Yessir,' the Shutzguard said.

They left Helsinki. Jack Ladd, looking like a large red Indian with a mobile face, went to sleep under the sheepskin rug. Gripenburg sat erect in the front seat. He was a Finno-Swede who understood all the polite rules of human behaviour and said that Jack Ladd violated all of them by his vulgar humour and lack of dignity. Wolfe looked at the Lieutenant's erect neck, and felt better about Jack Ladd.

They went along the main Vipuri road. They went through Loivisa, Hameena and the villages, and through Vipuri; and reached the beginnings of the Mannerheim line in the dark afternoon. They took the road between the railway lines, and passed the tank barriers, the cleared spaces, the camouflaged positions and the guard-posts.

They stopped at a farmhouse that was still warm with desertion, and had a line of frozen washing near its entrance. Jack Ladd and Wolfe dried the sweat out of their socks while Lieutenant Gripenburg used the field telephone attached to one of the walls. They went out again, and Gripenburg took them through a short fire-and-spruce forest to a track. He told them a Colonel was waiting to see them, and all they had to do was follow this track until they came to a shellcase.

'Where are you going?' Jack Ladd said indignantly.

Gripenburg said: 'There is a Christmas service in the hospital tonight. I arrange for it, and we can go there.'

'How far down is the shell?'

'Fifty metres. But stay on the track.'

'What do we do there?'

'There is a guard there. He will take you to the Colonel.'

Gripenburg went away.

Wolfe walked along the snow path with Jack Ladd close behind him. They both looked for the shell-case.

'That bloody Gripenburg,' Jack Ladd said.

'We came too far,' Wolfe said.

They walked back on the clean and even snow. Wolfe found it. The shell-case was mounted high on a stick. He knocked the cap of snow off it.

'That bloody Gripenburg,' Jack Ladd said again.

The track was camouflaged by two small spruce bows being pulled over it. Wolfe bent under the spruce and followed the path. It ran along the top of one of the oose ridges that are frequent in the Karelian Isthmus.

'What do we do now?' Jack Ladd had a locomotive complex that kept him in front of all things. His complex was resting awhile, and he did not mind asking Wolfe what came next.

'We follow the track,' Wolfe said.

'It's probably mined.'

'I don't think so.'

'It ought to be,' he said. 'It is close to the line. Look at this.'

A length of chicken wire covered the top of the track. Small pieces of fir-boughs were resting on it. It was good camouflage. The path wound steeply down the oose ridge. Wolfe slipped, and his arm went down into the deep snow of the ridge. His hand caught on a sharp stick.

'Look out for mines,' Jack Ladd said.

Wolfe pulled his arm out. The hand was bleeding.

'How did you do that?' Jack Ladd said.

'A stick.'

'The snow is clean,' he said. 'Don't worry about it.'

Wolfe said he could not worry about it. He was thinking of the fighting here: the Russians would come up this ridge, but there would be machine-gun nests on top and no man could get up here because the snow was too deep, even for skis. He wondered why it was undisturbed. The communiqués said the Russians were always shelling or bombing this part of the line. He could hear heavy 1.68 Vickers on the left in regular and long bursts. They were a long way away.

'They'll get this place one day,' Wolfe said.

'The Russians aren't near enough.'

'Shelling,' Wolfe said.

'They can't see what they're shooting.'

'They don't need to.'

'The Russians are no good unless they can see what they're doing.'

'Ho hum,' said Wolfe.

A Finn came out of the timber with a Thompson gun held across his front. He wore a white snow suit, and was bulky underneath it because he had on a fur coat. He was on long racing skis.

'Paivaa,' Wolfe said quickly.

'Paivaa,' the Finn said. He was waiting.

Wolfe handed him the passes. He looked at them carefully, at the text and at the pictures, comparing them with their faces. 'A. Wolfe,' he said. Wolfe said yes. 'J. Ladd,' he said. 'Yoh,' Jack Ladd said in Swedish. The guard said, 'I speak English.'

'Is that so?' Jack Ladd lifted his forehead.

'Yes. You go to the Colonel?'

'That's right.'

The Finn gave the passes back and jumped about-face on his long skis, executing the difficult stick manipulation. They followed him and he spoke back over his shoulder.

'I went to Columbia,' he said, and it sounded American. 'Class of 37.'

'What did you do there?' Jack Ladd asked him politely but without interest, because every Finn had been in America or had relatives there.

'Physical Education,' the Finn said.

'Is that so?'

The Finn went on silently until he lifted one of the sticks and pointed to the wire.

'It is my idea,' he said.

'You're pretty good,' Jack Ladd told him.

'Have the Russians been shelling here?' Wolfe asked him.

'No. They have not found our positions yet.'

'Where is the line? The Mannerheim Line?'

'All around you,' the Finn laughed. He stopped in front of a snow bank. Wolfe saw a pine-hut underneath the snow. There was a hollow entrance to it. He could see the wooden chimney of an oil stove coming out of the roof of snow. It was placed flat against a wide spruce, so that the smoke curled around the trunk, spreading out and being absorbed by the branches. The Finn opened a white-painted door and said to go inside. Jack Ladd said they would see him on the way back. They went through one air-lock, down a set of wooden steps in a fibre-walled hut. A colonel was sitting at an office table that had a 'phone and a lamp. He said how-do-you-do, and apologized for not speaking good English.

'What do you want to see here?' he said.

'Everything.'

'The Russians would also like to see everything,' he said with no humour.

'Haven't they found you?'

'No. We have been careful. We are cavalry too; very difficult to hide.'

'How much cavalry?' Jack Ladd sat on the bed.

'About 200. We are really mounted infantry.'

A young man, hard-faced and with hair cropped up the sides and the back, came in and saluted the Colonel. 'This is my Rittmeister,' the Colonel said. A Rittmeister was a Captain of Cavalry. 'These are English-Americans,' he told the Rittmeister.

'To fight?'

'No,' Wolfe said quickly. The Finns always assumed that. The Rittmeister was disappointed. He shook hands and said something to the Colonel in Finnish.

'He says that you must see his horse. Also he wants me to say that he threw with the Javelin in Los Angeles in 1935,' the Colonel said.

The Rittmeister nodded. He held his head stiffly. He said in careful English:

'What do you think of the Russians?'

'What do you think of them?' Wolfe said.

The Rittmeister crushed his square hands together. 'Pulp,' he said.

The Rittmeister was unhumorous like the Colonel. He was young, but Wolfe thought that he had been enveloped in solemnity at some time of his life. Probably all of it. But it was very coarse and heavy solemnity. He said in slow English:

'When are the British and Americans coming to fight?'

'Any day,' Jack Ladd told him.

'We will finish the Russians when they come,' he said.

'Perhaps they will not come,' Wolfe said.

'They have promised.'

Wolfe repeated syllabellatically: 'Perhaps they will not come.'

'They must come,' the Rittmeister said. 'The Russians cannot break the Isthmus in winter.' He paused to think of words. 'In summer they can break the Isthmus. We will need the English in summer.'

'You expect too much.'

'Yes,' he said. 'We expect much.'

Wolfe was going to correct him; Lieutenant Gripenburg came into the hut. He saluted the Colonel, whom he apparently knew, and said he had come to take the Engelska-Amerikansken to the hospital. Wolfe understood it.

'We would like to see the Line,' he said.

'To-morrow,' Gripenburg said.

'Now,' Jack Ladd said.

'It is too dark,' the Colonel told them. 'And we also go to the hospital.'

They went to the hospital. Wolfe was surprised that a hospital was so close to the front. It was a one-storey fibre building that was completely air-hidden by the spreading branches of big firs growing around it. There was white cheese-cloth over the whole roof. In the early moonlight it was a spider's web. The hospital was near a river. When they crossed the ice, the Colonel said they were technically out of the front area and only in a war area.

'What religion have you?' the Rittmeister said as Wolfe walked in with him.

'None,' Wolfe told him.

'You must have religion.'

'No.'

'This is a Lutheran service.'

'I don't mind,' Wolfe said.

He walked up the steps of the well-lit entrance. The smell of hospital came very thick. When he turned into a passage, all the pyramid of religion lay down there before him. By the candlelight he saw a pulpit under a Christmas tree. The candles were on the Christmas tree. Around the tree and at one end of the passage were wounded soldiers, nurses, and unwounded soldiers. They were all spread along the passage so that the wards could hear the service, and all the doors were open. Near the pulpit Wolfe saw a Minister dressed in black. He recognized the Minister because he was very well known as one of the secretaries of the Lapua Fascist Party. He looked white and benevolent and he kept his shoulders straight, though he was talking to the Matron of the hospital.

'I will stand with you,' the Rittmeister said. 'To explain.'

Wolfe thanked him flatly.

'He is starting,' the Rittmeister put up his finger. Wolfe looked at the Minister. He was standing under the candles with his hands outspread. There was silence, ordered and definite.

'In a few moments,' he said in Swedish, 'we will begin the service,' Wolfe could understand it because he intoned it slowly and clearly. Everybody talked again.

'There are three Russian prisoners in this room,' the Rittmeister pointed to the open door they were standing in. Wolfe looked around and saw a small grey room with three beds in it. The Russian in the centre bed was propped up and had all his head and eyes in bandages. The other on the far side was obviously unconscious and very yellow in the face. Wolfe looked hard at him and knew he was dying. The nearest Russian was a boy who had wide eyes that looked at Wolfe, who half-smiled at him. The boy smiled back suddenly, and with surprise.

'We shifted them in here so they can hear well,' the Rittmeister said.

'It is good of you,' Wolfe said.

'It was Mister Toivala, the Minister.'

The Rittmeister lifted his finger again. The Minister, Mister Toivala, had raised his hands and was saying, 'We will now begin. We will sing a hymn.' He gave the number. The Rittmeister opened a book which he had produced. It was a Finnish-sounding hymn and was about the moral right of being alive and owing this moral right to the Almighty. They all sang it except Jack Ladd and Wolfe.

It finished, and Mister Toivala gave a short talk to the hospital staff. It was in Finnish and Wolfe did not understand it. The round Matron prayed in mechanical Swedish, thanking the Lord for His guidance, for His trust in them to do their duty, for His inexorable pity.

Mister Toivala lifted his hands again. In the yellow light Wolfe saw the shadows under his eyes broaden and lengthen as he spoke. He was praying.

'Our God,' he said. 'Our God, for this Cause which You have given us to give our blood, we thank You. Here, gathered in Thy sight, we are in the presence of Life eternal. Our God, in this hour of struggle, against barbarism, against atheism, against Bolshevism and its hordes; our God we beseech Thee to rise again and in us, in a mighty sweep, destroy for ever this horde that time and time we have fought, but in vain. Our God, in us let Thyself live again as the Great God of Battle. Let Thyself smite his crops, drain his rivers, and flow blood into his soil that his children may never live and never rise again. Give him death and give him famine, and destroy this evil on earth. For what You have given us; for our victories, for their defeats, we thank Thee, Oh Lord, and know You will live in us, for Thou art our Father in Heaven, Hallowed be Thy Name.'

Wolfe heard a man coughing. There was silence for a moment. The Minister went on.

'Thy Kingdom come.'

'Thy Will,' Wolfe heard the cough again, and he knew the Russian was dying.

'be done on earth,

'As it is in Heaven,' the Russian coughed, and started to vomit in a rising belly sound that finished in a cough because he could not get the blood up.

'Give us this day our daily bread,' the Russian vomited and Wolfe could hear it spilling on the floor in a mess. The Minister shouted in a high-pitched voice,

'And forgive us our trespasses,

'As we forgive those who trespass against us,' the Russian coughed and vomited together. Wolfe heard it on the floor. No one moved, and Mister Toivala made himself heard above it.

'And lead us not into temptation,

'But deliver us from evil,

'For Thine is the Kingdom,' the Russian half-vomited with his mouth open, but he was dead before he could finish it. It all died inside him, and the noise became a choke. The Minister shouted, though there was silence, and he finished it:

'The power and the glory,

'For ever-and-ever,

'Amen,' he cried. 'Amen.'

Three nurses ran in behind Wolfe to the Russians' room. He could smell sourness already, and so could the other two. The boy was not smiling, but was white in the face, and his lips tight and was struggling to move. The other, with the bandages, was holding his head with all his fingers. The boy shouted something. He kept shouting it until the Rittmeister walked in and hit him across the face.

As the Rittmeister came out, wiping his hand, Wolfe saw the Minister bending over the dead Russian sprawled from the bed in his own mess. He felt the snow, and the smell, and heard a Chopin Mazurka and couldn't see a day ahead and felt nothing but Death being given to the questions of all peoples.

He turned around and walked between the dispersal of people to the entrance.

He put on his coat and walked out behind the Rittmeister and the Colonel and Jack Ladd and Lieutenant Gripenburg.

Outside, the Lieutenant started to talk, but the Colonel told him to be quiet. They crossed the ice of the river, and Jack Ladd took out a black cigar and bit the end off it, then remembered he could not smoke so near the front. He took it out of his mouth and said to the Rittmeister:

'What was that Russian saying when you slapped him?'

The Rittmeister did not say anything. They walked on quietly through the waiting forest, until the Rittmeister said: 'To-morrow you will see my horse.'

They slept in the farmhouse with Lieutenant Gripenburg. In the morning they returned to the Colonel's hut after they had eaten hard breakfast. The Colonel was waiting for them, and said he would show them the positions. The Rittmeister was there also, and he was undisturbed-looking again. He said he would like to show them his horse.

'Certainly,' Jack Ladd told him.

The Rittmeister went out to get his horse.

The Colonel said: 'He has a beautiful animal.'

He put his coat on, and they went out into the brief sun. They followed the Colonel down a new path that led beyond the hut into the thick timber. Wolfe began to see all the snow-huts and log cabins through the trees. The Colonel said that the log cabins were stables, the huts were for the men. He pointed to the trees above them, and said the boughs completely covered this from the air.

'Don't they see you cutting the trees down?' Jack Ladd said, because there were stacks of logs that were being used to build the huts.

'They were cut a long time ago,' the Colonel said. 'We have practised this war many times.'

The men were in white capes. They had stacked their rifles nearby. They were building a hut by placing logs in alternate positions. They put hay between each log and the next.

'Insulation,' the Colonel explained.

When the logs were laid, a boy with a short tomahawk hacked off the stray ends of hay and threw them inside the half-finished hut. It had already been cleared inside of snow; and green fir-boughs were laid there in herring-bone pattern.

'These are for our replacements,' the Colonel pointed to all the huts.

'Where are you going?' Jack Ladd said.

The Colonel shrugged. 'The Russians are trying to find a place where they can break through. That is their tactic. We go where they attack. But it will take them a long time here. There is no weak place on the Isthmus. We have improved it for twenty years. No army could get through here.'

'In summer also?'

'In summer also,' he said.

The Rittmeister came with his horse.

Wolfe saw it moving sideways down the narrow track. The Rittmeister was holding tightly but casually to a rope halter. He was trying to keep the horse on the path, so that it would not make fresh tracks that planes could see. The horse had a white sheet over its back for camouflage. As its shoulders rose with the high-rising legs, the sheet floated a little. A mist came off its neck, and its breath pushed itself into the cold air.

The men stopped working and moved back. The horse moved around in small circles. The Rittmeister moved it under a fir. The animal stood still for a moment and the Rittmeister pulled off the white cape. It was like uncovering a giant negro tied and straining at a stake. The muscles reflected the sharp light, very black.

The animal could not keep still. Its legs moved. It moved its head from side to side. Wolfe knew it was compressed with anger. The Rittmeister stood under it with his arms straining and his face tight and only looking at the horse and keeping it more or less in one place as its legs stamped around. The horse tried to break the Rittmeister's grip. The Rittmeister kept it in control.

Wolfe looked at the two, and did not want to say anything.

Jack Ladd said: 'Jesus Christ, look at that horse.'

'It is a great beast,' the Colonel said.

'Does he ride it?'

'It is wonderful to see,' the Colonel said.

'It is too wild for cavalry.' Jack Ladd was amazed.

'It is very fast and surefooted.' The Colonel did not look away from the horse. 'It is good for scouting. It moves so quickly that nothing can stop it, and it is difficult to shoot. Together, they are my best scouts.'

The red-rimmed eyes looked above Wolfe and showed no interest in anything. Sometimes they looked down at the Rittmeister pulling on the halter. Its ears moved forward and backward, or stood high like pointed cacti.

It reared high on its back legs and pawed the air with its forelegs. It whined at the same time. The Rittmeister did not move. He pulled the horse down as it tried to climb into the air again.

'No one goes near to it,' the Colonel said. 'He grooms it himself.'

'How does he ride it?'

'That is different. When he is on it, they fit well together. But like this they do not like each other. They do not like each other at all.'

The Rittmeister pushed the horse around with deliberate contempt. The horse lifted itself up again, straining the halter loose in the Rittmeister's hands. As it climbed it cried out. The Rittmeister stood

away from it and kicked it in the lower stomach and brought the
animal down in quick collapse.

'Come over,' the Rittmeister said quickly.

'No, thank you,' Jack Ladd said.

'He is all right,' the Rittmeister's square hands held the neck.

Wolfe shook his head.

The Rittmeister stood back again. He picked up and swept the
sheet over the horse. A zup-zup-zup followed an approaching whine,
and there was a burst. Wolfe was flat on his neck and back, and the
air rushed out of him. The movement of black body, or muscles and
legs and speed came over him as the explosion died out. Everything
went out of him until there was silence.

He stood up and was surprised that he could move. He was
swearing and getting the snow out of his neck. He heard Jack Ladd
saying:

'Are you all right?'

He said he was all right. The Colonel was shouting in Finnish to
the men and running for the snow shelter.

'Are they bombing?' Wolfe said as he ran.

'Shelling,' Jack Ladd said. He was laughing at Wolfe; at his
surprise.

'It's a fine thing to laugh,' Wolfe said. Jack Ladd laughed again.
They went into the hut with the Colonel.

'They've found you now Colonel,' Jack Ladd said.

'It may be a stray shot,' the Colonel said.

He told the men to remain under cover so that there would be no
movement outside.

Wolfe remembered the horse.

'What happened to it?' he asked Jack Ladd.

'What?'

'The horse.'

'You ought to know. It knocked you down and got away.'

The Colonel went out. They followed him. They heard crashing.

'That bloody horse,' Jack Ladd said.

Wolfe saw the Colonel moving from tree to tree towards some skis
sticking in the snow. Two men were already pulling on their skis.
Wolfe looked around for the horse. He could hear its heavy
movement.

He saw the Rittmeister. He was on skis and had a German

parabellum tucked in his belt. He was pushing very fast along the track with his sticks. The Colonel passed him and came back in a flush of snow. He called down the hut and four men came out.

'The horse will give us away.' He was waiting to get his breath back. 'They fire a shell where they think we are. They have a plane up to see if there is any movement.'

'Is there a plane up now?' Wolfe looked up and around.

'Yes. But east. It is not right here yet.'

The Colonel took the men into the timber. There was silence for a while. Wolfe heard the animal again. It came along the hard track in big strides. The white sheet obscured its movement. The Rittmeister skied out of the timber and stood in its path. He was holding his arms wide.

Wolfe waited for the horse to smash into the Rittmeister. It went up and over, and beyond the Rittmeister without touching him. The Rittmeister was still there with his arms outstretched.

Wolfe heard the plane then. The Rittmeister heard it also.

The Colonel was shouting, 'Get that horse. Get that horse.'

The Rittmeister revolved around and got the parabellum from his belt. Without raising it he fired once and twice in quick succession. The shots echoed a little.

Wolfe saw the shells hit the animal in mid-stride. It came down against a tree, kicking and screaming above the noise of the plane.

The Rittmeister was already up to it. His feet were in the skis at its head. The parabellum hung in his hand at his side. The Rittmeister fired into one of the open eyes.

The plane came over. The Rittmeister waited a moment. Then he fell down into the snow beside the horse where its blood was running in the snow.

There was no movement. The plane passed over and did not come back.

Midway!

Robert J. Casey

'Secure from Flight Quarters . . .'

DAY OF BATTLE

June 4, Thursday.
North of Midway Islands.

1.00. – Just learned that the Army planes from Midway located another part of the Jap invasion force late Wednesday afternoon. They reported four heavy ships, at least two of which were battle-ships. They damaged one and left it 'burning furiously'.

Another report came in to-night. One of our subs sank three Jap subs and three merchant ships with eleven torpedoes at Wake. The submarine skipper was complaining in his report that his periscope was getting so cloudy that he couldn't see through it. What might he have done if only he could have seen what he was doing!

6.00 a.m. – I got up for réveillé and looked out at a clotted sky, a black sea and odd grey moonlight.

If there is such a thing as a special atmosphere for battle, here it is!

Daybreak was late because, in deference to the land-based forces co-operating with us, we had gone back to 'war time'.

The day is warm and a little calmer – a fine day for whatever it is. If the Japs were 700 miles away as reported yesterday they must be about 350 miles nearer this morning and we, having travelled about 350 miles in their direction must be almost on top of them. Of course both fleets may have changed direction since yesterday noon – quite possibly have.

Mickey Reeves turned down my offer to act as tail-end Charlie in one of his fine SOC's. He told in extenuation of how they took an overweight pilot to Samoa on the Marshall Islands expedition. When it came time to return to the ship the wind had died and the SOC wouldn't take off. A message was sent to the admiral: 'SOC unable to take off account wind conditions. Extra weight one hundred gallons petrol and pilot's overweight equivalent twenty gallons petrol.'

Two days later the plane got back. A report was sent to Halsey who replied promptly: 'Hope you've recovered also your twenty-gallon pilot.'

8.20. – Donald Duck issued a call to quarters with the *beep-beep* that made it official. As we started for battle-stations we were informed that the Japs had just attacked Midway, 170 miles to the southwest of us. We didn't have to be told as we swung about into launching position that we were going to take a flying leap at their carriers.

As I went into the wardroom to get my gas mask and tin hat I met Commander Crenshaw. 'Okay,' he said, 'this is it. And don't go out without your rubbers.' I crawled up to the searchlight platform and saw us start the ride into battle at the fastest speed this force has worked up to date.

We were going so fast that our protective destroyer, half submerged and slapping green water over her bridge, had trouble keeping up with us. The sea was flat, but still she buried her nose in the green and tossed up a plume in her wake that looked like Old Faithful.

Behind us the sea was strange to look upon, crisscrossed by frothy white lines – miles of them in fanciful design, as wide and white as concrete roads – the boiling water left to mark the passage of heavy ships. From here the sea appears to be crowded with ships. Our little force has grown miraculously – and fortunately – through the addition of cruisers and such that have overtaken us in the night, and also through the companionship of the *Yorktown*'s force, the stacks of whose destroyers look like black stumps on the horizon.

The officers of the secondary battery in sky control a few feet beneath this platform just got the story of the Army's battleship attack as I heard it during the night. They passed it on with cheers.

8.45. – I'm beginning to have a great deal of respect for Admiral Spruance, who is conducting this expedition. It is getting more and more apparent as we steam towards the west that we haven't been detected. . . . It's a miracle, but that seems to be the way of it.

We have an inferior force. It's probably one of the largest the

United States ever sent anywhere in a gesture of anger; but what of it? About half the Jap navy – and not the worst end of it – is out there ahead.

Every one of the gun crews that I can see below me – hanging to the guns to keep from being blown away – now realizes that luck or superior information or something has given us a chance to get this war well on its way to a finish in the next couple of hours. If we can sink a couple of battleships and four carriers the sea road to Tokyo is open, and to dominate the Pacific we won't need much more equipment than what we happen to have on hand.

Of course the dice may not roll that way. But somehow optimism has replaced the casual gloom of yesterday's outlook. We believe in Santa Claus again. . . . And besides, Hirohito's carriers won't be expecting us.

The wind is stiffer up here than anywhere else on the ship and you can count on thirty knots of it no matter where you go. Even so the funnel fumes hang around here like a hearse plume. The heat is creating its own eddy currents, and breathing in this locality is getting very difficult.

The air beyond the light-brown haze of the stacks is strikingly clear although there is a thick cover of cloud overhead and the sun peeks through infrequently. The whole scene is blue and black, and the details of our carriers and cruisers draped on the starboard flank stand out like images in field glasses.

9.10. – We make a right-angle turn. The wind stiffens, if that were possible, and the SBD's and STB's go off.

It's much too windy for me to hear what's being said in sky control so I don't know whether or not any contact has been made with the Japs. Anyway, the haul isn't too far for these planes if they have to go all the way to Midway. It's comforting to see them up and something of a relief, too. It won't be long now one way or the other and if anything's coming to us we'll soon know it. If we don't get the Jap he'll certainly get us.

The white road in our wake goes straight back to the horizon, a four-lane highway on which ride two cruisers, fantastically unreal behind a curtain of exhaust fumes.

From here I can look down on the SOC's sitting in their cradles and definitely detached from the flight. . . . This is no work for children or fat men. Beyond the catapults the 5-inch guns are bunched together on the flight deck, all of them with their muzzles in the air expectant of attack. Experience shows that there's nothing wrong with that premise or the technique.

These guns are manned by marine crews who from a height present a change in colour from that of a region where the sailors operate. Here instead of blue dungarees is a vista of shiny OD, a mass of it and as motionless as Lorado Taft's statue of the 'March of Time'. Nothing is so immobile as a gunner awaiting a chance to work.

Shells stand nose-down in the fuse cutters, colourful shell and dull varnished brass bases. The guns, somehow, look bright and new — freshly painted barrels with a red ring around the muzzles, brass elevation gears burnished with grease.

Somebody might make a fine picture here of the strain before battle — the strain that is somehow never manifested save in a deathlike impassivity such as this. But I have no time to enlarge on the theme. The sky is filling with them. They circle the carriers, group themselves in two's and three's and quartet's, and finally wing along under the high clouds in squadrons of fifteen. They are joined by a few gooneys — little ones, the first we've seen in weeks.

Why we've delayed so long in uncorking these planes nobody has told me, but it's fairly obvious. It may be hard on Midway to let the Japs proceed with their attack in force, but it's going to be a lot easier to smash the carriers if the planes are busy somewhere else. It would seem that the carriers are sending up all they've got. The sky over towards the starboard horizon is filling up with little black crosses, so presumably the *Yorktown* is doing the same thing. Over the top and God bless!

From the signal yards the flags come down and the flags go up — red, yellow, blue, white, crossed, striped, checkered. Lads are running up and down the ladders of the foremast with dispatch blanks in their hands. It's all spectacular and beginning to be thrilling.

9.30. — We're out of the fog banks and into a region of brilliant sky and glowing blue sea. Everybody aboard ship stands motionless, each man prayerful after his fashion as the planes go quickly out of sight off our starboard quarters. Few men, after all, have had a chance to look upon a spectacle like this. In the nature of things few will look on anything like it again.

The ship's bell tinkles the hour. As if it made any difference to anybody.

10.50. – Everything is on its way now except for about ten fighters which loiter around us.

I went below to get my glasses and found everything shut up tight. Nobody's taking any chances with this ship no matter how far away or how preoccupied the Japs may be. I found a sailor with a chisel or a permit or something to prise a scuttle cover off one of the hatches and so got below. Everything was darker than a coal-mine and as stuffy as the inside of a rubber boot. Turret men and powder monkeys lay sprawled in the long passageways. A hell of a life. In the long vigils before battle they lie in the dark. During battles they go through a monotony of powder and shell handing. The most vital moments they will ever experience are also the most drab.

Below decks you got an idea of the ship's speed from the sound of the water tearing at her shell plates as it went by. It's a sound deeper throated than a rumble and not far short of terrifying.

On the way back I stopped on the well deck for a look over the side. Here, close to the skittering foam, you got a greater sense of motion than you'd ever experience in a fast aeroplane. We are doing everything the engines will let us do. We dive into it and we roll. And every time the ship changes course the port rail goes under the water and the well deck takes a frothy ocean.

The day has turned out to be beautiful.

A report has come in that the Jap attack is divided into two sections – the striking force against which our planes have just moved and a reserve force between fifty and a hundred miles behind the striking force. The general course of these ships is on a line to the west of us.

10.30. – We go into a terrific lateral-pass manoeuvre and the ships start running across each other's bows. Donald Duck raises his voice 'Anti-aircraft stations stand by to repel attack.'

I go back to my place on the foremast. Then comes the usual wait and study of the sky. You can't help but think that this fine day which you were finding so useful to our bombers is going to be just as helpful to Hirohito's bombers.

10.35. – Usual reports of approaching aircraft. . . . 'Unidentified plane bearing two-seveon-oh – fifty-two thousand. . . .' Everybody is tense of course, because sometimes these hysterical shouts turn out to make sense.

We are now leading the procession abreast of the destroyers. A

cruiser – floating arsenal of ack-ack – has come over alongside our
old carrier.

10.45. – Ten planes show up off the starboard bow. They may be
the *Yorktown*'s SBD's. As we glower at them we get the answer – the
step pyramid of the *Yorktown*'s bridge structure comes up over the
horizon. More planes are reported, but the *Yorktown* claims them for
her own and we withdraw from the contest.

We are still ploughing along at top speed. On the lower decks the
roar of the engines is so great that you have to shout to be heard a few
feet. The destroyers, if we keep on at this rate, will have to refuel tonight. One lone gooney is sailing along with us easily and hopefully.

At the moment the carrier nearest us has sent out fighters, dive
bombers and torpedo planes. If the *Yorktown* has contributed as many
as our old carrier, there ought to be about 180 planes on the way to
the attack, 105 of them bombers or torpedo carriers.

11.15. – A report has come in that one of our Fortresses has
attacked and damaged a carrier, presumably in the reserve group.
The attack on Midway has been driven off – eight planes shot down
over the island, the marines claiming a bag of thirty off shore.

It's odd how the battle is shaping up to fit the specifications of the
story the medical colonel told me when we went into Honolulu after
the Coral Sea. The Colonel said that the fight had already occurred.
I said it hadn't. Nature, as usual, is imitating art.

11.35. – We head now into the wind and it's very chilly. Some
fighter planes are coming in, presumably part of our protective patrol.
Against the sky they tumble along like a cloud of May flies. We're
making crochet patterns all over the sea again.

11.40. – There is some contact off the starboard quarter. Maybe
that's why the fighters come in. They shoot over the rim of the sea
and we continue our cotillion.

I'm getting sleepy. A grey half-moon hanging belatedly in the thin
blue sky reminds me so much of myself.

11.45. – Fighters come back to land on our carrier. Apparently a
false alarm.

12.00. – Mickey Reeves signalled me to come down to the bridge
for a sandwich. So I was right at headquarters when first reports
began to come in from our planes. The first message was brief. The
Jap carriers had been located, a little belatedly, and they were
virtually without air cover. . . . Apparently all their planes had been

sent out to make the conquest of Midway quick and easy. However, the squadron commander of the TBD unit reporting, said that his planes were virtually out of fuel.

'Request permission,' he called, 'to withdraw from action and refuel.'

The admiral's answer was terse:

'Attack at once.'

So I sat down in the chartroom to bite into a ham sandwich. The planes had begun to move in on the carriers. Whatever might be the result, we'd never be able to criticize the quality of our opportunity. . . .

I sat there thinking. The Jap air admiral undoubtedly had figured us as permanent fixtures in the southwest Pacific where last he had had word of us. So just about now he'd be looking up at the sky suddenly clouded with SBD's and asking himself the Japanese equivalent of 'Where the hell did those things come from?'

12.45. – Enemy planes reported off port at twelve miles. New alert sounds. The kids drop their food and sidle off to their guns. The Grummans once more leap off our carrier.

1.00. – Still no sign of the visitors. I guess the contact was another of those stories that breed so rapidly in times like this.

1.15. – Fifteen of the – 's bombers come over. The squadron is intact and in tight formation, its work, whatever it was, finished.

1.20. – The carriers swing round, apparently getting ready to take on returning planes which are now showing up in two's and three's. Everything is set to repel an attack, and with good reason. If these planes have failed in their mission or fought a draw or left the Jap carriers usable we may expect a quick and vicious attack in return. If by some remote juju we have put all four carriers out of commission we have just about gained mastery of the Pacific, including the Japanese side of the international date line, or so the more educated of my spies tell me.

I went back to the wardroom and contemplated this phenomenon. Presently the word filtered back to us that the attack had been a complete success. All the carriers had been hit and severely damaged. At least three of them were burning. One, apparently, had been sunk in the first two or three minutes of the engagement.

One battleship of the north group of the force that we had attacked was afire. A second battleship had been hit. Reports from the Army told of hits on two more battleships and another carrier. Discounting these messages to the fullest extent and recognizing how easy it is for one observer to duplicate the report of another, it was still obvious that we had had something of a field day, still obvious that the bulk of Japan's attacking planes must presently be going into the drink for want of any place to land.

BOMBS BURSTING IN AIR

I leaned back in the Morris chair and stretched out my legs and presently was sound asleep in that deep exhaustion that follows such moments of tension. I was aroused by the sound of some other chair-holders grabbing up their tin hats. I got out on to deck about *2.30*. The time is uncertain. My watch was smashed.

There was no time to climb up to the coop on the foremast. A spot of ack-ack had burst over to port near the horizon and the air in that direction seemed to be covered with planes. Word came from nowhere – by the telepathy of battles, I guess – that the *Yorktown* was being attacked. The battle was already on and it would necessarily be brief. The ack-ack was ragged but the thunderheads of it blackened the horizon.

We had no way of telling how many Jap planes came in on that raid but there couldn't have been many. The blasting was short-lived. The carrier came up towards us obviously in good order and such planes as we could pick up with ordinary field-glasses appeared to be ours.

A couple of heavy cruisers peeled off from our formation and streaked over towards the *Yorktown*. It seemed a little late for rescue work and a little unnecessary. The *Yorktown* had come through the assault without much aid and apparently wasn't needing any help to celebrate her escape. This, it seemed to me, might be like shooting stars over the rim of the sea.

As in the first attack this drama lasts only a matter of seconds. The black puffs attenuate and lose colour and mingle with the status clouds in the low distance. The fires of the burning planes are quickly out. The carrier has gone over the horizon again and the ocean is as it was before, save for one strange and terrifying thing – a column of smoke, like the greasy black cockade that marked Wotje after the

Marshall Islands raid, is rising straight into the air to reach at last the dim levels of the ack-ack bursts. Something is afire over there. Commander Crenshaw thinks that maybe a destroyer got hit. We cross our fingers and hope it wasn't the carrier. At any rate it's serious.

We keep on our course with every rivet straining and we cast no regretful or anxious glances at the horizon. We haven't time. We keep our necks pulled well down into our collars and mind our business. Whatever happened to the carrier may be happening to us in very short order. The Japs will never overlook the flagship as long as they have a plane left.

(Emphasis inserted at midnight: As long as they have a plane left!)

6.05. – An announcement was made over the loud-speaker to coagulate the rumours on which we have been subsisting since the planes went off this morning. We begin to realize that we have actually taken part in a decisive and important battle. Until now we have been kidding ourselves that this might be so. But now we know. Whatever else we may have done, we are now informed that we have 'attacked and severely damaged four enemy aircraft carriers. . . .' A haul in itself if the carriers have been smashed enough to put them into dry dock for a few months; a terrific victory if they have been smashed badly enough to keep them from getting back to Tokyo. . . . But there's a catch to this announcement and possibly an explanation for the smoke over on the horizon. . . . 'One of our aircraft carriers was attacked in two waves and badly damaged. We suffered severe losses in aeroplanes. . . .' Battles, you are learning, are merely encounters in which the victor's losses are a little less than those of the loser.

About 6.10 I came in off the deck to a dimly lighted wardroom for a cup of coffee. I needed it. A lot of officers were there, most of them munching sandwiches automatically and in silence. If they spoke at all it was with the voices of men dead for sleep. . . .

'We sent out fifty-three TBD's and we got back five.' 'They had to land in the water – no petrol.' 'If they attacked the carrier why don't they attack us? What's keeping them?' 'I guess most of their planes are in the drink, too.' 'If four carriers are smashed, their planes are going to have a hell of a time finding a place to land.' 'Is the carrier still afloat?' 'She's listing badly to starboard and down by the bow.'

For a victory feast this was certainly a depressing session.

Out on deck again at 6.30. Either we had altered our course a bit or the carrier had altered hers. The carrier was now well up over the horizon, an appalling mass of smoke rolling off her flight deck.

6.40. – Air alarm. I scrambled up to the searchlight platform again. As I passed the 20-mm battery, Mickey Reeves came out of the charthouse. 'Watch it on that side,' he ordered. 'They think they've got something coming in on the sun.'

It swung about immediately and careened towards me so that I was hanging to the ladder like a fly trying to get a hold on the ceiling. When I got to the platform we were leaving the burning carrier behind us. Another carrier, undamaged, and her cruisers in new perspective were jet black against the reddening sky.

Down at the 5-inch guns the Marine crews were staring into the sun, shading their eyes with their hands, their faces screwed into odd knots like those of characters in a Bellows drawing – alert but as usual immobile; concerned, perhaps, but not showing it.

One interesting thing occurred while I was looking at the guns: A carrier got lost. A moment ago she was there in plain sight. Now she was gone. And I wasn't the only person aboard who wondered about that.

7.30. – Lieutenant Dancey, my ex-cabin mate, came up the ladder bound for the fighting top. I crawled up after him and looked out upon a larger if no more watery world.

We had forgotten about the enemy plane at that time. It never showed up – if it ever existed – but as we took a long sweep on our zigzag, the wounded carrier did. Presently she rose over the rim like something in a magic-lantern show. Somebody apparently had tossed a miracle. She had straightened up. The list had been reduced so that it wasn't apparent through the glasses. The fire had gone out. Big, clean, beautiful, she filled a large section of our vision like a symmetrical island. She was like an island not only in her silhouette but in her immobility. Four cruisers stood by.

7.35. – Dancey asked for a report on operations in progress and that's how we learned that we still had twenty-four torpedo planes out working on what was left of the mess we produced this morning. They may have some trouble getting back before dark.

7.40. – The sun is getting low. The horizon is a band of glowing orange. And against it the battered carrier stands in her glorious aloofness. As we watch, four heavy cruisers steam off along the edge of the panorama towards the north and the destroyers follow. You look at all of this with a catch in your throat. And you brace yourself for the sentimental shock that must come presently when one of the destroyers turns about to put a tin fish into her. For there's no doubt now that the ship has been abandoned.

She was dead in the water, you could see that. You could guess at the sieve-like condition of a hull so battered that her engines were finished. . . . So we'd sink her as we'd sunk the *Lexington* only a couple of weeks ago. We stood by and waited for the drop of the trap.

But it didn't come. The ships held to their course away from the deserted hulk. The carrier, until our course for the recovery of planes took us over the horizon and dropped her from our vision, stood majestically on the rim of the sea, the blazing sun behind her like the burst of light at the climax of a grand opera, her head up.

7.45. – Once the carrier was out of sight we took our loss philosophically. After all, to trade one carrier for three wasn't bad business, and despite the confused reports of the operation it was quite likely that the proportions of the bargain were even greater. I mentioned to Commander Mayer that for the first time since December 7 we were now able to meet the Japs with the odds even – with the odds even despite the fact that they outnumbered us still in ships and outclassed us in main battery-fire power. For the first time since I began to ride with this task force we had arrived at a point where we could trade the Japs carrier for carrier and still have enough left to lick them.

Mayer nodded.

'All this has worked out like the war games,' he said. 'We've been over this problem right here in these same waters a dozen times. Somebody realized a long time ago that the best way to beat the Japs would be to let them pick the battleground – but make it our battleground that they picked. The Japs wanted another Tsushima, but we got it instead.'

8.30. – The carrier still close to us launches some fighters. About that time the missing one pokes her nose over the horizon dead ahead of us. How she got there is something I'll never know. Her reappearance is reported immediately to a lot of interested folks below.

The TBD's are coming in to land. They are well bunched but in no particular formation. The recently released fighters romp about here and there over them in the darkening sky like a flock of blackbirds.

I recall a comment of Ralph Morse about torpedo bomber pilots:

'They don't stand any watches. They don't have to go out and do patrol jobs. They don't have any dogfights to worry about. They may sit around playing poker for a month before they have to go out. . . . Then they go out and they don't come back.'

Note at midnight: These lads, however, came back in good order. And they brought a puzzle. One of our carriers had sent out twenty-four planes, including her remaining TBD's. Thirty-five came back. The explanation of course is that some of the homing pigeons were part of the outfit from the ship put out of action.

8.35. – The look-outs began their customary twilight field day.

'Large group planes bearing three-one-oh unidentified.' Seven fighters steak out to investigate that one.

'Aircraft two-five-three relative reported friendly.'

'Unidentified aircraft, sir, just passed overhead.'

8.45. – 'Only unidentified plane now in sky is at one-one-eight relative. . . . Sixty thousand yards.'

The last of the bombers is in. I am going below.

The wardroom gossip was brief considering that we had just taken part in a first-class battle and, not only that, had come out intact and with an amazing success where most of us had expected to be sunk.

Crowley contributed a bit of common sense for the consideration of tired officers. 'We have a lot of subs out there,' he said. 'It's to be expected that they are closing in on such ships as the bombers have partly wrecked and slowed down.'

The officers listened to him politely and without argument. Most of them had been awake for twenty-four hours. All of them had been under constant strain for a long nightmarish, if glorious, day. One by one they went to sleep in their chairs or staggered off somewhere to lie down.

The score, at present unverified and of problematical accuracy, is this:

The Navy claims two carriers badly damaged and two completely destroyed.

Reports from Midway say that Army bombers damaged two carriers – which isn't so confusing when you figure that they were probably working on the 'reserve force' somewhere, detached from the main striking force. The Army bag is also said to include one battleship afire and one with a brace of torpedoes in it. Three ships are on fire between here and Midway, one probably a heavy cruiser and others unidentified.

Fantastic as these figures would have seemed yesterday when we were counting heads of our force and rechecking the report of what the Japs were bringing to us, it's now obvious that Admiral Yamamoto's outfit has taken a severe trimming. The figures seem less outrageous when you figure what the results of the trimming have been on Jap manoeuvres. The big fleet is in full retreat, as it probably would never have to be if the Japs could muster any planes at all. That means that if they had five carriers as advertised, then at the moment five of the five aren't working. How many are actually sunk we don't know at present – possibly none. But they're out of action and it's obvious that the resulting disaster to the Jap fleet is little short of disastrous. To-morrow or next day may show the best part of this armada out of business, our mastery of the Pacific assured, the threat to Australia definitely removed, and this war on its way to a fine finish.

Seldom in the history of naval warfare has an admiral walked out so far into a trap with his chin so far out, and seldom in naval warfare has a surprise stroke by a working minority meant so much.

The warning net carried the chatter of amazed Japs all morning, along with the less amazed but colourful conversation of our pilots. One Jap apparently was trying to confuse the Americans, because after each of his messages in Japanese he would count up to five in English and say 'Acknowledge.' It was apparent that so far as the battle was concerned he was an outsider. He probably knew that the carriers were being attacked, but he pursued his job of patrolling with no thought that our bombers could have come from anywhere except Midway. Then suddenly he came out of a cloud or round a corner or something and a great light seemed to break upon him. He gasped, and when he spoke it was in the language with which he was most familiar – as one always does in shock. In his case it turned out to be good San Francisco high-school English:

'My God! The whole US fleet is out here!'

He was wrong of course, but as we are going now, nobody in the

Jap navy is likely to stay around here long enough to discover his
error.

This is quite likely to become one of the most amazing battles since
men began to set themselves up as naval experts. For example,
despite the fact that we were outclassed by the fleet the Japs sent
against us – they had a margin of four battleships and possibly three
carriers – our task forces in combination made up the biggest armed
force that the US ever turned loose upon the waters for an act of war.
We carried out our mission in good order, we took part in a major
engagement which we appear to have won handily. *And we haven't fired
a shot.* This is the first big naval battle fought entirely (or at least
brought to its crisis entirely) by aeroplanes.

Mickey Reeves mentioned that it would be a good subject for a
critique.

'Sure,' said Crowley, 'if you could find anybody who was there.'

There is plenty of basis for his cynicism. . . . 'They live the life of
Riley. . . . They go out. . . . They never come back. . . .'

After 11 p.m. we got a report from the TBD's that carried out the
late-afternoon expedition.

When they caught up with the Japs again, only one carrier was
present and that was afire. They worked on that briefly. Then they
saw a battleship and dropped the rest of their eggs on it. As they left,
fire was pouring out of its funnels and it was in obvious difficulties.

The submarine – also reported that she had put a couple of
torpedoes into a carrier of the *Soryu* class, and the story gets better
and better.

It will of course take a couple of days to sort out the casualty list.
For instance, the battleship reported by the late evening bombing
party may be a heavy cruiser. The three missing carriers may have
fallen out of formation or may have taken another course to keep far
over the horizon and well away from the beacon of a burning ship.
The *Soryu*-class carrier reported torpedoed by the sub may be one of
those reported damaged in previous communiqués. But at the worst
construction you can put on the results, the knock-over seems to have
been complete and startling.

I am going to bed. I am so damned tired that my legs are buckling
under me.

PURSUIT

June 5, Friday.
North of Midway. In pursuit of the Jap fleet. Calm, wet, misty.

Despite exhaustion I got little sleep. The lack of ventilation below made me come up for air at 3 a.m. Went out on deck again to give moral support to G.Q. Came in again. It was dark and rainy, and obviously there wasn't going to be much of a sunrise.

We got a report from Midway along with the morning news sheet. The attack had damaged only a power plant and some odds and ends of sheds. The runways, hangars and gas storage were untouched. Eight Jap planes were knocked down by ack-ack. The Army airmen, realizing the strength behind the Japanese push, had been prepared to operate with light bomb loads and count on returning to Honolulu to land. But there's been no necessity for that. They came down on Midway immediately after the first, and only, wave of the blitz.

All day we moved west without contact.

We got a bit of encouragement about the *Yorktown*. She's still afloat and promises to remain afloat. A fleet of minesweepers, Navy tugs and such craft is being rushed out from Pearl Harbour to tow her in.

6.20. – We start through the rain at top speed apparently headed for the kill. We may have trouble locating our quarry. The fog is so thick that we can't see the other ships running alongside us.

This battle has taken on an odd complexion. We have a very fine chance to annihilate what is left of the Jap force, but what Crowley calls the 'logistics' are beginning to enter into the problem. The destroyers are just about out of fuel. They can't tear along indefinitely at top speed and, for that matter, neither can we. Such manoeuvring as this pursuit of a defeated fleet after twenty minutes of contact could never have been foreseen even by the chief of staff of a madhouse. So fuel will have to be brought to us from Honolulu if the chase is to continue with any hope of success.

As matters stand we still have enough oil to last us a couple of days and a tanker is said to be on its way out.

Pursuit is further complicated by the fact that we are pretty vulnerable. We don't want to get too close to a battery of 16-inch guns by day, and we'd just as soon keep out of the reach of sneaking destroyers by night.

6.30. – After a dull, not to say comatose day, sixty SBD's were shot off to look over a new combination of Japs. A group apparently from the reserve is ahead of us. It is said to be composed of two *Isei*-class battleships, the Japs' second-best heavies, and two carriers, one of which is afire. The speed of this outfit is thirteen knots, which would indicate that something very serious is wrong with at least one of the ships.

In yesterday's bombing a lot of SBD's worked on a battleship in the northern group, dropped a few 500-pound bombs on the deck without damaging it in any vital spot. They climaxed their work with a couple of near misses that fixed up the big flatiron as the *Bismarck* had been fixed up for slaughter. They damaged the rudder and from that time on the big battleships steamed about in circles.

7.00. – Planes report contact.

8.45. – Eight SBD's come back with bombs.

9.05. – Fifty-two planes are still out and the sun is just about gone. A mob of men is standing silent on the decks hoping for a chance to welcome home the wanderer – an unusual and touching performance.

9.15. – In the wardroom. A voice: 'Is it getting dark out there?' Crowley: 'A little. They'll have to make a night landing.' Voice: 'Boy, I'm glad I'm not with them.'

9.30. – I went out on to the deck. It was pretty dark, with a dirty streak of orange ahead of the carrier. One by one the SBD's began to straggle in. By 9.35 the returning ones had turned on their running lights. They'd come across the southern sky from the west. After a while, when the black got blacker, the carrier turned on her searchlight and waved it about, picking up a heavy cruiser a couple of miles away and making it look like a white model of itself. Mast lights appeared on all ships at the edge of the formation. And it still looked like an impossible job to get the wanderers home.

The marine major looked at the lights and went in after his life-jacket. 'We may complete this recovery right square in the middle of the Jap fleet,' he said.

About fifteen minutes later, however, the last plane came in and a ripple of cheering ran around the decks. The searchlight of the second carrier made one brief sweep and another light came on. The two met vertically and came apart. A blazing white 'V' stood five thousand feet high in the black sky. The lights went out.

Taking inventory of the activities at the end of the second day, it would appear that there have been two forces of Jap ships engaged. (This aside from the train vessels which went out of the picture after the first attack by the PBY's and Flying Fortresses. Apparently they dropped back out of bombing range and so were well on their way home when the retreat started.) The northern group was the striking force. It consisted of two battleships, four carriers and assorted heavy cruisers and destroyers. Behind it at no great distance – possibly fifty to seventy-five miles – was a reserve force of two more battleships, one or possibly two carriers. The Army claims to have hit one carrier and two battleships of this group and the strafe is still on.

Admiral Nimitz issued a communiqué to-night: 'A battle is in progress off Midway Island. All armed services are engaged. One battleship and one carrier of the enemy fleet have been damaged.' Well, that's safe enough. Apparently Nimitz is taking no chances and is discounting in advance the messages that reach him from imaginative birdmen.

There may be good reason for his conservatism. We aren't completely in command of the situation yet, although we are looking upon a pretty good imitation of it. A carrier is reported to be coming down from Dutch Harbour to work on us. Nobody minds this, because with the carrier strength we have now we'd be more likely to go looking for the Jap than run away from him.

There is always, of course, the possibility of bad breaks. One can conceive of conditions under which the battered Japs might get free to Wake and thence to Japan, conditions under which they might lure us into a torpedo trap or something of the sort, or manoeuvre us into a position where the land planes could take care of us. (I mention this latter contingency just by way of imaginative flight, because we know where Wake is, just as well as they do.) But at the moment, however cock-eyed the reports, however lousy our reconnaissance work, however uncertain our next step in the attack, there is no doubt that we have gained a decisive and important victory.

10.00 p.m. – We are about to cross the 180th meridian headed due west, but are just going to ignore the loss of Saturday.

Midnight. – There have been no reports from the bombers that took after the Jap remnants last evening. However, Cincpac has ordered us to close in and polish off the leavings with light surface action.

We listen gravely and wonder. We certainly won't be sticking our necks out if the battleships are still doing well. We might carry on indefinitely, of course, slapping bombs at the retreating ships between here and, say, Marcus, and wearing them down to a point where we might go in and sink them with shell. But fuel is becoming a real problem. To-morrow the Japs will still be within Fortress bombing range, but it is quite likely that to-morrow will be the last day for all of us.

One interesting bit has come out of the reports from Midway. It becomes apparent that despite their heavy losses the Little Brown Brothers were pursuing their customary technique. With at least four carriers smashed and all their planes gone, they drove on to within fifty miles of Midway. At that point, apparently, Yamamoto found out that all his carriers were down and sent an urgent message to his alleged chiefs to pick up their marbles and get out while they were still in one piece. So they went.

Oddly nobody had paid much attention to the Jap cruiser force – that is, nobody but the SBD pilots who occasionally mention cruisers in their inventory. It now begins to be certain that two of the *Mogami* class (8,500 tons and well equipped) have been sunk. Others are reported afire here and there. And as Tom O'Connell points out, a cruiser fire never lasts long. She burns energetically two or three hours and then she sinks.

So we retire to our infrequent hay, pondering the wonder of it all.

June 6 (or is it?), Saturday. – At sea west of Midway. Sunny. Calm. Warmer.

We've headed a little southwest and are about 800 miles from Wake.

Shortly after breakfast the task-force air patrol spotted a carrier and six destroyers pursuing a southwesterly course at ten knots, 150 miles from here. The scouts reported a complete absence of enemy air protection – another indication of what we suspected yesterday, that all the Jap planes were destroyed in the first few hours of the attack, that the flight which attacked the *Yorktown* probably never found a carrier to land on.

We sent up some SOC's and then began a day of indubitably successful operation accompanied by cock-eyed reconnaissance.

At 11 o'clock the latest batch of scout planes reported that the carrier wasn't a carrier but a battleship. This bulletin was somewhat authenticated at noon when Donald Duck announced, 'We have just intercepted a message from the commander-in-chief of the Japanese fleet saying that he is being bombed.'

But after that the communications began to get mysteriouser and mysteriouser. Soon after noon came another report from a new bombing expedition: 'Have made hits on two ships. Carrier afire and seems badly damaged.' On the heels of that a cruiser plane reported sighting 'carrier and two heavy cruisers. The carrier was sunk,' he said. 'I saw it sink.'

Two of our SOC's, piloted by Mickey Reeves and Crowley, took off at 1.30 to look at what there was to see of the shambles. They were within twenty-five minutes' flying time of this scene when they were called back.

And as if that didn't add up to enough to muddle pretty nearly everybody, returning bombers reported that they'd had a field day with a battleship which they left well on its way to the bottom. We had only three torpedo planes left to send on the afternoon's mission, but apparently they did pretty well.

The best explanation anybody can give to all the odd reports is that the Japs split their force into two groups reasonably close together, a battleship and six destroyers in one section, a carrier without planes, accompanied by two heavy cruisers, in the other.

We sent out three bombing attacks to-day. The first one worked on the carrier and cruisers; the second, looking for the same target, came upon the battleship. The returning pilots report a highly successful operation. Eighteen hits were planted in the big flat-iron. The planes then stood off and watched preparations being made to abandon ship. They then landed several hits on the cruisers and used their remaining bombs to plaster destroyers. They came home convinced that they had left nothing afloat except men in life-jackets whom it was impossible to count, let alone pick up.

It is estimated on the basis of to-day's reports that between 18,000 and 20,000 men were killed in this brief battle. While we aren't wasting too much sympathy on our enemy at the moment, we are awed by the catastrophe that overtook him. There is chill in the thought that there, but for the Grace of God, go we. Had we been seen. . . . Had the Japs attacked us before making the try for Midway. . . .

Hiroshima The Fire

John Hersey

Immediately after the explosion, the Reverend Mr Kiyoshi Tanimoto, having run wildly out of the Matsui estate and having looked in wonderment at the bloody soldiers at the mouth of the dugout they had been digging, attached himself sympathetically to an old lady who was walking along in a daze, holding her head with her left hand, supporting a small boy of three or four on her back with her right, and crying, 'I'm hurt! I'm hurt! I'm hurt!' Mr Tanimoto transferred the child to his own back and led the woman by the hand down the street, which was darkened by what seemed to be a local column of dust. He took the woman to a grammar school not far away that had previously been designated for use as a temporary hospital in case of emergency. By this solicitous behavior, Mr Tanimoto at once got rid of his terror. At the school, he was much surprised to see glass all over the floor and fifty or sixty injured people already waiting to be treated. He reflected that, although the all-clear had sounded and he had heard no planes, several bombs must have been dropped. He thought of a hillock in the rayon man's garden from which he would get a view of the whole of Koi – of the whole of Hiroshima, for that matter – and he ran back up to the estate.

From the mound, Mr Tanimoto saw an astonishing panorama. Not just a patch of Koi, as he had expected, but as much of Hiroshima as he could see through the clouded air was giving off a thick, dreadful miasma. Clumps of smoke, near and far, had begun to push up through the general dust. He wondered how such extensive damage could have been dealt out of a silent sky; even a few planes, far up, would have been audible. Houses nearby were burning, and when huge drops of water the size of marbles began to fall, he half thought that they must be coming from the hoses of firemen fighting the blazes. (They were actually drops of condensed moisture falling from the turbulent tower of dust, heat, and fission fragments that had already risen miles into the sky above Hiroshima.)

Mr Tanimoto turned away from the sight when he heard Mr Matsuo call out to ask whether he was all right. Mr Matsuo had been safely cushioned within the falling house by the bedding stored in the front hall and had worked his way out. Mr Tanimoto scarcely answered. He had thought of his wife and baby, his church, his home, his parishioners, all of them down in that awful murk. Once more he began to run in fear – toward the city.

Mrs Hatsuyo Nakamura, the tailor's widow, having struggled up from under the ruins of her house after the explosion, and seeing Myeko, the youngest of her three children, buried breast-deep and unable to move, crawled across the debris, hauled at timbers, and flung tiles aside, in a hurried effort to free the child. Then, from what seemed to be caverns far below, she heard two small voices crying, '*Tasukete! Tasukete!* Help! Help!'

She called the names of her ten-year-old son and eight-year-old daughter: 'Toshio! Yaeko!'

The voices from below answered.

Mrs Nakamura abandoned Myeko, who at least could breathe, and in a frenzy made the wreckage fly above the crying voices. The children had been sleeping nearly ten feet apart, but now their voices seemed to come from the same place. Toshio, the boy, apparently had some freedom to move, because she could feel him undermining the pile of wood and tiles as she worked from above. At last she saw his head, and she hastily pulled him out by it. A mosquito net was wound intricately, as if it had been carefully wrapped, around his feet. He said he had been blown right across the room and had been on top of his sister Yaeko under the wreckage. She now said, from underneath, that she could not move, because there was something on her legs. With a bit more digging, Mrs Nakamura cleared a hole above the child and began to pull her arm. '*Itai!* It hurts!' Yaeko cried. Mrs Nakamura shouted, 'There's no time now to say whether it hurts or not,' and yanked her whimpering daughter up. Then she freed Myeko. The children were filthy and bruised, but none of them had a single cut or scratch.

Mrs Nakamura took the children out into the street. They had nothing on but underpants, and although the day was very hot, she worried rather confusedly about their being cold, so she went back into the wreckage and burrowed underneath and found a bundle of clothes she had packed for an emergency, and she dressed them in pants, blouses, shoes, padded-cotton air-raid helmets called *bokuzuki*, and even, irrationally, overcoats. The children were silent, except for the five-year-old, Myeko, who kept asking questions: 'Why is it night already? Why did our house fall down? What happened?' Mrs Nakamura, who did not know what had happened (had not the all-clear sounded?), looked around and saw through the darkness that all the houses in her neighborhood had collapsed. The house next door, which its owner had been tearing down to make way for a fire lane, was not very thoroughly, if crudely, torn down; its owner, who had been sacrificing his home for the community's safety, lay dead. Mrs Nakamoto, wife of the head of the local air-raid defense Neighborhood Association, came across the street with her head all bloody, and said that her baby was badly cut; did Mrs Nakamura have any bandage? Mrs Nakamura did not, but she crawled into the remains of her house again and pulled out some white cloth that she had been using in her work as a seamstress; ripped it into strips, and gave it to Mrs Nakamoto. While fetching the cloth, she noticed her sewing machine; she went back in for it and dragged it out. Obviously, she could not carry it with her, so she unthinkingly plunged her symbol of livelihood into the receptacle which for weeks had been her symbol of safety – the cement tank of water in front of her house, of the type every household had been ordered to construct against a possible fire raid.

A nervous neighbor, Mrs Hataya, called to Mrs Nakamura to run away with her to the woods in Asano Park – an estate, by the Kyo River not far off, belonging to the wealthy Asano family, who once owned the Toyo Kisen Kaisha steamship line. The park had been designated as an evacuation area for their neighborhood. Seeing fire breaking out in a nearby ruin (except at the very center, where the bomb itself ignited some fires, most of Hiroshima's citywide conflagration was caused by inflammable wreckage falling on cook-stoves and live wires), Mrs Nakamura suggested going over to fight it. Mrs Hataya said, 'Don't be foolish. What if planes come and drop more bombs?' so Mrs Nakamura started out for Asano Park with her children and Mrs Hataya, and she carried her rucksack of emergency clothing, a blanket, an umbrella, and a suitcase of things she had cached in her air-raid shelter. Under many ruins, as they hurried along, they heard muffled screams for help. The only building they saw standing on their way to Asano Park was the Jesuit mission house, alongside the Catholic kindergarten to which Mrs Nakamura had sent Myeko for a time. As they passed it, she saw Father Kleinsorge, in bloody underwear, running out of the house with a small suitcase in his hand.

Right after the explosion, while Father Wilhelm Kleinsorge, S.J., was wandering around in his underwear in the vegetable garden, Father Superior LaSalle came around the corner of the building in the darkness. His body, especially his back, was bloody; the flash had made him twist away from his window, and tiny pieces of glass had flown at him. Father Kleinsorge, still bewildered, managed to ask, 'Where are the rest?' Just then, the two other priests living in the mission house appeared – Father Cieslik, unhurt, supporting Father Schiffer, who was covered with blood that spurted from a cut above his left ear and who was very pale. Father Cieslik was rather pleased with himself, for after the flash he had dived into a doorway, which he had previously reckoned to be the safest place inside the building, and when the blast came, he was not injured. Father LaSalle told Father Cieslik to take Father Schiffer to a doctor before he bled to death, and suggested either Dr Kanda, who lived on the next corner, or Dr Fujii, about six blocks away. The two men went out of the compound and up the street.

The daughter of Mr Hoshijima, the mission catechist, ran up to Father Kleinsorge and said that her mother and sister were buried under the ruins of their house, which was at the back of the Jesuit compound, and at the same time the priests noticed that the house of the Catholic-kindergarten teacher at the front of the compound had collapsed on her. While Father LaSalle and Mrs Murata, the mission housekeeper, dug the teacher out, Father Kleinsorge went to the catechist's fallen house and began lifting things off the top of the pile. There was not a sound underneath; he was sure the Hoshijima women had been killed. At last, under what had been a corner of the kitchen, he saw Mrs Hoshijima's head. Believing her dead, he began to haul her out by the hair, but suddenly she screamed, '*Itai! Itai!*' It hurts! It hurts!' He dug some more and lifted her out. He managed, too, to find her daughter in the rubble and free her. Neither was badly hurt.

A public bath next door to the mission house had caught fire, but since there the wind was southerly, the priests thought their house would be spared. Nevertheless, as a precaution, Father Kleinsorge went inside to fetch some things he wanted to save. He found his room in a state of weird and illogical confusion. A first-aid kit was hanging undisturbed on a hook on the wall, but his clothes, which had been on other hooks nearby, were nowhere to be seen. His desk was in splinters all over the room, but a mere papier-mâché suitcase, which he had hidden under the desk, stood handle-side up, without a scratch on it, in the doorway of the room, where he could not miss it. Father Kleinsorge later came to regard this as a bit of Providential interference, inasmuch as the suitcase contained his breviary, the account books for the whole diocese, and a considerable amount of paper money belonging to the mission, for which he was responsible. He ran out of the house and deposited the suitcase in the mission air-raid shelter.

At about this time, Father Cieslik and Father Schiffer, who was still spurting blood, came back and said that Dr Kanda's house was ruined and that fire blocked them from getting out of what they supposed to be the local circle of destruction to Dr Fujii's private hospital, on the bank of the Kyo River.

Dr Masakazu Fukii's hospital was no longer on the bank of the Kyo River; it was in the river. After the overturn, Dr Fujii was so stupefied and so tightly squeezed by the beams gripping his chest that he was unable to move at first, and he hung there about twenty minutes in the darkened morning. Then a thought which came to him – that soon the tide would be running in through the estuaries and his head would be submerged – inspired him to fearful activity; he wriggled and turned and exerted what strength he could (though his left arm, because of the pain in his shoulder, was useless), and before long he had freed himself from the vise. After a few moments' rest, he climbed onto the pile of timbers and, finding a long one that slanted up to the riverbank, he painfully shinnied up it.

Dr Fujii, who was in his underwear, was now soaking and dirty.

His undershirt was torn and blood ran down it from bad cuts on his chin and back. In this disarray, he walked out onto Kyo Bridge, beside which his hospital had stood. The bridge had not collapsed. He could see only fuzzily without his glasses, but he could see enough to be amazed at the number of houses that were down all around. On the bridge, he encountered a friend, a doctor named Machii, and asked in bewilderment, 'What do you think it was?'

Dr Machii said, 'It must have been a *Molotoffano hanakago*' – a Molotov flower basket, the delicate Japanese name for the 'bread basket,' or self-scattering cluster of bombs.

At first, Dr Fujii could see only two fires, one across the river from his hospital site and one quite far to the south. But at the same time, he and his friend observed something that puzzled them, and which, as doctors, they discussed: although there were as yet very few fires, wounded people were hurrying across the bridge in an endless parade of misery, and many of them exhibited terrible burns on their faces and arms. 'Why do you suppose it is?' Dr Fujii asked. Even a theory was comforting that day, and Dr Machii stuck to his. 'Perhaps because it was a Molotov flower basket,' he said.

There had been no breeze earlier in the morning when Dr Fujii had walked to the railway station to see his friend off, but now brisk winds were blowing every which way; here on the bridge the wind was easterly. New fires were leaping up, and they spread quickly, and in a very short time terrible blasts of hot air and showers of cinders made it impossible to stand on the bridge any more. Dr Machii ran to the far side of the river and along a still unkindled street. Dr Fujii went down into the water under the bridge, where a score of people had already taken refuge, among them his servants, who had extricated themselves from the wreckage. From there, Dr Fujii saw a nurse hanging in the timbers of his hospital by her legs, and then another painfully pinned across the breast. He enlisted the help of some of the others under the bridge and freed both of them. He thought he heard the voice of his niece for a moment, but he could not find her; he never saw her again. Four of his nurses and the two patients in the hospital died, too. Dr Fujii went back into the water of the river and waited for the fire to subside.

* * *

The lot of Drs Fujii, Kanda, and Machii right after the explosion – and, as these three were typical, that of the majority of the physicians and surgeons of Hiroshima – with their offices and hospitals destroyed, their equipment scattered, their own bodies incapacitated in varying degrees, explained why so many citizens who were hurt went untended and why so many who might have lived died. Of a hundred and fifty doctors in the city, sixty-five were already dead and most of the rest were wounded. Of 1,780 nurses, 1,654 were dead or too badly hurt to work. In the biggest hospital, that of the Red Cross, only six doctors out of thirty were able to function, and only ten nurses out of more than two hundred. The sole uninjured doctor on the Red Cross Hospital staff was Dr Sasaki. After the explosion, he hurried to a storeroom to fetch bandages. This room, like everything he had seen as he ran through the hospital, was chaotic – bottles of medicines thrown off shelves and broken, salves spattered on the walls, instruments strewn everywhere. He grabbed up some bandages and an unbroken bottle of Mercurochrome, hurried back to the chief surgeon, and bandaged his cuts. Then he went out into the corridor and began patching up the wounded patients and the doctors and nurses there. He blundered so without his glasses that he took a pair off the face of a wounded nurse, and although they only approximately compensated for the errors of his vision, they were better than nothing. (He was to depend on them for more than a month.)

Dr Sasaki worked without method, taking those who were nearest him first, and he noticed soon that the corridor seemed to be getting more and more crowded. Mixed in with the abrasions and lacerations which most people in the hospital had suffered, he began to find dreadful burns. He realized then that casualties were pouring in from outdoors. There were so many that he began to pass up the lightly wounded; he decided that all he could hope to do was to stop people from bleeding to death. Before long, patients lay and crouched on the floors of the wards and the laboratories and all the other rooms, and in the corridors, and on the stairs, and in the front hall, and under the portecochère, and on the stone front steps, and in the driveway and courtyard, and for blocks each way in the streets outside. Wounded people supported maimed people; disfigured families leaned together. Many people were vomiting. A tremendous number of schoolgirls – some of those who had been taken from their classrooms to work outdoors, clearing fire lanes – crept into the hospital. In a city of two hundred and forty-five thousand, nearly a hundred thousand people had been killed or doomed at one blow; a hundred thousand more were hurt. At least ten thousand of the wounded made their way to the best hospital in town, which was altogether unequal to such a trampling, since it had only six hundred beds, and they had all been occupied. The people in the suffocating crowd inside the hospital wept and cried, for Dr Sasaki to hear, '*Sensei!* Doctor!,' and the less seriously wounded came and pulled at his sleeve and begged him to go to the aid of the worse wounded. Tugged here and there in his stockinged feet, bewildered by the numbers, staggered by so much raw flesh, Dr Sasaki lost all sense of profession and stopped working as a skillful surgeon and a sympathetic man; he became an automaton, mechanically wiping, daubing, winding, wiping, daubing, winding.

Some of the wounded in Hiroshima were unable to enjoy the questionable luxury of hospitalization. In what had been the personnel office of the East Asia Tin Works, Miss Sasaki lay doubled over, unconscious, under the tremendous pile of books and plaster and wood and corrugated iron. She was wholly unconscious (she later estimated) for about three hours. Her first sensation was of dreadful pain in her left leg. It was so black under the books and debris that the borderline between awareness and unconsciousness was fine; she apparently crossed it several times, for the pain seemed to come and go. At the moments when it was sharpest, she felt that her leg had been cut off somewhere below the knee. Later, she heard someone walking on top of the wreckage above her, and anguished voices spoke up, evidently from within the mess around her: 'Please help! Get us out!'

Father Kleinsorge stemmed Father Schiffer's spurting cut as well as he could with some bandages that Dr Fujii had given the priests a few days before. When he finished, he ran into the mission house again and found the jacket of his military uniform and an old pair of gray trousers. He put them on and went outside. A woman from next door ran up to him and shouted that her husband was buried under her house and the house was on fire; Father Kleinsorge must come and save him.

Father Kleinsorge, already growing apathetic and dazed in the presence of the cumulative distress, said, 'We haven't much time.' Houses all around were burning, and the wind was now blowing hard. 'Do you know exactly which part of the house he is under?' he asked.

'Yes, yes,' she said. 'Come quickly.'

They went around to the house, the remains of which blazed violently, but when they got there, it turned out that the woman had no idea where her husband was. Father Kleinsorge shouted several times, 'Is anyone there?' There was no answer. Father Kleinsorge said to the woman, 'We must get away or we will all die.' He went back to the Catholic compound and told the Father Superior that the fire was coming closer on the wind, which had swung around and was now from the north; it was time for everybody to go.

Just then, the kindergarten teacher pointed out to the priests Mr Fukai, the secretary of the diocese, who was standing in his window on the second floor of the mission house, facing in the direction of the explosion, weeping. Father Cieslik, because he thought the stairs unusable, ran around to the back of the mission house to look for a ladder. There he heard people crying for help under a nearby fallen roof. He called to passers-by running away in the street to help him lift it, but nobody paid any attention, and he had to leave the buried ones to die. Father Kleinsorge ran inside the mission house and scrambled up the stairs, which were awry and piled with plaster and lathing, and called to Mr Fukai from the doorway of his room.

Mr Fukai, a very short man of about fifty, turned around slowly, with a queer look, and said, 'Leave me here.'

Father Kleinsorge went into the room and took Mr Fukai by the collar of his coat and said, 'Come with me or you'll die.'

Mr Fukai said, 'Leave me here to die.'

Father Kleinsorge began to shove and haul Mr Fukai out of the room. Then the theological student came up and grabbed Mr Fukai's feet, and Father Kleinsorge took his shoulders, and together they carried him downstairs and outdoors. 'I can't walk!' Mr Fukai cried. 'Leave me here!' Father Kleinsorge got his paper suitcase with the money in it and took Mr Fukai up pickaback, and the party started for the East Parade Ground, their district's 'safe area.' As they went out of the gate, Mr Fukai, quite childlike now, beat on Father Kleinsorge's shoulders and said, 'I won't leave. I won't leave.' Irrelevantly, Father Kleinsorge turned to Father LaSalle and said, 'We have lost all our possessions but not our sense of humor.'

The street was cluttered with parts of houses that had slid into it, and with fallen telephone poles and wires. From every second or third house came the voices of people buried and abandoned, who invariably screamed, with formal politeness, '*Tasukete kure!* Help, if you please!' The priests recognized several ruins from which these cries came as the homes of friends, but because of the fire it was too late to help. All the way, Mr Fukai whimpered, 'Let me stay.' The party turned right when they came to a block of fallen houses that was one flame. At Sakai Bridge, which would take them across to the East Parade Ground, they saw that the whole community on the opposite side of the river was a sheet of fire; they dared not cross and decided to take refuge in Asano Park, off to their left. Father Kleinsorge, who had been weakened for a couple of days by his bad case of diarrhea, began to stagger under his protesting burden, and as he tried to climb up over the wreckage of several houses that blocked their way to the park, he stumbled, dropped Mr Fukai, and plunged down, head over heels, to the edge of the river. When he picked himself up, he saw Mr Fukai running away. Father Kleinsorge shouted to a dozen soldiers, who were standing by the bridge, to stop him. As Father Kleinsorge started back to get Mr Fukai, Father LaSalle called out, 'Hurry! Don't waste time!' So Father Kleinsorge just requested the soldiers to take care of Mr Fukai. They said they would, but the little, broken man got away from them, and the last the priests could see of him, he was running back toward the fire.

Mr Tanimoto, fearful for his family and church, at first ran toward them by the shortest route, along Koi Highway. He was the only person making his way into the city; he met hundreds and hundreds who were fleeing, and every one of them seemed to be hurt in some way. The eyebrows of some were burned off and skin hung from their faces and hands. Others, because of pain, held their arms up as if carrying something in both hands. Some were vomiting as they walked. Many were naked or in shreds of clothing. On some undressed bodies, the burns had made patterns – of undershirt straps

and suspenders and, on the skin of some women (since white repelled
the heat from the bomb and dark clothes absorbed it and conducted
it to their skin), the shapes of flowers they had had on their kimonos.
Many, although injured themselves, supported relatives who were
worse off. Almost all had their heads bowed, looked straight ahead,
were silent, and showed no expression whatever.

After crossing Koi Bridge and Kannon Bridge, having run the
whole way, Mr Tanimoto saw, as he approached the center, that all
the houses had been crushed and many were afire. Here the trees
were bare and their trunks were charred. He tried at several points to
penetrate the ruins, but the flames always stopped him. Under many
houses, people screamed for help, but no one helped; in general,
survivors that day assisted only their relatives or immediate neighbors, for they could not comprehend or tolerate a wider circle of
misery. The wounded limped past the screams, and Mr Tanimoto
ran past them. As a Christian he was filled with compassion for those
who were trapped, and as a Japanese he was overwhelmed by the
shame of being unhurt, and he prayed as he ran, 'God help them and
take them out of the fire.'

He thought he would skirt the fire, to the left. He ran back to
Kannon Bridge and followed for a distance one of the rivers. He tried
several cross streets, but all were blocked, so he turned far left and
ran out to Yokogawa, a station on a railroad line that detoured the
city in a wide semicircle, and he followed the rails until he came to a
burning train. So impressed was he by this time by the extent of the
damage that he ran north two miles to Gion, a suburb in the foothills.
All the way, he overtook dreadfully burned and lacerated people, and
in his guilt he turned to right and left as he hurried and said to some
of them, 'Excuse me for having no burden like yours.' Near Gion, he
began to meet country people going toward the city to help, and
when they saw him, several exclaimed, 'Look! There is one who is
not wounded.' At Gion, he bore toward the right bank of the main
river, the Ota, and ran down it until he reached fire again. There was
no fire on the other side of the river, so he threw off his shirt and
shoes and plunged into it. In midstream, where the current was fairly
strong, exhaustion and fear finally caught up with him – he had run
nearly seven miles – and he became limp and drifted in the water. He
prayed, 'Please, God, help me to cross. It would be nonsense for me

to be drowned when I am the only uninjured one.' He managed a few more strokes and fetched up on a spit downstream.

Mr Tanimoto climbed up the bank and ran along it until, near a large Shinto shrine, he came to more fire, and as he turned left to get around it, he met, by incredible luck, his wife. She was carrying their infant daughter. Mr Tanimoto was now so emotionally worn out that nothing could surprise him. He did not embrace his wife; he simply said, 'Oh, you are safe.' She told him that she had got home from her night in Ushida just in time for the explosion; she had been buried under the parsonage with the baby in her arms. She told how the wreckage had pressed down on her, how the baby had cried. She saw a chink of light, and by reaching up with a hand, she worked the hole bigger, bit by bit. After about half an hour, she heard the crackling noise of wood burning. At last the opening was big enough for her to push the baby out, and afterward she crawled out herself. She said she was now going out to Ushida again. Mr Tanimoto said he wanted to see his church and take care of the people of his Neighborhood Association. They parted as casually – as bewildered – as they had met.

Mr Tanimoto's way around the fire took him across the East Parade Ground, which, being an evacuation area, was now the scene of a gruesome review: rank on rank of the burned and bleeding. Those who were burned moaned, '*Mizu, mizu!* Water, water!' Mr Tanimoto found a basin in a nearby street and located a water tap that still worked in the crushed shell of a house, and he began carrying water to the suffering strangers. When he had given drink to about thirty of them, he realized he was taking too much time. 'Excuse me,' he said loudly to those nearby who were reaching out their hands to him and crying their thirst. 'I have many people to take care of.' Then he ran away. He went to the river again, the basin in his hand, and jumped down onto a sandpit. There he saw hundreds of people so badly wounded that they could not get up to go farther from the burning city. When they saw a man erect and unhurt, the chant began again: '*Mizu, mizu, mizu.*' Mr Tanimoto could not resist them; he carried them water from the river – a mistake, since it was tidal and brackish. Two or three small boats were ferrying hurt people across the river from Asano Park, and when one touched the spit, Mr Tanimoto again made his loud, apologetic speech and jumped into the boat. It took him across to the park. There, in the underbrush, he found some of his charges of the Neighborhood Association, who had come there by his previous instructions, and saw many acquaintances, among them Father Kleinsorge and the other Catholics. But he missed Fukai, who had been a close friend. 'Where is Fukai-*san*?' he asked.

'He didn't want to come with us,' Father Kleinsorge said. 'He ran back.'

When Miss Sasaki heard the voices of the people caught along with her in the dilapidation at the tin factory, she began speaking to them. Her nearest neighbor, she discovered, was a high-school girl who had been drafted for factory work, and who said her back was broken. Miss Sasaki replied, 'I am lying here and I can't move. My left leg is cut off.'

Some time later, she again heard somebody walk overhead and then move off to one side, and whoever it was began burrowing. The digger released several people, and when he had uncovered the high-school girl, she found that her back was not broken, after all, and she crawled out. Miss Sasaki spoke to the rescuer, and he worked toward her. He pulled away a great number of books, until he had made a tunnel to her. She could see his perspiring face as he said, 'Come out, Miss.' She tried. 'I can't move,' she said. The man excavated some more and told her to try with all her strength to get out. But books were heavy on her hips, and the man finally saw that a bookcase was leaning on the books and that a heavy beam pressed down on the bookcase. 'Wait,' he said. 'I'll get a crowbar.'

The man was gone a long time, and when he came back, he was ill-tempered, as if her plight were all her fault. 'We have no men to help you!' he shouted in through the tunnel. 'You'll have to get out by yourself.'

'That's impossible,' she said. 'My left leg . . .' The man went away.

Much later, several men came and dragged Miss Sasaki out. Her left leg was not severed, but it was badly broken and cut and it hung askew below the knee. They took her out into a courtyard. It was raining. She sat on the ground in the rain. When the downpour increased, someone directed all the wounded people to take cover in the factory's air-raid shelters. 'Come along,' a torn-up woman said to her. 'You can hop.' But Miss Sasaki could not move, and she just waited in the rain. Then a man propped up a large sheet of corrugated iron as a kind of lean-to, and took her in his arms and carried her to it. She was grateful until he brought two horribly wounded people – a woman with a whole breast sheared off and a man whose face was all raw from a burn – to share the simple shed with her. No one came back. The rain cleared and the cloudly afternoon was hot; before nightfall the three grotesques under the slanting piece of twisted iron began to smell quite bad.

The former head of the Nobori-cho Neighborhood Association to which the Catholic priests belonged was an energetic man named Yoshida. He had boasted, when he was in charge of the district air-raid defenses, that fire might eat away all of Hiroshima but it would never come to Nobori-cho. The bomb blew down his house, and a joist pinned him by the legs, in full view of the Jesuit mission house across the way and of the people hurrying along the street. In their confusion as they hurried past, Mrs Nakamura, with her children, and Father Kleinsorge, with Mr Fukai on his back, hardly saw him; he was just part of the general blur of misery through which they moved. His cries for help brought no response from them; there were so many people shouting for help that they could not hear him separately. They and all the others went along. Nobori-cho became absolutely deserted, and the fire swept through it. Mr Yoshida saw the wooden mission house – the only erect building in the area – go up in a lick of flame, and the heat was terrific on his face. Then flames came along his side of the street and entered his house. In a paroxysm of terrified strength, he freed himself and ran down the alleys of Nobori-cho, hemmed in by the fire he had said would never come. He began at once to behave like an old man; two months later his hair was white.

As Dr Fujii stood in the river up to his neck to avoid the heat of the fire, the wind blew stronger and stronger, and soon, even though the expanse of water was small, the waves grew so high that the people under the bridge could not longer keep their footing. Dr Fujii went close to the shore, crouched down, and embraced a large stone with his usable arm. Later it became possible to wade along the very edge

of the river, and Dr Fujii and his two surviving nurses moved about
two hundred yards upstream, to a sandpit near Asano Park. Many
wounded were lying on the sand. Dr Machii' was there with his
family; his daughter, who had been outdoors when the bomb burst,
was badly burned on her hands and legs but fortunately not on her
face. Although Dr Fujii's shoulder was by now terribly painful, he
examined the girl's burns curiously. Then he lay down. In spite of
the misery all around, he was ashamed of his appearance, and he
remarked to Dr Machii that he looked like a beggar, dressed as he
was in nothing but torn and bloody underwear. Later in the afternoon, when the fire began to subside, he decided to go to his parental
house, in the suburb of Nagatsuka. He asked Dr Machii to join him,
but the Doctor answered that he and his family were going to spend
the night on the spit, because of his daughter's injuries. Dr Fujii,
together with his nurses, walked first to Ushida, where, in the
partially damaged house of some relatives, he found first-aid materials
he had stored there. The two nurses bandaged him and he them.
They went on. Now not many people walked in the street, but a great
number sat and lay on the pavement, vomited, waited for death, and
died. The number of corpses on the way to Nagatsuka was more and
more puzzling. The Doctor wondered: Could a Molotov flower basket
had done all this?

Dr Fujii reached his family's house in the evening. It was five miles
from the center of town, but its roof had fallen in and the windows
were all broken.

All day, people poured into Asano Park. This private estate was far
enough away from the explosion so that its bamboos, pines, laurel,
and maples were still alive, and the green place invited refugees –
partly because they believed that if the Americans came back, they
would bomb only buildings; partly because the foliage seemed a
center of coolness and life, and the estate's exquisitely precise rock
gardens, with their quiet pools and arching bridges, were very
Japanese, normal, secure; and also partly (according to some who
were there) because of an irresistible, atavistic urge to hide under
leaves. Mrs Nakamura and her children were among the first to
arrive, and they settled in the bamboo grove near the river. They all
felt terribly thirsty, and they drank from the river. At once they were

nauseated and began vomiting, and they retched the whole day. Others were also nauseated; they all thought (probably because of the strong odor of ionization, an 'electric smell' given off by the bomb's fission) that they were sick from a gas the Americans had dropped. When Father Kleinsorge and the other priests came into the park, nodding to their friends as they passed, the Nakamuras were all sick and prostrate. A woman named Iwasaki, who lived in the neighborhood of the mission and who was sitting near the Nakamuras, got up and asked the priests if she should stay where she was or go with them. Father Kleinsorge said, 'I hardly know where the safest place is.' She stayed there, and later in the day, though she had no visible wounds or burns, she died. The priests went farther along the river and settled down in some underbrush. Father LaSalle lay down and went right to sleep. The theological student, who was wearing slippers, had carried with him a bundle of clothes, in which he had packed two pairs of leather shoes. When he sat down with the others, he found that the bundle had broken open and a couple of shoes had fallen out and now he had only two lefts. He retraced his steps and found one right. When he rejoined the priests, he said, 'It's funny, but things don't matter any more. Yesterday, my shoes were my most important possessions. Today, I don't care. One pair is enough.'

Father Cieslik said, 'I know. I started to bring my books along, and then I thought, "This is no time for books."'

When Mr Tanimoto, with his basin still in his hand, reached the park, it was very crowded, and to distinguish the living from the dead was not easy, for most of the people lay still, with their eyes open. To Father Kleinsorge, an Occidental, the silence in the grove by the river, where hundreds of gruesomely wounded suffered together, was one of the most dreadful and awesome phenomena of his whole experience. The hurt ones were quiet; no one wept, much less screamed in pain; no one complained; none of the many who died did so noisily; not even the children cried; very few people even spoke. And when Father Kleinsorge gave water to some whose faces had been almost blotted out by flash burns, they took their share and then raised themselves a little and bowed to him, in thanks.

Mr Tanimoto greeted the priests and then looked around for other friends. He saw Mrs Matsumoto, wife of the director of the Methodist School, and asked her if she was thirsty. She was, so he went to one of the pools in the Asano rock gardens and got water for her in his basin. Then he decided to try to get back to his church. He went into Nobori-cho by the way the priests had taken as they escaped, but he did not get far; the fire along the streets was so fierce that he had to turn back. He walked to the riverbank and began to look for a boat in which he might carry some of the most severely injured across the river from Asano Park and away from the spreading fire. Soon he found a good-sized pleasure punt drawn up on the bank, but in and around it was an awful tableau – five dead men, nearly naked, badly burned, who must have expired more or less all at once, for they were in attitudes which suggested that they had been working together to push the boat down into the river. Mr Tanimoto lifted them away from the boat, and as he did so, he experienced such horror at disturbing the dead – preventing them, he momentarily felt, from launching their craft and going on their ghostly way – that he said out loud, 'Please forgive me for taking this boat. I must use it for others, who are alive.' The punt was heavy, but he managed to slide it into the water. There were no oars, and all he could find for propulsion was a thick bamboo pole. He worked the boat upstream to the most crowded part of the park and began to ferry the wounded. He could pack ten or twelve into the boat for each crossing, but as the river was too deep in the center to pole his way across, he had to paddle with the bamboo, and consequently each trip took a very long time. He worked several hours that way.

Early in the afternoon, the fire swept into the woods of Asano Park. The first Mr Tanimoto knew of it was when, returning in his boat, he saw that a great number of people had moved toward the riverside. On touching the bank, he went up to investigate, and when he saw the fire, he shouted, 'All the young men who are not badly hurt come with me!' Father Kleinsorge moved Father Schiffer and Father LaSalle close to the edge of the river and asked people there to get them across if the fire came too near, and then joined Tanimoto's volunteers. Mr Tanimoto sent some to look for buckets and basins and told others to beat the burning underbrush with their clothes; when utensils were at hand, he formed a bucket chain from one of the pools in the rock garden. The team fought the fire for more than two hours, and gradually defeated the flames. As Mr Tanimoto's men worked, the frightened people in the park pressed closer and closer to the river, and finally the mob began to force some of the unfortunates who were on the very bank into the water. Among those driven into the river and drowned were Mrs Matsumoto, of the Methodist School, and her daughter.

When Father Kleinsorge got back after fighting the fire, he found Father Schiffer still bleeding and terribly pale. Some Japanese stood around and stared at him, and Father Schiffer whispered, with a weak smile, 'It is as if I were already dead.' 'Not yet,' Father Kleinsorge said. He had brought Dr Fujii's first-aid kit with him, and he had noticed Dr Kanda in the crowd, so he sought him out and asked him if he would dress Father Schiffer's bad cuts. Dr Kanda had seen his wife and daughter dead in the ruins of his hospital; he sat now with his head in his hands. 'I can't do anything,' he said. Father Kleinsorge bound more bandage around Father Schiffer's head, moved him to a steep place, and settled him so that his head was high, and soon the bleeding diminished.

The roar of approaching planes was heard about this time. Someone in the crowd near the Nakamura family shouted, 'It's some Grummans coming to strafe us!' A baker named Nakashima stood up and commanded, 'Everyone who is wearing anything white, take it off.' Mrs Nakamura took the blouses off her children, and opened her umbrella and made them get under it. A great number of people, even badly burned ones, crawled under bushes and stayed there until the hum, evidently of a reconnaissance or weather run, died away.

It began to rain. Mrs Nakamura kept her children under the umbrella. The drops grew abnormally large, and someone shouted, 'The Americans are dropping gasoline. They're going to set fire to us!' (This alarm stemmed from one of the theories being passed through the park as to why so much of Hiroshima had burned: it was that a single plane had sprayed gasoline on the city and then somehow set fire to it in one flashing moment.) But the drops were palpably water, and as they fell, the wind grew stronger and stronger, and suddenly – probably because of the tremendous convection set up by the blazing city – a whirlwind ripped through the park. Huge trees crashed down; small ones were uprooted and flew into the air. Higher, a wild array of flat things revolved in the twisting funnel – pieces of iron roofing, papers, doors, strips of matting. Father Kleinsorge put a piece of cloth over Father Schiffer's eyes, so that the feeble man would not think he was going crazy. The gale blew Mrs Murata, the mission housekeeper, who was sitting close by the river, down the embankment at a shallow, rocky place, and she came out with her bare feet bloody. The vortex moved out onto the river, where it sucked up a waterspout and eventually spent itself.

After the storm, Mr Tanimoto began ferrying people again, and Father Kleinsorge asked the theological student to go across and make his way out to the Jesuit Novitiate at Nagatsuka, about three miles from the center of town, and to request the priests there to come with help for Fathers Schiffer and LaSalle. The student got into Mr Tanimoto's boat and went off with him. Father Kleinsorge asked Mrs Nakamura if she would like to go out to Nagatsuka with the priests when they came. She said she had some luggage and her children were sick – they were still vomiting from time to time, and so, for that matter, was she – and therefore she feared she could not. He said he thought the fathers from the Novitiate could come back the next day with a pushcart to get her.

Later in the afternoon, when he went ashore for a while, Mr Tanimoto, upon whose energy and initiative many had come to depend, heard people begging for food. He consulted Father Kleinsorge, and they decided to go back into town to get some rice from Mr Tanimoto's Neighborhood Association shelter and from the mission shelter. Father Cieslik and two or three others went with them. At first, when they got among the row of prostrate houses, they did not know where they were; the change was too sudden, from a busy city of two hundred and forty-five thousand that morning to a mere pattern of residue in the afternoon. The asphalt of the streets was still so soft and hot from the fires that walking was uncomfortable. They encountered only one person, a woman, who said to them as they passed, 'My husband is in those ashes.' At the mission, where Mr Tanimoto left the party, Father Kleinsorge was dismayed to see the building razed. In the garden, on the way to the shelter. He noticed a pumpkin roasted on the vine. He and Father Cieslik tasted it and it was good. They were surprised at their hunger, and they ate quite a bit. They got out several bags of rice and gathered up several other cooked pumpkins and dug up some potatoes that were nicely baked under the ground, and started back. Mr Tanimoto rejoined them on the way. One of the people with him had some cooking utensils. In the park, Mr Tanimoto organized the lightly wounded women of his neighborhood to cook. Father Kleinsorge offered the Nakamura family some pumpkin, and they tried it, but they could not keep it on their stomachs. Altogether, the rice was enough to feed nearly a hundred people.

Just before dark, Mr Tanimoto came across a twenty-year-old girl, Mrs Kamai, the Tanimoto's next-door neighbor. She was crouching on the ground with the body of her infant daughter in her arms. The baby had evidently been dead all day. Mrs Kamai jumped up when she saw Mr Tanimoto and said, 'Would you please try to locate my husband?'

Mr Tanimoto knew that her husband had been inducted into the Army just the day before; he and Mrs Tanimoto had entertained Mrs Kamai in the afternoon, to make her forget. Kamai had reported to the Chugoku Regional Army Headquarters – near the ancient castle in the middle of town – where some four thousand troops were stationed. Judging by the many maimed soldiers Mr Tanimoto had seen during the day, he surmised that the barracks had been badly damaged by whatever it was that had hit Hiroshima. He knew he hadn't a chance of finding Mrs Kamai's husband, even if he searched, but he wanted to humor her. 'I'll try,' he said.

'You've got to find him,' she said. 'He loved our baby so much. I want him to see her once more.'

ACKNOWLEDGEMENTS

The Publishers wish to thank the following for their permission to use the material below:

Irwin Shaw, Jonathan Cape Ltd and John Farquharson Ltd for Chapter 21 of *The Young Lions;* J.G. Ballard, Victor Gollancz Ltd and Simon & Schuster, Inc. for Chapters 20-22 of *Empire of the Sun* © 1984 by J.G. Ballard; William Heinemann Ltd and A.P. Watt Ltd for an extract from *A Town Like Alice* by Nevil Shute; Evans Brothers Ltd for Chapters 1-3 of *The Man Who Never Was* by Ewen Montague; Dell for Chapter 20 of *From Here to Eternity* by James Jones; Harrap Ltd for Parts 2 & 3 of *Ill Met by Moonlight* by W. Stanley Moss; James A. Michener, William Collins, Sons & Co. Ltd and Macmillan Inc. for *The Landing on Kuralei* from *Tales of the South Pacific;* Macmillan Publishers Ltd and Mr J. Lovat Dickinson for Chapter 6 of *The Last Enemy* by Richard Hillary; Kurt Vonnegut, Jonathan Cape Ltd and Donald G. Farber for Chapter 2 of *Slaughterhouse Five;* The Peters, Fraser & Dunlop Group Ltd and Little, Brown and Company for an extract from *Officers and Gentlemen* by Evelyn Waugh, Copyright © 1955 by Evelyn Waugh; Chapter 2 of *The Naked and the Dead* by Norman Mailer. Reprinted by permission of the author and the author's agents Scott Meredith Literary Agency, Inc., 845 Third Avenue, New York, New York 10022; Charles J. Rolo and Russell & Vokening, Inc. for Chapters 15-17 of *Wingate's Raiders* © 1944 by Charles J. Rolo, renewed in 1969 by Charles J. Rolo; Bruce Marshall and Evans Brothers Ltd for Chapter 9 and part of Chapter 10 of *The White Rabbit;* Paul Brickhill and William Collins, Sons & Co. Ltd for an extract from *Reach for the Sky;* Lieut. Col. Graham Brooks, MC (Late RA) and Century Hutchinson Limited for *Shooting Party* from *Grand Party;* William Collins, Sons & Co. Ltd for Chapter 4 of *The Winds of War;* Cornelius Ryan and Victor Gollancz Ltd for *The Day*/Chapter 2 of *The Longest Day;* R.J. Minney and William Collins, Sons & Co. Ltd for Chapter 18 of *Carve Her Name with Pride;* Lindsay Baly for part of Chapter 2 of *Ironbottom Sound;* P.R. Reid and Hodder & Stoughton Lrd for Chapter 2 of *The Colditz Story;* Michael Joseph Ltd for Chapter 18 of *Enemy Coast Ahead* by Guy Gibson, VC; The Estate of Nella Last and the Falling Wall Press for *May 1941* from *Nella Last's War – A Mother's Diary;* Joseph Heller, Jonathan Cape Ltd and Simon & Schuster Inc. for Chapter 9 of *Catch 22.* Copyright © 1955, 61 by Joseph Heller; Martha Gelhorn, Virago and Bill Buford for *The Battle of the Bulge* from *The Face of War;* Raymond Paull and the Octopus Publishing Group, Australia for *The Invasion of Papua* from *Retreat from Kokoda;* The Estate of H.E. Bates and Laurence Pollinger Ltd for *No Trouble At All* from *The Stories of Flying Officer X;* Mrs Ronald Seth for Chapters 5 and 6 of *Stalingrad – Point of Return* by Ronald Seth; John Prebble and Curtis Brown Ltd for *The Soldier Looks for his Family;* Nancy Wake, Curtis Brown (Australia) Pty Ltd and Macmillan, Australia for Chapter 9 of *The White Mouse* published by the Macmillan Company of Australia Pty Ltd, Melbourne 1985; F.J. Salfeld for *Fear of Death;* The Estate of John Steinbeck, William Heinemann Ltd and Viking Penguin, Inc. for an extract from *The Moon is Down;* Cassell and Alfred A. Knopf, Inc. for Chapter 10 of *The Cruel Sea* by Nicholas Monsarrat; R.L. Crimp and Leo Cooper for *9th November – 8th December* from *Diary of a Desert Rat;* James Aldridge and Curtis Brown Ltd for Chapter 3 of *Of Many Men;* Robert J. Casey and Century Hutchinson Ltd for Book 6 of *Torpedo Junction;* John Hersey and Alfred A. Knopf, Inc. for Chapter 2 of *Hiroshima* copyright 1946, 1985 by John Hersey. Copyright renewed 1973 by John Hersey.

Every effort has been made to clear the copyright material in this book. The Publishers trust that their apologies will be accepted for any errors or omissions.